D1108294

Ex Libris
Raymond E. Nelsen

CANONS AND DECREES
OF THE
COUNCIL OF TRENT

CANONS AND DECREES
OF THE
COUNCIL OF TRENT

ORIGINAL TEXT
WITH ENGLISH TRANSLATION

BY

REV. H. J. SCHROEDER, O.P.

B. HERDER BOOK CO.
15 & 17 SOUTH BROADWAY, ST. LOUIS, MO.
AND
33 QUEEN SQUARE, LONDON, W. C.

Library of Congress Catalog Card Number: 41-21651

Printed in U. S. A.

NIHIL OBSTAT

Fr. Humbertus Kane, O.P.

Fr. Alexius Driscoll, O.P.

IMPRIMI POTEST

Fr. Petrus O'Brien, O.P.

Prior Provincialis

NIHIL OBSTAT

Sti. Ludovici, die 5. Septembris, 1941

A. A. Esswein,

Censor Deputatus

IMPRIMATUR

Sti. Ludovici, die 5. Septembris, 1941

✠ *Joannes J. Glennon,*

Archiepiscopus

Fourth Printing, 1960

Vail-Ballou Press, Inc., Binghamton and New York

TRANSLATOR'S FOREWORD

Some fifteen years ago the writer formed the intention of making accessible to English readers the disciplinary decrees of the ecumenical or general councils of the Church, a work which, with the exception of the Council of Trent, had up to that time received no attention. The fact that the last of these, that of the Vatican, did not issue any such decrees narrowed my field of labor to nineteen councils, leaving, nevertheless, a field still large enough to make anyone who has taken sufficient time to look carefully over the ground hesitant about undertaking the work. The results of these labors, covering the first eighteen councils, appeared in 1937 under the title, *Disciplinary Decrees of the General Councils*. The present volume covers the Council of Trent, giving the translation and text of its canons and decrees.

The original intention of limiting myself to the disciplinary decisions of the councils could not very well be carried out in the case of Trent without producing a one-sided work amounting almost to a monstrosity. In the list of general councils Trent holds the first place, not only because of its restatement of Catholic doctrine and its initiation of a genuine reform, but also because of its extraordinary influence both within and without the Church. Its purpose was twofold, to define the doctrines of the Church in reply to the heresies of the Protestants, and to bring about a thorough reform of the inner life of Christians. We have become so accustomed to look upon the two parts as one that either without the other seems incomplete. Moreover, it is scarcely necessary to state that the translation of these dogmatic decisions will be of immense advantage not only to the clergy but also and especially to the seminarian and the educated layman. In them the council proclaimed to the world the doctrines that were committed to the keeping of the Church on the day of Pentecost. They are a sign erected on everlasting foundations indicating to the passer-by the straight road along which the Church has traveled ever since that day and along which she will continue to travel till the day of judgment. She recognizes no detours, for these lead only to destruction. Again, many of the council's dogmatic decrees are gems, masterpieces of theology reduced to the briefest possible form, yet sufficiently complete to leave nothing wanting. I make mention particularly of the famous decree on justification, in the working out and formulation of which "the spirit of God is easily discernible." The council spent seven months of arduous labor in formulating that decree as we have it today. There had been no decisions on that point of Catholic doctrine by earlier councils by which to be guided or on which to lean. In the works of the Fathers we look in vain for a definite and satisfactory exposition. The older theologians incorporated what they had to say on that subject in their treatises on grace, while the controversial works of later Catholic writers were more or less tainted by the false doctrine of a twofold formal cause of justification, namely, the *justitia inhaerens* and the *justitia imputata*, a compromise contrivance designed to conciliate the heretics. In the reform decrees the reader will find the means employed by the Church to correct and remove prevailing moral evils and abuses.

The first English translation of the canons and decrees of the Council of Trent, so far as I am aware, was made by the Rev. J. Waterworth and published in London in 1848. As is well known, this work has been out of print and off the market for many years. As long as it was available it filled a real need. In 1687 there appeared an anonymous translation. But the work was so poorly done and so unfaithful to the original that it must be regarded as a travesty and burlesque rather than as a translation. Another rendition was made by T. A. Buckley and published in England in 1851. This I have not seen, and had it not been for an item in the catalogue of a London antiquarian some years ago, I would not know of its existence. Whether an English rendering of Trent has ever been made in this country, I do not know. A translation of the dogmatic decrees only was made by an Oxford convert in *Catholic Doctrine as Defined by the Council of Trent* (Philadelphia, 1869), which is a translation of a series of conferences delivered in Geneva by the Rev. A. Nampon, S.J., under the title, *Étude de la doctrine catholique dans le concile de Trente*.

The Latin text of the canons and decrees given in the second part of this book and upon which the accompanying translation is based, is that of the Neapolitan edition of 1859, which was made from the Roman edition of 1834 issued by the *Collegium Urbanum de Propaganda Fide*. In transcribing this text typographical errors were corrected by reference to the new edition of the Acts of the council sponsored by the *Görres-Gesellschaft* in so far as it was available and also to the edition of Le Plat (Antwerp, 1779). In the spelling of certain words changes were made to conform to current usage. In the translation I have endeavored to adhere to the text as closely as possible, that is, to make it as literal as the text would permit, without, however, making that adherence a slavish one. Only direct scriptural quotations, not paraphrases, are printed in italics. For the benefit of those who are interested in a wider acquaintance with pre-Tridentine legislation, references to provincial councils and to the *Corpus Juris Canonici* will be found more copious and more complete under the Latin text. The references to a few papal bulls are given to indicate the action of popes to enforce the decrees of Trent.

REV. H. J. SCHROEDER, O.P.

TABLE OF CONTENTS

SEVENTH SESSION

EIGHTH SESSION

NINTH SESSION

TENTH SESSION

ELEVENTH SESSION

TWELFTH SESSION

THIRTEENTH SESSION

FOURTEENTH SESSION

FIFTEENTH SESSION

SIXTEENTH SESSION

SEVENTEENTH SESSION

EIGHTEENTH SESSION

NINETEENTH SESSION

TWENTIETH SESSION

TWENTY-FIRST SESSION

TWENTY-SECOND SESSION

TWENTY-THIRD SESSION

TWENTY-FOURTH SESSION

TWENTY-FIFTH SESSION

INDEX RERUM ANALYTICUS

SESSIO SEPTIMA

SESSIO OCTAVA

SESSIO NONA

SESSIO DECIMA

SESSIO UNDECIMA

SESSIO DUODECIMA

SESSIO DECIMA TERTIA

SESSIO DECIMA QUARTA

SESSIO DECIMA QUINTA

SESSIO DECIMA SEXTA

SESSIO DECIMA SEPTIMA

SESSIO DECIMA OCTAVA

SESSIO DECIMA NONA

SESSIO VIGESIMA

SESSIO VIGESIMA PRIMA

SESSIO VIGESIMA SECUNDA

SESSIO VIGESIMA TERTIA

SESSIO VIGESIMA QUARTA

SESSIO VIGESIMA QUINTA

CONTINUATIO SESSIONIS

BULL OF THE CONVOCATION

OF THE HOLY ECUMENICAL

COUNCIL OF TRENT

under Pope Paul III

Paul, Bishop, servant of the servants of God, for a perpetual remembrance hereof

Recognizing at the very beginning of our pontificate, which the divine providence of Almighty God, not for any merit of our own, but by reason of its own great goodness, has committed to us, to what troubled times and to how many distresses in almost all affairs our pastoral solicitude and vigilance were called, we desired indeed to remedy the evils that have long afflicted and well-nigh overwhelmed the Christian commonwealth; but we also, as men *compassed with infirmity*,[1] felt our strength unequal to take upon ourselves such a burden. For while we realized that peace was necessary to free and preserve the commonwealth from the many dangers that threatened it, we found all filled with hatreds and dissensions, and particularly those princes, to whom God has entrusted almost the entire direction of affairs, at enmity with one another. Whilst we deemed it necessary for the integrity of the Christian religion and for the confirmation within us of the hope of heavenly things, that there be *one fold and one shepherd* [2] for the Lord's flock, the unity of the Christian name was well-nigh rent and torn asunder by schisms, dissensions and heresies. Whilst we desired the commonwealth to be safe and protected against the arms and insidious designs of the infidels, yet, because of our transgressions and the guilt of us all, indeed, because of the wrath of God hanging over us by reason of our sins, Rhodes had been lost, Hungary ravaged, war by land and sea intended and planned against Italy, and against Austria and Illyria, since the Turk, our godless and ruthless enemy, was never at rest and looked upon our mutual enmities and dissensions as his fitting oppor-

[1] Heb. 5:2.
[2] John 10:16.

tunity to carry out his designs with success. Wherefore, having been called, as we have said, in so great a tempest of heresies, discords and wars and in such restlessness of the waves to rule and pilot the bark of Peter, and not trusting sufficiently our own strength, we first of all *cast our cares upon the Lord*,[3] that He might sustain us and provide our soul with firmness and strength, our understanding with prudence and wisdom. Then, considering that our predecessors, endowed with admirable wisdom and sanctity, had often in the greatest dangers of the Christian commonwealth had recourse to ecumenical councils and general assemblies of bishops as the best and most suitable remedy, we also decided to hold a general council. When, on consulting the opinions of the princes whose consent in this matter we deemed particularly useful and expedient, we found them at that time not averse to so holy a work, we, as our letters and records attest, summoned an ecumenical council and a general assembly of those bishops and fathers, whose duty it is to attend, to be opened in the city of Mantua on the twenty-third of May in the year 1537 of our Lord's incarnation and the third of our pontificate; entertaining almost the assured hope that when we should be assembled there in the name of the Lord, He would, as He promised, *be in our midst* [4] and in His goodness and mercy dispel with ease by the breath of His mouth all the storms and dangers of the times. But, as the enemy of mankind always plots against pious enterprises, at the very outset, contrary to all our hopes and expectations, the city of Mantua was refused us, unless we subscribed to certain conditions which were totally irreconcilable with the ordinances of our predecessors, with the condition of the times, with our own dignity and liberty, and with that of the Apostolic See and the ecclesiastical name, as we have made known in other letters. Wherefore we were obliged to find another place and to choose another city, and since a convenient and suitable one did not immediately present itself, we were constrained to prorogue the celebration of the council to the following first day of November. In the meantime, the Turk, our cruel and everlasting enemy, having attacked Italy with a powerful fleet, captured, sacked and ravaged several cities on the shores of Apulia and carried off as booty the inhabitants, while we, in the greatest fear and general danger, were occupied in fortifying our shores and in furnishing assistance to the nearest neighboring localities. At the same time, however, we did not

---

[3] Ps. 54:23.
[4] Matt. 18:

neglect to consult and exhort the Christian princes to inform us what in their opinion would be a suitable place to hold the council, and since their opinions were various and uncertain, and there seemed to be needless delay, we, with the best intention and, we think, with prudence, chose Vicenza, a populous city, which by reason of the valor, esteem and power of the Venetians, who conceded it to us, offered not only free access but also and especially a free and safe place of residence for all. But since time had already far advanced and the choice of the new city had to be made known to all, the proximity of the first of November precluding any announcement of this change, and winter moreover was near, we were again obliged to prorogue the council to the following spring, that is, to the first of the next May. This having been firmly settled and decreed, we considered, while preparing ourselves and everything else to hold and celebrate that council successfully with the help of God, that it was a matter of prime importance both for the celebration of the council and for Christendom, that the Christian princes be united in peace and concord, and so we did not fail to implore and beseech our most beloved sons in Christ, Charles, ever august Emperor of the Romans, and Francis, the most Christian King, the two chief props and supports of the Christian name, to come together in a conference with us. Both of them we very often urged by letters, nuncios and legates *a latere* selected from the number of our venerable brethren, to lay aside their jealousies and animosities, to agree to an alliance and holy friendship, and to succor the tottering state of Christendom, for the preservation of which especially did God give them power; and in case of neglect to do this and of failure to direct all their counsels to the common welfare of Christendom, they would have to render to Him a strict and severe account. Yielding at last to our petitions they repaired to Nice, whither we also, for the cause of God and of bringing about peace, undertook a long and, to our advanced age, very fatiguing journey. Neither did we neglect in the meantime, as the time set for the council, namely, the first of May, approached, to send to Vicenza three legates *a latere*, men of the greatest worth and esteem, chosen from the number of our brethren, the cardinals of the holy Roman Church, to open the council, to receive the prelates coming from various parts, and to transact and attend to such matters as they should deem necessary, till we ourselves on our return from our journey and mission of peace should be able to direct everything with greater exactness. In the meantime we applied ourselves with all the zeal, love and energy of our soul to that holy and most necessary work, the establishment of peace among the princes. God is our witness, in whose goodness we trusted when we exposed ourselves to the dangers of the journey and of life. Our conscience is witness, and in this matter certainly cannot reproach us with having either neglected or not sought an opportunity to effect a reconciliation. Witnesses are the princes themselves, whom we so often and so urgently implored through our nuncios, letters, legates, admonitions, exhortations and entreaties of every kind to lay aside their jealousies and form an alliance, that with united zeal and action they might aid the Christian commonwealth, already reduced to the greatest immediate danger. Witnesses, moreover, are those vigils and anxieties, those labors and strenuous exertions of our soul by day and night, which we have endured to such large measure in this matter and cause. For all that, our counsels and labors have not yet produced the desired results; for so it pleased the Lord our God, who, however, we trust will yet look more favorably on our wishes. We ourselves have not in this matter, so far as we could, omitted anything pertaining to the duty of our pastoral office. If there be any who interpret our efforts for peace in any other sense, we are grieved indeed, but in our grief we nevertheless give thanks to Almighty God who, as an example and a lesson of patience to us, willed that His own Apostles should be *accounted worthy to suffer reproach for the name of Jesus who is our peace.*[5] However, though by reason of our sins a true and lasting peace between the two princes could not be effected in our meeting and conference at Nice, nevertheless, a truce of ten years was agreed upon; and hoping that as a result of this the holy council might be celebrated more beneficially and thus by its authority peace be permanently established, we urged the princes to come to the council themselves and to bring with them the prelates who had accompanied them and to summon those absent. On both these points, however, they excused themselves on the grounds that it was necessary for them to return to their kingdoms and that the prelates who had accompanied them, being wearied and exhausted by the journey and its expenses, must recover and recruit themselves, and they besought us to decree yet another prorogation of the time for the opening of the council. While we were rather unwilling to yield in this, we received in the meantime letters from our legates at Vicenza, announcing that though the day for the opening of the council had arrived, indeed had long

[5] Acts 5:41; Eph. 2:14.

since passed, hardly more than one or two prelates had repaired to Vicenza from foreign nations. Since we saw on receipt of this information that the council could under no circumstances be held at this time, we yielded to the princes and put off the time for the opening of the council till the following Easter, the feast of the resurrection of the Lord. The decretal letters concerning this our ordinance and prorogation were given and published at Genoa on the twenty-eighth of June in the year of the incarnation of our Lord 1538. This delay we granted the more readily because each of the princes promised to send ambassadors to us at Rome, that those things which remained for the perfect establishment of peace and which on account of the brevity of time could not be accomplished at Nice, might be considered and negotiated more conveniently in our presence at Rome. And for this reason also both requested that the peace negotiations might precede the celebration of the council, for with peace established the council would be much more beneficial and salutary to the Christian commonwealth. It was this hope for peace that moved us always to yield to the wishes of the princes, a hope that was greatly strengthened by the kind and friendly conference between those two princes after our departure from Nice, the news of which, giving us the greatest joy, confirmed us in the good hope, so that we believed God had at last listened to our prayers and received our earnest wishes for peace. This conclusion of peace, therefore, we earnestly desired and urged, and since it was the opinion not only of the two aforesaid princes but also of our most dear son in Christ, Ferdinand, King of the Romans, that the work of the council ought not to be undertaken till peace had been established, and all urged us by letters and through their spokesmen to decide on a further prorogation of the time, particularly insistent being the most illustrious Emperor, who declared that he had promised those who dissent from Catholic unity that he would consider the matter with us on their behalf to the end that some plan of agreement might be arranged, which could not be done satisfactorily before his return to Germany, and guided throughout by the same hope of peace and the wishes of such powerful princes, and above all, seeing that even on the said feast of the resurrection no other prelates had assembled at Vicenza, we, now avoiding the word prorogation, which has been so often repeated in vain, preferred to suspend the celebration of the general council during our own good pleasure and that of the Apostolic See. This we therefore did and dispatched letters concerning this suspension to each of the aforesaid princes on the tenth day of June, 1539, as may be clearly seen therein. This suspension having been made by force of circumstances, we looked forward to that more favorable time and to some conclusion of peace that would later bring dignity and numbers to the council as well as a more immediate safety to the Christian commonwealth. But the affairs of Christendom meanwhile became worse day by day. The Hungarians on the death of their king called in the Turks; King Ferdinand declared war against them; a portion of Belgium was incited to revolt against the Emperor, who, to crush that rebellion, traversed France into Belgium on the most friendly and peaceful terms with the most Christian King and with a great manifestation of mutual good will toward each other. Thence he returned to Germany where he began to hold diets of the princes and cities of Germany with a view to discuss that agreement of which he had spoken to us. But as the hope for peace was already on the wane and that method of providing and establishing unity by means of diets seemed rather adapted to produce greater discord, we were led to return to our former remedy of a general council, and through our legates, cardinals of the holy Roman Church, proposed this to the Emperor himself, which we also did later and especially in the Diet of Ratisbon, at which our beloved son, Gasparo Contarini, Cardinal of St. Praxedes, acted as our legate with great learning and integrity. For since, as we had previously feared, we might be petitioned by a decision of the diet to declare that certain articles maintained by the dissenters from the Church be tolerated till they be examined and decided upon by an ecumenical council, and since neither Christian and Catholic truth, nor our own dignity nor that of the Apostolic See would permit us to yield in this, we chose rather to command that it be proposed openly that a council be held as soon as possible. Neither did we ever have any other intention and wish than that an ecumenical and general council should be convened at the earliest opportunity. For we hoped that thereby peace might be restored to the Christian people and integrity to the Christian religion; yet we desired to hold that council with the good will and favor of the Christian princes. However, while looking forward to this will, while watching for the hidden time, *the time of thy good pleasure, O Lord,*[6] we were at last forced to conclude that all time is pleasing to God when there is question of deliberation on holy things and on such as pertain to Christian piety. Wherefore, beholding with

---

[6] Ps. 68:14.

the bitterest grief of our soul that the affairs of Christendom were daily becoming worse, Hungary oppressed by the Turks, Germany endangered, and all other states overwhelmed with apprehension and grief, we resolved to wait no longer for the consent of any prince, but to look solely to the will of the Almighty God and to the good of the Christian commonwealth. Wherefore, since the city of Vicenza was no longer at our disposal, and we desired in our choice of a new place for holding the council to have in mind both the common welfare of Christians and the conveniences of the German nation, and seeing that among the various places proposed these desired the city of Trent, we, though of opinion that everything could be transacted more conveniently in cisalpine Italy, nevertheless yielded with paternal charity to their desires. Accordingly, we have chosen the city of Trent as that in which the ecumenical council is to be held on the following first day of November, selecting that place as a convenient one in which the bishops and prelates from Germany and from the nations bordering on Germany can assemble very easily and those from France, Spain and other more remote provinces without difficulty. In fixing the day for the council, we considered that there should be time both for the publication of this our decree throughout the Christian nations and to make it possible for all the prelates to arrive. Our reason for not announcing the change of place of the council one year in advance, as has been prescribed by certain constitutions,[7] was this, that we were not willing that the hope of applying some remedy to the Christian commonwealth, afflicted as it is with so many disasters and calamities, should be delayed any longer, though we know the times and recognize the difficulties, and we understand that what may be looked for from our counsels is a matter of uncertainty. But since it is written: *Commit thy way to the Lord, and trust in him, and he will do it*,[8] we have resolved to trust in the clemency and mercy of God rather than distrust our own weakness, for in undertaking good works it often happens that where human counsels fail the divine power succeeds. Wherefore, relying on the authority of Almighty God, Father, Son, and Holy Ghost, and on that of His blessed Apostles Peter and Paul, which we also exercise on earth, and supported also by the advice and assent of our venerable brethren, the cardinals of the holy Roman Church, having removed and annulled

---

[7] Council of Constance, Sess. XXXIX, const. *Frequens*. Cf. my work, *Disciplinary Decrees of the General Councils* (St. Louis, 1937), pp. 447 f.

[8] Ps. 36:5.

the aforesaid suspension, which by the present we remove and annul, we announce, proclaim, convoke, ordain and decree a holy ecumenical and general council to be opened on the first day of November of the present year 1542 from the incarnation of the Lord in the city of Trent, for all nations a commodious, free and convenient place, to be there begun and prosecuted and with the help of God concluded and completed to His glory and praise and the welfare of the whole Christian people; and we summon, exhort and admonish, in whatever country they may be, all our venerable brethren, the patriarchs, archbishops, bishops, and our beloved sons, the abbots, as well as all others who by law or privilege have the right to sit in general councils and express their sentiments therein, enjoining and strictly commanding them by virtue of their oath to us and to this Holy See, and in virtue of holy obedience and under other penalties that by law or custom are usually imposed and proposed in the celebration of councils against absentees, that they attend and be present personally at this holy council, unless they should perchance be hindered by a just impediment, of which, however, they shall be obliged to give proof, in which case they must be represented by their lawful procurators and delegates. Also the aforesaid Emperor and the most Christian King, as well as the other kings, dukes and princes, whose presence, if ever, would certainly at this time be very salutary to the most holy faith of Christ and of all Christians, we beg and beseech by the bowels of the mercy of God and of our Lord Jesus Christ, the truth of whose faith and whose religion are now so violently assailed both from within and without, that if they wish the Christian commonwealth to be safe, if they feel themselves bound and under obligation to the Lord for His great favors toward them, they will not abandon His cause and interests but will come personally to the celebration of the holy council, where their piety and virtue would be greatly conducive to the common good, to their own and the welfare of others, temporal as well as spiritual. But if, which we do not wish, they themselves cannot appear, let them at least send distinguished men entrusted with authority, each of whom may represent in the council with prudence and dignity the person of his prince. But above all, and this is for them an easy matter, let them see to it that the bishops and prelates of their respective kingdoms and provinces proceed to the council without tergiversation and delay, a favor that God himself and we can in justice claim particularly from the prelates and princes of Germany; for since it is chiefly on their account and at their wishes that the council has been summoned, and in the very city that they desired, let them not regard it burdensome to celebrate and adorn it with their presence, so that, God going before us in our deliberations and holding before our minds the light of His wisdom and truth, we may in the holy ecumenical council, in a better and easier manner consider, and with the charity of all concurring to one end, ponder, discuss, execute and bring speedily and happily to the desired result whatever things pertain to the purity and truth of the Christian religion, to the restoration of what is good and the correction of bad morals, to the peace, unity and harmony of Christians among themselves, of the princes as well as of the people, and whatever is necessary to repulse those attacks of barbarians and infidels whereby they seek the overthrow of all Christendom. And that this our letter and its contents may come to the knowledge of all whom it concerns, and that no one may plead ignorance as an excuse, particularly since there may not perchance be free access to all to whom it ought to be especially communicated, we wish and command that it be read publicly and in a loud voice by the messengers of our court or by some public notaries in the Vatican Basilica of the Prince of the Apostles and in the Lateran Church, at a time when the people are accustomed to assemble there to hear divine services; and after having been read, let it be affixed to the doors of the said churches, also to the gates of the Apostolic Chancery and to the usual place in the Campo di Fiore, where it shall hang openly for some time for the perusal and cognizance of all; and when removed thence, copies of it shall still remain affixed in the same places. For by being thus read, published and affixed, we wish that each and all whom our aforesaid letter concerns be, after the interval of two months from the day of being published and affixed, so bound and obligated as if it had been read and published in their presence. We command and decree also that an unshaken and firm faith be given to transcripts thereof, written or subscribed by the hand of a notary public and authenticated by the seal of some person constituted in ecclesiastical dignity. Therefore, let no one infringe this our letter of summons, announcement, convocation, statute, decree, command, precept and supplication, or with foolhardy boldness oppose it. But if anyone shall presume to attempt this, let him know that he will incur the indignation of Almighty God and of His blessed Apostles

Peter and Paul. Given at Rome at Saint Peter's in the year 1542 of the Lord's incarnation on the twenty-second of May, in the eighth year of our pontificate.

Blosius.

Hier. Dand.

FIRST SESSION

OF THE

HOLY ECUMENICAL AND GENERAL

COUNCIL OF TRENT

celebrated under the sovereign pontiff, Paul III, on the thirteenth day of December in the year of the Lord 1545

DECREE CONCERNING THE OPENING OF THE COUNCIL

Does it please you, for the praise and glory of the holy and undivided Trinity, Father, Son, and Holy Ghost, for the advance and exaltation of the Christian faith and religion, for the extirpation of heresies, for the peace and unity of the Church, for the reform of the clergy and Christian people, for the suppression and destruction of the enemies of the Christian name, to decree and declare that the holy and general Council of Trent begins and has begun?

They answered: It pleases us.

ANNOUNCEMENT OF THE NEXT SESSION

And since the solemnity of the Nativity of our Lord Jesus Christ is near, and other festivals of the closing and opening year follow thereon, does it please you that the next ensuing session be held on the Thursday after the Epiphany, which will be the seventh of the month of January in the year of the Lord 1546?

They answered: It pleases us.

SECOND SESSION

celebrated on the seventh day of January, 1546

DECREE CONCERNING THE MANNER OF LIVING AND OTHER MATTERS TO BE OBSERVED DURING THE COUNCIL

The holy Council of Trent, lawfully assembled in the Holy Ghost and presided over by the same three legates of the Apostolic See, recognizing with the blessed Apostle James that *every best gift and every perfect gift is from above, coming down from the Father of lights,*[1] who, to those who ask of Him *wisdom, giveth to all abundantly and upbraideth them not;* [2] and knowing also that *the fear of the Lord is the beginning of wisdom,*[3] has ordained and decreed that each and all of the faithful of Christ assembled in the city of Trent be exhorted, as they are hereby exhorted, to amend themselves in the evils and sins hitherto committed and to walk henceforth in the fear of the Lord; *not to fulfil the lusts of the flesh,*[4] to be *instant in prayer,*[5] to confess more often, to receive the sacrament of the Eucharist, to frequent the churches, to observe, so far as each one is able, the commandments of the Lord, and to pray daily in private for peace among the Christian princes and for unity of the Church. The bishops, however, and all others constituted in the sacerdotal order, who are participating in the celebration of the ecumenical council in this city, are to apply themselves diligently to glorifying God, to offer up sacrifices, praises and prayers, to celebrate in accordance with their duty the sacrifice of the mass at least every Sunday, the day on which God made the light, rose from the dead, and poured forth the Holy Ghost upon the disciples; [6] making, as the same Holy Ghost commanded by the Apostle, *supplications, prayers, intercessions and thanksgivings* for our most holy Lord the Pope, for the Emperor, *for kings and others who are placed in high*

---

[1] James 1:17.
[2] *Idem,* 1:5.
[3] Ps. 110:10; Prov. 1:7; 9:10; Eccles. 1:16.
[4] Gal. 5:16.
[5] Rom. 12:12.
[6] Acts 2:1 ff.

stations, and for all men, that we may lead a quiet and peaceable life,[7] may enjoy peace and witness an increase of the faith. Furthermore, it exhorts that they fast at least every Friday in memory of the passion of the Lord and give alms to the poor. Every Thursday the mass of the Holy Ghost shall be celebrated in the cathedral with the litanies and other prayers assigned for this purpose; in the other churches there shall be said on the same day at least the litanies and the prayers. During the time that the sacred services are being performed, let there be no talking and idle conversation, but let mouth and mind be united with the celebrant. And since *it behooves bishops to be blameless, sober, chaste, ruling well their own household,*[8] it exhorts also that above all things each observe sobriety at table and moderation in diet; and further, since there idle conversations are often wont to arise, that the reading of the Scriptures be introduced at the tables, even at those of the bishops.[9] Let each one instruct and charge his servants not to be contentious, given to wine, disrespectful, covetous, arrogant, blasphemous and lovers of pleasure; finally, let them shun vice and embrace virtue, and in attire, in behavior and in all their actions let them manifest decorum as becomes the servants of the servants of God. Moreover, since it is the chief care, solicitude and intention of this holy council that the darkness of heresies, which for so many years has covered the earth, being dispelled, the light of Catholic truth may, with the aid of Jesus Christ, who is the true light,[10] shine forth in splendor and purity, and that those things that need reform may be reformed, the council exhorts all Catholics here assembled and who will be here assembled, especially those having a knowledge of the Sacred Scriptures, that by sedulous meditation they ponder diligently within themselves, by what ways and means the intention of the council can best be carried out and the desired result obtained; how the things to be condemned may be condemned more promptly and prudently and those to be approved may be approved, so that throughout the whole world all may with one voice and with the same profession of faith glorify God and the Father of our Lord Jesus Christ.[11]

In expressing opinions when the priests of the Lord are assembled in

[7] Cf. I Tim. 2:1 f.

[8] *Idem*, 3:2 ff.

[9] Cf. III Synod of Toledo (589), c.7 (c.11, D.XLIV); II Synod of Reims (813), c.17 (Hardouin IV, 1019) and *infra*, Sess. XXV, chap. 1 de ref.

[10] John 1:9.

[11] Rom. 15:6.

the place of benediction, in conformity with the decree of the Synod of Toledo,[12] no one ought to be boisterous by immoderate shouting or create disturbance by stamping, nor contentious in false, vain and obstinate disputations, but let whatever is said be so tempered with mildness that neither the hearers be offended nor the keenness of correct judgment warped by a disturbed mind.

Moreover, this holy council has ordained and decreed that if it should happen that some during the council do not sit in their proper places and also make known their mind by the word *Placet*, are present at the assemblies and perform any other acts whatsoever, no disadvantage shall thereby accrue to anyone, neither shall anyone thereby acquire a new right.[13]

ANNOUNCEMENT OF THE NEXT SESSION

After this the next session was announced for Thursday, the fourth day of the following February.

---

[12] Cf. XI Synod of Toledo (675), c. 1.

[13] Cf. Sess. XXV at the end.

THIRD SESSION

celebrated on the fourth day of February, 1546

DECREE CONCERNING THE SYMBOL OF FAITH

In the name of the holy and undivided Trinity, Father, Son, and Holy Ghost.

This holy, ecumenical and general Council of Trent, lawfully assembled in the Holy Ghost, the same three legates of the Apostolic See presiding, considering the magnitude of the matters to be dealt with, especially those comprised under the two heads, the extirpation of heresies and the reform of morals, for which purposes it was chiefly assembled, and recognizing with the Apostle that its *wrestling is not against flesh and blood, but against the spirits of wickedness in high places*,[1] exhorts with the same Apostle each and all above all things to be *strengthened in the Lord and in the might of his power, in all things taking the shield of faith, wherewith they may be able to extinguish all the fiery darts of the most wicked one, and to take the helmet of the hope of salvation and the sword of the spirit, which is the word of God.*[2] Wherefore, that this pious solicitude [of the council] may begin and continue by the grace of God, it ordains and decrees that before all else a confession of faith be set forth; following herein the examples of the Fathers, who in the more outstanding councils were accustomed at the beginning of their work to use this shield against heresies, with which alone they have at times drawn unbelievers to the faith, overcome heretics and confirmed the faithful. For this reason it has thought it well that the symbol of faith which the holy Roman Church uses as the cardinal principle wherein all who profess the faith of Christ necessarily agree and as the firm and sole foundation *against which the gates of hell shall never prevail*,[3] be expressed in the same words in which it is read in all the churches, which is as follows: *I believe in one God the Father Almighty, creator of heaven and earth, of all things visible and invisible; and in one Lord Jesus Christ, the only begotten*

[1] Eph. 6:12.
[2] *Ibid.*, 6:10, 16 f.
[3] Matt. 16:18.

Son of God and born of the Father before all ages; God of God, light of light, true God of true God; begotten, not made, consubstantial with the Father, by whom all things were made; who for us men and for our salvation descended from heaven, and was incarnate by the Holy Ghost of the Virgin Mary, and was made man; crucified also for us under Pontius Pilate, he suffered and was buried; and he arose on the third day according to the Scriptures, and ascended into heaven, sits at the right hand of the Father; and again he will come with glory to judge the living and the dead; of whose kingdom there shall be no end; and in the Holy Ghost the Lord and giver of life, who proceeds from the Father and the Son; who with the Father and the Son together is adored and glorified; who spoke by the prophets; and in one holy Catholic and Apostolic Church. I confess one baptism for the remission of sins; and I look for the resurrection of the dead, and the life of the world to come. Amen.

ANNOUNCEMENT OF THE NEXT SESSION

The same holy, ecumenical and general Council of Trent, lawfully assembled in the Holy Ghost, the same three legates of the Apostolic See presiding, understanding that many prelates in various localities are girded for their journey, and that some also are on their way here; and considering that the greater the attendance of Fathers in sanctioning and confirming all that will be decreed by the holy council, in so much greater esteem and respect will those decrees be held among all men, has ordained and decreed that the next session after the present one be held on the Thursday following the next *Laetare* Sunday. In the meantime, however, the discussion and examination of those things which the council shall deem necessary to discuss and examine, shall not be deferred.

FOURTH SESSION

celebrated on the eighth day of April, 1546

DECREE CONCERNING THE CANONICAL SCRIPTURES

The holy, ecumenical and general Council of Trent, lawfully assembled in the Holy Ghost, the same three legates of the Apostolic See presiding, keeps this constantly in view, namely, that the purity of the Gospel may be preserved in the Church after the errors have been removed. This [Gospel], of old promised through the Prophets in the Holy Scriptures,[1] our Lord Jesus Christ, the Son of God, promulgated first with His own mouth, and then commanded it to be preached by His Apostles to every creature [2] as the source at once of all saving truth and rules of conduct. It also clearly perceives that these truths and rules are contained in the written books and in the unwritten traditions, which, received by the Apostles from the mouth of Christ Himself, or from the Apostles themselves,[3] the Holy Ghost dictating, have come down to us, transmitted as it were from hand to hand. Following, then, the examples of the orthodox Fathers, it receives and venerates with a feeling of piety and reverence all the books both of the Old and New Testaments, since one God is the author of both; also the traditions, whether they relate to faith or to morals, as having been dictated either orally by Christ or by the Holy Ghost, and preserved in the Catholic Church in unbroken succession. It has thought it proper, moreover, to insert in this decree a list of the sacred books, lest a doubt might arise in the mind of someone as to which are the books received by this council.[4] They are the following: of the Old

---

[1] Jer. 31:22.

[2] Matt. 28:19 f.; Mark 16:15.

[3] See II Thess. 2:14; c.5, D.XI.

[4] For earlier lists, cf. Synod of Laodicea (end of IV cent.), c.60, the genuineness of which canon however is contested (Hefele-Leclercq, *Hist. des conciles*, I, 1026); Synod of Rome (382) under Pope Damasus (Denzinger, *Enchiridion*, no. 84); Synod of Hippo (393), c.36, which the III Synod of Carthage (397) made its own in c.47 (*idem*, no. 92); Innocent I in 405 to Exuperius, bishop of Toulouse (*idem*, no. 96); Eugene IV in the Council of Florence (Mansi, XXXI, 1736; Hardouin, IX, 1023 f.). The Tridentine list or decree was the first infallible and effectually promulgated declaration on the Canon of the Holy Scriptures.

Testament, the five books of Moses, namely, Genesis, Exodus, Leviticus, Numbers, Deuteronomy; Josue, Judges, Ruth, the four books of Kings, two of Paralipomenon, the first and second of Esdras, the latter of which is called Nehemias, Tobias, Judith, Esther, Job, the Davidic Psalter of 150 Psalms, Proverbs, Ecclesiastes, the Canticle of Canticles, Wisdom, Ecclesiasticus, Isaias, Jeremias, with Baruch, Ezechiel, Daniel, the twelve minor Prophets, namely, Osee, Joel, Amos, Abdias, Jonas, Micheas, Nahum, Habacuc, Sophonias, Aggeus, Zacharias, Malachias; two books of Machabees, the first and second. Of the New Testament, the four Gospels, according to Matthew, Mark, Luke and John; the Acts of the Apostles written by Luke the Evangelist; fourteen Epistles of Paul the Apostle, to the Romans, two to the Corinthians, to the Galatians, to the Ephesians, to the Philippians, to the Colossians, two to the Thessalonians, two to Timothy, to Titus, to Philemon, to the Hebrews; two of Peter the Apostle, three of John the Apostle, one of James the Apostle, one of Jude the Apostle, and the Apocalypse of John the Apostle. If anyone does not accept as sacred and canonical the aforesaid books in their entirety and with all their parts, as they have been accustomed to be read in the Catholic Church and as they are contained in the old Latin Vulgate Edition, and knowingly and deliberately rejects the aforesaid traditions, let him be anathema. Let all understand, therefore, in what order and manner the council, after having laid the foundation of the confession of faith, will proceed, and who are the chief witnesses and supports to whom it will appeal in confirming dogmas and in restoring morals in the Church.

DECREE CONCERNING THE EDITION AND USE OF THE SACRED BOOKS

Moreover, the same holy council considering that not a little advantage will accrue to the Church of God if it be made known which of all the Latin editions of the sacred books now in circulation is to be regarded as authentic, ordains and declares that the old Latin Vulgate Edition, which, in use for so many hundred years, has been approved by the Church, be in public lectures, disputations, sermons and expositions held as authentic, and that no one dare or presume under any pretext whatsoever to reject it.

Furthermore, to check unbridled spirits, it decrees that no one relying on his own judgment shall, in matters of faith and morals pertaining to the edification of Christian doctrine, distorting the Holy

Scriptures in accordance with his own conceptions,[5] presume to interpret them contrary to that sense which holy mother Church, to whom it belongs to judge of their true sense and interpretation,[6] has held and holds, or even contrary to the unanimous teaching of the Fathers, even though such interpretations should never at any time be published. Those who act contrary to this shall be made known by the ordinaries and punished in accordance with the penalties prescribed by the law.

And wishing, as is proper, to impose a restraint in this matter on printers also, who, now without restraint, thinking what pleases them is permitted them, print without the permission of ecclesiastical superiors the books of the Holy Scriptures and the notes and commentaries thereon of all persons indiscriminately, often with the name of the press omitted, often also under a fictitious press-name, and what is worse, without the name of the author, and also indiscreetly have for sale such books printed elsewhere, [this council] decrees and ordains that in the future the Holy Scriptures, especially the old Vulgate Edition, be printed in the most correct manner possible, and that it shall not be lawful for anyone to print or to have printed any books whatsoever dealing with sacred doctrinal matters without the name of the author, or in the future to sell them, or even to have them in possession, unless they have first been examined and approved by the ordinary, under penalty of anathema and fine prescribed by the last Council of the Lateran.[7] If they be regulars they must in addition to this examination and approval obtain permission also from their own superiors after these have examined the books in accordance with their own statutes. Those who lend or circulate them in manuscript before they have been examined and approved, shall be subject to the same penalties as the printers, and those who have them in their possession or read them, shall, unless they make known the authors, be themselves regarded as the authors. The approbation of such books, however, shall be given in writing and shall appear authentically at the beginning of the book, whether it be written or printed, and all this, that is, both the examination and approbation, shall be done gratuitously, so that what ought to be approved may be approved and what ought to be condemned may be condemned.

---

[5] St. Jerome, *Comment. on Galatians,* chap. 5, vers. 19–21, *PL,* XXVI, 445 (c. 27, C.XXIV, q. 3); c. 39 (§ 70) *ead.*

[6] Quinisext Council (692), c. 19 (Mansi, XI, 951; Hardouin, III, 1667).

[7] Cf. the bull "Inter sollicitudines," Schroeder, *Disciplinary Decrees of the General Councils,* p. 504.

Furthermore, wishing to repress that boldness whereby the words and sentences of the Holy Scriptures are turned and twisted to all kinds of profane usages, namely, to things scurrilous, fabulous, vain, to flatteries, detractions, superstitions, godless and diabolical incantations, divinations, the casting of lots and defamatory libels, to put an end to such irreverence and contempt, and that no one may in the future dare use in any manner the words of Holy Scripture for these and similar purposes, it is commanded and enjoined that all people of this kind be restrained by the bishops as violators and profaners of the word of God, with the penalties of the law and other penalties that they may deem fit to impose.

ANNOUNCEMENT OF THE NEXT SESSION

Likewise, this holy council ordains and decrees that the next session will be held and celebrated on the Thursday after the next most sacred feast of Pentecost.

FIFTH SESSION

celebrated on the seventeenth day of June, 1546

DECREE CONCERNING ORIGINAL SIN

That our Catholic faith, *without which it is impossible to please God,*[1] may, after the destruction of errors, remain integral and spotless in its purity, and that the Christian people may not be *carried about with every wind of doctrine,*[2] since that old serpent,[3] the everlasting enemy of the human race, has, among the many evils with which the Church of God is in our times disturbed, stirred up also not only new but also old dissensions concerning original sin and its remedy, the holy, ecumenical and general Council of Trent, lawfully assembled in the Holy Ghost, the same three legates of the Apostolic See presiding, wishing now to reclaim the erring and to strengthen the wavering, and following the testimonies of the Holy Scriptures, of the holy Fathers, of the most approved councils, as well as the judgment and unanimity of the Church herself, ordains, confesses and declares these things concerning original sin:

1. If anyone does not confess that the first man, Adam, when he transgressed the commandment of God in paradise, immediately lost the holiness and justice in which he had been constituted, and through the offense of that prevarication incurred the wrath and indignation of God, and thus death with which God had previously threatened him,[4] and, together with death, captivity under his power who thenceforth *had the empire of death, that is to say, the devil,*[5] and that the entire Adam through that offense of prevarication was changed in body and soul for the worse,[6] let him be anathema.

2. If anyone asserts that the transgression of Adam injured him alone and not his posterity,[7] and that the holiness and justice which he re-

---

1 Heb. 11:6.
2 Eph. 4:14.
3 Gen. 3:1 ff.; Apoc. 12:9; 20:2.
4 Gen. 2:17.
5 Heb. 2:14.
6 Cf. II Synod of Orange (529), c.1. Denzinger, no. 174.
7 See I Cor. 15:21 f.; II Synod of Orange, c.2. *Ibid.*, no. 175.

ceived from God, which he lost, he lost for himself alone and not for us also; or that he, being defiled by the sin of disobedience, has transfused only death and the pains of the body into the whole human race, but not sin also, which is the death of the soul, let him be anathema, since he contradicts the Apostle who says: *By one man sin entered into the world and by sin death; and so death passed upon all men, in whom all have sinned.*[8]

3. If anyone asserts that this sin of Adam, which in its origin is one, and by propagation, not by imitation, transfused into all, which is in each one as something that is his own, is taken away either by the forces of human nature or by a remedy other than the merit of the one mediator, our Lord Jesus Christ,[9] who has reconciled us to God in his own blood, *made unto us justice, sanctification and redemption;*[10] or if he denies that that merit of Jesus Christ is applied both to adults and to infants by the sacrament of baptism rightly administered in the form of the Church, let him be anathema; *for there is no other name under heaven given to men, whereby we must be saved.*[11] Whence that declaration: *Behold the Lamb of God, behold him who taketh away the sins of the world;*[12] and that other: *As many of you as have been baptized, have put on Christ.*[13]

4. If anyone denies that infants, newly born from their mothers' wombs, are to be baptized, even though they be born of baptized parents, or says that they are indeed *baptized for the remission of sins,*[14] but that they derive nothing of original sin from Adam which must be expiated by the laver of regeneration for the attainment of eternal life, whence it follows that in them the form of baptism for the remission of sins is to be understood not as true but as false, let him be anathema, for what the Apostle has said, *by one man sin entered into the world, and by sin death, and so death passed upon all men, in whom all have sinned,*[15] is not to be understood otherwise than as the Catholic Church has everywhere and always understood it. For in virtue of this rule of faith handed down from the apostles, even infants who could not as

---

[8] Rom. 5:12.
[9] See I Tim. 2:5.
[10] See I Cor. 1:30.
[11] Acts 4:12.
[12] John 1:29.
[13] Gal. 3:27.
[14] Acts 2:38.
[15] Rom. 5:12.

yet commit any sin of themselves, are for this reason truly baptized for the remission of sins, in order that in them what they contracted by generation may be washed away by regeneration.[16] For, *unless a man be born again of water and the Holy Ghost, he cannot enter into the kingdom of heaven.*[17]

5. If anyone denies that by the grace of our Lord Jesus Christ which is conferred in baptism, the guilt of original sin is remitted, or says that the whole of that which belongs to the essence of sin is not taken away, but says that it is only canceled or not imputed, let him be anathema. For in those who are born again God hates nothing, because *there is no condemnation to those who are* truly *buried together with Christ by baptism unto death,*[18] *who walk not according to the flesh,*[19] but, putting off the old man and putting on the new one who is created according to God,[20] are made innocent, immaculate, pure, guiltless and beloved of God, *heirs indeed of God, joint heirs with Christ;*[21] so that there is nothing whatever to hinder their entrance into heaven. But this holy council perceives and confesses that in the one baptized there remains concupiscence or an inclination to sin, which, since it is left for us to wrestle with, cannot injure those who do not acquiesce but resist manfully by the grace of Jesus Christ; indeed, he who shall have *striven lawfully shall be crowned.*[22] This concupiscence, which the Apostle sometimes calls sin,[23] the holy council declares the Catholic Church has never understood to be called sin in the sense that it is truly and properly sin in those born again, but in the sense that it is of sin and inclines to sin. But if anyone is of the contrary opinion, let him be anathema.

This holy council declares, however, that it is not its intention to include in this decree, which deals with original sin, the blessed and immaculate Virgin Mary, the mother of God, but that the constitutions of Pope Sixtus IV, of happy memory, are to be observed under the penalties contained in those constitutions, which it renews.[24]

---

[16] C. 153, D. IV de cons.
[17] John 3:5.
[18] Rom. 6:4; c. 13, D. IV de cons.
[19] Rom. 8:1.
[20] Eph. 4:22, 24; Col. 3:9 f.
[21] Rom. 8:17.
[22] See II Tim. 2:5.
[23] Rom. 6–8; Col. 3.
[24] Cc. 1, 2, Extrav. comm., De reliq. et venerat. sanct., III, 12.

DECREE CONCERNING REFORM

CHAPTER I

THE ESTABLISHMENT OF LECTURESHIPS IN HOLY SCRIPTURE AND THE LIBERAL ARTS

The same holy council, adhering to the pious decisions of the sovereign pontiffs and of approved councils,[25] and accepting and adding to them, that the heavenly treasure of the sacred books which the Holy Ghost has with the greatest liberality delivered to men may not lie neglected, has ordained and decreed that in those churches in which there exists a prebend or a benefice with an obligation attached, or other income by whatever name it may be known, set aside for instructors in sacred theology, the bishops, archbishops, primates, and other ecclesiastical superiors of those localities compel, even by a reduction of their revenues, those who hold such prebend, benefice or income, to expound and interpret the Holy Scriptures, either personally if they are competent, otherwise by a competent substitute to be chosen by the bishops, archbishops, primates, or other superiors of those places. In the future such prebend, benefice and income shall be conferred only on competent persons and those who can themselves discharge that office; a provision made otherwise shall be null and void. In metropolitan and cathedral churches, however, if the city be an outstanding and populous one, and also in collegiate churches that are situated in a prominent town, even though they do not belong to any diocese, provided the clergy there are numerous, where there is no prebend, benefice or income provided for this purpose, let the prebend that shall first become vacant in any manner whatever, except by resignation, and to which some other incompatible duty is not attached, be understood to be *ipso facto* and forever set aside and devoted to that purpose. And should it happen that in those churches there is not any or no sufficient income,[26] let the metropolitan or the bishop himself, by assigning thereto the revenues of some simple benefice, the duties connected with it being nevertheless discharged, or by contributions of the *beneficiati* of his city and diocese, or otherwise, as may be most

[25] C. 12 D. XXXVII; cc. 1, 4, 5, X, De magistr., V, 5. Cf. also Sess. XXIII, chap. 18 de ref.

[26] Sess. XXIV, chap. 15 de ref.

convenient, provide in such a way with the advice of the chapter that the instructions in Holy Scripture may be procured; so, however, that all other instructions, whether established by custom or any other agency, be by no means on that account omitted. Churches whose annual revenues are scanty and where the number of clergy and people is so small that instruction in theology cannot be conveniently had therein, may have at least a master, to be chosen by the bishop with the advice of the chapter, to teach grammar gratuitously to clerics and other poor students,[27] so that afterwards they may with the help of God pass on to the study of Holy Scripture. For this purpose let the revenues of some simple benefice be assigned to that master of grammar,[28] which he shall receive so long as he is engaged in teaching (provided, however, that that benefice be not deprived of the services due to it), or let some suitable remuneration be paid him out of the capitular or episcopal income, or finally, let the bishop himself devise some other arrangement suitable to his church and diocese, that this pious, useful and profitable provision may not under any feigned excuse be neglected. In the monasteries of monks also, where this can be conveniently done, let there be instructions in the Holy Scriptures.[29] If abbots prove negligent in this matter, let the bishops of the localities, as the delegates herein of the Apostolic See, compel them thereto by suitable measures. In the convents of other regulars in which studies can conveniently flourish, let there be likewise instructions in the Holy Scriptures, which shall be assigned by the general and provincial chapters to the more worthy masters. In the public gymnasia also where instructions so profitable and of all the most necessary have not thus far been instituted, let them be introduced by the piety and charity of the most religious princes and governments for the defense and increase of the Catholic faith and the preservation and propagation of wholesome doctrine, and where once instituted and neglected, let them be restored. And that under the semblance of piety impiety may not be disseminated, the same holy council has decreed that no one be admitted to this office of instructor, whether such instruction be public or private, who has not been previously examined and approved by the bishop of the locality as to his life, morals and knowledge; which, how-

---

[27] C. 1, X, De magistr., V, 5; Sess. XXIII, chap. 18 de ref.

[28] By the bull *In sacrosancta* of Pius IV (13 Nov., 1564) this master was bound to make a profession of faith.

[29] To which Paul V by the constitution *Apostolicae* (1610) added instructions in Hebrew, Greek and Arabic.

ever, is not to be understood of instructions in the monasteries of monks. Moreover, those who teach Holy Scripture, as long as they teach publicly in the schools, and also the students who study in those schools, shall fully enjoy and possess in case of absence all the privileges accorded by the common law with regard to the collection of the incomes of their prebends and benefices.[30]

Chapter II

PREACHERS OF THE WORD OF GOD AND QUESTORS OF ALMS

But since the preaching of the Gospel is no less necessary to the Christian commonwealth than the reading thereof, and since this is the chief duty of the bishops,[31] the same holy council has ordained and decreed that all bishops, archbishops, primates and all other prelates of the churches are bound personally, if not lawfully hindered, to preach the holy Gospel of Jesus Christ. But if it should happen that bishops and the others mentioned above are hindered by a legitimate impediment, they shall be bound, in accordance with the provision of the general council,[32] to appoint competent persons to discharge beneficially this office of preaching. If however anyone through contempt fails to observe this, let him be subject to severe punishment. Archpriests, priests and all who in any manner have charge of parochial and other churches to which is attached the *cura animarum,* shall at least on Sundays and solemn festivals,[33] either personally or, if they are lawfully impeded, through others who are competent, feed the people committed to them with wholesome words in proportion to their own and their people's mental capacity, by teaching them those things that are necessary for all to know in order to be saved, and by impressing upon them with briefness and plainness of speech the vices that they must avoid and the virtues that they must cultivate, in order that they may escape eternal punishment and obtain the glory of heaven. But if anyone of the above should neglect to discharge this duty, even on the plea that for some reason he is exempt from the jurisdiction of the bishop, even if the churches are said in some way to be exempt, or per-

---

[30] C.5, X, De magistr., V, 5.
[31] Cf. Sess. XXIV, chap. 4 de ref.; c.6, D.LXXXVIII.
[32] C.15, X, De off. jud. ord., I, 31 (IV Lat., c.10).
[33] Cf. Sess. XXIV, chap. cit.

haps annexed or united to some monastery that is outside the diocese, if the churches are really within their dioceses, let not the watchful and pastoral solicitude of the bishops be wanting, lest that be fulfilled: *The little ones have asked for bread, and there was none to break it unto them.*[34] Wherefore, if after having been admonished by the bishop they neglect their duty for a period of three months, let them be compelled by ecclesiastical censures or by other measures at the discretion of the bishop; and should he deem it expedient, let a fair remuneration be paid from the revenues of the benefices to another person to discharge that office, till the incumbent, having come to his senses, shall fulfil his own duty.

But if there should be found parochial churches subject to monasteries that are not in any diocese, and the abbots and regular prelates are negligent in the aforesaid matters, let them be compelled thereto by the metropolitans in whose provinces the dioceses are located, who in this matter shall act as delegates of the Apostolic See, and no custom, exemption, appeal, protest or counteraction shall impede the execution of this decree, till a competent judge, who shall proceed summarily and examine only into the truth of the fact, shall have taken the matter into consideration and given a decision. Regulars of whatever order, unless they have been examined by their superiors regarding life, morals and knowledge and approved by them, may not without their permission preach even in the churches of their order, and they must present themselves personally with this permission before the bishops and ask from these the blessing before they begin to preach. In churches, however, that are not of their orders they must, in addition to the permission of their superiors, have also that of the bishop, without which they may not under any circumstances preach in churches that do not belong to their orders.[35] This permission the bishops shall grant *gratis*. But if, which heaven avert, a preacher should spread errors or scandals among the people, let the bishop forbid him to preach, even though he preach in his own or in the monastery of another order. Should he preach heresies, let him proceed against him in accordance with the requirement of the law or the custom of the locality, even though that preacher should plead exemption by a general or special privilege; in which case the bishop shall proceed by Apostolic authority and as the delegate of the Apostolic See. But let bishops be careful that a preacher

[34] Lam. 4:4.
[35] C. 13 (§ 6), X, De haeret., V, 7; Sess. XXIV, chap. 4 de ref.

be not annoyed by false accusations or calumnies, or have just cause of complaint concerning such. Moreover, let bishops be on their guard not to permit anyone, whether of those who, being regulars in name, live outside their monasteries and the obedience of their religious institute, or secular priests, unless they are known to them and are of approved morals and doctrine, to preach in their city or diocese, even under pretext of any privilege whatsoever, till they have consulted the holy Apostolic See on the matter; from which See it is not likely that privileges of this kind are extorted by unworthy persons except by suppressing the truth or stating what is false.

Those soliciting alms, who are also commonly known as questors,[36] whatever their state, shall not in any manner presume to preach either *per se* or *per alium*, and shall, notwithstanding any privilege whatsoever, be absolutely restrained by suitable measures by the bishops and ordinaries of the localities.

ANNOUNCEMENT OF THE NEXT SESSION

This holy council also ordains and decrees that the next session be held and celebrated on the Thursday after the feast of the blessed Apostle James.

The session was afterwards prorogued to the thirteenth day of January, 1547.

[36] C. 14, X, De poenit. et remiss., V, 38; c. 11 (§ 2), VI°, De haeret., V, 2; c. 2, in Clem., De poenit. et remis., V, 9. By the bull of Pius V, *Etsi Dominici,* (1567) all indulgences which gave occasion for abuse by the questors were withdrawn.

SIXTH SESSION

celebrated on the thirteenth day of January, 1547

DECREE CONCERNING JUSTIFICATION

Introduction

Since there is being disseminated at this time, not without the loss of many souls and grievous detriment to the unity of the Church, a certain erroneous doctrine concerning justification, the holy, ecumenical and general Council of Trent, lawfully assembled in the Holy Ghost, the most reverend John Maria, Bishop of Praeneste de Monte, and Marcellus, priest of the Holy Cross in Jerusalem, cardinals of the holy Roman Church and legates Apostolic *a latere*, presiding in the name of our most holy Father and Lord in Christ, Paul III, by the providence of God, Pope, intends, for the praise and glory of Almighty God, for the tranquillity of the Church and the salvation of souls, to expound to all the faithful of Christ the true and salutary doctrine of justification, which the *Sun of justice*,[1] Jesus Christ, *the author and finisher of our faith* [2] taught, which the Apostles transmitted and which the Catholic Church under the inspiration of the Holy Ghost has always retained; strictly forbidding that anyone henceforth presume to believe, preach or teach otherwise than is defined and declared in the present decree.

Chapter I

THE IMPOTENCY OF NATURE AND OF THE LAW TO JUSTIFY MAN

The holy council declares first, that for a correct and clear understanding of the doctrine of justification, it is necessary that each one recognize and confess that since all men had lost innocence in the

[1] Mal. 4:2.
[2] Heb. 12:2.

prevarication of Adam,[3] having become unclean,[4] and, as the Apostle says, *by nature children of wrath*,[5] as has been set forth in the decree on original sin,[6] they were so far *the servants of sin*[7] and under the power of the devil and of death, that not only the Gentiles by the force of nature, but not even the Jews by the very letter of the law of Moses, were able to be liberated or to rise therefrom, though free will, weakened as it was in its powers and downward bent,[8] was by no means extinguished in them.

Chapter II

THE DISPENSATION AND MYSTERY OF THE ADVENT OF CHRIST

Whence it came to pass that the heavenly Father, *the Father of mercies and the God of all comfort*,[9] *when the blessed fulness of the time was come*,[10] sent to men Jesus Christ, His own Son, who had both before the law and during the time of the law been announced and promised to many of the holy fathers,[11] *that he might redeem the Jews who were under the law*,[12] and *that the Gentiles who followed not after justice*[13] might attain to justice, and that all men might receive the adoption of sons. Him has God *proposed* as a propitiator *through faith in his blood*[14] *for our sins, and not for our sins only, but also for those of the whole world.*[15]

Chapter III

WHO ARE JUSTIFIED THROUGH CHRIST

But though *He died for all*,[16] yet all do not receive the benefit of His death, but those only to whom the merit of His passion is com-

---

[3] Rom. 5:12; I Cor. 15:22.
[4] Is. 64:6.
[5] Eph. 2:3.
[6] Cf. Sess. V at the beginning.
[7] Rom. 6:17, 20.
[8] Cf. II Synod of Orange (529), c.25. Hardouin, II, 1101.
[9] See II Cor. 1:3.
[10] Gal. 4:4.
[11] Gen. 49:10, 18.
[12] Gal. 4:5.
[13] Rom. 9:30.
[14] *Ibid.*, 3:25; Dist. I De poenit., *passim.*
[15] See I John 2:2.
[16] See II Cor. 5:15.

municated; because as truly as men would not be born unjust, if they were not born through propagation of the seed of Adam, since by that propagation they contract through him, when they are conceived, injustice as their own, so if they were not born again in Christ, they would never be justified, since in that new birth there is bestowed upon them, through the merit of His passion, the grace by which they are made just. For this benefit the Apostle exhorts us always *to give thanks to the Father, who hath made us worthy to be partakers of the lot of the saints in light, and hath delivered us from the power of darkness, and hath translated us into the kingdom of the Son of his love, in whom we have redemption and remission of sins.*[17]

Chapter IV

A BRIEF DESCRIPTION OF THE JUSTIFICATION OF THE SINNER AND ITS MODE IN THE STATE OF GRACE

In which words is given a brief description of the justification of the sinner, as being a translation from that state in which man is born a child of the first Adam, to the state of grace and of the adoption of the sons of God through the second Adam, Jesus Christ, our Savior. This translation however cannot, since the promulgation of the Gospel, be effected except through the laver of regeneration or its desire, as it is written: *Unless a man be born again of water and the Holy Ghost, he cannot enter into the kingdom of God.*[18]

Chapter V

THE NECESSITY OF PREPARATION FOR JUSTIFICATION IN ADULTS, AND WHENCE IT PROCEEDS

It is furthermore declared that in adults the beginning of that justification must proceed from the predisposing grace of God through Jesus Christ, that is, from His vocation, whereby, without any merits on their part, they are called; that they who by sin had been cut off from God, may be disposed through His quickening and helping grace to convert themselves to their own justification by freely assenting to

---

[17] Col. 1:12-14.
[18] John 3:5.

and cooperating with that grace; so that, while God touches the heart of man through the illumination of the Holy Ghost, man himself neither does absolutely nothing while receiving that inspiration, since he can also reject it, nor yet is he able by his own free will and without the grace of God to move himself to justice in His sight. Hence, when it is said in the sacred writings: *Turn ye to me, and I will turn to you,*[19] we are reminded of our liberty; and when we reply: *Convert us, O Lord, to thee, and we shall be converted,*[20] we confess that we need the grace of God.

Chapter VI

THE MANNER OF PREPARATION

Now, they [the adults] are disposed to that justice when, aroused and aided by divine grace, receiving *faith by hearing,*[21] they are moved freely toward God, believing to be true what has been divinely revealed and promised, especially that the sinner is justified by God *by his grace, through the redemption that is in Christ Jesus;*[22] and when, understanding themselves to be sinners, they, by turning themselves from the fear of divine justice, by which they are salutarily aroused, to consider the mercy of God, are raised to hope, trusting that God will be propitious to them for Christ's sake; and they begin to love Him as the fountain of all justice, and on that account are moved against sin by a certain hatred and detestation, that is, by that repentance that must be performed before baptism;[23] finally, when they resolve to receive baptism, to begin a new life and to keep the commandments of God. Of this disposition it is written: *He that cometh to God, must believe that he is, and is a rewarder to them that seek him;*[24] and, *Be of good faith, son, thy sins are forgiven thee;*[25] and, *The fear of the Lord driveth out sin;*[26] and, *Do penance, and be baptized every one of you in the name of Jesus Christ, for the remission of your sins, and you shall receive the gift of the Holy Ghost;*[27] and,

---

[19] Zach. 1:3.
[20] Lam. 5:21.
[21] Rom. 10:17.
[22] *Ibid.*, 3:24.
[23] Cf. Sess. XIV, chap. 4.
[24] Heb. 11:6.
[25] Matt. 9:2; Mark 2:5.
[26] Ecclus. 1:27.
[27] Acts 2:38; cc. 13, 97, D. IV de cons.

Going, therefore, teach ye all nations, baptizing them in the name of the Father, and of the Son, and of the Holy Ghost, teaching them to observe all things whatsoever I have commanded you; [28] finally, *Prepare your hearts unto the Lord.*[29]

Chapter VII

IN WHAT THE JUSTIFICATION OF THE SINNER CONSISTS, AND WHAT ARE ITS CAUSES

This disposition or preparation is followed by justification itself, which is not only a remission of sins but also the sanctification and renewal of the inward man through the voluntary reception of the grace and gifts whereby an unjust man becomes just and from being an enemy becomes a friend, that he may be *an heir according to hope of life everlasting.*[30] The causes of this justification are: the final cause is the glory of God and of Christ and life everlasting; the efficient cause is the merciful God who *washes and sanctifies* [31] gratuitously, signing and anointing *with the holy Spirit of promise, who is the pledge of our inheritance;* [32] the meritorious cause is His most beloved only begotten, our Lord Jesus Christ, who, *when we were enemies,*[33] *for the exceeding charity wherewith he loved us,*[34] merited for us justification by His most holy passion on the wood of the cross and made satisfaction for us to God the Father; the instrumental cause is the sacrament of baptism, which is the sacrament of faith,[35] without which no man was ever justified; finally, the single formal cause is the justice of God, not that by which He Himself is just, but that by which He makes us just, that, namely, with which we being endowed by Him, are *renewed in the spirit of our mind,*[36] and not only are we reputed but we are truly called and are just, receiving justice within us, each one according to his own measure, which the Holy Ghost distributes to everyone as He wills,[37] and according to each one's disposition and cooperation. For

[28] Matt. 28:19 f.
[29] See I Kings 7:3.
[30] Tit. 3:7.
[31] See I Cor. 6:11.
[32] Eph. 1:13 f.
[33] Rom. 5:10.
[34] Eph. 2:4.
[35] C.76, D.IV de cons.
[36] Eph. 4:23.
[37] See I Cor. 12:11.

though no one can be just except he to whom the merits of the passion of our Lord Jesus Christ are communicated, yet this takes place in that justification of the sinner, when by the merit of the most holy passion, *the charity of God is poured forth by the Holy Ghost in the hearts* [38] of those who are justified and inheres in them; whence man through Jesus Christ, in whom he is ingrafted, receives in that justification, together with the remission of sins, all these infused at the same time, namely, faith, hope and charity. For faith, unless hope and charity be added to it, neither unites man perfectly with Christ nor makes him a living member of His body.[39] For which reason it is most truly said that *faith without works is dead* [40] and of no profit, and *in Christ Jesus neither circumcision availeth anything nor uncircumcision, but faith that worketh by charity*.[41] This faith, conformably to Apostolic tradition, catechumens ask of the Church before the sacrament of baptism, when they ask for the faith that gives eternal life, which without hope and charity faith cannot give. Whence also they hear immediately the word of Christ: *If thou wilt enter into life, keep the commandments.*[42] Wherefore, when receiving true and Christian justice, they are commanded, immediately on being born again, to preserve it pure and spotless, as *the first robe* [43] given them through Christ Jesus in place of that which Adam by his disobedience lost for himself and for us, so that they may bear it before the tribunal of our Lord Jesus Christ and may have life eternal.

Chapter VIII

HOW THE GRATUITOUS JUSTIFICATION OF THE SINNER BY FAITH IS TO BE UNDERSTOOD

But when the Apostle says that man is justified by faith and freely,[44] these words are to be understood in that sense in which the uninterrupted unanimity of the Catholic Church has held and expressed them, namely, that we are therefore said to be justified by faith, because faith

[38] Rom. 5:5.
[39] Cf. *infra*, chap. 10.
[40] James 2:17, 20.
[41] Gal. 5:6, 6:15.
[42] Matt. 19:17.
[43] Luke 15:22; c.31, D.II de poenit.
[44] Rom. 3:24; 5:1.

is the beginning of human salvation, the foundation and root of all justification, *without which it is impossible to please God* [45] and to come to the fellowship of His sons; and we are therefore said to be justified gratuitously, because none of those things that precede justification, whether faith or works, merit the grace of justification. For, *if by grace, it is not now by works, otherwise*, as the Apostle says, *grace is no more grace.*[46]

Chapter IX

AGAINST THE VAIN CONFIDENCE OF HERETICS

But though it is necessary to believe that sins neither are remitted nor ever have been remitted except gratuitously by divine mercy for Christ's sake, yet it must not be said that sins are forgiven or have been forgiven to anyone who boasts of his confidence and certainty of the remission of his sins,[47] resting on that alone, though among heretics and schismatics this vain and ungodly confidence may be and in our troubled times indeed is found and preached with untiring fury against the Catholic Church. Moreover, it must not be maintained, that they who are truly justified must needs, without any doubt whatever, convince themselves that they are justified, and that no one is absolved from sins and justified except he that believes with certainty that he is absolved and justified,[48] and that absolution and justification are effected by this faith alone, as if he who does not believe this, doubts the promises of God and the efficacy of the death and resurrection of Christ. For as no pious person ought to doubt the mercy of God, the merit of Christ and the virtue and efficacy of the sacraments, so each one, when he considers himself and his own weakness and indisposition, may have fear and apprehension concerning his own grace, since no one can know with the certainty of faith, which cannot be subject to error, that he has obtained the grace of God.

[45] Heb. 11:6.
[46] Rom. 11:6.
[47] Cf. *infra*, can. 12 and 13.
[48] *Infra*, can. 14.

CHAPTER X

THE INCREASE OF THE JUSTIFICATION RECEIVED

Having, therefore, been thus justified and made the friends and *domestics of God*,[49] advancing *from virtue to virtue*,[50] they are *renewed*, as the Apostle says, *day by day*,[51] that is, *mortifying the members* [52] of their flesh, and presenting them as instruments of justice unto sanctification,[53] they, through the observance of the commandments of God and of the Church, faith cooperating with good works, increase in that justice received through the grace of Christ and are further justified, as it is written: *He that is just, let him be justified still;* [54] and, *Be not afraid to be justified even to death;* [55] and again, *Do you see that by works a man is justified, and not by faith only?* [56] This increase of justice holy Church asks for when she prays: "Give unto us, O Lord, an increase of faith, hope and charity." [57]

CHAPTER XI

THE OBSERVANCE OF THE COMMANDMENTS AND THE NECESSITY AND POSSIBILITY THEREOF

But no one, however much justified, should consider himself exempt from the observance of the commandments; no one should use that rash statement, once forbidden by the Fathers under anathema, that the observance of the commandments of God is impossible for one that is justified. For God does not command impossibilities, but by commanding admonishes thee to do what thou canst and to pray for what thou canst not, and aids thee that thou mayest be able.[58] *His commandments are not heavy*,[59] and *his yoke is sweet and burden*

---

[49] Eph. 2:19.
[50] Ps. 83:8.
[51] See II Cor. 4:16.
[52] Col. 3:5.
[53] Rom. 6:13, 19.
[54] Apoc. 22:11.
[55] Ecclus. 18:22.
[56] James 2:24.
[57] Thirteenth Sunday after Pentecost.
[58] St. Augustine, *De natura et gratia*, c.43 (50), *PL*, XLIV, 271.
[59] See I John 5:3.

light.[60] For they who are the sons of God love Christ, but they who love Him, keep His commandments, as He Himself testifies; [61] which, indeed, with the divine help they can do. For though during this mortal life, men, however holy and just, fall at times into at least light and daily sins, which are also called venial, they do not on that account cease to be just, for that petition of the just, *forgive us our trespasses,*[62] is both humble and true; for which reason the just ought to feel themselves the more obliged to walk in the way of justice, for *being now freed from sin and made servants of God,*[63] they are able, *living soberly, justly and godly,*[64] to proceed onward through Jesus Christ, by whom they have access unto this grace.[65] For God does not forsake those who have been once justified by His grace, unless He be first forsaken by them. Wherefore, no one ought to flatter himself with faith alone, thinking that by faith alone he is made an heir and will obtain the inheritance, even though *he suffer* not *with Christ, that he may be also glorified with him.*[66] For even Christ Himself, as the Apostle says, *whereas he was the Son of God, he learned obedience by the things which he suffered, and being consummated, he became to all who obey him the cause of eternal salvation.*[67] For which reason the same Apostle admonishes those justified, saying: *Know you not that they who run in the race, all run indeed, but one receiveth the prize? So run that you may obtain. I therefore so run, not as at an uncertainty; I so fight, not as one beating the air, but I chastise my body and bring it into subjection; lest perhaps when I have preached to others, I myself should become a castaway.*[68] So also the prince of the Apostles, Peter: *Labor the more, that by good works you may make sure your calling and election. For doing these things, you shall not sin at any time.*[69] From which it is clear that they are opposed to the orthodox teaching of religion who maintain that the just man sins, venially at least, in every good work; [70] or, what is more intolerable, that he merits eternal punishment; and they also who assert that the just sin in all works, if, in order to arouse

[60] Matt. 11:30.
[61] John 14:23.
[62] Matt. 6:12.
[63] Rom. 6:18, 22.
[64] Tit. 2:12.
[65] Rom. 5:1 f.
[66] *Ibid.*, 8:17.
[67] Heb. 5:8 f.
[68] See I Cor. 9:24, 26 f.
[69] See II Pet. 1:10.
[70] Cf. *infra,* can. 25.

their sloth and to encourage themselves to run the race, they, in addition to this, that above all God may be glorified, have in view also the eternal reward,[71] since it is written: *I have inclined my heart to do thy justifications on account of the reward;*[72] and of Moses the Apostle says; that *he looked unto the reward.*[73]

CHAPTER XII

RASH PRESUMPTION OF PREDESTINATION IS TO BE AVOIDED

No one, moreover, so long as he lives this mortal life, ought in regard to the sacred mystery of divine predestination, so far presume as to state with absolute certainty that he is among the number of the predestined,[74] as if it were true that the one justified either cannot sin any more, or, if he does sin, that he ought to promise himself an assured repentance. For except by special revelation, it cannot be known whom God has chosen to Himself.

CHAPTER XIII

THE GIFT OF PERSEVERANCE

Similarly with regard to the gift of perseverance, of which it is written: *He that shall persevere to the end, he shall be saved,*[75] which cannot be obtained from anyone except from Him who is able to make him stand who stands,[76] that he may stand perseveringly, and to raise him who falls, let no one promise himself herein something as certain with an absolute certainty, though all ought to place and repose the firmest hope in God's help. For God, unless men themselves fail in His grace, as *he has begun a good work, so will he perfect it, working to will and to accomplish.*[77] Nevertheless, let those who think themselves to stand, take heed lest they fall,[78] and with fear and trembling work out their salvation,[79] in labors, in watchings, in almsdeeds, in prayer, in

[71] Cf. *infra*, can. 31.
[72] Ps. 118:112.
[73] Heb. 11:26.
[74] Cf. c.17, C.XXIV, q.3.
[75] Matt. 10:22; 24:13.
[76] Rom. 14:4.
[77] Phil. 1:6; 2:13.
[78] See I Cor. 10:12.
[79] Phil. 2:12.

fastings and chastity. For knowing that they are born again unto the hope of glory,[80] and not as yet unto glory, they ought to fear for the combat that yet remains with the flesh, with the world and with the devil, in which they cannot be victorious unless they be with the grace of God obedient to the Apostle who says: *We are debtors, not to the flesh, to live according to the flesh; for if you live according to the flesh, you shall die, but if by the spirit you mortify the deeds of the flesh, you shall live.*[81]

Chapter XIV

THE FALLEN AND THEIR RESTORATION

Those who through sin have forfeited the received grace of justification, can again be justified when, moved by God, they exert themselves to obtain through the sacrament of penance the recovery, by the merits of Christ, of the grace lost.[82] For this manner of justification is restoration for those fallen, which the holy Fathers have aptly called a second plank after the shipwreck of grace lost.[83] For on behalf of those who fall into sins after baptism, Christ Jesus instituted the sacrament of penance when He said: *Receive ye the Holy Ghost, whose sins you shall forgive, they are forgiven them, and whose sins you shall retain, they are retained.*[84] Hence, it must be taught that the repentance of a Christian after his fall is very different from that at his baptism, and that it includes not only a determination to avoid sins and a hatred of them, or *a contrite and humble heart,*[85] but also the sacramental confession of those sins, at least in desire, to be made in its season, and sacerdotal absolution, as well as satisfaction by fasts, alms, prayers and other devout exercises of the spiritual life, not indeed for the eternal punishment, which is, together with the guilt, remitted either by the sacrament or by the desire of the sacrament, but for the temporal punishment which, as the sacred writings teach, is not always wholly remitted, as is done in baptism, to those who, ungrateful to the grace of God which they have received, have grieved the Holy Ghost [86] and

[80] See I Pet. 1:3.
[81] Rom. 8:12 f.
[82] Cf. *infra*, can. 23 and 29.
[83] C.72, D.I de poenit.
[84] John 20:22 f.
[85] Ps. 50:19.
[86] Eph. 4:30.

have not feared to *violate the temple of God.*[87] Of which repentance it is written: *Be mindful whence thou art fallen; do penance, and do the first works;* [88] and again, *The sorrow that is according to God worketh penance, steadfast unto salvation;* [89] and again, *Do penance, and bring forth fruits worthy of penance.*[90]

Chapter XV

BY EVERY MORTAL SIN GRACE IS LOST, BUT NOT FAITH

Against the subtle wits of some also, who *by pleasing speeches and good words seduce the hearts of the innocent,*[91] it must be maintained that the grace of justification once received is lost not only by infidelity, whereby also faith itself is lost, but also by every other mortal sin, though in this case faith is not lost; thus defending the teaching of the divine law which excludes from the kingdom of God not only unbelievers, but also the faithful [who are] *fornicators, adulterers, effeminate, liers with mankind, thieves, covetous, drunkards, railers, extortioners,*[92] and all others who commit deadly sins, from which with the help of divine grace they can refrain, and on account of which they are cut off from the grace of Christ.

Chapter XVI

THE FRUITS OF JUSTIFICATION, THAT IS, THE MERIT OF GOOD WORKS, AND THE NATURE OF THAT MERIT

Therefore, to men justified in this manner, whether they have preserved uninterruptedly the grace received or recovered it when lost, are to be pointed out the words of the Apostle: *Abound in every good work, knowing that your labor is not in vain in the Lord.*[93] *For God is not unjust, that he should forget your work, and the love which you have shown in his name;* [94] and, *Do not lose your confidence, which*

[87] See I Cor. 3:17.
[88] Apoc. 2:5.
[89] See II Cor. 7:10.
[90] Matt. 3:2; 4:17; Luke 3:8.
[91] Rom. 16:18.
[92] See I Cor. 6:9 f.; I Tim. 1:9 f.
[93] See I Cor. 15:58.
[94] Heb. 6:10.

hath a great reward.[95] Hence, to those who work well *unto the end* [96] and trust in God, eternal life is to be offered, both as a grace mercifully promised to the sons of God through Christ Jesus, and as a reward promised by God himself, to be faithfully given to their good works and merits.[97] For this is the crown of justice which after his fight and course the Apostle declared was laid up for him, to be rendered to him by the just judge, and not only to him, but also to all that love his coming.[98] For since Christ Jesus Himself, as the head into the members and the vine into the branches,[99] continually infuses strength into those justified, which strength always precedes, accompanies and follows their good works, and without which they could not in any manner be pleasing and meritorious before God, we must believe that nothing further is wanting to those justified to prevent them from being considered to have, by those very works which have been done in God, fully satisfied the divine law according to the state of this life and to have truly merited eternal life, to be obtained in its [due] time, provided they depart [this life] in grace,[100] since Christ our Savior says: *If anyone shall drink of the water that I will give him, he shall not thirst forever; but it shall become in him a fountain of water springing up unto life everlasting.*[101] Thus, neither is our own justice established as our own from ourselves,[102] nor is the justice of God ignored or repudiated, for that justice which is called ours, because we are justified by its inherence in us, that same is [the justice] of God, because it is infused into us by God through the merit of Christ. Nor must this be omitted, that although in the sacred writings so much is attributed to good works, that even *he that shall give a drink of cold water to one of his least ones*, Christ promises, *shall not lose his reward;* [103] and the Apostle testifies that, *That which is at present momentary and light of our tribulation, worketh for us above measure exceedingly an eternal weight of glory;* [104] nevertheless, far be it that a Christian should either trust or glory in himself and not in the Lord,[105] whose bounty toward

[95] Heb. 10:35.
[96] Matt. 10:22.
[97] Rom. 6:22.
[98] See II Tim. 4:8.
[99] John 15:1 f.
[100] Apoc. 14:13.
[101] John 4:13 f.
[102] Rom. 10:3; II Cor. 3:5.
[103] Matt. 10:42; Mark 9:40.
[104] See II Cor. 4:17.
[105] See I Cor. 1:31; II Cor. 10:17.

all men is so great that He wishes the things that are His gifts to be their merits. And since *in many things we all offend*,[106] each one ought to have before his eyes not only the mercy and goodness but also the severity and judgment [of God]; neither ought anyone to judge himself, even though he be not conscious to himself of anything;[107] because the whole life of man is to be examined and judged not by the judgment of man but of God, *who will bring to light the hidden things of darkness, and will make manifest the counsels of the hearts, and then shall every man have praise from God*,[108] who, as it is written, *will render to every man according to his works*.[109]

After this Catholic doctrine on justification, which whosoever does not faithfully and firmly accept cannot be justified, it seemed good to the holy council to add these canons, that all may know not only what they must hold and follow, but also what to avoid and shun.

CANONS CONCERNING JUSTIFICATION

Canon 1. If anyone says that man can be justified before God by his own works, whether done by his own natural powers or through the teaching of the law,[110] without divine grace through Jesus Christ, let him be anathema.

Can. 2. If anyone says that divine grace through Christ Jesus is given for this only, that man may be able more easily to live justly and to merit eternal life, as if by free will without grace he is able to do both, though with hardship and difficulty, let him be anathema.

Can. 3. If anyone says that without the predisposing inspiration of the Holy Ghost[111] and without His help, man can believe, hope, love or be repentant as he ought,[112] so that the grace of justification may be bestowed upon him, let him be anathema.

Can. 4. If anyone says that man's free will moved and aroused by God, by assenting to God's call and action, in no way cooperates toward disposing and preparing itself to obtain the grace of justification, that it cannot refuse its assent if it wishes, but that, as something

---

106 James 3:2.
107 See I Cor. 4:3 f.
108 *Ibid.*, 4:5.
109 Matt. 16:27; Rom. 2:6; Apoc. 22:12.
110 Cf. *supra*, chaps. 1, 3.
111 *Ibid.*, chap. 5.
112 Rom. 5:5.

inanimate, it does nothing whatever and is merely passive, let him be anathema.

Can. 5. If anyone says that after the sin of Adam man's free will was lost and destroyed, or that it is a thing only in name, indeed a name without a reality, a fiction introduced into the Church by Satan, let him be anathema.

Can. 6. If anyone says that it is not in man's power to make his ways evil, but that the works that are evil as well as those that are good God produces, not permissively only but also *proprie et per se*, so that the treason of Judas is no less His own proper work than the vocation of St. Paul, let him be anathema.

Can. 7. If anyone says that all works done before justification, in whatever manner they may be done, are truly sins, or merit the hatred of God; that the more earnestly one strives to dispose himself for grace, the more grievously he sins, let him be anathema.

Can. 8. If anyone says that the fear of hell,[113] whereby, by grieving for sins, we flee to the mercy of God or abstain from sinning, is a sin or makes sinners worse, let him be anathema.

Can. 9. If anyone says that the sinner is justified by faith alone,[114] meaning that nothing else is required to cooperate in order to obtain the grace of justification, and that it is not in any way necessary that he be prepared and disposed by the action of his own will, let him be anathema.

Can. 10. If anyone says that men are justified without the justice of Christ,[115] whereby He merited for us, or by that justice are formally just, let him be anathema.

Can. 11. If anyone says that men are justified either by the sole imputation of the justice of Christ or by the sole remission of sins, to the exclusion of the grace and *the charity which is poured forth in their hearts by the Holy Ghost*,[116] and remains in them, or also that the grace by which we are justified is only the good will of God, let him be anathema.

Can. 12. If anyone says that justifying faith is nothing else than confidence in divine mercy,[117] which remits sins for Christ's sake, or that it is this confidence alone that justifies us, let him be anathema.

---

[113] Matt. 10:28; Luke 12:5.
[114] *Supra*, chaps. 7, 8.
[115] Gal. 2:16; *supra*, chap. 7.
[116] Rom. 5:5.
[117] *Supra*, chap. 9.

Can. 13. If anyone says that in order to obtain the remission of sins it is necessary for every man to believe with certainty and without any hesitation arising from his own weakness and indisposition that his sins are forgiven him, let him be anathema.

Can. 14. If anyone says that man is absolved from his sins and justified because he firmly believes that he is absolved and justified,[118] or that no one is truly justified except him who believes himself justified, and that by this faith alone absolution and justification are effected, let him be anathema.

Can. 15. If anyone says that a man who is born again and justified is bound *ex fide* to believe that he is certainly in the number of the predestined,[119] let him be anathema.

Can. 16. If anyone says that he will for certain, with an absolute and infallible certainty, have that great gift of perseverance even to the end, unless he shall have learned this by a special revelation,[120] let him be anathema.

Can. 17. If anyone says that the grace of justification is shared by those only who are predestined to life, but that all others who are called are called indeed but receive not grace, as if they are by divine power predestined to evil, let him be anathema.

Can. 18. If anyone says that the commandments of God are, even for one that is justified and constituted in grace,[121] impossible to observe, let him be anathema.

Can. 19. If anyone says that nothing besides faith is commanded in the Gospel, that other things are indifferent, neither commanded nor forbidden, but free; or that the ten commandments in no way pertain to Christians, let him be anathema.

Can. 20. If anyone says that a man who is justified and however perfect is not bound to observe the commandments of God and the Church, but only to believe,[122] as if the Gospel were a bare and absolute promise of eternal life without the condition of observing the commandments, let him be anathema.

Can. 21. If anyone says that Christ Jesus was given by God to men as a redeemer in whom to trust, and not also as a legislator whom to obey, let him be anathema.

---

118 *Supra*, chap. 9.
119 *Ibid.*, chap. 12.
120 *Ibid.*, chap. 13.
121 *Ibid.*, chap. 11.
122 Cf. chap. cit.

Can. 22. If anyone says that the one justified either can without the special help of God persevere in the justice received,[123] or that with that help he cannot, let him be anathema.

Can. 23. If anyone says that a man once justified can sin no more, nor lose grace,[124] and that therefore he that falls and sins was never truly justified; or on the contrary, that he can during his whole life avoid all sins, even those that are venial, except by a special privilege from God, as the Church holds in regard to the Blessed Virgin, let him be anathema.

Can. 24. If anyone says that the justice received is not preserved and also not increased before God through good works,[125] but that those works are merely the fruits and signs of justification obtained, but not the cause of its increase, let him be anathema.

Can. 25. If anyone says that in every good work the just man sins at least venially,[126] or, what is more intolerable, mortally, and hence merits eternal punishment, and that he is not damned for this reason only, because God does not impute these works unto damnation, let him be anathema.

Can. 26. If anyone says that the just ought not for the good works done in God [127] to expect and hope for an eternal reward from God through His mercy and the merit of Jesus Christ, if by doing well and by keeping the divine commandments they persevere to the end,[128] let him be anathema.

Can. 27. If anyone says that there is no mortal sin except that of unbelief,[129] or that grace once received is not lost through any other sin however grievous and enormous except by that of unbelief, let him be anathema.

Can. 28. If anyone says that with the loss of grace through sin faith is also lost with it, or that the faith which remains is not a true faith, though it is not a living one, or that he who has faith without charity is not a Christian, let him be anathema.

Can. 29. If anyone says that he who has fallen after baptism cannot by the grace of God rise again,[130] or that he can indeed recover again the

[123] *Supra*, chap. 13.
[124] *Ibid.*, chap. 14.
[125] *Ibid.*, chap. 10.
[126] *Ibid.*, chap. 11 at the end.
[127] *Ibid.*, chap. 16.
[128] Matt. 24:13.
[129] *Supra*, chap. 15.
[130] *Ibid.*, chap. 14.

lost justice but by faith alone without the sacrament of penance, contrary to what the holy Roman and Universal Church, instructed by Christ the Lord and His Apostles, has hitherto professed, observed and taught, let him be anathema.

Can. 30. If anyone says that after the reception of the grace of justification the guilt is so remitted and the debt of eternal punishment so blotted out to every repentant sinner, that no debt of temporal punishment remains to be discharged either in this world [131] or in purgatory before the gates of heaven can be opened,[132] let him be anathema.

Can. 31. If anyone says that the one justified sins when he performs good works with a view to an eternal reward,[133] let him be anathema.

Can. 32. If anyone says that the good works of the one justified are in such manner the gifts of God that they are not also the good merits of him justified; or that the one justified by the good works that he performs by the grace of God and the merit of Jesus Christ, whose living member he is, does not truly merit an increase of grace, eternal life, and in case he dies in grace, the attainment of eternal life itself and also an increase of glory, let him be anathema.

Can. 33. If anyone says that the Catholic doctrine of justification as set forth by the holy council in the present decree, derogates in some respect from the glory of God or the merits of our Lord Jesus Christ, and does not rather illustrate the truth of our faith and no less the glory of God and of Christ Jesus, let him be anathema.

DECREE CONCERNING REFORM

Chapter I

IT IS PROPER THAT PRELATES RESIDE IN THEIR CHURCHES; IF THEY ACT OTHERWISE, THE PENALTIES OF THE EARLIER LAWS ARE RENEWED AGAINST THEM AND NEW ONES ARE PRESCRIBED

The same holy council, the same legates of the Apostolic See presiding, wishing to restore a very much collapsed ecclesiastical discipline and to reform the depraved morals of the clergy and the Christian people, has deemed it proper to begin with those who preside over the

---

[131] Cf. Sess. XIV, chap. 8.
[132] Cf. Sess. XXV at the beginning.
[133] *Supra,* chap. 11 at the end.

major churches, for unblemished character in those who govern is the salvation of those governed.[134] Trusting therefore that by the mercy of our Lord and God and the prudent vigilance of the vicar of that God on earth, it will surely come about that for the government of the churches, a burden formidable even to the shoulders of angels, those who are most worthy, whose previous life in its every stage, from their youth to their riper years, laudably spent in the services of ecclesiastical discipline, bears testimony in their favor, will be chosen in accordance with the venerable ordinances of the holy Fathers,[135] it admonishes all who under whatever name or title are set over patriarchal, primatial, metropolitan and cathedral churches, and hereby wishes that they be considered admonished, that *taking heed to themselves and to the whole flock, wherein the Holy Ghost hath placed them to rule the Church of God which he hath purchased with his own blood*,[136] that *they be vigilant*, as the Apostle commands, *labor in all things and fulfil their ministry*.[137] Let them know, however, that they cannot fulfil this if like hirelings they desert the flocks committed to them [138] and do not attend to the guardianship of their sheep, whose blood will be required at their hands by the supreme judge; [139] since it is most certain that the shepherd's excuse will not be accepted if the wolf devours the sheep and he knows it not. And since there are some at this time, which is greatly to be deplored, who, forgetful even of their own salvation and preferring earthly things to the things of heaven and things human to things divine, wander about at divers courts or keep themselves occupied with the care of temporal affairs, their fold forsaken and their watchfulness over the sheep committed to them neglected, it has seemed good to the holy council to renew, as by virtue of the present decree it does renew, the old canons promulgated against non-residents,[140] which on account of the disorders of the times and of men have well-nigh fallen into desuetude; and furthermore, for a more faithful residence of the same and for the reform of morals in the Church, to ordain and decree in the manner following. If anyone, by whatever dignity, rank and pre-eminence distinguished, shall, by remaining outside of his

[134] C.5, D.LXI.
[135] C.4, D.LIX; cc.2, 6, 8, D.LXI.
[136] Acts 20:28.
[137] See II Tim. 4:5.
[138] John 10:12.
[139] Ezech. 33:6.
[140] C.20, C.VII, q.1 ff.; tit. X, De cler. non resid., III, 4 et in VI°, III, 3.

diocese for a continuous period of six months [141] without lawful impediment or just and reasonable causes,[142] be absent from a patriarchal, primatial, metropolitan or cathedral church, under whatever title, cause, name or right committed to him, he shall incur *ipso jure* the forfeiture of a fourth part of one year's revenues, to be applied by the ecclesiastical superior to the church treasury and to the poor of the locality. If he continues to absent himself for another six months, he shall *eo ipso* forfeit another fourth part of the revenues, to be applied in like manner.[143] If the contumacy proceed yet farther, that he may be subject to a severer penalty of the sacred canons, the metropolitan shall be bound to denounce the absent suffragan bishops, and the oldest resident suffragan bishop shall be bound under penalty, to be incurred *ipso facto*, of being forbidden entrance to the church,[144] to denounce the absent metropolitan to the Roman pontiff by letter or messenger within three months, that he, by the authority of his supreme see, may take action against the non-resident prelates, as the degree of contumacy of each may demand, and provide the churches with more useful pastors, as he shall know in the Lord to be salutary and expedient.

Chapter II

NO ONE HOLDING A BENEFICE THAT REQUIRES PERSONAL RESIDENCE MAY ABSENT HIMSELF EXCEPT FOR A JUST CAUSE TO BE APPROVED BY THE BISHOP, WHO SHALL THEN APPOINT A VICAR FOR THE *CURA ANIMARUM*, WITHDRAWING A PORTION OF THE REVENUES

Those inferior to bishops, who by title or *in commendam* hold any ecclesiastical benefices that by law or custom require personal residence, shall by appropriate measures be compelled by their ordinaries to reside therein, according as it seems expedient to them for the good government of the churches and the increase of divine worship, taking into account the character of places and persons, and to no one shall privileges or perpetual indults in favor of non-residence or the reception of revenues during absence be of avail; [145] temporary permissions

[141] C. 11, X, De cler. non resid., III, 4.
[142] Cf. Sess. XXIII, chap. 1 de ref.
[143] Cf. Sess. and chap. cit.
[144] Cf. Schroeder, *Disciplinary Decrees of the General Councils*, p. 353, no. 60.
[145] C. 15, VI°, De rescrip., I, 3.

and dispensations, however, granted solely on true and reasonable grounds and to be legally proved before the ordinary, shall remain in force; in which cases, nevertheless, it is the duty of the bishops, as delegated in this matter by the Apostolic See, to see to it that the *cura animarum* is in no way neglected by the appointment of competent vicars and the assignment of a suitable portion of the revenues; [146] no privilege or exemption whatever shall be of avail to anyone in this matter.

CHAPTER III

TRANSGRESSIONS OF SECULAR CLERICS AND OF REGULARS WHO LIVE OUTSIDE THEIR MONASTERIES, SHALL BE CORRECTED BY THE ORDINARY OF THE LOCALITY

The prelates of the churches shall apply themselves prudently and diligently to correct the excesses of their subjects, and no secular cleric under pretext of a personal privilege, or a regular living outside his monastery under pretext of a privilege of his order, shall, if he transgresses, be considered exempt from being visited, punished and corrected in accordance with the canonical enactments by the ordinary of the locality as delegated in this matter by the Apostolic See.[147]

CHAPTER IV

BISHOPS AND OTHER MAJOR PRELATES SHALL VISIT ALL CHURCHES AS OFTEN AS THIS IS NECESSARY; EVERYTHING THAT MIGHT HINDER THE EXECUTION OF THIS DECREE IS ABROGATED

Chapters of cathedral and of other major churches and the members thereof shall not by any exemptions, customs, judicial verdicts, oaths, agreements, which bind only the originators thereof and not also their successors, shield themselves so that they cannot even with Apostolic authority be visited, corrected and amended in accordance with the canonical statutes as often as shall be necessary by their own bishops and other major prelates, by themselves alone or with those whom they shall deem fit to accompany them.[148]

---

[146] C.34, VI°, De elect., I, 6.
[147] Cf. Sess. XIV, chap. 4 de ref.
[148] Cf. Sess. XXIV, chap. 3 de ref. and Sess. XXV, chap. 6 de ref.

Chapter V

BISHOPS SHALL NEITHER EXERCISE ANY PONTIFICAL FUNCTIONS NOR ORDAIN IN ANOTHER DIOCESE

No bishop is allowed under pretext of any privilege to exercise pontifical functions in the diocese of another, except with the expressed permission of the ordinary of the place, and for those persons only who are subject to the same ordinary.[149] If the contrary is done, the bishop is *ipso jure* suspended from the exercise of pontifical functions and those so ordained from the exercise of their orders.

ANNOUNCEMENT OF THE NEXT SESSION

Does it please you that the next following session be celebrated on Thursday after the first Sunday of the approaching Lent, which will be the third day of March?

They answered: It pleases us.

---

[149] Cf. Sess. XIV, chaps. 2, 3 de ref. and Sess. XXIII, chap. 8 de ref.

SEVENTH SESSION

celebrated on the third day of March, 1547

DECREE CONCERNING THE SACRAMENTS

Foreword

For the completion of the salutary doctrine on justification, which was promulgated with the unanimous consent of the Fathers in the last session, it has seemed proper to deal with the most holy sacraments of the Church, through which all true justice either begins, or being begun is increased, or being lost is restored. Wherefore, in order to destroy the errors and extirpate the heresies that in our stormy times are directed against the most holy sacraments, some of which are a revival of heresies long ago condemned by our Fathers, while others are of recent origin, all of which are exceedingly detrimental to the purity of the Catholic Church and the salvation of souls, the holy, ecumenical and general Council of Trent, lawfully assembled in the Holy Ghost, the same legates of the Apostolic See presiding, adhering to the teaching of the Holy Scriptures, to the Apostolic traditions, and to the unanimous teaching of other councils and of the Fathers, has thought it proper to establish and enact these present canons; hoping, with the help of the Holy Spirit, to publish later those that are wanting for the completion of the work begun.

CANONS ON THE SACRAMENTS IN GENERAL

Canon 1. If anyone says that the sacraments of the New Law were not all instituted by our Lord Jesus Christ, or that there are more or less than seven, namely, baptism, confirmation, Eucharist, penance, extreme unction, order and matrimony,[1] or that any one of these seven is not truly and intrinsically a sacrament, let him be anathema.

Can. 2. If anyone says that these sacraments of the New Law do not

[1] Eugene IV in *decr. ad Armenos* (Denzinger, no. 695); Pius IV in the bull *Injunctum nobis* (*idem*, no. 996).

differ from the sacraments of the Old Law, except that the ceremonies are different and the external rites are different, let him be anathema.

Can. 3. If anyone says that these seven sacraments are so equal to each other that one is not for any reason more excellent than the other, let him be anathema.

Can. 4. If anyone says that the sacraments of the New Law are not necessary for salvation but are superfluous, and that without them or without the desire of them men obtain from God through faith alone the grace of justification,[2] though all are not necessary for each one, let him be anathema.

Can. 5. If anyone says that these sacraments have been instituted for the nourishment of faith alone, let him be anathema.

Can. 6. If anyone says that the sacraments of the New Law do not contain the grace which they signify, or that they do not confer that grace on those who place no obstacles in its way,[3] as though they are only outward signs of grace or justice received through faith and certain marks of Christian profession, whereby among men believers are distinguished from unbelievers, let him be anathema.

Can. 7. If anyone says that grace, so far as God's part is concerned, is not imparted through the sacraments always and to all men even if they receive them rightly, but only sometimes and to some persons, let him be anathema.

Can. 8. If anyone says that by the sacraments of the New Law grace is not conferred *ex opere operato*, but that faith alone in the divine promise is sufficient to obtain grace, let him be anathema.

Can. 9. If anyone says that in three sacraments, namely, baptism, confirmation and order, there is not imprinted on the soul a character, that is, a certain spiritual and indelible mark, by reason of which they cannot be repeated,[4] let him be anathema.

Can. 10. If anyone says that all Christians have the power to administer the word and all the sacraments,[5] let him be anathema.

Can. 11. If anyone says that in ministers, when they effect and confer the sacraments, there is not required at least the intention of doing what the Church does,[6] let him be anathema.

Can. 12. If anyone says that a minister who is in mortal sin, though

[2] Cf. Sess. VI, chap. 7 and can. 9.
[3] Eugene IV in the decr. cited.
[4] *Ibid.*
[5] Cf. Sess. XIV, Penance, chap. 6, and Extr. Unct., chap. 3.
[6] Eugene IV in the decr. cited.

he observes all the essentials that pertain to the effecting or conferring of a sacrament,[7] neither effects nor confers a sacrament, let him be anathema.

Can. 13. If anyone says that the received and approved rites of the Catholic Church, accustomed to be used in the administration of the sacraments, may be despised or omitted by the ministers without sin and at their pleasure, or may be changed by any pastor of the churches to other new ones, let him be anathema.

CANONS ON BAPTISM

Canon 1. If anyone says that the baptism of John had the same effect as the baptism of Christ,[8] let him be anathema.

Can. 2. If anyone says that true and natural water is not necessary for baptism[9] and thus twists into some metaphor the words of our Lord Jesus Christ: *Unless a man be born again of water and the Holy Ghost,*[10] let him be anathema.

Can. 3. If anyone says that in the Roman Church, which is the mother and mistress of all churches, there is not the true doctrine concerning the sacrament of baptism,[11] let him be anathema.

Can. 4. If anyone says that the baptism which is given by heretics in the name of the Father, and of the Son, and of the Holy Ghost, with the intention of doing what the Church does, is not true baptism,[12] let him be anathema.

Can. 5. If anyone says that baptism is optional, that is, not necessary for salvation,[13] let him be anathema.

Can. 6. If anyone says that one baptized cannot, even if he wishes, lose grace, however much he may sin, unless he is unwilling to believe, let him be anathema.

Can. 7. If anyone says that those baptized are by baptism made debtors only to faith alone, but not to the observance of the whole law of Christ, let him be anathema.

Can. 8. If anyone says that those baptized are free from all the pre-

---

[7] Cf. c.98, C.I, q.1; cc.39, 149, D.IV de cons.
[8] Cf. c.135, D.IV de cons.
[9] Cf. c.5, X, De bapt., III, 42.
[10] John 3:5.
[11] C.9, X, De haeret., V, 7.
[12] Cc.97, 98, C.I, q.1.
[13] John 3:5.

cepts of holy Church, whether written or unwritten, so that they are not bound to observe them unless they should wish to submit to them of their own accord, let him be anathema.

Can. 9. If anyone says that the remembrance of the baptism received is to be so impressed on men that they may understand that all the vows made after baptism are void in virtue of the promise already made in that baptism, as if by those vows they detracted from the faith which they professed and from the baptism itself, let him be anathema.

Can. 10. If anyone says that by the sole remembrance and the faith of the baptism received, all sins committed after baptism are either remitted or made venial, let him be anathema.

Can. 11. If anyone says that baptism, truly and rightly administered, must be repeated in the one converted to repentance after having denied the faith of Christ among the infidels, let him be anathema.

Can. 12. If anyone says that no one is to be baptized except at that age at which Christ was baptized, or when on the point of death, let him be anathema.

Can. 13. If anyone says that children, because they have not the act of believing, are not after having received baptism to be numbered among the faithful, and that for this reason are to be rebaptized when they have reached the years of discretion; [14] or that it is better that the baptism of such be omitted than that, while not believing by their own act, they should be baptized in the faith of the Church alone, let him be anathema.

Can. 14. If anyone says that those who have been thus baptized when children, are, when they have grown up, to be questioned whether they will ratify what their sponsors promised in their name when they were baptized, and in case they answer in the negative, are to be left to their own will; neither are they to be compelled in the meantime to a Christian life by any penalty other than exclusion from the reception of the Eucharist and the other sacraments, until they repent, let him be anathema.

CANONS ON CONFIRMATION

Can. 1. If anyone says that the confirmation of those baptized is an empty ceremony and not a true and proper sacrament; or that of old it was nothing more than a sort of instruction, whereby those approach-

---

[14] Cf. c.139 D.IV de cons.

ing adolescence gave an account of their faith to the Church, let him be anathema.

Can. 2. If anyone says that those who ascribe any power to the holy chrism of confirmation, offer insults to the Holy Ghost, let him be anathema.

Can. 3. If anyone says that the ordinary minister of holy confirmation is not the bishop alone,[15] but any simple priest, let him be anathema.

DECREE CONCERNING REFORM

The same holy council, the same legates presiding therein, intending to continue, to the praise of God and the increase of the Christian religion, the work begun concerning residence and reform, has thought it well to decree as follows, saving always and in all things the authority of the Apostolic See.

Chapter I

THE COMPETENCY REQUIRED TO CONDUCT CATHEDRAL CHURCHES

No one shall be chosen to govern cathedral churches unless he is born of lawful wedlock, is of mature age, is known for his integrity of morals, and possesses the required knowledge,[16] in accordance with the constitution of Alexander III, which begins, "Cum in cunctis," promulgated in the Lateran Council.[17]

Chapter II

THOSE HOLDING SEVERAL CATHEDRAL CHURCHES ARE COMMANDED TO RESIGN IN A SPECIFIED MANNER AND TIME ALL BUT ONE

No one, by whatever dignity, rank or pre-eminence distinguished, shall presume, in contravention of the sacred canons,[18] to accept and to hold at the same time several metropolitan or cathedral churches, either by title or *in commendam* or under any other name, since he must be

---

[15] Cf. Sess. XXIII, chap. 4.

[16] Cf. Sess. XXII, chap. 2 de ref.

[17] C.7, X, De elect., I, 6.

[18] C.2, D.LXX; c.3, C.X, q.3; cc.1, 2, C.XXI, q.1; cc.5, 13, 28, X, De praeb., III, 5; c.32, VI°, De praeb., III, 4.

considered exceedingly fortunate who succeeds in ruling one church well, fruitfully and with due interest in the salvation of the souls committed to him. But those who now hold several churches contrary to the tenor of the present decree, shall be bound, retaining the one which they prefer, to resign the rest within six months if they are subject to free disposal by the Apostolic See, in other cases within a year; otherwise those churches, with the sole exception of the one last obtained, shall be *eo ipso* considered vacant.

Chapter III

BENEFICES ARE TO BE CONFERRED ONLY ON COMPETENT PERSONS

Inferior ecclesiastical benefices, especially those to which is attached the *cura animarum*, shall be conferred on worthy and competent persons and on such as can reside in the place and exercise personally the care of souls, in accordance with the constitution of Alexander III in the Lateran Council, which begins, "Quia nonnulli," [19] and that of Gregory X, published in the General Council of Lyons, which begins, "Licet canon." [20] A collation or provision made otherwise is absolutely null, and let the collating bishop know that he will incur the penalties of the constitution of the general council, which begins, "Grave nimis." [21]

Chapter IV

THE HOLDER OF SEVERAL BENEFICES CONTRARY TO THE CANONS SHALL BE DEPRIVED OF THEM

Whoever shall in the future presume to accept and to hold at the same time several charges or otherwise incompatible ecclesiastical benefices,[22] whether by way of union for life or by way of perpetual *commendam* or under any other name or title whatsoever, in contravention of the provision of the sacred canons and especially of the constitution of Innocent III, which begins, "De multa," [23] shall be *ipso jure* deprived

---

[19] C. 3, X, De cler. non resid., III, 4.
[20] C. 14, VI°, De elect., I, 16.
[21] C. 29, X, De praeb., III, 5.
[22] Cf. Sess. XXIV, chap. 17 de ref.
[23] C. 28, X, De praeb., III, 5.

of those benefices in accordance with the provisions of that constitution and also by virtue of the present canon.

Chapter V

HOLDERS OF SEVERAL BENEFICES TO WHICH IS ANNEXED THE *CURA ANIMARUM* MUST EXHIBIT THEIR DISPENSATIONS TO THE ORDINARY, WHO SHALL PROVIDE THE CHURCHES WITH A VICAR, ASSIGNING A SUITABLE PORTION OF THE REVENUES

Local ordinaries shall strictly compel all who hold several charges or otherwise incompatible ecclesiastical benefices to exhibit their dispensations, and adopt other procedures in accordance with the constitution of Gregory X, published in the General Council of Lyons, beginning with "Ordinarii," [24] which this holy council believes ought to be renewed and does renew; adding, moreover, that the ordinaries are by all means to provide, even by deputing competent vicars and assigning a suitable portion of the revenues, that the *cura animarum* be in no way neglected and that those benefices be by no means defrauded of the services due them; appeals, privileges and exemptions whatsoever, even with the appointment of special judges and their inhibitions, being of no avail to anyone in the aforesaid matter.

Chapter VI

WHAT UNIONS OF BENEFICES SHALL BE CONSIDERED VALID

Perpetual unions,[25] made within forty years, may be investigated by the ordinaries as delegates of the Apostolic See, and such as have been obtained through deceit or deception shall be declared null. Those however must be presumed to have been obtained surreptitiously which, having been granted within the aforesaid period, have not yet been carried into effect in whole or in part; those also which shall henceforth be made at the instance of any person, unless it is certain that they have been made for lawful and otherwise reasonable causes, which must be verified before the local ordinary, those persons being

[24] C.3, VI°, De off. ord., I, 16.

[25] Cf. Sess. XIV, chap. 9 de ref.; Sess. XXIV, chap. 13 de ref; Sess. XXV, chap. 9 de ref.

summoned whose interests are concerned; hence, unless the Apostolic See shall have declared otherwise, they shall be absolutely devoid of force.

Chapter VII

UNITED ECCLESIASTICAL BENEFICES MUST BE VISITED; THE *CURA ANIMARUM* THERETO IS TO BE EXERCISED ALSO BY PERPETUAL VICARS, WITH WHOSE APPOINTMENT A PORTION IS TO BE ASSIGNED EVEN FOR SPECIFIC PURPOSES

Ecclesiastical benefices having the *cura animarum*, which are found to have been always united or annexed to cathedral, collegiate or other churches, or to monasteries, benefices, colleges or to pious places of whatever sort,[26] shall be visited every year by the local ordinaries, who shall zealously see to it that the *cura animarum* is exercised in a praiseworthy manner by competent vicars, also perpetual, unless the ordinaries shall deem it expedient for the good government of the churches to provide otherwise, who shall be appointed to the same by the ordinaries with a portion consisting of a third part of the revenues,[27] or of a greater or less proportion, at the discretion of the ordinaries, also assigned for the specific purpose; appeals, privileges and exemptions, also with the appointment of special judges and their inhibitions, being of no avail to anyone in the aforesaid matter.

Chapter VIII

CHURCHES SHALL BE REPAIRED; THE *CURA ANIMARUM* DILIGENTLY DISCHARGED

The local ordinaries shall be bound to visit every year with Apostolic authority all churches in whatsoever manner exempt, and to provide by suitable legal remedies that those that need repair be repaired, and that they be not in any way defrauded of the *cura animarum* if such be annexed to them or of other services due them; [28] appeals, privileges, customs, even though immemorial, appointment of judges and their inhibitions, being absolutely excluded.

[26] Cf. Sess. XIV, chap. 9 de ref.
[27] Cf. *supra*, chap. 5 and Sess. XXV, chap. 16 de ref.
[28] Cc. 10–12, C.X, q. 1; Sess. XXI, chap. 8 de ref. and Sess. XXIV, chap. 9 de ref.

Chapter IX

THE RITE OF CONSECRATION IS NOT TO BE DELAYED

Those promoted to major churches shall receive the rite of consecration within the time prescribed by law,[29] and any delays granted extending beyond a period of six months, shall be of no avail to anyone.

Chapter X

WHEN A SEE IS VACANT, CHAPTERS SHALL NOT GRANT RELEASES TO ANYONE UNLESS HE BE PRESSED FOR TIME BECAUSE OF A BENEFICE OBTAINED OR ABOUT TO BE OBTAINED; VARIOUS PENALTIES AGAINST THOSE WHO ACT OTHERWISE

It shall not be lawful for chapters of churches, when a see is vacant, to grant, either by a provision of the common law or by virtue of a privilege or custom, permission to be ordained or dimissory letters or "reverends," as some call them, within a year from the day of the vacancy, to anyone who is not pressed for time by reason of an ecclesiastical benefice obtained or about to be obtained.[30] Otherwise, the contravening chapter shall be subject to ecclesiastical interdict, and those so ordained, if they are in minor orders, shall enjoy no clerical privilege, especially in criminal causes, while those in major orders shall be *ipso jure* suspended from the exercise thereof during the pleasure of the next prelate.

Chapter XI

AUTHORITY FOR PROMOTION WITHOUT A JUST CAUSE SHALL NOT AVAIL ANYONE

Authority for promotion by anyone shall be of no avail except to those who have a legitimate reason why they cannot be ordained by their own bishops, which must be expressed in writing; and then they shall not be ordained except by the bishop who resides in his own

---

[29] C.2, D.LXXV; c.1, D.C.

[30] C.3, VI°, De temp. ord., I, 9; cf. Sess. XXIII, chap. 10 de ref.

diocese,[31] or by one who exercises the pontifical functions for him, and after a careful examination.

Chapter XII

PERMISSION GRANTED FOR NON-PROMOTION SHALL NOT EXCEED ONE YEAR

Permission granted for not being promoted shall be good for one year only, except in the cases provided by law.[32]

Chapter XIII

WITH CERTAIN EXCEPTIONS, PERSONS, BY WHOMSOEVER PRESENTED, SHALL NOT BE APPOINTED WITHOUT BEING FIRST EXAMINED AND APPROVED BY THE ORDINARY

Those presented, elected or nominated by any ecclesiastical persons whatsoever, even by nuncios of the Apostolic See, shall not be appointed to, confirmed in or admitted to any ecclesiastical benefice,[33] even under the pretext of some privilege or immemorial custom, unless they shall have been first examined and found competent by the local ordinaries. And no one shall by recourse to an appeal be able to escape from being bound to undergo that examination. Those, however, are excepted who are presented, elected or nominated by universities or by colleges for general studies.[34]

Chapter XIV

THE CIVIL CAUSES OF EXEMPT PERSONS WHICH MAY BE TAKEN COGNIZANCE OF BY BISHOPS

In the causes of exempt persons the constitution of Innocent IV, beginning with "Volentes," published in the General Council of Lyons,[35]

[31] Cf. Sess. VI, chap. 5 de ref. and Sess. XIV, chap. 2 de ref.
[32] Cc. 14, 34, VI°, De elect., I, 6.
[33] Cf. Sess. XXV, chap. 9 de ref.
[34] Cf. Sess. XXIV, chap. 18 de ref.
[35] C. 1, VI°, De privil., V, 7.

shall be observed, which this holy council has thought ought to be renewed and does renew; adding moreover, that in civil causes relative to wages and to persons in distress, secular clerics and regulars living outside their monasteries, howsoever exempt, even though they have a special judge deputed by the Apostolic See, and in other causes if they have no such judge, may be brought before the local ordinaries as delegated in this matter by that See and be constrained and compelled by law to pay what they owe; no privileges, exemptions, appointment of conservators and their inhibitions, being of any avail whatever against the aforesaid.

Chapter XV

ORDINARIES SHALL SEE TO IT THAT ALL HOSPITALS, EVEN THOSE EXEMPT, ARE FAITHFULLY MANAGED BY THEIR ADMINISTRATORS

Ordinaries shall take care that all hospitals are faithfully and diligently managed by their administrators, by whatsoever name known and in whatsoever manner exempt,[36] observing the form of the constitution of the Council of Vienne, which begins, "Quia contingit," [37] which this holy council has thought ought to be renewed and does renew together with the restrictions therein contained.

ANNOUNCEMENT OF THE NEXT SESSION

This holy council has also ordained and decreed that the next session be held and celebrated on Thursday, the fifth day after the coming Sunday *in Albis*, which will be the twenty-first of April of the present year, 1547.

BULL AUTHORIZING THE TRANSFER OF THE COUNCIL

Paul, Bishop, servant of the servants of God, to our venerable brother John Maria, Bishop of Praeneste, and our beloved sons, Marcellus, priest of the Holy Cross in Jerusalem, and Reginald of St. Mary in

[36] Cf. Sess. XXV, chap. 8 de ref.
[37] C. 2, De relig. dom. in Clem., III, 11.

Cosmedin, deacon, cardinals, our legates *a latere* and of the Apostolic See, health and apostolic benediction.

We, by the providence of God, presiding over the government of the universal Church, though with merits unequal thereto, consider it a part of our office that when something of more than ordinary importance must be decided concerning the Christian commonwealth, it be done not only at an opportune time but also in a place at once convenient and suitable. Wherefore, when we lately, with the advice and consent of our venerable brethren, the cardinals of the holy Roman Church, on hearing that peace had been made between our most dear sons in Christ, Charles, ever august Emperor of the Romans, and Francis, the most Christian King of the French, raised and removed the suspension of the celebration of the holy, ecumenical and general council, which we had on another occasion, for reasons then stated, convoked with the same advice and consent in the city of Trent, and which was, for certain other reasons at that time also stated, suspended upon the same advice and consent to another more opportune and suitable time to be made known by us, being ourselves unable, because at that time lawfully hindered, to proceed personally to the aforesaid city and to be present at the council, we, by the same advice, appointed and deputed you as legates *a latere* on our behalf and on that of the Apostolic See in that council, and we sent you to that city as angels of peace, as is set forth more fully in our various letters dealing with this matter. Wishing now to provide opportunely that so holy a work as the celebration of this council may not through the inconvenience of the place or in any other manner be hindered or unduly delayed, we, by our own action and certain knowledge, with the plenitude of Apostolic authority and with the same advice and consent, grant to you all together or to two of you, in case the other should be detained by a lawful impediment or perchance be absent therefrom, by the tenor of these presents with Apostolic authority, full and unrestricted power and authority to transfer and change, whenever you shall deem it expedient, the aforesaid council from the city of Trent to any other more convenient, suitable and safer city which you shall judge appropriate; also to prohibit, even by ecclesiastical censures and penalties, the prelates and other members of that council to proceed therein to any further measures in the said city of Trent; further, to continue, hold and celebrate the same council in the other city to which it shall have been transferred and changed, and to summon to it the prelates and other members of the Council of Trent, even under penalty of perjury and other penalties named in the letters of the convocation of that council; also to preside and proceed in the council thus translated and changed in the name and by the authority aforesaid, and to perform, regulate, ordain and execute the other things mentioned above and the things necessary and suitable to it, in accordance with the contents and tenor of previous letters addressed to you on another occasion; declaring that we will hold as ratified and pleasing whatsoever shall be done, regulated and ordained by you in the aforesaid matters, and will, with God's help, see to it that it be inviolately observed; Apostolic constitutions and ordinances and other things whatsoever to the contrary notwithstanding. Therefore, let no one infringe this letter of our authorization or with foolhardy boldness go contrary to it. But if anyone shall presume to attempt this, let him know that he will incur the indignation of Almighty God and of the blessed Peter and Paul, His Apostles. Given at Rome at St. Peter's in the year of the Lord's incarnation 1547, on the twenty-fifth of February, in the eleventh year of our pontificate.

Fab. Bishop of Spol.
B. Motta.

EIGHTH SESSION

celebrated on the eleventh day of March, 1547

DECREE CONCERNING THE TRANSLATION OF THE COUNCIL

Does it please you to decree and declare that from the foregoing and other reports regarding that disease, it is so clearly and manifestly certain that the prelates cannot without danger to their lives remain in this city, and that therefore they cannot and ought not to be detained in it against their will? And considering, moreover, the withdrawal of many prelates since the last session, and the protests made in the general congregations by many other prelates wishing by all means to depart from here through fear of the disease, who cannot justly be detained and by whose departure the council would either be dissolved or, from the small number of prelates, its beneficial progress hindered; and considering also the imminent danger to life and the other manifestly true and legitimate reasons alleged in the congregations by some of the Fathers, does it please you likewise to decree and declare that for the preservation and prosecution of the council, and for the safety of the lives of the prelates, this council be transferred for a time to the city of Bologna as a place more suitable, more healthy and better adapted, and that the translation have effect from this day forth, that the session already announced for the twenty-first of April ought to be celebrated and be celebrated there on the day appointed; and that further matters be proceeded with in succession, till it shall seem expedient to our most holy Lord and to the holy council, with the advice of the most invincible Emperor, the most Christian King, and with the other Christian kings and princes, that this council may and ought to be brought back to this or to some other place?

They answered: It pleases us.

NINTH SESSION

celebrated at Bologna on the twenty-first day of April, 1547

DECREE CONCERNING THE PROROGATION OF THE SESSION

This holy, ecumenical and general council, which lately was assembled in the city of Trent and is now lawfully assembled in the Holy Ghost in Bologna, the same most reverend Lords, John Maria de Monte, Bishop of Praeneste, and Marcellus, priest of the Holy Cross in Jerusalem, cardinals of the holy Roman Church and legates Apostolic *a latere*, presiding in the name of our most holy Father and Lord in Christ, Paul III, by the providence of God, Pope, considering that on the eleventh day of the month of March of the present year, in a general and public session celebrated in the city of Trent and in the accustomed place, all formalities being observed in the accustomed manner, for reasons then pressing, urgent and legitimate, and also with the authority of the holy Apostolic See, which was granted specially to the same most reverend presidents, ordained and decreed that the council was to be transferred, as it has transferred it, from that place to this city, and likewise that the session announced there for this twenty-first day of April in order that decrees with regard to the sacraments and reform, with which it had intended to deal, might be enacted and promulgated, ought to be celebrated in this city of Bologna; and considering that some of the Fathers who have been accustomed to be present at this council being engaged in their own churches during these higher festival days of the great week [of Lent] and of the paschal solemnity, and some also, detained by other hindrances, have not yet arrived here, but who nevertheless, it is to be hoped, will shortly be present, and that for this reason it has happened that the matters regarding the sacraments and reform could not be examined and discussed in an assembly of prelates as numerous as the holy council desired; therefore, that everything may be done with mature deliberation, with due dignity and earnestness, it has decided and does decide that it is good, beneficial and expedient that the aforesaid session, which, as has been said, was to have been celebrated on this day, be deferred and prorogued, as it is now deferred and prorogued, for expediting the aforesaid matter, to the Thursday within the approaching octave of Pentecost; which day it has deemed and deems to be most convenient for the business to be transacted and most suitable especially for the Fathers who are absent; adding, however, that this holy council may and can, even in private congregation, limit and abridge that term at its will and pleasure, as it shall deem expedient for the business of the council.

TENTH SESSION

celebrated at Bologna on the second day of June, 1547

DECREE CONCERNING THE PROROGATION OF THE SESSION

Although this holy, ecumenical and general council has decreed that the session which was to have been celebrated in this illustrious city of Bologna on the twenty-first of the month of April last on the subject of the sacraments and reform, in accordance with the decree promulgated in public session in the city of Trent on the eleventh of March, should be deferred and prorogued to this present day for certain reasons, especially on account of the absence of some of the Fathers, who it was hoped would in a short time be present; wishing, however, even yet to deal kindly with those who have not come, the same holy council, lawfully assembled in the Holy Ghost, the same cardinals of the holy Roman Church and legates of the Apostolic See presiding, ordains and decrees that that session which it had decreed to celebrate on this the second day of the month of June of the present year 1547, be deferred and prorogued, as it does defer and prorogue it, to the Thursday after the feast of the Nativity of the Blessed Virgin Mary, which will be the fifteenth of the next month of September, for the disposition of the aforesaid and other matters; so, however, that the continuance of the discussion and examination of those things that relate to dogmas and reform shall not in the meantime be suspended, and that the holy council may and can freely, at its will and pleasure, even in private congregation, abridge and prorogue that term.

On the fourteenth day of September, 1547, in a general congregation held at Bologna, the session which was to have been held on the following day, was prorogued at the good pleasure of the holy council.

BULL OF THE RESUMPTION OF THE COUNCIL OF TRENT

under the Supreme Pontiff, Julius III

Julius, Bishop, servant of the servants of God, for a perpetual remembrance hereof

In order to put an end to the religious dissensions which for a long time have prevailed in Germany to the disturbance and scandal of the entire Christian world, it appears good, opportune and expedient to us, as also to our most dearly beloved son in Christ, Charles, ever august Emperor of the Romans, who has made this known to us by his letters and ambassadors, to bring back to the city of Trent the holy ecumenical and general council convoked by our predecessor, Pope Paul III, of happy memory, and begun, conducted and continued by us, who then enjoyed the honor of the cardinalate and, conjointly with two other cardinals of the holy Roman Church, presided in the name of our predecessor in the council, in which several public and solemn sessions were held and several decrees promulgated on the subjects of faith and reform, and also many other things relating to both subjects were examined and discussed. We, therefore, to whom, as reigning sovereign pontiff, it belongs to convoke and direct general councils, that we may, to the praise and glory of Almighty God, procure the peace of the Church and the increase of the Christian faith and of the orthodox religion, and may, as far as we are able, consider with paternal solicitude the tranquillity of Germany, a province which in times past was second to none in Christendom in cultivating true religion and the teaching of the holy councils and the holy Fathers, and in exhibiting due obedience and reverence to the supreme pontiffs, the vicars on earth of Christ our Redeemer, hoping that by the grace and bounty of God it will come about that all Christian kings and princes will approve, favor and aid our just and pious wishes in this matter, by the bowels of the mercy of our Lord Jesus Christ, exhort, command and admonish our venerable brethren the patriarchs, archbishops, bishops, our beloved sons the abbots and each and all of the others who by right, custom or privilege ought to be present at general councils, and whom our predecessor in his letters of convocation and in any others made and published with regard to this matter wished to be present at the council, to convene and assemble in the same city of Trent, since the lawful impediment no longer exists, and to apply themselves without delay to the continuation and prosecution of the council on the next first of May, which day we, after mature deliberation, of our own certain knowledge, with the plenitude of Apostolic authority, and with the advice and consent of our venerable brethren, the cardinals of the holy Roman Church, appoint and set aside for the resumption and continuation of the council in the state in which it now is. We shall make it our special care that our legates will be in the city at the same time, through whom, if on account of our age, state of health and the demands of the Apostolic See we shall be unable to be present personally, we shall under the guidance of the Holy Ghost preside over the council; any translation and suspension of the council and any other things whatsoever to the contrary notwithstanding, and especially those things which it was the will of our predecessor should not create any obstacles, as expressed in his letters aforesaid, which, with each and all of restrictions and decrees therein contained, we wish and decree to remain in force, and so far as there is need we hereby renew them; declaring, moreover, null and void whatever may be attempted knowingly or unknowingly by any person or by any authority to the contrary. Let no one, therefore, infringe this our letter of exhortation, summons, monition, ordinance, declaration, renewal, will and decrees, or with foolhardy boldness go contrary to it. But if anyone shall presume to attempt this, let him know that he will incur the indignation of Almighty God and of His blessed Apostles Peter and Paul. Given at Rome at St. Peter's in the year 1550 of our Lord's incarnation, on the fourteenth of December, in the first year of our pontificate.

M. Cardinal Crescen.
Rom. Amasaeus.

ELEVENTH SESSION OF THE COUNCIL OF TRENT

which is the first celebrated under the Supreme Pontiff,
Julius III, on the first day of May, 1551

DECREE CONCERNING THE RESUMPTION OF THE COUNCIL

Does it please you, for the praise and glory of the holy and undivided Trinity, Father, and Son, and Holy Ghost, for the increase and exaltation of the Christian faith and religion, that the holy, ecumenical and general Council of Trent be, in accordance with the form and tenor of the letters of our most holy Lord, resumed, and that further matters be proceeded with?

They answered: It pleases us.

ANNOUNCEMENT OF THE NEXT SESSION

Does it please you that the next session be held and celebrated on the following first of September?

They answered: It pleases us.

TWELFTH SESSION

which is the second under the Supreme Pontiff, Julius III, celebrated on the first day of September, 1551

DECREE CONCERNING THE PROROGATION OF THE SESSION

The holy, ecumenical and general Council of Trent, lawfully assembled in the Holy Ghost, the same legates and nuncios of the holy Apostolic See presiding, which had in the last session decreed that the following one was to be celebrated today and further matters to be proceeded with, yet by reason of the absence of the illustrious German nation, whose interests are chiefly to be considered, and also on account of the small attendance of the other Fathers, has hitherto delayed to proceed, now rejoicing in the Lord and giving due thanks to Almighty God for the recent arrival of our venerable brethren and sons in Christ, the Archbishops of Mainz and Trier, electoral princes of the Holy Roman Empire, and of many bishops of that country and of other provinces, and entertaining a firm hope that many other prelates both of Germany and of other nations, moved by the requirement of their office and by this example, will arrive in a few days, announces the next session for the fortieth day, which will be the eleventh of next October, to continue the council from the point where it now is; and since in the preceding sessions decrees were enacted concerning the seven sacraments of the New Law in general and baptism and confirmation in particular, it ordains and decrees that it will treat and discuss the sacrament of the most Holy Eucharist, and also, as regards reform, of the other matters which pertain to the easier and more convenient residence of prelates. It also admonishes and exhorts all the Fathers that, after the example of our Lord Jesus Christ, they in the meantime give themselves to fasting and prayer so far as human weakness will permit, so that God, who be praised forever, being at length appeased, may vouchsafe to bring back the hearts of men to the acknowledgment of His true faith, to the unity of holy mother Church and to the rule of righteous living.

THIRTEENTH SESSION

which is the third under the Supreme Pontiff, Julius III, celebrated on the eleventh day of October, 1551

DECREE CONCERNING THE MOST HOLY SACRAMENT OF THE EUCHARIST

The holy, ecumenical and general Council of Trent, lawfully assembled in the Holy Ghost, the same legate and nuncios of the holy Apostolic See presiding, though convened, not without the special guidance and direction of the Holy Ghost, for the purpose of setting forth the true and ancient doctrine concerning faith and the sacraments, and of applying a remedy to all the heresies and the other most grievous troubles by which the Church of God is now miserably disturbed and rent into many and various parts, yet, even from the outset, has especially desired that it might pull up by the roots the cockles [1] of execrable errors and schisms which the enemy has in these our troubled times disseminated regarding the doctrine, use and worship of the Sacred Eucharist, which our Savior left in His Church as a symbol of that unity and charity with which He wished all Christians to be mutually bound and united. Wherefore, this holy council, stating that sound and genuine doctrine of the venerable and divine sacrament of the Eucharist, which the Catholic Church, instructed by our Lord Jesus Christ Himself and by His Apostles, and taught by the Holy Ghost who always brings to her mind all truth,[2] has held and will preserve even to the end of the world, forbids all the faithful of Christ to presume henceforth to believe, teach or preach with regard to the most Holy Eucharist otherwise than is explained and defined in this present decree.

[1] Matt. 13:30.
[2] Luke 12:12; John 14:26; 16:13.

Chapter I

THE REAL PRESENCE OF OUR LORD JESUS CHRIST IN THE MOST HOLY SACRAMENT OF THE EUCHARIST

First of all, the holy council teaches and openly and plainly professes that after the consecration of bread and wine, our Lord Jesus Christ, true God and true man, is truly, really and substantially contained in the august sacrament of the Holy Eucharist under the appearance of those sensible things. For there is no repugnance in this that our Savior sits always at the right hand of the Father in heaven [3] according to the natural mode of existing, and yet is in many other places sacramentally present to us in His own substance by a manner of existence which, though we can scarcely express in words, yet with our understanding illumined by faith, we can conceive and ought most firmly to believe is possible to God.[4] For thus all our forefathers, as many as were in the true Church of Christ and who treated of this most holy sacrament, have most openly professed that our Redeemer instituted this wonderful sacrament at the last supper, when, after blessing the bread and wine, He testified in clear and definite words that He gives them His own body and His own blood. Since these words, recorded by the holy Evangelists [5] and afterwards repeated by St. Paul,[6] embody that proper and clearest meaning in which they were understood by the Fathers, it is a most contemptible action on the part of some contentious and wicked men to twist them into fictitious and imaginary tropes by which the truth of the flesh and blood of Christ is denied, contrary to the universal sense of the Church, which, as *the pillar and ground of truth*,[7] recognizing with a mind ever grateful and unforgetting this most excellent favor of Christ, has detested as satanical these untruths devised by impious men.

---

[3] Cf. Sess. III, the Symbol.
[4] Matt. 19:26; Luke 18:27.
[5] Matt. 26:26–28; Mark 14:22–24; Luke 22:19 f.
[6] See I Cor. 11:24 f.
[7] See I Tim. 3:15.

CHAPTER II

THE REASON FOR THE INSTITUTION OF THIS MOST HOLY SACRAMENT

Therefore, our Savior, when about to depart from this world to the Father, instituted this sacrament, in which He poured forth, as it were, the riches of His divine love towards men, *making a remembrance of his wonderful works*,[8] and commanded us in the participation of it to reverence His memory and *to show forth his death until he comes* [9] to judge the world. But He wished that this sacrament should be received as the spiritual food of souls,[10] whereby they may be nourished and strengthened, living by the life of Him who said: *He that eateth me, the same also shall live by me*,[11] and as an antidote whereby we may be freed from daily faults and be preserved from mortal sins. He wished it furthermore to be a pledge of our future glory and everlasting happiness, and thus be a symbol of that one body of which He is the head [12] and to which He wished us to be united as members by the closest bond of faith, hope and charity, that we might *all speak the same thing and there might be no schisms among us*.[13]

CHAPTER III

THE EXCELLENCE OF THE MOST HOLY EUCHARIST OVER THE OTHER SACRAMENTS

The most Holy Eucharist has indeed this in common with the other sacraments, that it is a symbol of a sacred thing and a visible form of an invisible grace; [14] but there is found in it this excellent and peculiar characteristic, that the other sacraments then first have the power of sanctifying when one uses them, while in the Eucharist there is the Author Himself of sanctity before it is used. For the Apostles had not yet received the Eucharist from the hands of the Lord, when He Him-

---

[8] Ps. 110:4.
[9] Luke 22:19; I Cor. 11:24–26.
[10] Matt. 26:26 f.
[11] John 6:58.
[12] See I Cor. 11:3; Eph. 5:23.
[13] See I Cor. 1:10.
[14] C.32, D.II de cons.

self told them that what He was giving them is His own body.[15] This has always been the belief of the Church of God, that immediately after the consecration the true body and the true blood of our Lord, together with His soul and divinity exist under the form of bread and wine, the body under the form of bread and the blood under the form of wine *ex vi verborum;*[16] but the same body also under the form of wine and the same blood under the form of bread and the soul under both, in virtue of that natural connection and concomitance whereby the parts of Christ the Lord, *who hath now risen from the dead, to die no more,*[17] are mutually united;[18] also the divinity on account of its admirable hypostatic union with His body and soul. Wherefore, it is very true that as much is contained under either form as under both.[19] For Christ is whole and entire under the form of bread and under any part of that form; likewise the whole Christ is present under the form of wine and under all its parts.

Chapter IV

TRANSUBSTANTIATION

But since Christ our Redeemer declared that to be truly His own body which He offered under the form of bread,[20] it has, therefore, always been a firm belief in the Church of God, and this holy council now declares it anew, that by the consecration of the bread and wine a change is brought about of the whole substance of the bread into the substance of the body of Christ our Lord, and of the whole substance of the wine into the substance of His blood.[21] This change the holy Catholic Church properly and appropriately calls transubstantiation.

[15] Matt. 26:26; Mark 14:22.
[16] Cf. *infra*, can. 1.
[17] Rom. 6:9.
[18] Cc.58, 71, 78, D.II de cons.
[19] Cf. *infra*, can. 3 and Sess. XXI, chap. 3.
[20] Luke 22:19; John 6:48 ff.; I Cor. 11:24.
[21] Cf. c.55, D.II de cons.; *infra*, can. 3.

Chapter V

THE WORSHIP AND VENERATION TO BE SHOWN TO THIS MOST HOLY SACRAMENT

There is, therefore, no room for doubt that all the faithful of Christ may, in accordance with a custom always received in the Catholic Church, give to this most holy sacrament in veneration the worship of *latria*, which is due to the true God.[22] Neither is it to be less adored for the reason that it was instituted by Christ the Lord in order to be received.[23] For we believe that in it the same God is present of whom the eternal Father, when introducing Him into the world, says: *And let all the angels of God adore him;*[24] whom the Magi, falling down, adored;[25] who, finally, as the Scriptures testify, was adored by the Apostles in Galilee.[26]

The holy council declares, moreover, that the custom that this sublime and venerable sacrament be celebrated with special veneration and solemnity every year on a fixed festival day,[27] and that it be borne reverently and with honor in processions through the streets and public places,[28] was very piously and religiously introduced into the Church of God. For it is most reasonable that some days be set aside as holy on which all Christians may with special and unusual demonstration testify that their minds are grateful to and mindful of their common Lord and Redeemer for so ineffable and truly divine a favor whereby the victory and triumph of His death are shown forth. And thus indeed did it behoove the victorious truth to celebrate a triumph over falsehood and heresy, that in the sight of so much splendor and in the midst of so great joy of the universal Church, her enemies may either vanish weakened and broken, or, overcome with shame and confounded, may at length repent.

---

[22] Cf. *infra*, can. 6.
[23] Matt. 26:26.
[24] Heb. 1:6.
[25] Matt. 2:11.
[26] *Ibid.*, 28:17; Luke 24:52.
[27] Cf. c.un. in Clem. De reliq. et venerat. sanct., III, 16.
[28] Cf. *infra*, can. 6.

CHAPTER VI

THE RESERVATION OF THE SACRAMENT OF THE HOLY EUCHARIST AND TAKING IT TO THE SICK

The custom of reserving the Holy Eucharist in a sacred place is so ancient [29] that even the period of the Nicene Council recognized that usage.[30] Moreover, the practice of carrying the Sacred Eucharist to the sick and of carefully reserving it for this purpose in churches, besides being exceedingly reasonable and appropriate, is also found enjoined in numerous councils [31] and is a very ancient observance of the Catholic Church. Wherefore, this holy council decrees that this salutary and necessary custom be by all means retained.

CHAPTER VII

THE PREPARATION TO BE EMPLOYED THAT ONE MAY RECEIVE THE SACRED EUCHARIST WORTHILY

If it is unbecoming for anyone to approach any of the sacred functions except in a spirit of piety, assuredly, the more the holiness and divinity of this heavenly sacrament are understood by a Christian, the more diligently ought he to give heed lest he receive it without great reverence and holiness, especially when we read those terrifying words of the Apostle: *He that eateth and drinketh unworthily, eateth and drinketh judgment to himself, not discerning the body of the Lord.*[32] Wherefore, he who would communicate, must recall to mind his precept: *Let a man prove himself.*[33] Now, ecclesiastical usage declares that such an examination is necessary in order that no one conscious to himself of mortal sin, however contrite he may feel, ought to receive the Sacred Eucharist without previous sacramental confession.[34] This the holy council has decreed to be invariably observed by all Christians, even by those priests on whom it may be incumbent by their office to

---

[29] C.93, D.II de cons.; c.6, C.XXVI, q.6; c.10, X, De celebr. miss., III, 41; *infra*, can. 7.

[30] Cf. I Council of Nicaea (325), c.13.

[31] Cf. c.63, D.L and c.1, X, De custod. eucharist., III, 44.

[32] See I Cor. 11:29.

[33] *Ibid.*, 11:28.

[34] Cf. *infra*, can. 11.

celebrate, provided the opportunity of a confessor is not wanting to them. But if in an urgent necessity a priest should celebrate without previous confession, let him confess as soon as possible.

Chapter VIII

ON THE USE OF THIS ADMIRABLE SACRAMENT

As to the use of this holy sacrament, our Fathers have rightly and wisely distinguished three ways of receiving it. They have taught that some receive it sacramentally only, as sinners; others spiritually only, namely, those who eating in desire the heavenly bread set before them, are by a lively *faith which worketh by charity* [35] made sensible of its fruit and usefulness; while the third class receives it both sacramentally and spiritually,[36] and these are they who so prove and prepare themselves beforehand that they approach this divine table clothed with the wedding garment.[37] As regards the reception of the sacrament, it has always been the custom in the Church of God that laics receive communion from priests, but that priests when celebrating communicate themselves,[38] which custom ought with justice and reason to be retained as coming down from Apostolic tradition.[39] Finally, the holy council with paternal affection admonishes, exhorts, prays and beseeches through the bowels of the mercy of our God, that each and all who bear the Christian name will now at last agree and be of one mind in this sign of unity, in this bond of charity, in this symbol of concord, and that, mindful of so great a majesty and such boundless love of our Lord Jesus Christ, who gave His own beloved soul as the price of our salvation and His own flesh to eat,[40] they may believe and venerate these sacred mysteries of His body and blood with such constancy and firmness of faith, with such devotion of mind, with such piety and worship, that they may be able to receive frequently that supersubstantial bread and that it may truly be to them the life of the soul and the perpetual health of their mind; that being invigorated by its strength, they may be able after the journey of this miserable pilgrimage to ar-

[35] Gal. 5:6.
[36] Cf. *infra*, can. 8.
[37] Matt. 22:11.
[38] Cf. c. 11, D. II de cons. and *infra*, can. 10.
[39] Heb. 5:3; 7:27.
[40] John 6:56 ff.

rive in their heavenly country, there to eat, without any veil, the same bread of angels [41] which they now eat under sacred veils.

But since it is not enough to declare the truth unless errors be exposed and repudiated, it has seemed good to the holy council to subjoin these canons, so that, the Catholic doctrine being already known, all may understand also what are the heresies which they ought to guard against and avoid.

CANONS ON THE MOST HOLY SACRAMENT OF THE EUCHARIST

Canon 1. If anyone denies that in the sacrament of the most Holy Eucharist are contained truly, really and substantially the body and blood together with the soul and divinity of our Lord Jesus Christ, and consequently the whole Christ,[42] but says that He is in it only as in a sign, or figure or force, let him be anathema.

Can. 2. If anyone says that in the sacred and holy sacrament of the Eucharist the substance of the bread and wine remains conjointly with the body and blood of our Lord Jesus Christ, and denies that wonderful and singular change of the whole substance of the bread into the body and the whole substance of the wine into the blood, the appearances only of bread and wine remaining, which change the Catholic Church most aptly calls transubstantiation,[43] let him be anathema.

Can. 3. If anyone denies that in the venerable sacrament of the Eucharist the whole Christ is contained under each form and under every part of each form when separated,[44] let him be anathema.

Can. 4. If anyone says that after the consecration is completed, the body and blood of our Lord Jesus Christ are not in the admirable sacrament of the Eucharist,[45] but are there only *in usu,* while being taken and not before or after, and that in the hosts or consecrated particles which are reserved or which remain after communion, the true body of the Lord does not remain, let him be anathema.

Can. 5. If anyone says that the principal fruit of the most Holy Eucharist is the remission of sins, or that other effects do not result from it,[46] let him be anathema.

---

[41] Ps. 77:25.
[42] Cf. *supra,* chap. 3.
[43] *Ibid.,* chap. 4.
[44] *Ibid.,* chap. 3 and Sess. XXI, chap. 3.
[45] *Supra,* chap. 3.
[46] *Ibid.,* chap. 2.

Can. 6. If anyone says that in the holy sacrament of the Eucharist, Christ, the only begotten Son of God, is not to be adored with the worship of *latria*,[47] also outwardly manifested, and is consequently neither to be venerated with a special festive solemnity, nor to be solemnly borne about in procession according to the laudable and universal rite and custom of holy Church, or is not to be set publicly before the people to be adored and that the adorers thereof are idolaters, let him be anathema.

Can. 7. If anyone says that it is not lawful that the Holy Eucharist be reserved in a sacred place, but immediately after consecration must necessarily be distributed among those present,[48] or that it is not lawful that it be carried with honor to the sick, let him be anathema.

Can. 8. If anyone says that Christ received in the Eucharist is received spiritually only and not also sacramentally and really,[49] let him be anathema.

Can. 9. If anyone denies that each and all of Christ's faithful of both sexes are bound, when they have reached the years of discretion, to communicate every year at least at Easter,[50] in accordance with the precept of holy mother Church, let him be anathema.

Can. 10. If anyone says that it is not lawful for the priest celebrating to communicate himself,[51] let him be anathema.

Can. 11. If anyone says that faith alone is a sufficient preparation for receiving the sacrament of the most Holy Eucharist,[52] let him be anathema. And lest so great a sacrament be received unworthily and hence unto death and condemnation, this holy council ordains and declares that sacramental confession, when a confessor can be had, must necessarily be made beforehand by those whose conscience is burdened with mortal sin, however contrite they may consider themselves. Moreover, if anyone shall presume to teach, preach or obstinately assert, or in public disputation defend the contrary, he shall be *eo ipso* excommunicated.

---

[47] *Supra*, chap. 5.
[48] *Ibid*., chap. 6.
[49] *Ibid*., chap. 8.
[50] Sess. XIV, Penance, can. 8.
[51] *Supra*, chap. 8.
[52] *Ibid*., chap. 7.

DECREE CONCERNING REFORM

Chapter I

BISHOPS SHALL APPLY THEMSELVES WITH PRUDENCE TO REFORM THE MORALS OF THEIR SUBJECTS; FROM THE CORRECTION OF THE BISHOPS THERE SHALL BE NO APPEAL

The same holy Council of Trent, lawfully assembled in the Holy Ghost, the same legate and nuncios of the Apostolic See presiding, having in mind to decide some things that relate to the jurisdiction of bishops, in order that, as was announced in the last session, they may the more willingly reside in the churches committed to them the more easily and conveniently they may be able to rule and keep in uprightness of life and of morals those subject to them, deems it appropriate in the first place to admonish them to bear in mind that they are shepherds and not oppressors and that they ought so to preside over those subject to them as not to lord it over them,[53] but to love them as children and brethren and to strive by exhortation and admonition to deter them from what is unlawful, that they may not be obliged, should they transgress, to coerce them by due punishments. In regard to those, however, who should happen to sin through human frailty, that command of the Apostle is to be observed, that they reprove, entreat, rebuke them in all kindness and patience,[54] since benevolence toward those to be corrected often effects more than severity, exhortation more than threat, and charity more than force.[55] But if on account of the gravity of the offense there is need of the rod, then is rigor to be tempered with gentleness, judgment with mercy, and severity with clemency, that discipline, so salutary and necessary for the people, may be preserved without harshness and they who are chastised may be corrected, or, if they are unwilling to repent, that others may by the wholesome example of their punishment be deterred from vices, since it is the duty of a shepherd, at once diligent and kind, to apply first of all mild anodynes to the disorders of his sheep, and afterwards, if the gravity of the disorder should demand it, to proceed to sharper and severer remedies; but if even these prove ineffective in removing the

---

[53] See I Pet. 5:2 f.; c.1–9, D.XLV.
[54] See II Tim. 4:2.
[55] C.6, D.XLV.

disorders, then he is to liberate the other sheep at least from the danger of contagion.[56] Since, therefore, those guilty of crimes, for the most part to avoid punishment and to evade the judgments of their bishops, pretend to have complaints and grievances and under the subterfuge of an appeal, impede the process of the judge, [this council] in order to prevent a remedy which was instituted for the protection of the innocent from being abused and utilized for the defense of wickedness,[57] and that their cunning and tergiversation may be thwarted, has ordained and decreed: That in causes relative to visitation and correction, or to competency and incompetency, as also in criminal causes, there shall before the definitive sentence be no appeal from the bishop or his vicar-general in spiritual matters by reason of an interlocutory judgment or any other grievance whatsoever; nor shall the bishop or his vicar be bound to take notice of an appeal of this kind since it is frivolous, but he may proceed to further measures notwithstanding that appeal or any inhibition emanating from the judge of appeal, as also every written statement and custom, even immemorial, to the contrary, unless a grievance of this kind cannot be repaired by the definitive sentence or there is no appeal from it,[58] in which cases the statutes of the ancient canons shall remain unimpaired.

Chapter II

WHEN AN APPEAL FROM THE BISHOP IN CRIMINAL CAUSES IS TO BE COMMITTED TO THE METROPOLITAN OR TO ONE OF THE NEAREST BISHOPS

An appeal in criminal causes from the sentence of the bishop or his vicar-general in spiritual matters, where there is room for appeal, shall, if it happens to be a case assigned by Apostolic authority locally, be committed to the metropolitan, or also to his vicar-general in spiritual matters; or if he be for some reason suspected, or be distant more than two legal days' journey, or if it be from him that the appeal is made,[59] the case shall be assigned to one of the nearest bishops or their vicars, but not to inferior judges.

---

[56] Cc. 16, 17, C.XXIV, q. 3.
[57] C. 3, X, De appell., II, 28.
[58] *Ibid.*, c. 59.
[59] C. 11, VI°, De rescrip., I, 3.

Chapter III

THE ACTS OF THE FIRST INSTANCE SHALL WITHIN THIRTY DAYS BE GIVEN GRATUITOUSLY TO THE ACCUSED APPELLANT

The accused who in a criminal cause appeals from the bishop or his vicar-general in spiritual matters, shall by all means produce before the judge to whom he has appealed, the acts of the first instance, and the judge, unless he has seen them, shall not proceed to his absolution. He from whom the appeal has been made shall, on demand of the appellant, furnish those acts gratuitously within thirty days; otherwise the case of an appeal of this kind shall be terminated without them according as justice may demand.

Chapter IV

IN WHAT MANNER CLERICS ARE ON ACCOUNT OF GRAVE CRIMES TO BE DEGRADED FROM SACRED ORDERS

Since ecclesiastics are sometimes guilty of crimes so grave that on account of their shocking wickedness they have to be deposed from sacred orders and handed over to the secular court, in which, according to the sacred canons, a certain number of bishops is required,[60] and if it should be difficult to assemble them all the due execution of the law would be retarded, whereas even when they are able to be present their residence would be interrupted; therefore, it is ordained and decreed that it shall be lawful for a bishop by himself or by his vicar-general in spiritual matters, even without the presence of other bishops, to proceed against a cleric, even if constituted in the priesthood, both in regard to his condemnation and to his verbal deposition, and he may by himself proceed also to actual and solemn degradation from ecclesiastical orders and grades, in the cases in which the presence of a specified number of other bishops is required by the canons after convoking and being assisted in this by a like number of abbots who have the right of using the miter and crosier by Apostolic privilege, if they can be found in the city or diocese and can conveniently be present; otherwise he may be assisted by other persons constituted in ecclesiastical dignity, who are outstanding by reason of their age and recommendable by their knowledge of law.

[60] C. 2, C. III, q. 8; cc. 1, 4-7, C. XV, q. 7.

Chapter V

THE BISHOP MAY TAKE SUMMARY COGNIZANCE OF FAVORS RELATIVE EITHER TO THE ABSOLUTION FROM CRIME OR THE REMISSION OF PUNISHMENT

And since it sometimes happens that under false pleas, which however appear probable enough, certain persons fraudulently obtain favors of the kind, whereby the punishments imposed on them by the just severity of their bishops are either wholly remitted or mitigated; and since it is a thing not to be tolerated that a lie, which is so exceedingly displeasing to God, should not only go unpunished, but should even obtain for him who tells it the pardon of another crime; it is therefore ordained and decreed as follows: a bishop residing in his own church may *per se ipsum,* as the delegate of the Apostolic See, and without judicial process, take cognizance of the cheating and stealing of a favor obtained under false pretences for the absolution of any public crime or delinquency, concerning which he himself had instituted an inquiry, or for the remission of a punishment to which he has himself condemned the criminal; and he shall not admit that favor after it shall have been lawfully established that it was obtained by the statement of what is false or by the suppression of what is true.[61]

Chapter VI

A BISHOP MAY NOT BE PERSONALLY CITED EXCEPT IN A CASE INVOLVING DEPOSITION OR DEPRIVATION

Since the subjects of a bishop, even though they may have been justly corrected, do nevertheless often bear toward him a violent hatred and, as if they had suffered some wrong at his hands, bring false accusations against him in order that they may annoy him by any means in their power,[62] the fear of which annoyance chiefly renders him more backward in inquiring into and punishing their delinquencies; therefore, in order that he may not be compelled to his own great disadvantage and that of his church to abandon the flock entrusted to him,

---

[61] Cc. 20, 22, X, De rescrip., I, 3.
[62] C. 21, C. II, q. 7.

and not without detriment to the episcopal dignity to wander from place to place, it is ordained and decreed: a bishop, even though he be proceeded against *ex officio*, or by way of inquiry or denunciation or accusation or in any other way, shall not be cited or warned to appear in person except for a cause for which he may be deposed from or deprived of his office.[63]

Chapter VII

QUALIFICATIONS OF WITNESSES AGAINST A BISHOP

In the matter of examination or information in a criminal cause or in an otherwise grave cause against a bishop, no witnesses shall be accepted unless their testimony is confirmed and they are of good life, of good esteem and reputation; and if they shall have made any deposition through hatred, rashness or self-interest, they shall be subject to severe penalties.

Chapter VIII

GRAVE EPISCOPAL CAUSES SHALL BE TAKEN COGNIZANCE OF BY THE SUPREME PONTIFF

Causes of bishops, when by reason of the nature of the crime charged against them they have to appear [in person], shall be taken before the supreme pontiff and be decided by him.[64]

DECREE

postponing the Definition of four Articles concerning the Sacrament of the Eucharist and granting Letters of Safe-conduct to the Protestants

The same holy council, desiring to root up from the field of the Lord all errors which have like thorns sprung up relative to this most holy sacrament, and to provide for the salvation of all the faithful, having devoutly offered daily prayers to Almighty God, among other articles pertaining to this sacrament which have been considered with the most careful examination of the Catholic truth, after many and

---

[63] Cf. Sess. XXIV, chap. 5 de ref.

[64] C.7, C.VI, q.4; Sess. XXIV, chap. cit.

most thorough discussions according to the importance of the matters have been held and the views also of the most eminent theologians have been ascertained, has also considered the following: Whether it is necessary to salvation and prescribed by divine law that all the faithful of Christ receive that venerable sacrament under both species; then, whether he receives less who communicates under one than he who communicates under both; further, whether holy mother Church errs when she permits the laity and priests when not celebrating to communicate under the form of bread only; finally, whether children also must communicate. But since those of the glorious province of Germany, who call themselves Protestants, desire to be heard by the holy council in regard to these articles before they are defined, and for this reason have asked of it a pledge that they may be permitted to come here in safety, sojourn in this city, speak and express freely their views before the council and then depart when they please, this holy council, though it has for many months looked forward with great eagerness to their arrival, nevertheless, like an affectionate mother that groans and labors, desiring and laboring tirelessly to the end that among those who bear the Christian name there may be no schisms, but that as all acknowledge the same God and Redeemer, so also may they confess the same, believe the same, know the same, trusting in the mercy of God and hoping that they may be brought back to the most holy and salutary union of one faith, hope and charity, willingly yielding to them in this matter, has, so far as it concerns [the council], given and granted, in accordance with their request, assurance of safety and good faith, which they call a safe-conduct, the tenor of which will be set forth below, and for their sake it has postponed the definition of those articles to the second session, which, that they may conveniently be present thereat, it has announced for the feast of the Conversion of St. Paul, which is the twenty-fifth day of the month of January of the following year. It was furthermore decided that in the same session the sacrifice of the mass will be treated of because of the close connection between the two subjects; meanwhile it will discuss the sacraments of penance and extreme unction in the next session. This it has decided to be held on the feast of St. Catherine, virgin and martyr, which will be the twenty-fifth of November, and at the same time, in both sessions, the matter of reform will be continued.

SAFE-CONDUCT GRANTED TO PROTESTANTS

The holy and general Council of Trent, lawfully assembled in the Holy Ghost, the same legate and nuncios of the holy Apostolic See presiding, grants, so far as it pertains to the council itself, to each and all persons throughout the whole of Germany, whether ecclesiastics or seculars, of whatever rank, station, condition and circumstances they may be, who may wish to come to this ecumenical and general council, security and full protection, which they call a safe-conduct, with each and all of the necessary and suitable clauses and decisions, even though they ought to be expressed specifically and not in general terms, and it is its wish that they be understood as so expressed, so that they may and shall enjoy full liberty to confer, make proposals and discuss those things that are to be discussed in the council; to come freely and safely to the ecumenical council, to remain and sojourn there and to propose therein, in writing as well as orally, as many articles as may seem good to them, to deliberate with the Fathers or with those who may have been chosen by the council and without any abuse and contumely dispute with them; they may also depart whenever they please. It has moreover seemed expedient to the holy council, that if for their greater liberty and safety they wish that certain judges be deputed on their behalf in regard to crimes that either have been committed or may be committed by them, they may themselves choose such as are favorably disposed toward them, even though the crimes should be of a grave nature or even savor of heresy.

FOURTEENTH SESSION

which is the fourth under the Supreme Pontiff, Julius III,
celebrated on the twenty-fifth day of November, 1551

THE MOST HOLY SACRAMENTS OF PENANCE AND EXTREME UNCTION

Though the holy, ecumenical and general Council of Trent, lawfully assembled in the Holy Ghost, the same legate and nuncios of the holy Apostolic See presiding, has in the decree on justification,[1] by reason of a certain necessity induced by the affinity of the subjects, given much consideration to the sacrament of penance, yet so great is in our days the number of errors relative to this sacrament, that it will be of no little general benefit to give to it a more exact and complete definition, in which all errors having under the guidance of the Holy Ghost been pointed out and refuted, Catholic truth may be made clear and resplendent, which [truth] this holy council now sets before all Christians to be observed for all time.

CHAPTER I

THE NECESSITY AND INSTITUTION OF THE SACRAMENT OF PENANCE

If in all those regenerated such gratitude were given to God that they constantly safeguarded the justice received in baptism by His bounty and grace, there would have been no need for another sacrament besides that of baptism to be instituted for the remission of sins.[2] But since God, *rich in mercy*,[3] *knoweth our frame*,[4] He has a remedy of life even to those who may after baptism have delivered themselves up to the servitude of sin and the power of the devil, namely, the sacrament of penance, by which the benefit of Christ's death is applied to those who have fallen after baptism. Penance was indeed necessary at all times for all men who had stained themselves by mortal sin,[5] even for those

[1] Cf. Sess. VI, chap. 14.
[2] Cf. *infra*, chap. 5, Penance.
[3] Eph. 2:4.
[4] Ps. 102:14.
[5] Sess. and chap. cited.

who desired to be cleansed by the sacrament of baptism, in order to obtain grace and justice; so that their wickedness being renounced and amended, they might with a hatred of sin and a sincere sorrow of heart detest so great an offense against God. Wherefore the Prophet says: *Be converted and do penance for all your iniquities, and iniquity shall not be your ruin.*[6] The Lord also said: *Except you do penance, you shall all likewise perish;*[7] and Peter the Prince of the Apostles, recommending penance to sinners about to receive baptism, said: *Do penance and be baptized every one of you.*[8] Moreover, neither before the coming of Christ was penance a sacrament nor is it such since His coming to anyone before baptism. But the Lord then especially instituted the sacrament of penance when, after being risen from the dead, He breathed upon His disciples, and said: *Receive ye the Holy Ghost, whose sins you shall forgive, they are forgiven them, and whose sins you shall retain, they are retained.*[9] The consensus of all the Fathers has always acknowledged that by this action so sublime and words so clear the power of forgiving and retaining sins was given to the Apostles and their lawful successors for reconciling the faithful who have fallen after baptism, and the Catholic Church with good reason repudiated and condemned as heretics the Novatians, who of old stubbornly denied that power of forgiving.[10] Therefore, this holy council, approving and receiving that perfectly true meaning of the above words of the Lord, condemns the grotesque interpretations of those who, contrary to the institution of this sacrament, wrongly contort those words to refer to the power of preaching the word of God and of making known the Gospel of Christ.

Chapter II

THE DIFFERENCES BETWEEN THE SACRAMENT OF PENANCE AND THAT OF BAPTISM

Besides, it is clear that this sacrament is in many respects different from baptism.[11] For apart from the fact that in matter and form, which constitute the essence of a sacrament, it differs very widely, it is be-

[6] Ezech. 18:30.
[7] Luke 13:5.
[8] Acts 2:38.
[9] John 20:22 f.; *infra,* can. 3, Penance.
[10] Eusebius, *Hist. eccl.,* VI, c.43.
[11] Cf. *infra,* can. 2 and Sess. VI, chap. 14.

yond question that the minister of baptism need not be a judge, since the Church exercises judgment on no one who has not entered it through the gate of baptism. *For what have I to do,* says St. Paul, *to judge them that are without?* [12] It is otherwise with regard to those who are of the household of the faith, whom Christ the Lord has once by the laver of baptism made members of His own body.[13] For these, if they should afterward have defiled themselves by some crime, He wished not to have cleansed by the repetition of baptism, since that is in no manner lawful in the Catholic Church, but to be placed as culprits before this tribunal that by the sentence of the priests they may be absolved, not only once but as often as, repentant of the sins committed, they should turn themselves thereto. Moreover, the fruit of baptism is one thing, that of penance another. For by baptism *we put on Christ* [14] and are made in Him an entirely new creature, receiving a full and complete remission of all sins; to which newness and integrity, however, we are by no means able to arrive by the sacrament of penance without many tears and labors on our part, divine justice demanding this, so that penance has rightly been called by the holy Fathers a laborious kind of baptism. This sacrament of penance is for those who have fallen after baptism necessary for salvation, as baptism is for those who have not yet been regenerated.

Chapter III

THE PARTS AND FRUITS OF THIS SACRAMENT

The holy council teaches furthermore, that the form of the sacrament of penance, in which its efficacy chiefly consists, are those words of the minister: *I absolve thee*, etc., to which are indeed laudably added certain prayers according to the custom of holy Church, which, however, do not by any means belong to the essence of the form nor are they necessary for the administration of the sacrament. But the acts of the penitent himself, namely, contrition,[15] confession and satisfaction, constitute the matter of this sacrament, which acts, inasmuch as they are by God's institution required in the penitent for the integrity of the

[12] See I Cor. 5:12.
[13] *Ibid.*, 12:13.
[14] Gal. 3:27.
[15] Cf. *infra,* chap. 4; Sess. VI, chap. 14, and *infra,* can. 4.

sacrament and for the full and complete remission of sins, are for this reason called the parts of penance. But that which is signified and produced by this sacrament is, so far as its force and efficacy are concerned, reconciliation with God, which sometimes, in persons who are pious and who receive this sacrament with devotion, is wont to be followed by peace and serenity of conscience with an exceedingly great consolation of spirit. The holy council, while declaring these things regarding the parts and effect of this sacrament, at the same time condemns the opinions of those who maintain that faith and the terrors that agitate conscience are parts of penance.

Chapter IV

CONTRITION

Contrition, which holds the first place among the aforesaid acts of the penitent, is a sorrow of mind and a detestation for sin committed with the purpose of not sinning in the future.[16] This feeling of contrition was at all times necessary for obtaining the forgiveness of sins and thus indeed it prepares one who has fallen after baptism for the remission of sins, if it is united with confidence in the divine mercy and with the desire to perform the other things that are required to receive this sacrament in the proper manner. The holy council declares therefore, that this contrition implies not only an abstention from sin and the resolution and beginning of a new life, but also a hatred of the old,[17] according to the statement: *Cast away from you all your transgressions by which you have transgressed, and make to yourselves a new heart and a new spirit.*[18] And certainly he who has pondered those lamentations of the saints: *To thee only have I sinned, and have done evil before thee;*[19] *I have labored in my groanings, every night I will wash my bed;*[20] *I will recount to thee all my years in the bitterness of my soul,*[21] and others of this kind, will easily understand that they issued from an overwhelming hatred of their past life and from a profound detestation of sins. The council teaches furthermore, that though it

[16] Cf. Sess. VI, chaps. 6, 14.
[17] *Infra*, can. 5.
[18] Ezech. 18:31.
[19] Ps. 50:6.
[20] Ps. 6:7.
[21] Is. 38:15.

happens sometimes that this contrition is perfect through charity and reconciles man to God before this sacrament is actually received, this reconciliation, nevertheless, is not to be ascribed to the contrition itself without a desire of the sacrament, which desire is included in it. As to imperfect contrition, which is called attrition, since it commonly arises either from the consideration of the heinousness of sin or from the fear of hell and of punishment, the council declares that if it renounces the desire to sin and hopes for pardon, it not only does not make one a hypocrite and a greater sinner, but is even a gift of God and an impulse of the Holy Ghost, not indeed as already dwelling in the penitent, but only moving him, with which assistance the penitent prepares a way for himself unto justice. And though without the sacrament of penance it cannot *per se* lead the sinner to justification, it does, however, dispose him to obtain the grace of God in the sacrament of penance. For, struck salutarily by this fear, the Ninivites, moved by the dreadful preaching of Jonas, did penance and obtained mercy from the Lord.[22] Falsely therefore do some accuse Catholic writers, as if they maintain that the sacrament of penance confers grace without any pious exertion on the part of those receiving it, something that the Church of God has never taught or ever accepted. Falsely also do they assert that contrition is extorted and forced, and not free and voluntary.

Chapter V

CONFESSION

From the institution of the sacrament of penance as already explained, the universal Church has always understood that the complete confession of sins was also instituted by the Lord and is by divine law necessary for all who have fallen after baptism;[23] because our Lord Jesus Christ, when about to ascend from earth to heaven, left behind Him priests, His own vicars,[24] as rulers and judges,[25] to whom all the mortal sins into which the faithful of Christ may have fallen should be brought in order that they may, in virtue of the power of the keys, pronounce the sentence of remission or retention of sins. For it is evi-

---

[22] Jonas 3:5; Matt. 12:41; Luke 11:32.
[23] Luke 5:14; 17:14; I John 1:9. Cf. *infra*, can. 6.
[24] Matt. 16:19; John 20:23.
[25] Cf. c.51, D.I de poenit.

dent that priests could not have exercised this judgment without a knowledge of the matter, nor could they have observed justice in imposing penalties, had the faithful declared their sins in general only and not specifically and one by one. From which it is clear that all mortal sins of which they have knowledge after a diligent self-examination, must be enumerated by the penitents in confession,[26] even though they are most secret and have been committed only against the two last precepts of the Decalogue;[27] which sins sometimes injure the soul more grievously and are more dangerous than those that are committed openly. Venial sins, on the other hand, by which we are not excluded from the grace of God and into which we fall more frequently,[28] though they may be rightly and profitably and without any presumption declared in confession, as the practice of pious people evinces, may, nevertheless, be omitted without guilt and can be expiated by many other remedies. But since all mortal sins, even those of thought, make men *children of wrath*[29] and enemies of God, it is necessary to seek pardon of all of them from God by an open and humble confession. While therefore the faithful of Christ strive to confess all sins that come to their memory, they no doubt lay all of them before the divine mercy for forgiveness; while those who do otherwise and knowingly conceal certain ones, lay nothing before the divine goodness to be forgiven through the priest; for if one sick be ashamed to make known his wound to the physician, the latter does not remedy what he does not know. It is evident furthermore, that those circumstances that change the species of the sin are also to be explained in confession, for without them the sins themselves are neither integrally set forth by the penitent nor are they known to the judges, and it would be impossible for them to estimate rightly the grievousness of the crimes and to impose the punishment due to the penitents on account of them. Hence it is unreasonable to teach that these circumstances have been devised by idle men, or that one circumstance only is to be confessed, namely, to have sinned against another. It is also malicious to say that confession, commanded to be made in this manner, is impossible, or to call it a torture of consciences; for it is known that in the Church nothing else is required of penitents than that each one, after he has diligently examined

---

[26] Cf. *infra*, can. 7.
[27] Deut. 5:21.
[28] Cf. Sess. VI, can. 23; c.20, D.III de poenit.
[29] Eph. 2:3.

himself and searched all the folds and corners of his conscience, confess those sins by which he remembers to have mortally offended his Lord and God; while the other sins of which he has after diligent thought no recollection, are understood to be in a general way included in the same confession; for which sins we confidently say with the Prophet: *From my secret sins cleanse me, O Lord.*[30] But the difficulty of such a confession and the shame of disclosing the sins might indeed appear a burdensome matter, if it were not lightened by so many and so great advantages and consolations, which are most certainly bestowed by absolution upon all who approach this sacrament worthily. Moreover, as regards the manner of confessing secretly to a priest alone, although Christ has not forbidden that one may in expiation for his crimes and for his own humiliation, for an example to others as well as for the edification of the Church thus scandalized, confess his offenses publicly, yet this is not commanded by divine precept; nor would it be very prudent to enjoin by human law that offenses, especially secret ones, should be divulged by a public confession. Wherefore, since secret sacramental confession, which holy Church has used from the beginning and still uses, has always been recommended by the most holy and most ancient Fathers with great and unanimous agreement, the empty calumny of those who do not fear to teach that it is foreign to the divine command, is of human origin and owes its existence to the Fathers assembled in the Lateran Council,[31] is convincingly disproved. For the Church did not through the Lateran Council decree that the faithful of Christ should confess, a thing that she recognized as of divine law and necessary, but that the precept of confession should be complied with by each and all at least once a year when they have attained the age of discretion. Hence this salutary custom of confessing during that sacred and most acceptable period of Lent is now observed in the whole Church to the great benefit of the souls of the faithful, which custom this holy council completely indorses and sanctions as pious and worthy of retention.

---

[30] Ps. 18:13.

[31] Cf. c. 12, X, De poenit., V, 38.

CHAPTER VI

THE MINISTER OF THIS SACRAMENT AND ABSOLUTION

With regard to the minister of this sacrament, the holy council declares false and absolutely foreign to the truth of the Gospel all doctrines which perniciously extend the ministry of the keys to all other men besides bishops and priests,[32] in the belief that those words of the Lord: *Whatsoever you shall bind upon earth, shall be bound also in heaven, and whatsoever you shall loose upon earth, shall be loosed also in heaven;* [33] and, *Whose sins you shall forgive, they are forgiven them, and whose sins you shall retain, they are retained*,[34] were, contrary to the institution of this sacrament, addressed indifferently and indiscriminately to all the faithful of Christ in such manner that everyone has the power of forgiving sins, public ones by way of rebuke, if the one rebuked complies, and secret ones by way of a voluntary confession made to anyone.[35] It [the council] teaches furthermore that even priests who are in mortal sin exercise, through the power of the Holy Ghost conferred in ordination,[36] as ministers of Christ the office of forgiving sins, and that the opinion of those is erroneous who maintain that bad priests do not possess this power. But although the absolution of the priest is the dispensation of another's bounty, yet it is not a bare ministry only, either of proclaiming the Gospel or of declaring that sins are forgiven, but it is after the manner of a judicial act,[37] by which sentence is pronounced by him as by a judge. The penitent, therefore, ought not so flatter himself on his own faith as to think that even though he have no contrition and there be wanting on the part of the priest the intention to act earnestly and absolve effectively, he is nevertheless really and in the sight of God absolved by reason of faith alone. For faith without penance effects no remission of sins, and he would be most negligent of his salvation who, knowing that a priest absolved him jokingly, would not diligently seek another who would act earnestly.

---

[32] *Infra*, can. 10.
[33] Matt. 16:19; 18:18.
[34] John 20:23.
[35] Cf. Sess. VII, Sacraments, can. 10.
[36] C.8, D.XIX; c.89, C.I, q.1.
[37] *Infra*, can. 9.

Chapter VII

THE RESERVATION OF CASES

Wherefore, since the nature of a judgment requires that sentence be imposed only on subjects, the Church of God has always maintained and this council confirms it as most true, that the absolution which a priest pronounces upon one over whom he has neither ordinary nor delegated jurisdiction ought to be invalid.[38] To our most holy Fathers it seemed to be a matter of great importance to the discipline of the Christian people, that certain more atrocious and grave crimes should be absolved not by all but only by the highest priests;[39] whence the sovereign pontiffs in virtue of the supreme authority given to them in the universal Church could with right reserve to their own exclusive judgment certain more grave cases of crimes.[40] And since all things that are from God are well ordered,[41] it is not to be doubted that the same may be lawfully done by all bishops, each in his own diocese,[42] unto edification however, not unto destruction, in virtue of the authority over their subjects that is given to them above other priests inferior in rank, especially in regard to those crimes that carry with them the censure of excommunication. That this reservation of crimes have effect not only in external administration but also in God's sight is in accord with divine authority. But that no one may on this account perish, it has always been very piously observed in the same Church of God that there be no reservation *in articulo mortis*,[43] and that all priests, therefore, may in that case absolve all penitents from all sins and censures; and since outside of this single instance priests have no power in reserved cases, let them strive to persuade penitents to do this one thing, betake themselves to superiors and lawful judges for the benefit of absolution.

---

[38] Cf. c.2, VI°, De poenit., V, 10.

[39] Cf. c.52, C.XVI, q.1; c.29, C.XVII, q.4 *et al.*

[40] Cf. cc.1, 3, 19, 22, 24, 32, X, De sent. excomm., V, 39; cc.11, 18, h.t. in VI°, V, 11; c.1, h.t. in Extrav. comm., V, 10 *et al.*

[41] Rom. 13:1.

[42] Cf. *infra*, Sess. XXIV, chap. 6 de ref.

[43] Cf. c.29, C.XVII, q.4; c.5, VI°, De poenis, V, 9; c.3, h.t. in Clem., V, 8; c.3, Extrav. comm., De privil., V, 7.

Chapter VIII

THE NECESSITY AND FRUIT OF SATISFACTION

Finally, in regard to satisfaction, which, of all the parts of penance, just as it is that which has at all times been recommended to the Christian people by our Fathers, so it is the one which chiefly in our age is under the high-sounding pretext of piety assailed by those who *have an appearance of piety, but have denied the power thereof*,[44] the holy council declares that it is absolutely false and contrary to the word of God, that the guilt is never remitted by the Lord without the entire punishment being remitted also.[45] For clear and outstanding examples are found in the sacred writings,[46] by which, besides divine tradition, this error is refuted in the plainest manner. Indeed the nature of divine justice seems to demand that those who through ignorance have sinned before baptism be received into grace in one manner, and in another those who, after having been liberated from the servitude of sin and of the devil, and after having received the gift of the Holy Ghost, have not feared knowingly to violate the temple of God [47] and to grieve the Holy Spirit.[48] And it is in keeping with divine clemency that sins be not thus pardoned us without any satisfaction, lest seizing the occasion and considering sins as trivial and offering insult and affront to the Holy Spirit,[49] we should fall into graver ones, *treasuring up to ourselves wrath against the day of wrath*.[50] For without doubt, these satisfactions greatly restrain from sin, check as it were with a bit, and make penitents more cautious and vigilant in the future; they also remove remnants of sin, and by acts of the opposite virtues destroy habits acquired by evil living. Neither was there ever in the Church of God any way held more certain to ward off impending chastisement by the Lord than that men perform with true sorrow of mind these works of penance.[51] Add to this, that while we by making satisfaction suffer for our sins, we are made conformable to Christ Jesus who satisfied for

---

[44] See II Tim. 3:5.
[45] Cf. Sess. VI, chap. 14, can. 30 and *infra*, can. 12.
[46] Gen. 3:16 ff.; Num. 12:14 f.; 20:11 f.; II Kings 12:13 f., etc.
[47] See I Cor. 3:17.
[48] Eph. 4:30.
[49] Heb. 10:29.
[50] Rom. 2:5; James 5:3.
[51] Matt. 3:2, 8; 4:17; 11:21.

our sins,[52] from whom is all our sufficiency,[53] having thence also a most certain pledge, that *if we suffer with him, we shall also be glorified with him.*[54] Neither is this satisfaction which we discharge for our sins so our own as not to be through Christ Jesus; for we who can do nothing of ourselves as of ourselves, can do all things with the cooperation of Him who strengthens us.[55] Thus man has not wherein to glory, but all our glorying is in Christ,[56] in whom we live,[57] in whom we merit, in whom we make satisfaction, *bringing forth fruits worthy of penance*,[58] which have their efficacy from Him, by Him are offered to the Father, and through Him are accepted by the Father. The priests of the Lord must therefore, so far as reason and prudence suggest, impose salutary and suitable satisfactions, in keeping with the nature of the crimes and the ability of the penitents; otherwise, if they should connive at sins and deal too leniently with penitents, imposing certain very light works for very grave offenses, they might become partakers in the sins of others. But let them bear in mind that the satisfaction they impose be not only for the protection of a new life and a remedy against infirmity, but also for the atonement and punishment of past sins; for the early Fathers also believed and taught that the keys of the priests were bestowed not to loose only but also to bind.[59] It was not their understanding, moreover, that the sacrament of penance is a tribunal of wrath or of punishments, as no Catholic ever understood that through our satisfactions the efficacy of the merit and satisfaction of our Lord Jesus Christ is either obscured or in any way diminished; [60] but since the innovators wish to understand it so, they teach, in order to destroy the efficacy and use of satisfaction, that a new life is the best penance.

Chapter IX

THE WORKS OF SATISFACTION

It [the council] teaches furthermore that the liberality of the divine munificence is so great that we are able through Jesus Christ to make

[52] Rom. 5:10.
[53] See II Cor. 3:5.
[54] Rom. 8:17.
[55] See II Cor. 3:5; Phil. 4:13.
[56] See I Cor. 1:31; II Cor. 10:17; Gal. 6:14.
[57] Acts 17:28.
[58] Matt. 3:8; Luke 3:8.
[59] Matt. 16:19; John 20:23; *infra*, can. 15.
[60] Cf. *infra*, can. 14.

satisfaction to God the Father not only by punishments voluntarily undertaken by ourselves to atone for sins, or by those imposed by the judgment of the priest according to the measure of our offense, but also, and this is the greatest proof of love, by the temporal afflictions imposed by God and borne patiently by us.

THE DOCTRINE OF THE SACRAMENT OF EXTREME UNCTION

It has seemed good to the holy council to add to the preceding doctrine on penance the following concerning the sacrament of extreme unction, which was considered by the Fathers as the completion not only of penance but also of the whole Christian life, which ought to be a continual penance. First therefore, with regard to its institution it declares and teaches that our most benevolent Redeemer, who wished to have His servants at all times provided with salutary remedies against all the weapons of all enemies,[61] as in the other sacraments He provided the greatest aids by means of which Christians may during life keep themselves free from every graver spiritual evil, so did He fortify the end of life by the sacrament of extreme unction as with the strongest defense. For though our adversary seeks and seizes occasions throughout our whole life to devour our souls in any manner,[62] yet there is no time when he strains more vehemently all the powers of his cunning to ruin us utterly, and if possible to make us even lose faith in the divine mercy, than when he perceives that the end of our life is near.

CHAPTER I

THE INSTITUTION OF THE SACRAMENT OF EXTREME UNCTION

This sacred unction of the sick was instituted by Christ our Lord as truly and properly a sacrament of the New Law, alluded to indeed by Mark[63] but recommended and announced to the faithful by James the Apostle and brother of the Lord. *Is any man*, he says, *sick among you? Let him bring in the priests of the Church and let them pray over him, anointing him with oil in the name of the Lord; and the prayer of faith shall save the sick man, and the Lord shall raise him up; and if he*

[61] Eph. 6:10 ff.
[62] See I Pet. 5:8.
[63] Mark 6:13.

be in sins, they shall be forgiven him.[64] In which words, as the Church has learned from Apostolic tradition received from hand to hand, he teaches the matter, form, proper administration and effect of this salutary sacrament. For the Church has understood that the matter is the oil blessed by the bishop, because the anointing very aptly represents the grace of the Holy Ghost with which the soul of the sick person is invisibly anointed. The form, furthermore, are those words: "By this unction, etc."

Chapter II

THE EFFECT OF THIS SACRAMENT

Moreover, the significance and effect of this sacrament are explained in these words: *And the prayer of faith shall save the sick man, and the Lord shall raise him up, and if he be in sins they shall be forgiven him.*[65] For the thing signified is the grace of the Holy Ghost whose anointing takes away the sins if there be any still to be expiated, and also the remains of sin and raises up and strengthens the soul of the sick person by exciting in him great confidence in the divine mercy, supported by which the sick one bears more lightly the miseries and pains of his illness and resists more easily the temptations of the devil who lies in wait for his heel;[66] and at times when expedient for the welfare of the soul restores bodily health.

Chapter III

THE MINISTER OF THIS SACRAMENT AND THE TIME WHEN IT OUGHT TO BE ADMINISTERED

And now, with regard to prescribing who ought to receive and administer this sacrament, this also was not obscurely expressed in the words cited above. For there it is also pointed out that the proper ministers of this sacrament are the priests of the Church; by which name in that place are to be understood not the elders by age or the highest in rank among the people, but either bishops or priests[67] rightly or-

[64] James 5:14 f.
[65] *Ibid.*, 5:15.
[66] Gen. 3:15.
[67] C.3, D.XCV and *infra*, Extr. Unct., can. 4.

dained by bishops with *the imposition of the hands of the priesthood.*[68] It is also declared that this anointing is to be applied to the sick, but especially to those who are in such danger as to appear to be at the end of life, whence it is also called the sacrament of the dying. If the sick should after the reception of this sacrament recover, they may again be strengthened with the aid of this sacrament when they fall into another similar danger of death. Wherefore, they are under no condition to be listened to who against so manifest and clear a statement of the Apostle James[69] teach that this anointing is either a human contrivance or is a rite received from the Fathers, having neither a command from God nor a promise of grace; nor those who declare that this has already ceased, as though it were to be understood only as referring to the grace of healing in the primitive Church; nor those who maintain that the rite and usage which the holy Roman Church observes in the administration of this sacrament are opposed to the expression of the Apostle James,[70] and therefore must be changed into some other; nor finally those who assert that this last anointing may without sin be despised by the faithful; for all these things are most clearly at variance with the manifest words of so great an Apostle. Assuredly, in reference to those things that constitute the substance of this sacrament, the Roman Church, the mother and mistress of all other churches, does not observe anything in administering this unction that has not been prescribed by the blessed James. Nor indeed can there be contempt for so great a sacrament without a grievous sin and offense to the Holy Ghost.

These things regarding the sacraments of penance and extreme unction this holy ecumenical council professes and teaches and proposes to all the faithful of Christ to be believed and held. And it submits the following canons to be inviolately observed, and forever anathematizes those who maintain the contrary.

CANONS CONCERNING THE MOST HOLY SACRAMENT OF PENANCE

Canon 1. If anyone says that in the Catholic Church penance is not truly and properly a sacrament instituted by Christ the Lord for recon-

[68] See I Tim. 4:14.
[69] James 5:14 f.
[70] *Infra,* Extr. Unct., can. 3.

ciling the faithful of God as often as they fall into sin after baptism,[71] let him be anathema.

Can. 2. If anyone, confounding the sacraments, says that baptism is itself the sacrament of penance,[72] as though these two sacraments were not distinct, and that penance therefore is not rightly called a second plank after shipwreck,[73] let him be anathema.

Can. 3. If anyone says that those words of the Lord Savior, *Receive ye the Holy Ghost, whose sins you shall forgive, they are forgiven them, and whose sins you shall retain, they are retained,*[74] are not to be understood of the power of forgiving and retaining sins in the sacrament of penance, as the Catholic Church has always understood them from the beginning, but distorts them, contrary to the institution of this sacrament, as applying to the authority of preaching the Gospel, let him be anathema.

Can. 4. If anyone denies that for the full and perfect remission of sins three acts are required on the part of the penitent, constituting as it were the matter of the sacrament of penance, namely, contrition, confession and satisfaction, which are called the three parts of penance;[75] or says that there are only two parts of penance, namely, the terrors of a smitten conscience convinced of sin and the faith received from the Gospel or from absolution, by which one believes that his sins are forgiven him through Christ, let him be anathema.

Can. 5. If anyone says that the contrition which is evoked by examination, recollection and hatred of sins,[76] whereby one recounts his years in the bitterness of his soul,[77] by reflecting on the grievousness, the multitude, the baseness of his sins, the loss of eternal happiness and the incurring of eternal damnation, with a purpose of amendment, is not a true and beneficial sorrow, does not prepare for grace, but makes a man a hypocrite and a greater sinner; finally, that this sorrow is forced and not free and voluntary, let him be anathema.

Can. 6. If anyone denies that sacramental confession was instituted by divine law or is necessary to salvation;[78] or says that the manner of confessing secretly to a priest alone, which the Catholic Church has

---

[71] Cf. *supra,* chap. 1.
[72] *Ibid.*
[73] C.72, D.I de poenit.
[74] Matt. 16:19; John 20:23 f.; cf. Sess. VI, chap. 14 and *supra,* chap. 1.
[75] *Supra,* chap. 3.
[76] *Ibid.*, chap. 4.
[77] Is. 38:15.
[78] *Supra,* chap. 5.

always observed from the beginning and still observes, is at variance with the institution and command of Christ and is a human contrivance, let him be anathema.

Can. 7. If anyone says that in the sacrament of penance it is not required by divine law for the remission of sins to confess each and all mortal sins which are recalled after a due and diligent examination,[79] also secret ones and those that are a violation of the two last commandments of the Decalogue,[80] as also the circumstances that change the nature of a sin, but that this confession is useful only to instruct and console the penitent and in olden times was observed only to impose a canonical satisfaction; or says that they who strive to confess all sins wish to leave nothing to the divine mercy to pardon; or finally, that it is not lawful to confess venial sins, let him be anathema.

Can. 8. If anyone says that the confession of all sins as it is observed in the Church is impossible and is a human tradition to be abolished by pious people;[81] or that each and all of the faithful of Christ of either sex are not bound thereto once a year in accordance with the constitution of the great Lateran Council,[82] and that for this reason the faithful of Christ are to be persuaded not to confess during Lent, let him be anathema.

Can. 9. If anyone says that the sacramental absolution of the priest is not a judicial act but a mere service of pronouncing and declaring to him who confesses that the sins are forgiven, provided only he believes himself to be absolved, even though the priest absolves not in earnest but only in jest;[83] or says that the confession of the penitent is not necessary in order that the priest may be able to absolve him, let him be anathema.

Can. 10. If anyone says that priests who are in mortal sin have not the power of binding and loosing,[84] or that not only priests are the ministers of absolution but that to each and all of the faithful of Christ was it said: *Whatsoever you shall bind upon earth, shall be bound also in heaven; and whatsoever you shall loose upon earth, shall be loosed in heaven;*[85] and *whose sins you shall forgive, they are forgiven them,*

---

[79] *Supra,* chap. 5.
[80] Deut. 5:21.
[81] *Supra,* chap. 5.
[82] *Ibid.,* chap. 5 at the end.
[83] *Ibid.,* chap. 6.
[84] *Ibid.,* chaps. 5–6.
[85] Matt. 16:19; 18:18.

and whose sins you shall retain, they are retained; [86] by virtue of which words everyone can absolve from sins, from public sins by reproof only, provided the one reproved accept correction, and from secret sins by voluntary confession, let him be anathema.

Can. 11. If anyone says that bishops have not the right to reserve cases to themselves except such as pertain to external administration, and that therefore the reservation of cases does not hinder a priest from absolving from reserved cases,[87] let him be anathema.

Can. 12. If anyone says that God always pardons the whole penalty together with the guilt and that the satisfaction of penitents is nothing else than the faith by which they perceive that Christ has satisfied for them,[88] let him be anathema.

Can. 13. If anyone says that satisfaction for sins, as to their temporal punishment, is in no way made to God through the merits of Christ by the punishments inflicted by Him and patiently borne, or by those imposed by the priest, or even those voluntarily undertaken, as by fasts, prayers, almsgiving or other works of piety, and that therefore the best penance is merely a new life,[89] let him be anathema.

Can. 14. If anyone says that the satisfactions by which penitents atone for their sins through Christ are not a worship of God but traditions of men, which obscure the doctrine of grace and the true worship of God and the beneficence itself of the death of Christ,[90] let him be anathema.

Can. 15. If anyone says that the keys have been given to the Church only to loose and not also to bind, and that therefore priests, when imposing penalties on those who confess, act contrary to the purpose of the keys and to the institution of Christ, and that it is a fiction that there remains often a temporal punishment to be discharged after the eternal punishment has by virtue of the keys been removed,[91] let him be anathema.

CANONS CONCERNING THE SACRAMENT OF EXTREME UNCTION

Canon 1. If anyone says that extreme unction is not truly and properly a sacrament instituted by Christ our Lord and announced by

---

[86] John 20:23.
[87] *Supra*, chap. 7.
[88] *Ibid.*, chap. 8.
[89] *Ibid.*, chaps. 8–9.
[90] *Ibid.*, chap. 8.
[91] *Ibid.*, chaps. 1, 8.

the blessed Apostle James,[92] but is only a rite received from the Fathers or a human invention, let him be anathema.

Can. 2. If anyone says that the anointing of the sick neither confers any grace nor remits sins nor comforts the sick, but that it has already ceased, as if it had been a healing grace only in the olden days,[93] let him be anathema.

Can. 3. If anyone says that the rite and usage of extreme unction which the holy Roman Church observes is at variance with the statement of the blessed Apostle James,[94] and is therefore to be changed and may without sin be despised by Christians, let him be anathema.

Can. 4. If anyone says that the priests of the Church, whom blessed James exhorts to be brought to anoint the sick, are not the priests who have been ordained by a bishop, but the elders in each community, and that for this reason a priest only is not the proper minister of extreme unction,[95] let him be anathema.

DECREE CONCERNING REFORM

Introduction

It is the office of the bishops to admonish their subjects of their duty, especially those appointed to the *cura animarum*

Since it is properly the office of bishops to reprove the transgressions of all their subjects, this especially must claim their attention, that clerics, particularly those appointed to the *cura animarum*, be not wicked, nor lead a disorderly life with their connivance.[96] For if they permit them to be given to evil and corrupt morals, how shall they reprove the lay people for their transgressions when these can by one word repulse them for permitting clerics to be worse than they?[97] And with what freedom shall priests be able to correct laics when they must answer silently to themselves that they have committed the same things that they censure?[98] Wherefore, bishops shall admonish their

[92] James 5:14 f.
[93] Cf. *supra*, Extr. Unct., chap. 2.
[94] James 5:14 f.
[95] *Ibid.; supra*, Extr. Unct., chap. 3.
[96] C.13, X, De off. jud. ord., I, 31; *supra*, Sess. VI, chap. 3 de ref.
[97] See I Cor. 9:27.
[98] C.6, D.XXV.

clergy, of whatever rank they may be, that in conduct, speech and knowledge they be a guide to the people of God committed to them;[99] being mindful of what is written: *Be holy, for I also am holy*.[100] And in accordance with the word of the Apostle, let them not give offense to any man, that their ministry may not be blamed; but in all things let them exhibit themselves as the ministers of God,[101] lest the saying of the prophet be fulfilled in them: *The priests of God defile the sanctuaries and despise the law*.[102] But that the bishops may be able to execute this more freely, and may not be hindered therein by any pretext whatsoever, the same holy, ecumenical and general Council of Trent, the same legate and nuncios of the Apostolic See presiding therein, has thought it proper that the following canons be established and decreed.

Chapter I

IF ANY, FORBIDDEN TO ADVANCE TO ORDERS, DO SO ADVANCE, IF INTERDICTED OR SUSPENDED, THEY ARE TO BE PUNISHED

Since it is more honorable and safe for a subject to serve in an inferior ministry and render due obedience to those placed over him than to the scandal of the superiors seek the dignity of a higher rank, to him to whom the advance to sacred orders has, for any reason whatsoever, even on account of secret crime, or in whatsoever manner, even extra-judicially, been denied by his own prelate, or who has been suspended from his orders or ecclesiastical rank or dignities, no permission granted against the will of that prelate to bring about his promotion or restoration to former orders, rank, dignities or honors, shall be of any avail.

---

[99] Cf. Sess. XXII, chap. 1 de ref.
[100] Lev. 11:44; 19:2; 20:7; I Pet. 1:16.
[101] See II Cor. 6:3 f.
[102] Ezech. 22:26; Soph. 3:4.

Chapter II

IF A BISHOP SHALL CONFER ANY ORDERS WHATSOEVER ON ONE NOT SUBJECT TO HIM, EVEN IF HE BE HIS OWN DOMESTIC, WITHOUT THE EXPRESSED CONSENT OF THAT PERSON'S PRELATE, BOTH SHALL BE SUBJECT TO THE PENALTY PRESCRIBED

Since some bishops of churches located *in partibus infidelium*, having neither clergy nor Christian people, being well-nigh wanderers and without a fixed residence, seeking not the things of Jesus Christ, but other sheep without the knowledge of their pastor,[103] and finding themselves forbidden by this holy council to exercise episcopal functions in the diocese of another without the expressed permission of the local ordinary,[104] and then only in regard to persons who are subject to that ordinary, do in their boldness, by evasion and in contempt of the law, choose as it were an episcopal see in a place which belongs to no diocese, and presume to mark with the clerical character and even promote to the sacred order of the priesthood any who come to them, even though they have no commendatory letters from their bishops or prelates, whence it happens very often that persons are ordained who are but little qualified, who are untrained and ignorant, and have been rejected by their own bishops as incompetent and unworthy, neither able to perform the divine offices nor to administer rightly the sacraments of the Church; none of the bishops, therefore, who are called titular, even though they reside or sojourn in a place within no diocese, even if it be exempt, or in a monastery of whatsoever order, may, by virtue of any privilege granted them for a time, promote those who come to them, or promote or ordain to any sacred or minor orders, or even to the first tonsure, the subject of another bishop, even under the pretext that he is his domestic and companion at table, without the expressed consent of or dimissory letters from that person's own bishop.[105] Those acting contrary to this shall be *ipso jure* suspended for one year from the exercise of pontifical functions, and the one so promoted shall likewise be suspended from the exercise of the orders as long as his own prelate shall see fit.

---

[103] Cf. *infra*, chap. 8 de ref.
[104] Cf. Sess. VI, chap. 5 de ref.
[105] *Ibid.* and Sess. XXIII, chaps. 3, 8, 10 de ref.

Chapter III

A BISHOP MAY SUSPEND HIS CLERICS WHO HAVE BEEN IMPROPERLY PROMOTED BY ANOTHER, IF HE SHOULD FIND THEM INCOMPETENT

A bishop may suspend for as long a time as he may see fit from the exercise of the orders received, and may prohibit from ministering or from exercising the functions of any order, any of his clerics, especially those who are in sacred orders, who have been promoted by any authority whatsoever without his previous examination and commendatory letters, even though they shall have been approved as competent by him who ordained them, but whom he himself shall find unfit and incapable to celebrate the divine offices or to administer the sacraments of the Church.[106]

Chapter IV

NO CLERIC SHALL BE EXEMPT FROM THE CORRECTION OF THE BISHOP, EVEN OUTSIDE THE TIME OF VISITATION

All prelates of churches who ought to apply themselves diligently to correct the excesses of their subjects,[107] and against whom no cleric is by the statutes of this council under pretext of any privilege whatsoever considered secure that he may not be visited, punished and corrected in accordance with the canons, shall, if they reside in their own churches, have the power, delegated for this purpose by the Apostolic See, to correct and punish, even outside the time of visitation, all secular clerics in whatever manner exempt, who would otherwise be subject to their jurisdiction, for their excesses, crimes and delinquencies as often as and whenever there shall be need; [108] no exemptions, declarations, customs, sentences, oaths, agreements, which bind only their authors, shall be of any avail to said clerics and their relations, chaplains, domestics, agents, or to any others whatsoever in view and in consideration of said exempt clerics.

---

[106] Cf. Sess. XXIII, chap. 8 de ref.
[107] Sess. VI, chap. 3 de ref.; c.13, X, De off. jud. ord., I, 31.
[108] Sess. cit., chap. 4 de ref.

Chapter V

THE JURISDICTION OF CONSERVATORS IS RESTRICTED WITHIN CERTAIN LIMITS

Moreover, since some who, under the pretext that divers wrongs and annoyances are inflicted on them in their goods, possessions and rights, obtain certain judges to be appointed by means of conservatory letters to protect and defend them against such annoyances and wrongs and to maintain and keep them in the real or quasi possession of their goods, property and rights without suffering them to be molested therein, in most cases wrest from such letters a meaning that is contrary to the intention of the donor, therefore, conservatory letters, whatever may be their clauses and decrees, whatever judges may be appointed, or under whatever other sort of pretext or color they may have been granted, shall avail absolutely no one, of whatever dignity and condition, even though a chapter, from being in criminal and mixed causes accused and summoned, examined and proceeded against before his own bishop or other ordinary superior, or from being freely summoned before the ordinary judge in those matters, even if any rights should come to him from a concession made to him. In civil causes also, if he be the plaintiff, it shall under no condition be lawful for him to bring anyone for judgment before his own conservatory judges. And if in those cases in which he shall be defendant, it should happen that the conservator chosen by him should be declared by the plaintiff to be suspected by him, or if any dispute shall have arisen between the judges themselves, the conservator and the ordinary, with regard to the competency of jurisdiction, the cause shall not be proceeded with until a decision shall have been made relative to said suspicion or competency of jurisdiction by arbiters legally chosen. Nor shall such conservatory letters be of any avail to the said party's domestics, who are in the habit of shielding themselves thereby, except to two only and then provided they live at his own cost. No one, moreover, shall enjoy the benefit of such letters more than five years. It shall also not be lawful for conservatory judges to have any fixed tribunal. With regard to causes that relate to wages and to destitute persons, the decree of this holy council shall remain in its full force.[109] General universities, however, colleges of doctors or scholars, places

[109] Cf. Sess. VII, chap. 14 de ref.

belonging to regulars, also hospitals in which hospitality is actually exercised, and persons belonging to such universities, colleges, places and hospitals, are not to be considered included in the present decree, but are and are to be understood as wholly exempt.

Chapter VI

A PENALTY IS DECREED AGAINST CLERICS WHO, CONSTITUTED IN SACRED ORDERS OR HOLDING BENEFICES, DO NOT WEAR CLOTHES CONFORMING TO THEIR ORDER

And since, though the habit does not make the monk,[110] it is necessary nevertheless that clerics always wear a dress conformable to their order, that by the propriety of their outward apparel they may show forth the inward uprightness of their morals, yet to such a degree have the contempt of religion and the boldness of some grown in these days, that esteeming but little their own dignity and the clerical honor, they even wear in public the dress of laymen, setting their feet in different paths, one of things divine, the other of the flesh. Wherefore, all ecclesiastical persons, howsoever exempt, who are either in sacred orders or in possession of dignities with or without jurisdiction, offices or whatsoever ecclesiastical benefices, if, after having been admonished by their bishops, even by a public edict, they do not wear a becoming clerical dress conformable to their order and dignity and in conformity with the ordinance and mandate of their bishop, may and ought to be compelled thereto by suspension from their orders, office, benefice and from the fruits, revenues and proceeds of those benefices; and also, if, after having been once rebuked, they offend again in the matter, even by deprivation of those offices and benefices; the constitution of Clement V published in the Council of Vienne, beginning "Quoniam," being hereby renewed and amplified.[111]

---

[110] C. 13, X, De regular., III, 31.
[111] C. 2, in Clem., De vit. et hon. cler., III, 1.

Chapter VII

THE ORDINATION OF VOLUNTARY HOMICIDES IS FORBIDDEN; HOW INVOLUNTARY HOMICIDES ARE TO BE ORDAINED

Since also he who has killed his neighbor on set purpose and by lying in wait for him, is to be taken away from the altar,[112] he who has voluntarily committed a homicide, even though that crime has neither been proved by ordinary judicial process nor is otherwise public, but is secret, can never be promoted to sacred orders; nor shall it be lawful to confer on him any ecclesiastical benefices, even though they have not annexed the *cura animarum;* but he shall be forever excluded from every ecclesiastical order, benefice and office. But if it be declared that the homicide was not committed intentionally but accidentally, or when repelling force with force that one might defend himself from death (in which case indeed a dispensation for the ministry of sacred orders and of the altar and for all benefices and dignities is in some manner due by right), the matter shall be referred to the local ordinary, or if need be to the metropolitan or to the nearest bishop, who may dispense only after having taken cognizance of the case and after the entreaties and allegations have been proved, and not otherwise.

Chapter VIII

NO ONE SHALL BY VIRTUE OF ANY PRIVILEGE PUNISH THE CLERICS OF ANOTHER

Furthermore, since there are persons, some of whom are true pastors and have their own sheep, who seek to rule over the sheep of others also,[113] and at times give their attention to the subjects of others to such an extent as to neglect the care of their own; no one, even though he enjoy the episcopal dignity, who may have the privilege of punishing the subjects of another, shall under any circumstances proceed against clerics not subject to him, especially such as are in sacred orders, even if guilty of crimes ever so atrocious, except with the intervention of the bishop of those clerics, if that bishop resides in his own church,

---

[112] Ex. 21:14; c. 1, X, De homicid., V, 12.

[113] Cf. *supra*, chap. 2 de ref. and Sess. VI, chap. 5 de ref.

or of the person that may be deputed by that bishop; otherwise the proceedings and all their consequences shall be entirely without effect.

Chapter IX

THE BENEFICES OF ONE DIOCESE SHALL NOT UNDER ANY PRETEXT BE UNITED TO THE BENEFICES OF ANOTHER

And since it is by a very good law that dioceses and parishes have been made distinct,[114] and to each flock has been assigned its proper pastor and to inferior churches their rectors, each to take care of his own sheep, so that ecclesiastical order may not be disturbed or one and the same church belong in some way to two dioceses, not without grave disadvantage to those subject thereto; the benefices of one diocese, even if they be parochial churches, perpetual vicariates, simple benefices, prestimonies or prestimonial portions, shall not be united *in perpetuum* to a benefice, monastery, college or even to a pious place of another diocese, not even for the purpose of augmenting divine worship or the number of beneficiaries, or for any other reason whatsoever; hereby explaining the decree of this holy council on the subject of unions of this kind.[115]

Chapter X

REGULAR BENEFICES SHALL BE CONFERRED ON REGULARS

Benefices of regulars that have been accustomed to be granted in title to professed regulars, shall, when they happen to become vacant by the death of the titular incumbent, or by his resignation or otherwise, be conferred on religious of the same order only [116] or on persons who shall be absolutely bound to take the habit and make profession, and on no others, that they may *not wear a garment that is woven of woolen and linen together.*[117]

---

[114] Cf. c.9, X, De his, quae fiunt a prael., III, 10 and Sess. XXIV, chap. 13 de ref.

[115] Cf. Sess. VII, chaps. 6 and 7 de ref.; Sess. XXIV, chaps. 13 and 15 de ref.

[116] Cf. Sess. XXV, chap. 21 de regular.; c.5, VI°, De praeb., III, 4; c.27, X, De elect., I, 6.

[117] Deut. 22:11.

Chapter XI

THOSE TRANSFERRED TO ANOTHER ORDER SHALL REMAIN IN THE ENCLOSURE UNDER OBEDIENCE, AND SHALL BE DISQUALIFIED TO HOLD SECULAR BENEFICES

Since regulars, transferred from one order to another, usually obtain permission easily from their superior to remain out of the monastery, whereby occasion is given to wandering about and apostatizing, no prelate or superior of any order shall by virtue of any authority whatsoever, admit anyone to the habit and to profession, unless he remain in the order to which he was transferred and perpetually in the cloister under obedience to his superior,[118] and one so transferred, even though he be a canon regular, shall be wholly disqualified to hold secular benefices, even with the *cura* annexed.

Chapter XII

NO ONE SHALL OBTAIN A RIGHT OF PATRONAGE EXCEPT BY MEANS OF A FOUNDATION OR AN ENDOWMENT

Moreover, no one, of whatever ecclesiastical or secular dignity, may or ought to procure or have a right of patronage for any reason whatever, except that he has founded and erected *de novo* a church, benefice or chapel; or has adequately endowed out of his own patrimonial resources one already erected but insufficiently endowed.[119] But in case of such foundation or endowment, appointments thereto shall be reserved to the bishop and not to some other inferior person.

---

[118] Cf. Sess. XXV, chap. 4 de regular.
[119] Cf. Sess. cit., chap. 9 de ref.

Chapter XIII

THE PRESENTATION MUST BE MADE TO THE ORDINARY, OTHERWISE IT AND THE APPOINTMENT ARE NULL

Furthermore, it shall not be lawful for a patron, under pretext of any privilege, to present anyone in any way to the benefices that are under his right of patronage except to the ordinary bishop of the locality, to whom the provision for or appointment to that benefice would by right belong if the privilege ceased; [120] otherwise the presentation and the appointment perchance following shall be null and shall be understood as such.

Chapter XIV

The holy council declares, moreover, that in the next session, which it has already decreed to be held on the twenty-fifth day of January of the following year, 1552, it will, besides treating of the sacrifice of the mass, also apply itself to and treat of the sacrament of order and continue the subject of reform.

---

[120] Cf. Sess. and chap. cited, and cc.8, 21, X, De jur. patr., III, 38.

FIFTEENTH SESSION

which is the fifth under the Supreme Pontiff, Julius III, celebrated on the twenty-fifth day of January, 1552

DECREE FOR PROROGUING THE SESSION

Since this holy and general council has during these days, in accordance with the decrees enacted in the last sessions, most accurately and diligently considered the things that relate to the most holy sacrifice of the mass and to the sacrament of order, in order that in the present session it might publish, as the Holy Ghost would have prompted, decrees on these matters and on the four articles concerning the most holy sacrament of the Eucharist, which had been finally deferred to this session; and since it was thought that those who call themselves Protestants, for whose sake it had deferred the publication of those articles, and to whom it had given the public faith or a safe-conduct that they might come here freely and without any delay,[1] would in the meantime have presented themselves at this holy council; seeing, however, that they have not yet come, and the holy council having been petitioned in their name that the publication which was to have been made on this day be deferred to the following session, an assured hope being expressed that they will doubtlessly be present long before that session upon receipt in the meantime of a safe-conduct in a more amplified form, the same holy council, lawfully assembled in the Holy Ghost, the same legate and nuncios presiding, desiring nothing more than to remove from among the illustrious German nation all dissensions and schisms regarding religion, and to provide for its tranquillity, peace and concord; being prepared, should they come, to receive them kindly and to listen to them favorably, and trusting that they will come not with the intention of obstinately assailing the Catholic faith but of learning the truth, and that they will at last, as becomes those zealous for evangelical truth, acquiesce in the decrees and discipline of holy mother Church, has deferred the next session for the publication and promulgation of the aforesaid matters to the feast of St. Joseph, which

[1] *Supra,* Sess. XIII at the end.

will be the nineteenth day of the month of March, in order that they may have sufficient time and leisure not only to come but also to propose before that day arrives whatever they may wish. And that all cause for further delay on their part may be removed, it freely gives and grants them the public faith or a safe-conduct, the contents and tenor of which is given below. But it ordains and decrees that in the meantime the sacrament of matrimony is to be considered, and it will give in the same session its decisions thereon, in addition to the publication of the above-mentioned decrees, also continuing the matter of reform.

SAFE-CONDUCT GIVEN TO THE PROTESTANTS

The holy, ecumenical and general Council of Trent, lawfully assembled in the Holy Ghost, the same legate and nuncios of the Apostolic See presiding, adhering to the safe-conduct given in the session before the last and amplifying it in the manner following, certifies to all men that by the tenor of these presents, it grants and fully concedes the public faith and the fullest and truest security, which they call a safe-conduct, to each and all priests, electors, princes, dukes, marquises, counts, barons, soldiers, the common people, and to all other persons of whatever state, condition or character they may be, of the German province and nation, to the cities and other places thereof, and to all other ecclesiastical and secular persons, especially those of the Confession of Augsburg, who shall come or be sent with them to this general Council of Trent, and to those who are going to come or have already come, by whatever name they are or may be designated, to come freely to this city of Trent, to remain, abide and sojourn here and to propose, speak and consider, examine and discuss any matters whatever with the council, and to present freely whatever they may think suitable, to set forth any articles whatever either in writing or orally, and to explain, establish and prove them by the Sacred Scriptures and by the words, decisions and arguments of the blessed Fathers, and also to reply, if need be, to the objections of the general council, and to dispute and confer charitably and respectfully and without hindrance with those who have been selected by the council, reproachful, vexatious and offensive language being absolutely put aside; and particularly, that the controverted matters shall be treated in this Council of Trent in accordance with Sacred Scripture and the traditions of the Apostles, the approved councils, the consensus of the Catholic Church and the authority of the holy Fathers; with this further addition, that they shall under no condition be punished by reason of religion or of offenses committed or that may be committed in regard thereto; and also that the divine offices shall not by reason of their presence, either upon the road or in any place of their journey, their stay or their return, or in the city of Trent itself, be in any way interrupted; and that on the conclusion of these matters or before their conclusion, whensoever it shall please them, if they should wish by the command and permission of their superiors to return to their homes, or if any one of them should so wish, they may at their pleasure return freely and securely, without restraint, formality or delay, without injury to their property and to the honor and persons of their attendants and vice versa; making known, however, their intention of withdrawing to those to be deputed by the council, so that at a convenient time, without deceit or fraud, provision may be made for their security. The holy council wishes also that all clauses whatsoever, which may be necessary and suitable for a complete, effective and sufficient security for coming, sojourning and returning, be included and contained, and to be considered as included, in this public faith and safe-conduct. For their greater security and for the sake of peace and reconciliation, it declares also that if, which God forbid, any one or several of them should, either on the way to Trent or while sojourning there or returning therefrom, perpetrate or commit an atrocious act, by which the benefit of this public faith and assurance granted to them might be annulled and cassated, it wishes and concedes that those discovered in such crime shall be forthwith punished by their own countrymen and not by others, with a condign chastisement and proper reparation, which the council on its part may justly approve and commend, the form, conditions and terms of the safe-conduct remaining entirely intact thereby. In like manner it wishes also that if, which God forbid, any one or several of this council should, either on the road or while sojourning or returning, perpetrate or commit an atrocious act by which the benefit of this public faith or assurance may be violated or in any manner annulled, those discovered in any such crime shall be forthwith punished by the council itself and not by others, with a condign chastisement and proper reparation, which the Germans of the Augsburg Confession here present may on their part approve and commend, the present form, conditions and terms of the safe-conduct remaining entirely intact thereby. The council wishes furthermore, that each and all of their ambassadors shall be allowed to go out of the city of Trent to take the fresh air as often as it shall be convenient or necessary and to return here; also freely to send or dispatch their messenger or messengers to any place whatsoever to attend to their necessary affairs and to receive those sent or dispatched or the one sent or dispatched as often as they may deem fit; so however that several or one of those appointed by the council may accompany them or him in order to provide for their safety. This safe-conduct and security shall be good and extend from and during the time that they shall have been taken under the protection of this council and its agents to their arrival at Trent, and during the entire time of their sojourn here; and further, after a sufficient hearing has been had, a period of twenty days having expired, when they themselves should desire, or the council on the conclusion of such hearing should give them notice to return, it will, all deceit and fraud being wholly excluded, reconduct them with the help of God from Trent to that place of safety which each may choose for himself. All of which it promises and pledges in good faith to be inviolately observed toward each and all of the faithful of Christ, toward all ecclesiastical and secular princes and all ecclesiastical and secular persons, of whatsoever state and condition they may be or by whatsoever name they may be known. Moreover, it promises in sincere and good faith, to the exclusion of fraud and deceit, that the council will neither openly nor secretly seek any occasion, nor make use of, nor permit anyone else to make use of, any authority, power, right or statute, privilege of laws or canons, or of any councils in whatever form of words expressed, especially those of Constance and Siena, in any way prejudicial to this public faith and the fullest security, and of the public and free hearing granted by this council to the above-named; these it abrogates in this respect and for this occasion. And if the holy council or any member thereof, or any of its adherents, of whatever condition, state or pre-eminence, shall violate, which may the Almighty prevent, in any point or clause whatever, the form and terms of the security and safe-conduct as set forth above, and a satisfactory reparation that in their judgment may be justly approved and commended shall not have forthwith followed, they may consider the council to have incurred all those penalties which by human and divine law or by custom the violators of such safe-conducts can incur, without any excuse or contrary allegation in this respect.

SIXTEENTH SESSION

which is the sixth and last under the Supreme Pontiff, Julius III, celebrated on the twenty-eighth day of April, 1552

DECREE SUSPENDING THE COUNCIL

The holy, ecumenical and general Council of Trent, lawfully assembled in the Holy Ghost, the most reverent Lords, Sebastian, Archbishop of Sipontum, and Aloysius, Bishop of Verona, Apostolic nuncios, presiding in their own names as well as in that of the most reverend and illustrious Lord, the legate Marcellus Crescentius, Cardinal of the holy Roman Church with the title of St. Marcellus, who is absent by reason of a very grave illness, doubts not that it is known to all Christians that this ecumenical Council of Trent was first convoked and assembled by Paul, of happy memory. Afterward at the instance of the most august Emperor, Charles V, reconvened by our most holy Lord Julius III, chiefly for the reason that it might restore religion, which was deplorably divided into various opinions in many parts of the world, especially in Germany, to its former state, and correct the abuses and most corrupt morals of the Christians. And since very many Fathers from different countries, regardless of personal hardships and dangers, had for this purpose willingly assembled, and the business progressed earnestly and happily in the midst of a great concourse of the faithful, and there was great hope that those Germans who had inaugurated those innovations would come to the council so disposed as to accept unanimously the true foundations of the Church, some light seemed at last to have dawned upon affairs, and the Christian commonwealth, before so depressed and afflicted, began to lift up its head. Then suddenly such tumults and wars were enkindled by the craftiness of the enemy of the human race, that the council was at much inconvenience compelled to pause as it were and to interrupt its course, so that all hope for further progress at that time was dissipated; and so far was the council from remedying the evils and troubles existing among the Christians, that, contrary to its intentions, it irritated rather than calmed the minds of many. Since, therefore, the holy council saw that all places, and especially Germany, were ablaze with arms and discords, that almost all the German bishops, especially the electoral princes, solicitous for their churches, had withdrawn from the council, it decided not to resist so great a necessity and to await better times, so that the Fathers who now could achieve nothing might return to their churches to take care of their sheep and no longer spend their time in useless inactivity. Hence, since the conditions of the times so require, it decrees that the progress of this ecumenical Council of Trent shall be suspended for two years, as it does suspend it by the present decree; with this understanding, however, that if peace is brought about sooner and the former tranquillity restored, which it trusts will, with the help of the all-good and great God, come about soon, the progress of the council shall be regarded as resumed from that time and as having its full validity, stability and authority. But if, which may God prevent, the aforesaid lawful impediments shall at the expiration of the time specified not have been removed, the suspension shall immediately upon their removal thereafter be considered *eo ipso* revoked, and the council shall be and shall be understood to be restored to its full power and authority without any new convocation thereof, provided the consent and authority of His Holiness and of the Apostolic See has been given to this decree.

In the meantime, however, this holy council exhorts all Christian princes and prelates to observe, and so far as it pertains to them, to cause to be observed in their kingdoms, dominions and churches each and all the things which have so far been ordained and decreed by this holy ecumenical council.

BULL
FOR THE CELEBRATION OF THE COUNCIL OF TRENT

under the Supreme Pontiff, Pius IV

Pius, Bishop, servant of the servants of God, for a perpetual remembrance hereof

Called by the divine providence of God to the government of the Church, though unequal to so great a burden, and immediately casting the eyes of our mind over every part of the Christian commonwealth, and beholding, not without great horror, how far and wide the pest of heresy and schism have penetrated and how much the morals of the Christian people are in need of reform, we began in accordance with the duty of our office to devote our care and thought to the means whereby we should be able to exterminate those heresies, destroy so great and pernicious a schism, and reform the morals so much corrupted and depraved. And since we understand that for the correction of these evils that remedy is the most suitable which this Holy See has been accustomed to apply, namely, an ecumenical and general council, we formed the resolution to assemble and with the help of God to celebrate one. The same had indeed already been summoned by our predecessor, Paul III, of happy memory, and Julius, his successor, but due to frequent hindrance and interruption by various causes, it could not be brought to a conclusion. For Paul, having convoked it at first in the city of Mantua, then in Vicenza, for reasons expressed in his letters first suspended it and afterwards transferred it to Trent; then, when for certain reasons the time of its celebration was postponed here also, it was at length, after the removal of the suspension, begun in the city of Trent. After a few sessions had been held, however, and some decrees enacted, the council for certain reasons and with the concurrence of Apostolic authority, transferred itself to Bologna.[1] But Julius, who succeeded him, recalled it to the city of Trent,[2] at which time some more decrees were enacted. But since new disturbances were stirred up in the neighboring parts of Germany, and a very grave war enkindled in Italy and France, the council was again suspended and postponed; the enemy of the human race exerting himself exceedingly and throwing hindrances and difficulties in the way to retard at least as long as possible, since he could not entirely prevent, such a great advantage to the Church. But how greatly the heresies in the meantime increased, multiplied and propagated, how widely the schism spread, we can neither ponder nor relate without the greatest sorrow of mind. But at length the good and merciful Lord, who is never so angry that He forgets mercy,[3] deigned to grant peace and unanimity to the Christian kings and princes. By this proffered opportunity we, relying on His mercy, entertained the strongest hope that by the same means of a council an end may be put to these grave evils in the Church. That

---

[1] *Supra*, Sess. VIII.
[2] *Ibid.*, Sess. XI.
[3] Hab. 3:2.

therefore schisms and heresies may be destroyed, morals corrected and reformed, and peace among the Christian princes preserved, we have judged that its celebration should no longer be deferred. Wherefore, after mature deliberation with our venerable brethren, the cardinals of the holy Roman Church, and having also made known our intention to our most dear sons in Christ, Ferdinand, Emperor-elect of the Romans, and other kings and princes, whom, as we expected from their great piety and wisdom, we found very well disposed to aid in the celebration of the council, we, to the praise, honor and glory of the Almighty God, for the benefit of the universal Church, with the advice and consent of the same venerable brethren, and relying on and supported by the authority of God Himself and of the blessed Apostles Peter and Paul, which we also exercise on earth, summon a holy, ecumenical and general council to the city of Trent for the next following most holy day of the Lord's resurrection, and ordain and decree that, all suspension being removed, it be celebrated there. Wherefore, we urgently exhort and admonish in the Lord and also strictly command in virtue of holy obedience, and in virtue also of the oath which they have taken, and under the penalties which they know are prescribed by the sacred canons against those who neglect to attend general councils, our venerable brethren wherever located, patriarchs, archbishops, bishops, and our beloved sons the abbots, and others who by common law, privilege or ancient custom are allowed to sit and express their opinion in a general council, unless they happen to be prevented by a legitimate impediment, which they must prove to the council by lawful procurators. We furthermore admonish each and all whom it does or may concern that they do not neglect to attend the council. Our most dear sons in Christ, the Emperor-elect of the Romans and other Christian kings and princes, whose presence at the council would be earnestly desired, we exhort and beseech that if they themselves should not be able to be present at the council, they at least send as their deputies prudent, reputable and pious men to be present in their name, who, animated by their piety, will see to it that the prelates of their kingdoms and dominions perform without refusal and delay their duty to God and the Church at this so urgent a time; neither do we doubt in the least that they will also see to it that a safe and free road through their kingdoms and dominions is open to the prelates, their attendants, followers and all others who are proceeding to or returning from the council, and that they will be received and treated in all places kindly and courteously, as we also will provide so far as it concerns us, for we have resolved to omit absolutely nothing that we, who have been placed in this position, can do toward the completion of so pious and salutary a work, seeking nothing else, as God knows, and in the celebration of the council having no other desire but the honor of God, the recovery and salvation of the scattered sheep, and the lasting peace and tranquillity of the Christian commonwealth. And that this document and its contents may come to the knowledge of all whom it concerns, and that no one may offer the excuse that he was ignorant of it, especially since there may not perhaps be safe access to all who ought to have knowledge of this letter, we wish and command that it be read publicly and in a loud voice by messengers of our court or by some public notaries in the Vatican Basilica of the Prince of the Apostles and in the Church of the Lateran, at a time when the people are accustomed to assemble there for the celebration of the masses; and that, after having been read, it be affixed to the doors of those churches, also to the Apostolic Chancery, and at the usual place in the Campo di Fiore, where it shall be left for some time that it may be read and made known to all. When it is removed, copies thereof shall remain affixed in the same places. For we wish that by this reading, publication and affixture each and all of those whom it includes, shall after two months from the day of publication and affixture be so obligated and bound as if it had been published and read in their presence. We also ordain and decree that unshaken faith be given to the transcripts thereof, written or subscribed by the hand of a public notary and provided with the seal and signature of some person constituted in ecclesiastical dignity. Therefore, let no one infringe this letter of our summons, statute, decree, admonition and exhortation, or with foolhardy boldness oppose it. But if anyone shall presume to attempt this, let him know that he will incur the indignation of Almighty God and of His blessed Apostles Peter and Paul. Given at Rome at Saint Peter's on the thirtieth of November in the year 1560 of the Lord's incarnation and in the first year of our pontificate.

Antonius Florebellus Lavellinus.
Barengus.

SEVENTEENTH SESSION

OF THE

HOLY, ECUMENICAL AND GENERAL

COUNCIL OF TRENT

which is the first under the Supreme Pontiff, Pius IV, celebrated on the eighteenth day of January, 1562

DECREE CONCERNING THE CELEBRATION OF THE COUNCIL

Does it please you, for the praise and glory of the holy and undivided Trinity, Father, Son, and Holy Ghost, for the increase and exaltation of the faith and of the Christian religion, that the holy, ecumenical and general Council of Trent, lawfully assembled in the Holy Ghost, all suspension being removed, be celebrated from this day on, which is the eighteenth of the month of January of the year 1562 after the Nativity of the Lord, consecrated to the chair at Rome of blessed Peter, the Prince of the Apostles, according to the form and tenor of the letter of our most holy Lord, the sovereign pontiff, Pius IV, and that, due order being observed, those things be considered therein which at the suggestion and under the presidency of the legates shall appear suitable and proper to the council for alleviating the calamities of these times, adjusting religious controversies, restraining deceitful tongues, correcting the abuses of depraved morals, and to bring about true and Christian peace in the Church?

They answered: It pleases us.

SUMMONING OF THE NEXT SESSION

Does it please you that the next following session be held and celebrated on the Thursday after the second Sunday of Lent, which will be on the twenty-sixth day of the month of February?

They answered: It pleases us.

EIGHTEENTH SESSION

which is the second under the Supreme Pontiff, Pius IV, celebrated on the twenty-sixth day of February, 1562

DECREE CONCERNING THE CHOICE OF BOOKS AND THE INVITATION OF ALL TO THE COUNCIL UNDER PUBLIC PROTECTION

The holy, ecumenical and general Council of Trent, lawfully assembled in the Holy Ghost, the same legates of the Apostolic See presiding, not confiding in human strength but relying on the power and support of our Lord Jesus Christ, who has promised to give to His Church a mouth and wisdom,[1] has in view above all to restore to its purity and splendor the doctrine of the Catholic faith, which in many places has become defiled and obscured by the opinions of many differing among themselves, and to bring back to a better mode of life morals which have deviated from ancient usage, and to *turn the heart of the fathers unto the children*,[2] and the heart of the children unto the fathers. Since therefore it has first of all observed that the number of suspected and pernicious books in which an impure doctrine is contained and disseminated far and wide has in these days exceedingly increased, for which reason indeed many censures have with pious zeal been issued in various provinces and especially in the fair city of Rome, and that as yet no salutary remedy has been of avail against so great and pernicious a disease; it has thought it proper that the Fathers chosen for this inquiry should consider carefully what ought to be done with regard to censures and books and at an opportune time report thereon to the council, so that it may more easily separate the various and strange doctrines as cockle from the wheat of Christian truth,[3] and may more conveniently deliberate and determine what seems better adapted to remove anxiety from the minds of many and to put an end to causes of complaints. It wishes, moreover, that all this be brought to the knowledge of all per-

---

1 Luke 21:15.
2 *Ibid.*, 1:17.
3 Matt. 13:30.

sons, as it also does by the present decree bring it, so that if anyone should consider himself in any manner concerned either in the matter of books and censures or in other things which it has declared beforehand are to be treated in this general council, he may not doubt that he will be courteously listened to by the holy council.

And since the same holy council heartily desires and earnestly beseeches God for the things that are for the peace of the Church,[4] so that all acknowledging our common mother on earth, who cannot forget those whom she has begotten,[5] we *may with one mind and one mouth glorify God and the Father of our Lord Jesus Christ*,[6] it invites and exhorts, by the bowels of the mercy of our same God and Lord, to concord and reconciliation all who do not hold communion with us, and to come to this holy council, to embrace *charity, which is the bond of perfection*, and to show forth the peace of Christ rejoicing in their hearts, wherein they are called in one body.[7] Wherefore, *hearing this voice*, not of man but of the Holy Ghost, let them not *harden their hearts*,[8] but, walking not after their own sense,[9] nor pleasing themselves,[10] let them be moved and converted by this so pious and salutary admonition of their own mother. For as the holy council invites them with all the kindness of charity, so will it receive them.

Moreover, the same holy council has decreed that the public faith can be granted in a general congregation, and that it shall have the same force, authority and obligation as if it had been given and decreed in public session.

SUMMONS FOR THE NEXT SESSION

The same holy Council of Trent, lawfully assembled in the Holy Ghost, the same legates of the Apostolic See presiding, ordains and decrees that the next following session be held and celebrated on the Thursday after the most sacred feast of the Ascension of the Lord, which will be on the fourteenth day of the month of May.

---

[4] Ps. 121:6.
[5] Is. 49:15.
[6] Rom. 15:6.
[7] Col. 3:14 f.
[8] Ps. 94:8; Heb. 3:8.
[9] Eph. 4:17.
[10] Rom. 15:1 ff.

SAFE-CONDUCT GRANTED TO THE GERMAN NATION IN A GENERAL CONGREGATION ON THE FOURTH DAY OF MARCH, 1562

The holy, ecumenical and general Council of Trent, lawfully assembled in the Holy Ghost, the same legates of the Apostolic See presiding, certifies to all men that by the tenor of these presents it grants and fully concedes the public faith and the fullest and truest security, which they call a safe-conduct, to each and all priests, electors, princes, dukes, marquises, counts, barons, soldiers, the common people, and to all other persons, of whatever state, condition or character they may be, the German province and nation, to the cities and other places thereof, and to all other ecclesiastical and secular persons, especially those of the Confession of Augsburg, who shall come or shall be sent with them to this general Council of Trent, and to those who are going to come or have already come, by whatever name they are or may be designated, to come freely to this city of Trent, to remain, abide and sojourn here, and to propose, speak and consider, examine and discuss any matters whatever with the council, to present freely whatever they may think suitable, to set forth any articles whatever either in writing or orally, and to explain, establish and prove them by the Sacred Scriptures and by the words, decisions, and arguments of the blessed Fathers, and also to reply, if need be, to the objections of the general council, and to dispute and confer charitably and respectfully and without hindrance with those who have been selected by the council, putting aside absolutely reproachful, vexatious and offensive language; and particularly, it certifies that the controverted matters shall be treated in this Council of Trent in accordance with Sacred Scriptures and the traditions of the Apostles, the approved councils, the consensus of the Catholic Church and the authority of the holy Fathers; with this further provision, it grants and entirely concedes that they shall under no condition be punished by reason of religion or of offenses committed or that may be committed in regard thereto; provided also that the divine offices shall not by reason of their presence, either upon the road or in any place of their journey, their stay or their return, or in the city of Trent itself, be in any way interrupted; and that on the conclusion of these matters or before their conclusion, whensoever it shall please them, if they should wish by the command and permission of their superiors to return to their homes, or if any one of them should so wish, they may at their pleasure return freely and securely, without restraint, formality or delay, without injury to their property and to the honor and persons of their attendants and vice versa; making known, however, their intention of withdrawing to those to be deputed by the council, so that at a convenient time, without deceit or fraud, provision may be made for their security. The holy council wishes also that all clauses whatsoever, which may be necessary and suitable for a complete, effective and sufficient security for coming, sojourning and returning, be included and contained, and to be considered as included, in this public faith and safe-conduct. For their greater security and for the sake of peace and reconciliation, it declares also that if, which God forbid, any one or several of them should either on the way to Trent or while sojourning in or returning therefrom, perpetrate or commit an atrocious act, by which the benefit of this public faith and assurance granted to them might be annulled and cassated, it wishes and concedes that those discovered in any such crime shall be forthwith punished by their own countrymen and not by others, with a condign chastisement and proper reparation, which the council on its part may justly approve and commend, the form, conditions and terms of the safe-conduct remaining entirely intact thereby. In like manner it wishes also that if, which God forbid, any one or several of this council should, either on the road or while sojourning or returning, perpetrate or commit an atrocious act by which the benefit of this public faith or assurance may be violated or in any manner annulled, those discovered in any such crime shall be forthwith punished by the council itself and not by others, with a condign chastisement and proper reparation, which the Germans of the Augsburg Confession here present may on their part approve and commend, the present form, conditions and terms of the safe-conduct remaining entirely intact thereby. The council wishes furthermore, that each and all of their ambassadors shall be allowed to go out of the city of Trent to take the fresh air as often as it shall be convenient or necessary and to return here; also freely to send or dispatch their messenger or messengers to any place whatsoever to attend to their necessary affairs and to receive those sent or dispatched or the one sent or dispatched as often as they may deem fit; so however that several or one of those appointed by the council may accompany them or him in order to provide for their safety. This safe-conduct and security shall be good and extend from and during the time that they shall have been taken under the protection of this council and its agents to their arrival at Trent, and during the entire time of their sojourn here; and further, after a sufficient hearing has been had, a period of twenty days having expired, when they themselves should desire, or the council on the conclusion of such hearing should give them notice to return, it will, all deceit and fraud being wholly excluded, reconduct them with the help of God from Trent to that place of safety which each may choose for himself. All of which it promises and pledges in good faith to be inviolately observed toward each and all of the faithful of Christ, toward all ecclesiastical and secular princes and all ecclesiastical and secular persons, of whatsoever state and condition they may be or by whatsoever name they may be known. Moreover, it promises in sincere and good faith, to the exclusion of fraud and deceit, that the council will neither openly nor secretly seek any occasion, nor make use of, nor permit anyone else to make use of, any authority, power, right or statute, privilege of laws or canons, or of any councils in whatever form of words expressed, especially those of Constance and Siena, in any way prejudicial to this public faith and the fullest security, and of the public and free hearing granted by this council to the above-named; these it abrogates in this respect and for this occasion. And if the holy council or any member thereof, or any of its adherents, of whatever condition, state or pre-eminence, shall violate, which may the Almighty prevent, in any point or clause whatever, the form and terms of the security and safe-conduct as set forth above, and a satisfactory reparation that in their judgment may be justly approved and commended shall not have forthwith followed, they may consider the council to have incurred all those penalties which by human and divine law or by custom the violators of such safe-conducts can incur, without any excuse or contrary allegation in this respect.

THE EXTENSION OF THE ABOVE TO OTHER NATIONS

The same holy council, lawfully assembled in the Holy Ghost, the same legates *de latere* of the Apostolic See presiding, grants the public faith or a safe-conduct under the same form and terms in which it is granted to the Germans, to each and all others who do not hold communion with us in matters of faith, of whatever kingdoms, nations, provinces, cities and places they may be, in which the contrary to that which the holy Roman Church holds is publicly and with impunity preached, taught or believed.

NINETEENTH SESSION

which is the third under the Supreme Pontiff, Pius IV, celebrated on the fourteenth day of May, 1562

DECREE FOR THE PROROGATION OF THE SESSION

The holy, ecumenical and general Council of Trent, lawfully assembled in the Holy Ghost, the same legates of the Apostolic See presiding, has for good and just reasons thought it fit to prorogue and does hereby prorogue to the Thursday after the next feast of Corpus Christi, which will be the fourth day of June, those decrees which were to have been drawn up and sanctioned today in the present session, and announces to all that the session will be held and celebrated on that day. In the meantime, supplication is to be made to God and the Father of our Lord Jesus Christ, the author of peace, that He may sanctify the hearts of all; that by His help the holy council may now and always be able to counsel and accomplish those things that will be for His praise and glory.

TWENTIETH SESSION

which is the fourth under the Supreme Pontiff, Pius IV,
celebrated on the fourth day of June, 1562

DECREE FOR THE PROROGATION OF THE SESSION

The holy, ecumenical and general Council of Trent, lawfully assembled in the Holy Ghost, the same legates of the Apostolic See presiding, has, by reason of various difficulties arising from various causes, and also to the end that all things may proceed in a more befitting manner and with greater deliberation, namely, that dogmas may be dealt with and ratified conjointly with what relates to reform, decreed that whatever seems good to be enacted, concerning both reform and dogma, shall be defined in the next session, which it announces to all for the sixteenth day of the following month of July; adding however, that this holy council may and can freely, at its will and pleasure, as it may judge expedient for the affairs of the council, shorten or extend that term also in a general congregation.

TWENTY-FIRST SESSION

which is the fifth under the Supreme Pontiff, Pius IV, celebrated on the sixteenth day of July, 1562

THE DOCTRINE OF COMMUNION UNDER BOTH KINDS AND THE COMMUNION OF LITTLE CHILDREN

The holy, ecumenical and general Council of Trent, lawfully assembled in the Holy Ghost, the same legates of the Apostolic See presiding, has thought fit that, since relative to the awe-inspiring and most holy sacrament of the Eucharist various monstrous errors are in different places circulated by the wiles of the evil spirit, by reason of which, in some provinces, many are seen to have fallen away from the faith and obedience of the Catholic Church, those things which relate to communion under both forms and to that of little children be explained in this place. Wherefore, it forbids all the faithful of Christ to presume henceforth to believe, teach or preach on these matters otherwise than is explained and defined in these decrees.

CHAPTER I

LAYMEN AND CLERICS WHEN NOT OFFERING THE SACRIFICE ARE NOT BOUND BY DIVINE LAW TO COMMUNION UNDER BOTH SPECIES

This holy council instructed by the Holy Ghost, who is *the spirit of wisdom and understanding, the spirit of counsel and godliness*,[1] and following the judgment and custom of the Church,[2] declares and teaches that laymen and clerics when not offering the sacrifice are bound by no divine precept to receive the sacrament of the Eucharist under both forms, and that there can be no doubt at all, *salva fide*, that communion under either form is sufficient for them to salvation. For though Christ the Lord at the last supper instituted and delivered to the

[1] Is. 11:2.

[2] Council of Constance, Sess. XIII (Denzinger, no. 626); cf. *infra*, can. 2.

Apostles this venerable sacrament under the forms of bread and wine,[3] yet that institution and administration do not signify that all the faithful are by an enactment of the Lord to receive under both forms. Neither is it rightly inferred from that discourse contained in the sixth chapter of John that communion under both forms was enjoined by the Lord, notwithstanding the various interpretations of it by the holy Fathers and Doctors. For He who said: *Except you eat the flesh of the Son of man and drink his blood, you shall not have life in you,*[4] also said: *He that eateth this bread shall live forever;*[5] and He who said: *He that eateth my flesh and drinketh my blood hath life everlasting,*[6] also said: *The bread that I will give is my flesh for the life of the world;*[7] and lastly, He who said: *He that eateth my flesh and drinketh my blood, abideth in me and I in him,*[8] said, nevertheless: *He that eateth this bread shall live forever.*[9]

Chapter II

THE POWER OF THE CHURCH CONCERNING THE DISPENSATION OF THE SACRAMENT OF THE EUCHARIST

It declares furthermore, that in the dispensation of the sacraments, *salva illorum substantia*, the Church may, according to circumstances, times and places, determine or change whatever she may judge most expedient for the benefit of those receiving them or for the veneration of the sacraments; and this power has always been hers. The Apostle seems to have clearly intimated this when he said: *Let a man so account of us as of the ministers of Christ, and the dispensers of the mysteries of God;*[10] and that he himself exercised this power, as in many other things so in this sacrament, is sufficiently manifest, for after having given some instructions regarding its use, he says: *The rest I will set in order when I come.*[11] Wherefore, though from the beginning of the Christian religion the use of both forms has not been infrequent, yet since that custom has been already very widely changed, holy mother

---

[3] Matt. 26:26–28; Mark 14:22–24; Luke 22:19 f.; I Cor. 11:24 f.
[4] John 6:54.
[5] *Ibid.*, 6:52.
[6] *Ibid.*, 6:55.
[7] *Ibid.*, 6:52.
[8] *Ibid.*, 6:57.
[9] *Ibid.*, 6:59.
[10] See I Cor. 4:1.
[11] *Ibid.*, 11:34.

Church, cognizant of her authority in the administration of the sacraments, has, induced by just and weighty reasons, approved this custom of communicating under either species and has decreed that it be considered the law, which may not be repudiated or changed at pleasure without the authority of the Church.

Chapter III

CHRIST, WHOLE AND ENTIRE, AND A TRUE SACRAMENT ARE RECEIVED UNDER EITHER SPECIES

It declares, moreover, that though our Redeemer at the last supper instituted and administered this sacrament to the Apostles under two forms, as has already been said, yet it must be acknowledged that Christ, whole and entire, and a true sacrament are received under either form alone,[12] and therefore, as regards its fruits, those who receive one species only are not deprived of any grace necessary to salvation.

Chapter IV

LITTLE CHILDREN ARE NOT BOUND TO SACRAMENTAL COMMUNION

Finally, the same holy council teaches that little children who have not attained the use of reason are not by any necessity bound to the sacramental communion of the Eucharist; for having been regenerated by the laver of baptism and thereby incorporated with Christ,[13] they cannot at that age lose the grace of the sons of God already acquired. Antiquity is not therefore to be condemned, however, if in some places it at one time observed that custom. For just as those most holy Fathers had acceptable ground for what they did under the circumstances, so it is certainly to be accepted without controversy that they regarded it as not necessary to salvation.

CANONS ON COMMUNION UNDER BOTH SPECIES AND THAT OF LITTLE CHILDREN

Canon 1. If anyone says that each and all the faithful of Christ are by a precept of God or by the necessity of salvation bound to receive

[12] Cf. Sess. XIII, chap. 3 and can. 3.
[13] Tit. 3:5.

both species of the most holy sacrament of the Eucharist,[14] let him be anathema.

Can. 2. If anyone says that the holy Catholic Church was not moved by just causes and reasons that laymen and clerics when not consecrating should communicate under the form of bread only,[15] or has erred in this, let him be anathema.

Can. 3. If anyone denies that Christ, the fountain and author of all graces, is received whole and entire under the one species of bread, because, as some falsely assert, He is not received in accordance with the institution of Christ under both species,[16] let him be anathema.

Can. 4. If anyone says that communion of the Eucharist is necessary for little children before they have attained the years of discretion,[17] let him be anathema.

The two articles proposed on another occasion but not yet discussed,[18] namely, whether the reasons which moved the holy Catholic Church to decree that laymen and priests not celebrating are to communicate under the one species of bread only, are so stringent that under no circumstances is the use of the chalice to be permitted to anyone; and whether, in case it appears advisable and consonant with Christian charity that the use of the chalice be conceded to a person, nation or kingdom, it is to be conceded under certain conditions, and what are those conditions, the same holy council reserves for examination and definition to another time, at the earliest opportunity that shall present itself.

DECREE CONCERNING REFORM

The same holy, ecumenical and general Council of Trent, lawfully assembled in the Holy Ghost, the same legates of the Apostolic See presiding, has judged it proper, to the praise of Almighty God and to the glory of holy Church, that what follows, relative to the matter of reform, be at present enacted.

---

[14] Cf. *supra*, chap. 1.
[15] *Ibid.*, chap. 2.
[16] *Ibid.*, chap. 3; Sess. XIII, chap. 3 and can. 3.
[17] *Supra*, chap. 4.
[18] Cf. pp. 85 f.

CHAPTER I

BISHOPS SHALL CONFER ORDERS AND GIVE DIMISSORY AND TESTIMONIAL LETTERS *GRATIS*; THEIR MINISTERS SHALL RECEIVE ABSOLUTELY NOTHING THEREFOR AND NOTARIES THAT WHICH IS PRESCRIBED IN THIS DECREE

Since the ecclesiastical order must be free from every suspicion of avarice, neither bishops nor others who confer orders, or their ministers, shall under any pretext whatever receive anything for the collation of any orders, not even for the clerical tonsure, or for dimissory or testimonial letters, or for the seal or for any other reason whatsoever, even though it should be offered voluntarily. Notaries, except in those places only where the laudable custom of receiving nothing does not prevail, may receive only the tenth part of a gold florin for each dimissory or testimonial letter, provided no salary is paid them for the discharge of the office. Further, no emolument from the income of the notary shall accrue either directly or indirectly to the bishop from the collation of orders, for in that case the council decrees that they are bound to give their labor wholly *gratis;* annulling and prohibiting absolutely in all localities taxes, statutes and customs to the contrary, even though immemorial, which might preferably be called abuses and corruptions tending to simoniacal depravity. Those who act otherwise, givers as well as receivers, shall, apart from the divine punishment, incur *ipso facto* the penalties prescribed by law.[19]

CHAPTER II

THOSE WHO HAVE NOT THE MEANS OF LIVELIHOOD ARE TO BE EXCLUDED FROM SACRED ORDERS

Since it is not becoming that those who are enrolled in the sacred ministry should, to the dishonor of the order, beg or engage in some improper business; and since it is known that very many in different localities are admitted to sacred orders with almost no selection, who by various methods of fraud and deception pretend to have an eccle-

[19] Cc.6, 8, 101, 107, 113, C.I, q.1; c.14, C.II, q.5; cc.4, 5, 11, 13, 30, X, De simonia, V, 3, etc.

siastical benefice or sufficient means, the holy council decrees that henceforth no secular cleric, though otherwise qualified as regards morals, knowledge and age, shall be promoted to sacred orders unless it be first legitimately established that he is in peaceful possession of an ecclesiastical benefice sufficient for a decent livelihood; and he may not resign that benefice without mentioning the fact that he was promoted by reason of the title thereof; neither shall that resignation be accepted unless it is certain that he can live suitably from other sources; a resignation made otherwise shall be void. As to those who have a patrimony or pension, only those may hereafter be ordained whom the bishop judges ought to be received in consideration of the need or benefit of his churches, having first informed himself that they really possess that patrimony or pension and that there are means sufficient for their subsistence. The same, moreover, may not under any condition be alienated, canceled or remitted without the permission of the bishop, until they have obtained a sufficient ecclesiastical benefice or have some other means whereby to live; the penalties of the ancient canons in respect hereto being renewed.[20]

Chapter III

THE MANNER OF INCREASING THE DAILY DISTRIBUTIONS IS PRESCRIBED; TO WHOM THEY SHALL BE DUE; THE CONTUMACY OF THOSE WHO DO NOT SERVE IS PUNISHED

Since benefices have been established for divine worship and for administering the ecclesiastical offices, to the end that divine worship may not be in any part curtailed, but may in all things receive due attention,[21] the holy council decrees that in churches, cathedral as well as collegiate, in which there are no daily distributions, or so meager that they are probably disregarded, a third part of the fruits and of all proceeds and revenues of dignities with and without jurisdiction as well as of canonries, portions and offices, shall be set apart and used for daily distributions, to be divided proportionately among those who possess dignities and others who are present at divine service in accordance with the proportion to be decided by the bishop, also as

---

[20] Cc. 2, 4, 16, 23, X, De praeb., III, 5; c. 37, h.t. in VI°, III, 4.
[21] C. 15, VI°, De rescrip., I, 3.

delegate of the Apostolic See, at the first distribution of the fruits; [22] with the retention, however, of the customs of those churches in which those who do not reside therein or do not serve receive nothing or less than a third; exemptions and other customs, even though immemorial, and appeals whatsoever notwithstanding. In case the contumacy of those who do not serve should increase, they may be proceeded against according to the provision of the law and the sacred canons.[23]

Chapter IV

WHEN ASSISTANTS ARE TO BE EMPLOYED IN THE *CURA ANIMARUM*. THE MANNER OF ERECTING NEW PARISHES IS SPECIFIED

In all parochial or baptismal churches in which the people are so numerous that one rector does not suffice to attend to the administration of the sacraments of the Church and divine worship, the bishops shall, also as delegates of the Apostolic See, compel the rectors, or those to whom it pertains, to associate with themselves in this office as many priests as are necessary to administer the sacraments and carry on divine worship. In those, moreover, to which, by reason of distance and hardship, the parishioners cannot come without great inconvenience to receive the sacraments and hear the divine offices, they may, even against the will of the rectors, establish new parishes, pursuant to the form of the constitution of Alexander III, which begins, "Ad audientiam." [24] To those priests who are first to be appointed to the newly erected churches, a suitable portion, decided by the bishop, shall be assigned from the fruits in whatever way belonging to the mother-church, and if it be necessary, he may compel the people to contribute what may be sufficient for the sustenance of those priests; every general or special reservation or attachment respecting the aforesaid churches notwithstanding. Neither can such ordinances and erections be invalidated or hindered by any provisions, even by virtue of resignation or by any other restrictions or hindrances.

---

[22] Cf. Sess. XXII, chap. 3 de ref. and Sess. XXIV, chap. 12 de ref.
[23] Cc. 16, 17, X, De cler. non resid., III, 4; Sess. XXIII, chap. 1 de ref.
[24] C. 3, X, De eccl. aedif., III, 48.

Chapter V

BISHOPS MAY FORM PERPETUAL UNIONS IN CASES PERMITTED BY LAW

Likewise, in order that the state of the churches in which the divine services are offered to God may be maintained in accordance with their dignity, the bishops may, also as delegates of the Apostolic See, according to the prescription of the law, form perpetual unions,[25] without detriment, however, to the incumbents, of any parochial and baptismal churches and of other benefices with or without the *cura* with those to which a *cura* is annexed, by reason of their poverty or in other cases permitted by law, even if those churches or benefices be generally or specially reserved or in any way attached. These unions shall not be revoked or suppressed by virtue of any provision whatever or by reason of resignation, restriction or hindrance.

Chapter VI

TO ILLITERATE RECTORS VICARS SHALL BE GIVEN WITH THE ASSIGNMENT OF A PORTION OF THE FRUITS; THOSE CONTINUING TO GIVE SCANDAL MAY BE DEPRIVED OF THEIR BENEFICES

Since illiterate and incompetent rectors of parochial churches are but little suited for sacred offices,[26] and others by the depravity of their lives corrupt rather than edify, the bishops may, also as delegates of the Apostolic See, give temporarily to such illiterate and incompetent rectors, if otherwise blameless, assistants or vicars, with a portion of the fruits sufficient for their maintenance or provide for them in some other manner, every appeal and exemption being set aside. But those who live a disgraceful and scandalous life, they shall, after admonishing them, restrain and punish; and if they should continue to be incorrigible in their wickedness, they shall have the authority to deprive them of

---

[25] C.8, X, De excess. prael., V, 31; Sess. XIV, chap. 9 de ref. and Sess. XXIV, chap. 13 de ref.

[26] C.1, D.XXXVI; c.1, D.XXXVIII; c.10, X, De renunc., I, 9.

their benefices in accordance with the prescriptions of the sacred canons,[27] every exemption and appeal being rejected.

Chapter VII

BISHOPS SHALL TRANSFER BENEFICES FROM CHURCHES WHICH CANNOT BE RESTORED; OTHERS THEY SHALL HAVE REPAIRED; WHAT IS TO BE OBSERVED IN THIS MATTER

Since great care is to be taken also lest those things which have been dedicated to sacred services may through the injury of time decay and pass away from the memory of men, the bishops may, also as delegates of the Apostolic See, after having summoned those who are interested, transfer simple benefices, even those having the right of patronage, from churches which have fallen into ruin by reason of age or otherwise and which cannot by reason of their poverty be restored, to the mother-churches or to others of the same or neighboring places as they shall judge suitable; and in these churches they shall erect altars or chapels under the same invocations, or transfer them with all the emoluments and obligations imposed on the former churches to altars or chapels already erected. Parochial churches, however, thus fallen into decay, they shall, even if they enjoy the right of patronage, have repaired and restored from the fruits and revenues in any way belonging to those churches.[28] If these are not sufficient, they shall compel by all suitable means the patrons and others who receive any revenues from the said churches, or, in their default, the parishioners, to provide for the repairs; every appeal, exemption and objection being set aside. But if they should all be too poor, then they are to be transferred to the mother-church or neighboring churches, with authority to convert both the said parochial churches and others that are in ruins to profane, though not to sordid uses, nevertheless erecting a cross there.

---

[27] Cc. 13-15, X, De vit. et hon. cler., III, 1.

[28] Cc. 1, 4, X, De eccl. aedif., III, 48. Cf. Sess. VII, chap. 8 de ref.

Chapter VIII

MONASTERIES HELD *IN COMMENDAM* IN WHICH REGULAR OBSERVANCE DOES NOT EXIST, AS WELL AS ALL BENEFICES SHALL BE VISITED BY THE BISHOPS ANNUALLY

It is proper that all things in a diocese pertaining to the worship of God be diligently watched over by the ordinary and, where necessary, set in order by him. Wherefore, monasteries held *in commendam*, also abbeys, priories and those called provostries, in which regular observance does not exist, also benefices with or without the *cura*, secular and regular, in whatever manner held *in commendam*, even if exempt, shall be visited annually by the bishops, also as delegates of the Apostolic See; [29] and the same bishops shall provide by suitable measures, even by the sequestration of revenues, that whatever needs to be renewed or repaired, be done, and that the care of souls, if those places or those annexed to them be charged therewith, and other services due to them be properly exercised; appeals, privileges, customs, even though prescribed from time immemorial, conservators, commissions of judges and their inhibitions notwithstanding. But if regular observance is therein maintained, the bishops shall by fatherly admonitions see to it that the superiors of those regulars observe and cause to be observed the manner of life required by the rules of their order and that they keep and govern those subject to them in their duty. If however, after having been admonished, they shall not within six months have visited or corrected them, then the bishops, also as delegates of the Apostolic See, may visit and correct them, just as the superiors themselves should do in accordance with their rules; all appeals, privileges and exemptions being absolutely set aside.

---

[29] Cf. Sess. VII, chap. 8 de ref.; Sess. XXIV, chap. 9 de ref. and Sess. XXV, chap. 20 de regular.

CHAPTER IX

THE NAME AND SERVICES OF QUESTORS OF ALMS IS ABOLISHED. THE ORDINARIES SHALL PUBLISH INDULGENCES AND SPIRITUAL GRACES. TWO OF THE CHAPTER SHALL WITHOUT FEE RECEIVE THE ALMS

Since many remedies heretofore applied by different councils, those of the Lateran [30] and Lyons as well as that of Vienne,[31] against the pernicious abuses of questors of alms,[32] have in later times become useless, and since their depravity is, to the great scandal and complaint of the faithful, found to be daily so much on the increase that there seems to be no longer any hope of their amendment left, it is decreed that in all parts of Christendom their name and service be henceforth absolutely abolished and in no wise shall they be permitted to exercise such an office; any privileges granted to churches, monasteries, hospitals, pious places, and to any persons of whatever rank, state and dignity, or any customs, even though immemorial, notwithstanding. With regard to indulgences or other spiritual graces of which the faithful of Christ ought not on this account to be deprived, it is decreed that they are in the future to be announced to the people at suitable times by the local ordinaries aided by two members of the chapter. To these also the authority is given to collect faithfully and without fee the alms and charitable contributions offered them, so that all may understand that these heavenly treasures of the Church are administered not for gain but for piety.

ANNOUNCEMENT OF THE NEXT SESSION

The holy, ecumenical and general Council of Trent, lawfully assembled in the Holy Ghost, the same legates of the Apostolic See presiding, has ordained and decreed that the next following session be held and celebrated on the Thursday after the octave of the feast of the Nativity of the Blessed Virgin Mary, which will be on the seventeenth of the month of September next; with the addition, however, that the

---

[30] C. 14, X, De poenit., V, 38.
[31] C. 2, in Clem., h.t. V, 9.
[32] Cf. Sess. V, chap. 2 de ref. and Sess. XXV, Decree on Indulgences.

same holy council freely may and can, according to its will and pleasure, as it shall judge expedient for the affairs of the council, limit or extend, even in a general congregation, the said term and also everyone that is hereafter set for any session.

TWENTY-SECOND SESSION

which is the sixth under the Supreme Pontiff, Pius IV, celebrated on the seventeenth day of September, 1562

DOCTRINE CONCERNING THE SACRIFICE OF THE MASS

That the ancient, complete and in every way perfect faith and teaching regarding the great mystery of the Eucharist in the Catholic Church may be retained, and with the removal of errors and heresies may be preserved in its purity, the holy, ecumenical and general Council of Trent, lawfully assembled in the Holy Ghost, the same legates of the Apostolic See presiding, instructed by the light of the Holy Ghost, teaches, declares and orders to be preached to the faithful the following concerning it, since it is the true and only sacrifice.

CHAPTER I

THE INSTITUTION OF THE MOST HOLY SACRIFICE OF THE MASS

Since under the former Testament, according to the testimony of the Apostle Paul, there was no perfection because of the weakness of the Levitical priesthood, there was need, God the Father of mercies so ordaining, *that another priest should rise according to the order of Melchisedech,*[1] our Lord Jesus Christ, who might perfect and lead to perfection as many as were to be sanctified. He, therefore, our God and Lord, though He was by His death about to offer Himself once upon the altar of the cross to God the Father that He might there accomplish an eternal redemption, nevertheless, that His priesthood might not come to an end with His death,[2] at the last supper, on the night He was betrayed, that He might leave to His beloved spouse the Church a visible sacrifice, such as the nature of man requires, whereby that bloody sacrifice once to be accomplished on the cross might be represented, the memory thereof remain even to the end of the world, and

[1] Heb. 7:11.
[2] *Ibid.*, 7:24.

its salutary effects applied to the remission of those sins which we daily commit, declaring Himself constituted *a priest forever according to the order of Melchisedech,*[3] offered up to God the Father His own body and blood under the form of bread and wine, and under the forms of those same things gave to the Apostles, whom He then made priests of the New Testament, that they might partake, commanding them and their successors in the priesthood by these words to do likewise: *Do this in commemoration of me,*[4] as the Catholic Church has always understood and taught. For having celebrated the ancient Passover which the multitude of the children of Israel sacrificed in memory of their departure from Egypt,[5] He instituted a new Passover, namely, Himself, to be immolated under visible signs by the Church through the priests in memory of His own passage from this world to the Father, when by the shedding of His blood He redeemed and *delivered us from the power of darkness and translated us into his kingdom.*[6] And this is indeed that clean oblation which cannot be defiled by any unworthiness or malice on the part of those who offer it; which the Lord foretold by Malachias was to be great among the Gentiles,[7] and which the Apostle Paul has clearly indicated when he says, that they who are defiled by partaking of the table of devils cannot be partakers of the table of the Lord,[8] understanding by table in each case the altar. It is, finally, that [sacrifice] which was prefigured by various types of sacrifices during the period of nature and of the law,[9] which, namely, comprises all the good things signified by them, as being the consummation and perfection of them all.

CHAPTER II

THE SACRIFICE OF THE MASS IS PROPITIATORY BOTH FOR THE LIVING AND THE DEAD

And inasmuch as in this divine sacrifice which is celebrated in the mass is contained and immolated in an unbloody manner the same

[3] Ps. 109:4.
[4] Luke 22:19; I Cor. 11:24 f.
[5] Ex. 13.
[6] Col. 1:13.
[7] Mal. 1:11.
[8] Cf. I Cor. 10:21.
[9] Gen. 4:4; 12:8, etc.

Christ who once offered Himself in a bloody manner on the altar of the cross, the holy council teaches that this is truly propitiatory and has this effect, that if we, contrite and penitent, with sincere heart and upright faith, with fear and reverence, draw nigh to God, *we obtain mercy and find grace in seasonable aid.*[10] For, appeased by this sacrifice, the Lord grants the grace and gift of penitence and pardons even the gravest crimes and sins. For the victim is one and the same, the same now offering by the ministry of priests who then offered Himself on the cross, the manner alone of offering being different. The fruits of that bloody sacrifice, it is well understood, are received most abundantly through this unbloody one, so far is the latter from derogating in any way from the former. Wherefore, according to the tradition of the Apostles,[11] it is rightly offered not only for the sins, punishments, satisfactions and other necessities of the faithful who are living, but also for those departed in Christ but not yet fully purified.

Chapter III

MASSES IN HONOR OF THE SAINTS

And though the Church has been accustomed to celebrate at times certain masses in honor and memory of the saints, she does not teach that sacrifice is offered to them but to God alone who crowned them; [12] whence, the priest does not say: "To thee, Peter or Paul, I offer sacrifice," [13] but, giving thanks to God for their victories, he implores their favor that they may vouchsafe to intercede for us in heaven whose memory we celebrate on earth.

Chapter IV

THE CANON OF THE MASS

And since it is becoming that holy things be administered in a holy manner, and of all things this sacrifice is the most holy, the Catholic Church, to the end that it might be worthily and reverently offered and

---

[10] Heb. 4:16.
[11] Cf. *infra,* can. 3, and Sess. XXV, decr. on Purgatory.
[12] *Ibid.,* can. 5, and Sess. XXV, Invocation of the Saints.
[13] St. Aug., *De civitate Dei,* VIII, c. 27.

received, instituted many centuries ago the holy canon,[14] which is so free from error that it contains nothing that does not in the highest degree savor of a certain holiness and piety and raise up to God the minds of those who offer. For it consists partly of the very words of the Lord, partly of the traditions of the Apostles, and also of pious regulations of holy pontiffs.

Chapter V

THE CEREMONIES AND RITES OF THE MASS

And since the nature of man is such that he cannot without external means be raised easily to meditation on divine things, holy mother Church has instituted certain rites, namely, that some things in the mass be pronounced in a low tone and others in a louder tone. She has likewise, in accordance with apostolic discipline and tradition, made use of ceremonies,[15] such as mystical blessings, lights, incense, vestments, and many other things of this kind, whereby both the majesty of so great a sacrifice might be emphasized and the minds of the faithful excited by those visible signs of religion and piety to the contemplation of those most sublime things which are hidden in this sacrifice.

Chapter VI

THE MASS IN WHICH THE PRIEST ALONE COMMUNICATES

The holy council wishes indeed that at each mass the faithful who are present should communicate, not only in spiritual desire but also by the sacramental partaking of the Eucharist, that thereby they may derive from this most holy sacrifice a more abundant fruit; if, however, that is not always done, it does not on that account condemn as private and illicit those masses in which the priest alone communicates sacramentally, but rather approves and commends them, since these masses also ought to be considered as truly common, partly because at them the people communicate spiritually and partly also because they are celebrated by a public minister of the Church, not for himself only but for all the faithful who belong to the body of Christ.

---

[14] C.6, X, De celebr. miss., III, 41.

[15] Cf. *infra*, can. 7.

Chapter VII

THE MIXTURE OF WATER WITH WINE IN THE OFFERING OF THE CHALICE

The holy council in the next place calls to mind that the Church has instructed priests to mix water with the wine that is to be offered in the chalice; [16] because it is believed that Christ the Lord did this, and also because from His side there came blood and water; [17] the memory of this mystery is renewed by this mixture, and since in the Apocalypse of St. John the "people" are called "waters," [18] the union of the faithful people with Christ their head is represented.

Chapter VIII

THE MASS MAY NOT BE CELEBRATED IN THE VERNACULAR. ITS MYSTERIES TO BE EXPLAINED TO THE PEOPLE

Though the mass contains much instruction for the faithful, it has, nevertheless, not been deemed advisable by the Fathers that it should be celebrated everywhere in the vernacular tongue. Wherefore, the ancient rite of each Church, approved by the holy Roman Church, the mother and mistress of all churches, being everywhere retained, that the sheep of Christ may not suffer hunger, or *the little ones ask for bread and there is none to break it unto them*,[19] the holy council commands pastors and all who have the *cura animarum* that they, either themselves or through others, explain frequently during the celebration of the mass some of the things read during the mass, and that among other things they explain some mystery of this most holy sacrifice, especially on Sundays and festival days.[20]

---

[16] Cc.4, 5, 7, D.II de cons.; c.6, X, De celebr. miss., III, 41. Cf. Denzinger, nos. 416, 698, 945.

[17] John 19:34.

[18] Apoc. 17:1, 15.

[19] Lam. 4:4.

[20] Cf. Sess. V, chap. 2 de ref., and Sess. XXIV, chap. 7 de ref.

CHAPTER IX

PRELIMINARY REMARKS ON THE FOLLOWING CANONS

Since many errors are at this time disseminated and many things taught and discussed by many persons that are in opposition to this ancient faith, which is founded on the holy Gospel, the traditions of the Apostles, and the teaching of the holy Fathers, the holy council, after many and grave deliberations concerning these matters, has resolved with the unanimous consent of all to condemn and eliminate from holy Church by means of the following canons whatever is opposed to this most pure faith and sacred doctrine.

CANONS ON THE SACRIFICE OF THE MASS

Canon 1. If anyone says that in the mass a true and real sacrifice is not offered to God; or that to be offered is nothing else than that Christ is given to us to eat, let him be anathema.

Can. 2. If anyone says that by those words, *Do this for a commemoration of me*,[21] Christ did not institute the Apostles priests;[22] or did not ordain that they and other priests should offer His own body and blood, let him be anathema.

Can. 3. If anyone says that the sacrifice of the mass is one only of praise and thanksgiving; or that it is a mere commemoration of the sacrifice consummated on the cross but not a propitiatory one;[23] or that it profits him only who receives, and ought not to be offered for the living and the dead, for sins, punishments, satisfactions, and other necessities, let him be anathema.

Can. 4. If anyone says that by the sacrifice of the mass a blasphemy is cast upon the most holy sacrifice of Christ consummated on the cross; or that the former derogates from the latter, let him be anathema.

Can. 5. If anyone says that it is a deception to celebrate masses in honor of the saints and in order to obtain their intercession with God, as the Church intends,[24] let him be anathema.

---

[21] Luke 22:19; I Cor. 11:25.
[22] Cf. *supra*, chap. 1.
[23] *Ibid.*, chap. 2.
[24] *Ibid.*, chap. 3.

Can. 6. If anyone says that the canon of the mass contains errors and is therefore to be abrogated,[25] let him be anathema.

Can. 7. If anyone says that the ceremonies, vestments, and outward signs which the Catholic Church uses in the celebration of masses, are incentives to impiety rather than stimulants to piety,[26] let him be anathema.

Can. 8. If anyone says that masses in which the priest alone communicates sacramentally are illicit and are therefore to be abrogated,[27] let him be anathema.

Can. 9. If anyone says that the rite of the Roman Church, according to which a part of the canon and the words of consecration are pronounced in a low tone, is to be condemned; or that the mass ought to be celebrated in the vernacular tongue only; [28] or that water ought not to be mixed with the wine that is to be offered in the chalice because it is contrary to the institution of Christ,[29] let him be anathema.

DECREE CONCERNING THE THINGS TO BE OBSERVED AND AVOIDED IN THE CELEBRATION OF MASS

What great care is to be taken that the holy sacrifice of the mass be celebrated with all religious devotion and reverence, each one may easily conceive who considers that in the sacred writings he is called accursed who does the work of God negligently.[30] And since we must confess that no other work can be performed by the faithful that is so holy and divine as this awe-inspiring mystery, wherein that life-giving victim by which we are reconciled to the Father is daily immolated on the altar by priests, it is also sufficiently clear that all effort and attention must be directed to the end that it be performed with the greatest possible interior cleanness and purity of heart and exterior evidence of devotion and piety.[31] Therefore, since either through the depravity of the times or through the indifference and corruption of men many things seem already to have crept in that are foreign to the dignity of so great a sacrifice, in order that the honor and worship due

---

[25] *Supra*, chap. 4.
[26] *Ibid.*, chap. 5.
[27] *Ibid.*, chap. 6.
[28] *Ibid.*, chap. 8.
[29] *Ibid.*, chap. 7.
[30] Jer. 48:10.
[31] Cf. Sess. XIII, chap. 7.

to it may for the glory of God and the edification of the faithful be restored, the holy council decrees that the local ordinaries shall be zealously concerned and be bound to prohibit and abolish all those things which either *covetousness, which is a serving of idols,*[32] or irreverence, which can scarcely be separated from ungodliness, or superstition, a false imitation of true piety, have introduced.

And that many things may be summed up in a few, they shall in the first place, as regards avarice, absolutely forbid conditions of compensations of whatever kind, bargains, and whatever is given for the celebration of new masses; also those importunate and unbecoming demands, rather than requests, for alms and other things of this kind which border on simoniacal taint or certainly savor of filthy lucre.

In the second place, that irreverence may be avoided, each in his own diocese shall forbid that any wandering or unknown priest be permitted to celebrate mass. Furthermore, they shall permit no one who is publicly and notoriously wicked either to minister at the altar or to be present at the sacred services; nor suffer the holy sacrifice to be celebrated by any seculars and regulars whatsoever in private houses or entirely outside the church and the oratories dedicated solely to divine worship and to be designated and visited by the same ordinaries; [33] or unless those present have first shown by their outward disposition and appearance that they are there not in body only but also in mind and devout affection of heart. They shall also banish from the churches all such music which, whether by the organ or in the singing, contains things that are lascivious or impure; likewise all worldly conduct, vain and profane conversations, wandering around, noise and clamor, so that the house of God may be seen to be and may be truly called a house of prayer.[34]

Finally, that no room may be given to superstition, they shall by ordinance and prescribed penalties provide that priests do not celebrate at other than proper hours; or make use of rites or ceremonies and prayers in the celebration of masses other than those that have been approved by the Church and have been received through frequent and praiseworthy usage. They shall completely banish from the Church the practice of any fixed number of masses and candles, which has its origin in superstitious worship rather than in true religion; and they

---

[32] Eph. 5:5.
[33] Cc. 12, 34, D.I de cons.
[34] Is. 56:7; Matt. 21:13.

shall instruct the people as to what the very precious and heavenly fruit of this most holy sacrifice is and whence especially it is derived. They shall also admonish their people to go frequently to their own parish churches, at least on Sundays and the greater feast days.[35] All these things, therefore, which have been summarily enumerated, are in such wise set before all local ordinaries, that by the authority given them by this holy council, and also as delegates of the Apostolic See, they may prohibit, command, reform and establish not only the things aforesaid but also whatsoever else shall seem to them to be connected therewith; and they may by ecclesiastical censures and other penalties, which in their judgment they may impose, compel the faithful to observe them inviolately; any privileges, exemptions, appeals and customs to the contrary notwithstanding.

DECREE CONCERNING REFORM

The same holy, ecumenical and general Council of Trent, lawfully assembled in the Holy Ghost, the same legates of the Apostolic See presiding, that the work of reform may be continued, has deemed it well that the following things be established in the present session.

CHAPTER I

DECREES CONCERNING THE LIFE AND CONDUCT OF CLERICS ARE RENEWED

There is nothing that leads others to piety and to the service of God more than the life and example of those who have dedicated themselves to the divine ministry.[36] For since they are observed to be raised from the things of this world to a higher position, others fix their eyes upon them as upon a mirror and derive from them what they are to imitate. Wherefore, clerics, called to have the Lord for their portion,[37] ought by all means so to regulate their life and conduct that in dress, behavior, gait, speech, and all other things nothing may appear but what is dignified, moderated, and permeated with piety; avoiding also minor offenses which in them would be grievous, so that their actions may

[35] C.35, D.I de cons.; cc.4, 5, C.IX, q.2; c.2, X, De paroch., III, 29.
[36] Cf. Sess. XXV, chap. 1 de ref.
[37] C.1, D.XXI.

inspire reverence. Since therefore the more these things contribute to usefulness and honor in the Church of God, so the more zealously must they be observed, the holy council ordains that those things which have in the past been frequently and wholesomely enacted by the supreme pontiffs and holy councils concerning adherence to the life, conduct, dress, and learning of clerics, as also the avoidance of luxury, feastings, dances, gambling, sports, and all sorts of crime and secular pursuits, shall in the future be observed under the same or greater penalties to be imposed at the discretion of the ordinary; [38] nor shall appeal suspend the execution of that which pertains to the correction of morals. If any of these things shall be found to have fallen into desuetude, the ordinaries shall make it their duty to restore their practice as soon as possible and enforce the careful observance by all, any customs to the contrary notwithstanding; lest they themselves, God being the avenger, may have to pay the penalty deserved by their neglect of the correction of their subjects.

Chapter II

WHO ARE TO BE PROMOTED TO CATHEDRAL CHURCHES

Everyone who is hereafter to be promoted to a cathedral church shall not only be qualified by birth, age, morals, and life, and in other respects as required by the sacred canons,[39] but shall also for the space of at least six months previously have been constituted in sacred orders. Information covering these points, in case the (Roman) Curia has no knowledge or only recent knowledge of the person, shall be obtained from the legates of the Apostolic See or from the nuncios of the provinces or from his ordinary, and in his default, from the nearest ordinaries. In addition, he shall possess such learning as will enable him to discharge the obligations of the office that is to be conferred on him. He shall, therefore, have been previously promoted by merit in a university of learning to the rank of master or doctor or licentiate in sacred theology or canon law, or shall be declared by the public testimony of some academy competent to teach others. If he be a regular he shall have a similar attestation from the superiors of his order. All the aforesaid persons from whom the information or testimony is to be

---

[38] Cf. tot. tit. de vit. et hon. cler. apud Greg., in VI° et in Clem. (III, 1).

[39] Cf. c.5, D.LI; cc.7, 19, X, De elect., I, 6; Sess. VII, chap. 1 de ref., and Sess. XXIV, chaps. 1, 12 de ref.

obtained, shall be bound to report on these matters faithfully and *gratis;* otherwise let them know that their consciences will be grievously burdened and that they will have God and their superiors as avengers.

Chapter III

DAILY DISTRIBUTIONS ARE TO BE MADE FROM THE THIRD PART OF ALL REVENUES; ON WHOM THE PORTION OF ABSENTEES FALLS; CERTAIN CASES EXCEPTED

Bishops, also as delegates of the Apostolic See, have the authority to divide the third part of the fruits and revenues of all dignities with and without jurisdiction and offices existing in cathedral and collegiate churches into distributions, to be assigned as they shall judge advisable; [40] so namely, that if their recipients should fail on any day to discharge personally the duty that devolves upon them in accordance with the form to be prescribed by the bishops, they shall forfeit the distribution of that day and in no manner acquire proprietorship thereof; but it should be applied to the administration of the church so far as there is need, or, in the judgment of the ordinary, to some other pious purpose. If, however, their contumacy should increase, they shall proceed against them according to the prescriptions of the sacred canons.[41] If anyone of the aforesaid dignitaries possesses neither by right nor by custom any jurisdiction, administration or office in cathedral or collegiate churches, but should there be outside the city in the diocese a *cura animarum* which he is willing to take upon himself, then he shall during the time that he resides in and administers the church with such *cura* be considered as though he were present and assisted at the divine offices in those cathedral and collegiate churches. These things are to be understood as applying to those churches only in which there is no custom or statute whereby the said dignitaries who do not serve, lose something which amounts to the third part of the fruits and revenues; any customs, even though immemorial, exemptions and constitutions, even though confirmed by oath or by any authority whatsoever, to the contrary notwithstanding.

---

[40] Cf. Sess. XXI, chap. 3 de ref.
[41] *Ibid.*

CHAPTER IV

THOSE NOT IN SACRED ORDER SHALL NOT HAVE A VOICE IN THE CHAPTER OF A CATHEDRAL OR COLLEGIATE CHURCH. THE QUALIFICATIONS AND DUTIES OF THOSE WHO HOLD BENEFICES THEREIN

Anyone engaged in the divine offices in a cathedral or collegiate church, whether secular or regular, who is not constituted at least in the subdiaconal order, shall not have a voice in the chapter of those churches, even though this may have been freely conceded to him by the others. Those who hold or shall hereafter hold in the said churches dignities with or without jurisdiction, offices, prebends, portions, or any other benefices whatsoever, to which are attached various obligations, namely, that some say or sing the masses, others the Gospel, others the Epistles, shall be bound, in the absence of a just impediment, to receive the required orders within a year, whatever privilege, exemption, prerogative or nobility of birth they may possess; otherwise they shall incur the penalties provided by the constitution of the Council of Vienne, which begins, "Ut ii, qui," [42] which is by the present decree renewed. The bishops shall compel them to exercise personally the aforesaid orders on the days specified, and to discharge all other duties required of them in the divine service under the same and even other more severe penalties which may be imposed at their discretion.[43] In the future such offices shall not be assigned except to those who are known to have attained the required age and the other qualifications; otherwise such assignments shall be null.

CHAPTER V

DISPENSATIONS OUTSIDE THE CURIA SHALL BE COMMITTED TO THE BISHOP AND EXAMINED BY HIM

Dispensations, by whatever authority to be granted, if they are to be sent outside the Roman Curia, shall be committed to the ordinaries of those who have obtained them. Those, however, which are granted as a favor shall not have effect until the ordinaries, as delegates of the

[42] C. 2, De aet. et qual. et ord. praef., in Clem., I, 6.
[43] Cf. Sess. XXIV, chap. 12 de ref.

Apostolic See, have established summarily only and extra-judicially that the terms of the petition are free from fraud and deception.

Chapter VI

LAST TESTAMENTS ARE TO BE ALTERED WITH CAUTION

In alterations of last testaments, which ought not to be made except for a just and necessary cause,[44] the bishops, as delegates of the Apostolic See, shall, before the alterations are put into execution, ascertain summarily and extra-judicially that nothing has been stated in the petition which suppresses what is true or suggests what is false.

Chapter VII

THE CHAPTER "ROMANA" IN *SEXTO*, CONCERNING APPEALS, IS RENEWED

Apostolic legates and nuncios, patriarchs, primates and metropolitans, in appeals brought before them, shall in all causes, both in admitting the appeals and in granting inhibitions after an appeal, be bound to observe the form and tenor of the sacred constitutions and particularly that of Innocent IV, which begins, "Romana";[45] any custom, even though immemorial, usage or privilege to the contrary notwithstanding. Otherwise the inhibitions and proceedings and all consequences thereof shall be *ipso jure* null.

Chapter VIII

BISHOPS SHALL EXECUTE THE PIOUS DISPOSITIONS OF ALL PERSONS; SHALL VISIT PIOUS PLACES IF NOT UNDER THE IMMEDIATE PROTECTION OF KINGS

The bishops, also as delegates of the Apostolic See, shall in the cases conceded by law be the executors of all pious dispositions, whether

---

[44] Cf. Sess. XXV, chap. 4 de ref.

[45] C.3, VI°, De appell., II, 15.

made by last will or among the living; they shall have the right to visit hospitals and all colleges and confraternities of laymen,[46] even those that are called schools or are known by some other name (not, however, those that are under the immediate protection of kings, except with their permission); also eleemosynary institutions known as loan or charity foundations, and all pious places by whatever name designated, even though the care of the aforesaid institutions be in the hands of laymen and the said pious places protected by the privilege of exemption; by virtue of their office they shall, moreover, take cognizance of and execute in accordance with the ordinances of the sacred canons all things that have been instituted for the worship of God or for the salvation of souls or for the support of the poor;[47] any custom, even though immemorial, privilege or statute whatsoever to the contrary notwithstanding.

Chapter IX

ADMINISTRATORS OF ALL PIOUS PLACES SHALL RENDER AN ACCOUNT TO THE ORDINARY, UNLESS IT IS OTHERWISE PROVIDED IN THE FOUNDATION

Administrators, whether ecclesiastical or lay, of the revenues of any church, also of cathedrals, hospitals,[48] confraternities, eleemosynary institutions known as loan foundations, and of all pious places, shall be bound to render to the ordinary each year an account of their administration, all customs and privileges to the contrary being set aside, unless perchance it be expressly provided otherwise in the institution and regulation of such a church or fund. But if by reason of custom, privilege or some local regulation their account has to be rendered to others deputed thereto, then the ordinary shall also be employed conjointly with them, and releases made otherwise shall be of no avail to the said administrators.

---

[46] C.2, in Clem., De relig. dom., III, 11.
[47] Cf. cc.3, 6, 17, 19, X, De test. et ult. volunt., III, 26.
[48] Cf. Sess. VII, chap. 15 de ref., and Sess. XXV, chap. 8 de ref.

Chapter X

NOTARIES SHALL BE SUBJECT TO THE EXAMINATION AND JUDGMENT OF THE BISHOPS

Since the incompetency of notaries causes very much harm and is the occasion of many lawsuits, the bishop, also as delegate of the Apostolic See, may by examination inquire into the fitness of all notaries, even though appointed by Apostolic, imperial or royal authority; and if found incompetent or at any time delinquent in office, he may forbid them either altogether or for a time to exercise the office in ecclesiastical and spiritual affairs, lawsuits and causes. No appeal on their part shall suspend the prohibition of the ordinary.

Chapter XI

USURPERS OF THE PROPERTY OF ANY CHURCH OR PIOUS PLACES ARE PUNISHED

If any cleric or laic, of whatever rank, even imperial or royal, should be so possessed by avarice, the root of all evil,[49] as to presume to convert to his own use and to usurp *per se vel alios*, by force or fear, or even by means of supposititious persons, whether clerical or lay, or by any fraud or colored pretext whatsoever, the prerogatives, properties, rents and rights, even those held in fee or under lease, revenues, profits, or any incomes whatsoever, belonging to any church or benefices, secular or regular, eleemosynary institutions or any other pious places, which ought to be used for the needs of the ministers and the poor, or to hinder them from being received by those to whom they by right belong, he shall be anathematized till he shall have restored integrally to the church and to its administrator or beneficiary the prerogatives, properties, effects, rights, fruits and revenues which he has seized or in whatever way they have come to him, even by way of gift from a supposititious person, and furthermore, till he shall have obtained absolution from the Roman pontiff. If he be a patron of that church, he shall, in addition to the aforesaid penalties, be *eo ipso* deprived of the right of patronage. The cleric who instigates or consents to an

---

[49] Cf. I Tim. 6:10.

execrable fraud and usurpation of this kind, shall be subject to the same penalties, and he shall be deprived of all benefices and be rendered unqualified to hold others; and even after complete satisfaction and absolution, he shall be suspended, at the discretion of his ordinary, from the exercise of his orders.

DECREE CONCERNING THE PETITION FOR THE CONCESSION OF THE CHALICE

Moreover, since the same holy council in the preceding session reserved to another and more convenient time the examination and definition of two articles which had been proposed on another occasion [50] and had then not yet been discussed, namely, whether the reasons which induced the holy Catholic Church to decide that lay people and also priests when not celebrating are to communicate under the one species of bread, are so to be retained that under no condition is the use of the chalice to be permitted to anyone; and whether in case, for reasons befitting and consonant with Christian charity, it appears that the use of the chalice is to be conceded to any nation or kingdom, it is to be conceded under certain conditions, and what are those conditions; it has now, in its desire to provide for the salvation of those on whose behalf the petition is made, decreed that the entire matter be referred to our most holy Lord [the Pope], as in the present decree it does refer it, who in accordance with his singular prudence will do what he shall judge beneficial for the Christian commonwealth and salutary for those who petition for the use of the chalice.

ANNOUNCEMENT OF THE NEXT SESSION

Moreover, the same holy Council of Trent announces the day of the next session to be the Thursday after the octave of All Saints, which will be the twelfth day of the month of November, and in it will deal with the sacrament of order and the sacrament of matrimony, etc.

The session was prorogued till the fifteenth day of July, 1563.

[50] Cf. Sess. XIII in the decree of prorogation and Sess. XXI, following can. 4.

TWENTY-THIRD SESSION

which is the seventh under the Supreme Pontiff, Pius IV, celebrated on the fifteenth day of July, 1563

THE TRUE AND CATHOLIC DOCTRINE CONCERNING THE SACRAMENT OF ORDER, DEFINED AND PUBLISHED BY THE HOLY COUNCIL OF TRENT IN THE SEVENTH SESSION IN CONDEMNATION OF CURRENT ERRORS

CHAPTER I

THE INSTITUTION OF THE PRIESTHOOD OF THE NEW LAW

Sacrifice and priesthood are by the ordinance of God so united that both have existed in every law. Since therefore in the New Testament the Catholic Church has received from the institution of Christ the holy, visible sacrifice of the Eucharist, it must also be confessed that there is in that Church a new, visible and external priesthood, into which the old has been translated.[1] That this was instituted by the same Lord our Savior, and that to the Apostles and their successors in the priesthood was given the power of consecrating, offering and administering His body and blood, as also of forgiving and retaining sins, is shown by the Sacred Scriptures and has always been taught by the tradition of the Catholic Church.

CHAPTER II

THE SEVEN ORDERS

But since the ministry of so holy a priesthood is something divine, that it might be exercised in a more worthy manner and with greater veneration, it was consistent that in the most well-ordered arrangement of the Church there should be several distinct orders of ministers, who by virtue of their office should minister to the priesthood, so distributed

[1] Heb. 7:12.

that those already having the clerical tonsure should ascend through the minor to the major orders.[2] For the Sacred Scriptures mention unmistakably not only the priests but also the deacons,[3] and teach in the most definite words what is especially to be observed in their ordination; and from the very beginning of the Church the names of the following orders and the duties proper to each one are known to have been in use, namely, those of the subdeacon, acolyte, exorcist, lector and porter, though these were not of equal rank; for the subdiaconate is classed among the major orders by the Fathers and holy councils,[4] in which we also read very often of other inferior orders.[5]

Chapter III

THE ORDER OF THE PRIESTHOOD IS TRULY A SACRAMENT

Since from the testimony of Scripture, Apostolic tradition and the unanimous agreement of the Fathers it is clear that grace is conferred by sacred ordination, which is performed by words and outward signs, no one ought to doubt that order is truly and properly one of the seven sacraments of holy Church. For the Apostle says: *I admonish thee that thou stir up the grace of God which is in thee by the imposition of my hands. For God has not given us the spirit of fear, but of power and of love and of sobriety.*[6]

Chapter IV

THE ECCLESIASTICAL HIERARCHY AND ORDINATION

But since in the sacrament of order, as also in baptism and confirmation, a character is imprinted which can neither be effaced nor taken away,[7] the holy council justly condemns the opinion of those who say that the priests of the New Testament have only a temporary power, and that those who have once been rightly ordained can again become laymen if they do not exercise the ministry of the word of God. And

[2] Cf. *infra*, can. 2 and chap. 17 de ref.
[3] Act 6:5; 21:8; I Tim. 3:8, 12.
[4] Cc. 11–13, D.XXXII; c.4, D.LX; c.9, X, De aet. et qual. et ord. praef., I, 14.
[5] Cf. Synods of Elvira (*ca.* 305), c.33; Antioch (341), c.10; cc.14, 16, D.XXXII; Denzinger, *Enchiridion*, nos. 45, 153–58.
[6] See II Tim. 1:6 f.
[7] Cf. Sess. VII, Sacraments, can. 9 and *infra*, can. 4.

if anyone should assert that all Christians without distinction are priests of the New Testament, or that they are all *inter se* endowed with an equal spiritual power, he seems to do nothing else than derange the ecclesiastical hierarchy,[8] which is *an army set in array;* [9] as if, contrary to the teaching of St. Paul, all are apostles, all prophets, all evangelists, all pastors, all doctors.[10] Wherefore, the holy council declares that, besides the other ecclesiastical grades, the bishops, who have succeeded the Apostles, principally belong to this hierarchial order, and have been placed, as the same Apostle says, by the Holy Ghost to rule the Church of God; [11] that they are superior to priests, administer the sacrament of confirmation,[12] ordain ministers of the Church, and can perform many other functions over which those of an inferior order have no power. The council teaches furthermore, that in the ordination of bishops, priests and the other orders, the consent, call or authority, whether of the people or of any civil power or magistrate is not required in such wise that without this the ordination is invalid; [13] rather does it decree that all those who, called and instituted only by the people or by the civil power or magistrate, ascend to the exercise of these offices, and those who by their rashness assume them, are not ministers of the Church, but are to be regarded as thieves and robbers, who have not entered by the door.[14] These are the things which in general it has seemed good to the holy council to teach to the faithful of Christ regarding the sacrament of order. The contrary, however, it has resolved to condemn in definite and appropriate canons in the following manner, in order that all, making use with the help of Christ of the rule of faith, may in the midst of the darkness of so many errors recognize more easily the Catholic truth and adhere to it.

CANONS ON THE SACRAMENT OF ORDER

Canon 1. If anyone says that there is not in the New Testament a visible and external priesthood,[15] or that there is no power of conse-

---

[8] Cf. *infra,* can. 6.
[9] Cant. 6:3, 9.
[10] See I Cor. 12:28 ff.; Eph. 4:11.
[11] Acts 20:28.
[12] Cf. Sess. VII, Confirmation, can. 3.
[13] Cf. Synod of Laodicea, can. 13.
[14] John 10:1.
[15] Cf. *supra,* chap. 1.

crating and offering the true body and blood of the Lord and of forgiving and retaining sins,[16] but only the office and bare ministry of preaching the Gospel; or that those who do not preach are not priests at all, let him be anathema.

Can. 2. If anyone says that besides the priesthood there are not in the Catholic Church other orders, both major and minor,[17] by which, as by certain steps, advance is made to the priesthood,[18] let him be anathema.

Can. 3. If anyone says that order or sacred ordination is not truly and properly a sacrament instituted by Christ the Lord,[19] or that it is some human contrivance devised by men unskilled in ecclesiastical matters, or that it is only a certain rite for choosing ministers of the word of God and of the sacraments, let him be anathema.

Can. 4. If anyone says that by sacred ordination the Holy Ghost is not imparted and that therefore the bishops say in vain: *Receive ye the Holy Ghost*, or that by it a character is not imprinted, or that he who has once been a priest can again become a layman, let him be anathema.

Can. 5. If anyone says that the holy unction which the Church uses in ordination is not only not required but is detestable and pernicious, as also are the other ceremonies of order, let him be anathema.

Can. 6. If anyone says that in the Catholic Church there is not instituted a hierarchy by divine ordinance, which consists of bishops, priests and ministers, let him be anathema.

Can. 7. If anyone says that bishops are not superior to priests, or that they have not the power to confirm and ordain, or that the power which they have is common to them and to priests, or that orders conferred by them without the consent or call of the people or of the secular power are invalid, or that those who have been neither rightly ordained nor sent by ecclesiastical and canonical authority, but come from elsewhere, are lawful ministers of the word and of the sacraments, let him be anathema.

Can. 8. If anyone says that the bishops who are chosen by the authority of the Roman pontiff are not true and legitimate bishops, but merely human deception, let him be anathema.

---

[16] Matt. 16:19; Luke 22:19 f.; cc.5, 6, C.XXIV, q.1.

[17] Cf. *supra*, chap. 2.

[18] Cc.2, 3, D.LXXVII; and *infra*, chap. 13 de ref.

[19] Cf. *supra*, chap. 3.

DECREE CONCERNING REFORM

The same holy Council of Trent, continuing the matter of reform, resolves and ordains that the things following be at present decreed.

Chapter I

THE NEGLIGENCE OF PASTORS OF CHURCHES IN THE MATTER OF RESIDENCE IS IN VARIOUS WAYS RESTRAINED. THE *CURA ANIMARUM* IS PROVIDED FOR

Since by divine precept it is enjoined on all to whom is entrusted the *cura animarum* to know their sheep,[20] to offer sacrifice for them, and to feed them by the preaching of the divine word, the administration of the sacraments, and the example of all good works, to exercise a fatherly care in behalf of the poor and other distressed persons and to apply themselves to all other pastoral duties, all of which cannot be rendered and fulfilled by those who do not watch over and are not with their flock, but desert it after the manner of hirelings,[21] the holy council admonishes and exhorts them that, mindful of the divine precepts and *made a pattern of the flock*,[22] they in judgment and in truth be shepherds and leaders. And lest those things that concern residence which have already been piously and with profit decreed under Paul III,[23] of happy memory, be understood in a sense foreign to the mind of the holy council, as if in virtue of that decree it were lawful to be absent during five continuous months, the holy council, adhering to that decree, declares that all who, under whatever name or title, even though they be cardinals of the holy Roman Church, preside over patriarchal, primatial, metropolitan and cathedral churches, are bound to personal residence in their church or diocese, where they are obligated to discharge the office committed to them and from which they may not absent themselves except for the reasons and in the manner subjoined. Since Christian charity, urgent necessity, due obedience, and manifest advantage to the Church or the commonwealth require and demand that some at times be absent, the same holy council decrees

[20] John 10:1–16; 21:15–17; Acts 20:28.
[21] John 10:12 f.
[22] See I Pet. 5:3.
[23] Cf. Sess. VI, chaps. 1, 2 de ref.

that these reasons for lawful absence must be approved in writing by the most blessed Roman pontiff, or by the metropolitan, or, in his absence, by the oldest resident suffragan bishop, whose duty it shall also be to approve the absence of the metropolitan; except when the absence is necessitated by some function or office of the state attached to the episcopal dignity, in which cases the absence being a matter of public knowledge and at times unexpected, it will not be necessary to make known to the metropolitan the reasons therefor. To him, however, in conjunction with the provincial council, it shall pertain to decide concerning the permissions granted by himself or by his suffragans and to see that no one abuses that right and that transgressors are punished in accordance with canonical prescriptions. Moreover, those who are about to depart should remember so to provide for their sheep that as far as possible they may not suffer any injury through their absence.[24] But since those who are absent only for a brief period appear in the sense of the ancient canons not to be absent, because they are soon to return, the holy council wishes that that period of absence in a single year, whether continuous or interrupted, ought, except for the reasons mentioned above, in no case to exceed two or at most three months, and that consideration be taken that it be made from a just cause and without any detriment to the flock. Whether this be the case, the council leaves to the conscience of those who depart, which it hopes will be religious and delicate, for hearts are open to God,[25] whose work they are bound at their peril not to do deceitfully.[26] Meanwhile it admonishes and exhorts them in the Lord, that unless their episcopal duties call them elsewhere in their diocese, they are on no account to absent themselves from their cathedral church during the periods of the Advent of the Lord, Quadragesima, the Nativity, Easter, Pentecost and Corpus Christi, on which days especially the sheep ought to be refreshed and to rejoice in the Lord at the presence of the shepherd.[27]

But if anyone, which it is hoped will never happen, shall have been absent in violation of the provision of this decree, the holy council ordains that in addition to the other penalties imposed upon and renewed against non-residents under Paul III,[28] and the guilt of mortal

---

[24] Cf. c.34, VI°, De elect., I, 6; Sess. VI, chap. 2 de ref. at the end.
[25] Ps. 7:10; Acts 1:24.
[26] Jer. 48:10.
[27] C.29, C.VII, q.1.
[28] Cf. Sess. VI, chap. 1 de ref.

sin which he incurs, he can acquire no proprietorship of any fruits in proportion to the time of his absence, and cannot, even though no other declaration follows the present one, retain them with a safe conscience, but is bound, even in his default, through his ecclesiastical superior, to apply them to the treasury of the churches or to the poor of the locality; every agreement or arrangement to which appeal is made for ill-gotten fruits, whereby the aforesaid fruits might be restored to him in whole or in part, being forbidden; any privileges whatsoever granted to any college or treasury to the contrary notwithstanding.

Absolutely the same, as regards the guilt, the loss of fruits, and the penalties, does the holy council declare and decree with reference to inferior pastors and to all others who hold any ecclesiastical benefice having the *cura animarum;* [29] so however, that should it happen that they are absent for a reason that has first been made known to and approved by the bishop, they shall leave a due allowance of the stipend to a competent vicar to be approved by the ordinary. The permission to go away, which is to be granted in writing and gratuitously, they shall not obtain for a period longer than two months except for a grave reason. In case they shall be summoned, even though not personally, by an edict, and should be contumacious, the ordinaries shall be at liberty to constrain them by ecclesiastical censures, by the sequestration and withdrawal of fruits and other legal means, even deprivation; and no privilege whatsoever, no concession, domestic position, exemption, not even by reason of some benefice, no contract or statute, even though confirmed by oath or by any authority whatsoever, no custom, even though immemorial, which is to be regarded rather as a corruption, no appeal or inhibition, even in the Roman Curia or by virtue of the constitution of Eugene,[30] shall be able to suspend the execution hereof.

Finally, the holy council commands that both the decree under Paul III [31] and this present one be published in the provincial and episcopal councils; for it desires that things which so intimately concern the office of pastors and the salvation of souls, be frequently impressed on the ears and mind of all, so that with the help of God they may not hereafter fall into decay either through the corrosive action of time, the forgetfulness of men or by desuetude.

---

[29] Sess. VI, chap. 2 de ref.
[30] Cf. c. 3, Extrav. comm.. De privil., V, 7.
[31] Cf. Sess. VI, chap. 1 de ref.

CHAPTER II

THOSE PLACED OVER CHURCHES SHALL RECEIVE CONSECRATION WITHIN THREE MONTHS; WHERE THE CONSECRATION IS TO TAKE PLACE

If those who, under whatever name or title, even though they be cardinals of the holy Roman Church, have been placed over cathedral or superior churches, shall not within three months have received consecration,[32] they shall be bound to restore the fruits received; if for three more months they shall have neglected to do this, they shall be *ipso jure* deprived of their churches. Their consecration, if performed outside the Roman Curia, shall take place in the church to which they have been promoted, or in the province if it can be conveniently done.

CHAPTER III

BISHOPS, EXCEPT IN CASE OF ILLNESS, SHALL CONFER ORDERS IN PERSON

Bishops shall confer orders themselves; but should they be prevented by illness, they shall not send their subjects to another bishop to be ordained unless they have first been examined and approved.[33]

CHAPTER IV

WHO MAY RECEIVE THE FIRST TONSURE

No one shall be admitted to the first tonsure who has not received the sacrament of confirmation; who has not been taught the rudiments of the faith; who does not know how to read and write,[34] and concerning whom there is not a probable conjecture that he has chosen this manner of life that he may render to God a faithful service and not to escape fraudulently from civil justice.

---

[32] C.2, D.LXXV; c.1, D.C.; Sess. VII, chap. 9 de ref.
[33] Cf. *infra*, chaps. 8, 10; III Synod of Carthage (397), c.22.
[34] Cf. c.4. VI° De temp. ord., I, 9.

Chapter V

WHEREWITH THOSE TO BE ORDAINED ARE TO BE PROVIDED

Those who are to be promoted to minor orders shall have a good testimonial from their pastor and from the master of the school in which they are educated. Those, however, who are to be raised to any one of the major orders, shall a month before the ordination repair to the bishop, who shall commission the pastor or another person whom he may deem more suitable, to make known publicly in the church the names and desire of those who wish to be promoted, to inform himself diligently from trustworthy sources regarding the birth, age, morals and life of those to be ordained,[35] and to transmit to the bishop as soon as possible testimonial letters containing the results of the inquiry.[36]

Chapter VI

THE AGE OF FOURTEEN YEARS IS REQUIRED FOR AN ECCLESIASTICAL BENEFICE; WHO IS TO ENJOY THE *PRIVILEGIUM FORI*

No one who has received the first tonsure or is constituted in minor orders shall be able to hold a benefice before his fourteenth year.[37] Furthermore, he shall not enjoy the *privilegium fori* unless he has an ecclesiastical benefice, or, wearing the clerical garb and tonsure, serves in some church by order of the bishop, or is in an ecclesiastical seminary or with the permission of the bishop in some school or university on the way, as it were, to the reception of major orders.[38] As regards married clerics, the constitution of Boniface VIII, which begins, "Clerici, qui cum unicis," [39] shall be observed, provided these clerics, being assigned by the bishop to the service or ministry of some church, serve or minister in that church and wear the clerical garb and tonsure; privilege or custom, even immemorial, shall avail no one in this matter.

---

[35] Cf. c.5, D.XXIV.
[36] Cf. *infra*, chap. 7.
[37] C.3, X, De aet. et qual. et ord. praef., I, 14.
[38] C.7, X, de cler. conjug., III, 3.
[39] C. un h.t. in VI°, III, 2.

CHAPTER VII

THOSE TO BE ORDAINED ARE TO BE EXAMINED BY MEN SKILLED IN DIVINE AND HUMAN LAW

The holy council, following the footsteps of the ancient canons, decrees that when the bishop has arranged to hold an ordination, all who wish to dedicate themselves to the sacred ministry shall be summoned to the city for the Wednesday before the ordination, or any other day which the bishop may deem convenient.[40] And calling to his assistance priests and other prudent men skilled in the divine law and experienced in the laws of the Church, the bishop shall carefully investigate and examine the parentage, person, age, education, morals, learning and faith of those who are to be ordained.[41]

CHAPTER VIII

HOW AND BY WHOM EACH ONE OUGHT TO BE ORDAINED

The conferring of sacred orders shall be celebrated publicly, at the times specified by law,[42] and in the cathedral church in the presence of the canons of the church, who are to be summoned for that purpose; but if celebrated in another place of the diocese, in the presence of the local clergy, the church holding the highest rank should always, so far as possible, be chosen. Each one shall be ordained by his own bishop.[43] But if anyone should ask to be promoted by another, this shall under no condition, even under the pretext of any general or special rescript or privilege, even at the times specified, be permitted him unless his probity and morals be recommended by the testimony of his ordinary.[44] Otherwise the one ordaining shall be suspended for a year from conferring orders, and the one ordained shall be suspended from exercising the orders received for as long a period as his ordinary shall see fit.

---

[40] C.5, D.XXIV.

[41] Cf. *supra*, chap. 5 de ref.

[42] Cf. c.7, D.LXXV; cc.1–3, X, De temp. ord., I, 11.

[43] Cc.1–4, D.LXXI; c.2, D.LXXII; cc.6, 7, 9, 10, C.IX, q.2; cc.1, 2, VI°, De temp. ord., I, 9.

[44] Cf. Sess. XIV, chaps. 2, 3 de ref.

Chapter IX

A BISHOP ORDAINING ONE OF HIS OWN HOUSEHOLD SHALL AT ONCE AND IN REALITY CONFER ON HIM A BENEFICE

A bishop may not ordain one of his household who is not his subject, unless he has lived with him for a period of three years and to the exclusion of fraud confers on him at once a benefice; [45] any custom, even though immemorial, to the contrary notwithstanding.

Chapter X

PRELATES INFERIOR TO BISHOPS SHALL NOT CONFER THE TONSURE OR MINOR ORDERS EXCEPT ON RELIGIOUS SUBJECT TO THEM; NEITHER THEY NOR ANY CHAPTER WHATSOEVER SHALL GRANT DIMISSORY LETTERS; A SEVERER PENALTY IS PRESCRIBED AGAINST THOSE WHO TRANSGRESS THE DECREE

It shall not be lawful in the future for abbots and any other persons, however exempt, residing within the limits of a diocese, even in case they are said to be of no diocese or exempt, to confer the tonsure or minor orders on anyone who is not a religious subject to them; nor shall abbots themselves and other exempt persons, or any colleges or chapters, even those of cathedral churches, grant dimissory letters to any secular clerics that they may be ordained by others. But the ordination of all these persons, when everything contained in the decrees of this holy council has been observed,[46] shall pertain to the bishops within the limits of whose diocese they are; any privileges, prescriptions or customs, even though immemorial, notwithstanding. It commands also that the penalty imposed on those who, contrary to the decree of this holy council under Paul III,[47] procure dimissory letters from the chapter during the vacancy of the episcopal see, be extended to those who shall obtain the said letters not from the chapter but from any other persons who during the vacancy of the see succeed to the juris-

[45] C. 2, X, De praeb., III, 5.
[46] Cf. *supra*, chaps. 5, 6 and *infra*, chaps. 11, 12 de ref.
[47] Cf. Sess. VII, chap. 10 de ref.

diction of the bishop in lieu of the chapter. Those who issue dimissory letters contrary to the form of this decree, shall be *ipso jure* suspended from their office and benefices for one year.

CHAPTER XI

THE INTERSTICES AND CERTAIN OTHER REGULATIONS TO BE OBSERVED IN THE RECEPTION OF MINOR ORDERS

The minor orders shall be conferred on those who understand at least the Latin language, observing the prescribed interstices,[48] unless the bishop should deem it more expedient to act otherwise, that they may be taught more accurately how great is the burden of this vocation and may in accordance with the direction of the bishop exercise themselves in each office,[49] and this in the church to which they will be assigned (unless they happen to be absent *causa studiorum*); and thus they shall ascend step by step, that with increasing age they may grow in worthiness of life and in learning, which especially the example of their good conduct, their assiduous service in the Church, their greater reverence toward priests and the superior orders, and a more frequent communion than heretofore of the body of Christ will prove. And since from here there is entrance to the higher orders and to the most sacred mysteries, no one shall be admitted to them whom the promise of knowledge does not show to be worthy of the major orders.[50] These, however, shall not be promoted to sacred orders till a year after the reception of the last of the minor orders, unless necessity or the need of the Church shall in the judgment of the bishop require otherwise.

CHAPTER XII

THE AGE REQUIRED FOR MAJOR ORDERS; ONLY THOSE WORTHY ARE TO BE ADMITTED

No one shall in the future be promoted to the subdiaconate before the twenty-second, to the diaconate before the twenty-third, and to

---

[48] Cf. *infra*, chap. 13.
[49] *Ibid.*, chap. 17 and c.3, D.LIX.
[50] Cc.1, 2, 4, D.LIX.

the priesthood before the twenty-fifth year of his age.[51] However, the bishops should know that not all who have attained that age are to be admitted to these orders, but those only who are worthy and whose upright life is as old age. Regulars likewise shall not be ordained below that age or without a careful examination by the bishop; all privileges whatsoever in this respect being completely set aside.

Chapter XIII

WHO MAY BE ORDAINED SUBDEACON AND DEACON; THEIR OBLIGATIONS; ON NO ONE SHALL TWO SACRED ORDERS BE CONFERRED THE SAME DAY

Those shall be ordained subdeacons and deacons who have a good testimonial,[52] have already been approved in minor orders, and are instructed in letters and in those things that pertain to the exercise of the orders. They should hope, with the help of God, to be able to live continently,[53] should serve the churches to which they will be assigned, understand that it is very highly becoming, since they serve at the altar, to receive holy communion at least on the Lord's days and on solemn festival days. Those who have been promoted to the sacred order of subdeacon shall not till they have completed at least one year therein be permitted to ascend to a higher order,[54] unless the bishop shall judge otherwise. Two sacred orders shall not be conferred on the same day, even to regulars,[55] any privileges and indults whatsoever to whomsoever granted to the contrary notwithstanding.

Chapter XIV

WHO ARE TO BE PROMOTED TO THE PRIESTHOOD; THE OFFICE OF THOSE SO PROMOTED

Those who have conducted themselves piously and faithfully in their performance of earlier functions and are accepted for the order

---

[51] C.3, De aet. et qual. et ord. praef. in Clem., I, 6.
[52] See I Tim. 3:7; c.3, D.LXXVII.
[53] Cf. c.1, D.XXVIII.
[54] Cf. *supra,* chap. 11 de ref.
[55] Cc.13, 15, X, De temp. ord., I, 11.

of priesthood, shall have a good testimonial [56] and be persons who not only have served in the office of deacon for one entire year, unless by reason of the advantage and need of the Church the bishop should judge otherwise, but who also by a previous careful examination have been found competent to teach the people those things which are necessary for all to know unto salvation, and competent also to administer the sacraments, and so conspicuous for piety and purity of morals that a shining example of good works and a guidance for good living may be expected from them. The bishop shall see to it that they celebrate mass at least on the Lord's days and on solemn festivals, but if they have the *cura animarum*, as often as their duty requires. To those who have been promoted *per saltum*,[57] the bishop may for a legitimate reason grant a dispensation, provided they have not exercised the ministry.

Chapter XV

NO ONE SHALL HEAR CONFESSIONS UNLESS APPROVED BY THE ORDINARY

Although priests receive by ordination the power of absolving from sins, nevertheless the holy council decrees that no one, even though a regular, can hear the confessions of seculars, even priests, and that he is not to be regarded as qualified thereto, unless he either holds a parochial benefice or is by the bishops, after an examination, if they should deem it necessary, or in some other manner, judged competent and has obtained their approval,[58] which shall be given gratuitously; any privileges and custom whatsoever, even immemorial, notwithstanding.

Chapter XVI

VAGRANTS AND PERSONS USELESS TO THE CHURCHES SHALL BE EXCLUDED FROM ORDERS

Since no one ought to be ordained who in the judgment of his bishop is not useful or necessary to his churches, the holy council, following

---

[56] Cf. I Tim. 3:7; c.3, D.LXXVII.
[57] C.un., D.LII.
[58] Cf. c.2, VI°, De poenit., V, 10; c.2, De sepult. in Clem., III, 7.

the footsteps of the sixth canon of the Council of Chalcedon,[59] decrees that no one shall in the future be ordained who is not assigned to that church or pious place for the need or utility of which he is promoted, where he may discharge his duties and not wander about without any fixed abode.[60] But if he shall desert that place without consulting the bishop, he shall be forbidden the exercise of the sacred orders. Furthermore, no cleric who is a stranger shall, without commendatory letters from his ordinary, be admitted by any bishop to celebrate the divine mysteries and to administer the sacraments.[61]

Chapter XVII

IN WHAT MANNER THE EXERCISE OF THE MINOR ORDERS IS TO BE RESTORED

That the functions of holy orders from the deacon to the porter, which have been laudably received in the Church from the times of the Apostles, and which have been for some time discontinued in many localities, may again be restored to use in accordance with the canons,[62] and may not be derided by the heretics as useless, the holy council, burning with the desire to restore the ancient usage, decrees that in the future such functions shall not be exercised except by those constituted in these orders, and it exhorts in the Lord each and all prelates of the churches and commands them that they make it their care to restore these functions, so far as it can be conveniently done, in cathedral, collegiate and parochial churches of their diocese, if the number of people and the revenues of the church are able to bear it. To those exercising these functions they shall assign salaries from a part of the revenues of some simple benefices or of the church treasury if the revenues are adequate, or from the revenues of both, and of these salaries they may, if they prove negligent, be deprived in whole or in part by the judgment of the bishop. In case there should not be at hand unmarried clerics to exercise the functions of the four minor orders, their place may be supplied by married clerics of approved life, pro-

---

[59] C. 1, D.LXX; c. ult., *ibid.*

[60] *Ibid.*, c. 2.

[61] Cc. 6, 7, 9, D.LXXI *et al.*

[62] C. 1, D.XXI; Denzinger, nos. 154–58.

vided they have not married a second time,[63] are competent to discharge the duties, and wear the tonsure and the clerical garb in church.

Chapter XVIII

DIRECTIONS FOR ESTABLISHING SEMINARIES FOR CLERICS, ESPECIALLY THE YOUNGER ONES; IN THEIR ERECTION MANY THINGS ARE TO BE OBSERVED; THE EDUCATION OF THOSE TO BE PROMOTED TO CATHEDRAL AND MAJOR CHURCHES

Since the age of youth, unless rightly trained, is inclined to follow after the pleasure of the world,[64] and unless educated from its tender years in piety and religion before the habits of vice take possession of the whole man, will never perfectly and without the greatest and well-nigh extraordinary help of Almighty God persevere in ecclesiastical discipline, the holy council decrees that all cathedral and metropolitan churches and churches greater than these shall be bound, each according to its means and the extent of its diocese, to provide for, to educate in religion, and to train in ecclesiastical discipline, a certain number of boys of their city and diocese, or, if they are not found there, of their province, in a college located near the said churches or in some other suitable place to be chosen by the bishop.[65] Into this college shall be received such as are at least twelve years of age, are born of lawful wedlock, who know how to read and write competently, and whose character and inclination justify the hope that they will dedicate themselves forever to the ecclesiastical ministry. It wishes, however, that in the selection the sons of the poor be given preference, though it does not exclude those of the wealthy class, provided they be maintained at their own expense and manifest a zeal to serve God and the Church. These youths the bishop shall divide into as many classes as he may deem proper, according to their number, age, and progress in ecclesiastical discipline, and shall, when it appears to him opportune, assign some of them to the ministry of the churches, the others he shall keep in the college to be instructed, and he shall replace by others those who have been withdrawn, so that the college may be a perpetual semi-

[63] Cf. tot. tit., X, De big. non ord., I, 21.
[64] Gen. 8:21; cf. c.5, D.XXVIII; c.1, C.XII, q.1.
[65] Cf. Sess. V, chap. 1 de ref.

nary of ministers of God. And that they may be the better trained in the aforesaid ecclesiastical discipline, they shall forthwith and always wear the tonsure and the clerical garb; they shall study grammar, singing, ecclesiastical computation, and other useful arts; shall be instructed in Sacred Scripture, ecclesiastical books, the homilies of the saints, the manner of administering the sacraments, especially those things that seem adapted to the hearing of confessions, and the rites and ceremonies. The bishop shall see to it that they are present every day at the sacrifice of the mass, confess their sins at least once a month, receive the body of our Lord Jesus Christ in accordance with the directions of their confessor, and on festival days serve in the cathedral and other churches of the locality. All these and other things beneficial and needful for this purpose each bishop shall prescribe with the advice of two of the senior and more reputable canons chosen by himself as the Holy Ghost shall suggest, and they shall make it their duty by frequent visitation to see to it that they are always observed. The disobedient and incorrigible, and the disseminators of depraved morals they shall punish severely, even with expulsion if necessary; and removing all obstacles, they shall foster carefully whatever appears to contribute to the advancement and preservation of so pious and holy an institution. And since for the construction of the college, for paying salaries to instructors and servants, for the maintenance of the youths and for other expenses, certain revenues will be necessary, the bishops shall, apart from those funds which are in some churches and localities set aside for the instruction and maintenance of youths, and which are *eo ipso* to be considered as applied to this seminary under the care of the bishop, with the advice of two of the chapter, of whom one shall be chosen by the bishop, the other by the chapter, and also of two of the clergy of the city, the choice of one of whom shall in like manner be with the bishop, the other with the clergy, deduct a certain part or portion from the entire revenues of the bishop and of the chapter, and of all dignities with and without jurisdiction, offices, prebends, portions, abbeys and priories of whatever order, even though regular, whatever their character and rank; also of hospitals which, according to the constitution of the Council of Vienne, which begins, "Quia contingit," [66] are conferred as title or with a view of administration; also of all benefices, even those of regulars, though they enjoy the

[66] C. 2, De relig. dom. in Clem., III, 11.

right of patronage, even if exempt, or belong to no diocese, or are annexed to other churches, monasteries, hospitals, or to any other pious places even though exempt; also of the treasuries of the churches and of other places, and of all other ecclesiastical revenues or incomes, even those of other colleges (in which, however, the seminaries of students and instructors promoting the common good of the Church are not actually included, for the council wishes these to be exempt, except with reference to such revenues as exceed the expense of the suitable maintenance of these seminaries), or associations or confraternities, which in some localities are called schools; and of all monasteries, except those of the mendicants, also of all tithes belonging in any way to laics, from which ecclesiastical maintenance is customarily paid, and of those also which belong to knights, of whatever military body or order they may be, the brethren of St. John of Jerusalem alone excepted; and the part or portion so deducted, as also some simple benefices, of whatever nature or rank, and prestimonies, or prestimonial portions as they are called, even before they become vacant, without prejudice, however, to the divine service or to those who hold them, they shall apply to and incorporate in this college. This shall have effect whether the benefices be reserved or assigned; and the unions and assignments of these benefices can be neither suspended through resignation nor in any way hindered, but they shall have their effect, any vacancy, even in the Curia, notwithstanding, or any constitution whatsoever. For the payment of this portion the local bishop shall by ecclesiastical censures and other legal means, even with the aid of the secular arm, should he deem it necessary, compel the possessors of benefices, dignities with and without jurisdiction, and each and all of the abovementioned, whether the revenues are for themselves or for the salaries which they perchance pay to others out of the said revenues, retaining, however, a portion equivalent to that which they have to pay on account of these salaries; any privileges, exemptions, even such as might require a special declaration of annulment, custom, even though immemorial, any appeal and allegation which might hinder the execution of any or all of the above, notwithstanding. But if it should happen that as a result of these unions or otherwise, the seminary should be found to be endowed in whole or in part, then the portion deducted from each benefice, as stated above, and incorporated by the bishop, shall be discontinued in whole or in part as circumstances may require. And if the prelates of cathedrals and other major churches should prove negligent in the erection of the seminary and its maintenance and should decline to pay their portion, it shall be the duty of the archbishop to rebuke the bishop sharply and compel him to comply with all the aforesaid matters, and of the provincial synod to rebuke sharply and compel in like manner the archbishop and superiors, and diligently to see to it that this holy and pious work be, wherever possible, expedited without delay. The bishop shall receive annually the accounts of the revenues of the seminary in the presence of two delegated by the chapter and of as many delegated by the clergy of the city.

Furthermore, in order that the establishment of schools of this kind may be procured at less expense, the holy council decrees that bishops, archbishops, primates and other local ordinaries urge and compel, even by the reduction of their revenues, those who hold the position of instructor and others to whose position is attached the function of reading or teaching, to teach those to be educated in those schools personally, if they are competent, otherwise by competent substitutes, to be chosen by themselves and to be approved by the ordinaries.[67] But if these in the judgment of the bishop are not qualified, they shall choose another who is competent, no appeal being permitted; and should they neglect to do this, then the bishop himself shall appoint one. The aforesaid instructors shall teach what the bishop shall judge expedient. In the future, however, those offices or dignities, which are called professorships, shall not be conferred except on doctors or masters or licentiates of Sacred Scripture or canon law and on other competent persons who can personally discharge that office; any appointment made otherwise shall be null and void, all privileges and customs whatsoever, even though immemorial, notwithstanding.

But if in any province the churches labor under such poverty that in some a college cannot be established, then the provincial synod or the metropolitan with two of the oldest suffragans shall provide for the establishment of one or more colleges, as he may deem advisable, at the metropolitan or at some other more convenient church of the province, from the revenues of two or more churches in each of which a college cannot be conveniently established, where the youths of those churches might be educated. In churches having extensive dioceses, however, the bishop may have one or more in the diocese, as he may

---

[67] Cf. Sess. V, chap. 1 de ref.

deem expedient; which, however, shall in all things be dependent on the one erected and established in the [metropolitan] city.

Finally, if either with regard to the unions or the appraisement or assignment or incorporation of portions, or for any other reason, any difficulty should happen to arise by reason of which the establishment or the maintenance of the seminary might be hindered or disturbed, the bishop with those designated above or the provincial synod, shall have the authority, according to the custom of the country and the character of the churches and benefices, to decide and regulate all matters which shall appear necessary and expedient for the happy advancement of the seminary, even to modify or augment, if need be, the contents hereof.

ANNOUNCEMENT OF THE NEXT SESSION

Moreover, the same holy Council of Trent announces the next session for the sixteenth day of the month of September, in which it will treat of the sacrament of matrimony and of other matters pertaining to the doctrine of faith, if there be any which can be disposed of; further, it will deal with the collation of bishoprics, dignities and other ecclesiastical benefices and with various articles of reform.

The session was prorogued to the eleventh day of November, 1563.

TWENTY-FOURTH SESSION

which is the eighth under the Supreme Pontiff, Pius IV, celebrated on the eleventh day of November, 1563

DOCTRINE OF THE SACRAMENT OF MATRIMONY

The perpetual and indissoluble bond of matrimony was expressed by the first parent of the human race, when, under the influence of the divine Spirit, he said: *This now is bone of my bones and flesh of my flesh. Wherefore a man shall leave father and mother and shall cleave to his wife, and they shall be two in one flesh.*[1] But that by this bond two only are united and joined together, Christ the Lord taught more plainly when referring to those last words as having been spoken by God, He said: *Therefore now they are not two, but one flesh*,[2] and immediately ratified the firmness of the bond so long ago proclaimed by Adam with these words: *What therefore God has joined together, let no man put asunder.*[3]

But the grace which was to perfect that natural love, and confirm that indissoluble union, and sanctify the persons married, Christ Himself, the instituter and perfecter of the venerable sacraments, merited for us by His passion, which Paul the Apostle intimates when he says: *Husbands love your wives, as Christ also loved the Church, and delivered himself up for it;*[4] adding immediately: *This is a great sacrament, but I speak in Christ and in the Church.*[5]

Since therefore matrimony in the evangelical law surpasses in grace through Christ the ancient marriages, our holy Fathers, the councils,[6] and the tradition of the universal Church, have with good reason always taught that it is to be numbered among the sacraments of the New Law; and since with regard to this teaching ungodly men of this age, raving madly, have not only formed false ideas concerning this

---

[1] Gen. 2:23 f. (Matt. 19:4 ff.; Mark 10:6 ff.; Eph. 5:31 f.).
[2] Matt. 19:6; Mark 10:8.
[3] Matt., *ibid.;* Mark 10:9.
[4] Eph. 5:25.
[5] *Ibid.*, 5:32.
[6] Eugene IV in *decr. ad Armenos* (Denzinger, no. 702).

venerable sacrament, but, introducing in conformity with their habit under the pretext of the Gospel a carnal liberty, have by word and writing asserted, not without great harm to the faithful of Christ, many things that are foreign to the teaching of the Catholic Church and to the usage approved of since the times of the Apostles, this holy and general council, desiring to restrain their boldness, has thought it proper, lest their pernicious contagion should attract more, that the principal heresies and errors of the aforesaid schismatics be destroyed by directing against those heretics and their errors the following anathemas.

CANONS ON THE SACRAMENT OF MATRIMONY

Canon 1. If anyone says that matrimony is not truly and properly one of the seven sacraments of the evangelical law, instituted by Christ the Lord,[7] but has been devised by men in the Church and does not confer grace, let him be anathema.

Can. 2. If anyone says that it is lawful for Christians to have several wives at the same time and that this is not forbidden by any divine law,[8] let him be anathema.

Can. 3. If anyone says that only those degrees of consanguinity and affinity which are expressed in Leviticus can hinder matrimony from being contracted and dissolve it when contracted,[9] and that the Church cannot dispense in some of them or declare that others hinder and dissolve it, let him be anathema.

Can. 4. If anyone says that the Church cannot establish impediments dissolving marriage,[10] or that she has erred in establishing them, let him be anathema.

Can. 5. If anyone says that the bond of matrimony can be dissolved on account of heresy,[11] or irksome cohabitation, or by reason of the voluntary absence of one of the parties, let him be anathema.

Can. 6. If anyone says that matrimony contracted but not consummated is not dissolved by the solemn religious profession of one of the parties,[12] let him be anathema.

Can. 7. If anyone says that the Church errs in that she taught and

---

[7] Cf. *supra,* note 1.
[8] Matt. 19:4–6, 9.
[9] Lev. 18:6 ff.
[10] Matt. 16:19; Sess. XXI, chap. 2.
[11] Cf. c.4, X, De consang., IV, 14; cc.6, 7, X, De divor., IV, 19.
[12] Cf. c.16, X, De sponsal., IV, 1.

teaches that in accordance with evangelical and apostolic doctrine the bond of matrimony cannot be dissolved by reason of adultery on the part of one of the parties, and that both, or even the innocent party who gave no occasion for adultery, cannot contract another marriage during the lifetime of the other, and that he is guilty of adultery who, having put away the adulteress, shall marry another, and she also who, having put away the adulterer, shall marry another,[13] let him be anathema.

Can. 8. If anyone says that the Church errs when she declares that for many reasons a separation may take place between husband and wife with regard to bed and with regard to cohabitation for a determinate or indeterminate period, let him be anathema.

Can. 9. If anyone says that clerics constituted in sacred orders or regulars who have made solemn profession of chastity can contract marriage, and that the one contracted is valid notwithstanding the ecclesiastical law or the vow, and that the contrary is nothing else than a condemnation of marriage, and that all who feel that they have not the gift of chastity, even though they have made such a vow, can contract marriage, let him be anathema, since God does not refuse that gift to those who ask for it rightly, neither does *he suffer us to be tempted above that which we are able.*[14]

Can. 10. If anyone says that the married state excels the state of virginity or celibacy, and that it is better and happier to be united in matrimony than to remain in virginity or celibacy,[15] let him be anathema.

Can. 11. If anyone says that the prohibition of the solemnization of marriages at certain times of the year is a tyrannical superstition derived from the superstition of the heathen,[16] or condemns the blessings and other ceremonies which the Church makes use of therein, let him be anathema.

Can. 12. If anyone says that matrimonial causes do not belong to ecclesiastical judges, let him be anathema.

---

[13] Matt. 5:32; 19:9; Mark 10:11 f.; Luke 16:18; I Cor. 7:10 f.; cc.5-8, 10, C.XXXII, q.7.
[14] Cf. I Cor. 10:13.
[15] Matt. 19:11 f.; I Cor. 7:25 f., 38, 40; c.12, C.XXXII, q.1; c.9, C.XXXIII, q.5; c.16, X, De sponsal., IV, 1.
[16] Cf. *infra,* chap. 10 de ref. matr.

DECREE CONCERNING THE REFORM OF MATRIMONY

CHAPTER I

THE FORM PRESCRIBED IN THE LATERAN COUNCIL FOR SOLEMNLY CONTRACTING MARRIAGE IS RENEWED; BISHOPS MAY DISPENSE WITH THE PUBLICATION OF THE BANNS; WHOEVER CONTRACTS MARRIAGE OTHERWISE THAN IN THE PRESENCE OF THE PASTOR AND OF TWO OR THREE WITNESSES, DOES SO INVALIDLY

Although it is not to be doubted that clandestine marriages made with the free consent of the contracting parties are valid and true marriages so long as the Church has not declared them invalid,[17] and consequently that those persons are justly to be condemned, as the holy council does condemn them with anathema, who deny that they are true and valid, and those also who falsely assert that marriages contracted by children [minors] without the consent of the parents are invalid, nevertheless the holy Church of God has for very just reasons at all times detested and forbidden them.[18] But while the holy council recognizes that by reason of man's disobedience those prohibitions are no longer of any avail, and considers the grave sins which arise from clandestine marriages, especially the sins of those who continue in the state of damnation, when having left the first wife with whom they contracted secretly, they publicly marry another and live with her in continual adultery, and since the Church which does not judge what is hidden, cannot correct this evil unless a more efficacious remedy is applied, therefore, following in the footsteps of the holy Lateran Council celebrated under Innocent III,[19] it commands that in the future, before a marriage is contracted, the proper pastor of the contracting parties shall publicly announce three times in the church, during the celebration of the mass on three successive festival days, between whom marriage is to be contracted; after which publications, if no legitimate impediment is revealed, the marriage may be proceeded with in the presence of the people, where the parish priest, after having

---

[17] C.2, X, De cland. desp., IV, 3.

[18] C.3, C.XXX, q.5; c.13, C.XXXII, q.2; c.2, C.XXXV, q.6; c.3, X, Qui matr. accus. poss., IV, 18.

[19] C.3, X, De cland. desp., IV, 3.

questioned the man and the woman and heard their mutual consent, shall either say: "I join you together in matrimony, in the name of the Father, and of the Son, and of the Holy Ghost," or he may use other words, according to the accepted rite of each province. But if at some time there should be a probable suspicion that a marriage might be maliciously hindered if so many publications precede it, then either one publication only may be made or the marriage may be celebrated forthwith in the presence of the parish priest and of two or three witnesses. Then before its consummation the publications shall be made in the church, so that if any impediments exist they may be the more easily discovered, unless the ordinary shall deem it advisable to dispense with the publications. which the holy council leaves to his prudence and judgment. Those who shall attempt to contract marriage otherwise than in the presence of the parish priest or of another priest authorized by the parish priest or by the ordinary and in the presence of two or three witnesses, the holy council renders absolutely incapable of thus contracting marriage and declares such contracts invalid and null, as by the present decree it invalidates and annuls them. Moreover, it commands that the parish priest or another priest who shall have been present at a contract of this kind with less than the prescribed number of witnesses, also the witnesses who shall have been present without the parish priest or another priest, and also the contracting parties themselves, shall at the discretion of the ordinary be severely punished. Furthermore, the same holy council exhorts the betrothed parties not to live together in the same house until they have received the sacerdotal blessing in the church; [20] and it decrees that the blessing is to be given by their own parish priest, and permission to impart it cannot be granted to any other priest except by the parish priest himself or by the ordinary, any custom, even though immemorial, which ought rather to be called a corruption, or any privilege notwithstanding. But if any parish priest or any other priest, whether regular or secular, should attempt to unite in marriage or bless the betrothed of another parish without the permission of their parish priest, he shall, even though he may plead that his action was based on a privilege or immemorial custom, remain *ipso jure* suspended until absolved by the ordinary of that parish priest who ought to have been present at the marriage or from whom the blessing ought to have been received. The parish priest

---

[20] Cc.2, 3, 5, C.XXX, q.5; c.19, C.XXXV, qq.2, 3.

shall have a book in which he shall record the names of the persons united in marriage and of the witnesses, and also the day on which and the place where the marriage was contracted, and this book he shall carefully preserve. Finally, the holy council exhorts the betrothed that before they contract marriage, or at least three days before its consummation, they carefully confess their sins and approach devoutly the most holy sacrament of the Eucharist. If any provinces have in this matter other laudable customs and ceremonies in addition to the aforesaid, the holy council wishes earnestly that they be by all means retained. And that these so salutary regulations may not remain unknown to anyone, it commands all ordinaries that they as soon as possible see to it that this decree be published and explained to the people in all the parish churches of their dioceses, and that this be done very often during the first year and after that as often as they shall deem it advisable. It decrees, moreover, that this decree shall begin to take effect in every parish at the expiration of thirty days, to be reckoned from the day of its first publication in that church.

Chapter II

BETWEEN WHOM SPIRITUAL RELATIONSHIP IS CONTRACTED

Experience teaches that by reason of the large number of prohibitions, marriages are often unknowingly contracted in prohibited cases in which either the parties continue to live, not without great sin, or the marriages are dissolved, not without great scandal. Wherefore, the holy council wishing to provide against this condition, and beginning with the impediment arising from spiritual relationship, decrees that in accordance with the prescriptions of the holy canons,[21] one person only, whether man or woman, or at most one man and one woman, shall act as sponsors in baptism for the one baptized, and spiritual relationship shall be contracted between these only and the one baptized, and his father and mother, and also between the one baptizing and the one baptized and the father and mother of the one baptized. Before the parish priest proceeds to confer baptism, he shall carefully inquire of those whom it concerns what person or persons they have chosen to act as sponsors at the font for the one to be baptized, and

---

[21] C. 101, D. IV de cons.; c. 3, VI°, De cogn. spirit., IV, 3.

he shall permit him or them only to act as such, shall record their names in the book, and shall teach them what relationship they have contracted, so that they may not have any excuse on the score of ignorance. If any others, besides those designated, should touch the one being baptized, they shall not in any way contract a spiritual relationship, any constitutions asserting the contrary notwithstanding.[22] If through the fault or negligence of the parish priest it should be done otherwise, he shall be punished at the discretion of the ordinary. That relationship also which is contracted in confirmation is not to be extended beyond him who confirms, the one confirmed, his father and mother, and the sponsor; [23] all impediments of this spiritual relationship between other persons being completely removed.

Chapter III

THE IMPEDIMENT OF PUBLIC HONESTY IS RESTRICTED WITHIN CERTAIN LIMITS

The holy council completely removes the impediment of justice arising from public honesty where the betrothals are for any reason not valid.[24] But where they are valid, the impediment shall not extend beyond the first degree, because in more remote degrees such a prohibition can no longer be observed without detriment.

Chapter IV

AFFINITY ARISING FROM FORNICATION IS RESTRICTED TO THE SECOND DEGREE

Moreover, the holy council, moved by the same and other very grave reasons, restricts the impediment which arises on account of the affinity contracted from fornication, and which dissolves the marriage afterward contracted,[25] to those only who are united in the first and second degree; in more remote degrees it ordains that affinity of this kind does not dissolve the marriage afterward contracted.

---

[22] Cc. 2, 5, C. XXX, q. 3; c. 3, X, De cogn. spirit., IV, 11; c. 1, h.t. in VI°, IV, 3.
[23] C. 2, C. XXX, q. 1; c. 1, VI°, De cogn. spirit., IV, 3.
[24] C. un., VI°, De sponsal., IV, 1.
[25] Cc. 19–24, C. XXXII, q. 7; tot. tit. X, De eo, qui cog. consang., IV, 13.

CHAPTER V

NO ONE IS TO MARRY WITHIN THE PROHIBITED DEGREES; IN WHAT MANNER DISPENSATION IS TO BE GRANTED THEREIN

If anyone should presume knowingly to contract marriage within the prohibited degrees, he shall be separated and shall have no hope of obtaining a dispensation; [26] and this shall apply much more to him who has dared not only to contract such a marriage but also to consummate it. If he has done this in ignorance and yet has neglected the solemnities required in the contraction of matrimony, he shall be subject to the same penalties; for he who has rashly despised the salutary precepts of the Church, is not worthy to enjoy without difficulty her beneficence. But if after the observance of the solemnities some impediment should afterward be discovered of which he probably had no knowledge, then he may more easily and gratuitously be granted a dispensation. In the contraction of marriages either no dispensation at all shall be granted or rarely, and then for a reason and gratuitously. In the second degree a dispensation shall never be granted except in the case of great princes and for a public cause.

CHAPTER VI

PUNISHMENTS AGAINST ABDUCTORS ARE PRESCRIBED

The holy council decrees that between the abductor and the one abducted there can be no marriage so long as she remains in the power of the abductor. But if the one abducted is separated from the abductor and is in a free and safe place, and consents to have him for her husband, the abductor may have her for his wife; [27] nevertheless, the abductor and all who have given him advice, aid and approval shall be *ipso jure* excommunicated and forever infamous and disqualified for all dignities of any kind; and if they be clerics, they shall forfeit all rank.[28] The abductor shall, moreover, be bound, whether he marries the one ab-

---

[26] C.3, X, De cland. desp., IV, 3; c. un. in Clem., De consang., IV, un.
[27] Cc.7, 11, C.XXXVI, q.2; c.7, X, De rapt., V, 17.
[28] Cc.2–6, 10, 11, C.XXXVI, q.2.

ducted or not, to bestow on her at the discretion of the judge a suitable endowment.[29]

Chapter VII

VAGRANTS ARE TO BE UNITED IN MATRIMONY WITH CAUTION

There are many who are vagrants and have no permanent abode, and, being of unprincipled character, after having abandoned their first wife, marry another, very often several in different localities, during the lifetime of the first. The holy council wishing to put an end to this evil, extends this fatherly admonition to all whom it may concern; namely, not to admit to marriage easily this class of vagrants; it also exhorts the civil magistrates to restrain them vigorously. But it commands parish priests not to be present at the marriage of such persons unless they have first made a diligent inquiry, and after having reported the matter to the ordinary, shall have obtained permission from him to do so.

Chapter VIII

CONCUBINAGE IS SEVERELY PUNISHED

It is a grave sin for unmarried men to have concubines, but it is a most grave sin, and one committed in singular contempt of this great sacrament, when married men live in this state of damnation and have the boldness at times to maintain and keep them in their homes even with their own wives. Wherefore, the holy council, in order to provide suitable remedies against this great evil, decrees that if these concubinaries, whether unmarried or married, whatever may be their state, dignity or profession, have not, after a threefold admonition in reference to this matter by the ordinary, also *ex officio*, put away their concubines and separated themselves from intimacy with them, they shall be punished with excommunication from which they shall not be absolved till they have in fact obeyed the admonition given them.[30] But if, regardless of censures, they shall continue in concubinage for a year, the ordinary shall proceed against them with a severity in keeping with the character of the crime. Women, whether married or

[29] Ex. 22:16 f., *cit.* in c. 1, X, De adult., V, 16.
[30] C. 2, X, De cohab. cler., III, 2; Sess. XXV, chap. 14 de ref.

unmarried, who live publicly with adulterers or concubinaries, if after a threefold admonition they do not obey, shall be punished severely in accordance with their guilt by the local ordinaries, even though not called upon by anyone to do so, *ex officio;* and if the ordinaries should deem it expedient, they shall be expelled, even with the aid of the secular arm, if need be, from the city or the diocese; the other penalties imposed on adulterers and concubinaries shall remain in force.

Chapter IX

TEMPORAL LORDS OR MAGISTRATES SHALL NOT ATTEMPT ANYTHING CONTRARY TO THE FREEDOM OF MARRIAGE

Worldly inclinations and desires very often so blind the mental vision of temporal lords and magistrates, that by threats and ill usage they compel men and women who live under their jurisdiction, especially the rich or those who expect a large inheritance, to contract marriage against their will with those whom these lords or magistrates propose to them. Wherefore, since it is something singularly execrable to violate the freedom of matrimony, and equally execrable that injustice should come from those from whom justice is expected,[31] the holy council commands all, of whatever rank, dignity and profession they may be, under penalty of anathema to be incurred *ipso facto*, that they do not in any manner whatever, directly or indirectly, compel their subjects or any others whomsoever in any way that will hinder them from contracting marriage freely.[32]

Chapter X

THE SOLEMNITIES OF MARRIAGES ARE FORBIDDEN AT CERTAIN TIMES

The holy council commands that from the Advent of our Lord Jesus Christ till the day of the Epiphany, and from Ash Wednesday till the octave of Easter inclusive, the old prohibitions of solemn nuptials be carefully observed by all; [33] at other times it permits marriages to be

[31] Cf. cc. 14, 17, 29, X, De sponsal., IV, 1.
[32] Cf. c.6, C.XXXVI, q.2.
[33] Cc.8–11, C.XXXIII, q.4; c.4, X, De feriis, II, 9.

celebrated solemnly and the bishops shall see to it that they are conducted with becoming modesty and propriety, for matrimony is a holy thing and is to be treated in a holy manner.

DECREE CONCERNING REFORM

The same holy council, continuing the matter of reform, decrees that the following be ordained in the present session.

Chapter I

NORMS OF PROCEDURE IN THE ELECTION OF BISHOPS AND CARDINALS

If in all ecclesiastical grades a prudent and enlightened attention is necessary in order that in the house of the Lord there be nothing disorderly and nothing unbecoming, much more ought we to strive that no error be committed in the election of him who is constituted above all grades. For the state and order of the entire household of the Lord will totter if what is required in the body be not found in the head. Hence, although the holy council has elsewhere decided to advantage a number of things concerning those to be promoted to cathedral and major churches,[34] yet it considers this office to be of such a nature that if viewed in its greatness, there can never be caution enough taken concerning it. Wherefore it decrees that as soon as a church becomes vacant, public and private supplications and prayers be made and be ordered throughout the city and diocese by the chapter, that clergy and people may implore God for a good shepherd. It moreover exhorts and admonishes each and all who in any manner have a right from the Apostolic See to participate in the promotion of those to be placed in authority, or who otherwise render assistance (due to the circumstances of the present time no change being made herein), that they above all bear in mind that they can do nothing more serviceable to the glory of God and the salvation of the people than to exert themselves to the end that good and competent shepherds be promoted to the government of the Church, and that they become partakers in the sins of others and sin mortally unless they strive diligently that those

---

[34] Cf. Sess. VI, chap. 1 de ref.; VII, chaps. 1, 3 de ref.; XXII, chap. 2 de ref.

be promoted whom they judge the more worthy and useful to the Church, not moved by entreaties or human affection, or the solicitations of rivals, but because their merits speak for them, whom they know to be persons of lawful wedlock, and whose life, age, learning and all other qualifications meet the requirements of the sacred canons and the decrees of this Council of Trent.[35] But since the taking of the important and competent testimony of upright and learned men regarding the aforesaid qualifications cannot by reason of the diversity of nations, peoples and customs be everywhere uniformly followed, the holy council commands that in the provincial synod to be held by the metropolitan, there be prescribed for each place and province a special or proper form of the examination, investigation or instruction to be made, such as shall appear most useful and suitable for these places and which is to be submitted to the approval of the most holy Roman pontiff; so however, that after the completion of the examination or investigation of the person to be promoted, it shall, after having been put in the form of a public document, be transmitted as soon as possible, with all the attestations and with the profession of faith made by the one to be promoted, to the most holy Roman pontiff, in order that the Roman pontiff himself, with a complete knowledge of the whole matter and of the persons before him, may for the benefit of the Lord's flock provide the churches more profitably if in the examination or investigation they have been found competent. All examinations, investigations, attestations and proofs of whatever kind and by whomever made, even though in the Roman Curia, concerning the qualifications of the one to be promoted and the condition of the church, shall be carefully examined by the cardinal, who shall report thereon to the consistory, and three other cardinals; and this report shall be authenticated by the signature of the cardinal making the report and of the three other cardinals, in which each of the four cardinals shall affirm that, after having given it his careful attention, he has found those to be promoted to possess the qualifications required by law and by this holy council and at the peril of his eternal salvation firmly believes that they are competent to be placed over churches; and the report having been made in one consistory, that the investigation may in the meantime receive more mature consideration, the decision shall be deferred to another consistory, unless the most blessed pontiff shall deem it

[35] Cf. preceding references.

expedient to act otherwise. Each and all of the particulars relative to the life, age, learning and the other qualifications of those who are to be appointed bishops, which have been determined elsewhere by this council, the same it decrees are to be required in the election of the cardinals of the holy Roman Church, even though they be deacons, whom the most holy Roman pontiff shall, in so far as it can be conveniently done, choose from all the nations of Christendom according as he finds them competent. Finally, the same holy council, moved by so many very grave afflictions of the Church, cannot but call to mind that nothing is more necessary to the Church of God than that the holy Roman pontiff apply that solicitude which by the duty of his office he owes the universal Church in a very special way by associating with himself as cardinals the most select persons only, and appoint to each church most eminently upright and competent shepherds; and this the more so, because our Lord Jesus Christ will require at his hands the blood of the sheep of Christ that perish through the evil government of shepherds who are negligent and forgetful of their office.

Chapter II

PROVINCIAL SYNODS ARE TO BE CELEBRATED EVERY THREE YEARS, DIOCESAN SYNODS EVERY YEAR; WHO ARE TO CONVOKE THEM AND WHO ARE TO BE PRESENT THEREAT

Provincial synods, wherever they have been omitted, shall be restored for the regulation of morals, the correction of abuses, the settlement of controversies, and for other purposes permitted by the sacred canons.[36] Wherefore the metropolitans in person, or if they are legitimately hindered, the oldest suffragan bishop, shall not neglect to convoke, each in his own province, a synod within a year at least from the termination of the present council and after that at least every third year, after the octave of the resurrection of our Lord Jesus Christ or at some other more convenient time, according to the custom of the province, and which all the bishops and others who by right or custom are under obligation to be present shall be absolutely bound to attend, those being excepted who at imminent danger would have to cross the sea. The bishops of the province shall not in the future be compelled

[36] Cf. cc.2–7, 9–14, D.XVIII *et al.;* c.25, X, De accus., V, 1.

under pretext of any custom whatsoever to go against their will to the metropolitan church. Those bishops likewise who are not subject to any archbishop shall once for all choose some neighboring metropolitan, at whose provincial synod they shall be obliged to be present with the other bishops, and whatever has been decided therein they shall observe and cause to be observed. In all other respects their exemption and privileges shall remain intact and entire. Diocesan synods also are to be celebrated annually; at which also all those exempt, who would otherwise by reason of the cessation of that exemption have to attend, and who are not subject to general chapters, shall be bound to assemble; those also who have charge of parochial or other secular churches, even though annexed, whoever they may be, must be present at the synod. But if the metropolitans and also the bishops and the others mentioned above prove negligent in these matters, they shall incur the penalties prescribed by the sacred canons.

Chapter III

IN WHAT MANNER PRELATES ARE TO MAKE THEIR VISITATION

Patriarchs, primates, metropolitans and bishops shall not neglect to visit their respective dioceses, either personally or, if they are lawfully hindered, through their vicar-general or visitor; [37] if by reason of its extent they are unable to make a visitation of the whole annually, they shall either themselves or through their visitors visit at least the greater part of it, so that the whole may be completed in two years. Metropolitans, even after a complete visitation of their own diocese, shall not visit the cathedral churches or the dioceses of the bishops of their province, except for a cause taken cognizance of and approved by the provincial synod. Archdeacons, deans and other inferiors shall visit those churches in which they have thus far been accustomed legally to make visitations, but from now on with the consent of the bishop, personally and with the aid of a notary. Also the visitors delegated by a chapter, where the chapter has the right of visitation, shall be first approved by the bishop; thereby, however, the bishop, or if he be hindered, his visitor, shall not be prohibited from visiting those same churches apart from these, and the archdeacons and other inferiors

[37] C. 11, C.X, q. 1.

shall be bound to render to him an account within a month of the visitation made by them, and to show him the depositions of witnesses and the entire proceedings; any custom, even though immemorial, and any exemptions and privileges whatsoever notwithstanding. But the chief purpose of all these visitations shall be, after the extirpation of heresies, to restore sound and orthodox doctrine, to guard good morals and to correct such as are evil, to animate the people by exhortations and admonitions with religion, peace and innocence, and to regulate the rest for the benefit of the faithful as the prudence of the visitors may suggest, allowance being made for place, time and occasion.[38] That these things may be more easily and happily accomplished, each and all of the aforesaid to whom the right of visitation belongs, are admonished to treat all with a fatherly love and Christian zeal, and therefore content with a modest train of horses and servants, let them strive to complete the visitation as speedily as possible, yet with due attention. Meanwhile they shall exercise care that they do not become troublesome or a burden to anyone by useless expenses, and neither shall they nor any one of theirs, either by way of compensation for the visitation or from wills made for pious purposes, except what is by right due to them from pious bequests, or under any other name, receive anything, be it money or gift of whatever kind or in whatever way offered,[39] any custom, even though immemorial, notwithstanding; with the exception, however, of food, which shall be furnished them and theirs frugally and in moderation during the time necessary for the visitation only and not beyond that.[40] It shall, however, be left to the option of those who are visited to pay, if they prefer, what in accordance with a fixed assessment they have been accustomed to pay in money heretofore, or to furnish the food; inviolate also shall remain the right of old agreements entered into with monasteries or other pious places or with churches not parochial. But in those places or provinces where it is the custom that neither food nor money or anything else be received by the visitors, but that all be done gratuitously, that practice shall continue there. But if anyone, which God forbid, shall presume to receive more in any of the cases mentioned above, in addition to the restitution of double the amount to be made within a month, he shall also incur without hope of pardon the other penalties contained in the

[38] C.1 (§ 4), VI°, De cens., III, 20.
[39] Cc.1, 7, 8, C.X, q.3; c.6, X, De cens., III, 39.
[40] C.6, VI°, De off. ord., I, 16.

constitution of the General Council of Lyons, which begins, "Exigit," [41] as well as those of the provincial synod at the discretion of that synod. Patrons shall not presume in any way to intrude themselves in those things that pertain to the administration of the sacraments; they shall not interfere with the visitation of the ornaments of the church, or its immovable properties, or the revenues of the buildings, except in so far as they are competent to do this by reason of the institution and foundation; but the bishops themselves shall attend to these things and shall see to it that the revenues of the buildings are devoted to purposes necessary and useful to the church according as they shall deem most expedient.

Chapter IV

BY WHOM AND WHEN THE OFFICE OF PREACHING IS TO BE DISCHARGED. THE PARISH CHURCH IS TO BE ATTENDED TO HEAR THE WORD OF GOD. NO ONE MAY PREACH WITHOUT THE PERMISSION OF THE BISHOP

Desiring that the office of preaching, which belongs chiefly to bishops, be exercised as often as possible for the welfare of the faithful, the holy council, for the purpose of accommodating to the use of the present time the canons published elsewhere on this subject under Paul III,[42] of happy memory, decrees that they themselves shall personally, each in his own church, announce the Sacred Scriptures and the divine law, or, if lawfully hindered, have it done by those whom they shall appoint to the office of preaching; but in other churches by the parish priests, or, if they are hindered, by others to be appointed by the bishop in the city or in any part of the diocese as they shall judge it expedient, at the expense of those who are bound or accustomed to defray it, and this they shall do at least on all Sundays and solemn festival days, but during the season of fasts, of Lent and of the Advent of the Lord, daily, or at least on three days of the week if they shall deem it necessary; otherwise, as often as they shall judge that it can be done conveniently. The bishop shall diligently admonish the people that each one is bound to be present at his own parish church, where it can be conveniently done, to hear the word of God.[43] But no one,

[41] C.2, VI°, De cens., III, 20.
[42] Cf. Sess. V, chap. 2 de ref.
[43] Cc.62, 63, D.I de cons.

whether secular or regular, shall presume to preach, even in churches of his own order, in opposition to the will of the bishop. The bishops shall also see to it that at least on Sundays and other festival days, the children in every parish be carefully taught the rudiments of the faith and obedience toward God and their parents by those whose duty it is, and who shall be compelled thereto, if need be, even by ecclesiastical censures; any privileges and customs notwithstanding. In other respects the things decreed under Paul III concerning the office of preaching shall remain in force.[44]

Chapter V

MAJOR CRIMINAL CAUSES AGAINST BISHOPS SHALL BE TAKEN COGNIZANCE OF BY THE SUPREME PONTIFF ONLY, MINOR ONES BY THE PROVINCIAL SYNOD

Graver criminal causes against bishops, also that of heresy, which may God prevent, which merit deposition or deprivation, shall be taken cognizance of and decided by the Roman pontiff only.[45] But if the cause be of such a nature that it must perforce be assigned out of the Roman Curia, it shall not be committed to anyone but metropolitans or bishops to be chosen by the most holy pope. This commission shall be both special and signed by the most holy pontiff's own hand, and he shall never grant more to them than this, that they take information only of the fact and draw up the process, which they shall transmit immediately to the Roman pontiff, the definitive sentence being reserved to His Holiness. The other things decreed elsewhere under Julius III,[46] of happy memory, concerning these matters, as also the constitution of the general council under Innocent III, which begins, "Qualiter et quando," [47] and which the holy council renews in the present decree, shall be observed by all. But the minor criminal causes of bishops shall be taken cognizance of and decided in the provincial synod only, or by persons commissioned by the provincial synod.

---

[44] Cf. Sess. V, chap. 2 de ref.
[45] Cf. Sess. XIII, chap. 8 de ref.
[46] Cf. Sess. XIII, chaps. 6, 7 de ref.
[47] C.24, X, De accus., V, 1.

CHAPTER VI

AUTHORITY IS GIVEN TO THE BISHOPS TO DISPENSE IN CASES OF IRREGULARITY AND SUSPENSION AND TO ABSOLVE FROM CRIMES

Bishops are authorized to dispense in all cases of irregularity and suspension resulting from a secret crime, except that arising from wilful homicide and those arising from crimes that have found their way before a tribunal, and to absolve gratuitously, after the imposition of a salutary penance, *per se* or through a vicar especially appointed for this purpose *in foro conscientiae* in all occult cases, even those reserved to the Apostolic See, all delinquents subject to them in their diocese. The same is permitted them only, but not their vicars, in the same forum with respect to the crime of heresy.

CHAPTER VII

THE EFFICACY OF THE SACRAMENTS SHALL BE EXPLAINED BY BISHOPS AND PARISH PRIESTS BEFORE THEY ARE ADMINISTERED TO THE PEOPLE. DURING THE CELEBRATION OF THE MASS THE SACRED SCRIPTURES ARE TO BE EXPLAINED

That the faithful may approach the sacraments with greater reverence and devotion of mind, the holy council commands all bishops that not only when they are themselves about to administer them to the people, they shall first, in a manner adapted to the mental ability of those who receive them, explain their efficacy and use, but also they shall see to it that the same is done piously and prudently by every parish priest, and in the vernacular tongue, if need be and if it can be done conveniently, in accordance with the form which will be prescribed for each of the sacraments by the holy council in a catechism, which the bishops shall have faithfully translated into the language of the people and explained to the people by all parish priests. In like manner shall they explain on all festivals or solemnities during the solemnization of the mass or the celebration of the divine offices, in the vernacular tongue, the divine commands and the maxims of salvation,[48] and leaving aside useless questions, let them strive to engraft these things on the hearts of all and instruct them in the law of the Lord.

Chapter VIII

PUBLIC SINNERS SHALL DO PUBLIC PENANCE, UNLESS THE BISHOP SHALL DETERMINE OTHERWISE. A PENITENTIARY IS TO BE INSTITUTED IN CATHEDRALS

The Apostle admonishes that those who sin publicly are to be reproved publicly.[49] When therefore anyone has publicly and in the sight of many committed a crime by which there is no doubt that others have been offended and scandalized, it is proper that a penance commensurate with his guilt be publicly imposed on him, so that those whom he by his example has led to evil morals, he may bring back to an upright life by the evidence of his correction. The bishop, however, should he judge it advisable, may commute this kind of public penance to one that is secret. In all cathedral churches where it can be conveniently done, let the bishop appoint a penitentiary united with the prebend that shall next become vacant, who shall be a master or doctor or licentiate in theology or canon law and forty years of age, or another who may be found to be more suitable for the character of the place and who, while he is hearing confessions in the church, shall be considered as present in the choir.

Chapter IX

BY WHOM THOSE SECULAR CHURCHES ARE TO BE VISITED THAT BELONG TO NO DIOCESE

What has elsewhere been ordained by this council under Paul III,[50] of happy memory, and lately under our most blessed Lord Pius IV,[51] regarding the attention to be given by ordinaries to the visitation of benefices, even of those exempt, the same is to be observed also with

[48] Cf. Sess. XXII, chap. 8.
[49] See I Tim. 5:20; c.19 (§ 1), C.II, q.1; c.1, X, De poenit., V, 38.
[50] Cf. Sess. VI, chap. 4 de ref. and VII, chap. 8 de ref.
[51] Cf. Sess. XXI, chap. 8 de ref.

regard to those secular churches which are said to be in no one's diocese, namely, that they be visited by the bishop whose cathedral church is the nearest, if that is agreed upon, otherwise by him, acting as delegate of the Apostolic See, who has once been chosen for this in the provincial synod by the prelate of that place; any privileges and customs whatsoever, even though immemorial, notwithstanding.

Chapter X

THE EXECUTION OF THE VISITATION SHALL NOT BE IMPEDED BY THE SUBJECTS

That the bishops may be better able to keep the people whom they rule in duty and obedience, they shall in all those things that concern visitation and the correction of the morals of their subjects, have the right and authority, also as delegates of the Apostolic See, to decree, regulate, punish and execute, in accordance with the prescriptions of the canons, those things which in their prudence shall appear to them necessary for the emendation of their subjects and for the good of their dioceses. And in these matters, where it is question of visitation and correction of morals, no exemption, inhibition, appeal or complaint, even though submitted to the Apostolic See, shall in any manner whatsoever hinder or suspend the execution of those things which shall have been commanded, decreed or adjudicated by them.[52]

Chapter XI

HONORARY TITLES OR SPECIAL PRIVILEGES SHALL NOT DETRACT IN ANY WAY FROM THE RIGHT OF BISHOPS. THE CHAPTER "CUM CAPELLA," CONCERNING PRIVILEGES, IS RENEWED

Since privileges and exemptions which are granted to many persons under various titles, are known to create confusion nowadays in the jurisdiction of bishops and to give to those exempt occasion for a more unrestrained life, the holy council decrees that whenever it should be thought proper for just, weighty and apparently necessary reasons that some persons be decorated with the honorary titles of Prothono-

[52] Cf. Sess. XIII, chap. 1 de ref., XIV, chap. 4 de ref., XXII, chap. 1 de ref.

tary, Acolyte, Count Palatine, Royal Chaplain, or other such titles of distinction, whether in or out of the Roman Curia, as also others granted to any monasteries or in any manner imparted, whether assumed under the name of servants to military orders, monasteries, hospitals, colleges, or under any other title, it is to be understood that by these privileges nothing is taken away from the ordinaries whereby those persons to whom such privileges have already been granted or to whom they may be granted in the future cease to be fully subject in all things to the ordinaries as delegates of the Apostolic See; and as regards Royal Chaplains, let them be subject in accordance with the constitution of Innocent III, which begins, "Cum capella;" [53] those persons, however, being excepted who are engaged in actual service in the aforesaid places or in military orders and who reside within their enclosures or houses and live under obedience to them, and those also who have lawfully and according to the rule of these military orders made profession, whereof the ordinary must be certified; notwithstanding any privileges whatsoever, even those of the order of St. John of Jerusalem and of other military orders. But those privileges which by virtue of the constitution of Eugene [54] they are accustomed to enjoy who reside in the Roman Curia or who are in the household of cardinals, are by no means to be understood as applying to those who hold ecclesiastical benefices in regard to those benefices, but they shall continue to be subject to the jurisdiction of the ordinaries; any inhibitions whatsoever notwithstanding.

Chapter XII

QUALIFICATIONS NECESSARY FOR THOSE WHO ARE TO BE PROMOTED TO THE DIGNITIES AND CANONRIES OF CATHEDRAL CHURCHES AND THE DUTIES OF THOSE SO PROMOTED

Since dignities, especially in cathedral churches, were instituted to maintain and promote ecclesiastical discipline, to the end that those who hold them might be distinguished for piety, be an example to others, and assist the bishops by their labor and service, it is but right that those who are called to them should be such as are able to perform their duty. Wherefore, in the future no one shall be promoted to any

[53] C. 16, X, De privil., V, 33.
[54] C. 3, h.t., Extrav. comm., V, 7; Sess. XXIII, chap. 1 de ref.

dignities whatsoever to which is annexed the *cura animarum*, who has not attained at least the twenty-fifth year of his age, is experienced in the clerical order, and is recommended by the learning necessary for the discharge of his office and the integrity of his morals, conformably to the constitution of Alexander III promulgated in the Council of the Lateran, which begins, "Cum in cunctis." [55] In like manner archdeacons, who are called the eyes of the bishop,[56] shall in all churches where it is possible be masters in theology, or doctors or licentiates in canon law. To other dignities or offices to which no *cura animarum* is annexed, clerics, in other respects qualified, shall not be promoted unless they are twenty-two years of age. Those also who are promoted to any benefices whatever having the *cura animarum*, shall within at least two months from the day of having taken possession be bound to make in the hands of the bishop, or, if he be hindered, in the presence of his vicar-general or official, a public profession of their orthodox faith and to promise solemnly and swear that they will persevere in their obedience to the Roman Church. But those who are promoted to canonries and dignities in cathedral churches, shall be bound to do this not only in the presence of the bishop or his official but also in the chapter; otherwise all those promoted as aforesaid shall not make the fruits their own, neither shall possession be of any avail to them. Furthermore, no one shall in the future be admitted to a dignity, canonry or portion unless he is either already constituted in the sacred order which that dignity, prebend or portion requires, or is of such an age as will qualify him for the reception of that order within the time prescribed by law and by this holy council.[57] In all cathedral churches all canonries and portions shall be attached to the order of the priesthood, deaconship or subdeaconship, and the bishop shall with the advice of the chapter designate and distribute, as he shall deem expedient, to which each of the sacred orders is for the future to be attached; so however that at least one half shall be priests and the rest deacons or subdeacons. But where the more laudable custom obtains that the greater part or all shall be priests, this shall by all means be observed. The holy council also exhorts that in provinces where it can be conveniently done, all dignities and at least one half of the canonries in cathedral and prominent collegiate churches be conferred only on

[55] C.7, X, De elect., I, 6; Sess. VII, chap. 1 de ref., XXII, chap. 2 de ref.
[56] C.7, X, De off. archid., I, 23.
[57] Cf. Sess. VII, chap. 12 de ref.

masters or doctors, or also on licentiates in theology or canon law. Moreover, those who hold dignities, canonries, prebends or portions in such cathedral or collegiate churches, shall not be permitted by virtue of any statute or custom to be absent from those churches more than three months of each year,[58] saving however the statutes of those churches which require a longer period of service; otherwise every offender shall for the first year be deprived of one half of the fruits which he has made his own even by reason of his prebend and residence. But if he be again guilty of the same negligence, he shall be deprived of all the fruits which he has acquired during that year, and if he should become more contumacious, he shall be proceeded against in accordance with the prescriptions of the sacred canons.[59] Those shall receive distributions who have been present at the appointed hours; the others shall, all collusion and remission being debarred, forfeit them in accordance with the decree of Boniface VIII, which begins, "Consuetudinem," [60] and which the holy council restores to practice; any statutes or customs whatsoever notwithstanding. All shall be obliged to perform the divine offices in person and not by substitutes; [61] also to assist and serve the bishop when celebrating or exercising other pontifical functions, and in the choir instituted for psalmody, to praise the name of God reverently, distinctly and devoutly in hymns and canticles. They shall, moreover, wear at all times, both in and out of church, a becoming dress, shall abstain from unlawful hunting, fowling, dancing, taverns and games, and so excel in integrity of morals that they may with justice be called counsellors of the Church.[62] With regard to matters that pertain to the proper manner of conducting the divine offices, the proper way of singing or modulating therein, the definite rule for assembling and remaining in choir, the things necessary for those who minister in the church, and such like, the provincial synod shall prescribe for each province a fixed form that will be beneficial to and in accordance with the usage of each province. In the meantime, the bishop, with the aid of no less than two canons, one chosen by himself, the other by the chapter, may provide in these matters as he may deem expedient.

---

[58] Cf. Sess. XXIII, chap. 1 de ref.

[59] Cf. tot. tit. X, De cler. non resid., III, 4.

[60] C. un. VI°, De cler. non resid., III, 3; cf. c.32, X, De praeb., III, 5.

[61] C.3, X, De cler. non resid., III, 4; c.30, De praeb., III, 5; Sess. XXII, chap. 4 de ref.

[62] Cf. tot. tit. X, De vit. et hon. cler., III, 1; in VI°, III, 1; in Clem., III, 1; in Extrav. comm., III, 1; tit. X, De cler. venat., V, 24.

Chapter XIII

HOW THE POORER CATHEDRAL AND PARISH CHURCHES ARE TO BE PROVIDED FOR. PARISHES ARE TO BE SEPARATED BY DEFINITE BOUNDARIES

Since the revenues of many cathedral churches are so limited and scanty that they are in no way in keeping with the episcopal dignity and insufficient for the needs of the churches, the provincial synod, having summoned those who are concerned, shall examine and consider carefully what churches it may be advisable by reason of their limited means and poverty to unite to others in the neighborhood or to provide with additional revenues;[63] and the completed documents concerning this matter it shall send to the supreme Roman pontiff, who being informed thereby shall, as he in his prudence may deem advisable, either unite the poorly provided churches or by additional revenues improve them. In the meantime, until the aforesaid provisions are carried into effect, the supreme pontiff may from certain benefices assist those bishops who by reason of the poverty of their diocese are in need of revenues; provided, however, these benefices are not *curae* or dignities or canonries and prebends, or monasteries in which there is regular observance, or which are subject to general chapters or to certain visitors. In parochial churches also in which the revenues are in like manner so small that they are insufficient to meet the necessary obligations, the bishop, if unable to meet the exigency by a union of benefices, not however those of regulars, shall see to it that by the assignment of first fruits or tithes or by the contributions and collections of the parishioners, or in some other way that he shall deem more profitable, as much be collected as may decently suffice for the needs of the rector and the parish. In all unions, however, whether to be made for the aforesaid or other reasons, parochial churches shall not be united to any monasteries whatsoever, or to abbeys or dignities, or prebends of a cathedral or collegiate church, or to other simple benefices, hospitals or military orders, and those so united shall be investigated again by the ordinary in accordance with the decree elsewhere enacted by this council under Paul III,[64] of happy memory, which is to be observed also and in like manner with regard to unions made

[63] Cf. Sess. VII, chaps. 6, 7 de ref., XIV, chap. 9 de ref., XXIV, chap. 15 de ref.
[64] Cf. Sess. VII, chap. 6 de ref.

since that time; notwithstanding whatever forms of words used therein, which shall be considered as sufficiently expressed here. Furthermore, all those cathedral churches whose revenues do not exceed in actual annual value the sum of one thousand ducats, and those parochial churches in which they do not exceed the sum of one hundred ducats, shall not in the future be burdened with taxes or reservations of revenues for this purpose. Also, in those cities and localities where the parochial churches have no definite boundaries, and whose rectors have not their own people whom they may rule but administer the sacraments indiscriminately to all who desire them, the holy council commands the bishops that, for the greater security of the salvation of the souls committed to them, they divide the people into definite and distinct parishes and assign to each its own and permanent parish priest, who can know his people and from whom alone they may licitly receive the sacraments; [65] or that they make other, more beneficial provisions as the conditions of the locality may require. They shall also see to it that the same is done as soon as possible in those cities and localities where there are no parish churches; any privileges and customs whatsoever, even though immemorial, notwithstanding.

Chapter XIV

NO ONE SHALL BE ADMITTED TO THE POSSESSION OF A BENEFICE OR OF DISTRIBUTIONS WHEN THE DISTRIBUTION OF THE FRUITS IS NOT APPLIED TO PIOUS PURPOSES

In many churches, cathedral as well as collegiate and parochial, it is understood to be the practice, derived either from their constitutions or from evil customs, that in the election, presentation, nomination, institution, confirmation, collation or other provision, or upon admission to the possession of a cathedral church or a benefice, of canonries or prebends, or to a portion of the revenues, or to the daily distributions, there are introduced certain conditions or deductions from the fruits, certain payments, promises, or unlawful compensations, or what in some churches is called mutual profits. Since the holy council abhors these practices, it commands the bishops that they prohibit all things

[65] Cf. Sess. XIV, chap. 9 de ref.

of this kind that are not applied to pious purposes and such methods of entering upon offices, which create a suspicion of simoniacal taint or sordid avarice, and that they examine carefully their statutes and customs in regard to the above matter, and retaining only what they approve as laudable, reject and abolish the rest as corrupt and scandalous. It also ordains that those who in any way act in contravention of what is contained in the present decree incur the penalties prescribed against simoniacs by the sacred canons and various constitutions of the supreme pontiffs,[66] all of which it renews; notwithstanding any statutes, constitutions and customs, even though immemorial and confirmed by Apostolic authority, in regard to which any deceit, fraud and defect of intention may be investigated by the bishop as delegate of the Apostolic See.

Chapter XV

METHOD OF INCREASING THE SCANTY PREBENDS OF CATHEDRAL AND PROMINENT COLLEGIATE CHURCHES

In cathedral and prominent collegiate churches where the prebends are numerous and in relation to the daily distributions so small that they do not suffice for the decent maintenance of the rank of the canons in keeping with the character of the place and persons,[67] the bishops may with the consent of the chapter combine them with some simple benefices, not however with those of regulars, or, if in this way it cannot be done, they may, with the consent of the patrons if the right of patronage belongs to laymen, reduce their number by suppressing some of them and apply the fruits and proceeds to the daily distributions of the remaining prebends; so however, that such a number remain as may conveniently serve for the celebration of divine service and be in keeping with the dignity of the church; [68] any statutes and privileges, or any reservation whether general or special, or any expectation notwithstanding. The aforesaid unions or suppressions shall not be frustrated or hindered by any provisions whatsoever, not even by virtue of resignation or any other derogations or suspensions.

---

[66] Cf. C.I, q.1; tot. tit. X, De sim., III, 5 et Extrav. comm., V, 1.
[67] Cf. chap. 13 de ref. of this sess.
[68] C.2, X, De instit., III, 7.

Chapter XVI

WHAT DUTY DEVOLVES UPON THE CHAPTER DURING THE VACANCY OF A SEE

When a see becomes vacant, the chapter shall, in those places where the duty of receiving the revenues devolves upon it, appoint one or more trustworthy and diligent stewards who shall take care of the ecclesiastical properties and revenues, of which they shall have to give an account to him whom it will concern. It shall also be strictly bound to appoint within eight days after the death of the bishop an official or vicar, or to confirm the incumbent, who shall be at least a doctor or licentiate in canon law, or otherwise as competent a person as is available. In case this is not done, the aforesaid appointment shall devolve upon the metropolitan.[69] But if the church is a metropolitan one or one exempt and the chapter should prove negligent as was said above, then the oldest suffragan bishop in the metropolitan church and the bishop nearest the exempt church shall have the authority to appoint a competent steward and vicar. The bishop who is promoted to the vacant church shall with regard to the matters that pertain to him demand from the steward, vicar and all other officials and administrators who were during the vacancy of the see appointed in his place by the chapter or others, even though they are members of the same chapter, an account of their office, jurisdiction, administration or any other functions, and he shall have the authority to punish those who have been delinquent in their office or administration, even if the aforesaid officials, having turned in their accounts, should have obtained from the chapter or those delegated by it a quittance or discharge. The chapter shall also be bound to render to the bishop an account of documents belonging to the church, if any have come into its possession.

Chapter XVII

THE CONFERRING OF SEVERAL BENEFICES ON AND THEIR RETENTION BY ONE PERSON IS RESTRICTED

Since ecclesiastical order is upset when one cleric holds the offices of several, the sacred canons have piously provided that no one ought

[69] Cf. c. ult. in VI°, De suppl. negl. prael., I, 8.

to be enrolled in two churches.[70] But since many, led by the passion of ungodly covetousness, deceiving themselves, not God, are not ashamed to evade by various species of deceit what has been beneficially established and to hold several benefices at the same time, the holy council, desiring to restore discipline in the government of the churches, by the present decree, which it commands to be observed by all persons by whatever title distinguished, even though it be the dignity of the cardinalate, ordains that in the future one ecclesiastical benefice only shall be conferred on a person. If that is not sufficient to provide him on whom it is conferred with a decent livelihood, then it is permissible to confer on him another simple benefice that will afford a sufficiency, provided both do not require personal residence. These provisions shall apply not only to cathedral churches but also to all other benefices, whether secular or regular, even those held *in commendam*, of whatever title or character they may be. Those who now hold several parochial churches, or one cathedral and one parochial church, shall be strictly bound, all dispensations and unions for life notwithstanding, retaining one parochial church only, or the cathedral church only, to resign the other parochial churches within a period of six months; [71] otherwise the parochial churches and also all the benefices which they hold shall be considered *ipso jure* vacant and as such shall be freely conferred on other competent persons; [72] neither can those who previously held them retain conscientiously the fruits after the time specified. The holy council desires, however, that provision be made in some convenient way, as the supreme pontiff may see fit, for the necessities of those who resign.

Chapter XVIII

ON THE VACANCY OF A PAROCHIAL CHURCH THE BISHOP SHALL APPOINT THERETO A VICAR UNTIL HE HAS PROVIDED A PARISH PRIEST. IN WHAT MANNER AND BY WHOM THOSE APPOINTED TO PAROCHIAL CHURCHES ARE TO BE EXAMINED

It is highly desirable for the salvation of souls that they be directed by worthy and competent parish priests. That this may be accom-

[70] Cf. Sess. VII, chap. 2 de ref.
[71] Cf. Sess. VII, chap. 4 de ref.
[72] Cf. c.4, Extrav. comm., De praeb., III, 2.

plished more diligently and effectively, the holy council decrees that when a parochial church becomes vacant, whether by death or resignation, also in the Curia, or in whatever other manner, it shall be the duty of the bishop immediately upon receipt of information regarding the vacancy of the church to appoint, if need be, a competent vicar to the same, with a suitable assignment, using his own judgment in the matter, of a portion of the fruits thereof, who shall discharge the duties in that church till it has been provided with a rector, even if it be said that the charge of the church belongs to the bishop himself and is administered by one or more, also in churches called patrimonial or receptive, in which it has been the custom of the bishop to assign the *cura animarum* to one or more, all of whom, it commands, are bound to the examination prescribed below,[73] also if the parochial church be generally or specially reserved or assigned, even by virtue of an indult or privilege in favor of cardinals of the holy Roman Church, or of abbots or chapters. Moreover, the bishop and he who has the right of patronage shall within ten days, or such other term as the bishop shall prescribe, designate in the presence of those to be delegated as examiners some competent clerics who are to rule the church. Furthermore, it shall be permitted to others also who may know any who are fit for the office to make known their names, so that a careful investigation may afterward be made as to the age, morals and sufficiency of each. But if in accordance with the custom of the country it should appear more suitable to the bishop or the provincial synod, those who wish to be examined may be summoned by a public notice. At the expiration of the time specified, all whose names have been entered shall be examined by the bishop,[74] or, if hindered, by his vicar-general, and by other examiners who shall not be fewer than three, to whose votes, in case they are equal or distributed singly, the bishop or his vicar may add his in favor of whomsoever he shall deem most fit. At least six examiners shall be proposed annually by the bishop or his vicar in the diocesan synod, and they must prove satisfactory to it and be approved by it. Upon a vacancy occurring in any church, the bishop shall select three out of that number who shall conduct the examination with him, and on a subsequent vacancy he shall select out of the six aforesaid the same or three others whom he may prefer. These examiners shall be masters or doctors or licentiates in theology or canon law, or other

[73] Cf. Sess. VII, chap. 13 de ref.
[74] Cf. Sess. XXV, chap. 9 de ref.

clerics, whether regulars, also of the mendicant orders, or seculars, who appear most competent for the purpose; and all shall take an oath on the holy Gospels of God, that, every human consideration being set aside, they will discharge their duty faithfully. Let them take heed, however, that they do not by reason of this examination receive anything whatever either before or after, otherwise both they themselves and the givers will be guilty of the vice of simony, from which they cannot be absolved till they have resigned the benefices which they in any manner whatever possessed before this act, and they shall, moreover, be rendered disqualified to possess others in the future.[75] In all these matters they shall be bound to render an account not only before God but also, if need be, to the provincial synod, by which, if it has been discovered that they have done anything in contravention of their duty, they can at its discretion be severely punished. On the completion of the examination they shall make known how many they have judged fit in the matter of age, morals, learning, prudence, and other qualifications suitable for ruling the vacant church, and from these the bishop shall choose him whom he shall judge the more competent, and to him and to none other shall the collation of the church be made by him to whom such collation pertains.[76] If the church is under ecclesiastical patronage and the appointment thereto belongs to the bishop and to no one else, he whom the patron shall judge the more worthy among those approved by the examiners, shall be bound to present himself to the bishop that he may be appointed by him.[77] But when the appointment is to be made by any other than the bishop, then the bishop only shall choose the worthier among those who are worthy, and the patron shall present him to the one to whom the appointment belongs. If, however, the church is under lay patronage, the one presented by the patron must be examined, as above, by those delegated thereto, and is not to be admitted unless found competent. In all the above-mentioned cases, to no other than to one of those examined and approved by the examiners as aforesaid and in accordance with the above rules shall the church be committed, and no devolution or appeal, even to the Apostolic See or the legates, vice-legates or nuncios of that See, or to any bishops or metropolitans, primates or patriarchs, shall hinder or suspend the execution of the report of the aforesaid examiners, otherwise

[75] Cf. c.5, D.XXIV.
[76] Cf. Sess. XXV, chap. 9 de ref.
[77] Cf. Sess. VII, chap. 13 de ref.; Sess. XIV, chap. 13 de ref.

the vicar whom the bishop has at his discretion already appointed for the time being to the vacant church or whom he may afterward appoint, shall not be removed from the charge and administration of that church until it has been provided for, either by the appointment of the vicar himself or of some other person who has been approved and chosen as stated above. All provisions or appointments made otherwise than in accordance with the above stated form shall be regarded as surreptitious; any exemptions, indults, privileges, anticipations, appropriations, new provisions, indults granted to any universities,[78] also for a certain sum, and any other impediments whatsoever in contravention of this decree, notwithstanding. If, however, the revenues of said parochial churches should be so scanty as not to bear the burden of all this examination, or if no one should care to undergo the examination, or if by reason of open factions or dissensions, which are met with in some localities, more grievous quarrels and disturbances might easily be stirred up, the ordinary may omit this formality and have recourse to a private examination, if in conformity with his conscience and with the advice of the examiners he shall deem this expedient. The other things, however, are to be observed as above prescribed. If the provincial synod should judge that in the above regulations concerning the form of examination something ought to be added or omitted, it shall have the authority to do so.

Chapter XIX

MANDATES CONCERNING PROMOTION, EXPECTANCIES, AND OTHER THINGS OF THIS KIND ARE ABOLISHED

The holy council decrees that mandates concerning promotion and favors which are called expectancies, shall no longer be granted to anyone, even to colleges, universities, senators, or to any individuals whatsoever, even under the name of an indult, or for a certain sum, or under any other pretext; neither shall it be permitted to anyone to make use of those thus far granted.[79] Neither shall mental reservations nor other favors whatsoever with regard to future vacancies, or indults respecting churches belonging to others, or monasteries, be

[78] Cf. Sess. XXV, chap. 9 de ref.

[79] Cf. Sess. XXV, chap. 9 de ref., and tot. tit. X, De conc. praeb. non vac., III, 8; in VI°, III, 7; in Clem., III, 3.

granted to anyone, not even to cardinals of the holy Roman Church, and those hitherto granted shall be considered abolished.

Chapter XX

THE MANNER OF CONDUCTING CAUSES PERTAINING TO THE ECCLESIASTICAL FORUM IS PRESCRIBED

All causes belonging in any way whatever to the ecclesiastical forum, even if they relate to benefices, shall be taken cognizance of in the first instance before the local ordinaries only, and shall be completely terminated within at least two years from the day that the suit was instituted; otherwise, at the expiration of that term the parties, or either of them, shall be free to have recourse to superior, but otherwise competent, judges, who shall take up the cause as it then stands and shall see to it that it is terminated as soon as possible. Before that term they shall neither be committed to others nor withdrawn; any appeals introduced by the parties shall not be received by any superior judges, neither shall any assignment or restriction be issued by them except upon a definitive sentence or one having the force of such a sentence, and the grievance arising therefrom cannot be repaired by an appeal from the definitive sentence. From the above are to be excepted those causes which according to the prescriptions of the canons are to be dealt with before the Apostolic See,[80] or which the supreme Roman pontiff shall for an urgent and reasonable cause judge advisable to assign or withdraw by a special rescript provided with the signature of His Holiness signed with his own hand. Furthermore, matrimonial and criminal causes shall not be left to the judgment of a dean, archdeacon or other inferiors, even in the course of their visitation, but shall be reserved to the examination and jurisdiction of the bishop only (even though there should at the time be a dispute, in whatever instance it may be, between the bishop and the dean or archdeacon or other inferiors regarding the examination of those causes), and if in the same matrimonial cause one of the parties should in the presence of the bishop really prove his poverty, he shall not be compelled to litigate his case either in the second or third instance outside the province, unless the other party is prepared to provide for his maintenance and

[80] Cf. c.7, C.VI, q.4; Sess. XXV, chap. 10 de ref.

bear the expenses of the trial. In like manner, legates, also those *de latere*, nuncios, ecclesiastical governors or others, shall not only not presume by virtue of any authority whatsoever to hinder bishops in the aforesaid causes, or in any manner take away the exercise of or disturb their jurisdiction, but they shall not even proceed against clerics or other ecclesiastical persons until the bishop has first been approached and has proved himself negligent in the matter; otherwise their proceedings and decisions avail nothing and they shall be bound to make satisfaction to the parties for the damage sustained. Moreover, if anyone should appeal in cases permitted by the law,[81] or make a complaint regarding some grievance, or otherwise by reason of the lapse of two years, as was said above, have recourse to another judge, he shall be bound to transfer at his own expense to the judge of appeal all the acts of the proceedings conducted in the presence of the bishop, having previously, however, notified the bishop, so that if anything appears suitable to him for the direction of the cause, he may communicate it to the judge of appeal. But if the appellee appears, he shall also be bound to bear his proportion of the expenses of transferring the acts if he wishes to use them, unless it is a local custom to act otherwise, namely, that the entire costs are borne by the appellant. Furthermore, the notary shall be bound on receipt of a suitable fee to furnish the appellant as soon as possible and within at least one month with a copy of the proceedings, and should he through delay in supplying such copy be guilty of fraud, he shall at the discretion of the ordinary be suspended from the administration of his office and shall be compelled to pay double the costs of the suit, which is to be divided between the appellant and the poor of the locality. But if the judge himself should be aware of this delay, or should participate therein, or should in any other way hinder the delivery of the entire proceedings to the appellant within the time specified above, he shall be bound to the same penalty of paying double the costs, as was stated above; any privileges, indults, agreements which bind only their authors, and any other customs whatsoever to the contrary in respect to all matters dealt with above, notwithstanding.

[81] Cf. tot. tit. X, De appell., II, 28; in VI°, II, 15; in Clem., II, 12.

Chapter XXI

IT IS DECLARED THAT BY CERTAIN WORDS USED ABOVE, THE USUAL MANNER OF TREATING MATTERS IN GENERAL COUNCILS IS NOT CHANGED

The holy council, desiring that no occasion for doubt arise at any future time from decrees which it has published, in explaining those words contained in a decree published in the first session under our most blessed Lord, Pius IV, namely, "which at the suggestion and under the presidency of the legates shall appear suitable and proper to the holy council for alleviating the calamities of these times, adjusting religious controversies, restraining deceitful tongues, correcting the abuses of depraved morals, and to bring about true Christian peace in the world," [82] declares that it was not its intention that by the foregoing words the usual manner of treating matters in general councils should in any part be changed, or that anything new besides that which has so far been established by the sacred canons or the prescriptions of general councils, should be added to or taken away from anyone.

ANNOUNCEMENT OF THE NEXT SESSION

Moreover, the same holy council ordains and decrees that the next session be held on the Thursday after the conception of the Blessed Virgin Mary, which will be the ninth day of the coming December, with the authority, however, of abbreviating that time. In this session will be considered the sixth chapter now deferred to it and the remaining chapters on reform which have already been set forth and other matters related thereto. If it appears opportune and time will permit, some dogmas may also be considered, as in their turn they will be proposed in the congregations.

The time appointed for the session was abridged.

---

[82] Cf. Sess. XVII at the beginning.

TWENTY-FIFTH SESSION

which is the ninth and last under the Supreme Pontiff, Pius IV, begun on the third and closed on the fourth day of December, 1563

DECREE CONCERNING PURGATORY

Since the Catholic Church, instructed by the Holy Ghost, has, following the sacred writings and the ancient tradition of the Fathers, taught in sacred councils and very recently in this ecumenical council that there is a purgatory,[1] and that the souls there detained are aided by the suffrages of the faithful and chiefly by the acceptable sacrifice of the altar, the holy council commands the bishops that they strive diligently to the end that the sound doctrine of purgatory, transmitted by the Fathers and sacred councils,[2] be believed and maintained by the faithful of Christ, and be everywhere taught and preached. The more difficult and subtle questions, however, and those that do not make for edification and from which there is for the most part no increase in piety, are to be excluded from popular instructions to uneducated people.[3] Likewise, things that are uncertain or that have the appearance of falsehood they shall not permit to be made known publicly and discussed. But those things that tend to a certain kind of curiosity or superstition, or that savor of filthy lucre, they shall prohibit as scandals and stumblingblocks to the faithful. The bishops shall see to it that the suffrages of the living, that is, the sacrifice of the mass,[4] prayers, alms and other works of piety which they have been accustomed to perform for the faithful departed, be piously and devoutly discharged in accordance with the laws of the Church, and that whatever is due on their behalf from testamentary bequests or other ways, be discharged by the priests and ministers of the Church and others who are bound to render this service not in a perfunctory manner, but diligently and accurately.

[1] Cf. Sess. VI, can. 30 and Sess. XXII, chap. 2 and can. 3.

[2] Cf. cc.4, 5, D.XXV; Eugene IV in the Council of Florence (Denzinger, *Enchiridion*, no. 693).

[3] See I Tim. 1:4; II Tim. 2:23; Tit. 3:9.

[4] Cf. *infra*, chap. 4 de ref.

ON THE INVOCATION, VENERATION, AND RELICS OF SAINTS, AND ON SACRED IMAGES

The holy council commands all bishops and others who hold the office of teaching and have charge of the *cura animarum*, that in accordance with the usage of the Catholic and Apostolic Church, received from the primitive times of the Christian religion, and with the unanimous teaching of the holy Fathers and the decrees of sacred councils, they above all instruct the faithful diligently in matters relating to intercession and invocation of the saints, the veneration of relics, and the legitimate use of images, teaching them that the saints who reign together with Christ offer up their prayers to God for men, that it is good and beneficial suppliantly to invoke them and to have recourse to their prayers, assistance and support in order to obtain favors from God through His Son, Jesus Christ our Lord, who alone is our redeemer and savior; [5] and that they think impiously who deny that the saints who enjoy eternal happiness in heaven are to be invoked, or who assert that they do not pray for men, or that our invocation of them to pray for each of us individually is idolatry, or that it is opposed to the word of God and inconsistent with the honor of the *one mediator of God and men, Jesus Christ*,[6] or that it is foolish to pray vocally or mentally to those who reign in heaven. Also, that the holy bodies of the holy martyrs and of others living with Christ, which were the living members of Christ and the temple of the Holy Ghost,[7] to be awakened by Him to eternal life and to be glorified, are to be venerated by the faithful,[8] through which many benefits are bestowed by God on men, so that those who maintain that veneration and honor are not due to the relics of the saints, or that these and other memorials are honored by the faithful without profit, and that the places dedicated to the memory of the saints for the purpose of obtaining their aid are visited in vain, are to be utterly condemned, as the Church has already long since condemned and now again condemns them. Moreover, that the images of Christ, of the Virgin Mother of God, and of the other saints are to be placed and retained especially in the churches, and that due honor and veneration is to be given them; not, however,

---

[5] Cf. Sess. XXII, chap. 3.
[6] See I Tim. 2:5.
[7] See I Cor. 3:16; 6:19; II Cor. 6:16.
[8] Cf. II Council of Nicaea (787), can. 7.

that any divinity or virtue is believed to be in them by reason of which they are to be venerated, or that something is to be asked of them, or that trust is to be placed in images, as was done of old by the Gentiles who placed their hope in idols; [9] but because the honor which is shown them is referred to the prototypes which they represent, so that by means of the images which we kiss and before which we uncover the head and prostrate ourselves, we adore Christ and venerate the saints whose likeness they bear. That is what was defined by the decrees of the councils, especially of the Second Council of Nicaea,[10] against the opponents of images.

Moreover, let the bishops diligently teach that by means of the stories of the mysteries of our redemption portrayed in paintings and other representations the people are instructed and confirmed in the articles of faith, which ought to be borne in mind and constantly reflected upon; also that great profit is derived from all holy images, not only because the people are thereby reminded of the benefits and gifts bestowed on them by Christ, but also because through the saints the miracles of God and salutary examples are set before the eyes of the faithful, so that they may give God thanks for those things, may fashion their own life and conduct in imitation of the saints and be moved to adore and love God and cultivate piety. But if anyone should teach or maintain anything contrary to these decrees, let him be anathema. If any abuses shall have found their way into these holy and salutary observances, the holy council desires earnestly that they be completely removed, so that no representation of false doctrines and such as might be the occasion of grave error to the uneducated be exhibited. And if at times it happens, when this is beneficial to the illiterate, that the stories and narratives of the Holy Scriptures are portrayed and exhibited, the people should be instructed that not for that reason is the divinity represented in picture as if it can be seen with bodily eyes or expressed in colors or figures. Furthermore, in the invocation of the saints, the veneration of relics, and the sacred use of images, all superstition shall be removed,[11] all filthy quest for gain eliminated, and all lasciviousness avoided, so that images shall not be painted and adorned with a seductive charm, or the celebration of saints and the visitation of relics be perverted by the people into

---

[9] Ps. 134:15 ff.
[10] Sess. III, IV, VI.
[11] Cf. c.ult., X, De reliq. et ven. sanct., III, 45.

boisterous festivities and drunkenness, as if the festivals in honor of the saints are to be celebrated with revelry and with no sense of decency.[12] Finally, such zeal and care should be exhibited by the bishops with regard to these things that nothing may appear that is disorderly or unbecoming and confusedly arranged, nothing that is profane, nothing disrespectful, since holiness becometh the house of God.[13] That these things may be the more faithfully observed, the holy council decrees that no one is permitted to erect or cause to be erected in any place or church, howsoever exempt, any unusual image unless it has been approved by the bishop; also that no new miracles be accepted[14] and no relics recognized[15] unless they have been investigated and approved by the same bishop, who, as soon as he has obtained any knowledge of such matters, shall, after consulting theologians and other pious men, act thereon as he shall judge consonant with truth and piety. But if any doubtful or grave abuse is to be eradicated, or if indeed any graver question concerning these matters should arise, the bishop, before he settles the controversy, shall await the decision of the metropolitan and of the bishops of the province in a provincial synod; so, however, that nothing new or anything that has not hitherto been in use in the Church, shall be decided upon without having first consulted the most holy Roman pontiff.

CONCERNING REGULARS AND NUNS

The same holy council, continuing the work of reform, has thought fit that the following matters be decided.

Chapter I

ALL REGULARS SHALL ADJUST THEIR LIFE IN ACCORDANCE WITH THE REQUIREMENTS OF THE RULE WHICH THEY HAVE PROFESSED; SUPERIORS SHALL SEDULOUSLY SEE TO IT THAT THIS IS DONE

Since the holy council is not ignorant of how great a splendor and usefulness accrues to the Church of God from monasteries piously

---

[12] C. 2, D.III de cons.
[13] Ps. 92:5.
[14] Cf. c. 1, X, De reliq. et ven. sanct., III, 45.
[15] Cf. c. ult., X, h.t., De reliq.

regulated and properly administered, it has, to the end that the old and regular discipline may be the more easily and promptly restored where it has collapsed, and may be the more firmly maintained where it has been preserved, thought it necessary to command, as by this decree it does command, that all regulars, men as well as women, adjust and regulate their life in accordance with the requirements of the rule which they have professed, and especially that they observe faithfully whatever pertains to the perfection of their profession, as the vows of obedience, poverty, and chastity,[16] and any other vows and precepts peculiar to any rule and order and belonging to the essence thereof, as well as the preservation of the common life, food and clothing. Superiors shall use all care and diligence, in general and provincial chapters as well as in their visitations, which they shall not neglect to make at the proper times, that these things are not departed from, for it is evident that they cannot make any relaxations in those things that pertain to the substance of the regular life. For if those things that constitute the basis and foundation of all regular discipline are not strictly observed, the whole edifice must necessarily fall.

Chapter II

PRIVATE OWNERSHIP IS ABSOLUTELY FORBIDDEN TO REGULARS

To no regular, therefore, whether man or woman, shall it be lawful to possess or to hold as his own or even in the name of the convent any movable or immovable property, of whatever nature it may be or in whatever manner acquired; [17] but the same shall be handed over immediately to the superior and be incorporated in the convent. Neither shall it in the future be lawful for superiors to grant immovable property to any regular, not even the usufruct or use, or the administration thereof or as *commendam.* But the administration of the property of monasteries or convents shall belong to the officials thereof only, who are removable at the will of their superiors. Superiors shall so permit the use of movable goods that the furniture is consistent with the state of poverty which they have professed; there shall be nothing superfluous, neither shall anything that is necessary be denied them. But should anyone be discovered or convicted of possessing something in

[16] Cf. c.1 (§ Quum igitur in primis), in Clem., De verb. sig., V, 11.
[17] Cf. cc.11, 13, C.XII, q.1; cc.2, 6, X. De statu monach., III, 35.

any other manner, he shall be deprived for two years of his active and passive voice and shall also be punished in accordance with the prescriptions of his rule and order.

CHAPTER III

ALL MONASTERIES, SAVE THOSE HEREIN EXCEPTED, MAY POSSESS IMMOVABLE PROPERTY. THE NUMBER OF PERSONS IN THEM IS TO BE DETERMINED BY THE AMOUNT OF REVENUES OR ALMS. NO MONASTERIES MAY BE ERECTED WITHOUT THE PERMISSION OF THE BISHOP

The holy council grants that all monasteries and houses, of men as well as of women, and of mendicants, even those that were forbidden by their constitutions or that had not received permission to this effect by Apostolic privilege, with the exception of the houses of the brethren of St. Francis,[18] the Capuchins, and those called Minor Observants, may in the future possess immovable property. But if any of the aforesaid places, to which it has been granted by Apostolic authority to possess such property, have been deprived thereof, it decrees that the same shall be wholly restored to them. But in the aforesaid monasteries and houses, of men as well as of women, whether they do or do not possess immovable properties, only such a number of persons shall be determined upon and retained in the future as can be suitably maintained either from the revenues of the monasteries or from the customary alms; [19] neither shall such places be erected in the future unless the permission of the bishop in whose diocese they are to be established has first been obtained.

[18] Cf. c.3 (§ Porro), VI°, De verb. sig., V, 12; c.1, h.t. in Clem., V, 11.

[19] Cf. c.9, X, De vit. et hon. cler., III, 1; c.1, X, De instit., III, 7; c. un. (§ 1), VI°, De stat. regul., III, 16.

CHAPTER IV

NO REGULAR SHALL WITHOUT THE PERMISSION OF HIS SUPERIOR ENTER THE SERVICE EITHER OF ANOTHER PLACE OR PERSON, OR WITHDRAW FROM HIS MONASTERY. WHEN ABSENT BY REASON OF STUDY HE SHALL RESIDE IN A MONASTERY

The holy council forbids that any regular under the pretext of preaching or lecturing or of any pious work, place himself at the service of any prelate, prince, university, community, or of any other person or place whatsoever without the permission of his superior,[20] any privilege or authority obtained from others regarding these matters shall avail him nothing. Should he act in contravention of this he shall at the discretion of his superior be punished as disobedient. Neither shall it be lawful for regulars to leave their convents, even under pretext of going to their superiors, unless they have been sent or summoned by them. Anyone discovered without having obtained the aforesaid command in writing, shall be punished by the local ordinaries as a deserter of his institute. Those who for reasons of study are sent to universities, shall reside in convents only, otherwise the ordinaries shall take action against them.

CHAPTER V

PROVISION IS MADE FOR THE ENCLOSURE OF NUNS, ESPECIALLY THOSE WHO RESIDE OUTSIDE THE CITIES

The holy council, renewing the constitution of Boniface VIII, which begins, "Periculoso," [21] commands all bishops that by the judgment of God to which it appeals and under threat of eternal malediction, they make it their special care that in all monasteries subject to them by their own authority and in others by the authority of the Apostolic See, the enclosure of nuns be restored wherever it has been violated and that it be preserved where it has not been violated; restraining with ecclesiastical censures and other penalties, every appeal being set aside, the disobedient and gainsayers, even summoning for this purpose, if need be,

[20] Cf. c.35, C.XVI, q.1; c.7, X, De off. jud. ord., I, 31; cc.3, 4, X, Ne cler. vel monach., III, 50; c.1 (§ 5), in Clem., De stat. monach., III, 10.

[21] C. un., VI°, De stat. regul., III, 16.

the aid of the secular arm. The holy council exhorts all Christian princes to furnish this aid, and binds thereto under penalty of excommunication to be incurred *ipso facto* all civil magistrates. No nun shall after her profession be permitted to go out of the monastery, even for a brief period under any pretext whatever, except for a lawful reason to be approved by the bishop; [22] any indults and privileges whatsoever notwithstanding. Neither shall anyone, of whatever birth or condition, sex or age, be permitted, under penalty of excommunication to be incurred *ipso facto*, to enter the enclosure of a monastery without the written permission of the bishop or the superior.[23] But the bishop or superior ought to grant permission in necessary cases only, and no other person shall in any way be able to grant it, even by virtue of any authority or indult already granted or that may be granted in the future. And since monasteries of nuns situated outside the walls of a city or town are often without any protection exposed to the rapacity and other crimes of evil men, the bishops and other superiors shall make it their duty to remove, if they deem it expedient, the nuns from those places to new or old monasteries within cities or more populous towns, summoning, if need be, the aid of the secular arm. Those who hinder or disobey them, they shall compel to submission by ecclesiastical censures.

Chapter VI

THE MANNER OF CHOOSING SUPERIORS

That all things may be done properly and without fraud in the election of superiors, temporary abbots and other officials and generals, as also abbesses and other superioresses, the holy council above all things strictly commands that all the aforesaid must be chosen by secret ballot, so that the names of individual voters may never become known. Neither shall it be lawful in the future to appoint provincials, abbots, priors, or any other titled persons whatsoever with a view of determining the election to be made, nor to add the votes and approvals of those absent. But if anyone should be elected contrary to the prescription of this decree, such an election shall be invalid, and he who has permitted himself to be chosen provincial, abbot, or prior in the afore-

---

[22] Cf. c. un., VI°, De stat. regular., III, 16.
[23] C. 8, X, De vit. et hon. cler., III, 1.

said manner, shall from that time on be disqualified to hold any offices whatsoever in the order; any faculties that have been granted in these matters shall be considered as *eo ipso* nullified, and should any others be granted in the future, they shall be regarded as surreptitious.

Chapter VII

WHO MAY BE ELECTED ABBESSES AND SUPERIORESSES BY WHATEVER NAME KNOWN AND HOW THEY ARE TO BE ELECTED. NO ONE SHALL BE APPOINTED OVER TWO MONASTERIES

No one shall be elected abbess or prioress, or by whatever other name the one appointed or the superioress may be known, who is less than forty years of age and who has not lived commendably during the eight years after having made her profession. If no one is found in a monastery possessing these qualifications, then one may be chosen from another of the same order. But if the superior who presides over the election should judge even this inconvenient, with the consent of the bishop or other superior one of those in the same monastery who is beyond her thirtieth year and has lived commendably at least five years since her profession may be chosen.[24] No one, however, shall be appointed over two monasteries. If anyone is in any way in possession of two or more, she shall, retaining one, be compelled to resign the remainder within six months, and in case she has not resigned within that period, all shall be *ipso jure* vacant. He who presides at the election, whether it be the bishop or other superior, shall not enter the enclosure of the monastery, but shall hear or receive the vote of each at the little window of the grating. In other matters the constitutions of each order or monastery shall be observed.

Chapter VIII

HOW THE GOVERNMENT OF MONASTERIES WHICH HAVE NO REGULARS AS ORDINARY VISITORS IS TO BE CONDUCTED

All monasteries which are not subject to general chapters or to bishops, and which have not regular visitors who belong to the order, but have been accustomed to be governed under the immediate protec-

[24] Cf. c.43, VI°, De elect., I, 6.

tion and direction of the Apostolic See, shall be bound within a year from the dissolution of the present council and thereafter every three years, to assemble in congregations in accordance with the form of the constitution of Innocent III published in the general council, which begins, "In singulis"; [25] and they shall there authorize certain regulars who shall deliberate and decide on the manner and order of establishing the aforesaid congregations and also the rules to be therein observed. But if they should prove negligent in these matters, then the metropolitan in whose province the aforesaid monasteries are located, as the delegate of the Apostolic See, shall convoke them for the above named purpose. If, however, there is not a sufficient number of such monasteries within the confines of one province to establish a congregation, the monasteries of two or three provinces may form one congregation. When these congregations have been established, their general chapters and the superiors and visitors elected by them shall have the same authority over the monasteries of their congregation and over the regulars residing therein as other superiors and visitors have in other orders, and they shall be bound to visit the monasteries of their congregation frequently, to apply themselves to their reform, and to observe whatever has been decreed in the sacred canons [26] and in this holy council. But if at the request of the metropolitan they fail to take steps to carry the aforesaid matters into effect, then they shall be subject to the bishops, as the delegates of the Apostolic See, in whose dioceses the aforesaid places are situated.

Chapter IX

MONASTERES OF NUNS IMMEDIATELY SUBJECT TO THE APOSTOLIC SEE SHALL BE SUPERVISED BY THE BISHOP; OTHERS, BY THOSE DELEGATED IN GENERAL CHAPTERS OR BY OTHER REGULARS

Monasteries of nuns which are immediately subject to the Apostolic See, also those known by the name of Chapters of St. Peter or of St. John or by any other name, shall be supervised by the bishops as delegates of that See, anything to the contrary notwithstanding. Those, however, that are supervised by persons delegated in general chapters or by other regulars, shall be left under their charge and protection.

---

[25] Cf. c.7, X, De stat. monach., III, 35.

[26] Cf. tot. tit. X, De stat. monach., III, 35, De stat. regul. in VI°, III, 16, De stat. monach. in Clem., III, 10.

Chapter X

NUNS SHALL CONFESS AND COMMUNICATE ONCE A MONTH. AN EXTRAORDINARY CONFESSOR SHALL BE PROVIDED FOR THEM BY THE BISHOP. AMONG THEM THE EUCHARIST SHALL NOT BE RESERVED OUTSIDE THE PUBLIC CHURCH

Bishops and other superiors of monasteries of nuns shall take special care that the nuns, as they are admonished in their constitutions, confess their sins and receive the most holy Eucharist at least once a month,[27] so that they may fortify themselves by that salutary safeguard valiantly to overcome all the assaults of the devil. In addition to the ordinary confessor, the bishop and other superiors shall provide twice or three times a year an extraordinary one, whose duty it shall be to hear the confessions of all. The holy council forbids, however, that the holy body of Christ be reserved within the choir or the enclosure of the monastery and not in the public church; any indult or privilege notwithstanding.

Chapter XI

THE BISHOP SHALL VISIT MONASTERIES TO WHICH IS ANNEXED THE *CURA* OF SECULARS BESIDES THOSE WHO BELONG TO THEIR HOUSEHOLD, AND HE SHALL, WITH CERTAIN EXCEPTIONS, EXAMINE THOSE WHO ARE TO EXERCISE THAT *CURA*

In monasteries or houses of men or women to which is annexed the *cura animarum* of secular persons other than those who belong to the household of those monasteries or places, those persons, whether regulars or seculars, who exercise that *cura* shall in all things that pertain to that *cura* and to the administration of the sacraments be subject immediately to the jurisdiction, visitation, and correction of the bishop in whose diocese they are located. Neither may anyone, not even such as are removable at any moment, be appointed thereto except with his consent and after having been previously examined by him or by his vicar; [28] the monastery of Cluny with its territories being excepted, and

[27] C. 1 (§ 2), in Clem., De stat. monach., III, 10.
[28] Cf. c. 11, C.XVIII, q. 2.

excepted also are those monasteries or places in which the abbots, generals, or heads of orders ordinarily have their principal residence, and other monasteries or houses in which abbots or other superiors of regulars exercise episcopal and temporal jurisdiction over the parish priests and parishioners; saving the right, however, of those bishops who exercise a greater jurisdiction over the places or persons named above.

CHAPTER XII

IN THE OBSERVANCE OF EPISCOPAL CENSURES AND DIOCESAN FEASTS, REGULARS SHALL ACT IN ACCORD WITH THE SECULAR CLERGY

Not only the censures and interdicts that have emanated from the Apostolic See but also those promulgated by the ordinaries, shall on the bishop's command be published and observed by the regulars in their churches.[29] The feast days also which the bishop shall command to be observed in his diocese, shall be observed by all those exempt, also by the regulars.[30]

CHAPTER XIII

DISPUTES CONCERNING PRECEDENCE THE BISHOP SHALL SETTLE IMMEDIATELY. EXEMPT PERSONS WHO DO NOT LIVE IN VERY STRICT ENCLOSURES, ARE OBLIGED TO ATTEND THE PUBLIC PRAYERS

All disputes concerning precedence which very often and not without grave scandal arise among ecclesiastics, both secular and regular, at public processions as well as the burial of the dead, as also in the matter of carrying the canopy and other things of this kind, the bishop shall settle to the exclusion of every appeal; anything to the contrary notwithstanding. All exempt persons, secular as well as regular clerics, also monks, summoned to public processions, shall be obliged to attend; those only being excepted who live permanently in strict enclosure.

---

[29] C. 1, in Clem., De sent. excomm., V, 10.
[30] C. 13, D. XII.

CHAPTER XIV

BY WHOM PUNISHMENT IS TO BE IMPOSED ON A REGULAR GUILTY OF A PUBLIC OFFENSE

A regular not subject to the bishop and living within the enclosure of a monastery, who has outside of that enclosure committed so notorious an offense as to be a scandal to the people, shall at the instance of the bishop be severely punished by his superior within the time specified by the bishop, and the superior shall report to the bishop concerning this punishment. Otherwise he shall be deprived of his office by his superior and the delinquent may be punished by the bishop.[31]

CHAPTER XV

PROFESSION SHALL NOT BE MADE EXCEPT AFTER ONE YEAR'S PROBATION AND ON THE COMPLETION OF THE SIXTEENTH YEAR

In no religious order whatever, whether of men or of women, shall profession be made before the completion of the sixteenth year, and no one shall be admitted to profession who has been under probation less than a year after the reception of the habit.[32] Any profession made sooner is null and imposes no obligation to the observance of any rule either of a religious body or an order, neither does it entail any other effects whatsoever.[33]

---

[31] Cf. c. ult., X, De stat. monach., III, 35.
[32] Cf. c. 1, C.XVII, q. 2; c. 16, X, De regular., III, 31; c. 2, h.t. in VI°, III, 14.
[33] Cf. c. 8, X, h.t., III, 31; c. 1, h.t., in VI°, III, 14.

Chapter XVI

A RENUNCIATION MADE OR AN OBLIGATION ASSUMED TWO MONTHS BEFORE PROFESSION IS NULL. THE PROBATION COMPLETED, THE NOVICES SHALL BE EITHER PROFESSED OR DISMISSED. IN THE PIOUS INSTITUTE OF CLERICS OF THE SOCIETY OF JESUS NOTHING NEW IS INTRODUCED. NO PART OF THE PROPERTY OF A NOVICE SHALL BE GIVEN TO THE MONASTERY BEFORE PROFESSION

Moreover, no renunciation or obligation previously made, even upon oath or in favor of any pious cause whatsoever, shall be valid, unless it be made with the permission of the bishop or his vicar within two months immediately preceding profession, and it shall not be understood otherwise to have effect unless the profession followed; but if made in any other manner, even with the express renunciation of this favor, also upon oath, it shall be invalid and of no effect. When novices have completed their novitiate, the superiors shall admit to profession those novices found qualified; the others they shall dismiss from the monastery. Hereby, however, the holy council does not intend to innovate or prohibit something that will hinder the order of clerics of the Society of Jesus from serving the Lord and His Church in accordance with their pious institute approved by the holy Apostolic See. Before the profession of a novice, whether male or female, nothing shall under any pretext whatever be given to the monastery from the property of the same, either by parents, relatives or guardians, except for food and clothing during the time of probation, lest the novice should be unable to leave for the reason that the monastery possesses the whole or greater part of his substance, and he would be unable easily to recover it in case he should leave. The holy council, therefore, commands under penalty of anathema both givers and receivers that this be in no wise done, and that to those who leave before profession everything that was theirs be restored. All of which, that it may be done properly, the bishop shall, if need be, enforce with ecclesiastical censures.

Chapter XVII

IF A GIRL WHO IS MORE THAN TWELVE YEARS OF AGE WISHES TO TAKE THE HABIT OF REGULARS, SHE SHALL BE EXAMINED BY THE ORDINARY, AND AGAIN BEFORE PROFESSION

The holy council, having in view the freedom of the profession of virgins who are to be dedicated to God, ordains and decrees that if a girl more than twelve years of age wishes to take the habit of regulars, she shall not take that habit, neither shall she nor any other at a later period make profession,[34] until the bishop, or, if he be absent or hindered, his vicar, or someone delegated by them at their expense, has carefully examined the wish of the virgin, whether she has been forced or enticed, or knows what she is doing; [35] and if her will is found to be pious and free and she has the qualifications required by the rule of that monastery and order, and also if the monastery is a suitable one for her, she shall be permitted freely to make profession. And that the bishop may not be ignorant of the time of the profession, the superioress of the monastery shall be bound to give him notice thereof a month beforehand; but if she fails to make the matter known to him, she shall be suspended from office for as long a period as the bishop shall deem proper.

Chapter XVIII

NO ONE SHALL, EXCEPT IN THE CASES PERMITTED BY LAW, COMPEL A WOMAN TO ENTER A MONASTERY OR PREVENT HER IF SHE WISHES TO ENTER. THE CONSTITUTIONS OF THE PENITENTS OR CONVERTS ARE TO BE OBSERVED

The holy council anathematizes each and all persons, of whatever character or rank they may be, whether clerics or laics, seculars or regulars, and with whatever dignity invested, who shall, except in the cases permitted by law,[36] in any way force any virgin or widow, or any other woman whatsoever, to enter a monastery against her will, or to take the habit of any religious order or to make profession; those also who give advice, aid or encouragement, as well as those who, knowing that she does not enter the monastery or receive the habit, or make profes-

[34] C. 12, X, De regular., III, 31.
[35] C. 10, C.XX, q. 1; c. 1, X, De regular., III, 31.
[36] Cf. cc. 18, 19, X, De conv. conjug., III, 32.

sion voluntarily, shall in any way take part in that act by their presence, consent or authority. Similarly does it anathematize those who shall in any way and without a just cause impede the holy wish of virgins or other women to take the veil or pronounce the vows.[37] Each and all of those things which must be done before profession or at the profession itself shall be observed not only in monasteries subject to the bishop but also in all others. From the above, however, are excepted the women who are called penitents or converts, whose own constitutions shall be observed.

Chapter XIX

HOW TO PROCEED IN THE CASE OF THOSE WHO DESERT AN ORDER

Any regular who shall pretend that he entered a religious order through compulsion and fear, or shall allege that he was professed before the proper age or something similar,[38] and wishes for some reason to lay aside the habit, or departs with the habit without the permission of his superior, shall not be listened to unless it be within five years only from the day of his profession, and not even then unless he has submitted to his superior and to the ordinary the reasons for his pretensions. But if before doing this he has of his own accord laid aside the habit, he shall under no circumstances be admitted to assign any reason whatever, but shall be compelled to return to his monastery and be punished as an apostate, and in the meantime he shall not have the benefit of any privilege of his order. Moreover, no regular shall in virtue of any authority whatsoever be transferred to an order less rigorous,[39] neither shall permission be granted to any regular to wear the habit of his order secretly.

Chapter XX

SUPERIORS OF ORDERS NOT SUBJECT TO BISHOPS SHALL VISIT AND CORRECT INFERIOR MONASTERIES, EVEN THOSE PROVISIONALLY COLLATED

Abbots who are heads of orders and other superiors of the aforesaid orders who are not subject to bishops but have a lawful jurisdiction

[37] C.2, C.XX, q.2; c.16, C.XXXII, q.2.
[38] C.8, C.XX, q.1; c.12, X, De regular., III, 31.
[39] Cf. Sess. XIV, chap. 11 de ref.

over other inferior monasteries or priories, shall, each in his own locality and order, visit *ex officio* those monasteries and priories that are subject to them, also if held *in commendam*. Since these are subject to the heads of their orders, the holy council declares that they are not to be included in what has been decided elsewhere concerning the visitation of monasteries held *in commendam*,[40] and all superiors of the monasteries of the aforesaid orders shall be bound to receive the above named visitors and to execute their commands. Those monasteries also which are the heads of orders shall be visited in accordance with the constitutions of the holy Apostolic See and of each order. And so long as such provisional collations continue, there shall be appointed by the general chapters or by the visitors of the orders cloistral priors, or subpriors in the priories that have a convent, who shall correct and exercise spiritual authority. In all other things the privileges and faculties of the above named orders, which concern their persons, places and rights, shall remain firm and undisturbed.

Chapter XXI

MONASTERIES SHALL BE CONFERRED ON REGULARS. HEAD OR PRINCIPAL MONASTERIES SHALL NOT IN THE FUTURE BE CONFERRED ON ANYONE *IN COMMENDAM*

Since most monasteries, also abbeys, priories, and provostries, have suffered no little loss both in spiritual and temporal things through the maladministration of those to whom they have been entrusted, the holy council desires to restore them entirely to a discipline becoming the monastic life. But the present state of the times is so adverse and so full of difficulties that a remedy cannot be applied to all at once, or a common one everywhere, as it desired. Nevertheless, that it may not omit anything that may in time provide advantageously for the aforesaid, it trusts in the first place that the most holy Roman pontiff will according to his piety and prudence make it his care, so far as he sees the times will permit, that regulars expressly professed in the same order and capable of guiding and governing the flock be placed over those monasteries which are now held *in commendam* and which have their own convents. Those which in the future become vacant shall be conferred only on regulars of approved virtue and holiness.[41] With regard

[40] Cf. Sess. XXI, chap. 8 de ref.
[41] Cf. Sess. XIV, chap. 10 de ref.

to those monasteries which are the head and chief ones of the orders, whether their filiations be called abbeys or priories, they who now hold them *in commendam* shall be bound, if a regular has not been appointed as successor thereto, to make within six months a solemn profession of the vows peculiar to those orders or to resign; otherwise the aforesaid places held *in commendam* shall be considered *ipso jure* vacant. But that in each and all of the aforesaid matters no fraud may be perpetrated, the holy council decrees that in the appointments to the monasteries mentioned the character of each person be expressly stated, and any appointment made otherwise shall be considered surreptitious and shall not be protected by any subsequent possession, even though this covers a period of three years.

CHAPTER XXII

WHAT HAS BEEN SAID CONCERNING THE REFORM OF REGULARS SHALL BE CARRIED INTO EXECUTION WITHOUT DELAY

The holy council commands that each and all of the matters contained in the foregoing decrees be observed in all convents and monasteries, colleges and houses of all monks and regulars whatsoever, as also of all religious virgins and widows, even though they live under the guidance of military orders, also that (of St. John) of Jerusalem, and by whatever name they may be designated, under whatever rule or constitutions and under whatever protection or administration they may be, or in whatever subjection to, union with, or dependence on any order whatsoever, whether of mendicants or non-mendicants, or of other regular monks or canons whatsoever; any privileges of each and all of those above mentioned in whatever form of words expressed, even those known as *mare magnum* and those obtained at their foundation, also constitutions and rules, even though subscribed to under oath, and also customs and prescriptions, even though immemorial, notwithstanding. But if there are regulars, men as well as women, who live under a stricter rule or statutes, except with regard to the permission to possess immovable property in common, the holy council does not intend to hinder them in their rule and observance. And since the holy council desires that each and all of the aforesaid matters be put into effect as soon as possible, it commands all bishops that in the monasteries subject to them and in all others specifically committed to them in the foregoing decrees, and all abbots, generals and other superiors of the aforesaid orders, that they put into execution the foregoing matters immediately. And if there be anything that is not put into execution, the provincial synods shall supplement and correct the negligence of the bishops. The negligence of the regulars, their provincial and general chapters, and in default of the general chapters, the provincial synods shall attend to by delegating certain persons of the same order. The holy council also exhorts and in virtue of holy obedience commands all kings, princes, governments and magistrates to deign to lend, as often as requested, their help and influence in support of the aforesaid bishops, abbots, generals, and other superiors in the execution of the reform indicated above, so that they may without hindrance properly put into effect the foregoing matters to the praise of Almighty God.

DECREE CONCERNING REFORM

Chapter I

CARDINALS AND ALL PRELATES OF THE CHURCHES SHALL HAVE PLAIN FURNITURE AND TABLE. THEY SHALL NOT ENRICH THEIR RELATIONS AND DOMESTICS FROM THE PROPERTY OF THE CHURCH

It is to be desired that those who assume the episcopal office know what are their duties, and understand that they have been called not for their own convenience, not for riches or luxury, but to labors and cares for the glory of God. For it is not to be doubted that the rest of the faithful will be more easily roused to religion and innocence, if they see those who are placed over them concentrate their thoughts not on the things of this world but on the salvation of souls and on their heavenly country. Since the holy council considers these things to be of the greatest importance in the restoration of ecclesiastical discipline, it admonishes all bishops that they reflect often on these things and also by the actions and behavior of their life, which is a sort of perpetual sermon, give evidence that their deportment is consistent with their office; but above all that they so regulate their whole conduct that others may derive therefrom examples of moderation, modesty, continency, and of that holy humility which recommends us so to God.[42] Wherefore, after the example of our Fathers in the Council of Carthage,[43] it commands not only that bishops be content with modest furniture and a frugal table, but also that they take heed that in the rest of their manner of living and in their whole house, nothing appears that is at variance with this holy ordinance, or that does not manifest simplicity, zeal for God and a contempt for vanities. But above all does it forbid them to attempt to enrich their relations or domestics from the revenues of the Church,[44] since the canons of the Apostles also forbid that ecclesiastical goods, which belong to God, be given to relations; [45] but if they are poor, let them distribute to them as poor, but they shall not alienate or waste these goods for their sake. Indeed, the holy council admonishes them to the utmost of its ability that they lay aside completely all this human affection of the flesh toward brothers, nephews, and relations, which is the nursery of many evils in the Church. And what has been said of bishops is to be observed not only by all who hold ecclesiastical benefices, whether secular or regular, according to the nature of the rank of each, but it decrees that it applies also to the cardinals of the holy Roman Church, for since the administration of the universal Church is supported by their advice to the most holy Roman pontiff, it can appear wicked if they do not shine in the splendor of the virtues and in discipline of life, which should justly draw upon them the eyes of all.

Chapter II

BY WHOM PARTICULARLY THE DECREES OF THE COUNCIL ARE TO BE SOLEMNLY RECEIVED AND TAUGHT

The distress of the times and the malice of increasing heresies make it necessary that nothing be left undone which may appear to be for the edification of the faithful and for the defense of the Catholic faith. Wherefore, the holy council commands patriarchs, primates, archbishops, bishops, and all others who by right or custom ought to be present at the provincial synod,[46] that in the very first provincial synod to be held after the close of the present council, they receive publicly

---

[42] Cf. Ps. 101:18; Ecclus. 3:20; 35:21; Matt. 18:3 f.
[43] C.7, D.XLI.
[44] C.23, C.XII, q.1; c.19, C.XII, q.2.
[45] Cf. Apost. can. 39.
[46] Cf. Sess. XXIV, chap. 2 de ref.

each and all of the matters which have been defined and decreed by this holy council; also that they promise and profess true obedience to the supreme Roman pontiff and at the same time publicly express their hatred of and anathematize all the heresies that have been condemned by the sacred canons and general councils and especially by this council. The same shall in the future be observed by all who are promoted to patriarchal, primatial, archiepiscopal and episcopal sees, in the first provincial synod at which they are present. But if anyone of all the aforesaid should refuse, which God forbid, the comprovincial bishops shall be bound under penalty of divine indignation to give notice thereof immediately to the supreme Roman pontiff, and shall in the meantime abstain from communion with that person. All others who now hold or hereafter will hold ecclesiastical benefices, whose duty it is to assemble in diocesan synod, shall do and observe in the first synod to be held the same as was prescribed above, otherwise they shall be punished in accordance with the prescriptions of the sacred canons. Furthermore, all those to whom pertains the care, visitation, and reform of universities and of [houses of] general studies, shall diligently see to it that the canons and decrees of this holy council are integrally received by the universities and that the masters, doctors, and others in those universities teach and interpret the things that are of Catholic faith in conformity therewith, and at the beginning of each year bind themselves by solemn oath to the observance of this ordinance; [47] and if there be any other matters in the aforesaid universities that need correction and reform, they shall for the advancement of religion and ecclesiastical discipline be reformed and put in order by those to whom it pertains. Those universities, however, that are immediately subject to the protection and visitation of the supreme Roman pontiff, His Holiness will provide for in the matters of visitation and reform through his delegates in the manner aforesaid and as shall seem to him most beneficial.

---

[47] Cf. Sess. V, chap. 1 de ref.

Chapter III

THE SWORD OF EXCOMMUNICATION IS NOT TO BE USED RASHLY. WHERE IN THINGS AND PERSONS THE END CAN BE OBTAINED, CENSURES ARE TO BE ABSTAINED FROM AND THE CIVIL AUTHORITY HAS NO RIGHT TO INTRUDE

Although the sword of excommunication is the nerve of ecclesiastical discipline and very salutary for holding the people in their duty, it is, however, to be used with moderation and great discretion, since experience teaches that if wielded rashly or for trifling reasons, it is more despised than feared and is productive of destruction rather than of salvation. Wherefore, those excommunications which after previous admonitions are customarily imposed for the purpose of eliciting a so-called disclosure, or by reason of properties squandered or alienated, shall be issued by absolutely no one but the bishop, and even then not except by reason of an unusual circumstance and after a diligent and very complete examination by the bishop of the cause which moves his mind thereto.[48] Neither shall he allow himself to be moved to their imposition by the authority of any secular person, even though a magistrate, but the entire matter shall be left to his own judgment and conscience, whether, after considering the circumstances, place, person or time, he shall himself deem it advisable to impose them. With regard to judicial causes, all ecclesiastical judges, of whatever dignity they may be, are commanded that both during the proceedings and in rendering decisions, they abstain from ecclesiastical censures or interdict whenever the action can in each stage of the process be completed by themselves through their own authority; but in civil causes belonging in any way to the ecclesiastical forum, they may, if they deem it advisable, proceed against all persons, also laics, and terminate suits by pecuniary fines, which shall as soon as they have been collected be without further ado assigned to the pious places of the locality, or by distress of property, or by restraint of the persons, to be effected by their own or other agents, or even by the deprivation of benefices and other legal means. But if the action against the guilty party cannot be completed in this way and there be contumacy toward the judge, he may then in addition to other penalties chastise them also with the sword of anathema, if he should deem it expedient. In criminal causes also where

[48] Cf. cc.8, 41, 42, C.XI, q.3; c.48, X, De sent. excomm., V, 39.

a suit can be completed as was stated above, censures are to be abstained from. But if that effect cannot be easily obtained, it shall be lawful for the judge to make use of this spiritual sword against delinquents, provided the nature of the offense, preceded by at least two admonitions, even by an edict, requires it. But it shall not be lawful for any civil magistrate to prohibit an ecclesiastical judge from excommunicating anyone, or to command him to revoke an excommunication that has been imposed, under the pretext that the contents of the present decree have not been observed, since the investigation of this matter does not pertain to seculars but to ecclesiastics. But every excommunicated person who after the legitimate admonitions does not repent, shall not only be excluded from the sacraments and from intercourse and from friendship with the faithful, but if, bound with censure, he shall with obdurate heart remain therein for a year, he may also be proceeded against as suspected of heresy.[49]

Chapter IV

WHERE THE NUMBER OF MASSES TO BE CELEBRATED IS TOO GREAT, BISHOPS, ABBOTS AND GENERALS OF ORDERS SHALL MAKE SUCH DISPOSITION AS THEY SHALL DEEM EXPEDIENT

It often happens in some churches that by reason of various bequests from deceased persons either so great a number of masses to be celebrated is left with them that it is not possible to take care of them on the particular days specified by the testators, or that the alms given for their celebration is so small that it is not easy to find one who is willing to accept this obligation; the result being that the pious intentions of the testators are defeated and occasion is given of burdening the consciences of those to whom the aforesaid obligations pertain. The holy council, desirous that these bequests for pious purposes be satisfied in the fullest and most useful manner possible, empowers bishops in the diocesan synod and likewise abbots and generals of orders in their general chapters, to decide with regard to the aforesaid churches, which they shall find to stand in need of regulation in this matter, whatever in their consciences they shall after a diligent examination of the circum-

[49] Cf. cc.18, 19, 25, 26, C.XI, q.3; cc.8, 9, 15, 18, 29–31, 38, 39, X, De sent. excomm., V, 39.

stances judge to be most beneficial for the honor and service of God and the good of the churches; [50] so, however, that a commemoration be always made of the departed who for the welfare of their souls have left those bequests for pious purposes.

Chapter V

FROM WELL ESTABLISHED FOUNDATIONS WITH AN OBLIGATION ANNEXED NOTHING SHALL BE REMOVED

Reason requires that from those things which have been well established nothing be withdrawn by contrary ordinances. When, therefore, in virtue of the erection or foundation of any benefices whatsoever or other constitutions, certain qualifications are required or certain obligations are attached to them, then in the collation of the benefices or in any other arrangement whatsoever nothing shall be taken from them. The same is to be observed in the matter of prebends for theologians, masters, doctors, priests, deacons, and subdeacons whenever they have been so established, so that in any provision nothing shall be altered with regard to their qualifications and orders, and any provision made otherwise shall be considered surreptitious.

Chapter VI

HOW THE BISHOP OUGHT TO ACT WITH REGARD TO THE VISITATION OF EXEMPT CHAPTERS

The holy council ordains that in all cathedral and collegiate churches the decree published under Paul III, of happy memory, which begins, "Capitula cathedralium," [51] be observed, not only when the bishop makes his visitation but also as often as he proceeds *ex officio* or at the request of one against anyone of those included in said decree; so, however, that when he institutes proceedings outside of visitation all the following particulars shall be observed, namely, that the chapter at the beginning of each year choose two of its members, with whose counsel and consent the bishop or his vicar shall be bound to proceed both in

---

[50] Cf. Sess. XXII, chap. 6 de ref.
[51] Cf. Sess. VI, chap. 4 de ref.; Sess. XIV, chap. 4 de ref.

shaping the process and in all other transactions connected therewith to the end of the action inclusively, in the presence, however, of the bishop's notary and in his residence or in the customary court of justice. These two, however, shall have only one vote, and one of them may cast his with the bishop. But if in any transaction or interlocutory or definitive sentence both should disagree with the bishop, then they shall within six days choose in union with the bishop a third party; and should they disagree also in the choice of that third party, the selection shall devolve on the nearest bishop and the point on which they disagreed shall be decided in favor of the opinion with which the third party agrees. Otherwise the proceedings and what followed therefrom shall be null and without effect in law. In criminal cases, however, arising from incontinency, of which mention has been made in the decree dealing with *concubinarii*,[52] and in the more outrageous crimes that demand deposition and degradation, where it is feared that judgment may be evaded by flight and the detention of the person is therefore necessary, the bishop may in the beginning proceed alone to a summary investigation and the necessary detention, observing, however, the above order in the rest. But in all cases consideration is to be given to this, that the delinquents be confined in a suitable place in keeping with the nature of the crime and the character of the persons. Moreover, everywhere there shall be given to the bishops the honor which is in keeping with their dignity; to them belongs the first seat in the choir, in the chapter, in processions, and in other public functions,[53] and the place which they themselves may select, and theirs shall be the chief authority in everything that is to be done. If they propose something to the canons for deliberation and the matter is not one that is of benefit to them or theirs, the bishops themselves shall convoke the chapter, examine the votes, and decide according to them.[54] But in the absence of the bishop this shall be done entirely by those of the chapter to whom it by law or custom pertains, and the vicar of the bishop is not to be admitted to this. In all other things the jurisdiction and power of the chapter, if it perchance has any, and the administration of properties shall be left absolutely unimpaired and intact. All those, however, who do not possess dignities and do not belong to the chapter, shall in ecclesiastical causes be subject to the bishop, notwithstanding, with re-

[52] Cf. Sess. XXIV, chap. 8 de ref. Matr. and chap. 14 *infra*.
[53] C. 10, D.XCV.
[54] Cf. cc. 4, 5, X, De his, quae fiunt a prael., III, 10.

gard to what has been said above, privileges, even those accruing from a foundation, or customs, even though immemorial, or judgments, oaths, pacts, which bind only the authors thereof; the privileges, however, which have been granted to universities of general studies or to the persons attached thereto, shall in all things remain intact. But each and all of these things shall not have effect in those churches in which the bishops or their vicars, in virtue of constitutions, privileges, customs, pacts, or any other right, possess a power, authority, and jurisdiction greater than that included in the present decree; these the holy council does not intend to impair.

Chapter VII

ACCESS AND REGRESS TO BENEFICES ARE ABOLISHED. HOW, TO WHOM AND FOR WHAT REASON A COADJUTOR IS TO BE GRANTED

Since whatever in the matter of ecclesiastical benefices has the appearance of hereditary succession is odious to the sacred constitutions and contrary to the decrees of the Fathers,[55] no access or regress to any ecclesiastical benefice of whatever kind shall in future, even with consent, be granted to anyone, and those thus far granted shall not be suspended, extended, or transferred. And this decree shall apply to all ecclesiastical benefices whatsoever and to all persons, even though distinguished with the dignity of the cardinalate. In the case of coadjutors with future succession also the same shall hereafter be observed, so that they shall not be permitted to anyone in any ecclesiastical benefices whatsoever. But if at any time urgent necessity or the manifest interest of a cathedral church or of a monastery should demand that a coadjutor be given to a prelate, he shall not be given with the right of future succession until the reason therefore has first been diligently investigated by the most holy Roman pontiff,[56] and until it is certain that he possesses all the qualifications which by law and by the decrees of this holy council are required in bishops and prelates; [57] otherwise the concessions made in these matters shall be considered surreptitious.

---

[55] Cf. cc.5, 7, C.VIII, q.1; cc.7, 10, 11, 13, X, De fil. presb., I, 17; cc.6, 15, X, De jur. patr., III, 38.

[56] Cf. Sess. XXI, chap. 6 de ref.; cc.1, 14, C.VII, q.1.

[57] Cf. Sess. VII, chaps. 1, 3 de ref. and XXII, chap. 2 de ref.

Chapter VIII

DUTY OF THE ADMINISTRATORS OF HOSPITALS. BY WHOM AND HOW THEIR NEGLIGENCE IS TO BE PUNISHED

The holy council admonishes all who hold ecclesiastical benefices, whether secular or regular, to accustom themselves, so far as their revenues will permit, to exercise with promptness and kindness the office of hospitality so often commended by the holy Fathers; [58] being mindful that those who love hospitality receive Christ in their guests.[59] Those who hold *in commendam*, by way of administration or under any other title whatsoever, or also have united to their own churches institutions commonly called hospitals, or other pious places established especially for the benefit of pilgrims, of the infirm, the aged or the poor, or if parish churches perchance united to hospitals or converted into hospitals have been handed over to their patrons to be administered by them, it strictly commands that they discharge the office and duty imposed on them and actually exercise the hospitality that they owe from the revenues set aside for that purpose, in accordance with the constitution of the Council of Vienne, renewed elsewhere by this same council under Paul III, of happy memory, which begins, "Quia contingit." [60] But if these hospitals were established to receive a certain class of pilgrims, infirm persons or others, and in the place in which they are located there are no such persons or very few to be found, it commands further that their revenues be diverted to some other pious purpose that is more closely related to their foundation and the more useful in respect of place and time, as shall appear most expedient to the ordinary, aided by two of the chapter experienced in the administration of property and to be chosen by himself; unless it has perchance been specified otherwise, even with regard to this event, in their foundation or institution, in which case the bishop shall see to it that what has been prescribed be observed, or if that is not possible he shall, as above, regulate the matter in a beneficial manner. If, therefore, any or all of the aforesaid, of whatever rank, order and dignity, even if they be laics, who have the administration of hospitals, not however subject to regulars where regular observance is in

---

[58] Cf. c.2, D.XLII; c. un. D.LXXXV; c.2, D.LXXXIX; c.30, C.XII, q.2.

[59] Matt. 25:35.

[60] Cf. Sess. VII, chap. 15 de ref.; c.2 in Clem., De relig. dom., III, 11.

force, shall, after having been admonished by the ordinary, actually neglect to discharge the duty of hospitality in the fulness to which they are bound, they may be compelled thereto not only by ecclesiastical censures and other legal means, but may also be deprived forever of the administration and care of the hospital and others shall be put in their place by those to whom this pertains. The aforesaid persons, moreover, shall be bound in conscience to the restitution of the revenues which they have received in violation of the institution of these hospitals, which shall not be pardoned by any remission or agreement; neither shall the administration or government of such places be in the future entrusted to one and the same person for a longer period than three years, unless it be otherwise provided for in their foundation; notwithstanding, with regard to all of the aforesaid, any union, exemption and custom, even though immemorial, to the contrary, or any privileges or indults whatsoever.

Chapter IX

HOW THE RIGHT OF PATRONAGE IS TO BE PROVED. ON WHOM THE OFFICE OF PATRONS MAY BE CONFERRED. ACCESSIONS PROHIBITED. BY WHOM THAT RIGHT MAY NOT BE ACQUIRED

Just as it is not equitable to take away the legitimate rights of patronage and to infringe upon the pious intentions of the faithful in their institution, so also is it not to be permitted that under this pretext ecclesiastical benefices be reduced to a state of servitude, as is impudently done by many. That, therefore, in all things a proper procedure may be observed, the holy council decrees that the title of the right of patronage is based on a foundation or on an endowment and is to be proved from an authentic document and by other proofs required by law;[61] or also by repeated presentations during a period of time so remote that it goes beyond the memory of man, or by other methods, as the law may direct. But in the case of those persons, communities or universities in which that right is for the most part usually presumed to have been acquired by usurpation, a more complete and more precise proof shall be required to establish the true title; and even the proof derived from immemorial time shall avail them nothing unless,

[61] Cf. Sess. XIV, chap. 12 de ref.; c. 25, X, De jur. patr., III, 38.

in addition to the other things necessary for it, it shall be proved from authentic documents that presentations have been made without interruption during a period of no less than fifty years, all of which have been carried into effect. All other rights of patronage relating to benefices, secular as well as regular, or parochial, or in regard to dignities, or any other benefices whatsoever in a cathedral or collegiate church, as also faculties and the privileges granted in virtue of patronage or with any other right whatsoever to nominate, elect, and present to the same when vacant, shall be understood as completely abrogated and nullified *in totum,* together with the quasi-possession that followed therefrom, and benefices of this kind shall be conferred as being free by their collators and such appointments shall have full effect; excepted are the rights of patronage that belong to cathedral churches and those that belong to the emperor, or to kings, or to those possessing supreme jurisdiction, and to other high and pre-eminent princes who have the rights of sovereignty within their own dominions, and those which have been granted in favor of general studies.[62] Moreover, it shall be lawful for the bishop to reject those presented by the patrons if they are incompetent. But if the appointment belongs to inferiors, they [the presentees] shall nevertheless be examined by the bishop, in accordance with what has elsewhere been decreed by this holy council; [63] otherwise the appointment made by inferiors shall be null and void. The patrons of benefices, however, of whatever order and dignity, also if they are communities, universities, colleges of clerics or laics, shall by no means or for any reason or under any pretext interfere with the receiving of the fruits, revenues and dues of any benefices whatsoever,[64] even if they are by virtue of foundation or endowment truly under their right of patronage, but they shall leave them to be distributed freely by the rector or the incumbent, any custom whatsoever notwithstanding. Neither shall they contrary to the prescriptions of the canons presume to transfer to others the said right of patronage under the title of sale or under any other title.[65] If they act otherwise, they shall be subject to the penalties of excommunication and interdict and shall be *ipso jure* deprived of that right of patronage. Furthermore, the accessions made by way of union of free benefices with

---

[62] Cf. Sess. XXIV, chap. 19 de ref.
[63] Cf. Sess. XIV, chap. 13 de ref. and XXIV, chap. 18 de ref.
[64] Cf. c. un., X, Ut eccles. benef. sine demin. confer., III, 12.
[65] Cc.6, 16, X, De jur. patr., III, 38.

churches that are subject to the right of patronage, even of laics, whether they are parochial churches or benefices of any other kind whatsoever, even simple benefices, or dignities, or hospitals, in such wise that the aforesaid free benefices are made to be of the same nature as those to which they are united and placed under the right of patronage, if they have not yet been carried into full effect, or shall in the future be made at the instance of any person, by whatever authority they shall have been granted, even the Apostolic, they shall, together with the unions themselves, be considered as having been obtained surreptitiously, notwithstanding any form of words therein or any derogation which might be considered as equivalent to being expressed; neither shall they be any more carried into execution, but the benefices so united shall, when vacant, be freely conferred as heretofore. Those, however, which have been made within the last forty years and have obtained their full effect and complete incorporation, shall nevertheless be inquired into and examined by the ordinaries as delegates of the Apostolic See, and those which are found to have been obtained surreptitiously or deceitfully shall together with the unions be declared null and the benefices shall be separated and conferred on others.[66] In like manner also all rights of patronage over churches and all other benefices, also over dignities formerly free, which were acquired within the last forty years, or that may in the future be acquired, whether through an increase in the endowment or in consequence of new construction or through some similar reason, even though with the authority of the Apostolic See, shall be carefully examined by the ordinaries as delegates aforesaid, who shall not in these matters be hindered by the authority or privileges of anyone; and those which they shall find to have been not legitimately established for a very manifest necessity of the church, benefice or dignity, they shall revoke *in totum*, and, without detriment to the incumbents thereof and after restoration to the patrons of whatever they may have given therefor, they shall restore benefices of this kind to their former state of liberty; any privileges, constitutions, and customs, even though immemorial, notwithstanding.

---

[66] Cf. Sess. VII, chap. 6 de ref.

Chapter X

JUDGES TO BE DELEGATED BY THE APOSTOLIC SEE ARE TO BE DESIGNATED BY THE SYNOD; BY THEM AND BY THE ORDINARIES CAUSES ARE TO BE TERMINATED SPEEDILY

Since by reason of the malicious suggestions of petitioners and sometimes by reason of the distance of places an adequate knowledge of the persons to whom causes are committed cannot be obtained, and hence local causes are at times referred to judges who are not altogether competent, the holy council decrees that in all provincial and diocesan synods some persons who possess the qualifications required by the constitution of Boniface VIII, which begins, "Statutum,"[67] and who are otherwise suited thereto be designated, so that to them also, besides the local ordinaries, may hereafter be committed ecclesiastical and spiritual causes and such as belong to the ecclesiastical forum which have to be referred to their districts. And if one of those designated should happen to die in the meantime, then the local ordinary shall with the advice of the chapter appoint another in his place till the next provincial or diocesan synod, so that each diocese may have at least four or even more approved and qualified persons, as specified above, to whom causes of this kind may be committed by any legate or nuncio and also by the Apostolic See. Moreover, after the designation has been made, which the bishops shall transmit at once to the supreme Roman pontiff, all assignments of other judges made to others than these shall be regarded as surreptitious. The holy council furthermore admonishes the ordinaries and all other judges to strive to terminate causes in as brief a time as possible,[68] and to meet in every way, either by prescribing a definite time or by some other available method, the artifices of the litigants, whether it be in delaying the admission of the suit or in any other part of the trial.

[67] C.11, VI°, De rescript., I, 3.

[68] Cf. cc.5, 10, X, De dolo et cont., II, 14; c.2, X, De sent. et re jud., II, 27; Sess. XXIV, chap. 20 de ref.

CHAPTER XI

VARIOUS LEASES OF ECCLESIASTICAL PROPERTY ARE FORBIDDEN; SOME ALREADY MADE ARE INVALIDATED

It usually brings great ruin on churches when their property is, to the disadvantage of those who succeed, leased to others on the present payment of a sum of money. Wherefore, all such leases, if made for payments in advance, shall be in no way considered valid to the disadvantage of those who succeed,[69] any indult or privilege whatsoever notwithstanding; neither shall such leases be confirmed in the Roman Curia or elsewhere. It shall furthermore not be lawful to lease ecclesiastical jurisdiction or the authority to nominate or delegate vicars in matters spiritual,[70] or for the lessees to exercise them *per se aut alios*, and any concessions made otherwise, even by the Apostolic See, shall be considered surreptitious. The holy council declares invalid, even if confirmed by Apostolic authority, leases of ecclesiastical goods made within thirty years, for a long time, or as they are designated in some localities, for twenty-nine or for twice twenty-nine years, which the provincial synod or its delegates shall judge to have been contracted to the detriment of the church and contrary to the prescriptions of the canons.[71]

CHAPTER XII

TITHES ARE TO BE PAID IN FULL; THOSE WHO WITHHOLD THEM ARE TO BE EXCOMMUNICATED. THE RECTORS OF POOR CHURCHES ARE TO BE PIOUSLY SUPPORTED

Those are not to be tolerated who strive by various devices to withhold the tithes due to the churches, or who rashly take possession of and apply to their own use tithes to be paid by others, since the payment of tithes is due to God, and those who refuse to pay them or hinder those who pay them usurp the property of others.[72] There-

---

69 C.6, C.X, q.2.
70 Cc.1, 2, X, ne prael. vices suas, V, 4.
71 Cf. c. un., De reb. eccl. non al. in Extrav. comm., III, 4.
72 Ex. 22:29; Lev. 27:30 f.; Num. 18:21 ff.; Tob. 1:6; Mal. 3:10; c.66, C.XVI, q.1; cc.6, 7, C.XVI, q.7; cc.14, 23, 26, X, De decimis, III, 30.

fore, the holy council commands all, of whatever rank or condition, on whom rests the obligation to pay tithes, that they in the future pay in full, to the cathedral or to whatever other churches or persons to whom they are legitimately due, the tithes to which they are bound by law. Those who withhold them or hinder their payment shall be excommunicated, and they shall not be absolved from this crime until full restitution has been made.[73] It further exhorts each and all in Christian charity and the duty they owe their pastors, that they do not regard it a burden to assist liberally, out of the things given them by God, the bishops and priests who preside over the poorer churches, for the honor of God and the maintenance of the dignity of their pastors who watch over them.

Chapter XIII

THE CATHEDRAL OR PARISH CHURCHES SHALL RECEIVE A FOURTH PART OF FUNERAL DUES

The holy council decrees that in whatever places it has for forty years been the custom to pay to the cathedral or parochial church a fourth of the funeral dues,[74] as they are called, but has subsequently by virtue of any privilege whatever been granted to other monasteries, hospitals, or any pious places whatsoever, the same shall in the future, with unimpaired right and in the same proportion as was formerly the custom, be paid to the cathedral or parochial church; all concessions, favors, privileges, even those called *mare magnum*, or any others notwithstanding.

Chapter XIV

THE MANNER OF PROCEEDING AGAINST CLERICS WHO KEEP CONCUBINES IS PRESCRIBED

How shameful and how unworthy it is of the name of clerics who have dedicated themselves to the service of God to live in the filth of impurity and unclean cohabitation, the thing itself sufficiently testifies by the common scandal of all the faithful and the supreme dis-

---

[73] Cf. c.5, C.XVI, q.7; cc.5, 22, 25, 32, X, De decimis, III, 30; c.1, in Clem., h.t., III, 8.

[74] Cf. c.8, X, De sepult., III, 28; c.2, h.t. in VI°, III, 12; c.2, h.t. in Clem., III, 7.

grace on the clerical order. Wherefore, that the ministers of the Church may be brought back to that continency and purity of life which is proper to them, and that for this reason the people may learn to reverence them the more, the more honorable they see them in their conduct, the holy council forbids all clerics whatsoever to presume to keep concubines or other women concerning whom suspicion can be had in their house or elsewhere, or to presume to have any association with them; otherwise they shall be punished with the penalties imposed by the sacred canons or the statutes of the churches.[75] But if after being admonished by their superiors they do not keep away from them, they shall be *ipso facto* deprived of the third part of the fruits, revenues and dues of all their benefices and of their salaries, which shall be applied to the treasury of the church or to another pious place according to the judgment of the bishop.[76] If, however, they should persist in the same crime with the same or another woman and not obey even the second admonition, then they shall not only forfeit *eo ipso* all the fruits and revenues of their benefices and their salaries, which shall be applied to the aforesaid places, but they shall also be suspended from the administration of the benefices for as long a period as the ordinary, also as the delegate of the Apostolic See, shall deem advisable; and if those so suspended shall still not put them away or shall still associate with them, then they shall be forever deprived of their ecclesiastical benefices, portions, offices and salaries of whatever kind, and shall be declared disqualified and unworthy to hold any honors, dignities, benefices and offices whatsoever in the future, until after a manifest amendment of life it appears good to their superiors on justifiable grounds to grant them a dispensation. But if, after having once put them away, they should presume to renew the interrupted intercourse or to take to themselves other scandalous women of this kind, they shall, in addition to the aforesaid penalties, be chastised with the sword of excommunication.[77] Nor shall any appeal or exemption hinder or suspend the aforesaid execution, and the investigation of all the aforesaid shall pertain not to the archdeacons, or to the deans or other inferiors, but to the bishops themselves, who may proceed summarily and solely in accordance with the truth of the fact ascertained. Clerics who have no ecclesiastical benefices or salaries shall be pun-

[75] Cf. tot. tit. X, De cohab. cler. et mul., III, 2.
[76] Cf. cc.4, 6, h.t.
[77] Cf. cc.2, 3, h.t.

ished in accordance with the character of their crime and contumacy and their persistence therein by the bishop himself with imprisonment, suspension from order, disqualification to hold benefices, or in other ways conformable to the sacred canons. Bishops also, if, which God forbid, they do not abstain from crime of this nature and, after being admonished by the provincial synod, do not amend, are *ipso facto* suspended; [78] and if they persist therein, they shall be reported by that synod to the most holy Roman pontiff, who shall punish them according to the nature of the crime, even with deprivation if necessary.

Chapter XV

FROM WHAT BENEFICES THE ILLEGITIMATE SONS OF CLERICS ARE EXCLUDED

That the memory of the incontinency of the fathers may be banished as far as possible from places consecrated to God, where purity and holiness are most especially becoming, it shall not be lawful for sons of clerics, not born in lawful wedlock, to hold in those churches in which their fathers have or had some ecclesiastical benefice, any benefice whatsoever, even though a different one, or to minister in any way in those churches, or to have salaries from the revenues of the benefices which their fathers hold or formerly have held.[79] But if a father and son shall be found at the present time to hold benefices in the same church, the son shall be compelled to resign his benefice, or within three months to exchange it for another in another church, otherwise he shall be *ipso jure* deprived of it and any dispensation in this matter shall be considered surreptitious. Furthermore, any reciprocal resignations made in the future by fathers who are clerics in favor of their sons that one may obtain the benefices of the other, shall in every respect be considered as an evasion of this decree and of the prescriptions of the canons; nor shall the collations that followed by virtue of resignations of this kind, or of any others whatsoever made fraudulently, be of any avail to sons of clerics.

---

[78] C.1, D.XXXIV; cc.13, 16, D.LXXXI.
[79] Cf. tot. tit. X, De fil. presb., I, 17.

Chapter XVI

BENEFICES WITH THE *CURA* ANNEXED SHALL NOT BE CONVERTED INTO SIMPLE BENEFICES. A SUITABLE PORTION SHALL BE ASSIGNED TO HIM TO WHOM THE *CURA ANIMARUM* HAS BEEN COMMITTED. VICARIATES SHALL COME TO AN END WHEN THE *CURA* IS REUNITED TO THE BENEFICE

The holy council decrees that secular ecclesiastical benefices, by whatever name they may be designated, which by virtue of their original institution or in any other manner whatever have the *cura animarum*, shall not in the future be converted into a simple benefice, even though a suitable portion be assigned to a perpetual vicar; notwithstanding any favors whatsoever which have not obtained their plenary effect. With regard to those, however, in which contrary to their institution or foundation the *cura animarum* has been transferred to a perpetual vicar, even though they are found to have been in this state from time immemorial, if a suitable portion of the fruits has not been assigned to the vicar of the church, by whatever name he may be designated, it shall be assigned as soon as possible and within a year at least from the end of the present council, as the ordinary shall see fit, in accordance with the form of the decree made under Paul III, of happy memory.[80] But if this cannot be conveniently done, or if within that term it has not been done, then as soon as the benefice or vicariate shall have become vacant either by the retirement or death of the vicar or rector, or in any other way, the benefice shall again receive the *cura animarum* and be restored to its former state, and the name of vicariate shall be discontinued.

---

[80] Cf. Sess. VII, chap. 7 de ref.

Chapter XVII

BISHOPS SHALL MAINTAIN THEIR DIGNITY WITH SERIOUSNESS OF MANNERS, AND SHALL NOT CONDUCT THEMSELVES WITH UNWORTHY SERVILITY TOWARD MINISTERS OF KINGS, PRINCES OR BARONS

The holy council cannot but be deeply distressed when it hears that some bishops, forgetful of their state, dishonor the episcopal dignity by conducting themselves, both in and out of the church, with an unbecoming servility toward the ministers of kings, princes and barons, and as inferior ministers of the altar not only most unworthily give them precedence but even serve them in person. Wherefore, the holy council, detesting these and similar things, renews all the sacred canons, general councils and other Apostolic ordinances that relate to the decorum and esteem of the episcopal dignity, and commands that in the future bishops abstain from such things, and that both in and out of the church, having before their eyes their rank and order, they bear in mind everywhere that they are fathers and pastors; the rest, princes as well as all others, it commands that they pay them paternal honor and due reverence.

Chapter XVIII

THE CANONS SHALL BE STRICTLY OBSERVED. IF AT ANY TIME A DISPENSATION IS TO BE GRANTED WITH REGARD TO THEM, IT SHALL BE DONE VALIDLY, WITH MATURE CONSIDERATION AND *GRATIS*

Just as the public good requires that the fetters of the law be at times relaxed in order that cases and necessities which arise may be met more fully for the common good, so to dispense too frequently from the law and to yield to petitioners by reason of precedent rather than through a certain discrimination of persons and things is nothing else than to open the way for each one to transgress the laws. Wherefore, be it known to all that the most sacred canons are to be accurately observed by all and, so far as this is possible, without distinction. But if an urgent and just reason and at times a greater good should require that one or another be dispensed, this is to be granted after the matter has been investigated and after the most mature deliberation and *gratis* by those to whom that dispensation pertains, and any dispensation granted otherwise shall be regarded as surreptitious.

CHAPTER XIX

DUELING IS PUNISHED WITH THE SEVEREST PENALTIES

The abominable practice of dueling, introduced by the contrivance of the devil, that by the cruel death of the body he may bring about also the destruction of the soul, should be utterly eradicated from the Christian world. Emperor, kings, dukes, princes, marquises, counts, and temporal rulers by whatever other name known, who shall within their territories grant a place for dueling between Christians, shall be *eo ipso* excommunicated and shall be understood to be deprived of the jurisdiction and dominion obtained from the Church over any city, castle or locality in which or at which they have permitted the duel to take place, and if they are fiefs they shall forthwith revert to their direct rulers. Those who entered the combat as well as those who are called their seconds shall incur the penalty of excommunication, the confiscation of all their property, and perpetual infamy, and are in conformity with the sacred canons to be punished as homicides, and if they are killed in the combat they shall be forever deprived of Christian burial.[81] Those also who give advice in the matter of a duel, whether in questions of right or of fact, or in any other way whatever persuade anyone thereto, as also those who are present, shall be bound by the fetters of excommunication and everlasting malediction; any privilege whatsoever or evil custom, even though immemorial, notwithstanding.

CHAPTER XX

THE RIGHTS OF THE CHURCH ARE RECOMMENDED TO THE PRINCES FOR OBSERVANCE AND PROTECTION

The holy council, desirous that ecclesiastical discipline be not only restored among the Christian people, but also forever preserved unimpaired against all obstacles, besides those things which it has or-

[81] Cf. c.22, C.II, q.5; tot. tit. X, De torneam., V, 13, De cler. pugn. in duello, V, 14, et De homicid., V, 12.

dained concerning ecclesiastical persons, has deemed it proper that secular princes also be admonished of their duty; being confident that as Catholics whom God has willed to be protectors of the holy faith and the Church,[82] they will not only allow that the Church be restored her right but also will lead back all their subjects to due reverence toward the clergy, parish priests and the higher orders, and will not permit their officials or inferior magistrates through any spirit of covetousness or imprudence to violate the immunity of the Church and of ecclesiastical persons, which has been established by the authority of God and the ordinances of the canons, but that they, together with the princes themselves, render due obedience to the sacred constitutions of the supreme pontiffs and councils. It ordains therefore and commands that the sacred canons and all the general councils, as also other Apostolic ordinances published in the interest of ecclesiastical persons, the liberty of the Church, and against the violators thereof, all of which it renews by the present decree, be accurately observed by all. And hence it admonishes the emperor, kings, states, princes, and each and all, of whatever state or dignity they may be, that the more bountifully they are adorned with temporal goods and with power over others, the more religiously should they respect those things that are of ecclesiastical right as ordinances of God and as covered by His protection; and that they suffer them not to be infringed by any barons, members of their families, governors, or other temporal lords or magistrates, and above all by the ministers of the princes, but that they punish severely those who obstruct her liberty, immunity and jurisdiction. To these they themselves should be an example in the matter of piety, religion and protection of the churches, in imitation of their predecessors, those most excellent and religious princes, who not only defended the Church against injuries by others but by their authority and munificence promoted her interests in a special manner. Wherefore, let each one discharge his duty sedulously in this matter so that divine worship may be celebrated devoutly and the prelates and other clerics may remain quietly and without hindrances in their residences and in the discharge of their duties for the benefit and edification of the people.

---

[82] Cf. c.20, C.XXIII, q.5.

CHAPTER XXI

IN ALL THINGS THE AUTHORITY OF THE APOSTOLIC SEE SHALL REMAIN INTACT

Lastly, the holy council declares that each and all of the things which under whatever clauses and words have been established in this holy council in the matter of reform of morals and ecclesiastical discipline, under the supreme pontiffs Paul III and Julius III, of happy memory, as well as under the most blessed Pius IV, have been so decreed that in these matters the authority of the Apostolic See is and is understood to be intact.[83]

DECREE CONCERNING THE CONTINUATION OF THE SESSION ON THE FOLLOWING DAY

Since all the things that were to be considered in the present session cannot by reason of the lateness of the hour be conveniently dispatched, the things that remain are deferred till tomorrow by continuing this same session, as was resolved by the Fathers in a general congregation.

CONTINUATION OF THE SESSION ON THE FOURTH DAY OF DECEMBER

DECREE CONCERNING INDULGENCES

Since the power of granting indulgences was conferred by Christ on the Church,[84] and she has even in the earliest times made use of that power divinely given to her, the holy council teaches and commands that the use of indulgences, most salutary to the Christian people and approved by the authority of the holy councils, is to be retained in the Church, and it condemns with anathema those who assert that they are useless or deny that there is in the Church the power of granting them. In granting them, however, it desires that in accordance with the ancient and approved custom in the Church moderation be observed, lest by too great facility ecclesiastical discipline be weakened. But desiring that the abuses which have become connected with them, and by reason of which this excellent name of in-

[83] Cf. Sess. VII de ref. at the beginning.
[84] Matt. 16:19; John 20:23.

dulgences is blasphemed by the heretics, be amended and corrected, it ordains in a general way by the present decree that all evil traffic in them, which has been a most prolific source of abuses among the Christian people, be absolutely abolished.[85] Other abuses, however, of this kind which have sprung from superstition, ignorance, irreverence, or from whatever other source, since by reason of the manifold corruptions in places and provinces where they are committed, they cannot conveniently be prohibited individually, it commands all bishops diligently to make note of, each in his own church, and report them in the next provincial synod,[86] so that after having been examined by the other bishops also they may forthwith be referred to the supreme Roman pontiff, by whose authority and prudence that may be ordained which is expedient for the universal Church; that thus the gift of holy indulgences may be dispensed to all the faithful piously, holily, and without corruption.

CONCERNING THE CHOICE OF FOODS; FASTS AND FESTIVAL DAYS

The holy council exhorts furthermore, and by the most holy Advent of our Lord and Savior conjures all pastors, that like good soldiers they sedulously commend to all the faithful all those things which the holy Roman Church, the mother and mistress of all churches, has decreed; also those things which have been established in this council and in the other ecumenical councils, and to make every effort that they comply with all these things, particularly those which tend to mortify the flesh, as the choice of foods and fasts, also those that serve to increase piety, as the devout and religious celebration of festival days; often admonishing the people to obey those placed over them, since those who hear them will hear God as a rewarder, while those who despise them will feel God as an avenger.[87]

CONCERNING THE INDEX OF BOOKS AND THE CATECHISM, BREVIARY AND MISSAL

The holy council in the second session,[88] celebrated under our most holy Lord, Pius IV, commissioned some Fathers to consider what

[85] C. 2, in Clem., De poenit. et remiss., V, 9.
[86] Cf. Sess. XXI, chap. 9 de ref.
[87] Luke 10:16; Heb. 13:17; c. 9, D. XCIII.
[88] Cf. Sess. XVIII at the beginning.

ought to be done concerning various censures and books either suspected or pernicious and to report to this holy council. Hearing now that they have put the finishing hand to this work, which, however, by reason of the variety and multitude of books the holy council cannot distinctly and easily estimate, it commands that whatever has been done by them be given over to the most holy Roman pontiff, that it may by his judgment and authority be completed and made public. The same it commands shall be done with regard to the catechism by the Fathers to whom it was assigned,[89] and likewise with regard to the missal and breviary.

CONCERNING THE PLACE OF AMBASSADORS

The holy council declares that by the place assigned to ambassadors, ecclesiastics as well as seculars, whether in the sessions, processions, or in any other acts whatsoever, no prejudice has been created with regard to any of them,[90] but that all their rights and prerogatives, as well as those of the emperor, their kings, states, and princes are unimpaired and intact and continue in the same state in which they were before the present council.

CONCERNING THE ACCEPTANCE AND OBSERVANCE OF THE DECREES OF THE COUNCIL

So great have been the misfortunes of these times and such the inveterate malice of the heretics, that in the statement of our faith there has been nothing so clearly and so certainly defined, which they at the instigation of the enemy of the human race have not defiled with some kind of error. For which reason the holy council has taken very special care to condemn and anathematize the chief errors of the heretics of our time and to transmit and teach the true and Catholic doctrine, as it has condemned, anathematized, and decreed. And since so many bishops, summoned from the various provinces of the Christian world, cannot for so long a time without great loss to the flock committed to them and without universal danger be absent from their churches, and since there is no hope that the heretics who have been so often invited, even provided with a safe-conduct which they de-

[89] Cf. Sess. XXIV, chap. 7 de ref.
[90] Cf. Sess. II at the end.

sired,[91] and have been so long expected, will come here later, and it is therefore necessary finally to bring this holy council to an end, it remains now that it admonish in the Lord all princes, which it hereby does, so to direct their activity as not to permit the things that it has established to be corrupted or mutilated by the heretics, but that they be devoutly received and faithfully observed by them and by all others. But if with regard to their acceptance any difficulty should arise, or something should turn up which requires explanation or definition, which does not appear probable, the holy council trusts that besides the other remedies established in this council, the most blessed Roman pontiff will see to it that for the glory of God and the tranquillity of the Church, the necessities of the provinces be provided for either by summoning, especially from those provinces where the difficulty has arisen, the persons whom he shall judge competent to discuss the matter, or by the celebration of a general council if he should deem it necessary, or in any other way as shall seem to him more suitable.

THE READING OF THE DECREES OF THE COUNCIL UNDER PAUL III AND JULIUS III IN THE SESSION

Since at different times under Paul III as well as under Julius III, of happy memory, many things relative to dogma and the reform of morals have been decreed and defined in this council,[92] the holy council wishes that they be now recited and read.

They were read.

THE END OF THE COUNCIL AND THE REQUEST FOR CONFIRMATION FROM OUR MOST HOLY LORD

Most illustrious Lords and most reverend Fathers, does it please you that to the praise of Almighty God an end be put to this holy ecumenical council and that the confirmation of each and all of the things which have been decreed and defined therein under the Roman pontiffs, Paul III and Julius III, of happy memory, as well as under our most holy Lord, Pius IV, be sought in the name of this holy council

---

[91] Cf. Sess. XIII, XV, XVIII.
[92] Cf. Sess. V–VII, XIII, XIV.

by the presidents and the legates of the Apostolic See from the most blessed Roman pontiff?

They replied: It pleases us.

Hereupon the most illustrious and most reverend Cardinal Morone, the first legate and president, blessing the holy council, said: After having given thanks to God, most reverend Fathers, go in peace.

They replied: Amen.

ACCLAMATIONS OF THE FATHERS AT THE CLOSE OF THE COUNCIL

The Cardinal of Lorraine: To the most blessed Pius, Pope and our Lord, pontiff of the holy universal Church, many years and eternal memory.

Reply of the Fathers: O Lord God, do Thou preserve very long, for many years, the most holy Father to thy Church.

The Cardinal: To the souls of the most blessed sovereign pontiffs, Paul III and Julius III, by whose authority this holy, general council was begun, peace from the Lord, and eternal glory, and happiness in the light of the saints.

Reply: Be their memory in benediction.

The Cardinal: May the memory of the Emperor Charles V and of the most serene kings, who have promoted and protected this universal council, be in benediction.

Reply: Amen, Amen.

The Cardinal: To the most serene Emperor Ferdinand, ever august, orthodox, and peaceful, and to all our kings, states, and princes, many years.

Reply: Preserve, O Lord, the pious and Christian Emperor; O, heavenly Emperor, protect earthly kings, the preservers of the right faith.

The Cardinal: To the legates of the Apostolic See, and the presidents of this council, many years and many thanks.

Reply: Many thanks; the Lord reward them.

The Cardinal: To the most reverend cardinals and most illustrious ambassadors.

Reply: Many thanks; many years.

The Cardinal: To the most holy bishops, life and a happy return to their churches.

Reply: To the heralds of truth perpetual memory; to the orthodox senate many years.

The Cardinal: The holy, ecumenical Council of Trent; let us confess its faith; let us always observe its decrees.

Reply: Let us always confess, always observe.

The Cardinal: We all believe thus, we all think the same, agreeing therein and embracing them, we all subscribe. This is the faith of blessed Peter and of the Apostles; this is the faith of the Fathers; this is the faith of the orthodox.

Reply: Thus we believe; thus we think; thus we subscribe.

The Cardinal: Adhering to these decrees, may we be made worthy of the mercies and grace of the first and great supreme priest, Jesus Christ God; our inviolate Lady, the holy Mother of God, and all the saints interceding.

Reply: So be it, so be it. Amen, Amen.

The Cardinal: Anathema to all heretics.

Reply: Anathema, anathema.

After this the legates presiding commanded all the Fathers under penalty of excommunication, that they before leaving the city of Trent subscribe with their own hand the decrees of the council, or approve them by some public instrument; all then subscribed, and they were in number two hundred and fifty-five, namely, four legates, two cardinals, three patriarchs, twenty-five archbishops, one hundred and sixty-eight bishops, seven abbots, thirty-nine procurators of absentees with lawful commission, seven generals of orders.

PRAISE BE TO GOD

It agrees with the original; in faith whereof we have subscribed:

I, Angelus Massarellus, Bishop of Telese, secretary of the holy Council of Trent.

I, Marcus Antonius Peregrinus, of Como, notary of the same council.

I, Cynthius Pamphilius, cleric of the diocese of Camerino, notary of the same council.

ORATION
delivered in the ninth and last Session of the
COUNCIL OF TRENT
celebrated on the third and fourth day of December, 1563
under the Supreme Pontiff, Pius IV,
by the most Reverend Jerome Ragazonus, of Venice,
Bishop of Nazianzus and Coadjutor of Famagusta

WHEREIN ALL THAT WAS DEFINED IN THE COUNCIL OF TRENT PERTAINING TO FAITH AND MORALS IS SUMMARIZED

"Hear these things, all ye nations; give ear all ye inhabitants of the world." [1]

The Council of Trent which was begun long ago, was for a time suspended, often postponed and dispersed, now at last through a singular favor of Almighty God and with a complete and wonderful accord of all ranks and nations has come to a close. This most happy day has dawned for the Christian people; the day in which the temple of the Lord, often shattered and destroyed, is restored and completed, and this one ship, laden with every blessing and buffeted by the worst and most relentless storms and waves, is brought safely into port. Oh, that those for whose sake this voyage was chiefly undertaken had decided to board it with us; that those who caused us to take this work in hand had participated in the erection of this edifice! Then indeed we would now have reason for greater rejoicing. But it is certainly not through our fault that it so happened.

For that reason we chose this city, situated at the entrance to Germany, situated almost at the threshold of their homes; we have, in order to give them no ground for suspicion that the place is not entirely free, employed no guard for ourselves; we granted them that public security which they requested and which they themselves had drawn up; for a long time we awaited them and never did we cease to exhort them and plead with them to come here and learn the truth. Indeed, even in their absence we were, I think, sufficiently concerned about them. For since in a twofold respect medicine had to be applied to their weak and infirm spirits, one, the explanation and confirmation of the teaching of the Catholic and truly evangelical faith in those matters upon which

[1] Ps. 48:2.

they had cast doubt and which at this time appeared opportune for the dispersion and destruction of all the darkness of errors; the other, the restoration of ecclesiastical discipline, the collapse of which they claim was the chief cause of their severance from us, we have amply accomplished both so far as was in our power and so far as the conditions of the times would permit.

At the beginning, after having in accordance with a laudable custom of our forefathers made a profession of faith, in order to lay a foundation, as it were, for subsequent transactions and to point out by what witnesses and evidence the definition of articles of faith must be supported, this holy council scrupulously and prudently enumerated, after the example of the most approved ancient councils, the books of the Old and New Testaments which must be accepted without a doubt; and that no difficulty might arise as regards the wording of various translations, it approved a trustworthy and certain translation from the Greek and Hebrew. Thereupon, attacking the pillar and bulwark of all heresies concerning the original corruption of human nature, it stated what the truth itself would express if it could speak. Then, with reference to justification, an important matter and assailed in a striking manner by heretics of ancient as well as modern times, it defined, with such wonderful order and admirable wisdom that the spirit of God is easily discerned therein, those things by which the most pernicious opinions of this kind might be refuted and the correct manner of thinking pointed out. Through this most extraordinary decree in the memory of man well-nigh all heresies are strangled and, as darkness before the sun, dispersed and dissipated, and the truth appears with such clearness and splendor that no one can any longer pretend not to see so great a light. Hereupon followed the consideration of the seven sacraments of the Church; first in general, then each one in particular. Who does not see here how exactly, how clearly, copiously, resplendently, and, what is most important, how truly the nature of these heavenly mysteries is summed up? Who can in this body of doctrine, so great and rich in content, in any way still wish for something which is to be observed or avoided? Who will in all this find room or occasion to go astray? Who finally can henceforth entertain any doubt as to the power and efficacy of these sacraments, since it is clear that that grace which daily like trickling water flows through them into the souls of the faithful was then so abundantly present in us? Thereupon followed the decisions concerning the most holy sacrifice of the mass, communion under both species and for little children, than which we have nothing holier, nothing more beneficial, so that they appear to have fallen from heaven rather than to have been composed by men. To these is added today the true teaching concerning purgatory, the veneration and invocation of saints, images and relics, whereby not only the deceptions and calumnies of heretics are opposed but also the consciences of pious Catholics fully satisfied.

These things, dealing with matters that pertain to our salvation and known as dogmas, have been successfully and happily accomplished, and in this respect nothing more will be expected of us at this time.

But since in the administration of some of the foregoing matters there were some things which were not rightly and properly observed, you have, most esteemed Fathers, very carefully provided that they be carried out in a correct and untarnished manner and in accordance with the usages and institutions of the Fathers. You have thereby removed from the celebration of the mass all superstition, all greed for lucre and all irreverence; forbidden vagrant, unknown and depraved priests to offer this holy sacrifice; removed its celebration from private homes and profane places to holy and consecrated sanctuaries; you have banished from the temple of the Lord the more effeminate singing and musical compositions, promenades, conversations and business transactions; you have thus prescribed for each ecclesiastical rank such laws as leave no room for the abuse of the orders divinely conferred. You have likewise removed some matrimonial impediments which seemed to give occasion for violating the precepts of the Church, and to those who do not enter the conjugal union legitimately you have closed the easy way of obtaining forgiveness. And what shall I say about furtive and clandestine marriages? For myself I feel that if there had been no other reason for convoking the council, and there were many and grave reasons, this one alone would have provided sufficient ground for its convocation. For since this is a matter that concerns all, and since there is no corner of the earth which this plague has not invaded, provision had to be made by which this common evil might be remedied by common deliberation. By your clear-sighted and well-nigh divine direction, most holy Fathers, the occasion for innumerable and grave excesses and crimes has been completely removed, and the government of the Christian commonweal most wisely provided for. To this is added the exceedingly salutary and necessary prohibition of many abuses connected with purgatory, the veneration and invocation of the saints, images and relics, and also indulgences, abuses which appeared to defile and deform in no small measure the beautiful aspect of these objects.

The other part, in which was considered the restoration of the tottering and well-nigh collapsed ecclesiastical discipline, was most carefully performed and completed. In the future only those who are known for their virtues, not for their ambition, who will serve the interests of the people, not their own, and who desire to be useful rather than invested with authority, will be chosen for the discharge of ecclesiastical offices. The word of God, which is more penetrating than any two-edged sword,[2] will be more frequently and more zealously preached and explained.

The bishops and others to whom the *cura animarum* has been committed, will remain with and watch over their flocks and not wander about outside the districts entrusted to them. Privileges will no longer avail anyone for an impure and wicked life or for evil and pernicious teaching; no crime will go unpunished, no virtue will be without its reward. The multitude of poor and mendicant priests have been very well provided for; everyone will be assigned to a definite church and to a prescribed field of labor whence he may obtain sustenance.

Avarice, than which there is no vice more hideous,[3] especially in the house of God, will be absolutely banished therefrom, and the sacraments, as is proper, will be dispensed gratuitously. From one Church many will be established and from many one, according as the welfare of the people and circumstances demand. Questors of alms, as they are called, who, seeking their own and not the things of Jesus Christ, have brought great injury, great dishonor upon our religion, will be completely removed from the memory of men, which must be regarded as a very great blessing. For from this our present calamity took its beginning; from it an endless evil did not cease to creep in by degrees and daily take a wider course, nor have precautionary and disciplinary measures of many councils thus far been able to suppress it. Wherefore, who will not agree that for this reason it was a very prudent undertaking to cut off this member, on whose restoration to health much labor had been vainly spent, lest it corrupt the remainder of the body?

Moreover, divine worship will be discharged more purely and promptly, and those who carry the vessels of the Lord will be so

---

[2] Heb. 4:12.

[3] Ecclus. 10:9.

chastened that they will move others to follow their example. In connection with this point plans were skillfully devised whereby those who are to be promoted to sacred orders might in every church be from their youth up instructed in the habits of Christian life and knowledge, so that in this way a sort of seminary of all virtues might be established. In addition, provincial synods were restored; visitations reintroduced for the welfare of the people, not for the disturbance and oppression of them; greater faculties granted to the pastors for guiding and feeding their flocks; public penance again put into practice; hospitality recommended to ecclesiastical persons as well as to pious foundations; in the bestowal upon priests of the *cura animarum* a memorable and well-nigh heavenly method was adopted; plurality of benefices abolished; the hereditary possession of the sanctuary of God prohibited; excommunication restricted and the manner of its imposition determined; first judgments assigned to the places where the disputes arise; duels forbidden; a sort of bridle put on the luxury, greed and licentiousness of all people, particularly the clergy, which cannot be easily shaken off; kings and princes diligently reminded of their duties, and other things of a similar nature were enacted with the greatest discernment. Who does not see that you, most illustrious Fathers, have also in these matters done your duty in the fullest measure? Oftentimes in earlier councils our faith was explained and morals corrected, but I do not know whether ever more carefully and more clearly. We had here, especially during these two years, from all peoples and nations by whom the truth of the Catholic religion is recognized, not only Fathers but also ambassadors. And what men! If we consider science, the most learned; practice, the most experienced; mental gifts, the most penetrating; piety, the most religious; and deportment, the most irreproachable. The number also was such that if the present distresses of the Christian world are considered, this assembly appears the largest in attendance of all that preceded it. Here the individual wounds of all were uncovered, morals exposed, nothing was concealed. The propositions and arguments of our adversaries were so treated that it appeared as if their case not ours was the point under consideration. Some things were discussed three and even four times; debates were carried on with the greatest vehemence, for the purpose, namely, that as gold is tried in the fire, so might the power and vigor of the truth be proved through such contests. For how could there be discords among those who have the same view and the same aim?

That being the case, though it was very much desired, as I said in the beginning, to discuss these things conjointly with those for whose sake they were chiefly discussed, nevertheless such provision was made for the welfare and salvation of the absentees that it appears it could not have been otherwise even if they had been present. Let them read with humility, as becomes a Christian, what we have defined concerning our faith, and if some light should come upon them, let them not turn away the face; if they should hear the voice of the Lord, let them not harden their hearts, and if they should wish to return to the common embrace of mother Church from which they severed themselves, they may rest assured that every indulgence and sympathy will be extended to them. But the best way, most esteemed Fathers, to win the minds of those who differ with us and to hold in the faith and duty those who are in union with us is this, that we in our churches translate into action the enactments which we have here expressed in language. Laws may be the best, they are, however, but mute entities. Of what avail to the Hebrew people were the laws that came from the mouth of God Himself? What advantage did the laws of Lycurgus bring to the Lacedaemonians, those of Solon to the Athenians, for the preservation of liberty, the sole purpose for which they were written? But why do I make mention of such alien and ancient instances? What further instructions and precepts for good and holy living can we or should we desire in the life and teaching of our Lord Christ? Likewise, what was omitted by our forefathers that belongs either to the true faith or to a commendable conduct? For a long time we have had the salutary medicine, properly mixed and prepared; but if it is to drive out disease it must be taken and through the veins find its way throughout the entire body. From this cup of salvation, dearest brethren, let us first satiate ourselves, and let us be living and vocal laws, a model and rule by which the actions and aspirations of others may be guided, and so each one may convince himself that nothing will be gained from the advantage and honor of the Christian commonweal unless he zealously contributes in so far as is in him.

If this was our solicitude in the past, it must be more scrupulously so in the future. For if after the example of our Master and Savior we must first do and then teach,[4] what can be our excuse if after we have taught we fail to practice our teaching? Who could endure and tolerate us if after we have pointed out that theft is forbidden we our-

---

[4] Acts 1:1.

selves steal? that adultery is forbidden and we ourselves commit adultery? It is certainly not proper that saints turn away from the holy council, the innocent and virtuous from the precepts of virtue and innocence, the strong and steadfast in the faith from the firmly established teaching of our faith. And such are we expected to be by our people, who, for a long time anxiously awaiting our return, have consoled themselves with the consideration that we on our return will with greater zeal repair this absence. This you will do, I hope, most holy Fathers, with zealous endeavor; and as you have done here so will you also at home render due service to God and to the people.

Now let us first of all, so far as time will permit, express and render our most fervent and undying thanks to the great and eternal God, who has recompensed us not according to the sins that we have committed nor according to our transgressions,[5] but in His great goodness has granted us not only to see this most joyful day, which many desired to see, but also to celebrate it with the full and unqualified consent and approval of the entire Christian people. Then we must give special and everlasting thanks to our great and illustrious pontiff, Pius IV, who, as soon as he had ascended the chair of St. Peter, was so kindled with the desire to reconvene this council that he directed to it all his energy and attention. He immediately dispatched as delegates the most experienced men to announce the council to those provinces and nations for whose benefit it was chiefly convoked. These traversed nearly all the countries of the North, entreated, implored and adjured; they promised every security and friendship, and even passed over into England. Later, since he could not himself be present at the council, as he so ardently wished, he sent legates distinguished for piety and learning, two of whom, whose memory is in benediction, he wished to be here on the day appointed, though scarcely any bishops had yet arrived. These, together with a third added shortly after, spent nine inactive months in this place waiting for the arrival of an adequate number of bishops to open the council. In the meantime the Pope himself did nothing and contemplated nothing other than that very many and very distinguished Fathers should come here as soon as possible and all kings and princes of Christendom should send their ambassadors, so that by the common desire and deliberation of all this common matter, the gravest and most important of all, might be fully considered. And what did he

[5] Ps. 102:10.

later omit in the way of attention, anxiety and expenses that seemed in any manner to contribute to the greatness, liberty and success of this council? Oh, the extraordinary piety and prudence of our pastor and father! Oh, the fullest happiness to him by whose authority and under whose protection this long tossed about and distracted council found stability and rest! You who have passed away, Paul III and Julius, you I ask, how long and with what yearning have you desired to see what we see! at what costs and labor have you brought this about! Wherefore, most holy and most blessed Pius, we truly and heartily congratulate you that the Lord has reserved to you such great joy, to your name such high honor, which is the greatest proof of God's benevolence toward you; and with united prayers and supplications we beseech Him that He will for the honor and ornament of His holy Church very speedily restore you to us in good health and preserve you for many years. To the most illustrious Emperor also we must by every right extend our thanks and congratulations. Having won as a basic point the good will of the most powerful rulers who were kindled with such wonderful zeal for the propagation of the Christian religion, he has kept this city free from all danger and by his vigilance has seen to it that we might enjoy a safe and undisturbed peace; by the constant presence of his three representatives, men of the highest character, which was almost a pledge to us, he brought great security to our minds. In conformity with his eminent piety he was singularly solicitous about our affairs. He spared no labor to bring out of the densest darkness in which they dwell those who differed from him and from us in matters of faith and to lead them to see the bright light of this holy council. We must, moreover, hold in grateful remembrance the exceedingly pious disposition of the Christian kings and princes in honoring this council with the presence of their highly esteemed ambassadors and in committing their power to your authority. Finally, who is it, most illustrious legates and cardinals, who does not acknowledge his great obligation to you? You have been the most trustful leaders and directors of our deliberations. With incredible patience and perseverance you have taken care that our freedom either in the discussions or the decisions might not appear to be infringed upon. You have spared no bodily labor, no mental effort, that the business which many others like you have attempted in vain might be brought to the desired termination as soon as possible. In this, you, most illustrious and distinguished Morone, must feel a special and peculiar joy, you who twenty years ago laid the first stone for this magnificent edifice, and now, after many other master-builders have been employed at this work, you have fortunately by your extraordinary and almost divine wisdom put the final hand to it. This remarkable and singular deed of yours will be forever celebrated in words and no age will ever maintain its silence regarding your renown. What shall I say about you, most holy Fathers? How well you have merited by these your most marvelous deliberations in the interests of the Christian state! What commendation, what glory will be given to the name of each one of you by the entire Christian people! All will acknowledge and proclaim you true fathers, true pastors; everyone will cheerfully reward you for the preservation of his life and the attainment of salvation. Oh, how happy and joyful will that day be for our people, when on our return home from erecting this temple of the Lord they can again for the first time see and embrace us!

But thou Lord, our God, grant that we may by noble needs justify so generous an opinion of ourselves, and that the seed which we have sown in Thy field may yield abundant fruit and Thy word issue forth as dew, and that what Thou hast promised may take place during our time, that there be one fold and one shepherd of all, and he preferably Pius IV, to the eternal glory of Thy name. Amen.

PETITION FOR THE CONFIRMATION OF THE COUNCIL

We, Alexander of Farnese, cardinal-deacon of St. Lawrence in Damasus, vice-chancellor of the holy Roman Church, do certify and attest that on this day, Wednesday, the twenty-sixth of January, 1564, in the fifth year of the pontificate of our most holy Lord Pius IV, by the providence of God, Pope, my most reverend Lords, the Cardinals Morone and Simoneta, lately returned from the holy Council of Trent, at which they had presided as legates of the Apostolic See, did in a secret consistory held at St. Peter's petition our most holy Lord as follows:

"Most blessed Father, in a decree regarding the close of the ecumenical Council of Trent, published on the fourth of December last, it was declared that through the legates and presidents of Your Holiness and of the holy Apostolic See, confirmation of each and all of the things which were therein established and defined under Paul III and Julius III, of happy memory, as well as under Your Holiness, should be requested in the name of the Council from Your Holiness. Wherefore, we, Cardinal John Morone and Cardinal Louis Simoneta, who were then legates and presidents, wishing to execute what is ordained in that decree, do humbly petition in the name of the said ecumenical Council of Trent that Your Holiness deign to confirm each and all of the things which have been decreed and defined therein under Paul III and Julius III, of happy memory, as well as under Your Holiness."

Upon hearing which His Holiness, after having seen and read the contents of the said decree, and after having obtained the advice of my most reverend Lords, the cardinals, replied in these words:

"We, yielding to the petition made to us by the aforesaid legates in the name of the ecumenical Council of Trent regarding the confirmation thereof, with Apostolic authority and with the advice and assent of our venerable brethren, the cardinals, having previously had mature deliberation with them, confirm each and all of the things which have been decreed and defined in said Council under our predecessors, Paul III and Julius III, of happy memory, as well as during the time of our pontificate, and we command that they be received and inviolately observed by all the faithful of Christ, in the name of the Father and of the Son and of the Holy Ghost. Amen."

Thus it is.

A. Farnese, Cardinal,
Vice-Chancellor.

BULL

OF OUR MOST HOLY LORD, PIUS IV, BY THE PROVIDENCE OF GOD, POPE, CONCERNING THE CONFIRMATION OF THE ECUMENICAL AND GENERAL COUNCIL OF TRENT

Pius, Bishop, servant of the servants of God, for a perpetual remembrance hereof

"Blessed be the God and Father of our Lord Jesus Christ, the Father of mercies and the God of all comfort," [1] who, having deigned to look upon His holy Church, agitated and tossed by so many storms and tempests and day by day more sorely distressed, has at length come to her aid with a suitable and longed-for remedy. To extirpate so many

[1] Cf. II Cor. 1:3.

and most destructive heresies, to reform morals and restore ecclesiastical discipline, to bring about peace and harmony among the Christian people, an ecumenical and general council had already a long time ago been summoned by our predecessor, Paul III, of happy memory, to meet in the city of Trent and had been begun by holding several sessions. Recalled by his successor Julius to the same city, it was, after the celebration of several sessions, by reason of various hindrances and difficulties that prevented its continuance, for a long time interrupted, not without the greatest grief on the part of all pious persons, since the Church day by day increased her prayers for the success of that remedy. But after having assumed the government of the Apostolic See, we, trusting in the divine mercy, undertook to accomplish, as our pastoral solicitude directed us, so necessary and salutary a work, and supported by the pious zeal of our most beloved son in Christ, Ferdinand, Emperor-elect of the Romans, and of other Christian kings, states and princes, we at length attained that for which we did not cease to labor in watchfulness day and night and for which we have assiduously besought the Father of lights. For since a very large assembly of bishops and other distinguished prelates, one worthy of an ecumenical council, had, by our letters of convocation and impelled also by their piety, gathered from all Christian nations in that city, together with very many other pious persons pre-eminent for their knowledge of sacred letters and divine and human law, under the presidency in that council of the legates of the Apostolic See, and since we so favored the freedom of the council that we by letters to our legates voluntarily left the council free to deal with matters properly reserved to the Apostolic See, those things which remained to be considered, defined and decreed regarding the sacraments and other matters which seemed necessary for the refutation of heresies, removal of abuses, and reform of morals, were dealt with and accurately and very deliberately defined, explained and decreed by the holy council with the fullest freedom and thoroughness. On the completion of these matters the council was brought to a close with so great unanimity on the part of all who participated therein, that it was manifest that such agreement was *the Lord's doing, and it was very wonderful in our eyes* [2] and in those of all. For this so singular favor of God we at once ordered public prayers in this fair city in which the clergy and people participated with great devotion,

---

[2] Ps. 117:23.

and we made it our care that praises and thanksgivings so justly due be paid to the divine majesty, since the close of the council has brought with it a great and well-nigh assured hope that greater fruits will day by day accrue to the Church from its decrees and constitutions. But since the holy council itself, in its reverence toward the Apostolic See and following in this also the footsteps of the ancient councils, has, in a decree made in public session, petitioned us for the confirmation of all its decrees made in our time and in that of our predecessors, we, having been made acquainted with the request of the council, first by the letters of our legates, then, on their return, by what they diligently reported in the name of the council, after mature deliberation thereon with our venerable brethren, the cardinals of the holy Roman Church, and, above all, having invoked the aid of the Holy Ghost, after we had ascertained that all those decrees were Catholic, useful and salutary to the Christian people, to the praise of Almighty God, with the advice and assent of our brethren aforesaid, have this day in our secret consistory confirmed by Apostolic authority each and all, and have decreed that they be received and observed by all the faithful of Christ, as we also, for the clearer knowledge of all men, do by the contents of this letter confirm them and decree that they be received and observed by all. Moreover, in virtue of holy obedience and under the penalties prescribed by the holy canons, and others more severe, even of deprivation, to be imposed at our discretion, we command each and all of our venerable brethren, patriarchs, archbishops, bishops, and all other prelates of churches, whatever may be their state, rank, order and dignity, even though distinguished with the honor of the cardinalate, to observe diligently the said decrees and ordinances in their churches, cities and dioceses both in and out of the court of justice, and to cause them to be observed inviolately, each by his own subjects whom it may in any way concern; restraining all opponents and obstinate persons by means of judicial sentences, censures and ecclesiastical penalties contained in those decrees, every appeal being set aside, calling in also, if need be, the aid of the secular arm. We admonish and by the bowels of the mercy of our Lord Jesus Christ conjure our most beloved son the Emperor-elect and the other Christian kings, states and princes, that they, with the same piety and zeal which they manifested through their ambassadors at the council, for the honor of God and the salvation of their people, in reverence also toward the Apostolic See and the holy council, support, if need be, with their aid and encouragement, the prelates in enforcing and observing the decrees of the council, and not to permit opinions contrary to the sound and salutary doctrine of the council to be received by the people under their jurisdiction, but to forbid them absolutely. Furthermore, to avoid the perversion and confusion which might arise if everyone were allowed to publish, as he saw fit, his commentaries on and interpretations of the decrees of the council, we by Apostolic authority forbid all persons, ecclesiastics, of whatever order, condition or rank they may be, as well as laics, with whatever honor and power invested, prelates, indeed, under penalty of being prohibited entrance into the church, and others, whoever they may be, under penalty of excommunication *latae sententiae*, to presume without our authority to publish in any form any commentaries, glosses, annotations, scholia on, or any kind of interpretation whatsoever of the decrees of this council, or to decide something under whatever name, even under pretext of greater corroboration or better execution of the decrees, or under any other color or pretext. But if anything therein should appear to anyone to have been expressed and defined in an obscure manner and for that reason stands in need of some interpretation or decision, *let him go up to the place which the Lord has chosen*,[3] namely, to the Apostolic See, the mistress of all the faithful, whose authority the holy council also has so reverently acknowledged. For if difficulties and controversies relative to those decrees shall arise, their explanation and decision we reserve to ourselves, as the holy council itself has also decreed; being prepared, as that council has justly confided to us, to provide for the necessities of all the provinces as it shall appear to us most suitable; at the same time we declare null and void whatever should be attempted to the contrary in these matters, whether knowingly or unknowingly, by any authority whatsoever. But that these things may come to the knowledge of all and that no one may plead ignorance as an excuse, we wish and command that this letter be read publicly and in a loud voice by some officials of our court in the Vatican Basilica of the Prince of the Apostles and in the Lateran Church at a time when the people are accustomed to assemble there for the celebration of the masses; and after having been read, let it be affixed to the doors of those churches and also to those of the Apostolic Chancery and at the usual place in the Campo di Fiore, and let it be left there for some time that it may be read and come to the knowledge

---

[3] Deut. 17:8.

of all; but when removed thence, copies being according to custom left there, let it be committed to the press in the fair city that it may be more conveniently made known throughout the provinces and kingdoms of Christendom. We command and decree also that an unwavering faith be given to the transcripts thereof, written or subscribed by the hand of a notary public and authenticated by the seal and signature of some person constituted in ecclesiastical dignity. Let no one, therefore, infringe this our letter of confirmation, admonition, inhibition, will, commands and decrees, or with foolhardy boldness oppose it. But if anyone shall presume to attempt this, let him know that he will incur the indignation of Almighty God and of His blessed Apostles Peter and Paul. Given at Rome at Saint Peter's in the year 1564 of the Lord's incarnation on the twenty-sixth of January, in the fifth year of our pontificate.

I, Pius, Bishop of the Catholic Church.

I, F. Card. Pisanus, Bishop of Ostia, Dean.
I, Fed. Card. Caesius, Bishop of Porto.
I, Jo. Card. Moronus, Bishop of Tusculum.
I, A. Card. Farnesius, Vice-Chancellor, Bishop of Sabina.
. . . .
I, R. Card. S. Angeli, Major Penitentiary.
. . . .
I, Jo. Card. S. Vitalis.
I, Jo. Michael Card. Sarasenus.
. . . .
I, Jo. B. Cicada, Card. S. Clementis.
I, Scipio Card. Pisarum.
I, Jo. Card. Romanus.
I, F. M. G. Card. Alexandrinus.
I, F. Clemens Card. Arae Coeli.
I, Jo. Card. Sabellus.
. . . .
I, B. Card. Salviatus.
I, Philip. Card. Aburd.
I, Lud. Card. Simoneta.
. . . .
I, F. Card. Pacieccus y de Tol.

I, M. A. Card. Amulius.
I, Jo. Franc. Card. de Gambara.
I, Carolus Card. Borromaeus.
I, M. S. Card. Constant.
I, Alph. Card. Gesualdus.
I, Hipp. Card. Ferrar.
I, Franciscus Card. Gonzaga.
. . . .
I, Gui. Asc. Diac. Card. Cam.
I, Vitellotius Card. Vitellius.
. . . .
. . . .

Ant. Florebellus Lavellinus.
H. Cumyn.

TEN RULES CONCERNING PROHIBITED BOOKS DRAWN UP BY THE FATHERS CHOSEN BY THE COUNCIL OF TRENT AND APPROVED BY POPE PIUS [1]

I

All books which have been condemned either by the supreme pontiffs or by ecumenical councils before the year 1515 and are not contained in this list, shall be considered condemned in the same manner as they were formerly condemned.

II

The books of those heresiarchs, who after the aforesaid year originated or revived heresies, as well as of those who are or have been the heads or leaders of heretics, as Luther, Zwingli, Calvin, Balthasar Friedberg, Schwenkfeld, and others like these, whatever may be their name, title or nature of their heresy, are absolutely forbidden. The books of other heretics, however, which deal professedly with religion are absolutely condemned. Those on the other hand, which do not deal with religion and have by order of the bishops and inquisitors been examined by Catholic theologians and approved by them, are permitted. Likewise, Catholic books written by those who afterward fell into heresy, as well as by those who after their fall returned to the bosom

[1] Cf. Sess. XXV, decree concerning the index of books.

of the Church, may be permitted if they have been approved by the theological faculty of a Catholic university or by the general inquisition.

III

The translations of writers, also ecclesiastical, which have till now been edited by condemned authors, are permitted provided they contain nothing contrary to sound doctrine. Translations of the books of the Old Testament may in the judgment of the bishop be permitted to learned and pious men only, provided such translations are used only as elucidations of the Vulgate Edition for the understanding of the Holy Scriptures and not as the sound text. Translations of the New Testament made by authors of the first class of this list shall be permitted to no one, since great danger and little usefulness usually results to readers from their perusal. But if with such translations as are permitted or with the Vulgate Edition some annotations are circulated, these may also, after the suspected passages have been expunged by the theological faculty of some Catholic university or by the general inquisition, be permitted to those to whom the translations are permitted. Under these circumstances the entire volume of the Sacred Books, which is commonly called the *biblia Vatabli*, or parts of it, may be permitted to pious and learned men. From the Bibles of Isidore Clarius of Brescia, however, the preface and introduction are to be removed, and no one shall regard its text as the text of the Vulgate Edition.

IV

Since it is clear from experience that if the Sacred Books are permitted everywhere and without discrimination in the vernacular, there will by reason of the boldness of men arise therefrom more harm than good, the matter is in this respect left to the judgment of the bishop or inquisitor, who may with the advice of the pastor or confessor permit the reading of the Sacred Books translated into the vernacular by Catholic authors to those who they know will derive from such reading no harm but rather an increase of faith and piety, which permission they must have in writing. Those, however, who presume to read or possess them without such permission may not receive absolution from their sins till they have handed them over to the ordinary. Bookdealers who sell or in any other way supply Bibles written in the vernacular to anyone who has not this permission, shall lose the price of the books, which is to be applied by the bishop to pious purposes, and in keeping with the nature of the crime they shall be subject to other penalties which are left to the judgment of the same bishop. Regulars who have not the permission of their superiors may not read or purchase them.

V

Those books which sometimes produce the works of heretical authors, in which these add little or nothing of their own but rather collect therein the sayings of others, as lexicons, concordances, apothegms, parables, tables of contents and such like, are permitted if whatever needs to be eliminated in the additions is removed and corrected in accordance with the suggestions of the bishop, the inquisitor and Catholic theologians.

VI

Books which deal in the vernacular with the controversies between Catholics and heretics of our time may not be permitted indiscriminately, but the same is to be observed with regard to them what has been decreed concerning Bibles written in the vernacular. There is no reason, however, why those should be prohibited which have been written in the vernacular for the purpose of pointing out the right way to live, to contemplate, to confess, and similar purposes, if they contain sound doctrine, just as popular sermons in the vernacular are not prohibited. But if hitherto in some kingdom or province certain books have been prohibited because they contained matter the reading of which would be of no benefit to all indiscriminately, these may, if their authors are Catholic, be permitted by the bishop and inquisitor after they have been corrected.

VII

Books which professedly deal with, narrate or teach things lascivious or obscene are absolutely prohibited, since not only the matter of faith but also that of morals, which are usually easily corrupted through the reading of such books, must be taken into consideration, and those who possess them are to be severely punished by the bishops. Ancient books written by heathens may by reason of their elegance and quality of style be permitted, but may by no means be read to children.

VIII

Books whose chief contents are good but in which some things have incidentally been inserted which have reference to heresy, ungodliness, divination or superstition, may be permitted if by the authority of the general inquisition they have been purged by Catholic theologians. The same decision holds good with regard to prefaces, summaries or annotations which are added by condemned authors to books not condemned. Hereafter, however, these shall not be printed till they have been corrected.

IX

All books and writings dealing with geomancy, hydromancy, aeromancy, pyromancy, oneiromancy, chiromancy, necromancy, or with sortilege, mixing of poisons, augury, auspices, sorcery, magic arts, are absolutely repudiated. The bishops shall diligently see to it that books, treatises, catalogues determining destiny by astrology, which in the matter of future events, consequences, or fortuitous occurrences, or of actions that depend on the human will, attempt to affirm something as certain to take place, are not read or possessed.[2] Permitted, on the other hand, are the opinions and natural observations which have been written in the interest of navigation, agriculture or the medical art.

X

In the printing of books or other writings is to be observed what was decreed in the tenth session of the Lateran Council under Leo X.[3] Wherefore, if in the fair city of Rome any book is to be printed, it shall first be examined by the vicar of the supreme pontiff and by the Master of the Sacred Palace or by the persons appointed by our most holy Lord. In other localities this approbation and examination shall pertain to the bishop or to one having a knowledge of the book or writing to be printed appointed by the bishop and to the inquisitor of the city or diocese in which the printing is done, and it shall be approved by the signature of their own hand, free of charge and without delay

---

[2] For the mode of procedure suggested to the bishops and local inquisitors, cf. the bull *Coeli et terrae*, of Sixtus V, 5 Jan., 1586.

[3] Fifth Lateran, Hardouin, IX, pp. 1775-77; Schroeder, *Disciplinary Decrees of the General Councils*, pp. 504, 644 f.

under the penalties and censures contained in the same decree, with the observance of this rule and condition that an authentic copy of the book to be printed, undersigned by the author's hand, remain with the examiner. Those who circulate books in manuscript form before they have been examined and approved, shall in the judgment of the Fathers delegated by the council be subject to the same penalties as the printers, and those who possess and read them shall, unless they make known the authors, be themselves regarded as the authors. The approbation of such books shall be given in writing and must appear authentically in the front of the written or printed book and the examination, approbation and other things must be done free of charge. Moreover, in all cities and dioceses the houses or places where the art of printing is carried on and the libraries offering books for sale, shall be visited often by persons appointed for this purpose by the bishop or his vicar and also by the inquisitor, so that nothing that is prohibited be printed, sold or possessed. All book-dealers and venders of books shall have in their libraries a list of the books which they have for sale subscribed by the said persons, and without the permission of the same appointed persons they may not under penalties of confiscation of the books and other penalties to be imposed in the judgment of the bishops and inquisitors, possess or sell or in any other manner whatsoever supply other books. Venders, readers and printers shall be punished according to the judgment of the same. If anyone brings into any city any books whatsoever he shall be bound to give notice thereof to the same delegated persons, or in case a public place is provided for wares of that kind, then the public officials of that place shall notify the aforesaid persons that books have been brought in. But let no one dare give to anyone a book to read which he himself or another has brought into the city or in any way dispose of or loan it, unless he has first exhibited the book and obtained the permission of the persons appointed, or unless it is well known that the reading of the book is permitted to all. The same shall be observed by heirs and executors of last wills, so, namely, that they exhibit the books left by those deceased, or a list of them, to the persons delegated and obtain from them permission before they use them or in any way transfer them to other persons. In each and all of such cases let a penalty be prescribed, covering either the confiscation of books or in the judgment of the bishops or inquisitors another that is in keeping with the degree of the contumacy or the character of the offense.

With reference to those books which the delegated Fathers have examined and expurgated or have caused to be expurgated, or under certain conditions have permitted to be printed again, the book-dealers as well as others shall observe whatever is known to have been prescribed by them. The bishops and general inquisitors, however, in view of the authority which they have, are free to prohibit even those books which appear to be permitted by these rules, if they should deem this advisable in their kingdoms, provinces or dioceses. Moreover, the secretary of those delegated has by order of our most holy Lord [the pope] to hand over in writing to the notary of the holy universal Roman inquisition the names of the books which have been expurgated by the delegated Fathers as well as the names of those to whom they committed this task.

Finally, all the faithful are commanded not to presume to read or possess any books contrary to the prescriptions of these rules or the prohibition of this list. And if anyone should read or possess books by heretics or writings by any author condemned and prohibited by reason of heresy or suspicion of false teaching, he incurs immediately the sentence of excommunication. He, on the other hand, who reads or possesses books prohibited under another name shall, besides incurring the guilt of mortal sin, be severely punished according to the judgment of the bishops.

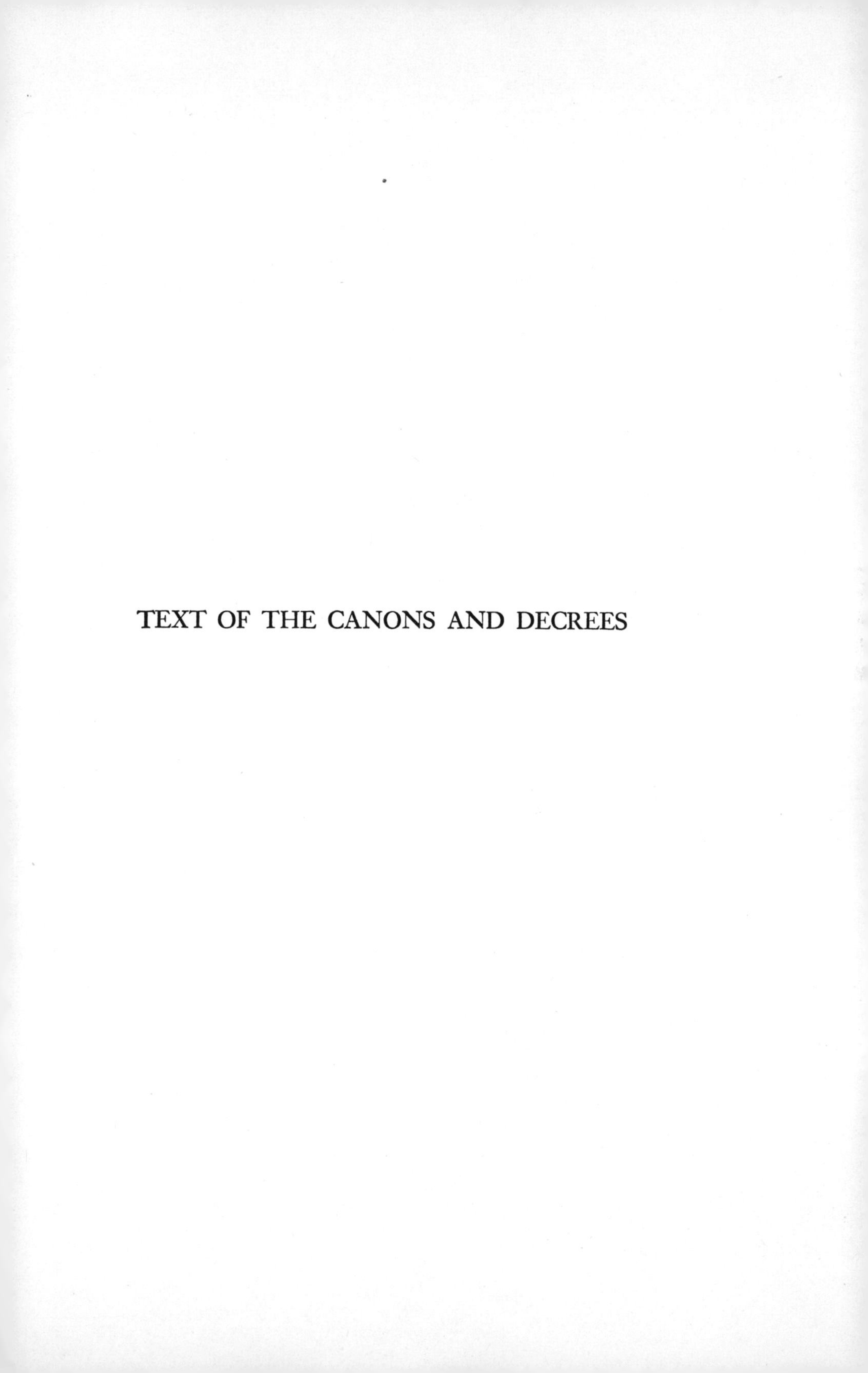

TEXT OF THE CANONS AND DECREES

BULLA INDICTIONIS
SACROSANCTI OECUMENICI
CONCILII TRIDENTINI
sub Paulo III Pont. Max.

PAULUS EPISCOPUS, SERVUS SERVORUM DEI, AD FUTURAM REI MEMORIAM

Initio nostri hujus pontificatus, quem non ob merita nostra, sed propter suam magnam bonitatem Dei omnipotentis providentia nobis commisit, cernentes jam tum, in quas perturbationes temporum quotque incommoda rerum fere omnium nostra pastoralis sollicitudo et vigilantia esset vocata, cupiebamus quidem mederi Christianae reipublicae malis, quibus illa jamdudum vexata et propemodum oppressa est; sed ipsi etiam, ut homines *circumdati infirmitate*,[1] ad tantum onus tollendum impares vires nostras esse sentiebamus. Nam cum pace opus esse intelligeremus ad liberandam et conservandam a plurimis impendentibus periculis rempublicam, omnia invenimus odiis et dissensionibus plena, dissentientibus praesertim principibus iis inter se, quibus summa rerum pene omnis a Deo permissa est. Cum *unum ovile et unum pastorem* [2] dominici esse gregis ad integritatem Christianae religionis et ad coelestium bonorum spem in nobis confirmandam necessarium duceremus: schismatis, dissidiis, haeresibus erat Christiani nominis divulsa jam pene et lacerata unitas. Cum tutam atque munitam ab infidelium armis atque insidiis rempublicam optaremus: nostris erratis nostraque cunctorum culpa, Dei videlicet ira peccatis nostris imminente, Rhodus fuerat amissa, Hungaria vexata, conceptum et meditatum contra Italiam, contraque Austriam et Illyricum terra marique bellum, cum impius et immitis hostis noster Turca nullo tempore requiesceret, nostrorumque inter se odia et dissensiones suam bene gerendae rei occasionem duceret. Igitur, ut dicebamus, in tanta haeresum, dissensionum bellorumque tempestate, tantisque excitatis fluctibus cum essemus ad moderandam

---

[1] Heb. 5:2.
[2] Joan. 10:16.

et gubernandam Petri naviculam vocati, nec viribus ipsi nostris satis fideremus, primum conjecimus in domino cogitatus nostros, ut ipse nos nutriret,[3] animumque nostrum firmitate et robore, mentem consilio sapientiaque instrueret. Deinde animo repetentes, majores nostros, sapientia admirabili et sanctitate praeditos, saepe in summis Christianae reipublicae periculis remedium optimum atque opportunissimum oecumenica concilia et episcoporum generales conventus adhibuisse: ipsi quoque animum ad generale habendum concilium adjecimus, exquisitisque principum sententiis, quorum nobis videbatur utilis in primis et opportuna ad hanc rem esse consensio, cum eos tunc non alienos ab hoc tam sancto opere invenissemus, oecumenicum concilium et generalem eorum episcoporum aliorumque patrum, ad quos pertineret, conventum in civitate Mantuae indiximus, anno incarnationis Domini, sicut litteris et monumentis nostris testatum est, millesimo quingentesimo trigesimo septimo, pontificatus nostri tertio, ad X. Kal. Jun. inchoandum; spem prope certam habentes fore, ut, cum illic in nomine Domini essemus congregati, ipse, sicut promisit, Dominus in medio nostrum adfuturus,[4] et bonitate ac misericordia sua omnes temporum procellas omniaque pericula spiritu oris sui facile depulsurus esset. Sed, ut semper insidiatur piis actionibus humani generis hostis, primum contra omnem spem et expectationem nostram denegata fuit nobis Mantuana civitas, nisi aliquas conditiones subiremus ab institutis majorum nostrorum, et conditione temporum, nostraque ac hujus Sanctae Sedis ac nominis ecclesiastici dignitate libertateque prorsus alienas, quas in aliis nostris litteris expressimus. Quapropter alium invenire locum aliamque deligere civitatem necesse habuimus, quae cum non statim nobis occurreret idonea et apta, ad sequentes Kal. Nov. prorogare concilii celebrationem fuimus coacti. Interim saevus et perpetuus hostis noster Turca, ingenti classe Italiam adortus, aliquot oppida in litoribus Apuliae cepit, vastavit, diripuit, praedas hominum abegit; nos in maximo timore et periculo omnium muniendis litoribus nostris, finitimisque auxilio juvandis fuimus occupati; nec tamen interea destitimus consulere et hortari Christianos principes, ut de idoneo ad habendum concilium loco quid sentirent nobis exponerent, quorum cum essent incertae variaeque sententiae, tempusque diutius, quam erat opus, videretur extrahi, nos optimo animo atque, ut arbitramur, etiam consilio, Vicentiam elegimus, urbem copiosam, et Venetorum, qui eam nobis concedebant, virtute, auctori-

[3] Ps. 54:23.
[4] Matt. 18:20.

tate, potentia cum aditum patentem, tum stationem omnibus liberam atque tutam in primis in se habentem. Sed cum jam tempus longius progressum esset, novaeque urbis electionem omnibus significari conveniret, jamque Kalendae Novembris appetentes facultatem hujus divulgationis excluderent, hiemsque esset propinqua, rursus altera prorogatione tempus concilii differre in proximum sequens ver, Maiique futuras Kalendas compulsi fuimus. Qua re firmiter constituta atque decreta, cum et nos ipsos, et cetera omnia ad eum bene agendum Deo juvante celebrandumque conventum pararemus, plurimum reputantes interesse cum celebrationis concilii, tum universae Christianae reipublicae, Christianos principes pace inter se et concordia consentire: carissimos in Christo filios nostros, Carolum Romanorum imperatorem semper augustum, et Christianissimum regem Franciscum, duo praecipua Christiani nominis firmamenta atque subsidia, orare atque obsecrare institimus, ut ad colloquium inter se et nobiscum una convenirent; quorum quidem apud utrumque litteris, nunciis, et a latere nostro missis ex venerabilium fratrum nostrorum numero legatis, saepissime egeramus, ut ex simultate et dissidiis ambo in unum foedus et piam amicitiam vellent convenire, labentibusque succurrere Christianis rebus; quarum servandarum cum esset illis potestas a Deo praecipue tributa, si id non agerent et ad commune Christianorum bonum sua consilia non dirigerent, acris et severa ratio eidem Deo ab ipsis reddenda esset. Qui aliquando precibus nostris annuentes Nicaeam se contulere, quo nos quoque longum iter, et senili aetati nostrae vehementer contrarium, Dei et pacis conciliandae causa suscepimus; neque praetermisimus interea, cum tempus concilii praestitutum, Kalendae videlicet Maiae, appropinquaret, tres legatos summae virtutis ac auctoritatis a latere nostro de numero eorumdem venerabilium fratrum nostrorum S. R. E. cardinalium Vicentiam mittere, qui initium concilii facerent, praelatosque undique venientes exciperent, et ea, quae judicarent esse opus, agerent et tractarent, quoad nos, ab itinere et negotio pacis reversi, omnia accuratius dirigere possemus. Interim vero in illud sanctum opus maximeque necessarium, tractationem videlicet pacis inter principes, incubuimus, et quidem omni animi studio, omni pietate ac diligentia. Testis est nobis Deus, cujus freti clementia nosmetipsos itineris et vitae periculo exposuimus; nostra testis conscientia, quae nihil habet in hac re quidem, in quo nos arguat aut praetermissae, aut non quaesitae ad pacificandum occasionis; principes ipsi testes, quos tam saepe tamque vehementer nunciis, litteris, legatis, monitis, hortatu, precibusque omnibus obsecraveramus, ut simultates deponerent, ut societatem coirent, ut Christianae reipublicae in maximum et propinquum jam adductae discrimen communibus studiis et subsidiis opitularentur; jam vero testes illae vigiliae atque curae, illi diurni nocturnique animi nostri labores gravesque sollicitudines, quas ob hanc rem et causam plurimas jam suscepimus. Nec tamen ad optatum exitum nostra consilia et acta adhuc perducta sunt. Ita enim visum Domino Deo est, quem tamen non desperamus aliquando optata nostra benignius respecturum. Ipsi quidem, quantum in nobis fuit, nihil, quod esset nostro pastorali officio debitum, in hac re omisimus. Quod si qui sunt, qui actiones pacis nostras in aliam interpretentur partem, dolemus quidem, sed tamen in dolore nostro gratias Deo omnipotenti agimus, qui ad exemplum et doctrinam patientiae nostrae suos voluit apostolos haberi dignos, qui pro nomine Jesu, qui pax nostra est, contumeliam paterentur.[5] Verum in illo congressu colloquioque nostro, quod Nicaeae habitum est, etsi, peccatis nostris impedientibus, inter duos principes vera et perpetua pax non potuit confici, induciae tamen decennales factae sunt, quarum opportunitate nos sperantes et sacrum concilium commodius celebratum iri, et deinde ex concilii auctoritate perfici posse pacem, apud principes institimus, ut et ipsi venirent ad concilium, et praelatos suos praesentes ducerent, absentesque accerserent. Qui cum de utroque se excusassent, quod et ipsis redire in regna sua tum necesse esset, et praelatos, quos secum habuissent itinere atque impendiis fessos atque exhaustos recreari et refici oporteret, nos hortati sunt, ut aliam quoque prorogationem temporis habendi concilii decerneremus. Qua in re concedenda cum essemus aliquantum difficiles, litteras interim a legatis nostris, qui Vicentiae erant, accepimus, transacto jam et longius praeterito concilii ineundi die unum vix aut alterum ex externis nationibus praelatum Vicentiam se contulisse. Quo nuncio accepto cum videremus, eo tempore nulla jam ratione haberi concilium posse, ipsis principibus concessimus, ut differretur tempus agendi concilii usque ad sanctum Pascha, diemque festum futurae dominicae resurrectionis. Cujus nostri praecepti expectationisque decretae litterae Genuae anno incarnationis Domini MDXXXVIII. IV. Kal. Jul. factae publicataeque sunt, atque hanc dilationem eo propensius fecimus, quod pollicitus est nobis uterque princeps, legatos suos Romam ad nos se missurum, ut ea, quae ad perfectionem pacis reliqua essent, neque Nicaeae ob brevitatem tem-

---

[5] Act. 5:41; Eph. 2:14.

poris potuerant omnia confici, Romae commodius coram nobis agerentur et tractarentur. Et ob hanc rationem etiam a nobis ambo petierunt, ut haec pacificationis procuratio concilii celebrationi praeponeretur, cum ipsum concilium pace facta multo deinde utilius et salutarius Christianae reipublicae futurum esset. Semper enim haec pacis spes nobis injecta principum nos voluntatibus assentiri hortata est; quam spem vehementer auxit post discessum a Nicaea nostrum ipsorum duorum principum inter se benevola amicaque congressio, quae, maxima nostra cum laetitia a nobis intellecta, confirmavit nos in bona spe, ut tandem aliquando nostras preces apud Deum exauditas et vota pacis accepta esse crederemus. Hanc igitur pacis conclusionem cum et expeteremus et urgeremus, nec solum duobus antedictis principibus, verum etiam carissimo in Christo filio nostro Ferdinando regi Romanorum videretur, actionem concilii, nisi pace facta, suscipi non oportere, cunctique a nobis per litteras suosque oratores contenderent, ut alias rursus temporis prorogationes faceremus, praecipue autem instaret serenissimus Caesar, promisisse se demonstrans iis, qui a catholica unitate dissentiunt, se operam suam apud nos interpositurum, ut aliqua concordiae ratio iniretur, quod ante suam in Germaniam profectionem apte non posset fieri: nos eadem semper spe pacis et tantorum principum voluntate adducti, cum praesertim cerneremus, ne ad dictum quidem resurrectionis festum alios praelatos Vicentiam convenisse, prorogationis nomen jam fugientes, quod tam saepe frustra fuerat repetitum, celebrationem generalis concilii ad nostrum et Sedis Apostolicae beneplacitum suspendere maluimus; itaque fecimus, et de suspensione hujusmodi litteras ad singulos supradictorum principum decima die Jun. MDXXXIX. dedimus, sicut ex illis perspicue potest intelligi. Ea itaque suspensione necessario per nos facta, dum tempus illud magis idoneum a nobis pacisque aliqua conclusio expectatur, quae et dignitatem postea frequentiamque concilio, et Christianae reipublicae praesentiorem salutem erat allatura, Christianae interea res in deterius quotidie prolapsae sunt, Hungaris rege [6] ipsorum mortuo Turcam vocantibus; Ferdinando rege bellum in eos movente; Belgis ad defectionem a Caesare ex parte quadam incitatis, cujus defectionis comprimendae causa per Galliam amicissime, et cum rege Christianissimo concordissime magno benevolae inter eos voluntatis indicio transiens in Belgas serenissimus Caesar, et illinc deinde in Germaniam profectus, conventus Germaniae princi-

[6] Joanne sc. Zapolya, qui 21 Julii, 1540, mortuus est.

pum et civitatum tractandae ejus, quam dixerat, concordiae causa habere coepit. Sed cum spe pacis jam deficiente ille quoque modus curandae in conventibus tractandaeque concordiae ad majores potius discordias concitandas aptus esse videretur, inducti fuimus ad pristinum concilii generalis remedium reverti, idque per legatos nostros S. R. E. cardinales [7] ipsi Caesari obtulimus; quod etiam postremo, et praecipue in Ratisponensi conventu egimus, cum illic dilectus filius noster Gasper tit. S. Praxedis cardinalis Contarenus summa doctrina et integritate legatum nostrum ageret. Nam cum, id quod ne accideret antea veriti eramus, ex ejus conventus sententia peteretur a nobis, ut ab ecclesia dissentientium quosdam articulos tolerandos declararemus, quoad per oecumenicum concilium illi excuterentur et deciderentur, idque nobis ut concederemus neque Christiana et catholica veritas, neque nostra et Sedis Apostolicae dignitas permitteret, palam potius concilium, ut quam primum fieret, proponi mandavimus. Neque vero in alia unquam sententia et voluntate fuimus, quam ut primo quoque tempore concilium oecumenicum et generale congregaretur. Sperabamus enim ex eo et pacem populo Christiano et Christianae religionis integritatem posse recuperari; verumtamen id cum bona gratia et voluntate Christianorum principum habere volebamus. Quam voluntatem dum expectamus, dum observamus tempus absconditum, tempus beneplaciti tui, o Deus,[8] aliquando tandem decernere compulsi sumus, omne esse tempus beneplacitum Deo, cum de rebus sanctis et ad Christianam pietatem pertinentibus concilia ineuntur. Quapropter videntes, maximo quidem animi nostri cum dolore, rem Christianam quotidie in pejus ruere, Hungaria a Turcis oppressa, Germanis periclitantibus, ceteris omnibus metu moeroreque afflictis, nullius jam principis consensum expectare, sed tantum Dei omnipotentis voluntatem et Christianae reipublicae utilitatem attendere constituimus. Itaque cum Vicentiam amplius non haberemus, cuperemusque cum universae Christianorum saluti, tum Germanicae nationis incommodis in eligendo per nos novi concilii habendi loco consulere, aliquotque locis propositis ipsam Tridentinam civitatem ab ipsis desiderari videremus: nos, etsi in citeriore Italia commodius omnia tractari posse judicabamus, ad eorum tamen postulationes nostram voluntatem paterna caritate defleximus. Itaque Tridentum civitatem elegimus, qua in civitate oecumenicum concilium ad proxime venturas Kal. Novembris haberetur; idoneum locum illum

[7] Per Farnesium sc. et Cervinum cardinales.
[8] Ps. 68:14.

statuentes, quo ex Germania quidem aliisque Germaniae finitimis nationibus facillime, ex Gallia, Hispania ceterisque provinciis remotioribus non difficiliter episcopi et praelati convenire possent. Dies autem concilii ea nobis spectata est, quae spatium in se haberet et publicandi per Christianas nationes nostri hujus decreti, et facultatis omnibus praelatis ad veniendum tribuendae. Quominus autem annuum tempus praefiniremus mutando concilii loco, sicut quibusdam constitutionibus alias praescriptum est,[9] ea res fuit in causa, quod longius extrahi spem sanandae aliqua in parte Christianae reipublicae, quae tot detrimentis et calamitatibus affecta est, noluimus; et tamen videmus tempora, agnoscimus difficultates, quid sperari possit ex consiliis nostris incertum esse intelligimus. Sed quia scriptum est: *Revela Domino viam tuam, et spera in eo, et ipse faciet,*[10] magis Dei clementiae et misericordiae confidere, quam nostrae imbecillitati diffidere constituimus. Saepe enim fit in bonis operibus incipiendis, ut quod humana consilia non valent divina virtus efficiat. Hujus igitur ipsius Dei omnipotentis, Patris et Filii et Spiritus Sancti, ac beatorum ejus Apostolorum Petri et Pauli auctoritate, qua nos quoque in terris fungimur, freti atque subnixi, de venerabilium item fratrum nostrorum S. R. E. cardinalium consilio et assensu, sublata amotaque suspensione, de qua supra commemoratum est, quam per praesentes tollimus et amovemus, sacrum oecumenicum et generale concilium in civitate Tridentina, loco commodo et libero omnibusque nationibus opportuno, ad Kal. proximas Novembris anni praesentis ab incarnatione Domini MDXLII. incipiendum, prosequendum, et eodem Domino adjuvante ad ipsius gloriam atque laudem et Christiani totius populi salutem absolvendum perficiendumque indicimus, annunciamus, convocamus, statuimus atque decernimus; omnes omnibus ex locis tam venerabiles fratres nostros patriarchas, archiepiscopos, episcopos, et dilectos filios abbates, quam alios quoscumque, quibus jure aut privilegio in conciliis generalibus residendi et sententias in eis dicendi permissa potestas est, requirentes, hortantes, admonentes, ac nihilominus eis vi jurisjurandi, quod nobis et huic Sanctae Sedi praestiterunt, ac sanctae virtute obedientiae, aliisque sub poenis jure aut consuetudine in celebrationibus conciliorum adversus non accedentes ferri et proponi solitis, mandantes arcteque praecipientes, ut ipsimet, nisi forte justo detineantur impedimento, de quo tamen

---

[9] Conc. Constantiense, Sess. XXXIX, const. *Frequens*. Mansi, *Concilia,* XXVII, 1159; Hardouin, *Concilia,* VIII, 856.
[10] Ps. 36:5.

fidem facere compellantur, aut certe per suos legitimos procuratores et nuncios sacro huic concilio omnino adesse et interesse debeant; supra autem dictos imperatorem, regemque Christianissimum, necnon ceteros reges, duces, principes, quorum praesentia, si alias unquam, hoc quidem tempore maxime sanctissimae Christi fidei et Christianorum omnium futura est salutaris, rogantes atque obsecrantes per viscera misericordiae Dei et Domini nostri Jesu Christi, cujus fidei veritas et religio et intus et extra graviter jam oppugnatur, ut, si salvam volunt Christianam esse rempubilicam, si se Domino obstrictos et obligatos pro maximis illius erga se beneficiis intelligunt, ne deserant ipsius Dei causam et negotium, ipsimet ad sacri concilii celebrationem veniant, in quo ipsorum pietas atque virtus communi utilitati, salutique suae, ac ceterorum, et temporali et aeternae plurimum est profutura. Sin autem, id quod nollemus, accedere ipsi non poterunt, at graves saltem viros legatos cum auctoritate mittant, qui personam principis sui quisque et cum prudentia et cum dignitate possint in concilio referre. In primis vero ut id curent, quod ipsis facillimum est, ut ex suis cujusque regnis ac provinciis episcopi et praelati sine tergiversatione et mora ad concilium proficiscantur, quod maxime quidem a praelatis principibusque Germaniae Deum ipsum, atque nos impetrare aequum est, ut, cum eorum praecipue causa ipsisque cupientibus concilium indictum sit, et in ea civitate indictum, quae ab eis est desiderata, non graventur ipsi sua cunctorum praesentia id celebrare et ornare, quo melius atque commodius quae ad integritatem et veritatem Christianae religionis, quae ad bonorum morum reductionem emendationemque malorum, quae ad Christianorum inter se tam principum, quam populorum pacem, unitatem concordiamque pertineant, et quae ad repellendos impetus barbarorum et infidelium, quibus illi universam Christianitatem obruere moliuntur, sint necessaria, Deo nostris consultationibus praeeunte et lumen sapientiae suae ac veritatis mentibus nostris praeferente, agi in dicto sacro oecumenico concilio et conspirante omnium caritate consuli, tractari, confici, ad optatosque exitus deduci quam primum et quam optime possint. Atque ut nostrae hae litterae, et quae in eis continentur, ad notitiam cunctorum, quorum oportet, perveniant, neve quis illorum ignorantiae excusationem praetendat, cum praesertim etiam non ad omnes eos, quibus nominatim illae essent intimandae, tutus forsitan pateat accessus: volumus et mandamus, ut in basilica Vaticana principis apostolorum et in ecclesia Lateranensi, cum ibi multitudo populi ad audiendam rem divinam congregari solita est, palam clara voce per curiae nostrae cursores aut notarios aliquos publicos legantur, lectaeque in valvis dictarum ecclesiarum, itemque cancellariae apostolicae portis, et Campi Florae solito loco affigantur, ubi ad lectionem et notitiam cunctorum aliquamdiu expositae pendeant; cumque inde amovebuntur, earum nihilominus exempla in eisdem locis remaneant affixa. Nos enim per lectionem, publicationem affixionemque hujusmodi omnes et quoscumque, quos antedictae nostrae litterae comprehendunt, post spatium duorum mensium a die litterarum publicationis et affixionis ita volumus obligatos esse atque adstrictos, ac si ipsismet illae coram lectae et intimatae essent; transumptis quidem earum, quae manu publici notarii scripta aut subscripta, et sigillo personae alicujus ecclesiastica in dignitate constitutae munita fuerint, ut fides certa et indubitata habeatur, mandamus atque decernimus. Nulli ergo omnino hominum liceat hanc paginam nostrae indictionis, annunciationis, convocationis, statuti, decreti, mandati, praecepti et obsecrationis infringere, vel ei ausu temerario contraire. Si quis autem hoc attentare praesumpserit, indignationem omnipotentis Dei, ac beatorum Petri et Pauli Apostolorum ejus se noverit incursurum. Datum Romae apud Sanctum Petrum anno incarnationis dominicae MDXLII. XI. Kal. Jun. pontificatus nostri anno VIII.

Blosius.
Hier. Dand.

SESSIO PRIMA

SACROSANCTI OECUMENICI ET GENERALIS

CONCILII TRIDENTINI
SUB PAULO III PONT. MAX.

celebrata

die XIII mensis Decembris anno Domini MDXLV

DECRETUM DE INCHOANDO CONCILIO

Placetne vobis ad laudem et gloriam sanctae et individuae Trinitatis, Patris et Filii et Spiritus Sancti, ad incrementum et exaltationem fidei et religionis Christianae, ad extirpationem haeresum, ad pacem et unionem ecclesiae, ad reformationem cleri et populi Christiani, ad depressionem et extinctionem hostium Christiani nominis, decernere et declarare, sacrum Tridentinum et generale concilium incipere et inceptum esse? *Responderunt:* Placet.

INDICTIO FUTURAE SESSIONIS

Et cum proxima sit celebritas Nativitatis Domini nostri Jesu Christi, et subsequantur aliae festivitates labentis et incipientis anni: placetne vobis primam futuram sessionem habendam esse die Jovis post Epiphaniam, quae erit septima mensis Januarii, anno Domini MDXLVI? *Responderunt:* Placet.

SESSIO SECUNDA

celebrata

die VII mensis Januarii, MDXLVI

DECRETUM DE MODO VIVENDI ET ALIIS IN CONCILIO SERVANDIS

Sacrosancta Tridentina synodus in Spiritu Sancto legitime congregata, in ea praesidentibus eisdem tribus Apostolicae Sedis legatis, agnoscens cum beato Jacobo Apostolo, quod *omne datum optimum et omne donum perfectum desursum est, descendens a patre luminum*,[1] qui iis, qui postulant a se sapientiam, *dat omnibus affluenter et non improperat eis;*[2] et simul sciens, quod *initium sapientiae est timor Domini:*[3] statuit et decrevit, omnes et singulos Christi fideles in civitate Tridentina congregatos exhortandos esse, prout exhortatur, ut se a malis et peccatis hactenus commissis emendare ac de cetero in timore Domini ambulare *et desideria carnis non perficere*,[4] orationibus instare, saepius confiteri, Eucharistiae sacramentum sumere, ecclesias frequentare, praecepta denique dominica, quantum quisque poterit, adimplere, necnon quotidie pro pace principum Christianorum et unitate ecclesiae privatim orare velint; episcopos vero et quoscumque alios in ordine sacerdotali constitutos, oecumenicum concilium in ea civitate concelebrantes, ut assidue in Dei laudibus incumbere, hostias, laudes et preces offerre, sacrificium missae quolibet saltem die dominico, in quo Deus lucem condidit et a mortuis resurrexit ac Spiritum Sanctum in discipulos infudit, peragere satagant, facientes, sicut idem Spiritus Sanctus per Apostolum praecipit, *obsecrationes, orationes, postulationes, gratiarum actiones* pro sanctissimo Domino nostro Papa, pro Imperatore, *pro regibus et ceteris, qui in sublimitate constituti sunt, et pro omnibus hominibus, ut quietam et tranquillam vitam agamus*,[5] pace fruamur et fidei incrementum videamus. Praeterea hortatur, ut jejunent saltem singulis sextis feriis in memoriam passionis Domini,

---

[1] Jac. 1:17.
[2] *Ibid.*, 1:5.
[3] Ps. 110:10; Prov. 1:7; 9:10; Ecclus. 1:16.
[4] Gal. 5:16.
[5] Cf. I Tim. 2:1 f.

et eleemosynas pauperibus erogent. In ecclesia autem cathedrali singulis quintis feriis celebretur missa de Spiritu Sancto cum litaniis et aliis orationibus ad hoc institutis; in aliis vero ecclesiis eadem die dicantur ad minus litaniae et orationes. Tempore autem quo sacra peraguntur, collocutiones et confabulationes non fiant, sed ore et animo celebranti assistatur.

Et quoniam *oportet episcopos esse irreprehensibiles, sobrios, castos, domui suae bene praepositos:* [6] hortatur etiam, ut ante omnia quilibet in mensa servet sobrietatem moderationemque ciborum; deinde, cum in eo loco saepe otiosi sermones oriri soleant, ut in ipsorum episcoporum mensis divinarum scripturarum lectio admisceatur.[7] Familiares vero suos unusquisque instruat et erudiat, ne sint rixosi, vinosi, impudici, cupidi, elati, blasphemi et voluptatum amatores; vitia demum fugiant et virtutes amplectantur et in vestitu et cultu et omnibus actibus honestatem prae se ferant, sicut decet ministros ministrorum Dei.

Ad haec cum hujus sacrosancti concilii praecipua cura, sollicitudo et intentio sit, ut propulsatis haeresum tenebris, quae per tot annos operuerunt terram, catholicae veritatis lux, Jesu Christo, qui vera lux est,[8] annuente, candor puritasque refulgeat et ea, quae reformatione egent, reformentur: ipsa synodus hortatur omnes catholicos hic congregatos et congregandos atque eos praesertim, qui sacrarum litterarum peritiam habent, ut sedula meditatione diligenter secum ipsi cogitent, quibus potissimum viis et modis ipsius synodi intentio dirigi et optatum effectum sortiri possit, quo maturius et consultius damnari damnanda, et probanda probari queant, ut per totum orbem omnes *uno ore* et eadem fidei confessione *glorificent Deum et Patrem Domini nostri Jesu Christi.*[9]

In sententiis vero dicendis juxta Toletani concilii statutum, in loco benedictionis considentibus Domini sacerdotibus, nullus debeat aut immodestis vocibus perstrepere aut tumultibus perturbare, nullis etiam falsis vanisve aut obstinatis disceptationibus contendere; sed quidquid dicatur, sic mitissima verborum prolatione temperetur, ut nec audientes offendantur, nec recti judicii acies perturbato animo inflectatur.[10]

---

[6] Cf. I Tim. 3:3 f.

[7] Hoc praeceptum conc. Toletani III (a.589), c.7 transiit in *Gratiani Decretum,* c.11, D.XLIV. Idem praecepit a.813 conc. Remense II, c.17. Hardouin IV, 1019.

[8] Joan. 1:9.

[9] Rom. 15:6.

[10] Desumpta est haec decreti pars fere ad verbum a conc. Toletano XI (a.675), c.1. Cf. *infra,* p. 553, lit. A et etiam c.4 conc. Toletani IV (a.633) apud Mansi, I, 10; X, 617; Hardouin, I, 6 ff.; III, 580.

Insuper ipsa sacra synodus statuit ac decrevit, quod si forte contigerit, aliquos debito in loco non sedere [11] et sententiam, etiam sub verbo *Placet*, proferre, congregationibus interesse et alios quoscumque actus facere, concilio durante, nulli propterea praejudicium generetur nullique novum jus acquiratur.

Deinde indicta fuit futura sessio ad diem Jovis quartam mensis Februarii proxime venturi.

---

[11] Cf. c.7, D.XVII et Sess. XXV in fin.

SESSIO TERTIA

celebrata

die IV mensis Februarii, MDXLVI

DECRETUM DE SYMBOLO FIDEI

In nomine sanctae et individuae Trinitatis, Patris et Filii et Spiritus Sancti. Haec sacrosancta oecumenica et generalis Tridentina synodus, in Spiritu Sancto legitime congregata, in ea praesidentibus eisdem tribus Apostolicae Sedis legatis, magnitudinem rerum tractandarum considerans, praesertim earum, quae duobus illis capitibus de extirpandis haeresibus et moribus reformandis continentur, quorum causa praecipue est congregata; agnoscens autem cum Apostolo, *non esse sibi colluctationem adversus carnem et sanguinem, sed adversus spirituales nequitias in coelestibus,*[1] cum eodem omnes et singulos in primis hortatur, ut *confortentur in Domino et in potentia virtutis ejus,*[2] *in omnibus sumentes scutum fidei, in quo possint omnia tela nequissimi ignea extinguere, atque galeam spei salutis accipiant cum gladio spiritus, quod est verbum Dei.*[3] Itaque ut haec pia ejus sollicitudo principium et progressum suum per Dei gratiam habeat, ante omnia statuit et decernit, praemittendam esse confessionem fidei, patrum exempla in hoc secuta, qui sacratioribus conciliis hoc scutum contra omnes haereses in principio suarum actionum apponere consuevere,[4] quo solo aliquando et infideles ad fidem traxerunt, haereticos expugnarunt et fideles confirmarunt. Quare symbolum fidei, quo sancta Romana ecclesia utitur tamquam principium illud, in quo omnes qui fidem Christi profitentur necessario conveniunt, ac fundamentum firmum et unicum contra

---

[1] Eph. 6:12.

[2] *Ibid.*, 6:10.

[3] *Ibid.*, 6:16 f.

[4] Plura fuerunt concilia quae professionem fidei in principio actionum emiserunt, ut Nicaenum I (a.325), Romanum I sub Julio I (a.337), Hipponen. (a.393), cujus decreta in Carthaginen. III (a.397) lecta et recepta sunt; Bracaren. III (a.675), Arelaten. VI (a.813). Plura etiam concilia Toletana, sc. IV (a.633), VI (a.638), XI (a.675), XIII (a.683), XVII (a.694), et alia a symbolo fidei initium sumpserunt. Non omittenda est hac in re professio fidei concilii generalis Lateranen. IV sub Innocentio III habiti. E contra, concilium Constantinopolitanum III (a.680) symbolum non in principio sed in actione XVII emisit.

quod *portae inferi nunquam praevalebunt,*[5] totidem verbis quibus in omnibus ecclesiis legitur, exprimendum esse censuit. Quod quidem ejusmodi est:

Credo in unum Deum, Patrem omnipotentem, factorem coeli et terrae, visibilium omnium et invisibilium. Et in unum Dominum Jesum Christum, Filium Dei unigenitum et ex Patre natum ante omnia saecula, Deum de Deo, lumen de lumine, Deum verum de Deo vero, genitum, non factum, consubstantialem Patri, per quem omnia facta sunt. Qui propter nos homines et propter nostram salutem descendit de coelis et incarnatus est de Spiritu Sancto ex Maria Virgine et homo factus est. Crucifixus etiam pro nobis sub Pontio Pilato, passus et sepultus est. Et resurrexit tertia die secundum scripturas et ascendit in coelum, sedet ad dexteram Patris. Et iterum venturus est cum gloria, judicare vivos et mortuos, cujus regni non erit finis. Et in Spiritum Sanctum, Dominum et vivificantem, qui ex Patre Filioque procedit. Qui cum Patre et Filio simul adoratur et conglorificatur, qui locutus est per prophetas. Et unam sanctam catholicam et apostolicam ecclesiam. Confiteor unum baptisma in remissionem peccatorum, et expecto resurrectionem mortuorum et vitam venturi saeculi. Amen.

INDICTIO FUTURAE SESSIONIS

Eadem sacrosancta oecumenica et generalis Tridentina synodus, in Spiritu Sancto legitime congregata, in ea praesidentibus eisdem tribus Apostolicae Sedis legatis, intelligens multos praelatos ex diversis partibus accinctos esse itineri, nonnullos etiam in via esse, quo huc veniant, cogitansque omnia ab ipsa sacra synodo decernenda eo majoris apud omnes existimationis et honoris videri posse, quo majori fuerint et pleniori patrum consilio et praesentia sancita et corroborata: statuit et decrevit, futuram sessionem post praesentem celebrandam esse die Jovis, quae subsequetur dominicam *Laetare* proxime futuram. Interim tamen non differri discussionem et examinationem eorum, quae ipsi synodo discutienda et examinanda videbuntur.

---

[5] Matt. 16:18.

SESSIO QUARTA
celebrata
die VIII mensis Aprilis, MDXLVI

DECRETUM DE CANONICIS SCRIPTURIS

Sacrosancta oecumenica et generalis Tridentina synodus, in Spiritu Sancto legitime congregata, praesidentibus in ea eisdem tribus Apostolicae Sedis legatis, hoc sibi perpetuo ante oculos proponens, ut sublatis erroribus puritas ipsa evangelii in ecclesia conservetur, quod promissum ante per prophetas in scripturis sanctis [1] Dominus noster Jesus Christus Dei Filius proprio ore primum promulgavit, deinde per suos apostolos tamquam fontem omnis et salutaris veritatis et morum disciplinae omni creaturae praedicari jussit; [2] perspiciensque hanc veritatem et disciplinam contineri in libris scriptis et sine scripto traditionibus, quae ipsius Christi ore ab apostolis acceptae, aut ab ipsis apostolis Spiritu Sancto dictante quasi per manus traditae [3] ad nos usque pervenerunt, orthodoxorum patrum exempla secuta, omnes libros tam veteris quam novi testamenti, cum utriusque unus Deus sit auctor, necnon traditiones ipsas, tum ad fidem tum ad mores pertinentes, tamquam vel oretenus a Christo, vel a Spiritu Sancto dictatas et continua successione in ecclesia catholica conservatas, pari pietatis affectu ac reverentia suscipit et veneratur. Sacrorum vero librorum indicem huic decreto adscribendum censuit,[4] ne cui dubitatio suboriri possit, quinam

---

[1] Jer. 31:22.

[2] Matt. 28:19 f.; Marc. 16:15.

[3] Cf. II Thess. 2:14; c.5, D.XI; c.6, X, De celebr. miss., III, 41; decretum V conc. Senonen. a.1528 Parisiis celebrati, apud Hardouin, IX, 1937; Hefele, *Conciliengeschichte*, IX, 635 f.

[4] Pro librorum sacrorum indicibus prioribus, cf. seq.: can. 85 (84) apostolorum (Hefele, I, 826). In hoc can. ex libris veteris testamenti omittuntur Tobias et Sapientia; ex illis novi testamenti Apocalypsis, sed adduntur duae epistolae Clementis I Papae et constitutiones apostolorum. Hos canones apost., non tamen constitutiones, confirmavit a.692 conc. Quinisextum sive Trullanum in can. 2 (*idem*, III, 330 f.). Conc. Laodicen., inter a.343 et 381 celebratum, in ultimo can. (60) libros utriusque testamenti enumerat, omissis tamen veteris testamenti Judith, Tobia, Sapientia, Ecclesiastico et Machabaeis, novi testamenti Apocalypsi (*idem*, I, 775). Conc. Hipponen. a.393 habitum, cujus canones conc. Carthaginen. III (a.397) suos fecit, in can. 36 omnes utriusque testamenti libros, qui nunc ab ecclesia catholica canonici habentur, recenset (*idem*, II, 59;

sint qui ab ipsa synodo suscipiuntur. Sunt vero infrascripti. Testamenti veteris: quinque Moysis, id est, Genesis, Exodus, Leviticus, Numeri, Deuteronomium; Josue, Judicum, Ruth, quatuor Regum, duo Paralipomenon, Esdrae primus et secundus, qui dicitur Nehemias, Tobias, Judith, Esther, Job, Psalterium Davidicum centum quinquaginta psalmorum, Parabolae, Ecclesiastes, Canticum Canticorum, Sapientia, Ecclesiasticus, Isaias, Jeremias cum Baruch, Ezechiel, Daniel, duodecim Prophetae minores, id est, Osea, Joel, Amos, Abdias, Jonas, Michaeas, Nahum, Habacuc, Sophonias, Aggaeus, Zacharias, Malachias, duo Machabaeorum primus et secundus. Testamenti novi: Quatuor Evangelia, secundum Matthaeum, Marcum, Lucam, et Joannem; Actus Apostolorum a Luca Evangelista conscripti, quatuordecim epistolae Pauli Apostoli, ad Romanos, duae ad Corinthios, ad Galatas, ad Ephesios, ad Philippenses, ad Colossenses, duae ad Thessalonicenses, duae ad Timotheum, ad Titum, ad Philemonem, ad Hebraeos; Petri Apostoli duae, Joannis Apostoli tres, Jacobi Apostoli una, Judae Apostoli una, et Apocalypsis Joannis Apostoli. Si quis autem libros ipsos integros cum omnibus suis partibus, prout in ecclesia catholica legi consueverunt et in veteri vulgata latina editione habentur, pro sacris et canonicis non susceperit, et traditiones praedictas sciens et prudens contempserit: anathema sit. Omnes itaque intelligant quo ordine et via ipsa synodus post jactum fidei confessionis fundamentum sit progressura, et quibus potissimum testimoniis ac praesidiis in confirmandis dogmatibus et instaurandis in ecclesia moribus sit usura.

DECRETUM DE EDITIONE ET USU SACRORUM LIBRORUM

Insuper eadem sacrosancta synodus considerans, non parum utilitatis accedere posse ecclesiae Dei, si ex omnibus latinis editionibus quae circumferuntur sacrorum librorum, quaenam pro authentica habenda sit innotescat: statuit et declarat, ut haec ipsa vetus et vulgata editio, quae longo tot saeculorum usu in ipsa ecclesia probata est, in publicis lectionibus, disputationibus, praedicationibus et expositionibus pro authentica habeatur, et quod nemo illam rejicere quovis praetextu audeat vel praesumat.

Denzinger, *Enchiridion*, n.92). Innocentii I Papae epist. ad Exuperium episc. Tolosan. (Denzinger, n.96). Decretum quod edidit Gelasius Papa ca. a.494 in synodo Romana, quodque ea in parte quae libros sacros enumerat decretum Damasi Papae renovat (Hardouin, II, 937; Denzinger, nn.84, 162). Bulla *Cantate Domino* ab Eugenio IV Papa in conc. Florentino edita. Hardouin, IX, 1021 ff.; Labbé, *Concilia*, XIII, 1204 ff.

Praeterea ad coercenda petulantia ingenia decernit, ut nemo suae prudentiae innixus, in rebus fidei et morum ad aedificationem doctrinae Christianae pertinentium, sacram scripturam ad suos sensus contorquens,[5] contra eum sensum quem tenuit et tenet sancta mater ecclesia, cujus est judicare de vero sensu et interpretatione scripturarum sanctarum, aut etiam contra unanimem consensum patrum ipsam scripturam sacram interpretari audeat,[6] etiamsi hujusmodi interpretationes nullo unquam tempore in lucem edendae forent. Qui contravenerint per ordinarios declarentur et poenis a jure statutis puniantur.

Sed et impressoribus modum in hac parte, ut par est, imponere volens, qui jam sine modo, hoc est, putantes sibi licere quidquid libet, sine licentia superiorum ecclesiasticorum ipsos sacrae scripturae libros et super illos adnotationes et expositiones quorumlibet indifferenter, saepe tacito, saepe etiam ementito praelo et, quod gravius est, sine nomine auctoris imprimunt, alibi etiam impressos libros hujusmodi temere venales habent: decernit et statuit, ut posthac sacra scriptura, potissimum vero haec ipsa vetus et vulgata editio quam emendatissime imprimatur, nullique liceat imprimere vel imprimi facere quosvis libros de rebus sacris sine nomine auctoris, neque illos in futurum vendere aut etiam apud se retinere, nisi primum examinati probatique fuerint ab ordinario, sub poena anathematis et pecuniae in canone concilii novissimi Lateranensis apposita.[7] Et si regulares fuerint, ultra examinationem et probationem hujusmodi licentiam quoque a suis superioribus impetrare teneantur, recognitis per eos libris juxta formam suarum ordinationum. Qui autem scripto eos communicant vel evulgant, nisi antea examinati probatique fuerint, eisdem poenis subjaceant, quibus impressores. Et qui eos habuerint vel legerint, nisi prodiderint auctorem, pro auctoribus habeantur. Ipsa vero hujusmodi librorum probatio in scriptis detur atque ideo in fronte libri vel scripti vel impressi authentice appareat. Idque totum, hoc est, et probatio et examen, gratis fiat, ut probanda probentur, et reprobentur improbanda.

Post haec temeritatem illam reprimere volens, qua ad profana quaeque convertuntur et torquentur verba et sententiae sacrae scripturae, ad scurrilia scilicet, fabulosa, vana, adulationes, detractiones, superstitiones, impias et diabolicas incantationes, divinationes, sortes, libellos etiam famosos: mandat et praecipit ad tollendam hujusmodi

---

[5] Cf. cc. 27, 39 (§ 70), C.XXIV, q. 3.
[6] Cf. conc. Trullan., c. 19. Mansi, XI, 951; Hardouin, III, 1667.
[7] Conc. Lateranen. V. Cf. *infra*, p. 553, lit. B.

irreverentiam et contemptum, ne de cetero quisquam quomodolibet verba scripturae sacrae ad haec et similia audeat usurpare, ut omnes hujus generis homines, temeratores et violatores verbi Dei, juris et arbitrii poenis per episcopos coerceantur.

INDICTIO FUTURAE SESSIONIS

Item haec sacrosancta synodus statuit et decernit, proximam futuram sessionem tenendam et celebrandam esse feria quinta post sacratissimum festum proximum Pentecostes.

SESSIO QUINTA
celebrata
die XVII mensis Junii, MDXLVI

DECRETUM DE PECCATO ORIGINALI

Ut fides nostra catholica, *sine qua impossibile est placere Deo*,[1] purgatis erroribus in sua sinceritate integra et illibata permaneat, et ne populus Christianus *omni vento doctrinae circumferatur*,[2] cum serpens ille antiquus,[3] humani generis perpetuus hostis, inter plurima mala quibus ecclesia Dei his nostris temporibus perturbatur, etiam de peccato originali ejusque remedio non solum nova, sed etiam vetera dissidia excitaverit: sacrosancta oecumenica et generalis Tridentina synodus, in Spiritu Sancto legitime congregata, praesidentibus in ea eisdem tribus Apostolicae Sedis legatis, jam ad revocandos errantes, et nutantes confirmandos accedere volens, sacrarum scripturarum et sanctorum patrum ac probatissimorum conciliorum testimonia et ipsius ecclesiae judicium et consensum secuta haec de ipso peccato originali statuit, fatetur ac declarat:

1. Si quis non confitetur,[4] primum hominem Adam, cum mandatum Dei in paradiso fuisset transgressus, statim sanctitatem et justitiam, in qua constitutus fuerat, amisisse incurrisseque per offensam praevaricationis hujusmodi iram et indignationem Dei atque ideo mortem, quam antea illi comminatus fuerat Deus, et cum morte captivitatem sub ejus potestate, *qui mortis* deinde *habuit imperium, hoc est diaboli*,[5] totumque Adam per illam praevaricationis offensam secundum corpus et animam in deterius commutatum fuisse;[6] anathema sit.

2. Si quis Adae praevaricationem sibi soli et non ejus propagini asserit nocuisse, et acceptam a Deo sanctitatem et justitiam, quam perdidit, sibi soli et non nobis etiam eum perdidisse; aut inquinatum

---

[1] Heb. 11:6.
[2] Eph. 4:14.
[3] Gen. 3:1 ff.; Apoc. 12:9; 20:2.
[4] Coelest. I Papae *epist. (21, c.4) ad episcopos Galliae a.431*. Denzinger, n.130.
[5] Heb. 2:14.
[6] Cf. conc. Arausican. II (a.529), c.1. Denzinger, n.174.

illum per inobedientiae peccatum mortem et poenas corporis tantum in omne genus humanum transfudisse, non autem et peccatum, quod mors est animae: [7] anathema sit, cum contradicat Apostolo dicenti: *Per unum hominem peccatum intravit in mundum, et per peccatum mors, et ita in omnes homines mors pertransiit, in quo omnes peccaverunt.*[8]

3. Si quis hoc Adae peccatum, quod origine unum est, et propagatione non imitatione transfusum omnibus inest unicuique proprium, vel per humanae naturae vires, vel per aliud remedium asserit tolli, quam per meritum unius mediatoris Domini nostri Jesu Christi,[9] qui nos Deo reconciliavit in sanguine suo, *factus nobis justitia, sanctificatio et redemptio;* [10] aut negat ipsum Christi Jesu meritum per baptismi sacramentum in forma ecclesiae rite collatum, tam adultis quam parvulis applicari: anathema sit. Quia *non est aliud nomen sub coelo datum hominibus, in quo oporteat nos salvos fieri.*[11] Unde illa vox: *Ecce agnus Dei, ecce qui tollit peccata mundi.*[12] Et illa: *Quicumque baptizati estis, Christum induistis.*[13]

4. Si quis parvulos recentes ab uteris matrum baptizandos negat, etiamsi fuerint a baptizatis parentibus orti, aut dicit in remissionem quidem peccatorum eos baptizari, sed nihil ex Adam trahere originalis peccati, quod regenerationis lavacro necesse sit expiari ad vitam aeternam consequendam,[14] unde fit consequens, ut in eis forma baptismatis in remissionem peccatorum non vera, sed falsa intelligatur: anathema sit. Quoniam non aliter intelligendum est id, quod dixit Apostolus: *Per unum hominem peccatum intravit in mundum, et per peccatum mors, et ita in omnes homines mors pertransiit, in quo omnes peccaverunt,*[15] nisi quemadmodum ecclesia catholica ubique diffusa semper intellexit. Propter hanc enim regulam fidei ex traditione apostolorum etiam parvuli, qui nihil peccatorum in semetipsis adhuc committere potuerunt, ideo in remissionem peccatorum veraciter baptizantur, ut in eis regeneratione mundetur, quod generatione contraxerunt.[16] *Nisi enim*

---

[7] Cf. conc. Arausican. II, c.2. Denzinger, n.175. Rouët de Journel, *Enchiridion patristicum* sub rubrica "Peccatum originale," p.770, n.302.
[8] Rom. 5:12.
[9] Cf. I Tim. 2:5.
[10] Cf. I Cor. 1:30.
[11] Act. 4:12.
[12] Joan. 1:29.
[13] Gal. 3:27.
[14] Conc. Milevitan. II (a.416), c.2. Denzinger, n.102. Transiit hoc cap. in *Decr. Grat.*, c.153, D.IV de cons.
[15] Rom. 5:12.
[16] C.153, D.IV de cons.

quis renatus fuerit ex aqua et Spiritu Sancto, non potest introire in regnum Dei.[17]

5. Si quis per Jesu Christi Domini nostri gratiam, quae in baptismate confertur, reatum originalis peccati remitti negat, aut etiam asserit, non tolli totum id, quod veram et propriam peccati rationem habet, sed illud dicit tantum radi aut non imputari: [18] anathema sit. In renatis enim nihil odit Deus, quia *nihil est damnationis iis,*[19] *qui vere consepulti sunt cum Christo per baptisma in mortem,*[20] *qui non secundum carnem ambulant,*[21] sed veterem hominem exuentes et novum, qui secundum Deum creatus est, induentes,[22] innocentes, immaculati, puri, innoxii ac Deo dilecti effecti sunt, *heredes quidem Dei, coheredes autem Christi,*[23] ita ut nihil prorsus eos ingressu coeli remoretur. Manere autem in baptizatis concupiscentiam vel fomitem, haec sancta synodus fatetur et sentit, quae cum ad agonem relicta sit, nocere non consentientibus et viriliter per Christi Jesu gratiam repugnantibus non valet. Quinimmo *qui legitime certaverit, coronabitur.*[24] Hanc concupiscentiam, quam aliquando Apostolus peccatum appellat,[25] sancta synodus declarat, ecclesiam catholicam nunquam intellexisse peccatum appellari, quod vere et proprie in renatis peccatum sit, sed quia ex peccato est et ad peccatum inclinat. Si quis autem contrarium senserit: anathema sit.

6. Declarat tamen haec ipsa sancta synodus, non esse suae intentionis comprehendere in hoc decreto, ubi de peccato originali agitur, beatam et immaculatam Virginem Mariam Dei genitricem, sed observandas esse constitutiones felicis recordationis Sixti Papae Quarti,[26] sub poenis in eis constitutionibus contentis, quas innovat.

---

[17] Joan. 3:5.
[18] Cf. Aug., *Contra duas epist. Pelagianorum,* lib. I, c. 13. Migne, *PL,* 44, p. 562.
[19] Rom. 8:1.
[20] *Ibid.,* 6:4; c. 13, D. IV de cons. (Leo I).
[21] *Ibid.,* 8:1.
[22] Eph. 4:22, 24; Col. 3:9 f.
[23] Rom. 8:17.
[24] Cf. II Tim. 2:5.
[25] Rom. 6–8; Col. 3.
[26] Sunt duae constitutiones Sixti V quae de conceptione b. Mariae Virginis agunt, sc. cc. 1, 2 in Extrav. comm., III, 12. Vide *infra,* pp. 554 f., litt. C et D.

DECRETUM DE REFORMATIONE

CAPUT I

DE INSTITUENDA LECTIONE SACRAE SCRIPTURAE ET LIBERALIUM ARTIUM

Eadem sacrosancta synodus, piis summorum pontificum et probatorum conciliorum constitutionibus inhaerens [27] easque amplectens et illis adjiciens, ne coelestis ille sacrorum librorum thesaurus, quem Spiritus Sanctus summa liberalitate hominibus tradidit, neglectus jaceat, statuit et decrevit quod in illis ecclesiis, in quibus praebenda aut praestimonium seu aliud quovis nomine nuncupatum stipendium pro lectoribus sacrae theologiae deputatum reperitur, episcopi, archiepiscopi, primates et alii locorum ordinarii eos, qui praebendam aut praestimonium seu stipendium hujusmodi obtinent, ad ipsius sacrae scripturae expositionem et interpretationem per se ipsos, si idonei fuerint, alioquin per idoneum substitutum, ab ipsis episcopis, archiepiscopis, primatibus et aliis locorum ordinariis eligendum, etiam per subtractionem fructuum, cogant et compellant. De cetero vero praebenda, praestimonium aut stipendium hujusmodi non nisi personis idoneis et quae per se ipsas id munus explicare possint, conferantur. Et aliter facta provisio nulla sit et invalida.

In ecclesiis autem metropolitanis vel cathedralibus, si civitas insignis vel populosa, ac etiam in collegiatis exsistentibus in aliquo insigni oppido, etiam nullius dioecesis, si ibi clerus numerosus fuerit, ubi nulla praebenda aut praestimonium seu stipendium hujusmodi deputatum reperitur, praebenda quomodocumque, praeterquam ex causa resignationis, primo vacatura, cui aliud onus incompatibile injunctum non sit, ad eum usum ipso facto perpetuo constituta et deputata intelligatur. Et quatenus in ipsis ecclesiis nulla vel non sufficiens praebenda foret,[28] metropolitanus vel episcopus ipse per assignationem fructuum alicujus simplicis beneficii, ejusdem tamen debitis supportatis oneribus, vel per contributionem beneficiatorum suae civitatis et dioecesis, vel alias, prout commodius fieri poterit, de capituli consilio ita provideat, ut ipsa sacrae scripturae lectio habeatur. Ita tamen, ut quaecumque aliae lectiones,

---

[27] Cf. c.12, D.XXXVII (Eugen. II); c.1, X, De magistr., V, 5 (Lat. III), c.4, *ibid.* (Lat. IV), c.5, *ibid.* (Honor. III); *infra*, Sess. XXIII, cap. 18 de ref.
[28] Cf. Sess. XXIV, cap. 15 de ref.

vel consuetudine vel quavis alia ratione institutae, propter id minime praetermittantur.

Ecclesiae vero quarum annui proventus tenues fuerint, et ubi tam exigua est cleri et populi multitudo, ut theologiae lectio in eis commode haberi non possit, saltem magistrum habeant [29] ab episcopo cum consilio capituli eligendum, qui clericos aliosque scholares pauperes grammaticam gratis doceat, ut deinceps ad ipsa sacrae scripturae studia (annuente Deo) transire possint. Ideoque illi magistro grammatices vel alicujus simplicis beneficii fructus, quos tamdiu percipiat, quamdiu in docendo perstiterit, assignentur,[30] dum tamen beneficium ipsum suo debito non fraudetur obsequio, vel ex capitulari vel episcopali mensa condigna aliqua merces persolvatur vel alias episcopus ipse aliquam rationem ineat suae ecclesiae et dioecesi accommodam, ne pia haec, utilis ac fructuosa provisio quovis quaesito colore negligatur.

In monasteriis quoque monachorum, ubi commode fieri queat, etiam lectio sacrae scripturae habeatur.[31] Qua in re si abbates negligentes fuerint, episcopi locorum, in hoc ut Sedis Apostolicae delegati, eos ad id opportunis remediis compellant.

In conventibus vero aliorum regularium, in quibus studia commode vigere possunt, sacrae scripturae lectio similiter habeatur, quae lectio a capitulis generalibus vel provincialibus assignetur dignioribus magistris.

In gymnasiis etiam publicis, ubi tam honorifica et ceterorum omnium maxime necessaria lectio hactenus instituta non fuerit, religiosissimorum principum ac rerum publicarum pietate et caritate, ad catholicae fidei defensionem et incrementum, sanaeque doctrinae conservationem et propagationem instituatur. Et ubi instituta foret et negligeretur, restituatur.

Et ne sub specie pietatis impietas disseminetur, statuit eadem sancta synodus, neminem ad hujusmodi lectionis officium tam publice quam privatim admittendum esse, qui prius ab episcopo loci de vita, moribus et scientia examinatus et approbatus non fuerit.[32] Quod tamen de lectoribus in claustris monachorum non intelligatur.

Docentes vero ipsam sacram scripturam, dum publice in scholis docuerint, et scholares, qui in ipsis scholis student, privilegiis omnibus

---

[29] Cf. *supra* adn. 27.

[30] Hic magister ex bulla Pii IV *In sacrosancta,* 1564, ad fidei professionem tenebatur.

[31] Cui addidit Paulus V const. *Apostolicae,* 1610, lectionem hebraicam, graecam et arabicam.

[32] Hinc emanavit bulla Pii IV de professione fidei, 13 Nov., 1564. Cf. *infra,* pp. 540 ff.

de perceptione fructuum praebendarum et beneficiorum suorum in absentia, a jure communi concessis, plene gaudeant et fruantur.[33]

Caput II

DE VERBI DEI CONCIONATORIBUS ET QUAESTORIBUS ELEEMOSYNARIIS

Quia vero Christianae reipublicae non minus necessaria est praedicatio evangelii quam lectio, et hoc est praecipuum episcoporum munus: [34] statuit et decrevit eadem sancta synodus, omnes episcopos, archiepiscopos, primates et omnes alios ecclesiarum praelatos teneri per se ipsos, si legitime impediti non fuerint, ad praedicandum sanctum Jesu Christi evangelium.

Si vero contigerit, episcopos et alios praedictos legitimo detineri impedimento, juxta formam generalis concilii [35] viros idoneos assumere teneantur ad hujusmodi praedicationis officium salubriter exequendum. Si quis autem hoc adimplere contempserit, districtae subjaceat ultioni.

Archipresbyteri quoque, plebani et quicumque parochiales vel alias, curam animarum habentes, ecclesias quocumque modo obtinent, per se vel alios idoneos, si legitime impediti fuerint, diebus saltem dominicis et festis solemnibus plebes sibi commissas pro sua et earum capacitate pascant salutaribus verbis, docendo ea, quae scire omnibus necessarium est ad salutem, annunciandoque eis cum brevitate et facilitate sermonis vitia, quae eos declinare, et virtutes, quas sectari oporteat, ut poenam aeternam evadere et coelestem gloriam consequi valeant. Id vero si quis eorum praestare negligat, etiamsi ab episcopi jurisdictione quavis ratione exemptum se esse praetenderet, etiamsi ecclesiae quovis modo exemptae dicerentur aut alicui monasterio, etiam extra dioecesim existenti, forsan annexae vel unitae, modo re ipsa in dioecesi sint, provida pastoralis episcoporum sollicitudo non desit, ne illud impleatur: *Parvuli petierunt panem, et non erat qui frangeret eis.*[36] Itaque ubi ab episcopo moniti, trium mensium spatio muneri suo defuerint, per censuras ecclesiasticas seu alias ad ipsius episcopi arbitrium cogantur, ita ut etiam, si ei sic expedire visum fuerit, ex beneficiorum fructibus alteri, qui id

---

[33] C.5, X, De magistr., V, 5 (Honor. III).
[34] Cf. Sess. XXIV, cap. 4 de ref.; c.6, D.LXXXVIII; conc. Remense II (a.813), cc.14, 15. Hardouin, IV, 1019.
[35] C. 15, X, De off. jud. ord., I, 31 (Lat. IV), *infra*, p. 557, lit. E.
[36] Thren. 4:4.

praestet, honesta aliqua merces persolvatur, donec principalis ipse resipiscens officium suum impleat.

Si quae vero parochiales ecclesiae reperiantur subjectae monasteriis in nulla dioecesi exsistentibus, si abbates et regulares praelati in praedictis negligentes fuerint, a metropolitanis, in quorum provinciis dioeceses ipsae sitae sunt, tamquam quoad hoc Sedis Apostolicae delegatis compellantur. Neque hujus decreti executionem consuetudo vel exemptio aut appellatio aut reclamatio sive recursus impedire valeat, quousque desuper a competenti judice, qui summarie et sola facti veritate inspecta procedat, cognitum et decisum fuerit.

Regulares vero cujuscumque ordinis, nisi a suis superioribus de vita, moribus et scientia examinati et approbati fuerint, ac de eorum licentia, etiam in ecclesiis suorum ordinum, praedicare non possint; cum qua licentia personaliter se coram episcopis praesentare et ab eis benedictionem petere teneantur antequam praedicare incipiant.

In ecclesiis vero quae suorum ordinum non sunt, ultra licentiam suorum superiorum etiam episcopi licentiam habere teneantur, sine qua in ipsis ecclesiis non suorum ordinum nullo modo praedicare possint.[37] Ipsam autem licentiam gratis episcopi concedant.

Si vero (quod absit) praedicator errores aut scandala disseminaverit in populum, etiamsi in monasterio sui vel alterius ordinis praedicet, episcopus ei praedicationem interdicat. Quod si haereses praedicaverit, contra eum secundum juris dispositionem aut loci consuetudinem procedat, etiamsi praedicator ipse generali vel speciali privilegio exemptum se esse praetenderet. Quo casu episcopus auctoritate apostolica et tamquam Sedis Apostolicae delegatus procedat. Curent autem episcopi, ne quis praedicator vel ex falsis informationibus vel alias calumniose vexetur justamve de eis conquerendi occasionem habeat.

Caveant praeterea episcopi, ne aliquem vel eorum, qui cum sint nomine regulares, extra claustra tamen et obedientiam religionum suarum vivunt, vel presbyterorum saecularium (nisi ipsis noti sint et moribus atque doctrina probati), etiam quorumlibet privilegiorum praetextu in sua civitate vel dioecesi praedicare permittant, donec ab ipsis episcopis super ea re sancta Sedes Apostolica consulatur, a qua privilegia hujusmodi nisi tacita veritate, et expresso mendacio, ab indignis extorqueri verisimile non est.

Quaestores vero eleemosynarii, qui etiam quaestuarii vulgo dicuntur,

---

[37] C. 13 (§ 6), X, De haeret., V, 7; Sess. XXIV, cap. 4 de ref.

cujuscumque conditionis exsistant, nullo modo nec per se nec per alium praedicare praesumant.[38] Et contrafacientes ab episcopis et ordinariis locorum, privilegiis quibuscumque non obstantibus, opportunis remediis omnino arceantur.

INDICTIO FUTURAE SESSIONIS

Item haec sacrosancta synodus statuit et decernit, primam futuram sessionem tenendam et celebrandam esse die Jovis feria quinta post festum beati Jacobi Apostoli.

Prorogata deinde fuit sessio ad diem XIII mensis Januarii, MDXLVII.

[38] C. 14, X, De poenit., V, 38 (Lat. IV); c. 11 (§ 2), De haeret. in VI°, V, 2 (Clem. IV); c. 2, De poenit. in Clem., V, 9. Per bullam Pii V *Etsi Dominici*, 8 Feb., 1567, sublatae sunt indulgentiae etiam perpetuae, quae quaestuandi occasionem praebeant.

SESSIO SEXTA

celebrata

die XIII mensis Januarii, MDXLVII

DECRETUM DE JUSTIFICATIONE

Prooemium

Cum hoc tempore non sine multarum animarum jactura et gravi ecclesiasticae unitatis detrimento, erronea quaedam disseminata sit de justificatione doctrina, ad laudem et gloriam omnipotentis Dei, ecclesiae tranquillitatem et animarum salutem sacrosancta oecumenica et generalis Tridentina synodus, in Spiritu Sancto legitime congregata, praesidentibus in ea nomine sanctissimi in Christo patris et domini nostri, domini Pauli, divina providentia Papae tertii, reverendissimis dominis, dominis Joanne Maria episcopo Praenestino de Monte et Marcello tit. S. Crucis in Jerusalem presbytero, S. R. E. cardinalibus et apostolicis de latere legatis, exponere intendit omnibus Christi fidelibus veram sanamque doctrinam ipsius justificationis, quam *sol justitiae* [1] Christus Jesus, fidei nostrae auctor et consummator,[2] docuit, apostoli tradiderunt et catholica ecclesia, Spiritu Sancto suggerente, perpetuo retinuit; districtius inhibendo ne deinceps audeat quisquam aliter credere, praedicare aut docere quam praesenti decreto statuitur ac declaratur.

Caput I

DE NATURAE ET LEGIS AD JUSTIFICANDOS HOMINES IMBECILLITATE

Primum declarat sancta synodus, ad justificationis doctrinam probe et sincere intelligendam oportere ut unusquisque agnoscat et fateatur, quod cum omnes homines in praevaricatione Adae innocentiam perdidissent,[3] facti immundi [4] et (ut Apostolus inquit) *natura filii irae*,[5]

[1] Mal. 4:2.
[2] Heb. 12:2.
[3] Rom. 5:12; I Cor. 15:22.
[4] Is. 64:6.
[5] Eph. 2:3.

quemadmodum in decreto de peccato originali exposuit,[6] usque adeo servi erant peccati [7] et sub potestate diaboli ac mortis, ut non modo gentes per viam naturae, sed ne Judaei quidem per ipsam etiam litteram legis Moysis inde liberari aut surgere possent, tametsi in eis liberum arbitrium minime extinctum esset, viribus licet attenuatum et inclinatum.[8]

Caput II

DE DISPENSATIONE ET MYSTERIO ADVENTUS CHRISTI

Quo factum est ut coelestis Pater, *Pater misericordiarum et Deus totius consolationis*,[9] Christum Jesum Filium suum, et ante legem et legis tempore multis sanctis patribus declaratum ac promissum, cum venit beata illa *plenitudo temporis*,[10] ad homines miserit, ut et Judaeos, *qui sub lege erant, redimeret*,[11] et *gentes, quae non sectabantur justitiam, justitiam apprehenderent*,[12] atque omnes adoptionem filiorum reciperent.[13] Hunc *proposuit Deus propitiatorem per fidem in sanguine ipsius*,[14] *pro peccatis nostris, non solum autem pro nostris, sed etiam pro totius mundi*.[15]

Caput III

QUI PER CHRISTUM JUSTIFICANTUR

Verum etsi ille *pro omnibus mortuus est*,[16] non omnes tamen mortis beneficium recipiunt, sed ii dumtaxat, quibus meritum passionis ejus communicatur. Nam sicut revera homines, nisi ex semine Adae propagati nascerentur, non nascerentur injusti, cum ea propagatione per ipsum, dum concipiuntur, propriam injustitiam contrahant; ita nisi in Christo renascerentur, nunquam justificarentur, cum ea renascentia per meritum passionis ejus gratia, qua justi fiunt, illis tribuatur. Pro

---

[6] Cf. Sess. V in princ.
[7] Rom. 6:20.
[8] Conc. Arausican. II (a.529), c.25. Hardouin, II, 1101.
[9] Cf. II Cor. 1:3.
[10] Gal. 4:4.
[11] *Ibid.*, 4:5.
[12] Rom. 9:30.
[13] Gal. 4:5.
[14] Rom. 3:25.
[15] Cf. I Joan. 2:2.
[16] Cf. II Cor. 5:15.

hoc beneficio Apostolus gratias nos semper agere hortatur *Patri, qui dignos nos fecit in partem sortis sanctorum in lumine, et eripuit de potestate tenebrarum, transtulitque in regnum Filii dilectionis suae, in quo habemus redemptionem et remissionem peccatorum.*[17]

Caput IV

INSINUATUR DESCRIPTIO JUSTIFICATIONIS IMPII, ET MODUS EJUS IN STATU GRATIAE

Quibus verbis justificationis impii descriptio insinuatur, ut sit translatio ab eo statu, in quo homo nascitur filius primi Adae, in statum gratiae et adoptionis filiorum Dei [18] per secundum Adam Jesum Christum salvatorem nostrum; quae quidem translatio post evangelium promulgatum sine lavacro regenerationis aut ejus voto fieri non potest, sicut scriptum est: *Nisi quis renatus fuerit ex aqua et Spiritu Sancto, non potest introire in regnum Dei.*[19]

Caput V

DE NECESSITATE PRAEPARATIONIS AD JUSTIFICATIONEM IN ADULTIS, ET UNDE SIT

Declarat praeterea, ipsius justificationis exordium in adultis a Dei per Christum Jesum praeveniente gratia sumendum esse, hoc est, ab ejus vocatione, qua nullis eorum exsistentibus meritis vocantur, ut qui per peccata a Deo aversi erant, per ejus excitantem atque adjuvantem gratiam ad convertendum se ad suam ipsorum justificationem, eidem gratiae libere assentiendo et cooperando, disponantur, ita ut tangente Deo cor hominis per Spiritus Sancti illuminationem neque homo ipse nihil omnino agat, inspirationem illam recipiens, quippe qui illam et abjicere potest, neque tamen sine gratia Dei movere se ad justitiam coram illo libera sua voluntate possit. Unde in sacris litteris cum dicitur: *Convertimini ad me, et ego convertar ad vos,*[20] libertatis nostrae ad-

---

[17] Col. 1:12–14.
[18] Rom. 8:23. Cf. Rouët de Journel, *Enchiridion patristicum* sub rubrica "Justificatio," p. 773, n.359.
[19] Joan. 3:5; cc.8, 149, D.IV de cons. (Aug.).
[20] Zach. 1:3; c.34, D.I de poenit.

monemur; cum respondemus: *Converte nos Domine ad te, et convertemur,*[21] Dei nos gratia praeveniri confitemur.

Caput VI

MODUS PRAEPARATIONIS

Disponuntur autem ad ipsam justitiam, dum excitati divina gratia et adjuti, fidem ex auditu concipientes,[22] libere moventur in Deum, credentes vera esse quae divinitus revelata et promissa sunt, atque illud in primis, a Deo justificari impium *per gratiam ejus, per redemptionem, quae est in Christo Jesu,*[23] et dum, peccatores se esse intelligentes, a divinae justitiae timore, quo utiliter concutiuntur, ad considerandam Dei misericordiam se convertendo, in spem eriguntur, fidentes, Deum sibi propter Christum propitium fore, illumque tamquam omnis justitiae fontem diligere incipiunt ac propterea moventur adversus peccata per odium aliquod et detestationem, hoc est, per eam poenitentiam quam ante baptismum agi oportet; denique dum proponunt suscipere baptismum, inchoare novam vitam et servare divina mandata. De hac dispositione scriptum est: *Accedentem ad Deum oportet credere, quia est et quod inquirentibus se remunerator sit,*[24] et: *Confide fili, remittuntur tibi peccata tua,*[25] et: *Timor Domini expellit peccatum,*[26] et: *Poenitentiam agite et baptizetur unusquisque vestrum in nomine Jesu Christi in remissionem peccatorum vestrorum, et accipietis donum Spiritus Sancti,*[27] et: *Euntes ergo docete omnes gentes, baptizantes eos in nomine Patris et Filii et Spiritus Sancti, docentes eos servare quaecumque mandavi vobis,*[28] Denique: *Praeparate corda vestra Domino.*[29]

---

[21] Thren. 5:21.
[22] Rom. 10:17.
[23] *Ibid.*, 3:24. Cf. Rouët de Journel, p. 773, n. 362; Denzinger, sub rubrica "Justificationis via," IX b, p. [27].
[24] Heb. 11:6.
[25] Matt. 9:2; Marc. 2:5.
[26] Ecclus. 1:27.
[27] Act. 2:38; cc. 13, 97, D. IV de cons.
[28] Matt. 28:19 f.
[29] Cf. I Reg. 7:3.

CAPUT VII

QUID SIT JUSTIFICATIO IMPII, ET QUAE EJUS CAUSAE

Hanc dispositionem seu praeparationem justificatio ipsa consequitur, quae non est sola peccatorum remissio, sed et sanctificatio et renovatio interioris hominis per voluntariam susceptionem gratiae et donorum, unde homo ex injusto fit justus et ex inimico amicus, ut sit *haeres secundum spem vitae aeternae.*[30] Hujus justificationis causae sunt: finalis quidem, gloria Dei et Christi ac vita aeterna; efficiens vero, misericors Deus, qui gratuito abluit et sanctificat,[31] signans et ungens [32] *Spiritu promissionis Sancto, qui est pignus haereditatis nostrae;* [33] meritoria autem dilectissimus unigenitus suus Dominus noster Jesus Christus, qui *cum essemus inimici,*[34] *propter nimiam caritatem, qua dilexit nos,*[35] sua sanctissima passione in ligno crucis nobis justificationem meruit et pro nobis Deo Patri satisfecit; instrumentalis item, sacramentum baptismi, quod est sacramentum fidei,[36] sine qua nulli unquam contigit justificatio. Demum unica formalis causa est justitia Dei, non qua ipse justus est, sed qua nos justos facit, qua videlicet ab eo donati renovamur spiritu mentis nostrae,[37] et non modo reputamur, sed vere justi nominamur et sumus, justitiam in nobis recipientes unusquisque suam secundum mensuram, quam Spiritus Sanctus partitur singulis prout vult,[38] et secundum propriam cujusque dispositionem et cooperationem. Quamquam enim nemo possit esse justus nisi cui merita passionis Domini nostri Jesu Christi communicantur, id tamen in hac impii justificatione fit, dum ejusdem sanctissimae passionis merito *per Spiritum Sanctum caritas Dei diffunditur in cordibus eorum* [39] qui justificantur atque ipsis inhaeret. Unde in ipsa justificatione cum remissione peccatorum haec omnia simul infusa accipit homo per Jesum Christum, cui inseritur: fidem, spem et caritatem. Nam fides, nisi ad eam spes accedat et caritas, neque unit perfecte cum Christo neque

---

[30] Tit. 3:7.
[31] Cf. I Cor. 6:11.
[32] Cf. II Cor. 1:21.
[33] Eph. 1:13 f.
[34] Rom. 5:10.
[35] Eph. 2:4.
[36] C.76, D.IV de cons. (Aug.).
[37] Eph. 4:23.
[38] Cf. I Cor. 12:11.
[39] Rom. 5:5.

corporis ejus vivum membrum efficit.[40] Qua ratione verissime dicitur, fidem sine operibus mortuam et otiosam esse,[41] et *in Christo Jesu neque circumcisionem aliquid valere, neque praeputium, sed fidem, quae per caritatem operatur.*[42] Hanc fidem ante baptismi sacramentum ex apostolorum traditione catechumeni ab ecclesia petunt, cum petunt fidem vitam aeternam praestantem, quam sine spe et caritate fides praestare non potest. Unde et statim verbum Christi audiunt: *Si vis ad vitam ingredi, serva mandata.*[43] Itaque veram et Christianam justitiam accipientes, eam ceu *primam stolam,*[44] pro illa, quam Adam sua inobedientia sibi et nobis perdidit, per Christum Jesum illis donatam, candidam et immaculatam jubentur statim renati conservare, ut eam perferant ante tribunal Domini nostri Jesu Christi et habeant vitam aeternam.[45]

Caput VIII

QUOMODO INTELLIGATUR, IMPIUM PER FIDEM ET GRATIS JUSTIFICARI

Cum vero Apostolus dicit, justificari hominem per fidem [46] et gratis,[47] ea verba in eo sensu intelligenda sunt, quem perpetuus ecclesiae catholicae consensus tenuit et expressit, ut scilicet per fidem ideo justificari dicamur, quia fides est humanae salutis initium, fundamentum et radix omnis justificationis, sine qua *impossibile est placere Deo* [48] et ad filiorum ejus consortium pervenire; gratis autem justificari ideo dicamur, quia nihil eorum, quae justificationem praecedunt, sive fides sive opera, ipsam justificationis gratiam promeretur; *Si enim gratia est, jam non ex operibus; alioquin* (ut idem Apostolus inquit) *gratia jam non est gratia.*[49]

[40] Cf. *infra,* cap. 10.
[41] Jac. 2:17, 20. Cf. Denzinger, *loc. cit.*
[42] Gal. 5:6, 6:15.
[43] Matt. 19:17.
[44] Luc. 15:22; cf. c.31, D.II de poenit. (Aug.).
[45] Cf. *Rituale Rom.* de ordine baptismi in fin.
[46] Rom. 5:1.
[47] *Ibid.,* 3:24.
[48] Heb. 11:6.
[49] Rom. 11:6.

Caput IX

CONTRA INANEM HAERETICORUM FIDUCIAM

Quamvis autem necessarium sit credere neque remitti neque remissa unquam fuisse peccata, nisi gratis divina misericordia propter Christum, nemini tamen fiduciam et certitudinem remissionis peccatorum suorum jactanti et in ea sola quiescenti peccata dimitti vel dimissa esse dicendum est, cum apud haereticos et schismaticos possit esse, immo nostra tempestate sit et magna contra ecclesiam catholicam contentione praedicetur vana haec et ab omni pietate remota fiducia. Sed neque illud asserendum est, oportere eos, qui vere justificati sunt, absque ulla omnino dubitatione apud semetipsos statuere, se esse justificatos, neminemque a peccatis absolvi ac justificari, nisi eum, qui certo credat, se absolutum et justificatum esse, atque hac sola fide absolutionem et justificationem perfici, quasi qui hoc non credit, de Dei promissis deque mortis et resurrectionis Christi efficacia dubitet. Nam sicut nemo pius de Dei misericordia, de Christi merito deque sacramentorum virtute et efficacia dubitare debet, sic quilibet, dum se ipsum suamque propriam infirmitatem et indispositionem respicit, de sua gratia formidare et timere potest, cum nullus scire valeat certitudine fidei, cui non potest subesse falsum, se gratiam Dei esse consecutum.

Caput X

DE ACCEPTAE JUSTIFICATIONIS INCREMENTO

Sic ergo justificati et amici Dei ac domestici facti,[50] euntes *de virtute in virtutem,*[51] renovantur (ut Apostolus inquit) *de die in diem,*[52] hoc est, mortificando membra carnis suae [53] et exhibendo ea arma justitiae in sanctificationem [54] per observationem mandatorum Dei et ecclesiae, in ipsa justitia per Christi gratiam accepta, cooperante fide bonis operibus, crescunt atque magis justificantur, sicut scriptum est: *Qui justus est, justificetur adhuc,*[55] et iterum: *Ne verearis usque ad mortem justi-*

---

[50] Eph. 2:19.
[51] Ps. 83:8.
[52] Cf. II Cor. 4:16.
[53] Col. 3:5.
[54] Rom. 6:13, 19.
[55] Apoc. 22:11.

ficari,[56] et rursus: *Videtis quoniam ex operibus justificatur homo et non ex fide tantum.*[57] Hoc vero justitiae incrementum petit sancta ecclesia cum orat: *Da nobis Domine fidei, spei et caritatis augmentum.*[58]

Caput XI

DE OBSERVATIONE MANDATORUM DEQUE ILLIUS NECESSITATE ET POSSIBILITATE

Nemo autem, quantumvis justificatus, liberum se esse ab observatione mandatorum putare debet, nemo temeraria illa et a patribus sub anathemate prohibita voce uti,[59] Dei praecepta homini justificato ad observandum esse impossibilia. Nam Deus impossibilia non jubet, sed jubendo monet, et facere quod possis et petere quod non possis, et adjuvat ut possis;[60] *cujus mandata gravia non sunt*,[61] *cujus jugum suave est et onus leve.*[62] Qui enim sunt filii Dei, Christum diligunt; qui autem diligunt eum (ut ipsemet testatur),[63] servant sermones ejus, quod utique cum divino auxilio praestare possunt. Licet enim in hac mortali vita quantumvis sancti et justi in levia saltem et quotidiana, quae etiam venialia dicuntur, peccata quandoque cadant, non propterea desinunt esse justi. Nam justorum illa vox est et humilis et verax: *Dimitte nobis debita nostra.*[64] Quo fit, ut justi ipsi eo magis se obligatos ad ambulandum in via justitiae sentire debeant, quo *liberati jam a peccato, servi autem facti Deo*,[65] *sobrie et juste et pie viventes*,[66] proficere possint per Christum Jesum, per quem accessum habuerunt in gratiam istam.[67] Deus namque sua gratia semel justificatos non deserit, nisi ab eis prius deseratur.[68] Itaque nemo sibi in sola fide blandiri debet, putans fide sola se haeredem esse constitutum haereditatemque consecuturum, etiamsi Christo non

---

[56] Ecclus. 18:22.
[57] Jac. 2:24.
[58] In oratione dominicae 13 post Pentecosten.
[59] Cf. conc. Arausican. II post cap. 25. Hardouin, II, 1101.
[60] S. Aug., *De natura et gratia*, c.43. Migne, *PL*, XLIV, 271.
[61] Cf. I Joan. 5:3.
[62] Matt. 11:30.
[63] Joan. 14:23.
[64] Matt. 6:12.
[65] Rom. 6:18, 22.
[66] Tit. 2:12.
[67] Rom. 5:2.
[68] S. Aug., *op. cit.*, c.26. *PL*, XLIV, 261.

compatiatur, ut et conglorificetur.[69] Nam et Christus ipse (ut inquit Apostolus), *cum esset Filius Dei, didicit ex iis, quae passus est, obedientiam, et consummatus factus est omnibus obtemperantibus sibi causa salutis aeternae.*[70] Propterea Apostolus ipse monet justificatos dicens: *Nescitis quod ii, qui in stadio currunt, omnes quidem currunt, sed unus accipit bravium? sic currite, ut comprehendatis. Ego igitur sic curro, non quasi in incertum, sic pugno, non quasi aërem verberans, sed castigo corpus meum et in servitutem redigo, ne forte, cum aliis praedicaverim, ipse reprobus efficiar.*[71] Item princeps apostolorum Petrus: *Satagite, ut per bona opera certam vestram vocationem et electionem faciatis; haec enim facientes non peccabitis aliquando.*[72] Unde constat, eos orthodoxae religionis doctrinae adversari, qui dicunt, justum in omni bono opere saltem venialiter peccare,[73] aut, quod intolerabilius est, poenas aeternas mereri; atque etiam eos, qui statuunt, in omnibus operibus justos peccare, si in illis suam ipsorum socordiam excitando et sese ad currendum in stadio cohortando, cum hoc, ut in primis glorificetur Deus, mercedem quoque intuentur aeternam, cum scriptum sit: *Inclinavi cor meum ad faciendas justificationes tuas propter retributionem,*[74] et de Moyse dicat Apostolus, quod aspiciebat in remuneratione.[75]

Caput XII

PRAEDESTINATIONIS TEMERARIAM PRAESUMPTIONEM CAVENDAM ESSE

Nemo quoque, quamdiu in hac mortalitate vivitur, de arcano divinae praedestinationis mysterio usque adeo praesumere debet, ut certo statuat se omnino esse in numero praedestinatorum,[76] quasi verum esset, quod justificatus aut amplius peccare non possit, aut, si peccaverit, certam sibi resipiscentiam promittere debeat. Nam nisi ex speciali revelatione sciri non potest, quos Deus sibi elegerit.

---

[69] Rom. 8:17.
[70] Heb. 5:8 f.
[71] Cf. I Cor. 9:24, 26 f.
[72] Cf. II Pet. 1:10.
[73] Cf. bullam *Exsurge Domine* Leonis X, art. 31 et 32. Denzinger, nn.771 f. et *infra*, can. 25.
[74] Ps. 118:112.
[75] Heb. 11:26.
[76] Cf. c.17, C.XXIV, q.3. Rouët de Journel, p. 774, n.365.

Caput XIII

DE PERSEVERANTIAE MUNERE

Similiter de perseverantiae munere, de quo scriptum est: *Qui perseveraverit usque in finem, hic salvus erit,*[77] quod quidem aliunde haberi non potest, nisi ab eo, qui potens est eum, qui stat, statuere,[78] ut perseveranter stet, et eum, qui cadit, restituere, nemo sibi certi aliquid absolute certitudine polliceatur, tametsi in Dei auxilio firmissimam spem collocare et reponere omnes debent. Deus enim, nisi ipsi illius gratiae defuerint, sicut coepit opus bonum, ita perficiet,[79] operans velle et perficere.[80] Verumtamen qui se existimant stare, videant ne cadant[81] et cum timore ac tremore salutem suam operentur,[82] in laboribus, in vigiliis, in eleemosynis, orationibus et oblationibus, in jejuniis et castitate.[83] Formidare enim debent, scientes, quod in spem gloriae[84] et nondum in gloriam renati sunt, de pugna, quae superest cum carne, cum mundo, cum diabolo, in qua victores esse non possunt, nisi cum Dei gratia Apostolo obtemperent dicenti: *Debitores sumus non carni, ut secundum carnem vivamus. Si enim secundum carnem vixeritis, moriemini. Si autem spiritu facta carnis mortificaveritis, vivetis.*[85]

Caput XIV

DE LAPSIS ET EORUM REPARATIONE

Qui vero ab accepta justificationis gratia per peccatum exciderunt, rursus justificari poterunt, cum excitante Deo per poenitentiae sacramentum merito Christi amissam gratiam recuperare procuraverint. Hic enim justificationis modus est lapsi reparatio, quam secundam post naufragium deperditae gratiae tabulam sancti patres apte nuncuparunt.[86] Etenim pro iis, qui post baptismum in peccata labuntur, Christus

---

77 Matt. 10:22; 24:13.
78 Rom. 14:4.
79 Phil. 1:6.
80 *Ibid.*, 2:13.
81 Cf. I Cor. 10:12.
82 Phil. 2:12.
83 Cf. II Cor. 6:5 f.
84 Cf. I Pet. 1:3.
85 Rom. 8:12 f.
86 Hieron. *epp. 84 ad Pammachium et Oceanum*, c.6 (c.72, D.I de poenit.), *PL*, XXII,

Jesus sacramentum instituit poenitentiae, cum dixit: *Accipite Spiritum Sanctum; quorum remiseritis peccata, remittuntur eis, et quorum retinueritis, retenta sunt.*[87] Unde docendum est, Christiani hominis poenitentiam post lapsum multo aliam esse a baptismali, eaque contineri non modo cessationem a peccatis et eorum detestationem, aut *cor contritum et humiliatum,*[88] verum etiam et eorumdem sacramentalem confessionem, saltem in voto et suo tempore faciendam, et sacerdotalem absolutionem, itemque satisfactionem per jejunia, eleemosynas, orationes et alia pia spiritualis vitae exercitia, non quidem pro poena aeterna, quae vel sacramento vel sacramenti voto una cum culpa remittitur, sed pro poena temporali, quae (ut sacrae litterae docent) non tota semper, ut in baptismo fit, dimittitur illis, qui gratiae Dei, quam acceperunt, ingrati Spiritum Sanctum contristaverunt [89] et templum Dei violare [90] non sunt veriti. De qua poenitentia scriptum est: *Memor esto, unde excideris, age poenitentiam, et prima opera fac,*[91] et iterum: *Quae secundum Deum tristitia est, poenitentiam in salutem stabilem operatur,*[92] et rursus: *Poenitentiam agite,*[93] et: *Facite fructus dignos poenitentiae.*[94]

Caput XV

QUOLIBET PECCATO MORTALI AMITTI GRATIAM, SED NON FIDEM

Adversus etiam hominum quorumdam callida ingenia, qui *per dulces sermones et benedictiones seducunt corda innocentium,*[95] asserendum est, non modo infidelitate, per quam et ipsa fides amittitur, sed etiam quocumque alio mortali peccato, quamvis non amittatur fides, acceptam justificationis gratiam amitti, divinae legis doctrinam defendendo, quae a regno Dei non solum infideles excludit, sed et fideles quoque *fornicarios, adulteros, molles, masculorum concubitores, fures,*

748; *122 ad Rusticum,* c.4, *PL,* XXII, 1045; *130 ad Demetridem,* c.9, *PL,* XXII, 1115; Tertul., *De poenitentia,* c.4, *PL,* I, 1343.

[87] Joan. 20:22 f.
[88] Ps. 50:19.
[89] Eph. 4:30.
[90] Cf. I Cor. 3:17.
[91] Apoc. 2:5.
[92] Cf. II Cor. 7:10.
[93] Matt. 3:2; 4:17.
[94] Luc. 3:8.
[95] Rom. 16:18.

avaros, ebriosos, maledicos, rapaces,[96] ceterosque omnes, qui letalia committunt peccata, a quibus cum divinae gratiae adjumento abstinere possunt [97] et pro quibus a Christi gratia separantur.

Caput XVI

DE FRUCTU JUSTIFICATIONIS, HOC EST, DE MERITO BONORUM OPERUM, DEQUE IPSIUS MERITI RATIONE

Hac igitur ratione justificatis hominibus, sive acceptam gratiam perpetuo conservaverint, sive amissam recuperaverint, proponenda sunt Apostoli verba: *Abundate in omni opere bono, scientes quod labor vester non est inanis in Domino.*[98] *Non enim injustus est Deus, ut obliviscatur operis vestri et dilectionis, quam ostendistis in nomine ipsius,*[99] et: *Nolite amittere confidentiam vestram, quae magnam habet remunerationem.*[100] Atque ideo bene operantibus usque in finem [101] et in Deo sperantibus proponenda est vita aeterna, et tamquam gratia filiis Dei per Christum Jesum misericorditer promissa, et tamquam merces ex ipsius Dei promissione bonis ipsorum operibus et meritis fideliter reddenda. Haec est enim illa corona justitiae, quam post suum certamen et cursum repositam sibi esse aiebat Apostolus a justo judice sibi reddendam, non solum autem sibi, sed et omnibus, qui diligunt adventum ejus.[102] Cum enim ille ipse Christus Jesus tamquam caput in membra et tamquam vitis in palmites [103] in ipsos justificatos jugiter virtutem influat, quae virtus bona eorum opera semper antecedit, comitatur et subsequitur, et sine qua nullo pacto Deo grata et meritoria esse possent: nihil ipsis justificatis amplius deesse credendum est, quominus plene illis quidem operibus, quae in Deo sunt facta, divinae legi pro hujus vitae statu satisfecisse et vitam aeternam, suo etiam tempore, si tamen in gratia decesserint,[104] consequendam vere promeruisse censeantur. Cum Christus salvator noster dicat: *Si quis biberit*

[96] Cf. I Cor. 6:9.
[97] Cf. II Cor. 12:9; Phil. 4:13.
[98] Cf. I Cor. 15:58.
[99] Heb. 6:10.
[100] *Ibid.*, 10:35.
[101] Matt. 10:22. Rouët de Journel, p. 773, n.354.
[102] Cf. II Tim. 4:8.
[103] Joan. 15:1 f.
[104] Cf. Apoc. 14:13.

ex aqua, quam ego dabo ei, non sitiet in aeternum, sed fiet in eo fons aquae salientis in vitam aeternam.[105] Ita neque propria nostra justitia tamquam ex nobis propria statuitur,[106] neque ignoratur aut repudiatur justitia Dei; [107] quae enim justitia nostra dicitur, quia per eam nobis inhaerentem justificamur, illa eadem Dei est, quia a Deo nobis infunditur per Christi meritum. Neque vero illud omittendum est, quod licet bonis operibus in sacris litteris usque adeo tribuatur, ut etiam qui uni ex minimis suis potum aquae frigidae dederit, promittat Christus eum non esse sua mercede cariturum,[108] et Apostolus testetur, *id quod in praesenti est momentaneum et leve tribulationis nostrae, supra modum in sublimitate aeternum gloriae pondus operari in nobis:* [109] absit tamen, ut Christianus homo in se ipso vel confidat vel glorietur et non in Domino,[110] cujus tanta est erga omnes homines bonitas, ut eorum velit esse merita, quae sunt ipsius dona.[111] Et quia *in multis offendimus omnes,*[112] unusquisque sicut misericordiam et bonitatem, ita severitatem et judicium ante oculos habere debet, neque se ipsum aliquis, etiam si nihil sibi conscius fuerit, judicare,[113] quoniam omnis hominum vita non humano judicio examinanda et judicanda est, sed Dei, *qui illuminabit abscondita tenebrarum et manifestabit consilia cordium, et tunc laus erit unicuique a Deo,*[114] *qui, ut scriptum est, reddet unicuique secundum opera sua.*[115]

Post hanc catholicam de justificatione doctrinam, quam nisi quisque fideliter firmiterque receperit, justificari non poterit,[116] placuit sanctae synodo hos canones subjungere, ut omnes sciant, non solum quid tenere et sequi, sed etiam quid vitare et fugere debeant.

---

[105] Joan. 4:13 f.
[106] Cf. II Cor. 3:5.
[107] Rom. 10:3.
[108] Matt. 10:42; Marc. 9:40.
[109] Cf. II Cor. 4:17.
[110] Cf. I Cor. 1:31; II Cor. 10:17.
[111] Coelest. I Papae *epist.* (21, c. 12) *ad episcopos Galliae a. 431. PL,* L, 536. Denzinger, n. 141.
[112] Jac. 3:2.
[113] Cf. I Cor. 4:3 f.
[114] *Ibid.*, 4:5.
[115] Matt. 16:27; Rom. 2:6; Apoc. 22:12.
[116] Cf. initium symboli Athanasii in *Breviario* ad Primam.

CANONES DE JUSTIFICATIONE

1. Si quis dixerit, hominem suis operibus,[117] quae vel per humanae naturae vires, vel per legis doctrinam fiant, absque divina per Christum Jesum gratia posse justificari coram Deo: anathema sit.

2. Si quis dixerit, ad hoc solum divinam gratiam per Christum Jesum dari, ut facilius homo juste vivere ac vitam aeternam promereri possit, quasi per liberum arbitrium sine gratia utrumque, sed aegre tamen et difficulter possit: anathema sit.

3. Si quis dixerit, sine praeveniente Spiritus Sancti inspiratione[118] atque ejus adjutorio hominem credere, sperare et diligere aut poenitere posse, sicut oportet, ut ei justificationis gratia conferatur: anathema sit.

4. Si quis dixerit, liberum hominis arbitrium a Deo motum et excitatum nihil cooperari assentiendo Deo excitanti atque vocanti, quo ad obtinendam justificationis gratiam se disponat ac praeparet, neque posse dissentire, si velit, sed velut inanime quoddam nihil omnino agere mereque passive se habere: anathema sit.

5. Si quis liberum hominis arbitrium post Adae peccatum amissum et extinctum esse dixerit, aut rem esse de solo titulo, immo titulum sine re, figmentum denique a satana invectum in ecclesiam: anathema sit.

6. Si quis dixerit, non esse in potestate hominis vias suas malas facere, sed mala opera ita ut bona Deum operari, non permissive solum, sed etiam proprie et per se, adeo ut sit proprium ejus opus non minus proditio Judae quam vocatio Pauli: anathema sit.

7. Si quis dixerit, opera omnia, quae ante justificationem fiunt, quacumque ratione facta sint, vere esse peccata vel odium Dei mereri, aut quanto vehementius quis nititur se disponere ad gratiam, tanto eum gravius peccare: anathema sit.

8. Si quis dexerit, gehennae metum, per quem ad misericordiam Dei de peccatis dolendo confugimus vel a peccando abstinemus, peccatum esse aut peccatores pejores facere: anathema sit.

9. Si quis dixerit, sola fide impium justificari,[119] ita ut intelligat, nihil aliud requiri quod justificationis gratiam consequendam cooperetur, et nulla ex parte necesse esse eum suae voluntatis motu praeparari atque disponi: anathema sit.

---

[117] Cf. *supra*, capp. 1, 3.
[118] *Ibid*., cap. 5.
[119] *Ibid*., capp. 7, 8.

10. Si quis dixerit, homines sine Christi justitia,[120] per quam nobis meruit, justificari, aut per eam ipsam formaliter justos esse: anathema sit.

11. Si quis dixerit, homines justificari vel sola imputatione justitiae Christi, vel sola peccatorum remissione, exclusa gratia et caritate, quae in cordibus eorum per Spiritum Sanctum diffundatur [121] atque illis inhaereat, aut etiam gratiam, qua justificamur, esse tantum favorem Dei: anathema sit.

12. Si quis dixerit, fidem justificantem nihil aliud esse quam fiduciam divinae misericordiae,[122] peccata remittentis propter Christum, vel eam fiduciam solam esse, qua justificamur: anathema sit.

13. Si quis dixerit, omni homini ad remissionem peccatorum assequendam necessarium esse, ut credat certo et absque ulla haesitatione propriae infirmitatis et indispositionis, peccata sibi esse remissa: anathema sit.

14. Si quis dixerit, hominem a peccatis absolvi ac justificari ex eo, quod se absolvi ac justificari certo credat,[123] aut neminem vere esse justificatum, nisi qui credit se esse justificatum, et hac sola fide absolutionem et justificationem perfici: anathema sit.

15. Si quis dixerit, hominem renatum et justicatum teneri ex fide ad credendum, se certo esse in numero praedestinatorum: [124] anathema sit.

16. Si quis magnum illud usque in finem perseverantiae donum se certo habiturum absoluta et infallibili certitudine dixerit, nisi hoc ex speciali revelatione didicerit: [125] anathema sit.

17. Si quis justificationis gratiam non nisi praedestinatis ad vitam contingere dixerit, reliquos vero omnes, qui vocantur, vocari quidem sed gratiam non accipere, utpote divina potestate praedestinatos ad malum: anathema sit.

18. Si quis dixerit, Dei praecepta homini etiam justificato et sub gratia constituto esse ad observandum impossibilia: [126] anathema sit.

19. Si quis dixerit, nihil praeceptum esse in evangelio praeter fidem, cetera esse indifferentia, neque praecepta, neque prohibita, sed libera, aut decem praecepta nihil pertinere ad Christianos: anathema sit.

---

[120] Gal. 2:16; *supra*, cap. 7.
[121] Rom. 5:5.
[122] *Supra*, cap. 9.
[123] Cf. cap. cit.
[124] Cf. *supra*, cap. 12.
[125] *Ibid.*, cap. 13.
[126] *Ibid.*, cap. 11.

20. Si quis hominem justificatum et quantumlibet perfectum dixerit non teneri ad observantiam mandatorum Dei et ecclesiae, sed tantum ad credendum,[127] quasi vero evangelium sit nuda et absoluta promissio vitae aeternae, sine conditione observationis mandatorum: anathema sit.

21. Si quis dixerit, Christum Jesum a Deo hominibus datum fuisse ut redemptorem, cui fidant, non etiam ut legislatorem, cui obediant: anathema sit.

22. Si quis dixerit, justificatum vel sine speciali auxilio Dei in accepta justitia perseverare posse, vel cum eo non posse: [128] anathema sit.

23. Si quis hominem semel justificatum dixerit amplius peccare non posse, neque gratiam amittere, atque ideo eum, qui labitur et peccat, nunquam vere fuisse justificatum; [129] aut contra, posse in tota vita peccata omnia, etiam venialia vitare, nisi ex speciali Dei privilegio, quemadmodum de beata Virgine tenet ecclesia: anathema sit.

24. Si quis dixerit, justitiam acceptam non conservari atque etiam non augeri coram Deo per bona opera, sed opera ipsa fructus solummodo et signa esse justificationis adeptae, non autem ipsius augendae causam: [130] anathema sit.

25. Si quis in quolibet bono opere justum saltem venialiter peccare dixerit, aut, quod intolerabilius est, mortaliter, atque ideo poenas aeternas mereri, tantumque ob id non damnari, quia Deus ea opera non imputet ad damnationem: anathema sit.

26. Si quis dixerit, justos non debere pro bonis operibus, quae in Deo fuerint facta, exspectare et sperare aeternam retributionem a Deo per ejus misericordiam et Jesu Christi meritum, si bene agendo et divina mandata custodiendo usque in finem perseveraverint: anathema sit.

27. Si quis dixerit, nullum esse mortale peccatum nisi infidelitatis,[131] aut nullo alio quantumvis gravi et enormi praeterquam infidelitatis peccato semel acceptam gratiam amitti: anathema sit.

28. Si quis dixerit, amissa per peccatum gratia simul et fidem semper amitti, aut fidem, quae remanet, non esse veram fidem, licet non sit viva, aut eum, qui fidem sine caritate habet, non esse Christianum: anathema sit.

29. Si quis dixerit, eum, qui post baptismum lapsus est, non posse per

---

[127] Cf. cap. 11.
[128] *Supra,* cap. 13. Cf. Rouët de Journel, p. 771, nn.318 f.
[129] *Ibid.*, cap. 14. Cf. Rouët de Journel, p. 774, n.364.
[130] *Supra,* cap. 10.
[131] *Ibid.*, cap. 15.

Dei gratiam resurgere;[132] aut posse quidem, sed sola fide, amissam justitiam recuperare sine sacramento poenitentiae, prout sancta Romana et universalis ecclesia, a Christo Domino et ejus apostolis edocta, hucusque professa est, servavit et docuit: anathema sit.

30. Si quis post acceptam justificationis gratiam cuilibet peccatori poenitenti ita culpam remitti et reatum aeternae poenae deleri dixerit, ut nullus remaneat reatus poenae temporalis, exsolvendae vel in hoc saeculo vel in futuro in purgatorio,[133] antequam ad regna coelorum aditus patere possit: anathema sit.

31. Si quis dixerit, justificatum peccare, dum intuitu aeternae mercedis bene operatur: anathema sit.

32. Si quis dixerit, hominis justificati bona opera ita esse dona Dei, ut non sint etiam bona ipsius justificati merita, aut ipsum justificatum bonis operibus, quae ab eo per Dei gratiam et Jesu Christi meritum, cujus vivum membrum est, fiunt, non vere mereri augmentum gratiae, vitam aeternam et ipsius vitae aeternae (si tamen in gratia decesserit) consecutionem, atque etiam gloriae augmentum: anathema sit.

33. Si quis dixerit, per hanc doctrinam catholicam de justificatione, a sancta synodo hoc praesenti decreto expressam, aliqua ex parte gloriae Dei vel meritis Jesu Christi Domini nostri derogari, et non potius veritatem fidei nostrae, Dei denique ac Christi Jesu gloriam illustrari: anathema sit.

DECRETUM DE REFORMATIONE

Caput I

PRAELATOS CONVENIT IN ECCLESIIS SUIS RESIDERE; SI SECUS FECERINT, JURIS ANTIQUI POENAE IN EOS INNOVANTUR, ET NOVAE DECERNUNTUR

Eadem sacrosancta synodus, eisdem praesidentibus Apostolicae Sedis legatis, ad restituendam collapsam admodum ecclesiasticam disciplinam, depravatosque in clero et populo Christiano mores emendandos se accingere volens, ab iis, qui majoribus ecclesiis praesunt, initium censuit esse sumendum. Integritas enim praesidentium salus est subditorum.[134] Confidens itaque, per Domini ac Dei nostri misericordiam providamque

---

[132] *Supra*, cap. 14.
[133] Cf. Sess. XIV, cap. 8 de poenit.
[134] C.5, D.LXI (Leo I).

ipsius Dei in terris vicarii sollertiam omnino futurum, ut ad ecclesiarum regimen (onus quippe angelicis humeris formidandum), qui maxime digni fuerint quorumque prior vita ac omnis aetas a puerilibus exordiis usque ad perfectiores annos per disciplinae stipendia ecclesiasticae laudabiliter acta testimonium praebeat, secundum venerabiles beatorum patrum sanctiones [135] assumantur: omnes patriarchalibus, primatialibus, metropolitanis et cathedralibus ecclesiis quibuscumque, quovis nomine ac titulo praefectos monet ac monitos esse vult, ut attendentes *sibi et universo gregi, in quo Spiritus Sanctus posuit eos, regere ecclesiam Dei, quam acquisivit sanguine suo*,[136] *vigilent*, sicut Apostolus praecipit, *in omnibus laborent et ministerium suum impleant*.[137] Implere autem illud se nequaquam posse sciant, si greges sibi commissos mercenariorum more deserant [138] atque ovium suarum, quarum sanguis de eorum est manibus a supremo judice requirendus,[139] custodiae minime incumbant, cum certissimum sit, non admitti pastoris excusationem, si lupus oves comedit et pastor nescit. Ac nihilominus quia nonnulli, quod vehementer dolendum est, hoc tempore reperiuntur, qui propriae etiam salutis immemores terrenaque coelestibus, ac divinis humana praeferentes, in diversis curiis vagantur, aut in negotiorum temporalium sollicitudine, ovili derelicto atque ovium sibi commissarum cura neglecta, se detinent occupatos: placuit sacrosanctae synodo, antiquos canones,[140] qui temporum atque hominum injuria pene in desuetudinem abierunt, adversus non residentes promulgatos innovare, quemadmodum virtute praesentis decreti innovat, ac ulterius pro firmiori eorumdem residentia et reformandis in ecclesia moribus in hunc, qui sequitur modum statuere atque sancire.

Si quis a patriarchali, primatiali, metropolitana seu cathedrali ecclesia, sibi quocumque titulo, causa, nomine seu jure commissa, quacumque ille dignitate, gradu et praeeminentia praefulgeat, legitimo impedimento seu justis et rationabilibus causis [141] cessantibus, sex mensibus [142] continuis extra suam dioecesim morando abfuerit, quartae partis fructuum

---

[135] Cf. c.4, D.LIX (Coelest. I); c.2, D.LXI (Hormisd.); c.6, *ibid.* (conc. Laodicen.); c.8, *ibid.* (Leo I).

[136] Act. 20:28.

[137] Cf. II Tim. 4:5.

[138] Joan. 10:12.

[139] Ezech. 33:6.

[140] Cf. c.20, C.VII, q.1 (Greg. I) ff.; tot. tit. X, De cler. non resid., III, 4 et in VI°, III, 3.

[141] Cf. Sess. XXIII, cap. 1 de ref.

[142] Cf. c.11, X, De cler. non resid., III, 4 (Innoc. III).

unius anni, fabricae ecclesiae et pauperibus loci per superiorem ecclesiasticum applicandorum, poenam ipso jure incurrat. Quod si per alios sex menses in hujusmodi absentia perseraverit, aliam quartam partem fructuum similiter applicandam eo ipso amittat. Crescente vero contumacia, ut severiori sacrorum canonum censurae subjiciatur, metropolitanus suffraganeos episcopos absentes, metropolitanum vero absentem suffrageneus episcopus antiquior residens sub poena interdicti ingressus ecclesiae eo ipso incurrenda infra tres menses per litteras seu nuncium Romano pontifici denunciare teneatur, qui in ipsos absentes, prout cujusque major aut minor contumacia exegerit, suae supremae Sedis auctoritate animadvertere et ecclesiis ipsis de pastoribus utilioribus providere poterit, sicut in Domino noverit salubriter expedire.

Caput II

NULLI BENEFICIUM EXIGENS PERSONALEM RESIDENTIAM OBTINENTI ABESSE LICET, NISI JUSTA DE CAUSA AB EPISCOPO APPROBANDA, QUI TUM ETIAM VICARIUM SUBDUCTA PARTE FRUCTUUM SUBSTITUAT OB CURAM ANIMARUM

Episcopis inferiores, quaevis beneficia ecclesiastica personalem residentiam de jure sive consuetudine exigentia, in titulum sive commendam obtinentes, ab eorum ordinariis, quemadmodum eis pro bono ecclesiarum regimine et divini cultus augmento, locorum et personarum qualitate pensata, expediens videbitur, opportunis juris remediis residere cogantur, nullique privilegia seu indulta perpetua de non residendo aut de fructibus in absentia percipiendis suffragentur.[143] Indulgentiis vero et dispensationibus temporalibus, ex veris et rationabilibus causis tantum concessis et coram ordinario legitime probandis, in suo robore permansuris; quibus casibus nihilominus officium sit episcoporum, tamquam in hac parte a Sede Apostolica delegatorum, providere, ut per deputationem idoneorum vicariorum et congruae portionis fructuum assignationem cura animarum nullatenus negligatur,[144] nemini quoad hoc privilegio seu exemptione quacumque suffragante.

---

[143] Cf. c. 15, VI°, De rescript., I, 3 (Bonif. VIII).
[144] Cf. c. 34, VI°, De elect., I, 6 (id.).

Caput III

EXCESSUS SAECULARIUM CLERICORUM ET REGULARIUM DEGENTIUM EXTRA MONASTERIA AB ORDINARIO LOCI CORRIGANTUR

Ecclesiarum praelati ad corrigendum subditorum excessus prudenter et diligenter intendant, et nemo saecularis clericus cujusvis personalis, vel regularis extra monasterium degens etiam sui ordinis privilegii praetextu tutus censeatur,[145] quominus, si deliquerit, ab ordinario loci, tamquam super hoc a Sede Apostolica delegato, secundum canonicas sanctiones visitari, puniri et corrigi valeat.

Caput IV

ECCLESIAS QUASCUMQUE EPISCOPI ET ALII MAJORES PRAELATI, QUOTIES OPUS FUERIT, VISITENT, OMNIBUS, QUAE HUIC DECRETO OBSTARE POSSENT, SUBLATIS

Capitula cathedralium et aliarum majorum ecclesiarum illorumque personae nullis exemptionibus, consuetudinibus, sententiis, juramentis, concordiis, quae tantum suos obligent auctores, non etiam successores, tueri se possint, quominus a suis episcopis et aliis majoribus praelatis per se ipsos solos vel illis, quibus sibi videbitur, adjunctis, juxta canonicas sanctiones toties quoties opus fuerit visitari, corrigi et emendari, etiam auctoritate apostolica, possint et valeant.[146]

Caput V

EPISCOPI IN ALIENA DIOECESI NEC PONTIFICALIA EXERCEANT, NEC ORDINES CONFERANT

Nulli episcopo liceat cujusvis privilegii praetextu pontificalia in alterius dioecesi exercere, nisi de ordinarii loci expressa licentia et in personas eidem ordinario subjectas tantum;[147] si secus factum fuerit, episcopus ab exercitio pontificalium, et sic ordinati ab executione ordinum sint ipso jure suspensi.

---

[145] Cf. Sess. XIV, cap. 4 de ref.
[146] Cf. Sess. XXIV, cap. 3 et Sess. XXV, cap. 6 de ref.
[147] Cf. Sess. XIV, capp. 2, 3 et Sess. XXIII, cap. 8 de ref.

INDICTIO FUTURAE SESSIONIS

Placetne vobis proximam futuram sessionem celebrari die Jovis feria quinta post primam dominicam subsequentis Quadragesimae, quae erit dies tertia mensis Martii? *Responderunt:* Placet.

SESSIO SEPTIMA
celebrata
die III mensis Martii, MDXLVII

DECRETUM DE SACRAMENTIS

Prooemium

Ad consummationem salutaris de justificatione doctrinae, quae in praecedenti proxima sessione uno omnium patrum consensu promulgata fuit, consentaneum visum est, de sanctissimis ecclesiae sacramentis agere, per quae omnis vera justitia vel incipit vel coepta augetur vel amissa reparatur. Propterea sacrosancta oecumenica et generalis Tridentina synodus, in Spiritu Sancto legitime congregata, praesidentibus in ea eisdem Apostolicae Sedis legatis, ad errores eliminandos et extirpandas haereses, quae circa ipsa sanctissima sacramenta hac nostra tempestate, tum de damnatis olim a patribus nostris haeresibus suscitatae, tum etiam de novo adinventae sunt, quae catholicae ecclesiae puritati et animarum saluti magnopere officiunt, sanctarum scripturarum doctrinae, apostolicis traditionibus atque aliorum conciliorum et patrum consensui inhaerendo, hos praesentes canones statuendos et decernendos censuit, reliquos, qui supersunt ad coepti operis perfectionem, deinceps, divino Spiritu adjuvante, editura.

CANONES DE SACRAMENTIS IN GENERE

1. Si quis dixerit, sacramenta novae legis non fuisse omnia a Jesu Christo Domino nostro instituta, aut esse plura vel pauciora quam septem,[1] videlicet baptismum, confirmationem, Eucharistiam, poenitentiam, extremam unctionem, ordinem et matrimonium, aut etiam aliquod horum septem non esse vere et proprie sacramentum: anathema sit.

2. Si quis dixerit, ea ipsa novae legis sacramenta a sacramentis anti-

[1] Eugen. IV in *decr. pro Armenis* (Denzinger, n.695); Pius IV in bulla *Injunctum nobis* (*idem*, n.996). Cf. Denzinger etiam sub rubrica "Sacramenta in genere," XII a, p. [40] et Rouët de Journel, *Enchiridion patristicum* sub eadem rubrica, p. 778, n.455.

quae legis non differre, nisi quia caeremoniae sunt aliae et alii ritus externi: anathema sit.

3. Si quis dixerit, haec septem sacramenta ita esse inter se paria, ut nulla ratione aliud sit alio dignius: anathema sit.

4. Si quis dixerit, sacramenta novae legis non esse ad salutem necessaria, sed superflua, et sine eis aut eorum voto per solam fidem homines a Deo gratiam justificationis adipisci,[2] licet omnia singulis necessaria non sint: anathema sit.

5. Si quis dixerit, haec sacramenta propter solam fidem nutriendam instituta fuisse: anathema sit.

6. Si quis dixerit, sacramenta novae legis non continere gratiam quam significant, aut gratiam ipsam non ponentibus obicem non conferre,[3] quasi signa tantum externa sint acceptae per fidem gratiae vel justitiae, et notae quaedam Christianae professionis, quibus apud homines discernuntur fideles ab infidelibus: anathema sit.

7. Si quis dixerit, non dari gratiam per hujusmodi sacramenta semper et omnibus, quantum est ex parte Dei, etiam si rite ea suscipiant, sed aliquando et aliquibus: anathema sit.

8. Si quis dixerit, per ipsa novae legis sacramenta ex opere operato non conferri gratiam, sed solam fidem divinae promissionis ad gratiam consequendam sufficere: anathema sit.

9. Si quis dixerit, in tribus sacramentis, baptismo scilicet, confirmatione et ordine, non imprimi characterem in anima, hoc est signum quoddam spirituale et indelebile, unde ea iterari non possunt: [4] anathema sit.

10. Si quis dixerit, Christianos omnes in verbo et omnibus sacramentis administrandis habere potestatem: [5] anathema sit.

11. Si quis dixerit, in ministris, dum sacramenta conficiunt et conferunt, non requiri intentionem, saltem faciendi quod facit ecclesia: [6] anathema sit.

12. Si quis dixerit, ministrum in peccato mortali exsistentem, modo omnia essentialia, quae ad sacramentum conficiendum aut conferendum pertinent, servaverit, non conficere aut conferre sacramentum: [7] anathema sit.

---

[2] Cf. Sess. VI, cap. 7 et can. 9, et Denzinger, XII b, p. [41].
[3] Eugen. IV in decr. cit.
[4] *Ibid.*
[5] Cf. Sess. XIV de poenit., cap. 6 et extr. unct., cap. 3.
[6] Eugen. IV in decr. cit.
[7] Cf. propositionem Joan. Wicleff in conc. Constantien. damnatam, apud Denzinger,

13. Si quis dixerit, receptos et approbatos ecclesiae catholicae ritus in solemni sacramentorum administratione adhiberi consuetos aut contemni, aut sine peccato a ministris pro libito omitti, aut in novos alios per quemcumque ecclesiarum pastorem mutari posse: anathema sit.

CANONES DE SACRAMENTO BAPTISMI

1. Si quis dixerit, baptismum Joannis habuisse eamdem vim cum baptismo Christi: [8] anathema sit.

2. Si quis dixerit, aquam veram et naturalem non esse de necessitate baptismi,[9] atque ideo verba illa Domini nostri Jesu Christi: *Nisi quis renatus fuerit ex aqua et Spiritu Sancto* [10] ad metaphoram aliquam detorserit: anathema sit.

3. Si quis dixerit, in ecclesia Romana, quae omnium ecclesiarum mater est et magistra, non esse veram de baptismi sacramento doctrinam: [11] anathema sit.

4. Si quis dixerit, baptismum, qui etiam datur ab haereticis in nomine Patris et Filii et Spiritus Sancti, cum intentione faciendi, quod facit ecclesia, non esse verum baptismum: [12] anathema sit.

5. Si quis dixerit, baptismum liberum esse, hoc est, non necessarium ad salutem: [13] anathema sit.

6. Si quis dixerit, baptizatum non posse, etiamsi velit, gratiam amittere, quantumcumque peccet, nisi nolit credere: anathema sit.

7. Si quis dixerit, baptizatos per baptismum ipsum solius tantum fidei debitores fieri, non autem universae legis Christi servandae: anathema sit.

8. Si quis dixerit, baptizatos liberos esse ab omnibus sanctae ecclesiae praeceptis, quae vel scripta vel tradita sunt, ita ut ea observare non teneantur, nisi se sua sponte illis submittere voluerint: anathema sit.

9. Si quis dixerit, ita revocandos esse homines ad baptismi suscepti memoriam, ut vota omnia, quae post baptismum fiunt, vi promissionis in baptismo ipso jam factae irrita esse intelligant, quasi per ea et fidei, quam professi sunt, detrahatur, et ipsi baptismo: anathema sit.

---

n.584. Rouët de Journel, p. 778, n.450. C.98, C.I, q.1 (Aug.); cc.39, 149, D.IV de cons. (Aug.).

[8] Cf. c.135, D.IV de cons. (Aug.). Rouët de Journel, p. 778, n.460.

[9] Cf. c.5, X, De bapt., III, 42 (Innoc. III). Rouët de Journel, p. 778, n.461.

[10] Joan. 3:5.

[11] C.9, X, De haeret., V, 7 (Luc. III).

[12] Cf. cc.97, 98, C.I, q.1 (Aug.).

[13] Joan. 3:5; c.142, D.IV de cons. (Aug.). Rouët de Journel, p. 778, n.470.

10. Si quis dixerit, peccata omnia, quae post baptismum fiunt, sola recordatione et fide suscepti baptismi vel dimitti vel venialia fieri: anathema sit.

11. Si quis dixerit, verum et rite collatum baptismum iterandum esse illi, qui apud infideles fidem Christi negaverit, cum ad poenitentiam convertitur: anathema sit.

12. Si quis dixerit, neminem esse baptizandum nisi ea aetate, qua Christus baptizatus est, vel in ipso mortis articulo: anathema sit.

13. Si quis dixerit, parvulos eo quod actum credendi non habent, suscepto baptismo inter fideles computandos non esse, ac propterea, cum ad annos discretionis pervenerint, esse rebaptizandos, aut praestare omitti eorum baptisma, quam eos non actu proprio credentes baptizari in sola fide ecclesiae: [14] anathema sit.

14. Si quis dixerit, hujusmodi parvulos baptizatos, cum adoleverint, interrogandos esse, an ratum habere velint, quod patrini eorum nomine, dum baptizarentur, polliciti sunt, et ubi se nolle responderint, suo esse arbitrio relinquendos nec alia interim poena ad Christianam vitam cogendos, nisi ut ab Eucharistiae aliorumque sacramentorum perceptione arceantur, donec resipiscant: anathema sit.

CANONES DE SACRAMENTO CONFIRMATIONIS

1. Si quis dixerit, confirmationem baptizatorum otiosam caeremoniam esse [15] et non potius verum et proprium sacramentum, aut olim nihil aliud fuisse quam catechesim quamdam, qua adolescentiae proximi fidei suae rationem coram ecclesia exponebant: anathema sit.

2. Si quis dixerit, injurios esse Spiritui Sancto eos, qui sacro confirmationis chrismati virtutem aliquam tribuunt: anathema sit.

3. Si quis dixerit, sanctae confirmationis ordinarium ministrum non esse solum episcopum,[16] sed quemvis simplicem sacerdotem: anathema sit.

DECRETUM DE REFORMATIONE

Eadem sacrosancta synodus eisdem praesidentibus et legatis, inceptum residentiae et reformationis negotium ad Dei laudem et

---

[14] Cf. c.139, D.IV de cons. (Aug.).

[15] Cf. Rouët de Journel, p. 779, n.476.

[16] Cf. Eugen. IV in decr. cit. (Denzinger, n.697); Sess. XXIII, cap. 4. Rouët de Journel, p. 779, n.479.

Christianae religionis incrementum prosequi intendens, ut sequitur statuendum censuit, salva semper in omnibus Sedis Apostolicae auctoritate.

Caput I

QUIS CAPAX REGIMINIS ECCLESIARUM CATHEDRALIUM

Ad cathedralium ecclesiarum regimen nullus nisi ex legitimo matrimonio natus et aetate matura, gravitate morum litterarumque scientia,[17] juxta constitutionem Alexandri III, quae incipit: *Cum in cunctis,*[18] in concilio Lateranensi promulgatam, praeditus assumatur.

Caput II

TENENTES PLURES CATHEDRALES ECCLESIAS JUBENTUR OMNES EXCEPTA UNA DIMITTERE CERTO MODO ET TEMPORE

Nemo, quacumque etiam dignitate, gradu aut praeeminentia praefulgens, plures metropolitanas seu cathedrales ecclesias in titulum sive commendam aut alio quovis nomine contra sacrorum canonum instituta [19] recipere et simul retinere praesumat, cum valde felix sit ille censendus, cui unam ecclesiam bene ac fructuose et cum animarum sibi commissarum salute regere contigerit. Qui autem plures ecclesias contra praesentis decreti tenorem nunc detinent, una, quam maluerint, retenta, reliquas infra sex menses, si ad liberam Sedis Apostolicae dispositionem pertineant, alias infra annum dimittere teneantur; alioquin ecclesiae ipsae, ultimo obtenta dumtaxat excepta, eo ipso vacare censeantur.

Caput III

HABILIBUS DUMTAXAT PERSONIS BENEFICIA CONFERANTUR

Inferiora beneficia ecclesiastica, praesertim curam animarum habentia, personis dignis et habilibus et quae in loco residere ac per se

[17] Sess. XXII, cap. 2 de ref. plus exigitur.

[18] C.7, X, De elect., I, 6. Cf. *infra*, p. 558, lit. F.

[19] Cf. c.2, D.LXX (conc. Placent.); c.3, C.X, q.3 (Toletan. XVI); c.1, C.XXI, q.1 (Nicaen. II); c.2, *ibid.* (Chalc.); c.5, X, De praeb., III, 5 (Lat. III), c.13, *ibid.* (Alex. III), c.28, *ibid.* (Lat. IV); c.32, VI°, De praeb., III, 4 (Bonif. VIII).

ipsos curam ipsam exercere valeant, juxta constitutionem Alexandri III in Lateranensi, quae incipit: *Quia nonnulli,*[20] et aliam Gregorii X in generali Lugdunensi concilio, quae incipit: *Licet canon,*[21] editam conferantur. Aliter autem facta collatio sive provisio omnino irritetur, et ordinarius collator poenas constitutionis concilii generalis, quae incipit: *Grave nimis,*[22] se noverit incursurum.

Caput IV

PLURIUM BENEFICIORUM RETENTOR CONTRA CANONES IIS PRIVATUR

Quicumque de cetero plura curata aut alias incompatibilia beneficia ecclesiastica [23] sive per viam unionis ad vitam, seu commendae perpetuae, aut alio quocumque nomine et titulo contra formam sacrorum canonum et praesertim constitutionis Innocentii III, quae incipit: *De multa,*[24] recipere ac simul retinere praesumpserit, beneficiis ipsis juxta ipsius constitutionis dispositionem ipso jure, etiam praesentis canonis vigore, privatus exsistat.

Caput V

PLURA BENEFICIA CURATA OBTINENTES ORDINARIO SUAS DISPENSATIONES EXHIBEANT, QUI DE VICARIO ECCLESIIS PROVIDEAT, CONGRUA PORTIONE FRUCTUUM ASSIGNATA

Ordinarii locorum quoscumque plura curata aut alias incompatibilia beneficia ecclesiastica obtinentes dispensationes suas exhibere districte compellant, et alias procedant juxta constitutionem Gregorii X in generali Lugdunensi concilio editam, quae incipit: *Ordinarii,*[25] quam eadem sancta synodus innovandam censet et innovat, addens insuper, quod ipsi ordinarii etiam per idoneorum vicariorum deputationem et congruae portionis fructuum assignationem omnino provideant, ut

---

[20] C. 3, X, De cler. non resid., III, 4 (Lat. III), *infra*, p. 558, lit. G.

[21] C. 14, VI°, De elect., I, 6 (Lugd. II), *infra*, p. 559, lit. H. Hunc canonem a Gregorio X in conc. Lugdunen. non editum fuisse, enodate indicavi in opere meo, *Disciplinary Decrees of the General Councils* (1937), pp. 327 ff.

[22] C. 29, X, De praeb., III, 5 (Lat. IV), *infra*, p. 559, lit. I.

[23] Cf. Sess. XXIV, cap. 17 de ref.

[24] C. 28, X, De praeb., III, 5 (Lat. IV), *infra*, p. 560, lit. J.

[25] C. 3, VI°, De off. ord., I, 16 (Lugd. II), *infra*, p. 561, lit. K. Idem de hoc canone dicendum est quod jam *supra* in adn. 21 notavi. Cf. *op. et loc. cit.*

animarum cura nullatenus negligatur et beneficia ipsa debitis obsequiis minime defraudentur; appellationibus, privilegiis et exemptionibus quibuscumque, etiam cum judicum specialium deputatione et illorum inhibitionibus in praemissis nemini suffragantibus.

Caput VI

QUAE BENEFICIORUM UNIONES VALIDAE CENSEANTUR

Uniones perpetuae [26] a quadraginta annis citra factae examinari ab ordinariis tamquam a Sede Apostolica delegatis possint, et quae per subreptionem vel per obreptionem obtentae fuerint, irritae declarentur; illae vero quae a dicto tempore citra concessae nondum in toto vel in parte sortitae sunt effectum, et quae deinceps ad cujusvis instantiam fient, nisi eas ex legitimis aut alias rationabilibus causis, coram loci ordinario, vocatis quorum interest, verificandis, factas fuisse constiterit, per subreptionem obtentae praesumantur, ac propterea, nisi aliter a Sede Apostolica declaratum fuerit, viribus omnino careant.

Caput VII

BENEFICIA ECCLESIASTICA UNITA VISITENTUR; PER VICARIOS ETIAM PERPETUOS CURA ANIMARUM EXERCEATUR; QUORUM DEPUTATIO FIAT CUM PORTIONE ASSIGNANDA, ETIAM SUPER RE CERTA

Beneficia ecclesiastica curata,[27] quae cathedralibus, collegiatis seu aliis ecclesiis vel monasteriis, beneficiis seu collegiis aut piis locis quibuscumque perpetuo unita et annexa reperiuntur, ab ordinariis locorum annis singulis visitentur, qui sollicite providere procurent, ut per idoneos vicarios, etiam perpetuos, nisi ipsis ordinariis pro bono ecclesiarum regimine aliter expedire videbitur, ab eis cum tertiae partis fructuum aut majori vel minori, arbitrio ipsorum ordinariorum, portione,[28] etiam super re certa assignanda, ibidem deputandos animarum cura laudabiliter exerceatur; appellationibus, privilegiis, exemptionibus, etiam cum

---

[26] Cf. Sess. XIV, cap. 9 de ref.; Sess. XXIV, cap. 13 de ref., et Sess. XXV, cap. 9 de ref.
[27] Cf. Sess. XIV, cap. cit.
[28] Cf. *supra*, cap. 5 et Sess. XXV, cap. 16 de ref.

judicum deputatione et illorum inhibitionibus quibuscumque in praemissis minime suffragantibus.

Caput VIII

ECCLESIAE REPARENTUR. CURA ANIMARUM SOLLICITE HABEATUR

Locorum ordinarii ecclesias quascumque quomodolibet exemptas auctoritate apostolica singulis annis visitare teneantur et opportunis juris remediis providere, ut quae reparatione indigent reparentur, et cura animarum, si qua illis immineat, aliisque debitis obsequiis minime defraudentur; [29] appellationibus, privilegiis, consuetudinibus, etiam ab immemorabili tempore praescriptis, judicum deputationibus et illorum inhibitionibus penitus exclusis.

Caput IX

MUNUS CONSECRATIONIS NON DIFFERENDUM

Ad majores ecclesias promoti munus consecrationis infra tempus a jure statutum suscipiant,[30] et prorogationes ultra sex menses concessae nulli suffragentur.

Caput X

SEDE VACANTE CAPITULA NULLI DENT REVERENDAS, NISI ARCTATO OCCASIONE OBTINENDI AUT OBTENTI BENEFICII; VARIAE CONTRAVENIENTIUM POENAE

Non liceat capitulis ecclesiarum, sede vacante, infra annum a die vacationis ordinandi licentiam aut litteras dimissorias seu reverendas, ut aliqui vocant, tam ex juris communis dispositione, quam etiam cujusvis privilegii aut consuetudinis vigore alicui, qui beneficii ecclesiastici recepti sive recipiendi occasione arctatus non fuerit, concedere; [31]

---

[29] Cf. c.10, C.X, q.1 (conc. Tarrac.), c.11, *ibid.* (Toletan. IV), c.12, *ibid.* (Brac. II); Sess. XXI, cap. 8 de ref., et Sess. XXIV, cap. 9 de ref.

[30] Id est, infra tres menses, c.2, D.LXXV (conc. Chalc.); c.1, D.C (Ravennen.). Falso hic can. posterior apud Gratianum Pelagio Papae sive I sive II attribuitur. Verius adscriberetur conc. memorato a.877 habito. Hardouin VI (P.I), p. 185 can. 1 et 2. Cf. Sess. XXIII, cap. 2 de ref.

[31] C.3, VI°, De temp. ord., I, 9 (Bonif. VIII). Cf. Sess. cit., cap. 10 de ref.

si secus fiat, capitulum contraveniens ecclesiastico subjaceat interdicto, et sic ordinati, si in minoribus ordinibus constituti fuerint, nullo privilegio clericali, praesertim in criminalibus, gaudeant; in majoribus vero ab executione ordinum ad beneplacitum futuri praelati sint ipso jure suspensi.

Caput XI

FACULTATES DE PROMOVENDO SINE JUSTA CAUSA NEMINI SUFFRAGENTUR

Facultates de promovendo a quocumque non suffragentur nisi habentibus legitimam causam, ob quam a propriis episcopis ordinari non possint, in litteris exprimendam; et tunc non ordinentur nisi ab episcopo in sua dioecesi residente,[32] aut pro eo pontificalia exercente, et diligenti praevio examine.

Caput XII

FACULTAS DE NON PROMOVENDO ANNUM NON EXCEDAT

Facultates de non promovendo, praeterquam in casibus a jure expressis concessae,[33] ad annum tantum suffragentur.

Caput XIII

A QUOCUMQUE PRAESENTATI NON INSTITUANTUR SINE PRAEVIO EXAMINE ORDINARII ET APPROBATIONE, CERTIS EXCEPTIS

Praesentati seu electi vel nominati a quibusvis ecclesiasticis personis, etiam Sedis Apostolicae nunciis, ad quaevis ecclesiastica beneficia non instituantur nec confirmentur neque admittantur,[34] etiam praetextu cujusvis privilegii seu consuetudinis, etiam ab immemorabili tempore praescriptae, nisi fuerint prius a locorum ordinariis examinati et idonei reperti; et nullus appellationis remedio se tueri possit, quominus examen subire teneatur. Praesentatis tamen,[35] electis seu nominatis ab universitatibus seu collegiis generalium studiorum exceptis.

[32] Cf. Sess. VI, cap. 5 de ref. et Sess. XIV, cap. 2 de ref.
[33] C. 14, VI°, De elect., I, 6 (Greg. X), c.34, *ibid.* (Bonif. VIII).
[34] Cf. Sess. XXV, cap. 9 de ref.
[35] Cf. Sess. XXIV, cap. 18 de ref.

Caput XIV

QUAENAM CAUSAE CIVILES AB EPISCOPIS COGNOSCI POSSINT

In exemptorum causis constitutio Innocentii IV, quae incipit: *Volentes,*[36] in generali Lugdunensi concilio edita servetur, quam eadem sacrosancta synodus innovandam censuit et innovat. Addendo insuper, quod in civilibus causis mercedum et miserabilium personarum clerici saeculares, aut regulares extra monasterium degentes, quomodolibet exempti, etiam si certum judicem a Sede Apostolica deputatum in partibus habeant, in aliis vero, si ipsum judicem non habuerint, coram locorum ordinariis, tamquam in hoc ab ipsa Sede delegatis, conveniri et jure medio ad solvendum debitum cogi et compelli possint. Privilegiis, exemptionibus, conservatorum deputationibus et eorum inhibitionibus adversus praemissa nequaquam valituris.

Caput XV

ORDINARII CURENT, UT HOSPITALIA QUAECUMQUE, ETIAM EXEMPTA, A SUIS ADMINISTRANTIBUS FIDELITER GUBERNENTUR

Curent ordinarii, ut hospitalia quaecumque a suis administratoribus,[37] quocumque illi nomine censeantur, etiam quomodolibet exemptis, fideliter et diligenter gubernentur, constitutionis concilii Viennensis, quae incipit: *Quia contingit,*[38] forma servata. Quam quidem constitutionem eadem sancta synodus innovandam duxit et innovat, cum derogationibus in ea contentis.

INDICTIO FUTURAE SESSIONIS

Item haec sacrosancta synodus statuit et decrevit, proximam futuram sessionem habendam et celebrandam esse die Jovis feria quinta post sequentem dominicam in Albis, quae erit vigesima prima mensis Aprilis praesentis anni MDXLVII.

---

[36] C. 1, VI°, De privil., V, 7, *infra,* p. 561, lit. L.
[37] Cf. Sess. XXV, cap. 8 de ref.
[38] C. 2, De relig. dom. in Clem., III, 11, *infra,* p. 562, lit. M.

BULLA

FACULTATIS TRANSFERENDI CONCILII

Paulus Episcopus, servus servorum Dei, venerabili fratri Joanni Mariae episcopo Praenestino, et dilectis filiis Marcello tit. S. Crucis in Jerusalem presbytero, ac Reginaldo S. Mariae in Cosmedin diacono cardinalibus, nostris et Apostolicae Sedis legatis de latere salutem et apostolicam benedictionem.

Regimini universalis ecclesiae, meritis licet imparibus, disponente Domino, praesidentes, nostri officii partes esse putamus, ut, si quid gravius causa reipublicae Christianae constituendum sit, id non modo tempore opportuno, verum etiam loco commodo et idoneo perficiatur. Cum itaque nos nuper, postquam suspensionem celebrationis sacri oecumenici et universalis concilii, alias per nos in civitate Tridentina ex causis tunc expressis de venerabilium fratrum nostrorum S. R. E. cardinalium consilio et assensu indicti, ex certis aliis etiam tunc expressis causis usque ad aliud opportunius et commodius tempus per nos declarandum de simili consilio et assensu factam, audita pace inter carissimos in Christo filios nostros, Carolum Rom. imperatorem semper augustum, et Franciscum Francorum regem Christianissimum conciliata, pari consilio et assensu sustuleramus et amoveramus, nequeuntes ipsi, tunc legitime impediti, ad dictam civitatem personaliter accedere et eidem concilio interesse, vos nostros et Apostolicae Sedis legatos de latere in eodem concilio de simili consilio constituerimus et deputaverimus, vosque ad eamdem civitatem tamquam pacis angelos destinaverimus, prout in diversis nostris desuper confectis litteris plenius continetur; nos, ne tam sanctum celebrationis concilii hujusmodi opus ex incommoditate loci, aut alias quovis modo impediatur aut plus debito differatur, opportune providere volentes, motu proprio et certa scientia, ac de apostolicae potestatis plenitudine, parique consilio et assensu vobis insimul, aut duobus ex vobis, reliquo legitimo impedimento detento, seu inde forte absente, quandocumque vobis videbitur, concilium praedictum de eadem civitate Tridentina ad quamcumque aliam commodiorem et opportuniorem seu tutiorem civitatem, de qua vobis etiam videbitur, transferendi et mutandi, ac illud in ipsa civitate Tridentina supprimendi et dissolvendi, necnon praelatis et aliis personis concilii hujusmodi, ne in eo ad ulteriora in dicta civitate Tridentina procedant, etiam sub censuris et poenis ecclesiasticis inhibendi, ac idem concilium in alia civitate hujusmodi, ad quam illud transferri et mutari contigerit, continuandi, tenendi et celebrandi, et ad illud praelatos et alias personas concilii Tridentini hujusmodi, etiam sub perjurii et aliis in litteris indictionis concilii hujusmodi expressis poenis, evocandi, eidemque sic translato et mutato concilii nomine et auctoritate praedictis praesidendi, ac in eo procedendi, ceteraque in praemissis et circa ea necessaria et opportuna alias juxta priorum vobis directarum litterarum continentiam et tenorem faciendi, statuendi, ordinandi et exsequendi, plenam et liberam apostolica auctoritate tenore praesentium concedimus potestatem et facultatem; ratum et gratum habituri quidquid per vos in praemissis factum, statutum, ordinatum executumve fuerit, idque facturi auctore Domino inviolabiliter observari; non obstantibus constitutionibus et ordinationibus apostolicis, ceterisque contrariis quibuscumque. Nulli ergo omnino hominum liceat hanc paginam nostrae concessionis infringere, vel ei ausu temerario contraire. Si quis autem hoc attentare praesumpserit, indignationem omnipotentis Dei ac beatorum Petri et Pauli Apostolorum ejus se noverit incursurum. Datum Romae apud S. Petrum anno incarnationis dominicae MDXLVII. VIII. Kalend. Mart. pontificatus nostri anno XI.

Fab. Episcopus Spol.
B. Motta.

SESSIO OCTAVA

celebrata

die XI mensis Martii, MDXLVII

DECRETUM DE TRANSLATIONE CONCILII

Placetne vobis decernere et declarare, de hujusmodi morbo ex praemissis et aliis allegatis ita manifeste et notorie constare, ut praelati in hac civitate sine vitae discrimine commorari et in ea idcirco inviti minime retineri possint et debeant? Itemque attento recessu multorum praelatorum post proxime praeteritam sessionem, et attentis protestationibus aliorum quamplurium praelatorum in congregationibus generalibus factis, hinc omnino timore ipsius morbi abire volentium, qui juste detineri non possunt et ex quorum discessu concilium vel dissolveretur vel ex paucitate praelatorum bonus ejus progressus impediretur, et attento etiam imminenti periculo vitae et aliis causis per aliquos ex patribus in ipsis congregationibus allegatis, utpote notorie veris et legitimis; placetne vobis similiter decernere et declarare, pro conservatione et prosecutione ipsius concilii, securitate vitae ipsorum praelatorum, concilium ipsum ad civitatem Bononiae velut ad locum magis paratum, salubrem et idoneum pro tempore transferendum esse et ex nunc transferri et ibidem sessionem jam indictam statuta die vigesima prima Aprilis celebrandam esse et celebrari, et successive ad ulteriora procedendum, donec sanctissimo domino nostro et sacro concilio expedire videbitur, ut ad hunc seu alium locum, communicato etiam consilio cum invictissimo Caesare et Christianissimo rege et aliis regibus ac principibus Christianis, ipsum concilium reduci possit et debeat? *Responderunt:* Placet.

SESSIO NONA

Bononiae celebrata
die XXI mensis Aprilis, MDXLVII

DECRETUM PROROGATIONIS SESSIONIS

Haec sacrosancta oecumenica et generalis synodus, quae dudum in civitate Tridentina congregata erat, nunc Bononiae in Spiritu Sancto legitime congregata, praesidentibus in ea nomine sanctissimi in Christo patris et domini nostri, domini Pauli divina providentia Papae III, eisdem reverendissimis dominis, D. Joanne Maria episcopo Praenestino de Monte, et Marcello tit. S. Crucis in Jerusalem presbytero, S. R. E. cardinalibus et apostolicis de latere legatis, considerans, quod die undecima mensis Martii praesentis anni in generali publica sessione, in eadem civitate Tridenti et in loco consueto celebrata, omnibusque agendis de more peractis, ex causis tunc instantibus, urgentibus et legitimis, interveniente etiam auctoritate sanctae Sedis Apostolicae, eisdem reverendissimis praesidentibus etiam specialiter concessa, decrevit et ordinavit concilium ex eo loco in hanc civitatem transferendum esse, sicuti transtulit, itemque sessionem pro praesenti die vigesima prima Aprilis illic indictam, ut de sacramentorum et reformationis materiis, de quibus tractandum proposuerat, canones sancirentur et promulgarentur, in hac ipsa civitate Bononiae celebrari debere; consideransque nonnullos ex patribus, qui in hoc concilio interesse consueverunt, his superioribus majoris hebdomadae et solemnitatis paschalis diebus in propriis ecclesiis occupatos, aliquos etiam aliis impedimentis detentos huc nondum accessisse, quos tamen brevi adfuturos sperandum est, ac propterea factum esse, ut non ea, quam sancta synodus desiderabat, praelatorum frequentia potuerint materiae ipsae sacramentorum et reformationis examinari et discuti: ut omnia maturo consilio, cum dignitate et gravitate debita fiant, bonum, opportunum et expediens censuit censetque, sessionem praedictam, quae hoc ipso die, ut praefertur, celebranda erat, ad diem Jovis infra octavam Pentecostes proxime futuram quoad ipsas materias expediendas differendam et prorogandam esse, quemadmodum differt ac prorogat; quam diem et rei gerendae maxime opportunam, et patribus praesertim absentibus percommodam judicavit et judicat: hoc tamen adjecto, quod terminum ipsum ipsa sancta synodus pro ejus arbitrio et voluntate, sicuti rebus concilii putaverit expedire, etiam in privata congregatione restringere et imminuere possit et valeat.

SESSIO DECIMA

Bononiae celebrata

die II mensis Junii, MDXLVII

DECRETUM PROROGATIONIS SESSIONIS

Quamvis haec sacrosancta oecumenica et generalis synodus sessionem, quae die vigesima prima mensis Aprilis proxime praeteriti super sacramentorum et reformationis materiis in hac inclyta civitate Bononiae ex decreto in urbe Tridentina in publica sessione die undecima mensis Martii promulgato celebranda erat, propter aliquas causas, ac praesertim propter absentiam nonnullorum patrum, quos brevi adfuturos sperabat, ad hunc praesentem diem differendam et prorogandam esse decreverit: volens tamen cum iis, qui non venerunt, etiam adhuc benigne agere, eadem sacrosancta synodus in Spiritu Sancto legitime congregata, praesidentibus in ea eisdem sanctae Romanae ecclesiae cardinalibus et Apostolicae Sedis legatis, statuit et decernit, sessionem ipsam, quam hac die secunda mensis Junii praesentis anni millesimi quingentesimi quadragesimi septimi celebrare decreverat, ad diem Jovis post festum Nativitatis beatae Mariae Virginis, quae erit decima quinta mensis Septembris proxime futuri, quoad praedictas et alias materias expediendas differendam et prorogandam esse, quemadmodum differt et prorogat; ita tamen, quod prosecutio discussionis et examinationis eorum, quae tam ad dogmata quam ad reformationem pertinent, interim non omittatur, et terminum ipsum ipsa sancta synodus pro ejus libito et voluntate etiam in privata congregatione abbreviare et prorogare libere possit et valeat.

Die XIV Septembris, MDXLVII, in congregatione generali Bononiae prorogata fuit sessio, quae futura erat die sequenti, ad beneplacitum sacri concilii.

BULLA

RESUMPTIONIS

CONCILII TRIDENTINI

sub Julio III Pont. Max.

Julius Episcopus, servus servorum Dei, ad futuram rei memoriam.

Cum ad tollenda religionis nostrae dissidia, quae in Germania longo tempore non sine totius Christiani orbis perturbatione et scandalo viguerunt, bonum, opportunum et expediens esse videatur, sicuti etiam carissimus in Christo filius noster Carolus Romanorum imperator semper augustus nobis per suas litteras et nuncios significari fecit, ut sacrum oecumenicum generale concilium per fel. rec. Paulum Papam III praedecessorem nostrum indictum, et per nos, tunc cardinalatus honore fungentes atque ipsius praedecessoris nomine una cum duobus aliis sanctae Romanae ecclesiae cardinalibus ipsi concilio praesidentes, inceptum, ordinatum et continuatum, in quo plures publicae et solemnes habitae fuerunt sessiones, pluraque tam in causa fidei quam reformationis promulgata decreta, multaque etiam ad utramque causam pertinentia examinata et discussa, ad civitatem Tridentinam reducatur: nos, ad quos, ut summos pro tempore pontifices, spectat generalia concilia indicere et dirigere, ut ecclesiae pacem et Christianae fidei atque orthodoxae religionis incrementum ad omnipotentis Dei laudem et gloriam procuremus, et, quantum in nobis est, tranquillitati ipsius Germaniae, quae sane provincia retroactis temporibus in vera religione, ac sacrorum conciliorum et sanctorum patrum doctrina excolenda, exhibendaque maximis pontificibus, Christi Redemptoris nostri in terra vicariis, debita obedientia et reverentia nulli Christianorum provinciae fuit unquam secunda, paterne consulamus; sperantes per ipsius Dei gratiam et benignitatem futurum, ut reges omnes ac principes Christiani justis piisque nostris hac in re votis annuant, faveant atque assistant: venerabiles fratres patriarchas, archiepiscopos, episcopos, et dilectos filios abbates, omnesque alios et singulos, qui de jure vel consuetudine vel privilegio conciliis generalibus interesse debent, quosque idem praedecessor noster in suis indictionis et aliis quibuscumque desuper confectis et publicatis litteris concilio interesse voluit, per viscera misericordiae Domini nostri Jesu Christi hortamur, requirimus et monemus, ut proximis futuris Kal. Maii, quem diem ad ipsum concilium in eo, in quo nunc reperitur, statu resumendum et prosequendum, praevia matura deliberatione et ex certa nostra scientia, et de apostolicae auctoritatis plenitudine ac venerabilium fratrum nostrorum sanctae Romanae ecclesiae cardinalium consilio et assensu statuimus et declaramus, in ipsa civitate Tridenti, legitimo cessante impedimento, convenire et se congregare, ac ipsius concilii continuationi et prosecutioni omni mora postposita incumbere velint. Nos enim operam sedulo daturi sumus, ut eodem tempore in eadem civitate nostri omnino adsint legati, per quos, si per aetatem nostram valetudinemque et Sedis Apostolicae necessitates personaliter adesse nequiverimus, Spiritu Sancto duce, ipsi concilio praesidebimus; quacumque ipsius concilii translatione et suspensione ceterisque contrariis non obstantibus quibuscumque, ac praesertim illis, quae idem praedecessor noster in suis litteris praedictis, quas cum omnibus et singulis in eis contentis clausulis et decretis in suo robore permanere volumus atque decernimus, et, quatenus opus sit, innovamus, voluit non obstare; irritum nihilominus decernentes et inane, si secus super his a quoquam quavis auctoritate, scienter vel ignoranter, contigerit attentari. Nulli ergo omnino hominum liceat hanc paginam nostrorum hortationis, requisitionis, monitionis, statuti, declarationis, innovationis, voluntatis et decretorum infringere vel ei ausu temerario contraire. Si quis autem hoc attentare praesumpserit, indignationem omnipotentis Dei ac beatorum Petri et Pauli Apostolorum ejus se noverit incursurum. Datum Romae apud S. Petrum anno incarnationis dominicae MDL. Kalendis Decembris pontificatus nostri anno I.

M. Cardinalis Crescen.
Rom. Amasaeus.

SESSIO UNDECIMA

SACROSANCTI OECUMENICI ET GENERALIS

CONCILII TRIDENTINI

QUAE EST PRIMA

SUB JULIO III PONT. MAX.

celebrata

Kalend. Maii, MDLI

DECRETUM DE RESUMENDO CONCILIO

Placetne vobis, ad laudem et gloriam sanctae et individuae Trinitatis, Patris et Filii et Spiritus Sancti, ad incrementum et exaltationem fidei et religionis Christianae, sacrum oecumenicum et generale concilium Tridentinum juxta formam et tenorem litterarum sanctissimi domini nostri resumi debere, et procedendum esse ad ulteriora? *Responderunt:* Placet.

INDICTIO FUTURAE SESSIONIS

Placetne vobis, proximam futuram sessionem habendam et celebrandam esse in futuris Kalend. Septembris? *Responderunt:* Placet.

SESSIO DUODECIMA

QUAE EST SECUNDA

SUB JULIO III PONT. MAX.

celebrata

die I Septembris, MDLI

DECRETUM PROROGATIONIS SESSIONIS

Sacrosancta oecumenica et generalis Tridentina synodus in Spiritu Sancto legitime congregata, praesidentibus in ea eisdem sanctae Sedis Apostolicae legato et nunciis, quae in proxime praeterita sessione sequentem hanc hodie habendam et ad ulteriora procedendum esse decreverat, cum ob inclytae germanicae nationis, cujus praecipue causa agitur, absentiam, ac non magnam ceterorum patrum frequentiam procedere hactenus distulerit, de venerabilium in Christo fratrum et filiorum suorum, Moguntini et Trevirensis archiepiscoporum ac sacri Romani imperii principum electorum, et complurium ipsius aliarumque provinciarum episcoporum sub hanc ipsam diem adventu in Domino exsultans, et dignas ipsi omnipotenti Deo agens gratias, firmamque spem concipiens, quamplurimos alios tam ipsius Germaniae quam aliarum nationum praelatos, et sui officii debito et hoc exemplo commotos, propediem esse venturos, futuram sessionem ad quadragesimam diem, quae erit undecima mensis Octobris proxime sequentis, indicit, et concilium ipsum in statu, in quo reperitur, prosequendo, cum in praeteritis sessionibus de septem sacramentis novae legis in genere, et in specie de baptismate et confirmatione definitum fuerit, statuit et decernit, de sanctissimae Eucharistiae sacramento, necnon, quod ad reformationem attinet, de reliquis, quae ad faciliorem et commodiorem praelatorum residentiam pertinent, agi et tractari debere; ac monet et hortatur omnes patres, ut interim Domini nostri Jesu Christi exemplo, quantum tamen humana fragilitas patietur, jejuniis et orationibus vacent, ut tandem placatus, qui in saecula sit benedictus, Deus corda hominum ad verae suae fidei agnitionem, et sanctae matris ecclesiae unitatem, ac recte vivendi normam reducere dignetur.

SESSIO DECIMA TERTIA

QUAE EST TERTIA

SUB JULIO III PONT. MAX.

celebrata

die XI Octobris, MDLI

DECRETUM DE SANCTISSIMO EUCHARISTIAE SACRAMENTO

Sacrosancta oecumenica et generalis Tridentina synodus, in Spiritu Sancto legitime congregata, praesidentibus in ea eisdem sanctae Sedis Apostolicae legato et nunciis, etsi in eum finem non absque peculiari Spiritus Sancti ductu et gubernatione convenerit, ut veram et antiquam de fide et sacramentis doctrinam exponeret, et ut haeresibus omnibus et aliis gravissimis incommodis, quibus Dei ecclesia misere nunc exagitatur et in multas ac varias partes scinditur, remedium afferret, hoc praesertim jam inde a principio in votis habuit, ut stirpitus convelleret zizania [1] exsecrabilium errorum et schismatum, quae inimicus homo his nostris calamitosis temporibus in doctrina fidei, usu et cultu sacrosanctae Eucharistiae superseminavit, quam alioqui Salvator noster in ecclesia sua tamquam symbolum reliquit ejus unitatis et caritatis, qua Christianos omnes inter se conjunctos et copulatos esse voluit. Itaque eadem sacrosancta synodus, sanam et sinceram illam de venerabili hoc et divino Eucharistiae sacramento doctrinam tradens, quam semper catholica ecclesia ab ipso Jesu Christo Domino nostro et ejus apostolis erudita, atque a Spiritu Sancto illi omnem veritatem in dies suggerente [2] edocta retinuit et ad finem usque saeculi conservabit, omnibus Christi fidelibus interdicit, ne posthac de sanctissima Eucharistia aliter credere, docere aut praedicare audeant, quam ut est hoc praesenti decreto explicatum atque definitum.

---

[1] Matt. 13:30.
[2] Luc. 12:12; Joan. 14:26; 16:13.

Caput I

DE REALI PRAESENTIA DOMINI NOSTRI JESU CHRISTI IN SANCTISSIMO EUCHARISTIAE SACRAMENTO

Principio docet sancta synodus et aperte ac simpliciter profitetur, in almo sanctae Eucharistiae sacramento post panis et vini consecrationem Dominum nostrum Jesum Christum verum Deum atque hominem vere, realiter ac substantialiter sub specie illarum rerum sensibilium contineri. Neque enim haec inter se pugnant, ut ipse Salvator noster semper ad dexteram Patris in coelis assideat [3] juxta modum exsistendi naturalem, et ut multis nihilominus aliis in locis sacramentaliter praesens sua substantia nobis adsit, ea exsistendi ratione, quam etsi verbis exprimere vix possumus, possibilem tamen esse Deo,[4] cogitatione per fidem illustrata assequi possumus et constantissime credere debemus. Ita enim majores nostri omnes, quotquot in vera Christi ecclesia fuerunt, qui de sanctissimo hoc sacramento disseruerunt, apertissime professi sunt, hoc tam admirabile sacramentum in ultima coena Redemptorem nostrum instituisse,[5] cum post panis vinique benedictionem se suum ipsius corpus illi praebere ac suum sanguinem disertis ac perspicuis verbis testatus est; quae verba a sanctis evangelistis commemorata [6] et a divo Paulo postea repetita,[7] cum propriam illam et apertissimam significationem prae se ferant, secundum quam a patribus intellecta sunt, indignissimum sane flagitium est ea a quibusdam contentiosis et pravis hominibus ad fictitios et imaginarios tropos, quibus veritas carnis et sanguinis Christi negatur, contra universum ecclesiae sensum detorqueri, quae, tamquam *columna et firmamentum veritatis*,[8] haec ab impiis hominibus excogitata commenta velut satanica detestata est, grato semper et memore animo praestantissimum hoc Christi beneficium agnoscens.

---

[3] Cf. Sess. III, decr. de symbolo fidei.
[4] Matt. 19:26; Luc. 18:27.
[5] C.6, X, De celebr. miss., III, 41 (Innoc. III). Rouët de Journel, *Enchiridion Patristicum* sub rubrica "Eucharistia," p. 779, nn.483–86; Denzinger, *Enchiridion,* XII f., p. [43].
[6] Matt. 26:26–28; Marc. 14:22–24; Luc. 22:19 f.
[7] Cf. I Cor. 11:24 f.
[8] Cf. I Tim. 3:15.

Caput II

DE RATIONE INSTITUTIONIS SANCTISSIMI HUJUS SACRAMENTI

Ergo Salvator noster, discessurus ex hoc mundo ad Patrem, sacramentum hoc instituit, in quo divitias divini sui erga homines amoris velut effudit, memoriam faciens mirabilium suorum,[9] et in illius sumptione colere nos sui memoriam praecepit, suamque annunciare mortem donec ipse ad judicandum mundum veniat.[10] Sumi autem voluit sacramentum hoc tamquam spiritualem animarum cibum,[11] quo alantur et confortentur viventes vita illius, qui dixit: *Qui manducat me et ipse vivet propter me*,[12] et tamquam antidotum, quo liberemur a culpis quotidianis, et a peccatis mortalibus praeservemur. Pignus praeterea id esse voluit futurae nostrae gloriae et perpetuae felicitatis, adeoque symbolum unius illius corporis, cujus ipse caput exsistit,[13] cuique nos, tamquam membra, arctissima fidei, spei et caritatis connexione adstrictos esse voluit, *ut id ipsum omnes diceremus, nec essent in nobis schismata.*[14]

Caput III

DE EXCELLENTIA SANCTISSIMAE EUCHARISTIAE SUPER RELIQUA SACRAMENTA

Commune hoc quidem est sanctissimae Eucharistiae cum ceteris sacramentis, symbolum esse rei sacrae et invisibilis gratiae formam visibilem; [15] verum illud in ea excellens et singulare reperitur, quod reliqua sacramenta tunc primum sanctificandi vim habent, cum quis illis utitur, at in Eucharistia ipse sanctitatis auctor ante usum est. Nondum enim Eucharistiam de manu Domini apostoli susceperant, cum vere tamen ipse affirmaret corpus suum esse quod praebebat; [16] et semper haec fides in ecclesia Dei fuit, statim post consecrationem verum Domini nostri corpus verumque ejus sanguinem sub panis et vini specie una cum

---

[9] Ps. 110:4.
[10] Luc. 22:19; I Cor. 11:24–26.
[11] Matt. 26:26 f.
[12] Joan. 6:58.
[13] Cf. I Cor. 11:3; Eph. 5:23.
[14] Cf. I Cor. 1:10.
[15] C.32, D.II de cons. (Aug.).
[16] Matt. 26:26; Marc. 14:22.

ipsius anima et divinitate exsistere; sed corpus quidem sub specie panis et sanguinem sub vini specie ex vi verborum, ipsum autem corpus sub specie vini et sanguinem sub specie panis, animamque sub utraque, vi naturalis illius connexionis et concomitantiae, qua partes Christi Domini, qui jam ex mortuis resurrexit non amplius moriturus,[17] inter se copulantur,[18] divinitatem porro, propter admirabilem illam ejus cum corpore et anima hypostaticam unionem. Quapropter verissimum est, tantumdem sub alterutra specie atque sub utraque contineri.[19] Totus enim et integer Christus sub panis specie et sub quavis ipsius speciei parte, totus item sub vini specie et sub ejus partibus exsistit.

Caput IV

DE TRANSSUBSTANTIATIONE

Quoniam autem Christus Redemptor noster corpus suum id, quod sub specie panis offerebat,[20] vere esse dixit, ideo persuasum semper in ecclesia Dei fuit, idque nunc denuo sancta haec synodus declarat, per consecrationem panis et vini conversionem fieri totius substantiae panis in substantiam corporis Christi Domini nostri, et totius substantiae vini in substantiam sanguinis ejus.[21] Quae conversio convenienter et proprie a sancta catholica ecclesia transsubstantiatio est appellata.

Caput V

DE CULTU ET VENERATIONE HUIC SANCTISSIMO SACRAMENTO EXHIBENDA

Nullus itaque dubitandi locus relinquitur, quin omnes Christi fideles pro more in catholica ecclesia semper recepto latriae cultum, qui vero Deo debetur, huic sanctissimo sacramento in veneratione exhibeant.[22] Neque enim ideo minus est adorandum, quod fuerit a Christo Domino,

---

[17] Rom. 6:9.

[18] C.58, D.II de cons. (Aug.), c.71, *ibid.* (Paschas.), c.78, *ibid.* (Missal. Ambros.).

[19] C.35, D.II de cons. (incert. auct.), c.77, *ibid.* (ex missal. Ambros. in praef. Dom. V post Epiph.), c.78, *ibid.* (Hilar.); cf. *infra,* can. 3 et Sess. XXI de comm., cap. 3. Rouët de Journel, p. 779, nn.491 f.

[20] Luc. 22:19; Joan. 6:48 f.; I Cor. 11:24.

[21] C.55, D.II de cons. (Ambros.); c.6, X, De celebr. miss., III, 41 (Innoc. III); *infra,* can. 2.

[22] Cf. *infra,* can. 6.

ut sumatur, institutum.[23] Nam illum eumdem Deum praesentem in eo adesse credimus, quem Pater aeternus introducens in orbem terrarum dicit: *Et adorent eum omnes angeli Dei,*[24] quem magi procidentes adoraverunt,[25] quem denique in Galilaea ab apostolis adoratum fuisse scriptura testatur.[26]

Declarat praeterea sancta synodus, pie et religiose admodum in Dei ecclesiam inductum fuisse hunc morem,[27] ut singulis annis peculiari quodam et festo die praecelsum hoc et venerabile sacramentum singulari veneratione ac solemnitate celebraretur, utque in processionibus reverenter et honorifice illud per vias et loca publica circumferretur.[28] Aequissimum est enim sacros aliquos statutos esse dies, cum Christiani omnes singulari ac rara quadam significatione gratos et memores testentur animos erga communem Dominum et Redemptorem pro tam ineffabili et plane divino beneficio, quo mortis ejus victoria et triumphus repraesentatur. Ac sic quidem oportuit victricem veritatem de mendacio et haeresi triumphum agere, ut ejus adversarii in conspectu tanti splendoris, et in tanta universae ecclesiae laetitia positi vel debilitati et fracti tabescant, vel pudore affecti et confusi aliquando resipiscant.

Caput VI

DE ASSERVANDO SACRAE EUCHARISTIAE SACRAMENTO, ET AD INFIRMOS DEFERENDO

Consuetudo asservandi in sacrario sanctam Eucharistiam adeo antiqua est,[29] ut eam saeculum etiam Nicaeni concilii agnoverit.[30] Porro deferri ipsam sacram Eucharistiam ad infirmos, et in hunc usum diligenter in ecclesiis conservari, praeterquam quod cum summa aequitate et ratione conjunctum est, tum multis in conciliis praeceptum invenitur, et vetustissimo catholicae ecclesiae more est observatum.[31] Quare haec

[23] Matt. 26:26.
[24] Heb. 1:6.
[25] Matt. 2:11.
[26] *Ibid.* 28:17; Luc. 24:52.
[27] Cf. *epist.* Urbani IV in Clem., c. un. De reliq. et ven. sanct., III, 16 relatam.
[28] Cf. *infra*, can. 6.
[29] C.93, D.II de cons. (Cap. reg. Franc.); c.10, X, De celebr. miss., III, 41 (Honor. III). Cf. *infra*, can. 7.
[30] C.9, C.XXVI, q.6 (Nicaen. I).
[31] Cf. conc. Ancyran. (a.314), c.6; c.10, C.XXVI, q.6 (Leo I); conc. Arausican. I (a.441), c.3; c.63, D.L, sc. conc. Agathen. (a.506), c.15; Statuta ecclesiae antiqua, c.76–78; c.1, X, De custod. Euchar., III, 44 (Lat. IV).

synodus retinendum omnino salutarem hunc et necessarium morem statuit.

Caput VII

DE PRAEPARATIONE, QUAE ADHIBENDA EST, UT DIGNE QUIS SACRAM EUCHARISTIAM PERCIPIAT

Si non decet ad sacras ullas functiones quempiam accedere nisi sancte, certe quo magis sanctitas et divinitas coelestis hujus sacramenti viro Christiano comperta est, eo diligentius cavere ille debet, ne absque magna reverentia et sanctitate ad id percipiendum accedat, praesertim cum illa plena formidinis verba apud Apostolum legamus: *Qui manducat et bibit indigne, judicium sibi manducat et bibit, non dijudicans corpus Domini.*[32] Quare communicare volenti revocandum est in memoriam ejus praeceptum: *Probet autem se ipsum homo.*[33] Ecclesiastica autem consuetudo declarat, eam probationem necessariam esse, ut nullus sibi conscius peccati mortalis, quantumvis sibi contritus videatur,[34] absque praemissa sacramentali confessione ad sacram Eucharistiam accedere debeat. Quod a Christianis omnibus, etiam ab iis sacerdotibus, quibus ex officio incubuerit celebrare, haec sancta synodus perpetuo servandum esse decrevit, modo non desit illis copia confessoris. Quod si necessitate urgente sacerdos absque praevia confessione celebraverit, quam primum confiteatur.

Caput VIII

DE USU ADMIRABILIS HUJUS SACRAMENTI

Quoad usum autem recte et sapienter patres nostri tres rationes hoc sanctum sacramentum accipiendi distinxerunt. Quosdam enim docuerunt sacramentaliter dumtaxat id sumere ut peccatores; alios tantum spiritualiter, illos nimirum, qui voto propositum illum coelestem panem edentes, fide viva, quae per dilectionem operatur,[35] fructum ejus et utilitatem sentiunt: tertios porro sacramentaliter simul et spirituali-

---

[32] Cf. I Cor. 11:29.
[33] *Ibid.*, 11:28.
[34] Cf. *infra*, can. 11.
[35] Gal. 5:6.

ter; [36] hi autem sunt, qui ita se prius probant et instruunt, ut vestem nuptialem induti ad divinam hanc mensam accedant.[37] In sacramentali autem sumptione semper in ecclesia Dei mos fuit, ut laici a sacerdotibus communionem acciperent; sacerdotes autem celebrantes se ipsos communicarent,[38] qui mos, tamquam ex traditione apostolica descendens,[39] jure ac merito retineri debet. Demum autem paterno affecto admonet sancta synodus, hortatur, rogat et obsecrat per viscera misericordiae Dei nostri, ut omnes et singuli, qui Christiano nomine censentur, in hoc unitatis signo, in hoc vinculo caritatis, in hoc concordiae symbolo jam tandem aliquando conveniant et concordent, memoresque tantae majestatis et tam eximii amoris Jesu Christi Domini nostri, qui dilectam animam suam in nostrae salutis pretium,[40] et carnem suam nobis dedit ad manducandum, haec sacra mysteria corporis et sanguinis ejus ea fidei constantia et firmitate, ea animi devotione, ea pietate et cultu credant et venerentur, ut panem illum supersubstantialem frequenter suscipere possint, et is vere eis sit animae vita et perpetua sanitas mentis, cujus vigore confortati ex hujus miserae peregrinationis itinere ad coelestem patriam pervenire valeant, eumdem panem angelorum,[41] quem modo sub sacris velaminibus edunt, absque ullo velamine manducaturi.

Quoniam autem non est satis veritatem dicere nisi detegantur et refellantur errores: placuit sanctae synodo hos canones subjungere, ut omnes, jam agnita catholica doctrina, intelligant quoque, quae ab illis haereses caveri vitarique debeant.

CANONES DE SANCTISSIMO EUCHARISTIAE SACRAMENTO

1. Si quis negaverit, in sanctissimae Eucharistiae sacramento contineri vere, realiter et substantialiter corpus et sanguinem una cum anima et divinitate Domini nostri Jesu Christi, ac proinde totum Christum; [42] sed dixerit tantummodo esse in eo, ut in signo, vel figura aut virtute: anathema sit.

2. Si quis dixerit, in sacrosancto Eucharistiae sacramento remanere

[36] Cf. *infra,* can. 8.
[37] Matt. 22:11.
[38] Cf. c.11, D.II de cons. (conc. Toletan. XII). *Infra,* can. 10.
[39] Heb. 5:3, 7:27.
[40] Joan. 6:56 ff.
[41] Ps. 77:25.
[42] Cf. *supra,* cap. 3.

substantiam panis et vini una cum corpore et sanguine Domini nostri Jesu Christi,[43] negaveritque mirabilem illam et singularem conversionem totius substantiae panis in corpus, et totius substantiae vini in sanguinem, manentibus dumtaxat speciebus panis et vini, quam quidem conversionem catholica ecclesia aptissime transsubstantiationem appellat: [44] anathema sit.

3. Si quis negaverit, in venerabili sacramento Eucharistiae sub unaquaque specie, et sub singulis cujusque speciei partibus, separatione facta, totum Christum contineri: [45] anathema sit.

4. Si quis dixerit, peracta consecratione in admirabili Eucharistiae sacramento non esse corpus et sanguinem Domini nostri Jesu Christi,[46] sed tantum in usu, dum sumitur, non autem ante vel post, et in hostiis seu particulis consecratis, quae post communionem reservantur vel supersunt, non remanere verum corpus Domini: anathema sit.

5. Si quis dixerit, vel praecipuum fructum sanctissimae Eucharistiae esse remissionem peccatorum,[47] vel ex ea non alios effectus provenire: anathema sit.

6. Si quis dixerit, in sancto Eucharistiae sacramento Christum unigenitum Dei Filium non esse cultu latriae etiam externo adorandum,[48] atque ideo nec festiva peculiari celebritate venerandum, neque in processionibus secundum laudabilem et universalem ecclesiae sanctae ritum et consuetudinem solemniter circumgestandum, vel non publice, ut adoretur, populo proponendum, et ejus adoratores esse idololatras: anathema sit.

7. Si quis dixerit, non licere sacram Eucharistiam in sacrario reservari, sed statim post consecrationem adstantibus necessario distribuendam; aut non licere, ut illa ad infirmos honorifice deferatur: [49] anathema sit.

8. Si quis dixerit, Christum in Eucharistia exhibitum spiritualiter tantum manducari, et non etiam sacramentaliter ac realiter: [50] anathema sit.

9. Si quis negaverit, omnes et singulos Christi fideles utriusque sexus,

---

[43] Cf. propositionem Joan. Wicleff in conc. Constantien. damnatam apud Denzinger, n.581.
[44] Cf. *supra*, cap. 4.
[45] Eugen. IV in *decr. pro Armenis*, Denzinger, n.698. Cf. *supra*, adn. 19 huj. sess.
[46] *Supra*, cap. 3.
[47] *Supra*, adn. 46 et cap. 2.
[48] *Ibid.*, cap. 5.
[49] *Ibid.*, cap. 6.
[50] *Ibid.*, cap. 8.

cum ad annos discretionis pervenerint, teneri singulis annis saltem in Paschate ad communicandum juxta praeceptum sanctae matris ecclesiae: [51] anathema sit.

10. Si quis dixerit, non licere sacerdoti celebranti se ipsum communicare: [52] anathema sit.

11. Si quis dixerit, solam fidem esse sufficientem praeparationem ad sumendum sanctissimae Eucharistiae sacramentum: [53] anathema sit. Et, ne tantum sacramentum indigne atque ideo in mortem et condemnationem sumatur, statuit atque declarat ipsa sancta synodus, illis, quos conscientia peccati mortalis gravat, quantumcumque etiam se contritos existiment, habita copia confessoris, necessario praemittendam esse confessionem sacramentalem. Si quis autem contrarium docere, praedicare vel pertinaciter asserere, seu etiam publice disputando defendere praesumpserit, eo ipso excommunicatus exsistat.

DECRETUM DE REFORMATIONE

Caput I

EPISCOPI PRUDENTER MORIBUS SUBDITORUM REFORMANDIS INVIGILENT; AB EORUM CORRECTIONE NON APPELLETUR

Eadem sacrosancta Tridentina synodus in Spiritu Sancto legitime congregata, praesidentibus in ea eisdem sanctae Sedis Apostolicae legato et nunciis, intendens nonnulla statuere, quae ad jurisdictionem pertinent episcoporum, ut juxta proximae sessionis decretum [54] illi in commissis sibi ecclesiis eo libentius resideant, quo facilius et commodius sibi subjectos regere et in vitae ac morum honestate continere potuerint: illud primum eos admonendos censet, ut se pastores, non percussores esse meminerint,[55] atque ita praeesse sibi subditis oportere, ut non in eis dominentur,[56] sed illos tamquam filios et fratres diligant, elaborentque, ut hortando et monendo ab illicitis deterreant, ne, ubi deliquerint, debitis eos poenis coercere cogantur. Quos tamen si quid per humanam fragilitatem peccare contigerit, illa Apostoli est ab eis ser-

[51] Cf. Sess. XIV de poenit., can. 8.
[52] *Supra*, cap. 8.
[53] *Ibid.*, cap. 7.
[54] Cf. Sess. XII sub fin.
[55] Cf. I Tim. 3:3; Tit. 1:7.
[56] Cf. I Pet. 5:2 f.; cc. 1–9, D. XLV.

vanda praeceptio, ut illos arguant, obsecrent, increpent in omni bonitate et patientia,[57] cum saepe plus erga corrigendos agat benevolentia quam austeritas, plus exhortatio quam comminatio, plus caritas quam potestas.[58] Sin autem ob delicti gravitatem virga opus fuerit, tunc cum mansuetudine rigor, cum misericordia judicium, cum lenitate severitas adhibenda est, ut sine asperitate disciplina populis salutaris ac necessaria conservetur, et qui correpti fuerint emendentur, aut, si resipiscere noluerint, ceteri salubri in eos animadversionis exemplo a vitiis deterreantur, cum sit diligentis et pii simul pastoris officium, morbis ovium levia primum adhibere fomenta; post, ubi morbi gravitas ita postulet, ad acriora et graviora remedia descendere; sin autem nec ea quidem proficiant illis submovendis, ceteras saltem oves a contagionis periculo liberare.[59] Cum igitur rei criminum plerumque ad evitandas poenas et episcoporum subterfugienda judicia querelas et gravamina simulent, et appellationis diffugio judicis processum impediant, ne remedio ad innocentiae praesidium instituto ad iniquitatis defensionem abutantur,[60] atque ut hujusmodi eorum calliditati et tergiversationi occurratur, ita statuit et decrevit: in causis visitationis et correctionis, sive habilitatis et inhabilitatis, necnon criminalibus, ab episcopo seu illius in spiritualibus vicario generali ante definitivam sententiam ab interlocutoria vel alio quocumque gravamine non appelletur, neque episcopus seu vicarius appellationi hujusmodi tamquam frivolae deferre teneatur, sed ea, ac quacumque inhibitione ab appellationis judice emanata, necnon omni stylo et consuetudine etiam immemorabili contraria non obstante, ad ulteriora valeat procedere, nisi gravamen hujusmodi per definitivam sententiam reparari vel ab ipsa definitiva appellari non possit,[61] quibus casibus sacrorum et antiquorum canonum statuta illibata persistant.

Caput II

IN CRIMINALIBUS APPELLATIO AB EPISCOPO QUANDO METROPOLITANO AUT UNI EX VICINIORIBUS COMMITTENDA SIT

A sententia episcopi vel ipsius in spiritualibus vicarii generalis, in criminalibus appellationis causa, ubi appellationi locus fuerit, si apos-

[57] Cf. II Tim. 4:2.
[58] Sunt verba Leonis III ex ejus epist. 82 desumpta et in c.6, D.XLV relata.
[59] C.16, C.XXIV, q.3 (Hieron.), c.17, *ibid.* (Aug.).
[60] Cf. c.3, X, De appell., II, 28 (Alex. III).
[61] Cf. c.59, *ibid.* (Innoc. III).

tolica auctoritate in partibus eam committi contigerit, metropolitano, seu illius etiam vicario in spiritualibus generali, aut, si ille aliqua de causa suspectus foret vel ultra duas legales diaetas distet,[62] seu ab ipso appellatum fuerit, uni ex vicinioribus episcopis seu illorum vicariis, non autem inferioribus judicibus, committatur.

Caput III

ACTA PRIMAE INSTANTIAE INTRA TRIGINTA DIES DENTUR GRATIS REO APPELLANTI

Reus, ab episcopo aut ejus vicario in spiritualibus generali in criminali causa appellans, coram judice, ad quem appellavit, acta primae instantiae omnino producat, et judex, nisi illis visis, ad ejus absolutionem minime procedat. Is autem, a quo appellatum fuerit, intra triginta dies acta ipsa postulanti gratis exhibeat; alioquin absque illis causa appellationis hujusmodi, prout justitia suaserit, terminetur.

Caput IV

QUA RATIONE CLERICI OB GRAVIA CRIMINA SACRIS EXAUCTORANDI

Cum vero tam gravia nonnunquam sint delicta ab ecclesiasticis commissa personis, ut ob eorum atrocitatem a sacris ordinibus deponendae, et curiae sint tradendae saeculari, in quo secundum sacros canones certus episcoporum numerus requiritur,[63] quos si omnes adhibere difficile esset, debita juris executio differretur, si quando autem intervenire possent, eorum residentia intermitteretur, propterea statuit et decrevit: episcopo per se seu illius vicario in spiritualibus generali contra clericum in sacris etiam presbyteratus ordinibus constitutum, etiam ad illius condemnationem necnon verbalem depositionem, et per se ipsum etiam ad actualem atque solemnem degradationem ab ipsis ordinibus et gradibus ecclesiasticis, in casibus, in quibus aliorum episcoporum praesentia in numero a canonibus definito requiritur, etiam absque illis procedere liceat, adhibitis tamen et in hoc sibi assistentibus totidem abbatibus usum mitrae et baculi ex privilegio apostolico habentibus, et in civitate

---

[62] Cf. c.11, VI°, De rescript., I, 3 (Bonif. VIII).
[63] C.2. C.III. q.8; cc.1 4-7, C.XV, q.7.

aut dioecesi reperiri et commode interesse possint; alioquin aliis personis in ecclesiastica dignitate constitutis, quae aetate graves ac juris scientia commendabiles exsistant.

Caput V

SUMMARIE COGNOSCAT EPISCOPUS DE GRATIIS AUT ABSOLUTIONEM CRIMINIS AUT REMISSIONEM POENAE RESPICIENTIBUS

Et quoniam per fictas causas, quae tamen satis probabiles videntur, interdum accidit, ut nonnulli ejusdem gratias extorqueant, per quas poenae illis episcoporum justa severitate inflictae aut remittuntur omnino, aut minuuntur, cum non ferendum sit, ut mendacium, quod tantopere Deo displicet,[64] non modo ipsum impunitum sit, verum etiam alterius delicti veniam impetret mentienti; idcirco, ut sequitur, statuit et decrevit: episcopus apud ecclesiam suam residens, de subreptione et obreptione gratiae, quae super absolutione alicujus publici criminis vel delicti, de quo ipse inquirere coeperat, aut remissione poenae, ad quam criminosus per eum condemnatus fuerit, falsis precibus impetratur, per se ipsum tamquam Sedis Apostolicae delegatus etiam summarie cognoscat, ipsamque gratiam, postquam per falsi narrationem aut veri taciturnitatem obtentam esse legitime constiterit, non admittat.[65]

Caput VI

NON CITETUR PERSONALITER EPISCOPUS, NISI DEPOSITIONIS AUT PRIVATIONIS CAUSA

Quoniam vero subditi episcopo, tametsi jure correpti fuerint, magnopere tamen eum odisse, et, tamquam injuria affecti sint, falsa illi crimina objicere solent, ut quoquo pacto possint, ei molestiam exhibeant,[66] cujus vexationis timor plerumque illum ad inquirenda et punienda eorum delicta segniorem reddit: idcirco, ne is magno suo et ecclesiae incommodo gregem sibi creditum relinquere, ac non sine episcopalis dignitatis diminutione vagari cogatur, ita statuit et decrevit: episcopus, nisi ob causam, ex qua deponendus sive privandus veniret,

[64] Ex. 23:1; Lev. 19:11 et al.
[65] Cf. cc. 20, 22, X, De rescript., I, 3 (Innoc. III).
[66] C. 21, C. II, q. 7.

etiam si ex officio, aut per inquisitionem, seu denunciationem vel accusationem, sive alio quovis modo procedatur, ut personaliter compareat, nequaquam citetur vel moneatur.[67]

Caput VII

QUALITATES TESTIUM CONTRA EPISCOPUM DESCRIBUNTUR

Testes in causa criminali ad informationem vel indicia seu alias in causa principali contra episcopum, nisi contestes et bonae conversationis, existimationis et famae fuerint, non recipiantur; et si odio, temeritate aut cupiditate aliquid deposuerint, gravibus poenis mulctentur.

Caput VIII

GRAVES EPISCOPORUM CAUSAE A PONT. MAX. COGNOSCANTUR

Causae episcoporum, cum pro criminis objecti qualitate comparere debeant, coram Pontifice Max. referantur, ac per ipsum terminentur.[68]

DECRETUM

PROROGATIONIS DEFINITIONIS QUATUOR ARTICULORUM DE SACRAMENTO EUCHARISTIAE, ET SALVI CONDUCTUS PROTESTANTIBUS DANDI

Eadem sancta synodus errores omnes, qui super hoc sanctissimo sacramento repullularunt, tamquam vepres ex agro dominico evellere, ac omnium fidelium saluti prospicere cupiens, quotidianis precibus Deo omnipotenti pie oblatis, inter alios ad hoc sacramentum pertinentes articulos diligentissima veritatis catholicae inquisitione tractatos, plurimis accuratissimisque pro rerum gravitate disputationibus habitis, cognitis quoque praestantissimorum theologorum sententiis, hos etiam tractabat: An necessarium sit ad salutem et divino jure praeceptum, ut singuli Christi fideles sub utraque specie ipsum venerabile sacramentum

---

[67] Cf. Sess. XXIV, cap. 5 de ref.
[68] C. 7, C. VI, q. 4 (conc. Sard.); cf. Sess. et cap. cit.

accipiant? et: Num minus sumat, qui sub altera, quam qui sub utraque communicat? et: An erravit sancta mater ecclesia, laicos et non celebrantes sacerdotes sub panis specie dumtaxat communicando? et: An parvuli etiam communicandi sint? Sed quoniam ex nobilissima Germaniae provincia ii, qui se protestantes nominant, super his ipsis articulis, antequam definiantur, audiri a sancta synodo cupiunt, et eam ob causam fidem publicam ab illa postularunt, ut ipsis tuto huc venire, et in hac urbe commorari ac libere coram synodo dicere atque proponere quae senserint, et postea, cum libuerit, recedere liceat: sancta ipsa synodus, licet magno desiderio eorum adventum multos antea menses exspectarit, tamen ut pia mater, quae ingemiscit et parturit, summopere id desiderans ac laborans, ut in iis, qui Christiano nomine censentur, nulla sint schismata, sed, quemadmodum eumdem omnes Deum et Redemptorem agnoscunt, ita idem dicant, idem credant, idem sapiant, confidens Dei misericordiae, et sperans fore, ut illi in sanctissimam et salutarem unius fidei, spei caritatisque concordiam redigantur, libenter eis in hac re morem gerens, securitatem et fidem, ut petierunt, publicam, quam salvum conductum vocant, quoad se pertinet, ejus, qui infra scriptus erit, tenoris dedit atque concessit, et eorum causa definitionem illorum articulorum ad secundam sessionem distulit; quam, ut illi commode ei interesse possint, in diem festum Conversionis D. Pauli, quae erit XXV die mensis Januarii anni sequentis, indixit. Illudque practcrea statuit, ut in eadem sessione de sacrificio missae agatur propter magnam utriusque rei connexionem, interea sessione proxima de poenitentiae et extremae unctionis sacramentis tractandum. Illam autem die festo divae Catherinae virginis et martyris, qui erit XXV Novembris, habendam esse decrevit, simulque, ut in utraque materiam reformationis prosequatur.

SALVUS CONDUCTUS
datus
PROTESTANTIBUS

Sacrosancta et generalis Tridentina synodus in Spiritu Sancto legitime congregata, praesidentibus in ea eisdem sanctae Sedis Apostolicae legato et nunciis, omnibus et singulis, sive ecclesiasticis sive saecularibus personis universae Germaniae, cujuscumque gradus, status, conditionis et qualitatis sint, quae ad oecumenicum hoc et generale concilium accedere voluerint, ut de iis rebus, quae in ipsa synodo tractari debent, omni libertate conferre, proponere et tractare, ac ad ipsum oecumenicum concilium libere et tuto venire et in eo manere et commorari, ac articulos, quot illis videbitur, tam scripto quam verbo offerre, proponere, et cum patribus, sive iis, qui ab ipsa sancta synodo delecti fuerint, conferre et absque ullis conviciis et contumeliis disputare, necnon, quando illis placuerit, recedere possint et valeant, publicam fidem et plenam securitatem, quam salvum conductum appellant, cum omnibus et singulis clausulis et decretis necessariis et opportunis, etiamsi specialiter et non per verba generalia exprimi deberent, quae pro expressis haberi voluit, quantum ad ipsam sanctam synodum spectat, concedit. Placuit praeterea sanctae synodo, ut, si pro majori libertate ac securitate eorum certos tam pro commissis, quam pro committendis per eos delictis judices eis deputari cupiant, illos sibi benevolos nominent, etiamsi delicta ipsa quantumcumque enormia ac haeresim sapientia fuerint.

SESSIO DECIMA QUARTA

QUAE EST QUARTA

SUB JULIO III PONT. MAX.

celebrata

die XXV Novembris, MDLI

DOCTRINA DE SANCTISSIMIS POENITENTIAE ET EXTREMAE UNCTIONIS SACRAMENTIS

Sacrosancta oecumenica et generalis Tridentina synodus in Spiritu Sancto legitime congregata, praesidentibus in ea eisdem sanctae Sedis Apostolicae legato et nunciis, quamvis in decreto de justificatione [1] multus fuerit de poenitentiae sacramento propter locorum cognationem necessaria quadam ratione sermo interpositus; tanta nihilominus circa illud nostra hac aetate diversorum errorum est multitudo, ut non parum publicae utilitatis retulerit, de eo exactiorem et pleniorem definitionem tradidisse, in qua demonstratis et convulsis Spiritus Sancti praesidio universis erroribus, catholica veritas perspicua et illustris fieret; quam nunc sancta haec synodus Christianis omnibus perpetuo servandam proponit.

Caput I

DE NECESSITATE ET INSTITUTIONE SACRAMENTI POENITENTIAE

Si ea in regeneratis omnibus gratitudo erga Deum esset, ut justitiam in baptismo ipsius beneficio et gratia susceptam constanter tuerentur, non fuisset opus, aliud ab ipso baptismo sacramentum ad peccatorum remissionem esse institutum.[2] Quoniam autem Deus, dives in misericordia,[3] *cognovit figmentum nostrum,*[4] illis etiam vitae remedium contulit, qui se postea in peccati servitutem et daemonis potestatem tradidissent, sacramentum videlicet poenitentiae, quo lapsis post baptismum

[1] Cf. Sess. VI, cap. 14.
[2] Cf. *infra,* cap. 5 de poenit.
[3] Eph. 2:4.
[4] Ps. 102:14.

beneficium mortis Christi applicatur. Fuit quidem poenitentia universis hominibus, qui se mortali aliquo peccato inquinassent, quovis tempore ad gratiam et justitiam assequendam necessaria,[5] illis etiam, qui baptismi sacramento ablui petivissent, ut perversitate abjecta et emendata tantam Dei offensionem cum peccati odio et pio animi dolore detestarentur. Unde Propheta ait: *Convertimini, et agite poenitentiam ab omnibus iniquitatibus vestris, et non erit vobis in ruinam iniquitas.*[6] Dominus etiam dixit: *Si poenitentiam non egeritis, omnes similiter peribitis.*[7] Et princeps apostolorum Petrus peccatoribus baptismo initiandis poenitentiam commendans dicebat: *Poenitentiam agite, et baptizetur unusquisque vestrum.*[8] Porro nec ante adventum Christi poenitentia erat sacramentum, nec est post adventum illius cuiquam ante baptismum. Dominus autem sacramentum poenitentiae tunc praecipue instituit, cum a mortuis excitatus insufflavit in discipulos suos, dicens: *Accipite Spiritum Sanctum; quorum remiseritis peccata, remittuntur eis, et quorum retinueritis, retenta sunt.*[9] Quo tam insigni facto et verbis tam perspicuis potestatem remittendi et retinendi peccata, ad reconciliandos fideles post baptismum lapsos, apostolis et eorum legitimis successoribus fuisse communicatam, universorum patrum consensus semper intellexit, et Novatianos, remittendi potestatem olim pertinaciter negantes, magna ratione ecclesia catholica tamquam haereticos explosit atque condemnavit.[10] Quare verissimum hunc illorum verborum Domini sensum sancta haec synodus probans et recipiens, damnat eorum commentitias interpretationes, qui verba illa ad potestatem praedicandi verbum Dei et Christi evangelium annunciandi contra hujusmodi sacramenti institutionem falso detorquent.

Caput II

DE DIFFERENTIA SACRAMENTI POENITENTIAE ET BAPTISMI

Ceterum hoc sacramentum multis rationibus a baptismo differre dignoscitur.[11] Nam praeterquam quod materia et forma, quibus sacra-

---

[5] Cf. Sess. VI, cap. 14. Rouët de Journel, *Enchiridion patristicum* sub rubrica "Poenitentia," p. 781, nn.531, 547; Denzinger, *Enchiridion*, XII i et XII k, pp. [45–47].
[6] Ezech. 18:30.
[7] Luc. 13:5.
[8] Act. 2:28; c.13 (§ 3), D.IV de cons. (Leo I).
[9] Joan. 20:22 f.; cf. *infra*, can. 3 de poenit. Rouët de Journel, p. 780, n.521.
[10] Eusebius, *Hist. eccl.*, VI, 43.
[11] Cf. Sess. VI, cap. 14 et *infra*, can. 2 de poenit.

menti essentia perficitur, longissime dissidet; constat certe, baptismi ministrum judicem esse non oportere, cum ecclesia in neminem judicium exerceat, qui non prius in ipsam per baptismi januam fuerit ingressus. *Quid enim mihi*, inquit Apostolus, *de iis, qui foris sunt, judicare?* [12] Secus est de domesticis fidei, quos Christus Dominus lavacro baptismi sui corporis membra semel effecit.[13] Nam hos, si se postea crimine aliquo contaminaverint, non jam repetito baptismo ablui, cum id in ecclesia catholica nulla ratione liceat, sed ante hoc tribunal tamquam reos sisti voluit, ut per sacerdotum sententiam non semel, sed quoties ab admissis peccatis ad ipsum poenitentes confugerint, possent liberari. Alius praeterea est baptismi, et alius poenitentiae fructus. Per baptismum enim Christum induentes nova prorsus in illo efficimur creatura,[14] plenam et integram peccatorum omnium remissionem consequentes: ad quam tamen novitatem et integritatem per sacramentum poenitentiae sine magnis nostris fletibus et laboribus, divina id exigente justitia, pervenire nequaquam possumus, ut merito poenitentia laboriosus quidam baptismus a sanctis patribus dicta fuerit.[15] Est autem hoc sacramentum poenitentiae lapsis post baptismum ad salutem necessarium, ut nondum regeneratis ipse baptismus.

Caput III

DE PARTIBUS ET FRUCTIBUS HUJUS SACRAMENTI

Docet praeterea sancta synodus, sacramenti poenitentiae formam, in qua praecipue ipsius vis sita est, in illis ministri verbis positam esse: *Ego te absolvo* etc., quibus quidem de ecclesiae sanctae more preces quaedam laudabiliter adjunguntur; ad ipsius tamen formae essentiam nequaquam spectant, neque ad ipsius sacramenti administrationem sunt necessariae. Sunt autem quasi materia hujus sacramenti ipsius poenitentis actus, nempe contritio,[16] confessio et satisfactio. Qui quatenus in poenitente ad integritatem sacramenti, ad plenamque et perfectam peccatorum remissionem ex Dei institutione requiruntur, hac ratione poenitentiae partes dicuntur. Sane vero res et effectus hujus sacramenti,

[12] Cf. I Cor. 5:12.
[13] *Ibid.*, 12:13.
[14] Gal. 3:27.
[15] Cf. Greg. Naz., *Oratio* "In sancta lumina," *PG*, XXXVI, 335 ff.; Joan. Damasc., *De fide orthodoxa*, IV, 9, *PG*, XCIV, 1118.
[16] Cf. Sess. VI, cap. 14 et *infra*, can. 4 de poenit.

quantum ad ejus vim et efficaciam pertinet, reconciliatio est cum Deo, quam interdum in viris piis et cum devotione hoc sacramentum percipientibus, conscientiae pax ac serenitas cum vehementi spiritus consolatione consequi solet. Haec de partibus et effectu hujus sacramenti sancta synodus tradens simul eorum sententias damnat, qui poenitentiae partes incussos conscientiae terrores et fidem esse contendunt.

Caput IV

DE CONTRITIONE

Contritio, quae primum locum inter dictos poenitentis actus habet, animi dolor ac detestatio est de peccato commisso, cum proposito non peccandi de cetero.[17] Fuit autem quovis tempore ad impetrandam veniam peccatorum hic contritionis motus necessarius, et in homine post baptismum lapso ita demum praeparat ad remissionem peccatorum, si cum fiducia divinae misericordiae et voto praestandi reliqua conjunctus sit, quae ad rite suscipiendum hoc sacramentum requiruntur. Declarat igitur sancta synodus, hanc contritionem non solum cessationem a peccato et vitae novae propositum et inchoationem,[18] sed veteris etiam odium continere, juxta illud: *Projicite a vobis omnes iniquitates vestras, in quibus praevaricati estis, et facite vobis cor novum et spiritum novum.*[19] Et certe, qui illos sanctorum clamores consideraverit: *Tibi soli peccavi, et malum coram te feci.*[20] *Laboravi in gemitu meo, lavabo per singulas noctes lectum meum.*[21] *Recogitabo tibi omnes annos meos in amaritudine animae meae,*[22] et alios hujus generis, facile intelliget, eos ex vehementi quodam anteactae vitae odio et ingenti peccatorum detestatione manasse. Docet praeterea, etsi contritionem hanc aliquando caritate perfectam esse contingat, hominemque Deo reconciliare, priusquam hoc sacramentum actu suscipiatur, ipsam nihilominus reconciliationem ipsi contritioni sine sacramenti voto, quod in illa includitur, non esse adscribendam. Illam vero contritionem imperfectam, quae attritio dicitur, quoniam vel ex turpitudinis peccati consideratione vel ex gehennae et poenarum metu communiter concipitur, si volunta-

---

[17] Cf. Sess. VI, capp. 6 et 14.
[18] Cf. *infra*, can. 5 de poenit.
[19] Ezech. 18:31.
[20] Ps. 50:6.
[21] Ps. 6:7.
[22] Is. 38:15.

tem peccandi excludat cum spe veniae, declarat non solum non facere hominem hypocritam et magis peccatorem, verum etiam donum Dei esse et Spiritus Sancti impulsum, non adhuc quidem inhabitantis, sed tantum moventis, quo poenitens adjutus viam sibi ad justitiam parat. Et quamvis sine sacramento poenitentiae per se ad justificationem perducere peccatorem nequeat, tamen eum ad Dei gratiam in sacramento poenitentiae impetrandam disponit. Hoc enim timore utiliter concussi Ninivitae ad Jonae praedicationem plenam terroribus poenitentiam egerunt, et misericordiam a Domino impetrarunt.[23] Quamobrem falso quidam calumniantur catholicos scriptores, quasi tradiderint, sacramentum poenitentiae absque bono motu suscipientium gratiam conferre, quod nunquam ecclesia Dei docuit neque sensit. Sed et falso docent, contritionem esse extortam et coactam, non liberam et voluntariam.

Caput V

DE CONFESSIONE

Ex institutione sacramenti poenitentiae jam explicata universa ecclesia semper intellexit, institutam etiam esse a Domino integram peccatorum confessionem,[24] et omnibus post baptismum lapsis jure divino necessariam exsistere, quia Dominus noster Jesus Christus, e terris ascensurus ad coelos, sacerdotes sui ipsius vicarios reliquit [25] tamquam praesides et judices,[26] ad quos omnia mortalia crimina deferantur, in quae Christi fideles ceciderint, quo pro potestate clavium remissionis aut retentionis peccatorum sententiam pronuncient. Constat enim, sacerdotes judicium hoc incognita causa exercere non potuisse, nec aequitatem quidem illos in poenis injungendis servare potuisse, si in genere dumtaxat, et non potius in specie ac sigillatim sua ipsi peccata declarassent. Ex his colligitur, oportere a poenitentibus omnia peccata mortalia, quorum post diligentem sui discussionem conscientiam habent, in confessione recenseri,[27] etiamsi occultissima illa sint et tantum adversus duo ultima decalogi praecepta commissa,[28] quae nonnunquam animum

---

[23] Jon. 3:5; Matt. 12:41; Luc. 11:32.

[24] Luc. 5:14, 17:14; Jac. 5:16; I Joan. 1:9; cf. *infra*, can. 6 de poenit. Rouët de Journel, p. 781, n.536.

[25] Matt. 16:19; Joan. 20:23.

[26] Cf. c.51, D.I de poenit. (Ambros.).

[27] Cf. *infra*, can. 7 de poenit.

[28] Deut. 5:21.

gravius sauciant, et periculosiora sunt iis, quae in manifesto admittuntur. Nam venialia, quibus a gratia Dei non excludimur et in quae frequentius labimur,[29] quamquam recte et utiliter citraque omnem praesumptionem in confessione dicantur, quod piorum hominum usus demonstrat: taceri tamen citra culpam, multisque aliis remediis expiari possunt. Verum, cum universa mortalia peccata, etiam cogitationis, homines irae filios [30] et Dei inimicos reddant, necessum est, omnium etiam veniam cum aperta et verecunda confessione a Deo quaerere. Itaque dum omnia, quae memoriae occurrunt, peccata Christi fideles confiteri student, procul dubio omnia divinae misericordiae ignoscenda exponunt. Qui vero secus faciunt et scienter aliqua retinent, nihil divinae bonitati per sacerdotem remittendum proponunt. Si enim erubescat aegrotus vulnus medico detegere, quod ignorat, medicina non curat. Colligitur praeterea, etiam eas circumstantias in confessione explicandas esse, quae speciem peccati mutant, quod sine illis peccata ipsa neque a poenitentibus integre exponantur, nec judicibus innotescant, et fieri nequeat, ut de gravitate criminum recte censere possint, et poenam, quam oportet, pro illis poenitentibus imponere. Unde alienum a ratione est docere, circumstantias has ab hominibus otiosis excogitatas fuisse, aut unam tantum circumstantiam confitendam esse, nempe peccasse in fratrem. Sed et impium est, confessionem, quae hac ratione fieri praecipitur, impossibilem dicere, aut carnificinam illam conscientiarum appellare; constat enim, nihil aliud in ecclesia a poenitentibus exigi, quam ut, postquam quisque diligentius se excusserit, et conscientiae suae sinus omnes et latebras exploraverit, ea peccata confiteatur, quibus se Dominum et Deum suum mortaliter offendisse meminerit; reliqua autem peccata, quae diligenter cogitanti non occurrunt, in universum eadem confessione inclusa esse intelliguntur; pro quibus fideliter cum Propheta dicimus: *Ab occultis meis munda me, Domine.*[31] Ipsa vero hujusmodi confessionis difficultas ac peccata detegendi verecundia gravis quidem videri posset, nisi tot tantisque commodis et consolationibus levaretur, quae omnibus digne ad hoc sacramentum accedentibus per absolutionem certissime conferuntur. Ceterum, quoad modum confitendi secreto apud solum sacerdotem, etsi Christus non vetuerit, quin aliquis in vindictam suorum scelerum et sui humiliationem, cum ob aliorum exemplum, tum ob ecclesiae of-

---

[29] Cf. Sess. VI, can. 23; c.20, D.III de poenit. (Aug.). Rouët de Journel, p. 782, n.548.
[30] Eph. 2:3.
[31] Ps. 18:13.

fensae aedificationem delicta sua publice confiteri possit: non est tamen hoc divino praecepto mandatum, nec satis consulte humana aliqua lege praeciperetur, ut delicta, praesertim secreta, publica essent confessione aperienda. Unde cum a sanctissimis et antiquissimis patribus magno unanimique consensu secreta confessio sacramentalis, qua ab initio ecclesia sancta usa est et modo etiam utitur, fuerit semper commendata, manifeste refellitur inanis eorum calumnia, qui eam a divino mandato alienam et inventum humanum esse, atque a patribus in concilio Lateranensi congregatis initium habuisse,[32] docere non verentur; neque enim per Lateranense concilium ecclesia statuit,[33] ut Christi fideles confiterentur, quod jure divino necessarium et institutum esse intellexerat, sed ut praeceptum confessionis saltem semel in anno ab omnibus et singulis, cum ad annos discretionis pervenissent, impleretur. Unde jam in universa ecclesia cum ingenti animarum fidelium fructu observatur mos ille salutaris confitendi sacro illo et maxime acceptabili tempore Quadragesimae, quem morem haec sancta synodus maxime probat et amplectitur tamquam pium et merito retinendum.

Caput VI

DE MINISTRO HUJUS SACRAMENTI ET ABSOLUTIONE

Circa ministrum autem hujus sacramenti declarat sancta synodus, falsas esse et a veritate evangelii penitus alienas doctrinas omnes, quae ad alios quosvis homines praeter episcopos et sacerdotes clavium ministerium perniciose extendunt,[34] putantes verba illa Domini: *Quaecumque alligaveritis super terram, erunt ligata et in coelo, et quaecumque solveritis super terram, erunt soluta et in coelo;*[35] et: *Quorum remiseritis peccata, remittuntur eis, et quorum retinueritis, retenta sunt,*[36] ad omnes Christi fideles indifferenter et promiscue contra institutionem hujus sacramenti ita fuisse dicta, ut quivis potestatem habeat remittendi peccata, publica quidem per correptionem, si correptus acquieverit, secreta vero per spontaneam confessionem cuicumque factam.[37] Docet quoque, etiam sacerdotes, qui peccato mortali tenentur, per virtutem

---

[32] Cf. *infra*, can. 8 et 14 de poenit.
[33] C. 12, X, De poenit., V, 38 (Lat. IV).
[34] Cf. *infra*, can. 10 de poenit.
[35] Matt. 16:19, 18:18.
[36] Joan. 20:23.
[37] Cf. Sess. VII, can. 10 de sacrament. Rouët de Journel, p. 781, n. 545.

Spiritus Sancti in ordinatione collatam tamquam Christi ministros functionem remittendi peccata exercere,[38] eosque prave sentire, qui in malis sacerdotibus hanc potestatem non esse contendunt. Quamvis autem absolutio sacerdotis alieni beneficii sit dispensatio, tamen non est solum nudum ministerium vel annunciandi evangelium, vel declarandi remissa esse peccata; sed ad instar actus judicialis, quo ab ipso velut a judice sententia pronunciatur.[39] Atque ideo non debet poenitens adeo sibi de sua ipsius fide blandiri, ut, etiamsi nulla illi adsit contritio, aut sacerdoti animus serio agendi et vere absolvendi desit, putet tamen se propter suam solam fidem vere et coram Deo esse absolutum. Nec enim fides sine poenitentia remissionem ullam peccatorum praestaret, nec is esset nisi salutis suae negligentissimus, qui sacerdotem joco se absolventem cognosceret, et non alium serio agentem sedulo requireret.

Caput VII

DE CASUUM RESERVATIONE

Quoniam igitur natura et ratio judicii illud exposcit, ut sententia in subditos dumtaxat feratur, persuasum semper in ecclesia Dei fuit, et verissimum esse synodus haec confirmat, nullius momenti absolutionem eam esse debere, quam sacerdos in eum profert, in quem ordinariam aut subdelegatam non habet jurisdictionem.[40] Magnopere vero ad Christiani populi disciplinam pertinere sanctissimis patribus nostris visum est, ut atrociora quaedam et graviora crimina non a quibusvis, sed a summis dumtaxat sacerdotibus absolverentur,[41] unde merito pontifices maximi pro suprema potestate sibi in ecclesia universa tradita causas aliquas criminum graviores suo potuerunt peculiari judicio reservare.[42] Neque dubitandum esset, quando omnia, quae a Deo sunt, ordinata sunt,[43] quin hoc idem episcopis omnibus in sua cuique dioecesi, in aedificationem tamen, non in destructionem liceat pro illis in subditos tradita supra reliquos inferiores sacerdotes auctoritate, praesertim quoad

[38] C.8, D.XIX (Anast. II); c.89, C.I, q.1 (Aug.).
[39] Cf. *infra*, can. 9 de poenit.
[40] C.2, VI°, De poenit., V, 10 (Bonif. VIII).
[41] C.52, C.XVI, q.1 (Greg. I); c.29, C.XVII, q.4 (Lat. II); Cyprian. *epp.* 17, 18 (ed. Hartel).
[42] Cf. c.29, C.XVII, q.4 (Lat. II); cc.1, 3, X, De sent. excomm., V, 39 (Alex. III), cc.19, 22, 24, *ibid.* (Clem. III), c.32, *ibid.* (Innoc. III); c.11 h.t. in VI°, V, 11 (Greg. X), c.18, *ibid.* (Bonif. VIII); c.1 h.t. in Extrav. comm., V, 10 (idem).
[43] Rom. 13:1.

illa, quibus excommunicationis censura annexa est.[44] Hanc autem delictorum reservationem consonum est divinae auctoritati non tantum in externa politia, sed etiam coram Deo vim habere. Verumtamen pie admodum, ne hac ipsa occasione aliquis pereat, in eadem ecclesia Dei custoditum semper fuit, ut nulla sit reservatio in articulo mortis,[45] atque ideo omnes sacerdotes quoslibet poenitentes a quibusvis peccatis et censuris absolvere possunt; extra quem articulum sacerdotes cum nihil possint in casibus reservatis, id unum poenitentibus persuadere nitantur, ut ad superiores et legitimos judices pro beneficio absolutionis accedant.[46]

Caput VIII

DE SATISFACTIONIS NECESSITATE ET FRUCTU

Demum quoad satisfactionem, quae ex omnibus poenitentiae partibus, quemadmodum a patribus nostris Christiano populo fuit perpetuo tempore commendata, ita una maxime nostra aetate summo pietatis praetextu impugnatur ab iis, qui *speciem pietatis habent, virtutem autem ejus abnegarunt*,[47] sancta synodus declarat, falsum omnino esse et a verbo Dei alienum, culpam a Domino nunquam remitti, quin universa etiam poena condonetur.[48] Perspicua enim et illustria in sacris litteris exempla reperiuntur,[49] quibus, praeter divinam traditionem, hic error quam manifestissime revincitur. Sane et divinae justitiae ratio exigere videtur, ut aliter ab eo in gratiam recipiantur qui ante baptismum per ignorantiam deliquerint; aliter vero, qui semel a peccati et daemonis servitute liberati, et accepto Spiritus Sancti dono, scientes templum Dei violare [50] et Spiritum Sanctum contristare non formidaverint.[51] Et divinam clementiam decet, ne ita nobis absque ulla satisfactione peccata dimittantur, ut, occasione accepta, peccata leviora putantes, velut injurii et contumeliosi Spiritui Sancto [52] in graviora labamur, thesauri-

[44] Cf. Sess. XXIV, cap. 6 de ref.

[45] Cf. c.5, VI°, De poenis, V, 9 (Bonif. VIII); c.3 h.t. in Clem., V, 8 (Clem. V); c.3, Extrav. comm., V, 7 (Eugen. IV).

[46] Quos casus reservare possint superiores regularium, cf. decretum Clementis VIII incipiens, *Sanctissimus*, 26 Maii, 1593.

[47] Cf. II Tim. 3:5.

[48] Cf. Sess. VI, cap. 14, can. 30 et *infra*, can. 12 de poenit.

[49] Gen. 3:16 ff.; Num. 12:14 f.; 20:11 f.; II Reg. 12:13 f., etc.

[50] Cf. I Cor. 3:17.

[51] Eph. 4:30.

[52] Heb. 10:29.

zantes nobis iram in die irae.[53] Procul dubio enim magnopere a peccato revocant, et quasi freno quodam coercent hae satisfactoriae poenae, cautioresque et vigilantiores in futurum poenitentes efficiunt; medentur quoque peccatorum reliquiis, et vitiosos habitus male vivendo comparatos contrariis virtutum actionibus tollunt. Neque vero securior ulla via in ecclesia Dei unquam existimata fuit ad amovendam imminentem a Domino poenam, quam ut haec poenitentiae opera homines cum vero animi dolore frequentent.[54] Accedit ad haec, quod, dum satisfaciendo patimur pro peccatis, Christo Jesu, qui pro peccatis nostris satisfecit,[55] ex quo omnis nostra sufficientia est,[56] conformes efficimur, certissimam quoque inde arrham habentes, quod, si compatimur,[57] et conglorificabimur. Neque vero ita nostra est satisfactio haec, quam pro peccatis nostris exsolvimus, ut non sit per Christum Jesum; nam qui ex nobis tamquam ex nobis nihil possumus, eo cooperante, qui nos confortat, omnia possumus.[58] Ita non habet homo unde glorietur; sed omnis gloriatio nostra in Christo est,[59] in quo vivimus,[60] in quo meremur, in quo satisfacimus, facientes fructus dignos poenitentiae,[61] qui ex illo vim habent, ab illo offeruntur Patri, et per illum acceptantur a Patre. Debent ergo sacerdotes Domini, quantum spiritus et prudentia suggesserit, pro qualitate criminum et poenitentium facultate salutares et convenientes satisfactiones injungere, ne, si forte peccatis conniveant et indulgentius cum poenitentibus agant, levissima quaedam opera pro gravissimis delictis injungendo, alienorum peccatorum participes efficiantur. Habeant autem prae oculis, ut satisfactio, quam imponunt, non sit tantum ad novae vitae custodiam et infirmitatis medicamentum, sed etiam ad praeteritorum peccatorum vindictam et castigationem: nam claves sacerdotum non ad solvendum dumtaxat, sed et ad legandum concessas [62] etiam antiqui patres et credunt et docent. Nec praeterea existimarunt, sacramentum poenitentiae esse forum irae vel poenarum, sicut nemo unquam catholicus sensit, ex hujusmodi nostris satisfactionibus vim meriti et satisfactionis Domini nostri Jesu Christi vel obscurari,[63] vel aliqua ex

[53] Rom. 2:5; Jac. 5:3.
[54] Matt. 3:2, 8; 4:17; 11:21, et al.
[55] Rom. 5:10.
[56] Cf. II Cor. 3:5.
[57] Rom. 8:17.
[58] Cf. II Cor. 3:5; Phil. 4:13.
[59] Cf. I Cor. 1:31; II Cor. 10:17; Gal. 6:14.
[60] Act. 17:28.
[61] Matt. 3:8; Luc. 3:8.
[62] Matt. 16:19; Joan. 20:23. Cf. *supra*, cap. 1 et *infra*, can. 3 et 15 de poenit.
[63] Cf. *infra*, can. 14 de poenit.

parte imminui; quod dum novatores intelligere volunt, ita optimam poenitentiam novam vitam esse docent, ut omnem satisfactionis vim et usum tollant.

Caput IX

DE OPERIBUS SATISFACTIONIS

Docet praeterea, tantam esse divinae munificentiae largitatem, ut non solum poenis sponte a nobis pro vindicando peccato susceptis, aut sacerdotis arbitrio pro mensura delicti impositis, sed etiam, quod maximum amoris argumentum est,[64] temporalibus flagellis a Deo inflictis et a nobis patienter toleratis apud Deum Patrem per Christum Jesum satisfacere valeamus.

DOCTRINA DE SACRAMENTO EXTREMAE UNCTIONIS

Visum est autem sanctae synodo, praecedenti doctrinae de poenitentia adjungere ea, quae sequuntur de sacramento extremae unctionis, quod non modo poenitentiae, sed et totius Christianae vitae, quae perpetua poenitentia esse debet, consummativum existimatum est a patribus. Primum itaque circa illius institutionem declarat et docet,[65] quod clementissimus Redemptor noster, qui servis suis quovis tempore voluit de salutaribus remediis adversus omnia omnium hostium tela esse prospectum,[66] quemadmodum auxilia maxima in sacramentis aliis praeparavit, quibus Christiani conservare se integros, dum viverent, ab omni graviori spiritus incommodo possint: ita extremae unctionis sacramento finem vitae tamquam firmissimo quodam praesidio munivit. Nam etsi adversarius noster occasiones per omnem vitam quaerat et captet, ut devorare animas nostras quoquo modo possit: [67] nullum tamen tempus est, quo vehementius ille omnes suae versutiae nervos intendat ad perdendos nos penitus, et a fiducia etiam, si possit, divinae misericordiae deturbandos, quam cum impendere nobis exitum vitae perspicit.

---

[64] C.42, D.III de poenit.
[65] Cf. *infra*, de extr. unct., can. 1.
[66] Eph. 6:10 ff.
[67] Cf. I Pet. 5:8.

CAPUT I

DE INSTITUTIONE SACRAMENTI EXTREMAE UNCTIONIS

Instituta est autem haec sacra unctio infirmorum tamquam vere et proprie sacramentum novi testamenti a Christo Domino nostro, apud Marcum quidem insinuatum,[68] per Jacobum autem Apostolum ac Domini fratrem fidelibus commendatum ac promulgatum. *Infirmatur*, inquit, *quis in vobis? inducat presbyteros ecclesiae, et orent super eum, ungentes eum oleo in nomine Domini; et oratio fidei salvabit infirmum, et alleviabit eum Dominus, et, si in peccatis sit, dimittentur ei.*[69] Quibus verbis, ut ex apostolica traditione per manus accepta ecclesia didicit, docet materiam, formam, proprium ministrum, et effectum hujus salutaris sacramenti. Intellexit enim ecclesia, materiam esse oleum ab episcopo benedictum, nam unctio aptissime Spiritus Sancti gratiam, qua invisibiliter anima aegrotantis inungitur, repraesentat; formam deinde esse illa verba: *Per istam unctionem* etc.

CAPUT II

DE EFFECTU HUJUS SACRAMENTI

Res porro et effectus hujus sacramenti illis verbis explicatur: *Et oratio fidei salvabit infirmum, et alleviabit eum Dominus; et, si in peccatis sit, dimittentur ei.*[70] Res etenim haec gratia est Spiritus Sancti,[71] cujus unctio delicta, si quae sint adhuc expianda, ac peccati reliquias abstergit, et aegroti animam alleviat et confirmat, magnam in eo divinae misericordiae fiduciam excitando, qua infirmus sublevatus et morbi incommoda ac labores levius fert, et tentationibus daemonis calcaneo insidiantis [72] facilius resistit, et sanitatem corporis interdum, ubi saluti animae expedierit, consequitur.

---

[68] Marc. 6:13. Rouët de Journel, p. 782, n.552; Denzinger, XII m, p. [48].
[69] Jac. 5:14 f.
[70] *Ibid.*, 5:15.
[71] Cf. *infra*, de extr. unct., can. 2.
[72] Gen. 3:15.

CAPUT III

DE MINISTRO HUJUS SACRAMENTI, ET TEMPORE, QUO DARI DEBEAT

Jam vero, quod attinet ad praescriptionem eorum, qui et suscipere et ministrare hoc sacramentum debent, haud obscure fuit illud etiam in verbis praedictis traditum. Nam et ostenditur illic, proprios hujus sacramenti ministros esse ecclesiae presbyteros, quo nomine eo loco non aetate seniores aut primores in populo intelligendi veniunt, sed aut episcopi, aut sacerdotes ab ipsis rite ordinati[73] *per impositionem manuum presbyteri.*[74] Declaratur etiam, esse hanc unctionem infirmis adhibendam, illis vero praesertim, qui tam periculose decumbunt, ut in exitu vitae constituti videantur, unde et sacramentum exeuntium nuncupatur. Quod si infirmi post susceptam hanc unctionem convaluerint, iterum hujus sacramenti subsidio juvari poterunt, cum in aliud simile vitae discrimen inciderint. Quare nulla ratione audiendi sunt qui contra tam apertam et dilucidam Apostoli Jacobi sententiam docent,[75] hanc unctionem vel figmentum esse humanum, vel ritum a patribus acceptum, nec mandatum Dei, nec promissionem gratiae habentem; et qui illam jam cessasse asserunt, quasi ad gratiam curationum dumtaxat in primitiva ecclesia referenda esset; et qui dicunt, ritum et usum, quem sancta Romana ecclesia in hujus sacramenti administratione observat, Jacobi Apostoli sententiae repugnare,[76] atque ideo in alium commutandum esse; et denique, qui hanc extremam unctionem a fidelibus sine peccato contemni posse affirmant. Haec enim omnia manifestissime pugnant cum perspicuis tanti Apostoli verbis. Nec profecto ecclesia Romana, aliarum omnium mater et magistra, aliud in hac administranda unctione, quantum ad ea, quae hujus sacramenti substantiam perficiunt, observat, quam quod beatus Jacobus praescripsit. Neque vero tanti sacramenti contemptus absque ingenti scelere et ipsius Spiritus Sancti injuria esse posset.

Haec sunt, quae de poenitentiae et extremae unctionis sacramentis sancta haec oecumenica synodus profitetur et docet, atque omnibus Christi fidelibus credenda et tenenda proponit. Sequentes autem canones inviolabiliter servandos esse tradit, et asserentes contrarium perpetuo damnat et anathematizat.

---

[73] C.3, D.XCV (Innoc. I) et *infra*, can. ult.
[74] Cf. I Tim. 4:14; c.6 (§ 5), D.XCV.
[75] Jac. 5:14 f.
[76] Cf. *infra*, de extr. unct., can. 3.

CANONES DE SANCTISSIMO POENITENTIAE SACRAMENTO

1. Si quis dixerit, in catholica ecclesia poenitentiam non esse vere et proprie sacramentum pro fidelibus, quoties post baptismum in peccata labuntur, ipsi Deo reconciliandis a Christo Domino nostro institutum: [77] anathema sit.

2. Si quis sacramenta confundens,[78] ipsum baptismum poenitentiae sacramentum esse dixerit, quasi haec duo sacramenta distincta non sint, atque ideo poenitentiam non recte secundam post naufragium tabulam appellari: [79] anathema sit.

3. Si quis dixerit, verba illa Domini Salvatoris: *Accipite Spiritum Sanctum; quorum remiseritis peccata, remittuntur eis, et quorum retinueritis, retenta sunt*,[80] non esse intelligenda de potestate remittendi et retinendi peccata in sacramento poenitentiae, sicut ecclesia catholica ab initio semper intellexit; detorserit autem contra institutionem hujus sacramenti ad auctoritatem praedicandi evangelium: anathema sit.

4. Si quis negaverit, ad integram et perfectam peccatorum remissionem requiri tres actus in poenitente,[81] quasi materiam sacramenti poenitentiae, videlicet contritionem, confessionem et satisfactionem, quae tres poenitentiae partes dicuntur; aut dixerit, duas tantum esse poenitentiae partes, terrores scilicet incussos conscientiae agnito peccato, et fidem conceptam ex evangelio vel absolutione, qua credit quis sibi per Christum remissa peccata: anathema sit.

5. Si quis dixerit, eam contritionem,[82] quae paratur per discussionem, collectionem et detestationem peccatorum, qua quis recogitat annos suos in amaritudine animae suae,[83] ponderando peccatorum suorum gravitatem, multitudinem, foeditatem, amissionem aeternae beatitudinis et aeternae damnationis incursum, cum proposito melioris vitae non esse verum et utilem dolorem, nec praeparare ad gratiam, sed facere hominem hypocritam et magis peccatorem; demum illam esse dolorem coactum, et non liberum ac voluntarium: anathema sit.

6. Si quis negaverit, confessionem sacramentalem vel institutam, vel ad salutem necessariam esse jure divino; [84] aut dixerit, modum secrete

---

[77] Cf. *supra*, cap. 1 de poenit.
[78] *Supra*, cap. cit.
[79] Cf. c.72, D.I de poenit. (Hieron.).
[80] Matt. 16:19; Joan. 20:23 f.; cf. Sess. VI, cap. 14 et *supra*, cap. 1 de poenit.
[81] Cf. *supra*, cap. 3 de poenit.
[82] *Ibid.*, cap. 4.
[83] Is. 38:15.
[84] *Supra*, cap. 5 de poenit.

confitendi soli sacerdoti, quem ecclesia catholica ab initio semper observavit et observat, alienum esse ab institutione et mandato Christi, et inventum esse humanum: anathema sit.

7. Si quis dixerit, in sacramento poenitentiae ad remissionem peccatorum necessarium non esse jure divino confiteri omnia et singula peccata mortalia, quorum memoria cum debita et diligenti praemeditatione habeatur, etiam occulta, et quae sunt contra duo ultima decalogi praecepta,[85] et circumstantias, quae peccati speciem mutant; sed eam confessionem tantum esse utilem ad erudiendum et consolandum poenitentem, et olim observatam fuisse tantum ad satisfactionem canonicam imponendam; aut dixerit, eos, qui omnia peccata confiteri student, nihil relinquere velle divinae misericordiae ignoscendum; aut demum, non licere confiteri peccata venialia; anathema sit.

8. Si quis dixerit, confessionem omnium peccatorum, qualem ecclesia servat, esse impossibilem, et traditionem humanam a piis abolendam; [86] aut ad eam non teneri omnes et singulos utriusque sexus Christi fideles juxta magni concilii Lateranensis constitutionem semel in anno,[87] et ob id suadendum esse Christi fidelibus, ut non confiteantur tempore Quadragesimae: anathema sit.

9. Si quis dixerit, absolutionem sacramentalem sacerdotis non esse actum judicialem, sed nudum ministerium pronunciandi et declarandi remissa esse peccata confitenti, modo tantum credat se esse absolutum, aut sacerdos non serio, sed joco absolvat; [88] aut dixerit non requiri confessionem poenitentis, ut sacerdos ipsum absolvere possit: anathema sit.

10. Si quis dixerit, sacerdotes, qui in peccato mortali sunt, potestatem ligandi et solvendi non habere; aut non solos sacerdotes esse ministros absolutionis, sed omnibus et singulos Christi fidelibus esse dictum: *Quaecumque ligaveritis super terram, erunt ligata et in coelo, et quaecumque solveritis super terram, erunt soluta et in coelo;* [89] et: *Quorum remiseritis peccata, remittuntur eis, et quorum retinueritis, retenta sunt,*[90] quorum verborum virtute quilibet absolvere possit peccata, publica quidem per correptionem dumtaxat, si correptus acquieverit, secreta vero per spontaneam confessionem: [91] anathema sit.

---

[85] Cf. *supra,* cap. 5 et Deut. 5:21.
[86] Cf. cap. cit.
[87] C. 12, X, De poenit., V, 38 (Lat. IV); *infra,* p. 564, lit. N.
[88] *Supra,* cap. 6 de poenit.
[89] Matt. 16:19; 18:18.
[90] Joan. 20:23.
[91] Cf. *supra,* capp. 5 et 6 de poenit.

11. Si quis dixerit, episcopos non habere jus reservandi sibi casus, nisi quoad externam politiam, atque ideo casuum reservationem non prohibere, quominus sacerdos a reservatis vere absolvat: [92] anathema sit.

12. Si quis dixerit, totam poenam simul cum culpa remitti semper a Deo, satisfactionemque poenitentium non esse aliam quam fidem, qua apprehendunt Christum pro eis satisfecisse: [93] anathema sit.

13. Si quis dixerit, pro peccatis, quoad poenam temporalem, minime Deo per Christi merita satisfieri poenis ab eo inflictis, et patienter toleratis vel a sacerdote injunctis, sed neque sponte susceptis, ut jejuniis, orationibus, eleemosynis, vel aliis etiam pietatis operibus, atque ideo optimam poenitentiam esse tantum novam vitam: [94] anathema sit.

14. Si quis dixerit, satisfactiones, quibus poenitentes per Christum Jesum peccata redimunt, non esse cultus Dei, sed traditiones hominum, doctrinam de gratia, et verum Dei cultum atque ipsum beneficium mortis Christi obscurantes: [95] anathema sit.

15. Si quis dixerit, claves ecclesiae esse datas tantum ad solvendum, non etiam ad ligandum, et propterea sacerdotes, dum imponunt poenas confitentibus, agere contra finem clavium et contra institutionem Christi; et fictionem esse, quod, virtute clavium sublata poena aeterna, poena temporalis plerumque exsolvenda remaneat: [96] anathema sit.

CANONES DE SACRAMENTO EXTREMAE UNCTIONIS

1. Si quis dixerit, extremam unctionem non esse vere et proprie sacramentum a Christo Domino nostro institutum [97] et a beato Jacobo Apostolo promulgatum,[98] sed ritum tantum acceptum a patribus, aut figmentum humanum: anathema sit.

2. Si quis dixerit, sacram infirmorum unctionem non conferre gratiam, nec remittere peccata, nec alleviare infirmos, sed jam cessasse, quasi olim tantum fuerit gratia curationum: [99] anathema sit.

3. Si quis dixerit, extremae unctionis ritum et usum,[100] quem observat

---

[92] *Ibid.*, cap. 7.
[93] *Ibid.*, cap. 8.
[94] *Ibid.*, capp. 8 et 9.
[95] *Ibid.*, cap. 8.
[96] *Ibid.*, capp. 1 et 8 sub fin.
[97] Cf. *supra*, de extr. unct. in princ. et cap. 1.
[98] Jac. 5:14 f.
[99] *Supra*, de extr. unct., cap. 2.
[100] *Ibid.*, cap. 3.

sancta Romana ecclesia, repugnare sententiae beati Jacobi Apostoli,[101] ideoque eum mutandum, posseque a Christianis absque peccato contemni: anathema sit.

4. Si quis dixerit, presbyteros ecclesiae, quos beatus Jacobus adducendos esse ad infirmum inungendum hortatur,[102] non esse sacerdotes ab episcopo ordinatos, sed aetate seniores in quavis communitate, ob idque proprium extremae unctionis ministrum non esse solum sacerdotem: [103] anathema sit.

DECRETUM DE REFORMATIONE

PROOEMIUM

EPISCOPORUM MUNUS EST, SUBDITOS, PRAESERTIM AD ANIMARUM CURAM CONSTITUTOS, ADMONERE OFFICII SUI

Cum proprie episcoporum munus sit, subditorum omnium vitia redarguere,[104] hoc illis praecipue cavendum erit, ne clerici, praesertim ad animarum curam constituti, criminosi sint, neve inhonestam vitam ipsis conniventibus ducant. Nam si eos pravis et corruptis moribus esse permittant, quo pacto laicos de ipsorum vitiis redarguent,[105] qui uno ab eis sermone convinci possent, quod clericos ipsis patiantur esse deteriores? Qua etiam libertate laicos corripere poterunt sacerdotes, cum tacite sibi ipsi respondeant, eadem se admisisse, quae corripiunt? [106] Monebunt propterea episcopi suos clericos, in quocumque ordine fuerint,[107] ut conversatione, sermone et scientia commisso sibi Dei populo praeeant, memores ejus, quod scriptum est: *Sancti estote, quia et ego sanctus sum.*[108] Et juxta Apostoli vocem nemini dent ullam offensionem, ut non vituperetur ministerium eorum; sed in omnibus exhibeant se sicut ministros Dei,[109] ne illud Prophetae dictum impleatur in eis: *Sacerdotes Dei contaminant sancta, et reprobant legem.*[110] Ut

---

[101] Jac. 5:14 f.
[102] *Ibid.*
[103] *Supra*, de extr. unct., cap. 3.
[104] Cf. c.13, X, De off. jud. ord., I, 31 (Lat. IV); Sess. VI, cap. 3 de ref.
[105] Cf. I Cor. 9:27.
[106] Sunt verba Hieronymi in c.6, D.XXV relata; c.2, D.LXI (Hormisd.); c.2, D.LXXXII (Innoc. I).
[107] Cf. Sess. XXII, cap. 1 de ref.
[108] Lev. 11:44; 19:2; 20:7; I Pet. 1:16.
[109] Cf. II Cor. 6:3 f.
[110] Ezech. 22:26; Soph. 3:4.

autem ipsi episcopi id liberius exsequi, ac quoquam praetextu desuper impediri nequeant, eadem sacrosancta oecumenica et generalis Tridentina synodus, praesidentibus in ea eisdem Apostolicae Sedis legato et nunciis, hos, qui sequuntur, canones statuendos et decernendos duxit.

Caput I

SI PROHIBITI ASCENDERE AD ORDINES ASCENDANT, SI INTERDICTI, SI SUSPENSI, PUNIANTUR

Cum honestius ac tutius sit subjecto, debitam praepositis obedientiam impendendo in inferiori ministerio deservire, quam cum praepositorum scandalo graduum altiorum appetere dignitatem, ei, cui ascensus ad sacros ordines a suo praelato ex quacumque causa, etiam ob occultum crimen, quomodolibet, etiam extrajudicialiter, fuerit interdictus, aut qui a suis ordinibus seu gradibus, vel dignitatibus ecclesiasticis fuerit suspensus, nulla contra ipsius praelati voluntatem concessa licentia de se promoveri faciendo, aut ad priores ordines, gradus, dignitates sive honores restitutio suffragetur.

Caput II

SI EPISCOPUS QUOSCUMQUE ORDINES CONTULERIT SIBI NON SUBDITO, ETIAM FAMILIARI, SINE EXPRESSO PROPRII PRAELATI CONSENSU, UTERQUE DECRETAE POENAE SUBJACEAT

Et quoniam nonnulli episcopi ecclesiarum, quae in partibus infidelium consistunt, clero carentes et populo Christiano, cum fere vagabundi sint et permanentem sedem non habeant, non quae Jesu Christi, sed alienas oves inscio proprio pastore quaerentes,[111] dum per hanc sanctam synodum se pontificalia officia in alterius dioecesi, nisi de loci ordinarii expressa licentia, et in personas eidem ordinario subjectas tantum exercere prohibitos vident, in legis fraudem et contemptum quasi episcopalem cathedram in loco nullius dioecesis sua temeritate eligunt, et quoscumque ad se venientes, etiamsi suorum episcoporum seu praelatorum litteras commendatitias non habeant, clericali cha-

[111] Cf. *infra*, cap. 8 et Sess. VI, cap. 5 de ref.

ractere insignire, et ad sacros etiam presbyteratus ordines promovere praesumunt, quo plerumque fit, ut minus idonei, et rudes ac ignari, et qui a suo episcopo tamquam inhabiles et indigni rejecti fuerint, ordinati nec divina officia peragere, nec ecclesiastica sacramenta recte valeant ministrare: nemo episcoporum, qui titulares vocantur, etiamsi in loco nullius dioecesis, etiam exempto, aut aliquo monasterio cujusvis ordinis resederint aut moram traxerint, vigore cujusvis privilegii sibi de promovendo quoscumque ad se venientes pro tempore concessi, alterius subditum, etiam praetextu familiaritatis continuae commensalitatis suae, absque sui proprii praelati expresso consensu aut litteris dimissoriis [112] ad aliquos sacros aut minores ordines vel primam tonsuram promovere seu ordinare valeat. Contra faciens ab exercitio pontificalium per annum, taliter vero promotus ab executione ordinum sic susceptorum, donec suo praelato visum fuerit, ipso jure sint suspensi.

Caput III

EPISCOPUS SUOS CLERICOS AB ALIO MALE PROMOTOS SUSPENDERE POTEST, SI MINUS IDONEOS REPERERIT

Episcopus quoscumque suos clericos, praesertim in sacris constitutos, absque suo praecedenti examine et commendatitiis litteris quacumque auctoritate promotos, licet tamquam habiles ab eo, a quo ordinati sunt, probatos, quos tamen ad divina officia celebranda seu ecclesiastica sacramenta ministranda minus idoneos et capaces repererit, a susceptorum ordinum exercitio ad tempus, de quo ei videbitur, suspendere, et illis, ne in altari aut aliquo ordine ministrent, interdicere possit.[113]

Caput IV

NULLUS CLERICUS EXIMATUR A CORRECTIONE EPISCOPI, ETIAM EXTRA VISITATIONEM

Omnes ecclesiarum praelati, qui ad corrigendos subditorum excessus diligenter intendere debent,[114] et a quibus nullus clericus per

---

[112] Cf. Sess. VI, cap. 5 et Sess. XXIII, capp. 3, 8, 10 de ref.; conc. Aurelianen. III (a.538), c.15; Moguntien. (a.888), c.14; cf. etiam tot. tit. de temp. ord. in VI°.

[113] Cf. cap. prox. antec. et Sess. XXIII, cap. 8 de ref.

[114] Cf. *supra*, de ref. in princ. et Sess. VI, cap. 3 de ref.; c.13, X, De off. jud. ord., I, 31 (Lat. IV).

hujus sanctae synodi statuta cujusvis privilegii praetextu tutus censetur, quominus juxta canonicas sanctiones visitari, puniri et corrigi possit, si in ecclesiis suis resederint, quoscumque saeculares clericos, qualitercumque exemptos, qui alias suae jurisdictioni subessent, de eorum excessibus, criminibus et delictis, quoties et quando opus fuerit, etiam extra visitationem, tamquam ad hoc Apostolicae Sedis delegati, corrigendi et castigandi facultatem habeant: [115] quibuscumque exemptionibus, declarationibus, consuetudinibus, sententiis, juramentis, concordiis, quae suos tantum obligent auctores, ipsis clericis, ac eorum consanguineis, capellanis, familiaribus, procuratoribus, et aliis quibuslibet, ipsorum exemptorum contemplatione et intuitu minime suffragantibus.

Caput V

CONSERVATORUM JURISDICTIO CERTIS FINIBUS CONCLUDITUR

Insuper, cum nonnulli, qui sub praetextu, quod super bonis et rebus ac juribus suis diversae eis injuriae ac molestiae inferantur, certos judices per litteras conservatorias deputari obtinent, qui illos a molestiis et injuriis hujusmodi tueantur ac defendant, et in possessione seu quasi bonorum, rerum ac jurium suorum manu teneant et conservent, neque super illis eos molestari permittant, ejusmodi litteras in plerisque contra concedentis mentem in reprobum sensum detorqueant: idcirco nemini omnino, cujuscumque dignitatis et conditionis sit, etiamsi capitulum fuerit, conservatoriae litterae, cum quibuscumque clausulis aut decretis, et quorumcumque judicum deputatione, quocumque etiam alio praetextu aut colore concessae, suffragentur ad hoc, ut coram suo episcopo sive alio superiore ordinario in criminalibus et mixtis causis accusari et conveniri, ac contra eum inquiri et procedi non possit, aut quominus, si qua jura ei ex concessione competierint, super illis libere valeat apud judicem ordinarium conveniri. In civilibus etiam causis, si ipse actor exstiterit, aliquem ei apud suos conservatores judices in judicium trahere minime liceat. Quod si in iis causis, in quibus ipse reus fuerit, contigerit, ut electus ab eo conservator ab actore suspectus esse dicatur, aut si qua inter ipsos judices, conservatorem et ordinarium, controversia super competentia jurisdictionis orta fuerit, nequaquam in causa procedatur, donec per

---

[115] Cf. Sess. VI, cap. 4 de ref. et Sess. XXIV, cap. 5 de ref.

arbitros in forma juris electos super suspicione aut jurisdictionis competentia fuerit judicatum. Familiaribus vero ejus, qui hujusmodi litteris conservatoriis tueri se solent, nihil illae prosint, praeterquam duobus dumtaxat, si tamen illi propriis ejus sumptibus vixerint. Nemo etiam similium litterarum beneficio ultra quinquennium gaudere possit. Non liceat quoque conservatoribus judicibus ullum habere tribunal erectum. In causis vero mercedum aut miserabilium personarum hujus sanctae synodi super hoc decretum [116] in suo robore permaneat. Universitates autem generales, ac collegia doctorum seu scholarium, et regularia loca, necnon hospitalia actu hospitalitatem servantia, ac universitatum, collegiorum, locorum et hospitalium hujusmodi personae in praesenti canone minime comprehensae, sed exemptae omnino sint et esse intelligantur.

Caput VI

POENA DECERNITUR IN CLERICOS, QUI IN SACRIS CONSTITUTI AUT BENEFICIA POSSIDENTES, ORDINI SUO CONGRUENTE VESTE NON UTUNTUR

Quia vero, etsi habitus non facit monachum,[117] oportet tamen clericos vestes proprio congruentes ordini semper deferre,[118] ut per decentiam habitus extrinseci morum honestatem intrinsecam ostendant, tanta autem hodie aliquorum inolevit temeritas religionisque contemptus, ut propriam dignitatem et honorem clericalem parvi pendentes vestes etiam publice deferant laicales, pedes in diversis ponentes, unum in divinis, alterum in carnalibus: propterea omnes ecclesiasticae personae quantumcumque exemptae, quae aut in sacris fuerint, aut dignitates, personatus, officia aut beneficia qualiacumque ecclesiastica obtinuerint, si postea, quam ab episcopo suo etiam per edictum publicum moniti fuerint, honestum habitum clericalem, illorum ordini ac dignitati congruentem, et juxta ipsius episcopi ordinationem et mandatum non detulerint, per suspensionem ab ordinibus ac officio, et beneficio ac fructibus, reditibus et proventibus ipsorum beneficiorum, necnon, si semel correpti denuo in hoc deliquerint,

---

[116] Cf. Sess. VII, cap. 14 de ref.

[117] Sunt verba Innocentii III in c. 13, X, De regular., III, 31 relata.

[118] Cf. c. ult., D. XLI; conc. Matisconen. (a. 581), c. 5; Nicaen. II (a. 787), c. 16; Lateranen. IV (a. 1215), c. 16. Cf. etiam const. Sixti V, *Cum sacrosanctam*, 9 Jan., 1589.

etiam per privationem officiorum et beneficiorum hujusmodi coerceri possint et debeant, constitutionem Clementis V in concilio Viennensi editam, quae incipit: *Quoniam,*[119] innovando et ampliando.

Caput VII

VOLUNTARII HOMICIDAE NUNQUAM, CASUALES QUOMODO ORDINANDI

Cum etiam qui per industriam occiderit proximum suum et per insidias, ab altari avelli debeat,[120] qui sua voluntate homicidium perpetraverit,[121] etiamsi crimen id nec ordine judiciario probatum, nec alia ratione publicum, sed occultum fuerit, nullo tempore ad sacros ordines promoveri possit, nec illi aliqua ecclesiastica beneficia, etiamsi curam non habeant animarum, conferri liceat, sed omni ordine, ac beneficio et officio ecclesiastico perpetuo careat. Si vero homicidium non ex proposito, sed casu, vel vim vi repellendo, ut quis se a morte defenderet, fuisse commissum narretur, quam ob causam etiam ad sacrorum ordinum et altaris ministerium, et beneficia quaecumque ac dignitates jure quodammodo dispensatio debeatur, committatur loci ordinario, aut ex causa metropolitano seu viciniori episcopo, qui non nisi causa cognita et probatis precibus ac narratis, nec aliter, dispensare possit.

Caput VIII

NULLI ALIENOS CLERICOS EX PRIVILEGIO PUNIRE LICEAT

Praeterea, quia nonnulli, quorum etiam aliqui veri sunt pastores ac proprias oves habent, alienis etiam ovibus praeesse quaerunt, et ita alienis subditis quandoque intendunt, ut suorum curam negligant;[122] quicumque, etiam episcopali praeditus dignitate, qui alienos subditos puniendi privilegium habuerit, contra clericos sibi non subjectos,

---

[119] C.2, De vit. et hon. cler., in Clem., III, 1; *infra,* p. 565, lit. O.
[120] Ex. 21:14 in c.1, X, De homicid., V, 12 citatus.
[121] Extendit illud ad abortum procurantes const. Sixti V *Effraenatam,* 29 Oct., 1588, quam Gregorius XIV per const. *Sedes Apostolica,* 31 Maii, 1591, ad foetum animatum restrinxit. Tempore antiquo damnatum fuit hoc crimen in conc. Ancyr. (a.314), c.21; in *epist.* 188, quae est canonica prima, Basilii Magni, can. 2; conc. Ilerden. (a.524 vel 546), c.2; Quinisext. (a.692), c.91. Cf. etiam conc. Eliberitan. (*ca.* a.305), c.63.
[122] *Supra,* cap. 2 de ref. et Sess. VI, cap. 5 de ref.

praesertim in sacris constitutos, quorumcumque etiam atrocium criminum reos, nisi cum proprii ipsorum clericorum episcopi, si apud ecclesiam suam resederit, aut personae ab ipso episcopo deputandae interventu nequaquam procedere debeat; alias processus et inde secuta quaecumque viribus omnino careant.

Caput IX

BENEFICIA UNIUS DIOECESIS NULLA DE CAUSA UNIANTUR BENEFICIIS ALTERIUS

Et quia jure optimo distinctae fuerunt dioeceses et parochiae,[123] ac unicuique gregi proprii attributi pastores et inferiorum ecclesiarum rectores, qui suarum quisque ovium curam habeant, ut ordo ecclesiasticus non confundatur, aut una et eadem ecclesia duarum quodammodo dioecesum fiat non sine gravi eorum incommodo, qui illi subditi fuerint: beneficia unius dioecesis, etiamsi parochiales ecclesiae, vicariae perpetuae, aut simplicia beneficia, seu praestimonia aut praestimoniales portiones fuerint, etiam ratione augendi cultum divinum aut numerum beneficiatorum aut alia quacumque de causa, alterius dioecesis beneficio, aut monasterio, seu collegio vel loco etiam pio perpetuo non uniantur; decretum hujus sanctae synodi super hujusmodi unionibus in hoc declarando.[124]

Caput X

REGULARIA BENEFICIA REGULARIBUS CONFERANTUR

Regularia beneficia, in titulum regularibus professis provideri consueta, cum per obitum, aut resignationem vel alias illa in titulum obtinentis vacare contigerit, religiosis tantum illius ordinis,[125] vel iis, qui habitum omnino suscipere et professionem emittere teneantur, et non aliis, ne vestem lino lanaque contextam induant, [126] conferantur.

---

[123] Cf. c.9, X, De his, quae fiunt a prael., III, 10 (Innoc. III); Sess. XXIV, cap. 13 de ref. sub fin.

[124] Cf. Sess. VII, capp. 6 et 7 de ref. et Sess. XXIV, capp. 13 et 15 de ref.

[125] Cf. Sess. XXV, cap. 21 de ref.; c.27, X, De elect., I, 6 (Innoc. III); c.5, VI°, De praeb., III, 4 (Bonif. VIII).

[126] Deut. 22:11.

Caput XI

TRANSLATI AD ALIUM ORDINEM IN CLAUSTRO SUB OBEDIENTIA MANEANT, ET BENEFICIORUM SAECULARIUM INCAPACES EXSISTANT

Quia vero regulares, de uno ad alium ordinem translati, facile a suo superiore licentiam standi extra monasterium obtinere solent, ex quo vagandi et apostatandi occasio tribuitur; nemo cujuscumque ordinis praelatus vel superior vigore cujusvis facultatis aliquem ad habitum et professionem admittere possit, nisi ut in ordine ipso, ad quem transfertur, sub sui superioris obedientia in claustro perpetuo maneat,[127] ac taliter translatus, etiamsi canonicorum regularium fuerit, ad beneficia saecularia, etiam curata, omnino incapax exsistat.

Caput XII

NEMO NISI EX FUNDATIONE VEL DOTATIONE JUS PATRONATUS OBTINEAT

Nemo etiam cujusvis dignitatis ecclesiasticae vel saecularis, quacumque ratione, nisi ecclesiam, beneficium aut capellam de novo fundaverit et construxerit, seu jam erectam, quae tamen sine sufficienti dote fuerit, de suis propriis et patrimonialibus bonis competenter dotaverit; jus patronatus impetrare aut obtinere possit aut debeat.[128] In casu autem fundationis aut dotationis hujusmodi institutio episcopo, et non alteri inferiori reservetur.

Caput XIII

PRAESENTATIO FIAT ORDINARIO; ALIAS PRAESENTATIO ET INSTITUTIO SIT NULLA

Non licet praeterea patrono cujusvis privilegii praetextu aliquem ad beneficia sui juris patronatus, nisi episcopo loci ordinario, ad quem provisio seu institutio ipsius beneficii, cessante privilegio, jure pertine-

---

[127] Cf. Sess. XXV, cap. 4 de regular.
[128] Cf. *ibid.*, cap. 9 de ref.

ret, quoquo modo praesentare; [129] alias praesentatio ac institutio forsan secutae nullae sint et esse intelligantur.

Caput XIV

Declarat praeterea sancta synodus, in futura sessione, quam ad XXV diem Jan. subsequentis anni MDLII habendam esse jam decrevit, una cum sacrificio missae agendum et tractandum etiam esse de sacramento ordinis, et prosequendam esse materiam reformationis.

---

[129] Cf. Sess. XXV, cap. 9 et cc. 8, 21, X, De jur. patr., III, 38 (Alex. III).

SESSIO DECIMA QUINTA

QUAE EST QUINTA

SUB JULIO III PONT. MAX.

celebrata

die XXV Januarii, MDLII

DECRETUM PROROGATIONIS SESSIONIS

Cum ex eo, quod proximis sessionibus decretum fuit, sancta haec et universalis synodus per hos dies accuratissime diligentissimeque tractaverit ea, quae ad sanctissimum missae sacrificium et ad sacramentum ordinis spectant, ut hodierna sessione, quemadmodum Spiritus Sanctus suggessisset, decreta de his rebus et quatuor praeterea articulos ad sanctissimum Eucharistiae sacramentum pertinentes in hanc tandem sessionem dilatos publicaret; atque interim adfuturos esse putaverit ad hoc sacrosanctum concilium eos, qui se protestantes vocant, quorum causa eorum publicationem articulorum distulerat, et ut libere ac sine cunctatione ulla huc venirent, fidem eis publicam sive salvum conductum concesserat: [1] tamen, cum illi nondum venerint, et eorum nomine supplicatum huic sanctae synodo fuerit, ut publicatio, quae hodierno die facienda fuerat, in sequentem sessionem differatur, certa spe allata adfuturos eos esse omnino multo ante illam sessionem, salvo conductu amplioris formae interim accepto, eadem sancta synodus in Spiritu Sancto legitime congregata, iisdem legato et nunciis praesidentibus, nihil magis optans, quam ex praestantissima natione Germanica omnes de religione dissensiones et schismata tollere, ac ejus quieti, paci otioque consulere, parata ipsos, si venerint, et humaniter excipere et benigne audire, confidensque, eos non fidei catholicae pertinaciter oppugnandae, sed veritatis cognoscendae studio esse venturos, et, ut evangelicae veritatis studiosos decet, sanctae matris ecclesiae decretis ac disciplinae ad extremum esse acquieturos, sequentem sessionem ad edenda et publicanda ea, quae supra commemorata sunt, in diem festum sancti Josephi, qui erit die XIX, mensis Martii,

---

[1] *Supra*, Sess. XIII sub fin.

distulit, ut illi satis temporis et spatii habeant non solum ad veniendum, verum etiam ad ea, quae voluerint, antequam is dies veniat, proponenda. Quibus ut omnem diutius cunctandi causam adimat, fidem publicam sive salvum conductum ejus, qui recitabitur, tenoris et sententiae libenter dat et concedit. Interea vero de matrimonii sacramento agendum, et de eo, praeter superiorum decretorum publicationem, definiendum esse, eadem sessione statuit et decernit, et prosequendam esse materiam reformationis.

SALVUS CONDUCTUS
datus
PROTESTANTIBUS

Sacrosancta oecumenica et generalis Tridentina synodus in Spiritu Sancto legitime congregata, praesidentibus in ea eisdem sanctae Sedis Apostolicae legato et nunciis, inhaerendo salvo conductui in penultima sessione dato, et illum juxta tenorem infrascriptum ampliando, universis fidem facit, quod omnibus et singulis sacerdotibus, electoribus, principibus, ducibus, marchionibus, comitibus, baronibus, nobilibus, militaribus, popularibus, et aliis quibuscumque viris, cujuscumque status et conditionis aut qualitatis exsistant, Germanicae provinciae et nationis civitatibus, et aliis locis ejusdem, et omnibus aliis ecclesiasticis et saecularibus, praesertim Augustanae confessionis, personis, qui aut quae una cum ipsis ad hoc generale Tridentinum concilium venient aut mittentur, ac profecturi sunt, aut hucusque venerunt, quocumque nomine censeantur aut valeant nuncupari, tenore praesentium publicam fidem et plenissimam verissimamque securitatem, quam salvum conductum appellant, libere ad hanc civitatem Tridentinam veniendi, ibidemque manendi, standi, morandi, proponendi, loquendi, una cum ipsa synodo de quibuscumque negotiis tractandi, examinandi, discutiendi, et omnia, quaecumque ipsis libuerit, ac articulos quoslibet tam scripto quam verbo libere offerendi, propalandi, eosque scripturis sacris, et beatorum patrum verbis, sententiis et rationibus declarandi, adstruendi et persuadendi, et, si opus fuerit, etiam ad objecta concilii generalis respondendi, et cum iis, qui a concilio delecti fuerint, disputandi christiane aut caritative absque omni impedimento conferendi, opprobriis, conviciis ac contumeliis penitus semotis; et signanter, quod causae controversae secundum sacram scripturam et apostolorum traditiones, probata concilia et catholicae ecclesiae consensum et sanctorum patrum auctoritates in praedicto concilio Tridentino tractentur; illo etiam addito, ut religionis praetextu aut delictorum circa eam commissorum aut committendorum minime puniantur, impartitur ac omnino concedit, sic etiam, ut propter illorum praesentiam neque in itinere aut quocumque locorum eundo, manendo aut redeundo, nec in ipsa civitate Tridentina a divinis officiis quovis modo cessetur; et ut his peractis vel non peractis, quandocumque ipsis libuerit, aut majorum suorum mandato et assensu ad propria reverti optabunt, aut aliquis eorum optabit, mox absque ulla renitentia et occasione aut mora, salvis rebus eorum et suorum pariter honore et personis vice versa possint juxta beneplacitum libere et secure redire, de scientia tamen ab eadem synodo deputandorum, ut tunc opportune eorum securitati absque dolo et fraude provideatur. Vult etiam sancta synodus in hac publica fide salvoque conductu omnes quascumque clausulas includi ac contineri ac pro inclusis haberi, quae pro plena, efficaci et sufficienti securitate in eundo, stando et redeundo necessariae et opportunae fuerint. Illud etiam ad majorem securitatem et pacis et conciliationis bonum exprimens, quod, si quispiam aut illorum aliqui sive in itinere Tridentum veniendo sive ibidem morando aut redeundo aliquod enorme, quod absit, egerint aut commiserint, quo posset hujus fidei publicae et assecurationis beneficium eis concessum annullari aut cassari, vult et concedit, ut in hujusmodi facinore deprehensi ab ipsis dumtaxat, et non ab aliis, condigna animadversione cum emenda sufficienti per partem ipsius synodi merito approbanda et laudanda mox puniantur; illorum assecurationis forma, conditionibus et modis omnino manentibus illibatis. Pariformiter etiam vult, ut, si quisquam vel aliqui ex ipsa synodo sive in itinere aut manendo aut redeundo aliquod enorme, quod absit, egerint aut commiserint, quo posset hujus fidei publicae et assecurationis beneficium violari aut quoquo modo tolli, in hujusmodi facinore deprehensi ab ipsa synodo dumtaxat, et non ab aliis, condigna animadversione et emenda sufficienti per partem dominorum Germanorum Augustanae confessionis tunc hic praesentium merito laudanda et approbanda mox puniantur, praesenti assecurationis forma, conditionibus et modis omnino manentibus illibatis. Vult praeterea ipsa synodus, quod liceat ipsis ambasciatoribus omnibus et singulis toties, quotiescumque opportunum fuerit seu necessarium, ad auram capiendam exire de civitate Tridentina et reverti ad eamdem, necnon nuncium vel nuncios suos ad quaecumque loca pro suis necessariis negotiis ordinandis libere mittere seu destinare, ac ipsos missos seu destinatos seu missum et destinatum suscipere toties quoties eis videbitur expedire, ita quod aliqui vel aliquis per deputandos concilii socientur, qui eorum securitati provideant vel provideat. Qui quidem salvus conductus et securitas stare ac durare debeat a tempore et per tempus, quo in ipsius synodi et suorum tuitionis curam ipsos suscipi contigerit et usque ad Tridentum perduci, ac toto tempore mansionis eorum ibidem, et rursum post sufficientem audientiam habitam, spatio viginti dierum praemisso, cum ipsi petierint, aut concilium habita hujusmodi audientia ipsis recessum indixerit, a Tridento usque in quem quisque elegerit sibi locum tutum, Deo favente, restituet, dolo et fraude prorsus exclusis. Quae quidem omnia pro universis et singulis Christi fidelibus pro omnibus principibus tam ecclesiasticis quam saecularibus quibuscumque, atque omnibus aliis ecclesiasticis et saecularibus personis, cujuscumque status et conditionis exsistant aut quocumque nomine censeantur, inviolabiliter observanda esse promittit et bona fide spondet. Insuper omni fraude et dolo exclusis vera et bona fide promittit, ipsam synodum nullam vel manifeste vel occulte occasionem quaesituram, aut aliqua auctoritate, potentia, jure vel statuto, privilegio legum vel canonum, aut quorumcumque conciliorum, praesertim Constantiensis et Senensis, quacumque forma verborum expressa, in aliquod hujus fidei publicae et plenissimae assecurationis, ac publicae et liberae audientiae ipsis per ipsam synodum concessae praejudicium quovis modo usuram, aut quemquam uti permissuram, quibus in hac parte pro hac vice derogat. Quod si sancta synodus, aut aliquis ex ea vel suis, cujuscumque conditionis, vel status aut praeeminentiae exsistens, praescriptae assecurationis et salvi conductus formam et modum in quocumque puncto vel clausula violaverit, quod tamen avertere dignetur omnipotens, et sufficiens emenda non fuerit mox subsecuta ipsorum arbitrio merito approbanda et laudanda, habeant ipsam synodum et habere poterunt incidisse in omnes poenas, quas jure divino et humano aut consuetudine hujusmodi salvorum conductuum violatores incurrere possunt, absque omni excusatione aut quavis in hac parte contradictione.

SESSIO DECIMA SEXTA

QUAE EST SEXTA ET ULTIMA

SUB JULIO III PONT. MAX.

celebrata

die XXVIII Aprilis, MDLII

DECRETUM SUSPENSIONIS CONCILII

Sacrosancta oecumenica et generalis Tridentina synodus in Spiritu Sancto legitime congregata, praesidentibus in ea reverendissimis dominis Sebastiano archiepiscopo Sipontino, et Aloysio episcopo Veronensi, apostolicis nunciis, tam eorum proprio, quam reverendissimi et illustrissimi domini Marcelli tit. S. Marcelli sanctae Romanae ecclesiae cardinalis Crescentii legati ob adversam ejus gravissimam valetudinem absentis nomine, non dubitat Christianis omnibus patere, hoc concilium oecumenicum Tridentum primo a Paulo fel. rec. convocatum et collectum fuisse; deinde a sanctissimo domino nostro Julio III efflagitante Carolo quinto augustissimo imperatore ea praecipue de causa fuisse restitutum, ut religionem in multis orbis partibus et praesertim in Germania in diversas opiniones miserabiliter distractam, in statum pristinum revocaret, abusus et mores Christianorum corruptissimos emendaret, cumque ad hoc agendum quamplurimi patres nulla laborum suorum periculorumque habita ratione e diversis regionibus alacriter confluxissent, resque strenue magno fidelium concursu feliciterque procederet, ac spes esset non levis, illos Germanos, qui eas novitates excitarant, in concilium venturos, sic animatos, ut veris ecclesiae rationibus unanimiter acquiescerent, lux denique quaedam rebus affulsisse videretur, caputque attollere inciperet profligata antea et afflicta respublica Christiana: ii repente tumultus, ea bella hostis generis humani versutia exarserunt, ut concilium velut haerere ac suum cursum interrumpere satis incommode cogeretur, spesque omnis ulterioris progressus hoc in tempore tolleretur; tantumque aberat, ut sancta synodus Christianorum malis et incommodis mederetur, ut multorum mentes praeter sui animi sententiam irritaret potius quam placaret. Cum igitur ipsa sancta synodus omnia et praecipue Germaniam armis ardere et discordiis videret, omnes fere episcopos Germanos, praesertim principes electores, suis consultum ecclesiis e concilio abiisse: decrevit tantae necessitati non reluctari, et ad meliora tempora rejicere, ut patres, quod eis nunc agere non licet, suis ovibus prospectum ad suas ecclesias regredi valerent, ne diutius utrobique inutili otio conterantur. Atque ita, quoniam sic temporum conditio tulit, hujus oecumenici concilii Tridentini progressum per biennium suspendendum fore decernit, prout praesenti decreto suspendit; ea tamen lege, ut, si citius pacata res sit ac tranquillitas pristina revertatur, quod sperat Dei Optimi Maximi beneficio non longo forsan spatio futurum, ipsius concilii progressus eodemmet tempore suam vim, firmitatem vigoremque habere censeatur. Sin autem, quod Deus avertat, peracto biennio praedicta legitima impedimenta non fuerint submota, cum primum cessaverint, talis suspensio eo ipso sublata esse intelligatur, ac suus vigor et robur concilio sit restitutum et esse intelligatur sine alia nova concilii convocatione, accedente ad hoc decretum, consensu et auctoritate Sanctitatis suae et sanctae Sedis Apostolicae.

Interea tamen eadem sancta synodus exhortatur omnes principes Christianos et omnes praelatos, ut observent, et respective, quatenus ad eos spectat, observare faciant in suis regnis, dominiis et ecclesiis omnia et singula, quae per hoc sacrum oecumenicum concilium fuerunt hactenus statuta et decreta.

BULLA
CELEBRATIONIS
CONCILII TRIDENTINI
sub Pio IV Pont. Max.

PIUS EPISCOPUS, SERVUS SERVORUM DEI, AD PERPETUAM REI MEMORIAM

Ad ecclesiae regimen, licet tanto oneri impares, sola Dei dignatione vocati, statim circumferentes mentis oculos per omnes reipublicae Christianae partes, cernentesque non sine magno horrore, quam longe lateque pestis haeresum et schismatis pervasisset, et quanta Christiani populi mores correctione indigerent, in eam curam et cogitationem pro suscepti muneris officio incumbere coepimus, quemadmodum ipsas haereses exstirpare, tantumque et tam perniciosum schisma tollere, moresque adeo corruptos et depravatos emendare possemus. Cum autem intelligeremus, ad haec sananda mala aptissimum esse remedium, quod sancta haec Sedes adhibere consuevisset, oecumenici generalisque concilii, ejus congregandi et Deo juvante celebrandi consilium cepimus. Indictum illud quidem antea fuit a fel. rec. Paulo III et ejus successore Julio praedecessoribus nostris, sed variis de causis saepius impeditum et interpellatum perfici non potuit. Siquidem Paulus, cum id primo in urbem Mantuam,[1] deinde Vicentiam indixisset, quasdam ob causas in litteris ejus expressas id primo suspendit, postea Tridentum transtulit; deinde cum quibusdam de causis ibi quoque ejus celebrandi tempus dilatum fuisset, tandem suspensione sublata in eadem civitate Tridentina inchoatum fuit. Verum sessionibus aliquot habitis et nonnullis decretis factis, ipsum se postea concilium aliquibus de causis, accedente etiam Sedis Apostolicae auctoritate, Bononiam transtulit.[2] Julius autem, qui ei successit, in eamdem civitatem Tridentinam id revocavit,[3] quo quidem tempore facta alia quaedam decreta sunt. Sed cum novi in propinquis Germaniae locis tumultus excitati fuissent, et bellum in Italia et Gallia gravissimum exarsisset, rursus concilium suspensum et dilatum fuit, adnitente nimirum humani generis hoste aliasque ex aliis difficultates et impedimenta objiciente, ut tantum ecclesiae commodum, quod prorsus auferre non poterat, saltem quam diutissime retardaret. Quantopere vero interea auctae fuerint et multiplicatae ac propagatae haereses, quantopere schisma creverit, sine maximo animi dolore nec meminisse possumus nec referre. Sed tandem pius et misericors Dominus, qui nunquam ita irascitur, ut misericordiae obliviscatur,[4] regibus et principibus Christianis pacem et unanimitatem donare dignatus est. Qua nos occasione oblata maximam in spem venimus, ipsius misericordia freti, fore, ut his tantis quoque ecclesiae malis eadem concilii via finis imponatur. Nos itaque ad schisma haeresesque tollendas, ad corrigendos et reformandos mores, ad pacem inter Christianos principes conservandam, celebrationem ejus non esse duximus diutius differendam. Habita igitur cum

---

[1] Cf. bullam convocationis, in qua Paulus id pluribus exponit.
[2] Cf. Sess. VIII.
[3] Cf. Sess. XI.
[4] Hab. 3:2.

venerabilibus fratribus nostris sanctae Romanae ecclesiae cardinalibus deliberatione matura, factis etiam concilii nostri certioribus carissimis in Christo filiis nostris Ferdinando Romanorum imperatore electo et aliis regibus atque principibus, quos quidem, sicut de eorum summa pietate et sapientia nobis pollicebamur, paratissimos ad ipsius concilii celebrationem adjuvandam invenimus, ad Dei omnipotentis laudem, honorem et gloriam, atque universalis ecclesiae utilitatem, de eorumdem fratrum nostrorum consilio et assensu sacrum oecumenicum et generale concilium ex auctoritate ejusdem Dei et beatorum Petri et Pauli Apostolorum, qua nos quoque in terris fungimur, freti et subnixi, in civitate Tridentina ad sanctissimum diem resurrectionis dominicae proxime futurum indicimus, et ibi celebrandum sublata suspensione quacumque statuimus atque decernimus. Quocirca venerabiles fratres nostros omnibus ex locis patriarchas, archiepiscopos, episcopos, et dilectos filios abbates ceterosque, quibus in concilio generali sedere et sententiam dicere jure communi vel ex privilegio vel ex antiqua consuetudine licet, vehementer in Domino hortamur et monemus, atque etiam districte praecipiendo mandamus in virtute sanctae obedientiae, in vi quoque juramenti, quod praestiterunt, et sub poenis, quas in eos, qui ad concilia generalia convenire neglexerint, sacris sciunt esse canonibus constitutas, ut ad concilium ibi celebrandum conveniant intra eam diem, nisi forte impedimento fuerint legitimo praepediti; quod tamen impedimentum per legitimos procuratores synodo probare debebunt. Monemus praeterea omnes et singulos, quorum interest interesseve poterit, ut in concilio adesse ne negligant. Carissimos vero in Christo filios nostros Romanorum imperatorem electum ceterosque reges et principes, quos optandum sane esset concilio interesse posse, hortamur et rogamus, ut, si ipsi concilio interesse non potuerint, at oratores suos, prudentes, graves et pios viros utique mittant, qui ipsorum nomine illi intersint, curentque diligenter pro sua pietate, ut ex eorum regnis atque dominiis praelati sine recusatione ac mora tam necessario tempore Deo et ecclesiae officium suum praestent, eosdem etiam curaturos esse minime dubitantes, ut per ipsorum regna et dominia tutum ac liberum iter praelatis, eorumque familiaribus, comitibus, et aliis omnibus ad concilium euntibus et ab illo redeuntibus pateat, benigneque ac comiter omnibus in locis recipiantur atque tractentur, sicut, quod ad nos attinet, ipsi quoque curabimus; qui nihil omnino praetermittere decrevimus, quod ad tam pium et salutare opus perficiendum a nobis in hoc loco constitutis praestari possit, nihil, ut Deus scit, quaerentes aliud, nihil propositum habentes in hoc concilio celebrando, nisi honorem ipsius Dei, dispersarum ovium reductionem ac salutem, et perpetuam Christianae reipublicae tranquillitatem ac quietem. Ut vero hae litterae et quae in eis continentur ad omnium, quorum oportet, notitiam perveniant, nec quisquam ea excusatione uti possit, quod illa ignoraverit, praesertim cum non ad omnes, quos de his litteris certiores fieri oporteret, tutus forsitan pateat aditus: volumus et mandamus, ut in basilica Vaticana principis apostolorum, et in ecclesia Lateranensi tunc, cum in eis populus, ut missarum solemnibus intersit, congregari solet, palam clara voce a curiae nostrae cursoribus seu notariis aliquibus publicis recitentur, et postquam recitatae furerint, ad valvas earum ecclesiarum, itemque cancellariae apostolicae et in loco solito Campi Florae affigantur, ibique, quo legi et omnibus innotescere possint, aliquandiu relinquantur. Cum autem inde amovebuntur, earum exempla in eisdem locis affixa remaneant. Nos enim per recitationem hanc, publicationem et affixionem omnes et singulos, qui his litteris comprehenduntur, post duos menses a die publicationis et affixionis earum volumus perinde adstrictos et obligatos esse, ac si ipsismet illae coram editae et lectae fuissent. Transumptis quoque earum, quae manu publici alicujus notarii scripta subscriptave, et sigillo ac subscriptione alicujus personae in dignitate ecclesiastica constitutae munita fuerint, ut sine dubitatione ulla fides habeatur, mandamus atque decernimus. Nulli ergo omnino hominum licet hanc paginam nostrae indictionis, statuti, decreti, praecepti, admonitionis et adhortationis infringere, vel ei ausu temerario contraire. Si quis autem hoc attentare praesumpserit, indignationem omnipotentis Dei, ac beatorum Petri et Pauli Apostolorum ejus se noverit incursurum. Datum Romae apud S. Petrum anno incarnationis dominicae MDLX. III. Kalend. Decembris, pontificatus nostri anno primo.

Antonius Florebellus Lavellinus.
Barengus.

SESSIO DECIMA SEPTIMA

SACROSANCTI OECUMENICI ET GENERALIS

CONCILII TRIDENTINI

QUAE EST PRIMA

SUB PIO IV PONT. MAX.

celebrata

die XVIII Januarii, MDLXII

DECRETUM DE CELEBRANDO CONCILIO

Placetne vobis, ad laudem et gloriam sanctae et individuae Trinitatis, Patris et Filii et Spiritus Sancti, ad incrementum et exaltationem fidei et religionis Christianae, sacrum oecumenicum et generale concilium Tridentinum in Spiritu Sancto legitime congregatum ab hodierno die, qui est decimus octavus mensis Jan. anni a Nativitate Domini millesimi quingentesimi sexagesimi secundi, cathedrae Romanae b. Petri apostolorum principis consecrato, sublata quacumque suspensione, juxta formam et tenorem litterarum sanctissimi domini nostri Pii IV Pont. Max. celebrari, et in eo ea debito servato ordine tractari, quae proponentibus legatis ac praesidentibus ad horum temporum levandas calamitates, sedandas de religione controversias, coercendas linguas dolosas, depravatorum morum abusus corrigendos, ecclesiae veram atque Christianam pacem conciliandam apta et idonea ipsi sanctae synodo videbuntur? *Responderunt:* Placet.

INDICTIO FUTURAE SESSIONIS

Placetne vobis, proximam futuram sessionem habendam et celebrandam esse feria quinta post secundam dominicam Quadragesimae, quae erit die vigesima sexta mensis Februarii? *Responderunt:* Placet.

SESSIO DECIMA OCTAVA

QUAE EST SECUNDA

SUB PIO IV PONT. MAX.

celebrata

die XXVI Februarii, MDLXII

DECRETUM DE LIBRORUM DELECTU, ET OMNIBUS AD CONCILIUM FIDE PUBLICA INVITANDIS

Sacrosancta oecumenica et generalis Tridentina synodus in Spiritu Sancto legitime congregata, praesidentibus in ea eisdem Apostolicae Sedis legatis, non humanis quidem viribus confisa, sed Domini nostri Jesu Christi, qui os et sapientiam ecclesiae suae daturum se promisit,[1] ope et auxilio freta, illud praecipue cogitat, ut catholicae fidei doctrinam, multorum inter se dissidentium opinionibus pluribus locis inquinatam et obscuratam, in suam puritatem et splendorem aliquando restituat, et mores, qui a veteri instituto deflexerunt, ad meliorem vitae rationem revocet, corque patrum ad filios [2] et cor filiorum ad patres convertat. Cum itaque omnium primum animadverterit, hoc tempore suspectorum ac perniciosorum librorum, quibus doctrina impura continetur et longe lateque diffunditur, numerum nimis excrevisse, quod quidem in causa fuit, ut multae censurae in variis provinciis et praesertim in alma urbe Roma pio quodam zelo editae fuerint, neque tamen huic tam magno ac pernicioso morbo salutarem ullam profuisse medicinam: censuit, ut delecti ad hanc disquisitionem patres de censuris librisque quid facto opus esset diligenter considerarent,[3] atque etiam ad eamdem sanctam synodum suo tempore referrent, quo facilius ipsa possit varias et peregrinas doctrinas tamquam zizania [4] a Christianae veritatis tritico separare, deque his commodius deliberare et statuere, quae ad scrupulum ex complurium animis eximendum et tollendas multarum querelarum causas magis opportuna videbuntur. Haec au-

---

[1] Luc. 21:15.
[2] *Ibid.*, 1:17.
[3] Cf. Sess. XXV circa fin. de indice libr.
[4] Matt. 13:30.

tem omnia ad notitiam quorumcumque deducta esse vult, prout etiam praesenti decreto deducit, ut, si quis ad se pertinere aliquo modo putaverit, quae vel de hoc librorum et censurarum negotio, vel de aliis, quae in hoc generali concilio tractanda praedixit, non dubitet a sancta synodo se benigne auditum iri.

Quoniam vero eadem sancta synodus ex corde optat Deumque enixe rogat quae ad pacem sunt ecclesiae,[5] ut universi communem matrem in terris agnoscentes, quae quos peperit oblivisci non potest,[6] unanimes uno ore glorificemus Deum et Patrem Domini nostri Jesu Christi,[7] per viscera misericordiae ejusdem Dei et Domini nostri omnes, qui nobiscum communionem non habent, ad concordiam et reconciliationem, et ut ad hanc sanctam synodum veniant, invitat atque hortatur, utque caritatem, quod est vinculum perfectionis,[8] amplectantur, pacemque Christi exultantem in cordibus suis prae se ferant, in quam vocati sunt in uno corpore. Hanc ergo non humanam, sed Spiritus Sancti vocem audientes ne obdurent corda sua,[9] sed in suo sensu non ambulantes,[10] neque sibi placentes,[11] ad tam piam et salutarem matris suae admonitionem excitentur et convertantur. Omnibus enim caritatis officiis sancta synodus eos ut invitat, ita complectetur.

Insuper eadem sancta synodus decrevit, fidem publicam in congregatione generali concedi posse, et eamdem vim habituram, ejusdemque roboris et momenti futuram ac si in publica sessione data et decreta fuisset.

INDICTIO FUTURAE SESSIONIS

Eadem sacrosancta Tridentina synodus, in Spiritu Sancto legitime congregata, praesidentibus in ea eisdem Apostolicae Sedis legatis, statuit et decernit, proximam futuram sessionem habendam et celebrandam esse feria quinta post sacratissimum festum Ascensionis Domini, quae erit die decima quarta mensis Maii.

---

[5] Ps. 121:6.
[6] Is. 49:15.
[7] Rom. 15:6.
[8] Col. 3:14 f.
[9] Ps. 94:8; Heb. 3:8.
[10] Eph. 4:17.
[11] Rom. 15:1–3.

SALVUS CONDUCTUS
concessus
GERMANICAE NATIONI

IN CONGREGATIONE GENERALI DIE IV, MARTII, MDLXII

Sacrosancta oecumenica et generalis Tridentina synodus in Spiritu Sancto legitime congregata, praesidentibus in ea eisdem Apostolicae Sedis legatis, universis fidem facit, quod omnibus et singulis sacerdotibus, electoribus, principibus, ducibus, marchionibus, comitibus, baronibus, nobilibus, militaribus, popularibus et aliis quibuscumque viris, cujuscumque status et conditionis aut qualitatis exsistant, Germanicae provinciae et nationis civitatibus, ac aliis locis ejusdem, et omnibus aliis ecclesiasticis et saecularibus, praesertim Augustanae confessionis, personis, qui aut quae una cum ipsis ad hoc generale Tridentinum concilium venient aut mittentur, ac profecturi sunt aut hucusque venerunt, quocumque nomine censeantur aut valeant nuncupari, tenore praesentium publicam fidem et plenissimam verissimamque securitatem, quam salvum conductum appellant, libere ad hanc civitatem Tridentinam veniendi, ibidemque manendi, standi, morandi, proponendi, loquendi, una cum ipsa synodo de quibuscumque negotiis tractandi, examinandi, discutiendi, et omnia, quaecumque ipsis libuerit, ac articulos quoslibet tam scripto quam verbo libere offerendi, propalandi, eosque scripturis sacris et beatorum patrum verbis, sententiis et rationibus declarandi, adstruendi et persuadendi, et, si opus fuerit, etiam ad objecta concilii generalis respondendi et cum iis, qui a concilio delecti fuerint, disputandi aut caritative absque omni impedimento conferendi, opprobriis, conviciis ac contumeliis penitus semotis; et signanter, quod causae controversae secundum sacram scripturam et apostolorum traditiones, probata concilia et catholicae ecclesiae consensum et sanctorum patrum auctoritates in praedicto concilio Tridentino tractentur; illo etiam addito, ut religionis praetextu aut delictorum circa eam commissorum aut committendorum minime puniantur, impertitur ac omnino concedit; sic etiam, ut propter illorum praesentiam neque in itinere aut quocumque locorum eundo, manendo aut redeundo, nec in ipsa civitate Tridentina a divinis officiis quovis modo cessetur, et ut his peractis vel non peractis, quandocumque ipsis libuerit, aut majorum suorum mandato et assensu ad propria reverti optabunt aut aliquis eorum optabit, mox absque ulla renitentia et occasione aut mora, salvis rebus eorum et suorum pariter honore et personis vice versa, possint juxta beneplacitum libere et secure redire, de scientia tamen ab eadem synodo deputandorum, ut tunc opportune eorum securitati absque dolo et fraude provideatur. Vult etiam sancta synodus in hac publica fide salvoque conductu omnes quascumque clausulas includi et contineri ac pro inclusis haberi, quae pro plena, efficaci et sufficienti securitate in eundo, stando et redeundo necessariae et opportunae fuerint. Illud etiam ad majorem securitatem et pacis ac conciliationis bonum exprimens, quod, si quispiam aut illorum aliqui, sive in itinere Tridentum veniendo sive ibidem morando aut redeundo aliquod enorme, quod absit, egerint aut commiserint, quo posset hujus fidei publicae et assecurationis beneficium eis concessum annullari aut cassari, vult et concedit, ut in hujusmodi facinore deprehensi ab ipsis dumtaxat, et non ab aliis, condigna animadversione cum emenda sufficienti per partem ipsius synodi merito approbanda et laudanda mox puniantur; illorum assecurationis forma, conditionibus et modis omnino manentibus illibatis. Pariformiter etiam vult, ut, si quisquam vel aliqui ex ipsa synodo sive in itinere aut manendo aut redeundo aliquod enorme, quod absit, egerint aut commiserint, quo posset hujus fidei publicae et assecurationis beneficium violari aut quoquo modo tolli, in hujusmodi facinore deprehensi ab ipsa synodo dumtaxat, et non ab aliis, condigna animadversione et emenda sufficienti per partem dominorum Germanorum Augustanae confessionis tunc hic praesentium merito laudanda et approbanda mox puniantur, praesenti assecurationis forma, conditionibus et modis omnino manentibus illibatis. Vult praeterea ipsa synodus, quod liceat ipsis ambasciatoribus omnibus et singulis toties, quotiescumque opportunum fuerit seu necessarium, ad auram capiendam exire de civitate Tridentina et reverti ad eamdem, necnon nuncium vel nuncios suos ad quaecumque loca pro suis necessariis negotiis ordinandis libere mittere seu destinare, ac ipsos missos seu destinatos seu missum et destinatum suscipere toties quoties eis videbitur expedire, ita quod aliqui vel aliquis per deputandos concilii socientur, qui eorum securitati provideant vel provideat. Qui quidem salvus conductus et securitates stare ac durare debeant et a tempore et per tempus, quo in ipsius synodi et suorum tuitionis curam ipsos suscipi contigerit et usque ad Tridentum perduci, ac toto tempore mansionis eorum ibidem, et rursum post sufficientem audientiam habitam, spatio viginti dierum praemisso, cum ipsi petierint aut concilium habita hujusmodi audientia ipsis recessum indixerit a Tridento usque in quem quisque elegerit sibi locum tutum Deo favente restituet, dolo et fraude prorsus exclusis. Quae quidem omnia pro universis et singulis Christi fidelibus, pro omnibus principibus tam ecclesiasticis quam saecularibus quibuscumque, atque omnibus aliis ecclesiasticis et saecularibus personis, cujuscumque status et conditionis exsistant, aut quocumque nomine censeantur, inviolabiliter observanda esse promittit et bona fide spondet. Insuper omni fraude et dolo exclusis vera et bona fide promittit, ipsam synodum nullam vel manifeste vel occulte occasionem quaesituram, aut aliqua auctoritate, potentia, jure vel statuto, privilegio legum vel canonum, aut quorumcumque conciliorum, praesertim Constantiensis et Senensis, quacumque forma verborum expressa, in aliquod hujus fidei publicae et plenissime assecurationis, ac publicae et liberae audientiae ipsis per ipsam synodum concessae praejudicium quovis modo usuram aut quemquam uti permissuram, quibus in hac parte pro hac vice derogat. Quod si sancta synodus, aut aliquis ex ea vel suis, cujuscumque conditionis vel status aut praeeminentiae exsistens, praescriptae assecurationis et salvi conductus formam et modum in quocumque puncto vel clausula violaverit, quod tamen avertere dignetur Omnipotens, et sufficiens emenda non fuerit mox subsecuta ipsorum arbitrio merito approbanda et laudanda, habeant ipsam synodum et habere poterunt incidisse in omnes poenas, quas jure divino et humano aut consuetudine hujusmodi salvorum conductuum violatores incurrere possunt, absque omni excusatione aut quavis in hac parte contradictione.

EXTENSIO AD ALIAS NATIONES

Eadem sacrosancta synodus in Spiritu Sancto legitime congregata, praesidentibus in ea eisdem Apostolicae Sedis de latere legatis, omnibus et singulis aliis, qui nobiscum in iis, quae sunt fidei, communionem non habent, ex quibuscumque regnis, nationibus, provinciis, civitatibus ac locis, in quibus publice et impune praedicatur vel docetur sive creditur contrarium ejus, quod sancta Romana sentit ecclesia, dat fidem publicam sive salvum conductum sub eadem forma et eisdem verbis, quibus datur Germanis.

SESSIO DECIMA NONA

QUAE EST TERTIA

SUB PIO IV PONT. MAX.

celebrata

die XIV Maii, MDLXII

DECRETUM PROROGATIONIS SESSIONIS

Sacrosancta oecumenica et generalis Tridentina synodus in Spiritu Sancto legitime congregata, praesidentibus in ea eisdem Apostolicae Sedis legatis, decreta ea, quae hodie in praesenti sessione statuenda ac sancienda erant, justis nonnullis ac honestis causis in feriam quintam post proximam solemnitatem Corporis Christi, quae erit pridie Nonas Junii, proroganda esse censuit ac prorogat, dictaque die sessionem habendam esse ac celebrandam omnibus indicit. Interea rogandus est Deus et Pater Domini nostri Jesu Christi auctor pacis, ut sanctificet corda omnium, quo adjuvante sancta synodus et nunc et semper meditari atque peragere valeat quae ad ejus laudem et gloriam pertineant.

SESSIO VIGESIMA

QUAE EST QUARTA

SUB PIO IV PONT. MAX.

celebrata

die IV Junii, MDLXII

DECRETUM PROROGATIONIS SESSIONIS

Sacrosancta oecumenica et generalis Tridentina synodus in Spiritu Sancto legitime congregata, praesidentibus in ea eisdem Apostolicae Sedis legatis, propter varias difficultates ex diversis causis exortas, atque etiam ut congruentius majorique cum deliberatione omnia procedant, nempe ut dogmata cum iis, quae ad reformationem spectant, simul tractentur et sanciantur, ea, quae statuenda videbuntur tam de reformatione quam de dogmatibus in proxima sessione, quam omnibus indicit in diem sextam decimam subsequentis mensis Julii, definienda esse decrevit; hoc tamen adjecto, quod dictum terminum ipsa sancta synodus pro ejus arbitrio et voluntate, sicuti rebus concilii putaverit expedire, etiam in generali congregatione, restringere et prorogare libere possit et valeat.

SESSIO VIGESIMA PRIMA

QUAE EST QUINTA

SUB PIO IV PONT. MAX.

celebrata

die XVI Julii, MDLXII

DOCTRINA DE COMMUNIONE SUB UTRAQUE SPECIE ET PARVULORUM

Sacrosancta oecumenica et generalis Tridentina synodus in Spiritu Sancto legitime congregata, praesidentibus in ea eisdem Apostolicae Sedis legatis, cum de tremendo et sanctissimo Eucharistiae sacramento varia diversis in locis errorum monstra nequissimi daemonis artibus circumferantur, ob quae in nonnullis provinciis multi a catholicae ecclesiae fide atque obedientia videantur discessisse, censuit ea, quae ad communionem sub utraque specie et parvulorum pertinent, hoc loco exponenda esse. Quapropter cunctis Christi fidelibus interdicit, ne posthac de iis aliter vel credere vel docere vel praedicare audeant, quam est his decretis explicatum atque definitum.

Caput I

LAICOS ET CLERICOS NON CONFICIENTES NON ADSTRINGI JURE DIVINO AD COMMUNIONEM SUB UTRAQUE SPECIE

Itaque sancta ipsa synodus a Spiritu Sancto, qui spiritus est sapientiae et intellectus, spiritus consilii et pietatis,[1] edocta, atque ipsius ecclesiae judicium et consuetudinem secuta,[2] declarat ac docet, nullo divino praecepto laicos et clericos non conficientes obligari ad Eucharistiae sacramentum sub utraque specie sumendum, neque ullo pacto, salva fide, dubitari posse, quin illis alterius speciei communio ad salutem sufficiat. Nam, etsi Christus Dominus in ultima coena venerabili

[1] Is. 11:2.

[2] Conc. Constantien., Sess. XIII (Denzinger, n.626); *infra*, can. 2.

hoc sacramentum in panis et vini speciebus instituit et apostolis tradidit,[3] non tamen illa institutio et traditio eo tendunt, ut omnes Christi fideles statuto Domini ad utramque speciem accipiendam adstringantur. Sed neque ex sermone illo apud Joannem VI recte colligitur, utriusque speciei communionem a Domino praeceptam esse, utcumque juxta varias sanctorum patrum et doctorum interpretationes intelligatur. Namque qui dixit: *Nisi manducaveritis carnem filii hominis et biberitis ejus sanguinem, non habebitis vitam in vobis*,[4] dixit quoque: *Si quis manducaverit ex hoc pane, vivet in aeternum.*[5] Et qui dixit: *Qui manducat meam carnem et bibit meum sanguinem, habet vitam aeternam*,[6] dixit etiam: *Panis, quem ego dabo, caro mea est pro mundi vita.*[7] Et denique qui dixit: *Qui manducat meam carnem et bibit meum sanguinem, in me manet et ego in illo*,[8] dixit nihilominus: *Qui manducat hunc panem, vivet in aeternam.*[9]

Caput II

ECCLESIAE POTESTAS CIRCA DISPENSATIONEM SACRAMENTI EUCHARISTIAE

Praeterea declarat, hanc potestatem perpetuo in ecclesia fuisse, ut in sacramentorum dispensatione, salva illorum substantia, ea statueret vel mutaret, quae suscipientium utilitati seu ipsorum sacramentorum venerationi pro rerum, temporum et locorum varietate magis expedire judicaret. Id autem Apostolus non obscure visus est innuisse, cum ait: *Sic nos existimet homo ut ministros Christi et dispensatores mysteriorum Dei*,[10] atque ipsum quidem hac potestate usum esse satis constat cum in multis aliis, tum in hoc ipso sacramento, cum, ordinatis nonnullis circa ejus usum: *Cetera*, inquit, *cum venero disponam.*[11] Quare agnoscens sancta mater ecclesia hanc suam in administratione sacramentorum auctoritatem, licet ab initio Christianae religionis non infrequens utriusque speciei usus fuisset, tamen progressu temporis

[3] Matt. 26:26–28; Marc. 14:22–24; Luc. 22:19 f.; I Cor. 11:24 f.
[4] Joan. 6:54.
[5] *Ibid.*, 6:52.
[6] *Ibid.*, 6:55.
[7] *Ibid.*, 6:52.
[8] *Ibid.*, 6:57.
[9] *Ibid.*, 6:59.
[10] Cf. I Cor. 4:1.
[11] *Ibid.*, 11:34.

latissime jam mutata illa consuetudine, gravibus et justis causis adducta hanc consuetudinem sub altera specie communicandi approbavit,[12] et pro lege habendam decrevit, quam reprobare aut sine ipsius ecclesiae auctoritate pro libito mutare non licet.

Caput III

TOTUM ET INTEGRUM CHRISTUM AC VERUM SACRAMENTUM SUB QUALIBET SPECIE SUMI

Insuper declarat, quamvis Redemptor noster, ut antea dictum est, in suprema illa coena hoc sacramentum in duabus speciebus instituerit et apostolis tradiderit, tamen fatendum esse, etiam sub altera tantum specie totum atque integrum Christum verumque sacramentum sumi,[13] ac propterea, quod ad fructum attinet, nulla gratia necessaria ad salutem eos defraudari, qui unam speciem solam accipiunt.

Caput IV

PARVULOS NON OBLIGARI AD COMMUNIONEM SACRAMENTALEM

Denique eadem sancta synodus docet,[14] parvulos usu rationis carentes nulla obligari necessitate ad sacramentalem Eucharistiae communionem, siquidem per baptismi lavacrum regenerati[15] et Christo incorporati adeptam jam filiorum Dei gratiam in illa aetate amittere non possunt. Neque ideo tamen damnanda est antiquitas, si eum morem in quibusdam locis aliquando servavit. Ut enim sanctissimi illi patres sui facti probabilem causam pro illius temporis ratione habuerunt, ita certa eos nulla salutis necessitate id fecisse sine controversia credendum est.

CANONES DE COMMUNIONE SUB UTRAQUE SPECIE ET PARVULORUM

1. Si quis dixerit, ex Dei praecepto vel necessitate salutis omnes et singulos Christi fideles utramque speciem sanctissimi Eucharistiae sacramenti sumere debere: [16] anathema sit.

---

[12] Conc. Constantien., *supra*, adn. 2.
[13] Cf. Sess. XIII, cap. 3 et can. 3.
[14] Cf. *infra*, can. 4.
[15] Tit. 3:5.
[16] *Supra*, huj. sess. cap. 1.

2. Si quis dixerit, sanctam ecclesiam catholicam non justis causis et rationibus adductam fuisse, ut laicos atque etiam clericos non conficientes sub panis tantummodo specie communicaret,[17] aut in eo errasse: anathema sit.

3. Si quis negaverit, totum et integrum Christum omnium gratiarum fontem et auctorem sub una panis specie sumi, quia, ut quidam falso asserunt, non secundum ipsius Christi institutionem sub utraque specie sumatur: [18] anathema sit.

4. Si quis dixerit, parvulis, antequam ad annos discretionis pervenerint, necessariam esse Eucharistiae communionem: [19] anathema sit.

Duos vero articulos alias propositos,[20] nondum tamen excussos, videlicet: an rationes, quibus sancta catholica ecclesia adducta fuit, ut communicaret laicos atque etiam non celebrantes sacerdotes sub una tantum panis specie, ita sint retinendae, ut nulla ratione calicis usus cuiquam sit permittendus; et: an, si honestis et Christianae caritati consentaneis rationibus concedendus alicui vel nationi vel regno calicis usus videatur, sub aliquibus conditionibus concedendus sit, et quaenam sint illae, eadem sancta synodus in aliud tempus, oblata sibi quam primum occasione, examinandos atque definiendos reservat.

DECRETUM DE REFORMATIONE

Eadem sacrosancta oecumenica et generalis Tridentina synodus, in Spiritu Sancto legitime congregata, praesidentibus in ea eisdem Apostolicae Sedis legatis, ad Dei omnipotentis laudem et sanctae ecclesiae ornamentum ea, quae sequuntur, de reformatione negotio in praesenti statuenda esse censuit.

Caput I

EPISCOPI GRATIS CUM ORDINES CONFERANT, TUM DIMISSORIAS ET TESTIMONIALES LITTERAS DENT, PRO QUIBUS EORUM MINISTRI NIHIL PRORSUS, NOTARII AUTEM QUOD IN DECRETO PRAEFINITUM EST, ACCIPIANT

Quoniam ab ecclesiastico ordine omnis avaritiae suspicio abesse debet, nihil pro collatione quorumcumque ordinum, etiam clericalis

[17] *Ibid.*, cap. 2.
[18] *Ibid.*, cap. 3 et Sess. XIII, cap. 3 et can. 3.
[19] Cf. *supra*, can. 4.
[20] Cf. Sess. XIII decr. ult.

tonsurae, nec pro litteris dimissoriis aut testimonialibus, nec pro sigillo, nec alia quacumque de causa, etiam sponte oblatum, episcopi et alii ordinum collatores aut eorum ministri quovis praetextu accipiant. Notarii vero in iis tantum locis, in quibus non viget laudabilis consuetudo nihil accipiendi, pro singulis litteris dimissoriis aut testimonialibus decimam tantum unius aurei partem accipere possint, dummodo eis nullum salarium sit constitutum pro officio exercendo; nec episcopo ex notarii commodis aliquod emolumentum ex eisdem ordinum collationibus directe vel indirecte provenire possit. Tunc enim gratis operam suam eos praestare omnino teneri decernit, contrarias taxas, ac statuta et consuetudines etiam immemorabiles quorumcumque locorum, quae potius abusus et corruptelae simoniacae pravitati faventes nuncupari possunt, penitus cassando et interdicendo, et qui secus fecerint, tam dantes quam accipientes ultra divinam ultionem poenas a jure [21] inflictas ipso facto incurrant.

Caput II

ARCENTUR A SACRIS ORDINIBUS QUI NON HABENT UNDE VIVERE POSSINT

Cum non deceat eos, qui divino ministerio adscripti sunt, cum ordinis dedecore mendicare, aut sordidum aliquem quaestum exercere, compertumque sit, complures plerisque in locis ad sacros ordines nullo fere delectu admitti, qui variis artibus ac fallaciis confingunt se beneficium ecclesiasticum aut etiam idoneas facultates obtinere: statuit sancta synodus, ne quis deinceps clericus saecularis, quamvis alias sit idoneus moribus, scientia et aetate, ad sacros ordines promoveatur, nisi prius legitime constet, eum beneficium ecclesiasticum, quod sibi ad victum honeste sufficiat, pacifice possidere. Id vero beneficium resignare non possit, nisi facta mentione, quod ad illius beneficii titulum sit promotus, neque ea resignatio admittatur, nisi constito, quod aliunde vivere commode possit; et aliter facta resignatio nulla sit. Patrimonium vero vel pensionem obtinentes ordinari posthac non possint, nisi illi, quos episcopus judicaverit assumendos pro necessitate vel

---

[21] C.6, C.I, q.1 (Gelas.), c.8, *ibid.* (conc. Chalc.), c.101, *ibid.* (Toletan. XI), c.107, *ibid.* (Nicol. II in conc. Rom.), c.113, *ibid.* (Greg. VII in conc. Rom.); conc. Aurelianen. II (a.533), c.3; Bracaren. II (a.572), c.3; Toletan. VIII (a.653), c.3; cc.4, 5, X, De Sim., V, 3 (Greg. I), cc.11, 13, *ibid.* (Alex. III), c.30, *ibid.* (Innoc. III).

commoditate ecclesiarum suarum; eo quoque prius perspecto, patrimonium illud vel pensionem vere ab eis obtineri, taliaque esse, quae eis ad vitam sustentandam satis sint. Atque illa deinceps sine licentia episcopi alienari aut exstingui vel remitti nullatenus possint, donec beneficium ecclesiasticum sufficiens sint adepti, vel aliunde habeant unde vivere possint; antiquorum canonum poenas super his innovando.[22]

Caput III

RATIO DISTRIBUTIONES QUOTIDIANAS AUGENDI PRAESCRIBITUR; QUIBUS DEBEANTUR; NON SERVIENTIUM CONTUMACIA PUNITUR

Cum beneficia ad divinum cultum atque ecclesiastica munia obeunda sint constituta, ne qua in parte minuatur divinus cultus, sed ei debitum omnibus in rebus obsequium praestetur: [23] statuit sancta synodus in ecclesiis tam cathedralibus quam collegiatis, in quibus nullae sunt distributiones quotidianae vel ita tenues, ut verisimiliter negligantur, tertiam partem fructuum et quorumcumque proventuum et obventionum tam dignitatum quam canonicatuum, personatuum, portionum et officiorum separari debere et in distributiones quotidianas converti, quae inter dignitates obtinentes et ceteros divinis interessentes proportionabiliter juxta divisionem ab episcopo, etiam tamquam Apostolicae Sedis delegato, in ipsa prima fructuum deductione faciendam dividantur,[24] salvis tamen consuetudinibus earum ecclesiarum, in quibus non residentes seu non servientes nihil vel minus tertia parte percipiunt; non obstantibus exemptionibus, ac aliis consuetudinibus, etiam immemorabilibus, et appellationibus quibuscumque. Crescenteque non servientium contumacia liceat contra eos procedere juxta juris ac sacrorum canonum dispositionem.[25]

---

[22] C.1, D.LXX (conc. Chalc.), c.2, *ibid.* (Urban. II); c.2, X, De praeb., III, 5 (Epitom. Nov. Jul.), c.4, *ibid.* (Lat. III), cc.16, 23, *ibid.* (Innoc. III); c.37 h.t. in VI°, III, 4 (Bonif. VIII).
[23] C.15, VI°, De rescript., I, 3 (idem).
[24] Cf. Sess. XXII, cap. 3 de ref. et Sess. XXIV, cap. 12 de ref.
[25] Cf. cc.16, 17, X, De cler. non resid., III, 4 (Greg. IX) et Sess. XXIII, cap. 1 de ref.

Caput IV

COADJUTORES CURAE ANIMARUM QUANDO SINT ASSUMENDI. RATIO NOVAS PAROCHIAS ERIGENDI TRADITUR

Episcopi, etiam tamquam Apostolicae Sedis delegati, in omnibus ecclesiis parochialibus vel baptismalibus, in quibus populus ita numerosus sit, ut unus rector non possit sufficere ecclesiasticis sacramentis ministrandis et cultu divino peragendo, cogant rectores, vel alios, ad quos pertinet, sibi tot sacerdotes ad hoc munus adjungere, quot sufficiant ad sacramenta exhibenda et cultum divinum celebrandum. In iis vero, in quibus ob locorum distantiam sive difficultatem parochiani sine magno incommodo ad percipienda sacramenta et divina officia audienda accedere non possunt, novas parochias etiam invitis rectoribus juxta formam constitutionis Alexandri III, quae incipit: *Ad audientiam*,[26] constituere possint. Illis autem sacerdotibus, qui de novo erunt ecclesiis noviter erectis praeficiendi, competens assignetur portio arbitrio episcopi ex fructibus ad ecclesiam matricem quomodocumque pertinentibus, et, si necesse fuerit, compellere possit populum ea subministrare, quae sufficiant ad vitam dictorum sacerdotum sustentandam; quacumque reservatione generali vel speciali vel affectione super dictis ecclesiis non obstantibus. Neque hujusmodi ordinationes et erectiones possint tolli nec impediri ex quibuscumque provisionibus, etiam vigore resignationis, aut quibusvis aliis derogationibus vel suspensionibus.

Caput V

POSSUNT EPISCOPI FACERE UNIONES PERPETUAS IN CASIBUS A JURE PERMISSIS

Ut etiam ecclesiarum status, ubi sacra Deo officia ministrantur, ex dignitate conservetur, possint episcopi, etiam tamquam Apostolicae Sedis delegati, juxta formam juris, sine tamen praejudicio obtinentium, facere uniones perpetuas [27] quarumcumque ecclesiarum parochialium et baptismalium, et aliorum beneficiorum curatorum vel non cura-

[26] C. 3, X, De eccl. aedif., III, 48, *infra*, p. 566, lit. P.
[27] Cf. c. 8, X, De excess. prael., V, 31 (Coelest. III); Sess. XIV, cap. 9 de ref. et Sess. XXIV, cap. 13 de ref.

torum cum curatis propter earum paupertatem et in ceteris casibus a jure permissis, etiam si dictae ecclesiae vel beneficia essent generaliter vel specialiter reservata aut qualitercumque affecta. Quae uniones etiam non possint revocari, nec quoquo modo infringi vigore cujuscumque provisionis, etiam ex causa resignationis, aut derogationis aut suspensionis.

Caput VI

IMPERITIS PAROCHIS VICARII ASSIGNATA PARTE FRUCTUUM DEPUTENTUR; IN SCANDALO PERSEVERANTES PRIVARI BENEFICIIS POSSINT

Quia illiterati et imperiti parochialium ecclesiarum rectores sacris minus apti sunt officiis,[28] et alii propter eorum vitae turpitudinem potius destruunt quam aedificant, episcopi, etiam tamquam Apostolicae Sedis delegati, eisdem illiteratis et imperitis, si alias honestae vitae sint, coadjutores aut vicarios pro tempore deputare, partemque fructuum eisdem pro sufficienti victu assignare, vel aliter providere possint, quacumque appellatione et exemptione remota. Eos vero, qui turpiter et scandalose vivunt, postquam praemoniti fuerint, coerceant ac castigent, et, si adhuc incorrigibiles in sua nequitia perseverent, eos beneficiis juxta sacrorum canonum constitutiones, exemptione et appellatione quacumque remota, privandi facultatem habeant.[29]

Caput VII

EPISCOPI TRANSFERANT BENEFICIA EX ECCLESIIS, QUAE NEQUEUNT RESTAURARI; ALIAS VERO REPARARI CURENT; QUID IN HOC SERVANDUM SIT

Cum illud quoque valde curandum sit, ne ea, quae sacris ministeriis dicata sunt, temporum injuria obsolescant et ex hominum memoria excidant, episcopi, etiam tamquam Apostolicae Sedis delegati, transferre possint beneficia simplicia, etiam juris patronatus, ex ecclesiis, quae vetustate vel alias collapsae sint, et ob eorum inopiam nequeant instaurari, vocatis iis, quorum interest, in matrices aut alias ecclesias

[28] Cf. c. 1, D. XXXVI (Gelas.); c. 1, D.XXXVIII (conc. Toletan. IV); c. 10, X, De renunc., I, 9 (Innoc. III).
[29] Cf. cc. 13–15, X, De vit. et hon. cler., III, 1 (Lat. IV).

locorum eorumdem seu viciniorum arbitrio suo; atque in eisdem ecclesiis erigant altaria vel capellas sub eisdem invocationibus, vel in jam erecta altaria vel capellas transferant cum omnibus emolumentis et oneribus prioribus ecclesiis impositis. Parochiales vero ecclesias, etiamsi juris patronatus sint, ita collapsas refici et instaurari procurent ex fructibus et proventibus quibuscumque ad easdem ecclesias quomodocumque pertinentibus.[30] Qui si non fuerint sufficientes, omnes patronos et alios, qui fructus aliquos ex dictis ecclesiis provenientes percipiunt, aut, in illorum defectum, parochianos omnibus remediis opportunis ad praedicta cogant, quacumque appellatione, exemptione et contradictione remota. Quod si nimia egestate omnes laborent, ad matrices seu viciniores ecclesias transferantur, cum facultate tam dictas parochiales quam alias ecclesias dirutas in profanos usus non sordidos, erecta tamen ibi cruce, convertendi.

Caput VIII

MONASTERIA COMMENDATA, IN QUIBUS NON VIGET REGULARIS OBSERVANTIA, ET BENEFICIA QUAECUMQUE QUOTANNIS AB EPISCOPIS VISITENTUR

Quaecumque in dioecesi ad Dei cultum spectant, ab ordinario diligenter curari, atque iis, ubi oportet, provideri aequum est. Propterea commendata monasteria, etiam abbatiae, prioratus et praepositurae nuncupatae, in quibus non viget regularis observantia, necnon beneficia tam curata quam non curata, saecularia et regularia, qualitercumque commendata, etiam exempta, ab episcopis, etiam tamquam Apostolicae Sedis delegatis, annis singulis visitentur;[31] curentque iidem episcopi congruentibus remediis, etiam per sequestrationem fructuum, ut quae renovatione indigent aut restauratione reficiantur, et cura animarum, si qua illis vel eorum annexis immineat, aliaque debita obsequia recte exerceantur; appellationibus quibuscumque, privilegiis, consuetudinibus, etiam immemorabili tempore praescriptis, conservatoriis, judicum deputationibus, et eorum inhibitionibus non obstantibus. Et, si in eis vigeret observantia regularis,[32] provideant

---

[30] C. I, X, De eccl. aedif., III, 48 (conc. Moguntien.), c.4, *ibid.* (Alex. III); cf. Sess. VII, cap. 8 de ref.

[31] Cf. Sess. et cap. cit.; Sess. XXIV, cap. 9 de ref. et Sess. XXV de regular., cap. 20; c. 10, C.X, q. 1 (conc. Tarraconen.).

[32] Cf. Sess. XXV, cap. cit.

episcopi paternis admonitionibus, ut eorum regularium superiores juxta eorum regularia instituta debitam vivendi rationem observent et observari faciant, et sibi subditos in officio contineant ac moderentur. Quod si admoniti intra sex menses eos non visitaverint vel correxerint, tunc iidem episcopi, etiam ut delegati Sedis Apostolicae, eos visitare possint et corrigere, prout ipsi superiores possent juxta eorum instituta; quibuscumque appellationibus, privilegiis et exemptionibus penitus remotis et non obstantibus.

Caput IX

QUAESTORUM ELEEMOSYNARUM NOMEN ET USUS TOLLITUR. INDULGENTIAS ET SPIRITUALES GRATIAS ORDINARII PUBLICENT. DUO DE CAPITULO ELEEMOSYNAS GRATIS ACCIPIANT

Cum multa a diversis antea conciliis, tam Lateranensi [33] ac Lugdunensi, quam Viennensi,[34] adversus pravos eleemosynarum quaestorum [35] abusus remedia tunc adhibita posterioribus temporibus reddita fuerint inutilia, potiusque eorum malitia ita quotidie magno fidelium omnium scandalo et querela excrescere deprehendatur, ut de eorum emendatione nulla spes amplius relicta videatur: statuit, ut posthac in quibuscumque Christianae religionis locis eorum nomen atque usus penitus aboleatur, nec ad officium hujusmodi exercendum ullatenus admittantur; non obstantibus privilegiis, ecclesiis, monasteriis, hospitalibus, piis locis et quibusvis cujuscumque gradus, status et dignitatis personis concessis, aut consuetudinibus etiam immemorabilibus. Indulgentias vero aut alias spirituales gratias, quibus non ideo Christi fideles decet privari, deinceps per ordinarios locorum, adhibitis duobus de capitulo, debitis temporibus populo publicandas esse decernit. Quibus etiam eleemosynas atque oblata sibi caritatis subsidia, nulla prorsus mercede accepta, fideliter colligendi facultas datur, ut tandem coelestes hos ecclesiae thesauros non ad quaestum, sed ad pietatem exerceri omnes vere intelligant.

---

[33] C. 14, X, De poenit., V, 38 (Lat. IV).
[34] C. 2 h.t. in Clem., V, 9.
[35] Cf. Sess. V, cap. 2 de ref. et Sess. XXV decr. de indulg.

INDICTIO FUTURAE SESSIONIS

Sacrosancta oecumenica et generalis Tridentina synodus, in Spiritu Sancto legitime congregata, praesidentibus in ea eisdem Apostolicae Sedis legatis, statuit et decrevit, proximam futuram sessionem habendam et celebrandam esse feria quinta post octavam festi Nativitatis beatae Mariae Virginis, quae erit decima septima mensis Septembris proxime futuri; hoc tamen adjecto, quod dictum terminum, ac unicuique sessioni in posterum praefigendum, ipsa sancta synodus pro ejus arbitrio et voluntate, sicuti rebus concilii putaverit expedire, etiam in generali congregatione restringere et prorogare libere possit et valeat.

SESSIO VIGESIMA SECUNDA

QUAE EST SEXTA

SUB PIO IV PONT. MAX.

celebrata

die XVII Septembris, MDLXII

DOCTRINA DE SACRIFICIO MISSAE

Sacrosancta oecumenica et generalis Tridentina synodus in Spiritu Sancto legitime congregata, praesidentibus in ea eisdem Apostolicae Sedis legatis, ut vetus, absoluta atque omni ex parte perfecta de magno Eucharistiae mysterio in sancta catholica ecclesia fides atque doctrina retineatur, et in sua puritate propulsatis erroribus atque haeresibus conservetur, de ea, quatenus verum et singulare sacrificium est, Spiritus Sancti illustratione edocta haec, quae sequuntur, docet, declarat et fidelibus populis praedicanda decernit.

Caput I

DE INSTITUTIONE SACROSANCTI MISSAE SACRIFICII

Quoniam sub priori testamento, teste Apostolo Paulo, propter Levitici sacerdotii imbecillitatem consummatio non erat, oportuit, Deo Patre misericordiarum ita ordinante, *sacerdotem alium secundum ordinem Melchisedech surgere,*[1] Dominum nostrum Jesum Christum, qui posset omnes, quotquot sanctificandi essent, consummare et ad perfectum adducere. Is igitur Deus et Dominus noster, etsi semel se ipsum in ara crucis morte intercedente Deo Patri oblaturus erat, ut aeternam illic redemptionem operaretur, quia tamen per mortem sacerdotium ejus extinguendum non erat,[2] in coena novissima, qua nocte tradebatur, ut dilectae sponsae suae ecclesiae visibile, sicut hominum natura exigit, relinqueret sacrificium, quo cruentum illud

---

[1] Heb. 7:11. Rouët de Journel, *Enchiridion patristicum* sub rubrica "Eucharistia," p. 780, n.515; Denzinger, *Enchiridion*, XII h, p. [44].
[2] Heb. 7:24.

semel in cruce peragendum repraesentaretur, ejusque memoria in finem usque saeculi permaneret,[3] atque illius salutaris virtus in remissionem eorum, quae a nobis quotidie committuntur, peccatorum applicaretur, sacerdotem secundum ordinem Melchisedech se in aeternum constitutum declarans,[4] corpus et sanguinem suum sub speciebus panis et vini Deo patri obtulit, ac sub earumdem rerum symbolis apostolis, quos tunc novi testamenti sacerdotes constituebat, ut sumerent, tradidit, et eisdem eorumque in sacerdotio successoribus, ut offerent, praecepit per haec verba: *Hoc facite in meam commemorationem*,[5] uti semper catholica ecclesia intellexit et docuit. Nam celebrato veteri pascha, quod in memoriam exitus de Aegypto multitudo filiorum Israel immolabat,[6] novum instituit pascha se ipsum, ab ecclesia per sacerdotes sub signis visibilibus immolandum in memoriam transitus sui ex hoc mundo ad Patrem, quando per sui sanguinis effusionem nos redemit eripuitque de potestate tenebrarum [7] et in regnum suum transtulit. Et haec quidem illa munda oblatio est, quae nulla indignitate aut malitia offerentium inquinari potest; quam Dominus per Malachiam [8] nomini suo, quod magnum futurum esset in gentibus, in omni loco mundam offerendam praedixit, et quam non obscure innuit Apostolus Paulus Corinthiis scribens,[9] cum dicit, non posse eos, qui participatione mensae daemoniorum polluti sint, mensae Domini participes fieri, per mensam altare utrobique intelligens. Haec denique illa est, quae per varias sacrificiorum naturae et legis tempore similitudines figurabatur,[10] utpote quae bona omnia per illa significata velut illorum omnium consummatio et perfectio complectitur.

Caput II

SACRIFICIUM MISSAE EST PROPITIATORIUM TAM PRO VIVIS QUAM PRO DEFUNCTIS

Et quoniam in divino hoc sacrificio, quod in missa peragitur, idem ille Christus continetur et incruente immolatur, qui in ara crucis semel

[3] Cf. I Cor. 11:24 f.
[4] Ps. 109:4.
[5] Luc. 22:19; I Cor. *loc. cit.*
[6] Ex. 13.
[7] Col. 1:13.
[8] Mal. 1:11.
[9] Cf. I Cor. 10:21.
[10] Gen. 4:4, 12:8 et al.; cf. Rouët de Journel, p. 780, n. 514.

se ipsum cruente obtulit, docet sancta synodus, sacrificium istud vere propitiatorium esse, per ipsumque fieri, ut, si cum vero corde et recta fide, cum metu et reverentia, contriti ac poenitentes ad Deum accedamus, *misericordiam consequamur et gratiam inveniamus in auxilio opportuno.*[11] Hujus quippe oblatione placatus Dominus gratiam et donum poenitentiae concedens, crimina et peccata etiam ingentia dimittit. Una enim eademque est hostia, idem nunc offerens sacerdotum ministerio, qui se ipsum tunc in cruce obtulit, sola offerendi ratione diversa. Cujus quidem oblationis cruentae, inquam, fructus per hanc incruentam uberrime percipiuntur, tantum abest, ut illi per hanc quovis modo derogetur. Quare non solum pro fidelium vivorum peccatis, poenis, satisfactionibus et aliis necessitatibus, sed et pro defunctis in Christo nondum ad plenum purgatis rite juxta apostolorum traditionem offertur.[12]

Caput III

DE MISSA IN HONOREM SANCTORUM

Et quamvis in honorem et memoriam sanctorum nonnullas interdum missas ecclesia celebrare consueverit, non tamen illis sacrificium offerri docet, sed Deo soli, qui illos coronavit; [13] unde nec sacerdos dicere solet: Offero tibi sacrificium, Petre vel Paule, sed, Deo de illorum victoriis gratias, eorum patrocinia implorat, ut ipsi pro nobis intercedere dignentur in coelis, quorum memoriam facimus in terris.

Caput IV

DE CANONE MISSAE

Et cum sancta sancte administrari conveniat, sitque hoc omnium sanctissimum sacrificium, ecclesia catholica, ut digne reverenterque offerretur ac perciperetur, sacrum canonem multis ante saeculis instituit [14] ita ab omni errore purum, ut nihil in eo contineatur, quod non maxime sanctitatem ac pietatem quamdam redoleat, mentesque offerentium in Deum erigat. Is enim constat cum ex ipsis Domini verbis,

---

[11] Heb. 4:16.
[12] Cf. *infra*, can. 3 et Sess. XXV, decr. de purgatorio.
[13] *Ibid.*, can. 5 et Sess. cit., decr. de invocat. sanct.
[14] Cf. c.6, X, De celebr. miss., III, 41 (Innoc. III).

tum ex apostolorum traditionibus ac sanctorum quoque pontificum piis institutionibus.

Caput V

DE MISSAE CAEREMONIIS ET RITIBUS

Cumque natura hominum ea sit, ut non facile queat sine adminiculis exterioribus ad rerum divinarum meditationem sustolli, propterea pia mater ecclesia ritus quosdam, ut scilicet quaedam submissa voce, alia vero elatiore in missa pronunciarentur, instituit, caeremonias item adhibuit,[15] ut mysticas benedictiones, lumina, thymiamata, vestes aliaque id genus multa ex apostolica disciplina et traditione, quo et majestas tanti sacrificii commendaretur, et mentes fidelium per haec visibilia religionis et pietatis signa ad rerum altissimarum, quae in hoc sacrificio latent, contemplationem excitarentur.

Caput VI

DE MISSA, IN QUA SOLUS SACERDOS COMMUNICAT

Optaret quidem sacrosancta synodus, ut in singulis missis fideles adstantes non solum spirituali affectu, sed sacramentali etiam Eucharistiae perceptione communicarent, quo ad eos sanctissimi hujus sacrificii fructus uberior proveniret; nec tamen, si id non semper fiat, propterea missas illas, in quibus solus sacerdos sacramentaliter communicat, ut privatas et illicitas damnat, sed probat atque adeo commendat, siquidem illae quoque missae vere communes censeri debent; partim, quod in eis populus spiritualiter communicet, partim vero, quod a publico ecclesiae ministro non pro se tantum, sed pro omnibus fidelibus, quid ad corpus Christi pertinent, celebrentur.

Caput VII

DE AQUA MISCENDA VINO IN CALICE OFFERENDO

Monet deinde sancta synodus, praeceptum esse ab ecclesia sacerdotibus, ut aquam vino in calice offerendo miscerent,[16] tum quod Chris-

---

[15] Cf. *infra,* can. 7.

[16] Cc.4, 5, 7, D.II de cons; c.6, X, De celebr. miss., III, 41. Cf. *decr. Eugen. IV pro Armenis* apud Denzinger, n.698. Vide etiam *idem,* nn.416, 945.

tum Dominum ita fecisse credatur, tum etiam quia e latere ejus aqua simul cum sanguine exierit; [17] quod sacramentum hac mixtione recolitur, et, cum aquae in Apocalypsi beati Joannis populi dicantur,[18] ipsius populi fidelis cum capite Christo unio repraesentatur.

Caput VIII

MISSA VULGARI LINGUA NON CELEBRETUR. EJUS MYSTERIA POPULO EXPLICENTUR

Etsi missa magnam contineat populi fidelis eruditionem, non tamen expedire visum est patribus, ut vulgari passim lingua celebraretur. Quamobrem, retento ubique cujusque ecclesiae antiquo et a sancta Romana ecclesia omnium ecclesiarum matre et magistra probato ritu, ne oves Christi esuriant, neve parvuli panem petant [19] et non sit qui frangat eis, mandat sancta synodus pastoribus [20] et singulis curam animarum gerentibus, ut frequenter inter missarum celebrationem vel per se vel per alios ex iis, quae in missa leguntur, aliquid exponant, atque inter cetera sanctissimi hujus sacrificii mysterium aliquod declarent, diebus praesertim dominicis et festis.

Caput IX

PROLEGOMENON CANONUM SEQUENTIUM

Quia vero adversus veterem hanc in sacrosancto evangelio, apostolorum traditionibus sanctorumque patrum doctrina fundatam fidem hoc tempore multi disseminati sunt errores, multaque a multis docentur et disputantur, sancta synodus, post multos gravesque his de rebus mature habitos tractatus, unanimi omnium consensu quae huic purissimae fidei sacraeque doctrinae adversantur damnare et a sancta ecclesia eliminare per subjectos hos canones constituit.

---

[17] Joan. 19:34.
[18] Apoc. 17:1, 15.
[19] Thren. 4:4.
[20] Cf. Sess. V, cap. 2 de ref. et Sess. XXIV, cap. 7 de ref.

CANONES DE SACRIFICIO MISSAE

1. Si quis dixerit, in missa non offerri Deo verum et proprium sacrificium, aut quod offerri non sit aliud quam nobis Christum ad manducandum dari: anathema sit.

2. Si quis dixerit, illis verbis: *Hoc facite in meam commemorationem,*[21] Christum non instituisse apostolos sacerdotes,[22] aut non ordinasse, ut ipsi aliique sacerdotes offerrent corpus et sanguinem suum: anathema sit.

3. Si quis dixerit, missae sacrificium tantum esse laudis et gratiarum actionis, aut nudam commemorationem sacrificii in cruce peracti, non autem propitiatorium; [23] vel soli prodesse sumenti, neque pro vivis et defunctis pro peccatis, poenis, satisfactionibus et aliis necessitatibus offerri debere: anathema sit.

4. Si quis dixerit, blasphemiam irrogari sanctissimo Christi sacrificio in cruce peracto per missae sacrificium, aut illi per hoc derogari: anathema sit.

5. Si quis dixerit, imposturam esse missas celebrare in honorem sanctorum [24] et pro illorum intercessione apud Deum obtinenda, sicut ecclesia intendit: anathema sit.

6. Si quis dixerit, canonem missae errores continere,[25] ideoque abrogandum esse: anathema sit.

7. Si quis dixerit, caeremonias, vestes et externa signa, quibus in missarum celebratione ecclesia catholica utitur, irritabula impietatis esse magis quam officia pietatis: [26] anathema sit.

8. Si quis dixerit, missas, in quibus solus sacerdos sacramentaliter communicat,[27] illicitas esse ideoque abrogandas: anathema sit.

9. Si quis dixerit, ecclesiae Romanae ritum, quo submissa voce pars canonis et verba consecrationis proferuntur, damnandum esse; aut lingua tantum vulgari missam celebrari debere; [28] aut aquam non miscendam esse vino in calice offerendo,[29] eo quod sit contra Christi institutionem: anathema sit.

---

[21] Luc. 22:19; I Cor. 11:25.
[22] Cf. *supra,* cap. 1.
[23] *Ibid.,* cap. 2. Rouët de Journel, p. 780, n.520.
[24] *Ibid.,* cap. 3.
[25] *Ibid.,* cap. 4.
[26] *Ibid.,* cap. 5.
[27] *Ibid.,* cap. 6.
[28] *Ibid.,* cap. 8.
[29] *Ibid.,* cap. 7.

DECRETUM DE OBSERVANDIS ET EVITANDIS IN CELEBRATIONE MISSAE

Quanta cura adhibenda sit, ut sacrosanctum missae sacrificium omni religionis cultu ac veneratione celebretur, quivis facile existimare poterit, qui cogitarit, maledictum in sacris litteris eum vocari, qui facit opus Dei negligenter.[30] Quod si necessario fatemur, nullum aliud opus adeo sanctum ac divinum a Christi fidelibus tractari posse, quam hoc ipsum tremendum mysterium, quo vivifica illa hostia, qua Deo Patri reconciliati sumus, in altari per sacerdotes quotidie immolatur: satis etiam apparet, omnem operam et diligentiam in eo ponendam esse, ut quanta maxima fieri potest interiori cordis munditia et puritate atque exteriori devotionis ac pietatis specie peragatur.[31] Cum igitur multa jam sive temporum vitio, sive hominum incuria et improbitate irrepsisse videantur, quae a tanti sacrificii dignitate aliena sunt, ut ei debitus honor et cultus ad Dei gloriam et fidelis populi aedificationem restituatur, decernit sancta synodus, ut ordinarii locorum episcopi ea omnia prohibere atque e medio tollere sedulo curent ac teneantur, quae vel avaritia, idolorum servitus,[32] vel irreverentia, quae ab impietate vix sejuncta esse potest, vel superstitio, verae pietatis falsa imitatrix, induxit.

Atque ut multa paucis comprehendantur, in primis, quod ad avaritiam pertinet, cujusvis generis mercedum conditiones, pacta, et quidquid pro missis novis celebrandis datur, necnon importunas atque illiberales eleemosynarum exactiones potius quam postulationes, aliaque hujusmodi, quae a simoniaca labe vel certe a turpi quaestu non longe absunt, omnino prohibeant.

Deinde, ut irreverentia vitetur, singuli in suis dioecesibus interdicant, ne cui vago et ignoto sacerdoti missas celebrare liceat. Neminem praeterea, qui publice et notorie criminosus sit, aut sancto altari ministrare, aut sacris interesse permittant; neve patiantur privatis in domibus,[33] atque omnino extra ecclesiam, et ad divinum tantum cultum dedicata oratoria, ab eisdem ordinariis designanda et visitanda, sanctum hoc sacrificium a saecularibus aut regularibus quibuscumque peragi, ac nisi prius intersint decenter composito corporis habitu

[30] Jer. 48:10.
[31] Cf. Sess. XIII, cap. 7.
[32] Eph. 5:5.
[33] Cf. c.12, D.I de cons. (conc. Moguntien.), c.34, *ibid.* (Trullan.).

declaraverint, se mente etiam ac devoto cordis affectu, non solum corpore, adesse. Ab ecclesiis vero musicas eas, ubi sive organo sive cantu lascivum aut impurum aliquid miscetur, item saeculares omnes actiones, vana atque adeo profana colloquia, deambulationes, strepitus, clamores arceant, ut domus Dei vere domus orationis [34] esse videatur ac dici possit.

Postremo, ne superstitionis locus aliquis detur, edicto et poenis propositis caveant, ne sacerdotes aliis quam debitis horis celebrent, neve ritus alios aut alias caeremonias et preces in missarum celebratione adhibeant praeter eas, quae ab ecclesia probatae ac frequenti et laudabili usu receptae fuerint. Quarumdam vero missarum et candelarum certum numerum, qui magis a superstitioso cultu quam a vera religione inventus est, omnino ab ecclesia removeant, doceantque populum, quis sit et a quo potissimum proveniat sanctissimi hujus sacrificii tam pretiosus ac coelestis fructus. Moneant etiam eumdem populum, ut frequenter ad suas parochias, saltem diebus dominicis et majoribus festis, accedant.[35] Haec igitur omnia, quae summatim enumerata sunt, omnibus locorum ordinariis ita proponuntur, ut non solum ea ipsa, sed quaecumque alia huc pertinere visa fuerint, ipsi pro data sibi a sacrosancta synodo potestate, ac etiam ut delegati Sedis Apostolicae prohibeant, mandent, corrigant, statuant, atque ad ea inviolate servanda censuris ecclesiasticis aliisque poenis, quae illorum arbitrio constituentur, fidelem populum compellant; non obstantibus privilegiis, exemptionibus, appellationibus ac consuetudinibus quibuscumque.

DECRETUM DE REFORMATIONE

Eadem sacrosancta oecumenica et generalis Tridentina synodus, in Spiritu Sancto legitime congregata, praesidentibus in ea eisdem Apostolicae Sedis legatis, ut reformationis negotium prosequatur, haec in praesenti sessione statuenda censuit.

---

[34] Is. 56:7; Matt. 21:13.

[35] Cf. c.35, D.I de cons. (conc. Agathen.); cc.4, 5, C.IX, q.2 (Nanneten.); c.2, X, De paroch., III, 29 (idem).

Caput I

DECRETA DE VITA ET HONESTATE CLERICORUM INNOVANTUR

Nihil est, quod alios magis ad pietatem et Dei cultum assidue instruat, quam eorum vita et exemplum, qui se divino ministerio dedicarunt.[36] Cum enim a rebus saeculi in altiorem sublati locum conspiciantur, in eos tamquam in speculum reliqui oculos conjiciunt, ex iisque sumunt quod imitentur. Quapropter sic decet omnino clericos in sortem Domini vocatos [37] vitam moresque suos omnes componere, ut habitu, gestu, incessu, sermone, aliisque omnibus rebus nil nisi grave, moderatum ac religione plenum prae se ferant; levia etiam delicta, quae in ipsis maxima essent, effugiant, ut eorum actiones cunctis afferant venerationem. Cum igitur, quo majore in ecclesia Dei et utilitate et ornamento haec sunt, ita etiam diligentius sint observanda, statuit sancta synodus, ut quae alias a summis pontificibus et a sacris conciliis de clericorum vita, honestate, cultu doctrinaque retinenda, ac simul de luxu, comessationibus, choreis, aleis, lusibus, ac quibuscumque criminibus, necnon saecularibus negotiis fugiendis copiose ac salubriter sancita fuerunt, eadem in posterum iisdem poenis, vel majoribus arbitrio ordinarii imponendis observentur; [38] nec appellatio executionem hanc, quae ad morum correctionem pertinet, suspendat. Si qua vero ex his in desuetudinem abiisse compererint, ea quam primum in usum revocari et ab omnibus accurate custodiri studeant; non obstantibus consuetudinibus quibuscumque, ne subditorum neglectae emendationis ipsi condignas Deo vindice poenas persolvant.

Caput II

QUINAM AD CATHEDRALES ECCLESIAS ASSUMENDI

Quicumque posthac ad ecclesias cathedrales erit assumendus, is non solum natalibus, aetate, moribus et vita ac aliis, quae a sacris canonibus requiruntur,[39] plene sit praeditus, verum etiam in sacro ordine

[36] Cf. Sess. XXV, cap. 1 de ref.
[37] Cf. c. 1, D. XXI (Isid.).
[38] Cf. tot. tit. de vit. et hon. cler. apud Greg., in VI° et in Clem. (III, 1), et Sess. XXV in princ.
[39] C. 5, D. LI (conc. Toletan. IV); c. 7, X, De elect., I, 6 (Lat. III), c. 19, *ibid.* (Innoc. III); Sess. VII, cap. 1 de ref. et Sess. XXIV, capp. 1 et 12 de ref.

antea saltem sex mensium spatio constitutus. Quarum rerum instructio, si ejus notitia nulla aut recens in curia fuerit, a Sedis Apostolicae legatis seu nunciis provinciarum, aut ejus ordinario, eoque deficiente a vicinioribus ordinariis sumatur. Scientia vero praeter haec ejusmodi polleat, ut muneris sibi injungendi necessitati possit satisfacere. Ideoque antea in universitate studiorum magister sive doctor aut licentiatus in sacra theologia vel jure canonico merito sit promotus, aut publico alicujus academiae testimonio idoneus ad alios docendos ostendatur. Quod si regularis fuerit, a superioribus suae religionis similem fidem habeat. Praedicti autem omnes, unde instructio seu testificatio erit sumenda, haec fideliter et gratis referre teneantur; alioquin eorum conscientias graviter oneratas esse scient, ac Deum et superiores suos habebunt ultores.

Caput III

STATUENDAE DISTRIBUTIONES QUOTIDIANAE EX TERTIA PARTE QUORUMCUMQUE FRUCTUUM; PORTIO ABSENTIUM QUIBUS CEDAT; CERTI CASUS EXCEPTI

Episcopi, etiam tamquam delegati apostolici, ex fructibus et proventibus quibuscumque omnium dignitatum, personatuum et officiorum, in ecclesiis cathedralibus vel collegiatis exsistentium, tertiam partem in distributiones eorum arbitrio assignandas dividere possint,[40] ut scilicet qui eas obtinent, si personaliter competens sibi servitium juxta formam ab eisdem episcopis praescribendam quolibet die statuto non impleverint, illius diei distributionem amittant, nec ejus quoquo modo dominium acquirant, sed fabricae ecclesiae, quatenus indigeat, aut alteri pio loco arbitrio ordinarii applicetur. Crescente vero contumacia contra eos juxta sacrorum canonum constitutiones procedant.[41] Quod si alicui ex praedictis dignitatibus in ecclesiis cathedralibus vel collegiatis de jure seu consuetudine jurisdictio, administratio vel officium non competat, sed extra civitatem in dioecesi cura animarum immineat, cui is, qui dignitatem obtinet, incumbere voluerit, tunc pro tempore, quo in curata ecclesia resederit ac ministraverit, tamquam praesens sit ac divinis intersit, in ecclesiis cathedralibus ac col-

---

[40] Cf. Sess. XXI, cap. 3 de ref.
[41] Cf. Sess. et cap. cit.

legiatis habeatur. Haec in iis tantum ecclesiis constituta intelligantur, in quibus nulla est consuetudo vel statutum, ut dictae dignitates non servientes aliquid amittant, quod ad tertiam partem dictorum fructuum et proventuum ascendat; non obstantibus consuetudinibus, etiam immemorabilibus, exemptionibus et constitutionibus, etiam juramento et quavis auctoritate firmatis.

Caput IV

IN ECCLESIA CATHEDRALI VEL COLLEGIATA SACRO ORDINE NON INITIATI VOCEM IN CAPITULO NON HABEANT. QUALITATES ET ONERA OBTINENTIUM BENEFICIA IN ILLIS

Quicumque in cathedrali vel collegiata, saeculari vel regulari ecclesia, divinis mancipatus officiis, in subdiaconatus ordine saltem constitutus non sit, vocem in hujusmodi ecclesiis in capitulo non habeat, etiamsi hoc sibi ab aliis libere fuerit concessum. Ii vero, qui dignitates, personatus, officia, praebendas, portiones ac quaelibet alia beneficia in dictis ecclesiis obtinent aut in posterum obtinebunt, quibus onera varia sunt annexa, videlicet ut alii missas, alii evangelium, alii epistolas dicant seu cantent, quocumque ii privilegio, exemptione, praerogativa, generis nobilitate sint insigniti, teneantur justo impedimento cessante infra annum ordines suscipere requisitos; alioquin poenas incurrant juxta constitutionem concilii Viennensis, quae incipit: *Ut ii, qui,*[42] quam praesenti decreto innovat. Cogantque episcopi eos diebus statutis dictos ordines per se ipsos exercere,[43] ac cetera omnia officia, quae debent, in cultu divino praestare, sub eisdem et aliis etiam gravioribus poenis, arbitrio eorum imponendis. Nec aliis in posterum fiat provisio, nisi iis, qui jam aetatem et ceteras habilitates integre habere dignoscantur; aliter irrita sit provisio.

---

[42] C. 2, De aet. et qual. et ord. praef. in Clem., I, 6, *infra,* p. 566, lit. Q.
[43] Cf. Sess. XXIV, cap. 12 de ref.

Caput V

DISPENSATIONES EXTRA CURIAM EPISCOPO COMMITTANTUR ET AB EO EXAMINENTUR

Dispensationes, quacumque auctoritate concedendae, si extra Romanam curiam committendae erunt, committantur ordinariis illorum, qui eas impetraverint; eae vero, quae gratiose concedentur, suum non sortiantur effectum, nisi prius ab eisdem tamquam delegatis apostolicis summarie tantum et extrajudicialiter cognoscatur, expressas preces subreptionis vel obreptionis vitio non subjacere.

Caput VI

CIRCUMSPECTE COMMUTANDAE ULTIMAE VOLUNTATES

In commutationibus ultimarum voluntatum, quae non nisi ex justa et necessaria causa fieri debent,[44] episcopi, tamquam delegati Sedis Apostolicae, summarie et extrajudicialiter cognoscant, nihil in precibus tacita veritate vel suggesta falsitate fuisse narratum, priusquam commutationes praedictae executioni demandentur.

Caput VII

INNOVATUR CAP. *ROMANA* DE APPELLATIONIBUS IN SEXTO

Legati et nuncii apostolici, patriarchae ac primates et metropolitani in appellationibus ad eos interpositis in quibusvis causis, tam in admittendis appellationibus quam in concedendis inhibitionibus post appellationem servare teneantur formam et tenorem sacrarum constitutionum, et praesertim Innocentii IV, quae incipit: *Romana;*[45] quacumque consuetudine, etiam immemorabili, aut stylo vel privilegio in contrarium non obstantibus. Aliter inhibitiones et processus et inde secuta quaecumque sint ipso jure nulla.

[44] Cf. Sess. XXV, cap. 4 de ref.
[45] C. 3, VI°, De appell., II, 15, *infra*, p. 567, lit. R.

Caput VIII

EPISCOPI PIAS OMNIUM DISPOSITIONES EXSEQUANTUR; QUAECUMQUE PIA LOCA VISITENT, DUMMODO NON SUB IMMEDIATA REGUM PROTECTIONE SINT

Episcopi,[46] etiam tamquam Sedis Apostolicae delegati, in casibus a jure concessis omnium piarum dispositionum tam in ultima voluntate quam inter vivos sint executores; habeant jus visitandi hospitalia, collegia quaecumque ac confraternitates laicorum, etiam quas scholas sive quocumque alio nomine vocant (non tamen quae sub regum immediata protectione sunt, sine eorum licentia), eleemosynas montis pietatis sive caritatis, et pia loca omnia, quomodocumque nuncupentur, etiamsi praedictorum locorum cura ad laicos pertineat, atque eadem pia loca exemptionis privilegio sint munita; ac omnia, quae ad Dei cultum aut animarum salutem seu pauperes sustentandos instituta sunt, ipsi ex officio suo juxta sacrorum canonum statuta cognoscant et exequantur,[47] non obstantibus quacumque consuetudine, etiam immemorabili, privilegio aut statuto.

Caput IX

ADMINISTRATORES QUORUMCUMQUE PIORUM LOCORUM REDDANT RATIONEM ORDINARIO, NISI ALITER IN FUNDATIONE SIT CAUTUM

Administratores tam ecclesiastici quam laici fabricae cujusvis ecclesiae, etiam cathedralis, hospitalis,[48] confraternitatis, eleemosynae montis pietatis et quorumcumque piorum locorum,[49] singulis annis teneantur reddere rationem administrationis ordinario; consuetudinibus et privilegiis quibuscumque in contrarium sublatis, nisi secus forte in institutione et ordinatione talis ecclesiae seu fabricae expresse cautum esset. Quod si ex consuetudine aut privilegio, aut ex constitutione aliqua loci aliis ad id deputatis ratio reddenda esset, tunc cum

---

[46] Cf. c.2, De relig. dom. in Clem., III, 11.
[47] Cf. c.6, X, De test. et ult. vol., III, 26 (conc. Moguntien.), cc.3, 17, 19, *ibid.* (Greg. IX).
[48] Cf. Sess. VII, cap. 15 de ref.
[49] Cf. c.2 De relig. dom. in Clem., III, 11 et Sess. XXV, cap. 8 de ref.

iis adhibeatur etiam ordinarius, et aliter factae liberationes dictis administratoribus minime suffragentur.

Caput X

NOTARII EPISCOPORUM EXAMINI ET JUDICIO SUBJACEANT

Cum ex notariorum imperitia plurima damna et multarum occasio litium oriatur, possit episcopus quoscumque notarios, etiamsi apostolica, imperiali aut regia auctoritate creati fuerint, etiam tamquam delegatus Sedis Apostolicae, examinatione adhibita eorum sufficientiam scrutari, illisque non idoneis repertis, aut quandocumque in officio delinquentibus, officii ejus in negotiis, litibus et causis ecclesiasticis ac spiritualibus exercendi usum perpetuo aut ad tempus prohibere. Neque eorum appellatio interdictionem ordinarii suspendat.

Caput XI

BONORUM CUJUSCUMQUE ECCLESIAE AUT PII LOCI OCCUPATORES PUNIUNTUR

Si quem clericorum vel laicorum, quacumque is dignitate, etiam imperiali aut regali, praefulgeat, in tantum malorum omnium radix cupiditas occupaverit,[50] ut alicujus ecclesiae, seu cujusvis saecularis vel regularis beneficii, montium pietatis, aliorumque piorum locorum jurisdictiones, bona, census ac jura, etiam feudalia et emphyteutica, fructus, emolumenta, seu quascumque obventiones, quae in ministrorum et pauperum necessitates converti debent, per se vel alios vi vel timore incusso, seu etiam per suppositas personas clericorum aut laicorum, seu quacumque arte aut quocumque quaesito colore in proprios usus convertere, illosque usurpare praesumpserit, seu impedire, ne ab iis, ad quos jure pertinent, percipiantur, is anathemati tamdiu subjaceat, quamdiu jurisdictiones, bona, res, jura, fructus et reditus, quos occupaverit, vel qui ad eum quomodocumque, etiam ex donatione suppositae personae, pervenerit, ecclesiae ejusque administratori sive beneficiato integre restituerit, ac deinde a Romano pontifice absolutionem obtinuerit. Quod si ejusdem ecclesiae patronus fuerit,

---

[50] Cf. I Tim. 6:10.

etiam jure patronatus ultra praedictas poenas eo ipso privatus exsistat. Clericus vero, qui nefandae fraudis et usurpationis hujusmodi fabricator seu consentiens fuerit, eisdem poenis subjaceat, necnon quibuscumque beneficiis privatus sit, et ad quaecumque alia beneficia inhabilis efficiatur, et a suorum ordinum executione etiam post integram satisfactionem et absolutionem sui ordinarii arbitrio suspendatur.

DECRETUM SUPER PETITIONE CONCESSIONIS CALICIS

Insuper, cum eadem sacrosancta synodus superiori sessione duos articulos alias propositos,[51] et tum nondum discussos, videlicet: an rationes, quibus sancta catholica ecclesia adducta fuit, ut communicaret laicos atque etiam non celebrantes sacerdotes sub una panis specie, ita sint retinendae, ut nulla ratione calicis usus cuiquam sit permittendus; et, an, si honestis et Christianae caritati consentaneis rationibus concedendus alicui vel nationi vel regno calicis usus videatur, sub aliquibus conditionibus concedendus sit, et quaenam illae sint, in aliud tempus oblata sibi occasione examinandos atque definiendos reservaverit: nunc, eorum, pro quibus petitur, saluti optime consultum volens, decrevit, integrum negotium ad sanctissimum dominum nostrum esse referendum, prout praesenti decreto refert, qui pro sua singulari prudentia id efficiat, quod utile reipublicae Christianae et salutare petentibus usum calicis fore judicaverit.

INDICTIO FUTURAE SESSIONIS

Insuper eadem sacrosancta Tridentina synodus diem futurae sessionis ad feriam quintam post octavam festivitatis omnium sanctorum, quae erit dies duodecima mensis Novembris, indicit, et in ea decernetur de sacramento ordinis, et de sacramento matrimonii, etc.

Prorogata fuit sessio usque ad diem XV Julii, MDLXIII.

---

[51] Cf. Sess. XIII in decr. prorog. et Sess. XXI post can. 4.

SESSIO VIGESIMA TERTIA

QUAE EST SEPTIMA

SUB PIO IV PONT. MAX.

celebrata

die XV Julii, MDLXIII

VERA ET CATHOLICA DOCTRINA DE SACRAMENTO ORDINIS, AD CONDEMNANDOS ERRORES NOSTRI TEMPORIS, A SANCTA SYNODO TRIDENTINA DECRETA ET PUBLICATA SESSIONE SEPTIMA

CAPUT I

DE INSTITUTIONE SACERDOTII NOVAE LEGIS

Sacrificium et sacerdotium ita Dei ordinatione conjuncta sunt, ut utrumque in omni lege exstiterit. Cum igitur in novo testamento sanctum Eucharistiae sacrificium visibile ex Domini institutione catholica ecclesia acceperit, fateri etiam oportet, in ea novum esse visibile et externum sacerdotium, in quod vetus translatum est.[1] Hoc autem ab eodem Domino Salvatore nostro institutum esse, atque apostolis eorumque successoribus in sacerdotio potestatem traditam consecrandi, offerendi et ministrandi corpus et sanguinem ejus, necnon et peccata dimittendi et retinendi, sacrae litterae ostendunt[2] et catholicae ecclesiae traditio semper docuit.

CAPUT II

DE SEPTEM ORDINIBUS

Cum autem divina res sit tam sancti sacerdotii ministerium consentaneum fuit, quo dignius et majori cum veneratione exerceri posset,

[1] Heb. 7:12.

[2] Matt. 16:19; 26:26–28; Marc. 14:22–24; Luc. 22:19 f.; Joan. 20:22 f.; I Cor. 11:24 f.

ut in ecclesiae ordinatissima dispositione plures et diversi essent ministrorum ordines, qui sacerdotio ex officio deservirent, ita distributi, ut qui jam clericali tonsura insigniti essent per minores ad majores ascenderent.[3] Nam non solum de sacerdotibus, sed et de diaconis sacrae litterae apertam mentionem faciunt,[4] et quae maxime in illorum ordinatione attendenda sunt gravissimis verbis docent, et ab ipso ecclesiae initio sequentium ordinum nomina, atque uniuscujusque eorum propria ministeria, subdiaconi scilicet, acolythi, exorcistae, lectoris et ostiarii in usu fuisse cognoscuntur, quamvis non pari gradu; nam subdiaconatus ad majores ordines a patribus et sacris conciliis refertur, in quibus et de aliis inferioribus frequentissime legimus.[5]

Caput III

ORDINEM VERE ESSE SACRAMENTUM

Cum scripturae testimonio, apostolica traditione et patrum unanimi consensu perspicuum sit, per sacram ordinationem, quae verbis et signis exterioribus perficitur, gratiam conferri, dubitare nemo debet, ordinem esse vere et proprie unum ex septem sanctae ecclesiae sacramentis. Inquit enim Apostolus: *Admoneo te, ut resuscites gratiam Dei, quae est in te per impositionem manuum mearum. Non enim dedit nobis Deus spiritum timoris, sed virtutis et dilectionis et sobrietatis.*[6]

Caput IV

DE ECCLESIASTICA HIERARCHIA ET ORDINATIONE

Quoniam vero in sacramento ordinis, sicut et in baptismo et confirmatione character imprimitur, qui nec deleri nec auferri potest,[7]

[3] Cf. *infra,* can. 2 et cap. 17 de ref.

[4] Act. 6:5; 21:8; I Tim. 3:8–12.

[5] Cf. Tertul., *De praescr.*, c.41; Cyprian., *Epp.* 29, 38 (ed. Hartel); *Epist.* Cornelii I ad Fabium episc. Antiochenum a.251 (Denzinger, n.45); conc. Eliberitan. (*ca.* a.305), c.33; Antiochen. (a.341), c.10; Statuta eccl. antiq. (Denzinger, nn.153–58); cc.11, 12, D.XXXII (Urban. II), c.13, *ibid.* (conc. Carthag. V), c.14, *ibid.* (Leo IX), c.16, *ibid.* (Nicaen. I); c.4, D.LX (Urban. II); c.9, X, De aet. et qual. et ord. praef., I, 14 (Innoc. III).

[6] Cf. II Tim. 1:6 f. Rouët de Journel, *Enchiridion patristicum* sub rubrica "Ordo," p. 782, n.553.

[7] Cf. Sess. VII, can. 9 de sacr. in genere et *infra,* can. 4. Rouët de Journel, p. 782, n.567.

merito sancta synodus damnat eorum sententiam, qui asserunt, novi testamenti sacerdotes temporariam tantummodo potestatem habere, et semel rite ordinatos iterum laicos effici posse, si verbi Dei ministerium non exerceant. Quod si quis omnes Christianos promiscue novi testamenti sacerdotes esse, aut omnes pari inter se potestate spirituali praeditos affirmet, nihil aliud facere videtur, quam ecclesiasticam hierarchiam,[8] quae est ut *castrorum acies ordinata,*[9] confundere; perinde ac si contra beati Pauli doctrinam omnes apostoli, omnes prophetae, omnes evangelistae, omnes pastores, omnes sint doctores.[10] Proinde sacrosancta synodus declarat, praeter ceteros ecclesiasticos gradus episcopos, qui in apostolorum locum successerunt, ad hunc hierarchicum ordinem praecipue pertinere, et positos, sicut idem Apostolus ait, a Spiritu Sancto regere ecclesiam Dei,[11] eosque presbyteris superiores esse, ac sacramentum confirmationis conferre,[12] ministros ecclesiae ordinare, atque alia pleraque peragere ipsos posse, quarum functionum potestatem reliqui inferioris ordinis nullam habent. Docet insuper sacrosancta synodus, in ordinatione episcoporum, sacerdotum et ceterorum ordinum nec populi, nec cujusvis saecularis potestatis et magistratus consensum sive vocationem sive auctoritatem ita requiri, ut sine ea irrita sit ordinatio; [13] quin potius decernit, eos, qui tantummodo a populo aut saeculari potestate ac magistratu vocati et instituti ad haec ministeria exercenda ascendunt, et qui ea propria temeritate sibi sumunt, omnes non ecclesiae ministros, sed fures et latrones per ostium non ingressos habendos esse.[14]

Haec sunt, quae generatim sacrae synodo visum est Christi fideles de sacramento ordinis docere. His autem contraria certis et propriis canonibus in hunc, qui sequitur, modum damnare constituit, ut omnes adjuvante Christo fidei regula utentes in tot errorum tenebris catholicam veritatem facilius agnoscere et tenere possint.

---

[8] Cf. *infra,* can. 6.
[9] Cant. 6:3, 9.
[10] Cf. I Cor. 12:28 ff.; Eph. 4:11.
[11] Act. 20:28.
[12] Cf. Sess. VII de confirm., can. 3.
[13] Conc. Laodicen. (a.343–381), c.13.
[14] Joan. 10:1.

CANONES DE SACRAMENTO ORDINIS

1. Si quis dixerit, non esse in novo testamento sacerdotium visibile et externum,[15] vel non esse potestatem aliquam consecrandi et offerendi verum corpus et sanguinem Domini, et peccata remittendi et retinendi,[16] sed officium tantum et nudum ministerium praedicandi evangelium; vel eos, qui non praedicant, prorsus non esse sacerdotes: anathema sit.

2. Si quis dixerit, praeter sacerdotium non esse in ecclesia catholica alios ordines,[17] et majores et minores, per quos velut per gradus quosdam in sacerdotium tendatur: [18] anathema sit.

3. Si quis dixerit, ordinem sive sacram ordinationem non esse vere et proprie sacramentum a Christo Domino institutum,[19] vel esse figmentum quoddam humanum, excogitatum a viris rerum ecclesiasticarum imperitis, aut esse tantum ritum quemdam eligendi ministros verbi Dei et sacramentorum: anathema sit.

4. Si quis dixerit, per sacram ordinationem non dari Spiritum Sanctum, ac proinde frustra episcopos dicere: *Accipe Spiritum Sanctum;* aut per eam non imprimi characterem; vel eum, qui sacerdos semel fuit, laicum rursus fieri posse: anathema sit.

5. Si quis dixerit, sacram unctionem, qua ecclesia in sancta ordinatione utitur, non tantum non requiri, sed contemnendam et perniciosam esse, similiter et alias ordinis caeremonias: anathema sit.

6. Si quis dixerit, in ecclesia catholica non esse hierarchiam divina ordinatione institutam, quae constat ex episcopis, presbyteris et ministris: anathema sit.

7. Si quis dixerit, episcopos non esse presbyteris superiores, vel non habere potestatem confirmandi et ordinandi; vel eam, quam habent, illis esse cum presbyteris communem; vel ordines ab ipsis collatos sine populi vel potestatis saecularis consensu aut vocatione irritos esse; aut eos, qui nec ab ecclesiastica et canonica potestate rite ordinati, nec missi sunt, sed aliunde veniunt, legitimos esse verbi et sacramentorum ministros: anathema sit.

8. Si quis dixerit, episcopos, qui auctoritate Romani pontificis as-

---

[15] Cf. *supra,* cap. 1.
[16] Matt. 16:19; Luc. 22:19 f.; c.5, C.XXIV, q.1 (Leo I), c.6, *ibid.* (Aug.).
[17] Cf. *supra,* cap. 2.
[18] C.2, D.LXXVII (Zosim.), c.3, *ibid.* (Siric.); cf. *infra,* cap. 13 de ref.
[19] Cf. *supra,* cap. 3.

sumuntur, non esse legitimos et veros episcopos, sed figmentum humanum: anathema sit.

DECRETUM DE REFORMATIONE

Eadem sacrosancta Tridentina synodus, reformationis materiam prosequens, haec, quae sequuntur, in praesenti decernenda esse statuit et decernit.

CAPUT I

RECTORUM ECCLESIARUM IN RESIDENDO NEGLIGENTIA VARIE COERCETUR; ANIMARUM CURAE PROVIDETUR

Cum praecepto divino mandatum sit omnibus, quibus animarum cura commissa est, oves suas agnoscere,[20] pro his sacrificium offerre, verbique divini praedicatione, sacramentorum administratione ac bonorum omnium operum exemplo pascere, pauperum aliarumque miserabilium personarum curam paternam gerere, et in cetera munia pastoralia incumbere, quae omnia nequaquam ab iis praestari et impleri possunt, qui gregi suo non invigilant neque assistunt, sed mercenariorum more deserunt: [21] sacrosancta synodus eos admonet et hortatur, ut divinorum praeceptorum memores factique forma gregis [22] in judicio et veritate pascant et regant. Ne vero ea, quae de residentia sancte et utiliter jam antea sub fel. rec. Paulo III sancita fuerunt,[23] in sensus a sacrosanctae synodi mente alienos trahantur, ac si vigore illius decreti quinque mensibus continuis abesse liceat, illis inhaerendo declarat sacrosancta synodus, omnes patriarchalibus, primatialibus, metropolitanis ac cathedralibus ecclesiis quibuscumque quocumque nomine et titulo praefectos, etiamsi sanctae Romanae ecclesiae cardinales sint, obligari ad personalem in sua ecclesia vel dioecesi residentiam, ubi injuncto sibi officio defungi teneantur, neque abesse posse, nisi ex causis et modis infra scriptis.

Nam cum Christiana caritas, urgens necessitas, debita obedientia ac evidens ecclesiae vel reipublicae utilitas aliquos nonnunquam abesse postulent et exigant, decernit eadem sacrosancta synodus, has legitime

[20] Joan. 10:1–16; 21:15–17; Act. 20:28.
[21] Joan. 10:12 f.
[22] Cf. I Pet. 5:3.
[23] Cf. Sess. VI, capp. 1 et 2 de ref.

absentiae causas a beatissimo Romano pontifice, aut metropolitano vel, eo absente, suffraganeo episcopo antiquiori residente, qui idem metropolitani absentiam probare debebit, in scriptis esse approbandas, nisi cum absentia inciderit propter aliquod munus et reipublicae officium episcopatibus adjunctum, cujus quoniam causae sunt notoriae et interdum repentinae, ne eas quidem significari metropolitano necesse erit. Ad eumdem tamen cum concilio provinciali spectabit judicare de licentiis a se vel a suffraganeo datis, et videre, ne quis eo jure abutatur, et ut poenis canonicis errantes puniantur. Interea meminerint discessuri, ita ovibus suis providendum, ut, quantum fieri poterit, ex ipsorum absentia nullum damnum accipiant.[24] Quoniam autem qui aliquantisper tantum absunt ex veterum canonum sententia non videntur abesse, quia statim reversuri sunt: [25] sacrosancta synodus vult, illud absentiae spatium singulis annis, sive continuum sive interruptum, extra praedictas causas nullo pacto debere duos aut ad summum tres menses excedere, et haberi rationem, ut id aequa ex causa fiat et absque ullo gregis detrimento; quod an ita sit, abscedentium conscientiae relinquit, quam sperat religiosam et timoratam fore, cum Deo corda pateant,[26] cujus opus non fraudulenter agere [27] suo periculo tenentur. Eosdem interim admonet et in Domino hortatur, ne per illius temporis spatium dominici Adventus, Quadragesimae, Nativitatis, Resurrectionis Domini, Pentecostes item et Corporis Christi diebus, quibus refici maxime et in Domino gaudere pastoris praesentia oves debeant, ipsi ab ecclesia sua cathedrali ullo pacto absint,[28] nisi episcopalia munia in sua dioecesi eos alio vocent.

Si quis autem, quod utinam nunquam eveniat, contra hujus decreti dispositionem abfuerit, statuit sacrosancta synodus, praeter alias poenas adversus non residentes sub Paulo III impositas et innovatas,[29] ac mortalis peccati reatum, quem incurrit, eum pro rata temporis

---

[24] C.34, VI°, De elect., I, 6 (Bonif. VIII); Sess. VI, cap. 2 de ref. in fin.

[25] Cf. conc. Sardicen. cc.11 et 12 (al. 14 et 15), quibus episcopo per tres hebdomadas a propria dioecesi abesse concedebatur.

[26] Ps. 7:10; Act. 1:24.

[27] Jer. 48:10.

[28] C.29, C.VII, q.1 clericum ad triennium a communione suspendebat, qui diebus solemnibus, sc. Nativitatis, Epiphaniae, Paschatis, vel Pentecostis sine justa causa ab ecclesia sua defuerit. Apud Gratianum et alios hoc cap. sub nomine can. 64 conc. Agathensis laudatur. At hoc concilium non nisi 47 canones edidit; reliqui omnes recentiori manu ex conciliis posterioribus adjecti fuerunt. Probabiliter referendus est textus praesens ad can. 15 conc. Arvernensis a.535 habiti. Cf. Hardouin II, p. 1003, adn. post can. 47. De conc. Arvernensi, *idem*, II, pp. 1179 ff.

[29] Cf. Sess. VI, cap. 1 de ref.

absentiae fructus suos non facere, nec tuta conscientia, alia etiam declaratione non secuta, illos sibi detinere posse, sed teneri, aut ipso cessante, per superiorem ecclesiasticum, illos fabricae ecclesiarum aut pauperibus loci erogare, prohibita quacumque conventione vel compositione, quae pro fructibus male perceptis appellatur, ex qua etiam praedicti fructus in totum, aut pro parte ei remitterentur; non obstantibus quibuscumque privilegiis cuicumque collegio aut fabricae concessis.

Eadem omnino, etiam quoad culpam, amissionem fructuum et poenas, de curatis inferioribus [30] et aliis quibuscumque, qui beneficium aliquod ecclesiasticum curam animarum habens obtinent, sacrosancta synodus declarat et decernit; ita tamen, ut, quandocumque eos causa prius per episcopum cognita et probata, abesse contigerit, vicarium idoneum ab ipso ordinario approbandum cum debita mercedis assignatione relinquant. Discedendi autem licentiam in scriptis gratisque concedendam ultra bimestre tempus nisi ex gravi causa non obtineant. Quod si per edictum citati, etiam non personaliter, contumaces fuerint, liberum esse vult ordinariis, per censuras ecclesiasticas et sequestrationem et subtractionem fructuum, aliaque juris remedia, etiam usque ad privationem, compellere, nec executionem hanc quolibet privilegio, licentia, familiaritate, exemptione, etiam ratione cujuscumque beneficii, pactione, statuto, etiam juramento vel quacumque auctoritate confirmato, consuetudine, etiam immemorabili, quae potius corruptela censenda est, sive appellatione aut inhibitione, etiam in Romana curia, vel vigore Eugenianae constitutionis [31] suspendi posse.

Postremo tam decretum illud sub Paulo III,[32] quam hoc ipsum in conciliis provincialibus et episcopalibus publicari sancta synodus praecipit. Cupit enim quae adeo ex pastorum munere animarumque salute sunt frequenter omnium auribus mentibusque infigi, ut in posterum Deo juvante nulla temporum injuria aut hominum oblivione aut desuetudine aboleantur.

---

[30] Sess. VI, cap. 2 de ref.
[31] C. 3, Extrav. comm., De privil., V, 7, *infra*, p. 568, lit. S.
[32] Cf. Sess. cit., cap. 1 de ref.

Caput II

ECCLESIIS PRAEFECTI CONSECRATIONIS MUNUS INTRA TRES MENSES SUSCIPIANT; CONSECRATIO QUO LOCO PERAGENDA

Ecclesiis cathedralibus seu superioribus quocumque nomine ac titulo praefecti, etiamsi sanctae Romanae ecclesiae cardinales sint, si munus consecrationis intra tres menses non susceperint,[33] ad fructuum perceptorum restitutionem teneantur; si intra totidem menses postea id facere neglexerint, ecclesiis ipso jure sint privati. Consecratio vero, si extra curiam Romanam fiat, in ecclesia, ad quam promoti fuerint, aut in provincia, si commode fieri poterit, celebretur.

Caput III

EPISCOPI EXTRA AEGRITUDINEM PER SE ORDINES CONFERANT

Episcopi per semetipsos ordines conferant. Quod si aegritudine fuerint impediti, subditos suos non aliter quam jam probatos et examinatos ad alium episcopum ordinandos dimittant.[34]

Caput IV

QUI PRIMA TONSURA INITIANDI

Prima tonsura non initientur qui sacramentum confirmationis non susceperint, et fidei rudimenta edocti non fuerint, quique legere et scribere nesciant,[35] et de quibus probabilis conjectura non sit, eos non saecularis judicii fugiendi fraude, sed, ut Deo fidelem cultum praestent, hoc vitae genus elegisse.

Caput V

ORDINANDI QUIBUS INSTRUCTI ESSE DEBEANT

Ad minores ordines promovendi bonum a parocho et a magistro scholae, in qua educantur, testimonium habeant. Hi vero, qui ad

[33] Hoc temporis spatium a conc. Chalcedonen. in can. 25 praescriptum fuit (c.2, D.LXXV). Vide etiam c.2 conc. Ravennen. (a.877) in c.1 (§ 1), D.C (Hardouin, VI, P. I, p. 185), et Sess. VII, cap. 9 de ref.
[34] Cf. *infra*, capp. 8 et 10; conc. Carthag. III (a. 397), c.22. Hardouin, I, 963.
[35] C. ult. VI°, De temp. ord., I, 9 (Bonif. VIII).

singulos majores erunt assumendi, per mensem ante ordinationem episcopum adeant, qui parocho aut alteri, cui magis expedire videbitur, committat, ut nominibus ac desiderio eorum, qui volent promoveri, publice in ecclesia propositis, de ipsorum ordinandorum natalibus, aetate, moribus et vita a fide dignis diligenter inquirat,[36] et litteras testimoniales, ipsam inquisitionem factam continentes, ad ipsum episcopum quam primum transmittat.[37]

Caput VI

AETAS QUATUORDECIM ANNORUM AD BENEFICIUM ECCLESIASTICUM REQUIRITUR; QUIS PRIVILEGIO FORI GAUDERE DEBEAT

Nullus prima tonsura initiatus aut etiam in minoribus ordinibus constitutus, ante decimum quartum annum beneficium possit obtinere.[38] Is etiam fori privilegio non gaudeat,[39] nisi beneficium ecclesiasticum habeat, aut clericalem habitum et tonsuram deferens alicui ecclesiae ex mandato episcopi inserviat, vel in seminario clericorum aut in aliqua schola vel universitate de licentia episcopi quasi in via ad majores ordines suscipiendos versetur. In clericis vero conjugatis servetur constitutio Bonifacii VIII, quae incipit: *Clerici, qui cum unicis*,[40] modo hi clerici, alicujus ecclesiae servitio vel ministerio ab episcopo deputati, eidem ecclesiae serviant vel ministrent, et clericali habitu et tonsura utantur; nemini quoad hoc privilegio vel consuetudine, etiam immemorabili, suffragante.

Caput VII

EXAMINANDI SUNT ORDINANDI A VIRIS PERITIS JURIS DIVINI ET HUMANI

Sancta synodus antiquorum canonum [41] vestigiis inhaerendo decernit, ut, quando episcopus ordinationem facere disposuerit, omnes, qui ad sacrum ministerium accedere voluerint, feria quarta ante ipsam ordinationem, vel quando episcopo videbitur, ad civitatem evocentur.

---

[36] C.5, D.XXIV, qui est cap. 11 conc. Nanneten. a.658 habiti.
[37] Cf. *infra*, cap. 7.
[38] Cf. c.3, X, De aet. et qual. et ord. praef., I, 14 (Alex. III).
[39] C.7, X, De cler. conjug., III, 3 (Innoc. III).
[40] C. un. h.t. in VI°, III, 2, *infra*, p. 569, lit. T.
[41] Cf. *supra*, adn. 36.

Episcopus autem, sacerdotibus et aliis prudentibus viris peritis divinae legis ac in ecclesiasticis sanctionibus exercitatis sibi adscitis, ordinandorum genus, personam, aetatem, institutionem, mores, doctrinam et fidem diligenter investiget et examinet.[42]

Caput VIII

QUOMODO ET A QUO UNUSQUISQUE PROMOVERI DEBEAT

Ordinationes sacrorum ordinum statutis a jure temporibus [43] ac in cathedrali ecclesia, vocatis praesentibusque ad id ecclesiae canonicis, publice celebrentur; si autem in alio dioecesis loco, praesente clero loci, dignior, quantum fieri poterit, ecclesia semper adeatur. Unusquisque autem a proprio episcopo ordinetur.[44] Quod si quis ab alio promoveri petat, nullatenus id ei, etiam cujusvis generalis aut specialis rescripti vel privilegii praetextu, etiam statutis temporibus, permittatur, nisi ejus probitas ac mores ordinarii sui testimonio commendentur.[45] Si secus fiat, ordinans a collatione ordinum per annum, et ordinatus a susceptorum ordinum executione, quamdiu proprio ordinario videbitur expedire, sit suspensus.

Caput IX

EPISCOPUS FAMILIAREM ORDINANS CONFERAT STATIM BENEFICIUM RE IPSA

Episcopus familiarem suum non subditum ordinare non possit, nisi per triennium secum fuerit commoratus et beneficium, quacumque fraude cessante, statim re ipsa illi conferat; [46] consuetudine quacumque, etiam immemorabili, in contrarium non obstante.

[42] *Supra,* cap. 5 de ref.
[43] Cf. c.7, D.LXXV (Gelas.) et cc.1–3, X, De temp. ord., I, 11 (Alex. III).
[44] Cf. c.1, D.LXXI (conc. Sardicen.), c.2, *ibid.* (Innoc. I), c.3, *ibid.* (Nicaen. I), c.4, *ibid.* (conc. Chalc.); c.2, D.LXXII (Carthag. III); cc.6, 7, C.IX, q.2 (Antiochen.), c.9, *ibid.* (Constantinopolitan. I), c.10, *ibid.* (Urban. II); c.1, VI°, De temp. ord., I, 9 (Clem. IV), c.2, *ibid.* (Lugd. II).
[45] Cf. Sess. XIV, capp. 2 et 3 de ref.
[46] Cf. c.2, X, De praeb., III, 5.

Caput X

EPISCOPIS INFERIORES PRAELATI TONSURAM VEL MINORES ORDINES NE CONFERANT, NISI REGULARIBUS SIBI SUBDITIS; NEC IPSI AUT CAPITULA QUAECUMQUE DIMISSORIAS CONCEDANT; GRAVIORI IN DECRETUM PECCANTIBUS POENA STATUTA

Abbatibus ac aliis quibuscumque quantumvis exemptis non liceat in posterum intra fines alicujus dioecesis consistentibus, etiamsi nullius dioecesis vel exempti esse dicantur, cuiquam, qui regularis subditus sibi non sit, tonsuram vel minores ordines conferre; nec ipsi abbates et alii exempti, aut collegia vel capitula quaecumque, etiam ecclesiarum cathedralium, litteras dimissorias aliquibus clericis saecularibus, ut ab aliis ordinentur, concedant. Sed horum omnium ordinatio, servatis omnibus, quae in hujus sanctae synodi decretis continentur,[47] ad episcopos, intra quorum dioecesis fines exsistant, pertineat; non obstantibus quibusvis privilegiis, praescriptionibus aut consuetudinibus, etiam immemorabilibus. Poenam quoque impositam iis, qui contra hujus sanctae synodi sub Paulo III decretum [48] a capitulo episcopali sede vacante litteras dimissorias impetrant, ad illos, qui easdem litteras non a capitulo, sed ab aliis quibusvis in jurisdictione episcopi loco capituli sede vacante succedentibus obtinerent, mandat extendi. Concedentes autem dimissorias contra formam decreti ab officio et beneficio per annum sint ipso jure suspensi.

Caput XI

INTERSTITIA IN SUSCEPTIONE MINORUM ORDINUM, ET CERTA ALIA PRAECEPTA OBSERVANDA

Minores ordines iis, qui saltem latinam linguam intelligant, per temporum interstitia,[49] nisi aliud episcopo expedire magis videretur, conferantur, ut eo accuratius quantum sit hujus disciplinae pondus possint edoceri, ac in unoquoque munere juxta praescriptum episcopi se exerceant,[50] idque in ea, cui adscripti erunt, ecclesia (nisi forte ex

---

[47] Cf. *supra*, capp. 5 et 6 de ref. et *infra*, 11 et 12.
[48] Sess. VII, cap. 10 de ref.
[49] Cf. *infra*, cap. 13.
[50] *Ibid.*, cap. 17 et c.3, D.LIX (Greg. I).

causa studiorum absint), atque ita de gradu in gradum ascendant, ut in iis cum aetate vitae meritum et doctrina major accrescat quod et bonorum morum exemplum, et assiduum in ecclesia ministerium, atque major erga presbyteros et superiores ordines reverentia, et crebrior, quam antea, corporis Christi communio maxime comprobabunt. Cumque hinc ad altiores gradus et sacratissima mysteria sit ingressus, nemo iis initietur, quem non scientiae spes majoribus ordinibus dignum ostendat.[51] Hi vero non nisi post annum a susceptione postremi gradus minorum ordinum ad sacros ordines promoveantur, nisi necessitas aut ecclesiae utilitas judicio episcopi aliud exposcat.

Caput XII

AETAS AD MAJORES ORDINES REQUISITA; DIGNI DUMTAXAT ASSUMENDI

Nullus in posterum ad subdiaconatus ordinem ante vigesimum secundum, ad diaconatus ante vigesimum tertium, ad presbyteratus ante vigesimum quintum aetatis suae annum promoveatur.[52] Sciant tamen episcopi, non singulos in ea aetate constitutos debere ad hos ordines assumi, sed dignos dumtaxat, et quorum probata vita senectus sit.[53] Regulares quoque nec in minori aetate, nec sine diligenti episcopi examine ordinentur; privilegiis quibuscumque quoad hoc penitus exclusis.

Caput XIII

SUBDIACONI ET DIACONI ORDINATIO QUALIS, ET EORUM MUNUS; NULLI ORDINES SACRI DUO CONFERANTUR EODEM DIE

Subdiaconi et diaconi ordinentur habentes bonum testimonium,[54] et in minoribus ordinibus jam probati, ac litteris et iis, quae ad ordinem exercendum pertinent, instructi. Qui sperent Deo auctore se continere posse,[55] ecclesiis, quibus adscribentur, inserviant, sciantque

[51] Cc. 1, 2, D. LIX (Zosim.), c. 4, *ibid.* (Coelest. I).

[52] C. ult., De aet. et qual. et ord. praef. in Clem., I, 6 subdiaconatum 18, diaconatum 20 et praesbyteratum 25 anno suscipi posse decreverat. Cap. 20 conc. Toletan. IV (a. 633) requirebat 30 annos ad presbyteratum.

[53] Sap. 4:9.

[54] Cf. I Tim. 3:7, c. 3, D. LXXVII (Siric.) et conc. Toletan. IV, c. 19.

[55] Cf. c. 1, D. XXVIII (Greg. I).

maxime decere, si saltem diebus dominicis et solemnibus, cum altari ministraverint, sacram communionem perceperint. Promoti ad sacrum subdiaconatus ordinem, si per annum saltem in eo non sint versati,[56] ad altiorem gradum, nisi aliud episcopo videatur, ascendere non permittantur. Duo sacri ordines non eodem die, etiam regularibus, conferantur;[57] privilegiis ac indultis quibusvis concessis non obstantibus quibuscumque.

Caput XIV

QUINAM AD PRESBYTERATUM ASSUMENDI; ET ASSUMPTORUM MUNUS

Qui pie et fideliter in ministeriis ante actis se gesserint, [et ad presbyteratus ordinem assumuntur, bonum] [58] habeant testimonium, et hi sint, qui non modo in diaconatu ad minus annum integrum, nisi ob ecclesiae utilitatem ac necessitatem aliud episcopo videtur, ministraverint, sed etiam ad populum docendum ea, quae scire omnibus necessarium est ad salutem ac administranda sacramenta, diligenti examine praecedente idonei comprobentur, atque ita pietate ac castis moribus conspicui, ut praeclarum bonorum operum exemplum et vitae monita ab eis possint expectari. Curet episcopus, ut ii saltem diebus dominicis et festis solemnibus, si autem curam habuerint animarum, tam frequenter, ut suo muneri satisfaciant, missas celebrent. Cum promotis per saltum,[59] si non ministraverint, episcopus ex legitima causa possit dispensare.

Caput XV

NULLUS CONFESSIONES AUDIAT, NISI AB ORDINARIO APPROBATUS

Quamvis presbyteri in sua ordinatione a peccatis absolvendi potestatem accipiant, decernit tamen sancta synodus, nullum, etiam regularem, posse confessiones saecularium, etiam sacerdotum, audire, nec ad id idoneum reputari, nisi aut parochiale beneficium, aut ab episcopis per examen, si illis videbitur esse necessarium, aut alias idoneus judice-

---

[56] Cf. *supra*, cap. 11 de ref.
[57] Cc. 13, 15, X, De temp. ord., I, 11 (Innoc. III).
[58] Dubitatur num verba haec pars sint textus originalis.
[59] C. un., D. LII (Alex. II).

tur,[60] et approbationem, quae gratis detur, obtineat; privilegiis et consuetudine quacumque, etiam immemorabili, non obstantibus.

Caput XVI

ARCENTUR AB ORDINIBUS ECCLESIIS INUTILES ET VAGI

Cum nullus debeat ordinari, qui judicio sui episcopi non sit utilis aut necessarius suis ecclesiis, sancta synodus, vestigiis sexti canonis concilii Chalcedonensis inhaerendo,[61] statuit, ut nullus in posterum ordinetur, qui illi ecclesiae aut pio loco, pro cujus necessitate aut utilitate assumitur, non adscribatur, ubi suis fungatur muneribus, nec incertis vagetur sedibus.[62] Quod si locum inconsulto episcopo deseruerit, ei sacrorum exercitium interdicatur. Nullus praeterea clericus peregrinus sine commendatitiis sui ordinarii litteris ab ullo episcopo ad divina celebranda et sacramenta administranda admittatur.[63]

Caput XVII

QUA RATIONE EXERCITIA MINORUM ORDINUM REPETENDA

Ut sanctorum ordinum a diaconatu ad ostiariatum functiones, ab apostolorum temporibus in ecclesia laudabiliter receptae, et pluribus in locis aliquamdiu intermissae, in usum juxta sacros canones revocentur,[64] nec ab haereticis tamquam otiosae traducantur, illius pristini moris restituendi desiderio flagrans sancta synodus decernit, ut in posterum hujuscemodi ministeria non nisi per constitutos in dictis ordinibus exerceantur, omnesque et singulos praelatos ecclesiarum in Domino hortatur et illis praecipit, ut quantum fieri commode poterit, in ecclesiis cathedralibus, collegiatis et parochialibus suae dioecesis, si populus frequens et ecclesiae proventus id ferre queant, hujusmodi

---

[60] Cf. c.2, VI°, De poenit., V, 10 (Bonif. VIII) et c.2 de sepult. in Clem., III, 7 (idem).

[61] C.1, D.LXX, *infra*, p. 570, lit. U; c. ult., *ibid.* (conc. Placent.). Interdicta fuit ordinatio absoluta etiam ab Alexandro III in c.5 Lat. III, et ab Innocentio III in c.16, X, De praeb., III, 5. Hac de re cf. Fuchs, *Der Ordinationstitel von seiner Entstehung bis auf Innozenz III* (Bonn, 1930).

[62] Cf. c.9 conc. Melfitan. (a.1089) sub Urbano II habiti. Hardouin VI, P.II, p. 1686.

[63] Cf. c.6, D.LXXI (conc. Carthag. a.348), c.7, *ibid.* (Chalc.), c.9, *ibid.* (Antiochen.) et al.

[64] Plura de his omnibus ex Isidoro Hispalensi exhibet c.1, D.XXI. Cf. etiam Denzinger, nn.154–58 et Eisenhofer, *Handbuch d. kath. Liturgik*, II, 389 ff.

functiones curent restituendas, et ex aliqua parte redituum aliquorum simplicium beneficiorum vel fabricae ecclesiae, si proventus suppetant, aut utriusque illorum eas functiones exercentibus stipendia assignent, quibus, si negligentes fuerint, ordinarii judicio aut ex parte mulctari aut in totum privari possint. Quod si ministeriis quatuor minorum ordinum exercendis clerici caelibes praesto non erunt, suffici possint etiam conjugati vitae probatae, dummodo non bigami,[65] ad ea munia obeunda idonei, et qui tonsuram et habitum clericalem in ecclesia gestent.

Caput XVIII

FORMA ERIGENDI SEMINARIUM CLERICORUM, PRAESERTIM TENUIORUM; IN CUJUS ERECTIONE PLURIMA OBSERVANDA; DE EDUCATIONE PROMOVENDORUM IN CATHEDRALIBUS ET MAJORIBUS ECCLESIIS

Cum adolescentium aetas, nisi recte instituatur, prona sit ad mundi voluptates sequendas,[66] et, nisi a teneris annis ad pietatem et religionem informetur, antequam vitiorum habitus totos homines possideat, nunquam perfecte ac sine maximo ac singulari propemodum Dei omnipotentis auxilio in disciplina ecclesiastica perseveret; sancta synodus statuit, ut singulae cathedrales, metropolitanae atque his majores ecclesiae pro modo facultatem et dioecesis amplitudine certum puerorum ipsius civitatis et dioecesis, vel ejus provinciae, si ibi non reperiantur, numerum in collegio ad hoc prope ipsas ecclesias vel alio in loco convenienti ab episcopo eligendo alere, ac religiose educare et ecclesiasticis disciplinis instituere teneantur.[67] In hoc vero collegio recipiantur qui ad minimum duodecim annos et ex legitimo matrimonio nati sint, ac legere et scribere competenter noverint, et quorum indoles et voluntas spem afferat, eos ecclesiasticis ministeriis perpetuo inservituros. Pauperum autem filios praecipue eligi vult; nec tamen ditiorum excludit, modo suo sumptu alantur, et studium prae se ferant Deo et ecclesiae inserviendi. Hos pueros episcopus in tot classes, quod ei videbitur, divisos juxta eorum numerum, aetatem ac in disciplina ecclesiastica progressum, partim, cum ei opportunum videbitur, ecclesiarum ministerio addicet, partim in collegio erudiendos retinebit; aliosque in locum eductorum sufficiet, ita ut hoc collegium Dei mi-

[65] Cf. tot. tit. X, De big. non ord., I, 21.
[66] Gen. 8:21. Cf. c.5, D.XXVIII (conc. Toletan. II) et c.1, C.XII, q.1 (Toletan. IV).
[67] Cf. Sess. V, cap. 1 de ref.

nistrorum perpetuum seminarium sit. Ut vero in eadem disciplina ecclesiastica commodius instituantur, tonsura statim atque habitu clericali semper utentur; grammatices, cantus, computi ecclesiastici, aliarumque bonarum artium disciplinam discent, sacram scripturam, libros ecclesiasticos, homilias sanctorum, atque sacramentorum tradendorum, maxime quae ad confessiones audiendas videbuntur opportuna, et rituum ac caeremoniarum formas ediscent. Curet episcopus, ut singulis diebus missae sacrificio intersint, ac saltem singulis mensibus confiteantur peccata, et juxta confessoris judicium sumant corpus Domini nostri Jesu Christi; cathedrali et aliis loci ecclesiis diebus festis inserviant. Quae omnia atque alia ad hanc rem opportuna et necessaria episcopi singuli cum consilio duorum canonicorum seniorum et graviorum, quos ipsi elegerint, prout Spiritus Sanctus suggesserit, constituent, eaque ut semper observentur saepius visitando operam dabunt. Dyscolos et incorrigibiles ac malorum morum seminatores acriter punient, eos etiam, si opus fuerit, expellendo, omniaque impedimenta auferentes, quaecumque ad conservandum et augendum tam pium et sanctum institutum pertinere videbuntur diligenter curabunt.

Et quia ad collegii fabricam instituendam et ad mercedem praeceptoribus et ministris solvendam, et ad alendam juventutem et ad alios sumptus certi reditus erunt necessarii, ultra ea, quae ad instituendos vel alendos pueros sunt in aliquibus ecclesiis et locis destinata, quae eo ipso huic seminario sub eadem episcopi cura applicata censeantur, iidem episcopi cum consilio duorum de capitulo, quorum alter ab episcopo, alter ab ipso capitulo eligatur, itemque duorum de clero civitatis, quorum quidem alterius electio similiter ad episcopum, alterius vero ad clerum pertineat, ex fructibus integris mensae episcopalis et capituli, et quarumcumque dignitatum, personatuum, officiorum, praebendarum, portionum, abbatiarum et prioratuum, cujuscumque ordinis, etiam regularis, aut qualitatis vel conditionis fuerint, et hospitalium, quae dantur in titulum vel administrationem juxta constitutionem concilii Viennensis, quae incipit: *Quia contingit*,[68] et beneficiorum quorumcumque, etiam regularium, etiamsi juris patronatus cujuscumque fuerint, etiamsi exempta, etiamsi nullius dioecesis, vel aliis ecclesiis, monasteriis et hospitalibus, et aliis quibusve locis piis etiam exemptis annexa, et ex fabricis ecclesiarum et aliorum locorum, etiam ex quibuscumque aliis ecclesiasticis reditibus seu proventibus,

---

[68] C. 2 de relig. dom. in Clem., III, 11, *infra*, p. 562, lit. M.

etiam aliorum collegiorum (in quibus tamen seminaria discentium vel docentium ad commune ecclesiae bonum promovendum actu non habentur; haec enim exempta esse voluit,[69] praeterquam ratione redituum, qui superflui essent ultra convenientem ipsorum seminariorum sustentationem) seu corporum vel confraternitatum, quae in nonnullis locis scholae appellantur, et omnium monasteriorum, non tamen mendicantium, etiam ex decimis quacumque ratione ad laicos, ex quibus subsidia ecclesiastica solvi solent, et milites cujuscumque militiae aut ordinis pertinentibus (fratribus S. Joannis Hierosolymitani dumtaxat exceptis), partem aliquam vel portionem detrahent; et eam portionem sic detractam, necnon beneficia aliquot simplicia, cujuscumque qualitatis et dignitatis fuerint, vel etiam praestimonia vel praestimoniales portiones nuncupatas, etiam ante vacationem, sine cultus divini et illa obtinentium praejudicio huic collegio applicabunt et incorporabunt. Quod locum habeat etiamsi beneficia sint reservata vel affecta; nec per resignationem ipsorum beneficiorum uniones et applicationes suspendi vel ullo modo impediri possint, sed omnino, quacumque vacatione, etiamsi in curia, effectum suum sortiantur, et quacumque constitutione non obstante. Ad hanc autem portionem solvendam beneficiorum, dignitatum, personatuum et omnium et singulorum supra commemoratorum possessores non modo pro se sed pro pensionibus, quas aliis forsan ex dictis fructibus solverent, retinendo tamen pro rata quidquid pro dictis pensionibus illis erit solvendum, ab episcopo loci per censuras ecclesiasticas ac alia juris remedia compellantur, etiam vocato ad hoc, si videbitur, auxilio brachii saecularis; quibusvis quoad omnia et singula supra dicta privilegiis, exemptionibus, etiamsi specialem derogationem requirerent, consuetudine etiam immemorabili, quavis appellatione et allegatione, quae executionem impediat, non obstantibus. Succedente vero casu, quo per uniones effectum suum sortientes vel aliter seminarium ipsum in totum vel in partem dotatum reperiatur, tunc portio ex singulis beneficiis ut supra detracta et incorporata ab episcopo, prout res ipsa exegerit, in totum vel pro parte remittatur. Quod si cathedralium et aliarum majorum ecclesiarum praelati in hac seminarii erectione ejusque conservatione negligentes fuerint, ac suam portionem solvere detrectaverint, episcopum archiepiscopus, archiepiscopum et superiores synodus provincialis acriter corripere, eosque ad omnia supra dicta cogere debeat, et ut quam

[69] Id est, illa, in quibus ejusmodi seminaria jam actu habentur, concilium exempta esse voluit.

primum hoc sanctum et pium opus, ubicumque fieri poterit, promoveatur studiose curabit. Rationes autem redituum hujus seminarii episcopus annis singulis accipiat, praesentibus duobus a capitulo et totidem a clero civitatis deputatis.

Deinde, ut cum minori impensa hujusmodi scholis instituendis provideatur,[70] statuit sancta synodus, ut episcopi, archiepiscopi, primates et alii locorum ordinarii, scholasterias obtinentes et alios, quibus est lectionis vel doctrinae munus annexum, ad docendum in ipsis scholis instituendos per se ipsos, si idonei fuerint, alioquin per idoneos substitutos ab eisdem scholasticis eligendos et ab ordinariis approbandos, etiam per subtractionem fructuum cogant et compellant. Quod si judicio episcopi digni non fuerint, alium, qui dignus sit, nominent, omni appellatione remota. Quod si neglexerint, episcopus ipse deputet. Docebunt autem praedicti, quae videbuntur episcopo expedire.

De cetero vero officia vel dignitates illae, quae scholasteriae dicuntur, non nisi doctoribus vel magistris aut licentiatis in sacra pagina aut in jure canonico, et aliis personis idoneis et qui per se ipsos id munus explere possint, conferantur, et aliter facta provisio nulla sit et invalida; non obstantibus quibusvis privilegiis et consuetudinibus, etiam immemorabilibus.

Si vero in aliqua provincia ecclesiae tanta paupertate laborent, ut collegium in aliquibus erigi non possit, synodus provincialis, vel metropolitanus cum duobus antiquioribus suffraganeis, in ecclesia metropolitana vel alia provinciae ecclesia commodiori unum aut plura collegia, prout opportunum judicabit, ex fructibus duarum aut plurium ecclesiarum, in quibus singulis collegium commode institui non potest, erigenda curabit, ubi pueri illarum ecclesiarum educentur.

In ecclesiis autem amplas dioeceses habentibus possit episcopus unum vel plura in dioecesi, prout sibi opportunum videbitur, habere seminaria, quae tamen ab illo uno, quod in civitate erectum et constitutum fuerit, in omnibus dependeant.

Postremo, si vel pro unionibus, seu pro portionum taxatione vel assignatione et incorporatione, aut qualibet alia ratione difficultatem aliquam oriri contigerit, ob quam hujus seminarii institutio vel conservatio impediretur aut perturbaretur, episcopus cum supra deputatis, vel synodus provincialis, pro regionis more, pro ecclesiarum et beneficiorum qualitate, etiam supra scripta, si opus fuerit, moderando aut

---

[70] Cf. Sess. V, cap. 1 de ref.

augendo, omnia et singula, quae ad felicem hujus seminarii profectum necessaria et opportuna videbuntur, decernere ac providere valeat.

INDICTIO FUTURAE SESSIONIS

Insuper eadem sacrosancta Tridentina synodus proximam futuram sessionem in diem decimam sextam mensis Septembris indicit, in qua agetur de sacramento matrimonii, et de aliis, si qua erunt ad doctrinam fidei pertinentia, quae expediri possint; item de provisionibus episcopatuum, dignitatum aliorumque beneficiorum ecclesiasticorum, ac de diversis reformationis articulis.

Prorogata fuit sessio usque ad diem XI Novembris, MDLXIII.

SESSIO VIGESIMA QUARTA

QUAE EST OCTAVA

SUB PIO IV PONT. MAX.

celebrata

die XI Novembris, MDLXIII

DOCTRINA DE SACRAMENTO MATRIMONII

Matrimonii perpetuum indissolubilemque nexum primus humani generis parens divini Spiritus instinctu pronunciavit, cum dixit: *Hoc nunc os ex ossibus meis, et caro de carne mea. Quamobrem relinquet homo patrem suum et matrem, et adhaerebit uxori suae et erunt duo in carne una.*[1]

Hoc autem vinculo duos tantummodo copulari et conjungi, Christus Dominus apertius docuit, cum postrema illa verba tamquam a Deo prolata referens dixit: *Itaque jam non sunt duo, sed una caro,* statimque ejusdem nexus firmitatem ab Adamo tanto ante pronunciatam his verbis confirmavit: *Quod ergo Deus conjunxit, homo non separet.*[2]

Gratiam vero, quae naturalem illum amorem perficeret, et indissolubilem unitatem confirmaret conjugesque sanctificaret, ipse Christus venerabilium sacramentorum institutor atque perfector sua nobis passione promeruit, quod Paulus Apostolus innuit dicens: *Viri, diligite uxores vestras, sicut Christus dilexit ecclesiam, et se ipsum tradidit pro ea,*[3] mox subjungens: *Sacramentum hoc magnum est, ego autem dico in Christo, et in ecclesia.*[4]

Cum igitur matrimonium in lege evangelica veteribus connubiis per Christum gratia praestet, merito inter novae legis sacramenta annumerandum sancti patres nostri,[5] concilia [6] et universalis ecclesiae tra-

[1] Gen. 2:23 f. (Matt. 19:4 ff.; Marc. 10:6 ff.; Eph. 5:31 f.).
[2] Matt. 19:6; Marc. 10:8 f.; cf. c.19, C.XXVII, q.2 (Greg. I).
[3] Eph. 5:25.
[4] *Ibid.*, 5:32.
[5] Quorum testimonia numero 18 collegit Rouët de Journel, *Enchiridion patristicum* sub rubrica "Matrimonium," p. 782, n.570.
[6] Cf. Denzinger, *Enchiridion* sub rubrica "Matrimonium," XII o, p. [50].

ditio semper docuerunt, adversus quam impii homines hujus saeculi insanientes non solum perperam de hoc venerabili sacramento senserunt, sed de more suo praetextu evangelii libertatem carnis introducentes, multa ab ecclesiae catholicae sensu et ab apostolorum temporibus probata consuetudine aliena, scripto et verbo asseruerunt non sine magna Christi fidelium jactura; quorum temeritati sancta et universalis synodus cupiens occurrere, insigniores praedictorum schismaticorum haereses et errores, ne plures ad se trahat perniciosa eorum contagio, exterminandos duxit, hos in ipsos haereticos eorumque errores decernens anathematismos.

CANONES DE SACRAMENTO MATRIMONII

1. Si quis dixerit, matrimonium non esse vere et proprie unum ex septem legis evangelicae sacramentis a Christo Domino institutum,[7] sed ab hominibus in ecclesia inventum, neque gratiam conferre: anathema sit.

2. Si quis dixerit, licere Christianis plures simul habere uxores,[8] et hoc nulla lege divina esse prohibitum: anathema sit.

3. Si quis dixerit, eos tantum consanguinitatis et affinitatis gradus, qui Levitico exprimuntur,[9] posse impedire matrimonium contrahendum et dirimere contractum, nec posse ecclesiam in nonnullis illorum dispensare, aut constituere, ut plures impediant et dirimant: anathema sit.

4. Si quis dixerit, ecclesiam non potuisse constituere impedimenta matrimonium dirimentia,[10] vel in iis constituendis errasse: anathema sit.

5. Si quis dixerit, propter haeresim,[11] aut molestam cohabitationem, aut affectatam absentiam a conjuge dissolvi posse matrimonii vinculum: anathema sit.

6. Si quis dixerit, matrimonium ratum non consummatum per solemnem religionis professionem alterius conjugum non dirimi:[12] anathema sit.

---

[7] Cf. adn. 1.
[8] Matt. 16:4–6, 9; cf. c. 1–9, C. XXXII, q. 7.
[9] Lev. 18:6 ff.
[10] Matt. 16:19; Sess. XXI, cap. 2.
[11] Cf. c. 4, X, De consang., IV, 14 (Innoc. III); c. 6, X, De divor., IV, 19 (Urban. III), c. 7, *ibid.* (Innoc. III).
[12] Cf. c. 16, X, De spons., IV, 1 (Alex. III).

7. Si quis dixerit, ecclesiam errare, cum docuit et docet juxta evangelicam et apostolicam doctrinam, propter adulterium alterius conjugum matrimonii vinculum non posse dissolvi, et utrumque, vel etiam innocentem, qui causam non dedit, non posse altero conjuge vivente aliud matrimonium contrahere, moecharique eum, qui dimissa adultera aliam duxerit, et eam, quae dimisso adultero alii nupserit: [13] anathema sit.

8. Si quis dixerit, ecclesiam errare, cum ob multas causas separationem inter conjuges quoad thorum seu quoad cohabitationem ad certum incertumve tempus fieri posse decernit: anathema sit.

9. Si quis dixerit, clericos in sacris ordinibus constitutos, vel regulares, castitatem solemniter professos, posse matrimonium contrahere, contractumque validum esse non obstante lege ecclesiastica vel voto, et oppositum nil aliud esse quam damnare matrimonium, posseque omnes contrahere matrimonium, qui non sentiunt se castitatis, etiamsi eam voverint, habere donum: anathema sit, cum Deus id recte petentibus non deneget, nec patiatur nos supra id, quod possumus, tentari.[14]

10. Si quis dixerit, statum conjugalem anteponendum esse statui virginitatis vel coelibatus, et non esse melius ac beatius manere in virginitate aut coelibatu, quam jungi matrimonio: [15] anathema sit.

11. Si quis dixerit, prohibitionem solemnitatis nuptiarum certis anni temporibus superstitionem esse tyrannicam ab ethnicorum superstitione profectam; [16] aut benedictiones et alias caeremonias, quibus ecclesia in illis utitur, damnaverit: anathema sit.

12. Si quis dixerit, causas matrimoniales non spectare ad judices ecclesiasticos: anathema sit.

---

[13] Matt. 5:32; 19:9; Marc. 10:11 f.; Luc. 16:18; I Cor. 7:10 f. Cf. c.5 (conc. Carthag. XI [a.407], apud codicem canonum eccl. Africanae c.102, Hardouin, I, 923); c.6 (Aug.), c.7 (Hieron.), c.8 (conc. Eliberitan.), c.10 (Aug.), C.XXXII, q.7.

[14] Cf. I Cor. 10:13.

[15] Matt. 19:11 f.; I Cor. 7:25 f., 38, 40; c.12, C.XXXII, q.1; c.9, C.XXXIII, q.5; c.16, X, De spons., IV, 1. Rouët de Journel, p. 783, n.582.

[16] Cf. *infra*, cap. 10 de ref. matr.

DECRETUM DE REFORMATIONE MATRIMONII

Caput I

MATRIMONII SOLEMNITER CONTRAHENDI FORMA IN CONCILIO LATERANENSI PRAESCRIPTA INNOVATUR. QUOAD PROCLAMATIONES DISPENSARE POSSIT EPISCOPUS. QUI ALITER QUAM PRAESENTIBUS PAROCHO ET DUOBUS VEL TRIBUS TESTIBUS CONTRAHIT, NIHIL AGIT

Tametsi dubitandum non est, clandestina matrimonia, libero contrahentium consensu facta, rata et vera esse matrimonia,[17] quamdiu ecclesia ea irrita non fecit, et proinde jure damnandi sunt illi, ut eos sancta synodus anathemate damnat, qui ea vera ac rata esse negant, quique falso affirmant, matrimonia a filiis familias sine consensu parentum contracta irrita esse, et parentes ea rata vel irrita facere posse: nihilominus sancta Dei ecclesia ex justissimis causis illa semper detestata est atque prohibuit.[18] Verum, cum sancta synodus animadvertat, prohibitiones illas propter hominum inobedientiam jam non prodesse, et gravia peccata perpendat, quae ex eisdem clandestinis conjugiis ortum habent, praesertim vero eorum, qui in statu damnationis permanent, dum priore uxore, cum qua clam contraxerant, relicta cum alia palam contrahunt, et cum ea in perpetuo adulterio vivunt; cui malo cum ab ecclesia, quae de occultis non judicat, succurri non possit, nisi efficacius aliquod remedium adhibeatur, idcirco sacri Lateranensis concilii[19] sub Innocentio III celebrati vestigiis inhaerendo praecipit, ut in posterum, antequam matrimonium contrahatur, ter a proprio contrahentium parocho tribus continuis diebus festivis in ecclesia inter missarum solemnia publice denuncietur, inter quos matrimonium sit contrahendum; quibus denunciationibus factis, si nullum legitimum opponatur impedimentum, ad celebrationem matrimonii in facie ecclesiae procedatur, ubi parochus, viro et muliere interrogatis, et eorum mutuo consensu intellecto, vel dicat: *Ego vos in matrimonium conjungo in nomine Patris et Filii et Spiritus Sancti*, vel aliis utatur verbis, juxta receptum uniuscujusque provinciae ritum.

---

[17] Cf. c.2, X, De clan. desp., IV, 3 (Alex. III).

[18] Cf. c.3, C.XXX, q.5 (Nicol. I); c.4, *ibid.* (Leo I), c.5, *ibid.* (Stat. eccl. antiq.); c.13, C.XXXII, q.2 (Ambros.); c.2, C.XXXV, q.6 et c.3, X, qui matr. accus. poss., IV, 18 (Coelest. III).

[19] C.3, X, De clan. desp., IV, 3 (Lat. IV), *infra*, p. 570, lit. V.

Quod si aliquando probabilis fuerit suspicio, matrimonium malitiose impediri posse, si tot praecesserint denunciationes, tunc vel una tantum denunciatio fiat, vel saltem parocho et duobus vel tribus testibus praesentibus matrimonium celebretur. Deinde ante illius consummationem denunciationes in ecclesia fiant, ut, si aliqua subsunt impedimenta, facilius detegantur, nisi ordinarius ipse expedire judicaverit, ut praedictae denunciationes remittantur, quod illius prudentiae et judicio sancta synodus relinquit. Qui aliter, quam praesente parocho vel alio sacerdote, de ipsius parochi seu ordinarii licentia, et duobus vel tribus testibus matrimonium contrahere attentabunt, eos sancta synodus ad sic contrahendum omnino inhabiles reddit, et hujusmodi contractus irritos et nullos esse decernit, prout eos praesenti decreto irritos facit et annullat. Insuper parochum vel alium sacerdotem, qui cum minore testium numero, et testes, qui sine parocho vel sacerdote hujusmodi contractui interfuerint, necnon ipsos contrahentes graviter arbitrio ordinarii puniri praecipit. Praeterea eadem sancta synodus hortatur, ut conjuges ante benedictionem sacerdotalem,[20] in templo suscipiendam, in eadem domo non cohabitent, statuitque benedictionem a proprio parocho fieri, neque a quoquam, nisi ab ipso parocho vel ab ordinario licentiam ad praedictam benedictionem faciendam alii sacerdoti concedi posse, quacumque consuetudine, etiam immemorabili, quae potius corruptela dicenda est, vel privilegio non obstante. Quod si quis parochus vel alius sacerdos, sive regularis sive saecularis sit, etiamsi id sibi ex privilegio vel immemorabili consuetudine licere contendat, alterius parochiae sponsos sine illorum parochi licentia matrimonio conjungere aut benedicere ausus fuerit, ipso jure tamdiu suspensus maneat, quamdiu ab ordinario ejus parochi, qui matrimonio interesse debebat seu a quo benedictio suscipienda erat, absolvatur. Habeat parochus librum, in quo conjugum et testium nomina, diemque et locum contracti matrimonii describat, quem diligenter apud se custodiat.

Postremo sancta synodus conjuges hortatur, ut antequam contrahant, vel saltem triduo ante matrimonii consummationem, sua peccata diligenter confiteantur, et ad sanctissimum Eucharistiae sacramentum pie accedant. Si quae provinciae aliis ultra praedictas laudabilibus consuetudinibus et caeremoniis hac in re utuntur, eas omnino retineri sancta synodus vehementer optat. Ne vero haec tam salubria prae-

---

[20] Cf. c. 2, C. XXX, q. 5 (Cap. Reg. Fr.), c. 3, *ibid.* (Nicol. I), c. 5, *ibid.* (Stat. eccl. antiq.); c. 19, C. XXXV, qq. 2 et 3 (Cap. Reg. Fr.).

cepta quemquam lateant, ordinariis omnibus praecipit, ut, quam primum potuerint, curent hoc decretum populo publicari ac explicari in singulis suarum dioecesum parochialibus ecclesiis, idque in primo anno quam saepissime fiat, deinde vero quoties expedire viderint.

Decernit insuper, ut hujusmodi decretum in unaquaque parochia suum robur post triginta dies habere incipiat, a die primae publicationis in eadem parochia factae numerandos.

Caput II

INTER QUOS COGNATIO SPIRITUALIS CONTRAHATUR

Docet experientia, propter multitudinem prohibitionum multoties in casibus prohibitis ignoranter contrahi matrimonia, in quibus vel non sine magno peccato perseveratur, vel ea non sine magno scandalo dirimuntur. Volens itaque sancta synodus huic incommodo providere, et a cognationis spiritualis impedimento incipiens, statuit, ut unus tantum, sive vir sive mulier, juxta sacrorum canonum instituta,[21] vel ad summum unus et una baptizatum de baptismo suscipiant, inter quos ac baptizatum ipsum et illius patrem et matrem, necnon inter baptizantem et baptizatum, baptizatique patrem ac matrem tantum spiritualis cognatio contrahatur.

Parochus, antequam ad baptismum conferendum accedat, diligenter ab eis, ad quos spectabit, sciscitetur, quem vel quos elegerint, ut baptizatum de sacro fonte suscipiant, et eum vel eos tantum ad illum suscipiendum admittat, et in libro eorum nomina describat, doceatque eos quam cognationem contraxerint, ne ignorantia ulla excusari valeant. Quod si alii ultra designatos baptizatum tetigerint, cognationem spiritualem nullo pacto contrahant, constitutionibus in contrariam facientibus non obstantibus.[22] Si parochi culpa vel negligentia secus factum fuerit, arbitrio ordinarii puniatur. Ea quoque cognatio, quae ex confirmatione contrahitur, confirmantem et confirmatum illiusque patrem et matrem ac tenentem non egrediatur; [23] omnibus inter alias personas hujus spiritualis cognationis impedimentis omnino sublatis.

---

[21] Cf. c.101, D.IV de cons. (cap. incert.); c.3, VI°, De cogn. spirit., IV, 3 (Bonif. VIII).

[22] Cf. c.2, C.XXX, q.3 (Zachar.), c.5, *ibid.* (Paschal. II); c.3, X, De cogn. spirit., IV, 11 (Alex. III) et c.1 h.t. in VI°, IV, 3 (Bonif. VIII).

[23] Cf. c.2, C.XXX, q.1 (conc. Compendien.), et c.1 h.t. in VI° cit.

Caput III

PUBLICAE HONESTATIS IMPEDIMENTUM CERTIS LIMITIBUS COARCTATUR

Justitiae publicae honestatis impedimentum,[24] ubi sponsalia quacumque ratione valida non erunt, sancta synodus prorsus tollit. Ubi autem valida fuerint, primum gradum non excedant, quoniam in ulterioribus gradibus jam non potest hujusmodi prohibitio absque dispendio observari.

Caput IV

AFFINITAS EX FORNICATIONE AD SECUNDUM GRADUM RESTRINGITUR

Praeterea sancta synodus, eisdem et aliis gravissimis de causis adducta, impedimentum,[25] quod propter affinitatem ex fornicatione contractam inducitur et matrimonium postea factum dirimit, ad eos tantum qui in primo et secundo gradu conjunguntur, restringit; in ulterioribus vero gradibus statuit, hujusmodi affinitatem matrimonium postea contractum non dirimere.

Caput V

NE QUIS INTRA GRADUS PROHIBITOS CONTRAHAT, QUAVE RATIONE IN ILLIS DISPENSANDUM

Si quis intra gradus prohibitos scienter matrimonium contrahere praesumpserit,[26] separetur et spe dispensationis consequendae careat; idque in eo multo magis locum habeat, qui non tantum matrimonium contrahere, sed etiam consummare ausus fuerit. Quod si ignoranter id fecerit, siquidem solemnitates requisitas in contrahendo matrimonio neglexerit, eisdem subjiciatur poenis; non enim dignus est qui eccle-

---

[24] C. un VI°, De spon., IV, 1 (Bonif. VIII).

[25] Cf. c.19, C.XXXII, q.7 (conc. Compendien.), c.20, *ibid.* (Moguntien.), c.21, *ibid.* (Vermerien.), c.22, *ibid.* (cap. incert.), c.23, *ibid.* (Burch. Worm.), c.24, *ibid.* (conc. Vermerien.), et tot. tit. X, De eo, qui cognov. consang., IV, 13.

[26] Cf. c.3 (§ 1), X, De clan. desp., IV, 3 (Lat. IV); c. un. de consang. in Clem., IV, un. (conc. Viennen.).

siae benignitatem facile experiatur, cujus salubria praecepta temere contempsit. Si vero solemnitatibus adhibitis impedimentum aliquod postea subesse cognoscatur, cujus ille probabilem ignorantiam habuit, tunc facilius cum eo et gratis dispensari poterit. In contrahendis matrimoniis vel nulla omnino detur dispensatio, vel raro, idque ex causa et gratis concedatur. In secundo gradu nunquam dispensetur nisi inter magnos principes et ob publicam causam.

Caput VI

IN RAPTORES ANIMADVERTITUR

Decernit sancta synodus, inter raptorem et raptam, quamdiu ipsa in potestate raptoris manserit, nullum posse consistere matrimonium. Quod si rapta, a raptore separata et in loco tuto et libero constituta, illum in virum habere consenserit, eam raptor in uxorem habeat,[27] et nihilominus raptor ipse ac omnes illi consilium, auxilium et favorem praebentes, sint ipso jure excommunicati ac perpetuo infames, omniumque dignitatum incapaces, et, si clerici fuerint, de proprio gradu decidant.[28] Teneatur praeterea raptor mulierem raptam, sive eam uxorem duxerit sive non duxerit, decenter arbitrio judicis dotare.[29]

Caput VII

VAGI MATRIMONIO CAUTE JUNGENDI

Multi sunt, qui vagantur et incertas habent sedes, et, ut improbi sunt ingenii, prima uxore relicta aliam et plerumque plures illa vivente diversis in locis ducunt. Cui morbo cupiens sancta synodus occurrere, omnes, ad quos spectat, paterne monet, ne hoc genus hominum vagantium ad matrimonium facile recipiant. Magistratus etiam saeculares hortatur, ut eos severe coerceant; parochus autem praecipit, ne illorum matrimoniis intersint, nisi prius diligentem inquisitionem fecerint et, re ad ordinarium delata, ab eo licentiam id faciendi obtinuerint.

---

[27] Cf. cc.7, 11, C.XXXVI, q.2; c.7, X, De rapt., V. 17 (Innoc. III).
[28] Cf. c.3, C.XXXVI, q.1 (conc. Aurelianen.) et tot. quaest. 2 ejusdem causae.
[29] Ex. 22:16 f. in c.1, X, De adult., V, 16 cit.

Caput VIII

CONCUBINATUS POENIS GRAVISSIMIS PUNITUR

Grave peccatum est, homines solutos concubinas habere, gravissimum vero et in hujus magni sacramenti singularem contemptum admissum, uxoratos quoque in hoc damnationis statu vivere, ac audere eas quandoque domi etiam cum uxoribus alere et retinere. Quare, ut huic tanto malo sancta synodus opportunis remediis provideat, statuit hujusmodi concubinarios, tam solutos quam uxoratos, cujuscumque status, dignitatis et conditionis exsistant, si, postquam ab ordinario, etiam ex officio, ter admoniti ea de re fuerint,[30] concubinas non ejecerint, seque ab earum consuetudine non sejunxerint, excommunicatione feriendos esse, a qua non absolvantur, donec re ipsa admonitioni factae paruerint. Quod si in concubinatu per annum censuris neglectis permanserint, contra eos ab ordinario severe pro qualitate criminis procedatur. Mulieres, sive conjugatae sive solutae, quae cum adulteris seu concubinariis publice vivunt, si ter admonitae non paruerint, ab ordinariis locorum, nullo etiam requirente, ex officio graviter pro modo culpae puniantur, et extra oppidum vel dioecesim, si id eisdem ordinariis videbitur, invocato, si opus fuerit, brachio saeculari, ejiciantur; aliis poenis contra adulteros et concubinarios inflictis in suo robore permanentibus.

Caput IX

NE DOMINI TEMPORALES AUT MAGISTRATUS QUIDPIAM LIBERTATI MATRIMONII CONTRARIUM MOLIANTUR

Ita plerumque temporalium dominorum ac magistratuum mentis oculos terreni affectus atque cupiditates excaecant, ut viros et mulieres sub eorum jurisdictione degentes, maxime divites vel spem magnae hereditatis habentes, minis et poenis adigant cum iis matrimonium invitos contrahere, quos ipsi domini vel magistratus illis praescripserint. Quare, cum maxime nefarium sit, matrimonii libertatem violare, et ab eis injurias nasci, a quibus jura expectantur,[31] praecipit

[30] Cf. c. 2, X, De cohab. cler., III, 2 (Eugen. II) et Sess. XXV, cap. 14 de ref.
[31] Cf. c. 14, X, De spons., IV, 1 (Alex. III), c. 17, *ibid.* (Luc. III), c. 29, *ibid.* (Greg. IX).

sancta synodus omnibus, cujuscumque gradus, dignitatis et conditionis exsistant, sub anathematis poena, quam ipso facto incurrant, ne quovis modo directe vel indirecte subditos suos vel quoscumque alios cogant, quominus libere matrimonia contrahant.[32]

Caput X

NUPTIARUM SOLEMNITATES CERTIS TEMPORIBUS PROHIBENTUR

Ab Adventu Domini nostri Jesu Christi usque in diem Epiphaniae, et a feria quarta Cinerum usque in octavam Paschatis inclusive, antiquas solemnium nuptiarum prohibitiones diligenter ab omnibus observari sancta synodus praecipit;[33] in aliis vero temporibus nuptias solemniter celebrari permittit, quas episcopi, ut ea qua decet modestia et honestate fiant, curabunt. Sancta enim res est matrimonium, et sancte tractandum.

DECRETUM DE REFORMATIONE

Eadem sacrosancta synodus, reformationis materiam prosequens, haec in praesenti sessione statuenda decernit.

Caput I

NORMA PROCEDENDI AD CREATIONEM EPISCOPORUM ET CARDINALIUM

Si in quibuslibet ecclesiae gradibus providenter scienterque curandum est, ut in Domini domo nihil sit inordinatum nihilque praeposterum, multo magis elaborandum est, ut in electione ejus, qui supra omnes gradus constituitur, non erretur. Nam totius familiae Domini status et ordo nutabit, si quod requiritur in corpore non inveniatur in capite.[34] Unde, etsi alias sancta synodus de promovendis ad cathedrales et superiores ecclesias nonnulla utiliter decrevit,[35] hoc tamen munus hujusmodi esse censet, ut, si pro rei magnitudine expendatur,

[32] Cf. c.6, C.XXXVI, q.2 (conc. Paris. III).

[33] Cf. cc.8, 9, C.XXXIII, q.4 (conc. Laodicen.), c.10, *ibid.* (Salegunst.), c.11, *ibid.* (Nicol. I); c.4, X, De fer., II, 9 (Clem. III).

[34] Desumptum est hoc prooemium fere ad verbum a Leonis I epistola ad episcopos Mauritaniae, cf. c.5, D.LXI.

[35] Cf. Sess. VI, cap. 1 de ref.; Sess. VII, capp. 1, 3 de ref., et Sess. XXII, cap. 2 de ref.

nunquam satis cautum de eo videri possit. Itaque statuit, ut, cum primum ecclesia vacaverit, supplicationes ac preces publice privatimque habeantur, atque a capitulo per civitatem et dioecesim indicantur, quibus clerus populusque bonum a Deo pastorem valeat impetrare. Omnes vero et singulos, qui ad promotionem praeficiendorum quodcumque jus quacumque ratione a Sede Apostolica habent, aut alioquin operam suam praestant, nihil in iis pro praesenti temporum ratione innovando, hortatur et monet, ut in primis meminerint, nihil se ad Dei gloriam et populorum salutem utilius posse facere, quam si bonos pastores et ecclesiae gubernandae idoneos promoveri studeant, eosque alienis peccatis communicantes mortaliter peccare, nisi quos digniores et ecclesiae magis utiles ipsi judicaverint, non quidem precibus vel humano affecto aut ambientium suggestionibus, sed eorum exigentibus meritis, praefici diligenter curaverint, et quos ex legitimo matrimonio natos, et vita, aetate, doctrina atque aliis omnibus qualitatibus praeditos sciant, quae juxta sacros canones et Tridentinae hujus synodi decreta requiruntur.[36] Quoniam vero in sumendo de praedictis omnibus qualitatibus gravi idoneoque bonorum et doctorum virorum testimonio non uniformis ratio ubique ex nationum, populorum ac morum varietate potest adhiberi, mandat sancta synodus, ut in provinciali synodo per metropolitanum habenda praescribatur quibusque locis et provinciis propria examinis seu inquisitionis aut instructionis faciendae forma, sanctissimi Romani pontificis arbitrio approbanda, quae magis eisdem locis utilis atque opportuna esse videbitur; ita tamen, ut, cum deinde hoc examen seu inquisitio de persona promovenda perfecta fuerit, ea in instrumentum publicum redacta cum toto testimonio ac professione fidei ab eo facta,[37] quam primum ad sanctissimum Romanum pontificem omnino transmittatur, ut ipse summus pontifex, plena totius negotii ac personarum notitia habita, pro gregis dominici commodo de illis, si idonei per examen seu per inquisitionem factam reperti fuerint, ecclesiis possit utilius providere. Omnes vero inquisitiones, informationes, testimonia ac probationes quaecumque de promovendi qualitatibus et ecclesiae statu a quibuscumque etiam in Romana curia habitae, per cardinalem, qui relationem facturus erit in consistorio, et alios tres cardinales diligenter examinentur, ac relatio ipsa cardinalis relatoris et trium cardinalium subscriptione roboretur,

---

[36] Cf. c.7, X, De elect., I, 6 (Lat. III) et adn. praec.

[37] Formam hujus professionis dedit et observari jussit Pius IV per const. *Injunctum nobis* die 13 Nov., 1564, *infra*, p. 540 relatam. Habetur etiam apud Denzinger, nn.994 ff.

in qua ipsi singuli quatuor cardinales affirment, se, adhibita accurata diligentia, invenisse promovendos qualitatibus a jure et ab hac sancta synodo requisitis praeditos, ac certo existimare sub periculo salutis aeternae, idoneos esse qui ecclesiis praeficiantur; ita ut relatione in uno consistorio facta, quo maturius interea de ipsa inquisitione cognosci possit, in aliud consistorium judicium differatur, nisi aliud beatissimo pontifici videbitur expedire. Ea vero omnia et singula, quae de episcoporum praeficiendorum vita, aetate, doctrina et ceteris qualitatibus alias in eadem synodo constituta sunt, decernit eadem, etiam in creatione sanctae Romanae ecclesiae cardinalium, etiam si diaconi sint, exigenda, quos sanctissimus Romanus pontifex ex omnibus Christianitatis nationibus, quantum commode fieri poterit, prout idoneos repererit, assumet. Postremo eadem sancta synodus, tot gravissimis ecclesiae incommodis commota, non potest non commemorare, nihil magis ecclesiae Dei esse necessarium, quam ut beatissimus Romanus pontifex, quam sollicitudinem universae ecclesiae ex muneris sui officio debet, eam hic potissimum impendat, ut lectissimos tantum sibi cardinales adsciscat, et bonos maxime atque idoneos pastores singulis ecclesiis praeficiat, idque eo magis, quod ovium Christi sanguinem, quae ex malo negligentium et sui officii immemorum pastorum regimine peribunt, Dominus noster Jesus Christus de manibus ejus sit requisiturus.[38]

Caput II

SYNODI PROVINCIALES QUOLIBET TRIENNIO, DIOECESANAE QUOTANNIS CELEBRENTUR; QUI EAS COGERE, QUIVE ILLIS INTERESSE DEBEANT

Provincilia concilia, sicubi omissa sunt, pro moderandis moribus, corrigendis excessibus, controversiis componendis, aliisque ex sacris canonibus permissis renoventur.[39] Quare metropolitani per se ipsos, seu, illis legitime impeditis, coepiscopus antiquior, intra annum ad minus a fine praesentis concilii, et deinde quolibet saltem triennio post octavam Paschae Resurrectionis Domini nostri Jesu Christi, seu

---

[38] Ezech. 3:18–21; 33:6–9; Act. 20:26 f.

[39] Cf. c.2, D.XVIII (Leo I), c.3, *ibid.* (conc. Nicaen. I), c.4, *ibid.* (Antiochen.), c.5, *ibid.* (Laodicen.), c.6, *ibid.* (Chalc.), c.7, *ibid.* (Nicaen. II), c.9, *ibid.* (Stat. eccl. antiq.), c.10, *ibid.* (Carthag. V), c.12, *ibid.* (Arelaten. II), c.13, *ibid.* (Agathen.), c.14, *ibid.* (Tarraconen.); c.25, X, De accus., V, 1 (Innoc. III).

alio commodiori tempore pro more provinciae, non praetermittat synodum in provincia sua cogere, quo episcopi omnes et alii, qui de jure vel consuetudine interesse debent, exceptis iis, quibus cum imminenti periculo transfretandum esset, convenire omnino teneantur. Nec episcopi comprovinciales praetextu cujuslibet consuetudinis ad metropolitanam ecclesiam in posterum accedere inviti compellantur. Itidem episcopi, qui nulli archiepiscopo subjiciuntur, aliquem vicinum metropolitanum semel eligant, in cujus synodo provinciali cum aliis interesse debeant, et quae ibi ordinata fuerint observent ac observari faciant. In reliquis omnibus eorum exemptio et privilegia salva atque integra maneant. Synodi quoque dioecesanae quotannis celebrentur, ad quas exempti etiam omnes, qui alias, cessante exemptione, interesse deberent, nec capitulis generalibus subduntur, accedere teneantur; ratione tamen parochialium aut aliarum saecularium ecclesiarum, etiam annexarum, debeant ii, qui illarum curam gerunt, quicumque illi sint, synodo interesse. Quod si in his tam metropolitani quam episcopi et alii supra scripti negligentes fuerint, poenas sacris canonibus sancitas incurrant.[40]

Caput III

QUA RATIONE VISITATIO PER PRAELATOS FACIENDA

Patriarchae, primates, metropolitani et episcopi propriam dioecesim per se ipsos aut, si legitime impediti fuerint,[41] per suum generalem vicarium aut visitatorem, si quotannis totam propter ejus latitudinem visitare non poterunt, saltem majorem ejus partem, ita tamen, ut tota biennio per se vel visitatores suos compleatur, visitare non praetermittant. A metropolitanis vero, etiam post plene visitatam propriam dioecesim, non visitentur cathedrales ecclesiae, neque dioeceses suorum comprovincialium, nisi causa cognita et probata in concilio provinciali. Archidiaconi autem, decani et alii inferiores in iis ecclesiis, ubi hactenus visitationem exercere legitime consueverunt, debeant quidem, assumpto notario, de consensu episcopi deinceps per se ipsos tantum ibidem visitare. Visitatores etiam a capitulo deputandi, ubi capitulum jus visitandi habet, prius ab episcopo approbentur; sed non ideo episcopus vel, eo impedito, ejus visitator, easdem ecclesias

---

[40] Cf. D.XVIII fere per totum.
[41] Cf. c.11, C.X, q.1 (conc. Toletan. IV).

seorsum ab his visitare prohibeatur, cui ipsi archidiaconi vel alii inferiores visitationis factae infra mensem rationem reddere et depositiones testium ac integra acta ei exhibere teneantur; non obstantibus quacumque consuetudine, etiam immemorabili, atque exemptionibus et privilegiis quibuscumque. Visitationum autem omnium istarum praecipuus sit scopus,[42] sanam orthodoxamque doctrinam expulsis haeresibus inducere, bonos mores tueri, pravos corrigere, populum cohortationibus et admonitionibus ad religionem, pacem innocentiamque accendere, cetera, prout locus, tempus et occasio feret, ex visitantium prudentia ad fidelium fructum constituere. Quae ut facilius feliciusque succedant, monentur praedicti omnes et singuli, ad quos visitatio spectat, ut paterna caritate Christianoque zelo omnes amplectantur, ideoque modesto contenti equitatu famulatuque studeant quam celerrime, debita tamen cum diligentia, visitationem ipsam absolvere. Interimque caveant, ne inutilibus sumptibus cuiquam graves onerosive sint,[43] neve ipsi aut quisquam suorum quidquam procurationis causa pro visitatione, etiam testamentorum ad pios usus, praeter id, quod ex relictis piis jure debetur, aut alio quovis nomine, nec pecuniam, nec munus, quodcumque sit, etiam qualitercumque offeratur, accipiant; non obstante quacumque consuetudine, etiam immemorabili, exceptis tamen victualibus,[44] quae sibi ac suis frugaliter moderateque pro temporis tantum necessitate et non ultra erunt ministranda. Sit tamen in optione eorum, qui visitantur, si malint solvere id, quod erat ab ipsis antea solvi certa pecunia taxata consuetum, an vero praedicta victualia subministrare; salvo item jure conventionum antiquarum cum monasteriis aliisve piis locis aut ecclesiis non parochialibus inito, quod illaesum permaneat. In iis vero locis seu provinciis, ubi consuetudo est, ut nec victualia, nec pecunia, nec quidquam aliud a visitatoribus accipiatur, sed omnia gratis fiant, ibi id observetur. Quod si quispiam, quod absit, aliquid amplius in supra dictis omnibus casibus accipere praesumpserit, is, praeter dupli restitutionem intra mensem faciendam, aliis etiam poenis juxta constitutionem concilii generalis Lugdunensis, quae incipit: *Exigit*,[45] necnon et aliis poenis in synodo provinciali arbitrio synodi absque ulla spe veniae mulctetur. Patroni vero in iis, quae ad sacramentorum ad-

[42] C. 1 (§ 4), VI, De cens., III, 20 (Innoc. IV).
[43] Cf. c. 1, C. X, q. 3 (conc. Bracaren. II), c. 7, *ibid.* (Cabilonen. II), c. 8, *ibid.* (Toletan. VIII) et c. 6, X, De cens., III, 39 (Lat. III).
[44] Cf. c. 6, VI°, De off. ord., I, 16 (Bonif. VIII).
[45] C. 2, VI°, De cens., III, 20, *infra*, p. 571, lit. W.

ministrationem spectant, nullatenus se praesumant ingerere, neque visitationi ornamentorum ecclesiae, aut bonorum stabilium seu fabricarum proventibus immisceant, nisi quatenus id eis ex institutione ac fundatione competat; sed episcopi ipsi haec faciant et fabricarum reditus in usus ecclesiae necessarios et utiles, prout sibi expedire magis visum fuerit, expendi curent.

Caput IV

PRAEDICATIONIS MUNUS, A QUIBUS ET QUANDO OBEUNDUM. ECCLESIA PAROCHIALIS AD AUDIENDUM VERBUM DEI ADEUNDA. NULLUS CONTRADICENTE EPISCOPO PRAEDICET

Praedicationis munus, quod episcoporum praecipuum est, cupiens sancta synodus quo frequentius possit ad fidelium salutem exerceri, canones alias super hoc editos sub fel. rec. Paulo III [46] aptius praesentium temporum usui accommodando, mandat, ut in ecclesia sua ipsi per se, aut, si legitime impediti fuerint, per eos, quos ad praedicationis munus assument, in aliis autem ecclesiis per parochos, sive iis impeditis, per alios ab episcopo impensis eorum, qui eas praestare vel tenentur vel solent, deputandos in civitate aut in quacumque parte dioecesis censebunt expedire, saltem omnibus dominicis et solemnibus diebus festis, tempore autem jejuniorum, Quadragesimae et Adventus Domini quotidie, vel saltem tribus in hebdomada diebus, si ita oportere duxerint, sacras scripturas divinamque legem annuncient, et alias quotiescumque id opportune fieri posse judicaverint. Moneatque episcopus populum diligenter, teneri unumquemque parochiae suae interesse, ubi commode id fieri potest, ad audiendum verbum Dei.[47] Nullus autem saecularis sive regularis, etiam in ecclesiis suorum ordinum, contradicente episcopo, praedicare praesumat. Iidem etiam saltem dominicis et aliis festivis diebus pueros in singulis parochiis fidei rudimenta et obedientiam erga Deum et parentes diligenter ab iis, ad quos spectabit, doceri curabunt, et, si opus sit, etiam per censuras ecclesiasticas compellent, non obstantibus privilegiis et con-

---

[46] Cf. Sess. V, cap. 2 de ref.
[47] Cf. c.61, D.I de cons. (can. Apost. 10), c.63, *ibid.* (Stat. eccl. antiq.); c.25 conc. Tolosan. (a.1229)

suetudinibus. In reliquis ea, quae de praedicationis munere sub eodem Paulo III decreta fuerunt,[48] suum robur obtineant.

Caput V

CAUSAE CRIMINALES CONTRA EPISCOPOS MAJORES A SOLO SUMMO PONTIFICE, MINORES A CONCILIO PROVINCIALI COGNOSCANTUR

Causae criminales graviores contra episcopos, etiam haeresis, quod absit, quae depositione aut privatione dignae sunt, ab ipso tantum summo Romano pontifice cognoscantur et terminentur.[49] Quod si ejusmodi sit causa, quae necessario extra Romanam curiam sit committenda, nemini prorsus ea committatur, nisi metropolitanis aut episcopis a beatissimo Papa eligendis. Haec vero commissio et specialis sit et manu ipsius sanctissimi pontificis signata, nec unquam plus his tribuat, quam ut solam facti instructionem sumant processumque conficiant, quem statim ad Romanum pontificem transmittant, reservata eidem Sanctissimo sententia definitiva. Cetera, alias sub fel. rec. Julio III super his decreta,[50] necnon et constitutio sub Innocentio III in concilio generali, quae incipit: *Qualiter et quando*,[51] quam sancta synodus in praesenti innovat, ab omnibus observetur. Minores vero criminales causae episcoporum in concilio tantum provinciali cognoscantur et terminentur, vel a deputandis per concilium provinciale.

Caput VI

DATUR EPISCOPIS POTESTAS CIRCA IRREGULARITATUM ET SUSPENSIONUM DISPENSATIONES ET CRIMINUM ABSOLUTIONES

Liceat episcopis in irregularitatibus omnibus et suspensionibus, ex delicto occulto provenientibus, excepta ea, quae oritur ex homicidio voluntario, et exceptis aliis deductis ad forum contentiosum, dispensare, et in quibuscumque casibus occultis, etiam Sedi Apostolicae reservatis, delinquentes quoscumque sibi subditos in dioecesi sua per

---

[48] Cf. Sess. V, cap. 2 de ref.
[49] Cf. Sess. XIII, cap. 8 de ref.
[50] Cf. Sess. cit., capp. 6 et 7 de ref.
[51] C. 24, X, De accus., V, 1, *infra*, p. 571, lit. X.

se ipsos aut vicarium ad id specialiter deputandum in foro conscientiae gratis absolvere, imposita poenitentia salutari. Idem et in haeresis crimine in eodem foro conscientiae eis tantum, non eorum vicariis, sit permissum.

Caput VII

SACRAMENTORUM VIRTUS, ANTEQUAM POPULO ADMINISTRENTUR, AB EPISCOPIS ET PAROCHIS EXPLICETUR. INTER MISSARUM SOLEMNIA SACRAE PAGINAE EXPLANENTUR

Ut fidelis populus ad suscipienda sacramenta majori cum reverentia atque animi devotione accedat, praecipit sancta synodus episcopis omnibus, ut non solum, cum haec per se ipsos erunt populo administranda, prius illorum vim et usum pro suscipientium captu explicent, sed etiam idem a singulis parochis pie prudenterque, etiam lingua vernacula, si opus sit et commode fieri poterit, servari studeant, juxta formam a sancta synodo in catechesi singulis sacramentis praescribendam, quam episcopi in vulgarem linguam fideliter verti atque a parochis omnibus populo exponi curabunt; necnon ut inter missarum solemnia aut divinorum celebrationem sacra eloquia et salutis monita eadem vernacula lingua singulis diebus festivis vel solemnibus explanent,[52] eadem in omnium cordibus, postpositis inutilibus quaestionibus,[53] inserere, atque eos in lege Domini erudire studeant.

Caput VIII

PUBLICE PECCANTES PUBLICE POENITEANT, NISI EPISCOPO ALITER VIDEATUR. POENITENTIARIUS IN CATHEDRALIBUS INSTITUENDUS

Apostolus monet, publice peccantes palam esse corripiendos.[54] Quando igitur ab aliquo publice et in multorum conspectu crimen commissum fuerit, unde alios scandalo offensos commotosque fuisse non sit dubitandum, huic condignam pro modo culpae poenitentiam publice injungi oportet, ut quo exemplo suo ad malos mores provo-

[52] Cf. Sess. XXII, cap. 8 de sacrific. miss.
[53] Cf. I Tim. 1:4; II Tim. 2:23; Tit. 3:9.
[54] Cf. I Tim. 5:20; c.19 (§ 1), C.II, q.1 (Aug.); c.1, X, De poenit., V, 38.

cavit, suae emendationis testimonio ad rectam revocet vitam. Episcopus tamen publicae hoc poenitentiae genus in aliud secretum poterit commutare, quando ita magis judicaverit expedire. In omnibus etiam cathedralibus ecclesiis, ubi id commode fieri poterit, poenitentiarius aliquis cum unione praebendae proxime vacaturae ab episcopo instituatur, qui magister sit vel doctor aut licentiatus in theologia vel jure canonico, et annorum quadraginta, seu alius, qui aptior pro loci qualitate reperiatur, qui, dum confessiones in ecclesia audiet, interim praesens in choro censeatur.

Caput IX

A QUO VISITARI DEBEANT ECCLESIAE SAECULARES NULLIUS DIOECESIS

Quae alias sub fel. rec. Paulo III [55] et nuper sub beatissimo domini nostri Pio IV [56] in hoc eodem concilio de adhibenda ab ordinariis diligentia in beneficiorum, etiam exemptorum, visitatione constituta sunt, eadem etiam in iis ecclesiis saecularibus observentur, quae in nullius dioecesi esse dicuntur, ut ab episcopo, cujus cathedralis ecclesia est proximior, si id constet, alioquin ab eo, qui semel in concilio provinciali a praelato loci illius electus fuerit,[57] tamquam Sedis Apostolicae delegato, visitentur; non obstantibus privilegiis et consuetudinibus quibuscumque, etiam immemorabilibus.

Caput X

EXECUTIO VISITATIONIS A SUBDITIS NE SUSPENDATUR

Episcopi, ut aptius quem regunt populum possint in officio atque obedientia continere, in omnibus iis, quae ad visitationem ac morum correctionem subditorum suorum spectant, jus et potestatem habeant, etiam tamquam Apostolicae Sedis delegati, ea ordinandi, moderandi, puniendi et exequendi juxta canonum sanctiones, quae illis ex prudentia sua pro subditorum emendatione ac dioecesis suae utilitate necessaria videbuntur. Nec in his, ubi de visitatione aut morum cor-

---

[55] Cf. Sess. VI, cap. 4 de ref. et Sess. VII, cap. 8 de ref.
[56] Sess. XXI, cap. 8 de ref.
[57] Cf. cap. 2 huj. sess. in medio.

rectione agitur,[58] exemptio aut ulla inhibitio, appellatio seu querela, etiam ad Sedem Apostolicam interposita, executionem eorum, quae ab his mandata, decreta aut judicata fuerint, quoquo modo impediat aut suspendat.

Caput XI

HONORARII TITULI AUT PRIVILEGIA PARTICULARIA EPISCOPORUM JURI NIHIL DETRAHANT

Quoniam privilegia et exemptiones, quae variis titulis plerisque conceduntur, hodie perturbationem in episcoporum jurisdictione excitare et exemptis occasionem laxioris vitae praebere dignoscuntur, decernit sancta synodus, ut, si quando justis, gravibus et fere necessariis suadentibus causis aliquos honorariis titulis protonotariatus, acolythatus, comitis palatini, capellani regii aut aliis hujusmodi in Romana curia vel extra insignibus decorandos esse placuerit, necnon alios, cuicumque monasterio oblatos vel quomodocumque addictos, aut sub nomine servientium militiis seu monasteriis, hospitalibus, collegiis aut quocumque alio titulo assumi, nihil ex iis privilegiis detractum esse ordinariis intelligatur, quominus ii, quibus ea jam concessa sunt, vel in posterum concedi contigerit, ipsis ordinariis tamquam Apostolicae Sedis delegatis plene in omnibus, et, quoad capellanos regios, juxta constitutionem Innocentii III, quae incipit: *Cum capella*,[59] subjecti exsistant; exceptis tamen iis, qui praedictis locis aut militiis actu serviunt et intra eorum septa ac domos resident subque eorum obedientia vivunt, sive iis, qui legitime et secundum regulam earumdem militiarum professionem fecerint, de qua ordinario constare debeat; non obstantibus privilegiis quibuscumque, etiam religionis sancti Joannis Jerosolymitani et aliarum militiarum. Quae vero privilegia residentibus in curia Romana vigore Eugenianae constitutionis [60] aut familiaritatis cardinalium competere solent, ea in iis, qui beneficia ecclesiastica obtinent, ratione praedictorum beneficiorum minime intelligantur, sed ordinarii jurisdictioni subjecti permaneant, non obstantibus quibuscumque inhibitionibus.

---

[58] Cf. Sess. XIII, cap. 1 de ref.; Sess. XIV, cap. 4 de ref.; Sess. XXII, cap. 1 de ref.

[59] C.16, X, De privil., V, 33, *infra*, p. 573, lit. Y.

[60] C.3 h.t. in Extrav. comm., V, 7, quod ordinarii procedere non possunt in suos subditos pro suis negotiis Romam euntes, etc. Cf. Sess. XXIII, cap. 1 de ref.

Caput XII

QUALES ESSE DEBEANT PROMOVENDI AD DIGNITATES ET CANONICATUS CATHEDRALIUM ECCLESIARUM, QUIDVE PROMOTI PRAESTARE TENEANTUR

Cum dignitates in ecclesiis, praesertim cathedralibus, ad conservandam augendamque ecclesiasticam disciplinam fuerint institutae, ut qui eas obtinerent pietate praecellerent, aliisque exemplo essent atque episcopos opera et officio juvarent, merito qui ad eas vocantur tales esse debent, qui suo muneri respondere possint. Nemo igitur deinceps ad dignitates quascumque, quibus animarum cura subest, promoveatur,[61] nisi qui saltem vigesimum quintum suae aetatis annum attigerit et, in clericali ordine versatus, doctrina ad suum munus exsequendum necessaria ac morum integritate commendetur, juxta constitutionem Alexandri III in concilio Lateranensi promulgatam, quae incipit: *Cum in cunctis.*[62] Archidiaconi etiam, qui oculi dicuntur episcopi,[63] sint in omnibus ecclesiis, ubi fieri poterit, magistri in theologia, seu doctores aut licentiati in jure canonico. Ad ceteras autem dignitates vel personatus, quibus animarum cura nulla subest, clerici alioquin idonei et viginti duobus annis non minores adsciscantur. Provisi etiam de beneficiis quibuscumque curam animarum habentibus teneantur a die adeptae possessionis ad minus intra duos menses in manibus ipsius episcopi vel, eo impedito, coram generali ejus vicario seu officiali, orthodoxae suae fidei publicam facere professionem, et in ecclesiae Romanae obedientia se permansuros spondeant ac jurent.[64] Provisi autem de canonicatibus et dignitatibus in ecclesiis cathedralibus non solum coram episcopo seu ejus officiali, sed etiam in capitulo idem facere teneantur; alioquin praedicti omnes provisi ut supra fructus non faciant suos, nec illis possessio suffragetur. Neminem etiam deinceps ad dignitatem, canonicatum aut portionem recipiant, nisi qui eo ordine sacro aut sit initiatus, quem illa dignitas, praebenda aut portio requirit, aut in tali aetate, ut infra tempus a jure et ab hac sancta synodo statutum initiari valeat.[65] In omnibus vero ecclesiis cathedrali-

---

[61] Cf. Sess. XXII, cap. 2 de ref.

[62] C.7 (praesertim § 2), X, De elect., I, 6, *infra*, p. 573, lit. Z. Cf. Sess. VII, cap. 1 de ref.

[63] Cf. c.7, X, De off. archid., I, 23 (Innoc. III). Vide etiam cc.6, 11, D.XCIII et *Constitutiones Apost.*, lib. II, c.44.

[64] Cf. huj. sess. adn. 37.

[65] Cf. c.34, VI°, De elect., I, 6 (Bonif. VIII); Sess. VII, cap. 12 de ref.

bus omnes canonicatus ac portiones habeant annexum ordinem presbyterii, diaconatus vel subdiaconatus; episcopus autem cum consilio capituli designet ac distribuat, prout viderit expedire, quibus quisque ordo ex sacris annexus in posterum esse debeat; ita tamen, ut dimidia saltem pars presbyteri sint, ceteri vero diaconi aut subdiaconi. Ubi vero consuetudo laudabilior habet, ut plures vel omnes sint presbyteri, omnino observetur. Hortatur etiam sancta synodus, ut in provinciis, ubi id commode fieri potest, dignitates omnes et saltem dimidia pars canonicatuum in cathedralibus ecclesiis et collegiatis insignibus conferantur tantum magistris vel doctoribus, aut etiam licentiatis in theologia vel jure canonico. Praeterea obtinentibus in eisdem cathedralibus aut collegiatis dignitates, canonicatus, praebendas aut portiones non liceat vigore cujuslibet statuti aut consuetudinis ultra tres menses ab eisdem ecclesiis quolibet anno abesse,[66] salvis nihilominus earum ecclesiarum constitutionibus, quae longius servitii tempus requirunt; alioquin primo anno privetur unusquisque dimidia parte fructuum, quos ratione etiam praebendae ac residentiae, fecit suos. Quod si iterum eadem fuerit usus negligentia, privetur omnibus fructibus, quos eodem anno lucratus fuerit. Crescente vero contumacia, contra eos juxta sacrorum canonum constitutiones procedatur.[67] Distributiones vero qui statis horis interfuerint recipiant; [68] reliqui, quavis collusione aut remissione exclusa, his careant juxta Bonifacii VIII decretum, quod incipit: *Consuetudinem*,[69] quod sancta synodus in usum revocat, non obstantibus quibuscumque statutis et consuetudinibus. Omnes vero divina per se [70] et non per substitutos compellantur obire officia, et episcopo celebranti aut alia pontificalia exercenti assistere et inservire, atque in choro ad psallendum instituto hymnis et canticis Dei nomen reverenter, distincte devoteque laudare. Vestitu insuper decenti tam in ecclesia quam extra assidue utantur; [71] ab illicitisque venationibus, aucupiis, choreis, tabernis lusibusque abstineant, atque ea morum integritate polleant, ut merito ecclesiae senatus dici possint.

---

66 Cf. Sess. XXIII, cap. 1 de ref.

67 Cf. tot. tit. X, De cler. non resid., III, 4. Cap. ult. ejusdem tit. dat episcopo potestatem hujusmodi contumaces beneficiis spoliandi, nisi excusationem rationabilem ostenderint.

68 Cf. c.32, X, De praeb., III, 5 (Honor. III).

69 C. un. VI°, De cler. non resid., III, 3, *infra*, p. 574, lit. AC.

70 Cf. c.3, X, De cler. non resid., III, 4 (Lat. III); c.30, X, De praeb., III, 5 (Innoc. III); Sess. XXII, cap. 4 de ref.

71 Cf. tot. tit. X, De vit. et hon. cler., III, 1; in VI°, III, 1; in Clem., III, 1; in Extrav. comm., III, 1, et tit. X, De cler. venant., V, 24.

Cetera, quae ad debitum in divinis officiis regimen spectant, deque congrua in his canendi seu modulandi ratione, de certa lege in choro conveniendi et permanendi, simulque de omnibus ecclesiae ministris, quae necessaria erunt, et si qua hujusmodi, synodus provincialis pro cujusque provinciae utilitate et moribus certam cuique formulam praescribet. Interea vero episcopus non minus quam cum duobus canonicis, quorum unus ab episcopo, alter a capitulo eligatur, in iis, quae expedire videbuntur, poterit providere.

Caput XIII

QUOMODO TENUIORIBUS CATHEDRALIBUS ECCLESIIS ET PAROCHIIS CONSULENDUM. PAROCHIAE CERTIS FINIBUS DISTINGUENDAE

Quoniam pleraeque cathedrales ecclesiae tam tenuis reditus sunt et angustae, ut episcopali dignitati nullo modo respondeant, neque ecclesiarum necessitati sufficiant, examinet concilium provinciale, vocatis iis quorum interest, et diligenter expendat, quas propter angustias tenuitatemque vicinis unire [72] vel novis proventibus augere expediat; confectaque de praemissis instrumenta ad summum Romanum pontificem mittat, quibus instructus summus pontifex ex prudentia sua, prout expedire judicaverit, aut tenues invicem uniat aut aliqua accessione ex fructibus audeat. Interim vero, donec praedicta effectum sortiantur, hujusmodi episcopis, qui fructuum subventione pro dioecesis suae tenuitate indigent, poterit de beneficiis aliquibus, dum tamen curata non sint, nec dignitates seu canonicatus et praebendae, nec monasteria, in quibus viget regularis observantia vel quae capitulis generalibus et certis visitatoribus subduntur, a summo Romano pontifice provideri. In parochialibus etiam ecclesiis, quarum fructus aeque adeo exigui sunt, ut debitis nequeant oneribus satisfacere, curabit episcopus, si per beneficiorum unionem, non tamen regularium, id fieri non possit, ut primitiarum vel decimarum assignatione, aut per parochianorum symbola ac collectas, aut qua commodiori ei videbitur ratione tantum redigatur, quod pro rectoris ac parochiae necessitate decenter sufficiat. In unionibus vero quibuslibet, seu ex supradictis, seu aliis causis faciendis, ecclesiae parochiales monasteriis quibuscumque, aut abbatiis, seu dignitatibus sive praeben-

[72] Cf. Sess. VII, capp. 6, 7 de ref.; Sess. XIV, cap. 9 de ref.; Sess. XXIV, cap. 15 de ref.

dis ecclesiae cathedralis vel collegiatae, sive aliis beneficiis simplicibus, aut hospitalibus militiisve non uniantur, et quae unitae sunt revideantur ab ordinariis juxta alias decretum in eadem synodo sub fel. rec. Paulo III,[73] quod etiam in unitis ab eo tempore citra aeque observetur; non obstantibus in iis quibuscumque verborum formis, quae hic pro sufficienter expressis habeantur. Ad haec in posterum omnes hae cathedrales ecclesiae, quarum reditus summam ducatorum mille, et parochiales, quae summam ducatorum centum secundum verum annuum valorem non excedunt, nullis pensionibus aut reservationibus fructuum graventur. In iis quoque civitatibus ac locis, ubi parochiales ecclesiae certos non habent fines, nec earum rectores proprium populum, quem regant, sed promiscue petentibus sacramenta administrantur, mandat sancta synodus episcopis pro tutiori animarum eis commissarum salute, ut distincto populo in certas propriasque parochias unicuique suum perpetuum peculiaremque parochum assignent,[74] qui eas cognoscere valeat, et a quo solo licite sacramenta suscipiant, aut alio utiliori modo, prout loci qualitas exegerit, provideant.[75] Idemque in iis civitatibus ac locis, ubi nullae sunt parochiales, quam primum fieri curent, non obstantibus quibuscumque privilegiis et consuetudinibus, etiam immemorabilibus.

Caput XIV

NE QUIS ADMITTATUR AD POSSESSIONEM BENEFICII AUT DISTRIBUTIONEM CUM FRUCTUUM DISTRIBUTIONE IN USUS NON PIOS CONVERTENDA

In pluribus ecclesiis, tam cathedralibus quam collegiatis et parochialibus, ex earum constitutionibus aut ex prava consuetudine observari intelligitur, ut in electione, praesentatione, nominatione, institutione, confirmatione, collatione vel alia provisione sive admissione ad possessionem alicujus cathedralis ecclesiae, vel beneficii, canonicatuum, aut praebendarum vel partem proventuum, seu ad distributiones quotidianas, certae conditiones seu deductiones ex fructibus, solutiones, promissiones, compensationesve illicitae, aut etiam quae in aliquibus ecclesiis dicuntur turnorum lucra, interponantur. Haec cum

[73] Cf. Sess. VII, cap. 6 de ref.
[74] Cf. Sess. XIV, cap. 9 de ref.
[75] Cf. Sess. XXI, cap. 4 de ref.

sancta synodus detestetur, mandat episcopis, ut, quaecumque hujusmodi in usus pios non convertuntur, atque ingressus eos, qui simoniacae labis aut sordidae avaritiae suspicionem habent, fieri non permittant, ipsique diligenter de eorum constitutionibus sive consuetudinibus super praedictis cognoscant, et illis tantum, quas ut laudabiles probaverint, exceptis, reliquas ut pravas ac scandalosas rejiciant et aboleant. Eos vero, qui adversus haec in praesenti decreto comprehensa quavis ratione commiserint, poenis contra simoniacos editis sacris canonibus et variis summorum pontificum constitutionibus,[76] quas omnes innovat, teneri decernit; non obstantibus quibuscumque statutis, constitutionibus, consuetudinibus, etiam immemorabilibus, etiam apostolica auctoritate confirmatis, de quarum surreptione, obreptione et intentionis defectu episcopus, tamquam Apostolicae Sedis delegatus, cognoscere possit.

Caput XV

RATIO AUGENDI TENUES PRAEBENDAS ECCLESIARUM CATHEDRALIUM ET COLLEGIATARUM INSIGNIUM

In ecclesiis cathedralibus et collegiatis insignibus,[77] ubi frequentes adeoque tenues sunt praebendae simul cum distributionibus quotidianis, ut sustinendo decenti canonicorum gradui pro loci et personarum qualitate non sufficiant, liceat episcopis cum consensu capituli vel aliquot simplicia beneficia, non tamen regularia, iis unire, vel, si hac ratione provideri non possit, aliquibus ex iis suppressis cum patronorum consensu, si de jure patronatus laicorum sint, quarum fructus et proventus reliquarum praebendarum distributionibus quotidianis applicentur, eas ad pauciorem numerum reducere; ita tamen, ut tot supersint, quae divino cultui celebrando ac dignitati ecclesiae commode valeant respondere;[78] non obstantibus quibuscumque constitutionibus et privilegiis, aut quacumque reservatione generali vel speciali aut affectione. Neque praedictae uniones aut suppressiones

---

[76] Cf. C.I, q.1 fere per tot. et tot. tit. X, De sim., III, 5 et Extrav. comm., V, 1.
[77] Cf. huj. sess. cap. 13 de ref.
[78] Cf. c.2, X, De institut., III, 7 (Eugen. III); Sess. XXI, cap. 3 de ref. et Sess. XXII, cap. 3 de ref.

tolli seu impediri possint ex quibuscumque provisionibus, etiam vigore resignationis, aut quibusvis aliis derogationibus vel suspensionibus.

Caput XVI

QUID MUNERIS INCUMBAT CAPITULO SEDE VACANTE

Capitulum sede vacante, ubi fructuum percipiendorum ei munus incumbit, oeconomum unum vel plures fideles ac diligentes decernat, qui rerum ecclesiasticarum et proventuum curam gerant, quorum rationem ei, ad quem pertinebit, sint reddituri. Item officialem seu vicarium infra octo dies post mortem episcopi constituere, vel existentem confirmare omnino teneatur, qui saltem in jure canonico sit doctor vel licentiatus, vel alias, quantum fieri poterit, idoneus. Si secus factum fuerit, ad metropolitanum deputatio hujusmodi devolvatur.[79] Et si ecclesia ipsa metropolitana fuerit aut exempta, capitulumque, ut praefertur, negligens fuerit, tunc antiquior episcopus ex suffraganeis in metropolitana, et propinquior episcopus in exempta oeconomum et vicarium idoneos possit constituere. Episcopus vero ad eamdem ecclesiam vacantem promotus, ex iis, quae ad eum spectant, ab eisdem oeconomo, vicario et aliis quibuscumque officialibus et administratoribus, qui sede vacante fuerunt a capitulo vel ab aliis in ejus locum constituti, etiamsi fuerint ex eodem capitulo, rationem exigat officiorum, jurisdictionis, administrationis aut cujuscumque eorum muneris, possitque eos punire, qui in eorum officio seu administratione deliquerint, etiamsi praedicti officiales redditis rationibus a capitulo vel a deputatis ab eodem absolutionem aut liberationem obtinuerint. Eidem quoque episcopo teneatur capitulum de scripturis ad ecclesiam pertinentibus, si quae ad capitulum pervenerunt, rationem reddere.

Caput XVII

BENEFICIORUM COLLATIONI ET PLURIUM RETENTIONI MODUS STATUITUR

Cum ecclesiasticus ordo pervertatur, quando unus plurium officia occupat clericorum, sancte sacris canonibus cautum fuit, neminem

---

[79] Cf. c. ult. VI°, De suppl. negl. prael., I, 8 (Bonif. VIII).

oportere in duabus ecclesiis conscribi.[80] Verum quoniam multi improbae cupiditatis affectu se ipsos, non Deum, decipientes, ea quae bene constituta sunt, variis artibus eludere et plura simul beneficia obtinere non erubescunt: sancta synodus debitam regendis ecclesiis disciplinam restituere cupiens, praesenti decreto, quod in quibuscumque personis, quocumque titulo, etiamsi cardinalatus honore fulgeant, mandat observari, statuit, ut in posterum unum tantum beneficium ecclesiasticum singulis conferatur. Quod quidem, si ad vitam ejus, cui confertur, honeste sustentandam non sufficiat, liceat nihilominus aliud simplex sufficiens, dummodo utrumque personalem residentiam non requirat, eidem conferri. Haecque non modo ad cathedrales ecclesias, sed etiam ad alia omnia beneficia, tam saecularia quam regularia quaecumque, etiam commendata, pertineant, cujuscumque tituli ac qualitatis exsistant. Illi vero, qui in praesenti plures parochiales ecclesias, aut unam cathedralem et aliam parochialem obtinent, cogantur omnino,[81] quibuscumque dispensationibus ac unionibus ad vitam non obstantibus, una tantum parochiali vel sola cathedrali retenta, alias parochiales infra spatium sex mensium dimittere. Alioquin tam parochiales quam beneficia omnia, quae obtinent, ipso jure vacare censeantur,[82] ac tamquam vacantia libere aliis idoneis conferantur, nec ipsi antea illa obtinentes tuta conscientia fructus post dictum tempus retineant. Optat autem sancta synodus, ut resignantium necessitatibus commoda aliqua ratione, prout summo pontifici videbitur, provideatur.

Caput XVIII

ECCLESIA PAROCHIALI VACANTE DEPUTANDUS AB EPISCOPO VICARIUS, DONEC ILLI PROVIDEATUR DE PAROCHO. NOMINATI AD PAROCHIALES QUA FORMA ET A QUIBUS EXAMINARI DEBENT

Expedit maxime animarum saluti, a dignis atque idoneis parochis gubernari. Id ut diligentius ac rectius perficiatur,[83] statuit sancta synodus, ut, cum parochialis ecclesiae vacatio, etiamsi cura ecclesiae vel episcopo incumbere dicatur et per unum vel plures administretur,

---

[80] Cf. Sess. VII, cap. 2 de ref.
[81] C. 28, X, De praeb., III, 5 et Sess. cit., cap. 4 de ref.
[82] Cf. c. 4, Extrav. comm., De praeb., III, 2 (Joan. XXII).
[83] Cf. const. *In conferendis* Pii V, 18 Mart., 1567.

etiam in ecclesiis patrimonialibus seu receptivis nuncupatis, in quibus consuevit episcopus uni vel pluribus curam animarum dare, quos omnes ad infra scriptum examen teneri mandat,[84] per obitum vel resignationem, etiam in curia seu aliter quomodocumque contigerit, etiamsi ipsa parochialis ecclesia reservata vel affecta fuerit generaliter vel specialiter, etiam vigore indulti seu privilegii in favorem sanctae Romanae ecclesiae cardinalium seu abbatum vel capitulorum; debeat episcopus statim, habita notitia vacationis ecclesiae, si opus fuerit, idoneum in ea vicarium cum congrua ejus arbitrio fructuum portionis assignatione constituere, qui onera ipsius ecclesiae sustineat, donec ei de rectore provideatur. Porro episcopus et qui jus patronatus habet, intra decem dies vel aliud tempus ab episcopo praescribendum idoneos aliquot clericos ad regendam ecclesiam coram deputandis examinatoribus nominet. Liberum sit tamen etiam aliis, qui aliquos ad id aptos noverint, eorum nomina deferre, ut possit postea de cujuslibet aetate, moribus et sufficientia fieri diligens inquisitio. Et si episcopo aut synodo provinciali pro regionis more videbitur magis expedire, per edictum etiam publicum vocentur qui volent examinari. Transacto constituto tempore omnes, qui descripti fuerint, examinentur ab episcopo [85] sive, eo impedito, ab ejus vicario generali atque ab aliis examinatoribus non paucioribus quam tribus, quorum votis, si pares aut singulares fuerint, accedere possit episcopus vel vicarius, quibus magis videbitur. Examinatores autem singulis annis in dioecesana synodo ab episcopo vel ejus vicario ad minus sex proponantur, qui synodo satisfaciant et ab ea probentur. Advenienteque vacatione cujuslibet ecclesiae tres ex illis eligat episcopus, qui cum eo examen perficiant; indeque succendente alia vacatione aut eosdem, aut alios tres, quos maluerit, ex praedictis illis sex eligat. Sint vero hi examinatores magistri seu doctores aut licentiati in theologia aut jure canonico, vel alii clerici seu regulares, etiam ex ordine mendicantium aut etiam saeculares, qui ad id videbuntur magis idonei, jurentque omnes ad sancta Dei evangelia, se quacumque humana affectione postposita fideliter munus executuros. Caveantque, ne quidquam prorsus occasione hujus examinis nec ante nec post accipiant; [86] alioquin simoniae vitium tam ipsi quam alii dantes incurrant, a quo absolvi nequeant nisi dimissis beneficiis, quae quomodocumque etiam antea obtinebant, et

---

[84] Cf. Sess. VII, cap. 13 de ref.
[85] Cf. Sess. XXV, cap. 9 de ref.
[86] Cf. c.5 (§ 1), D.XXIV (conc. Nanneten.).

ad alia in posterum inhabiles reddantur. Et de his omnibus non solum coram Deo, sed etiam in synodo provinciali, si opus erit, rationem reddere teneantur, a qua, si quid contra officium eos fecisse compertum fuerit, graviter ejus arbitrio puniri possint. Peracto deinde examine renuncientur quotcumque ab his idonei judicati fuerint aetate, moribus, doctrina, prudentia et aliis rebus ad vacantem ecclesiam gubernandam opportunis. Ex hisque episcopus eum eligat,[87] quem ceteris magis idoneum judicaverit, atque illi, et non alteri, collatio ecclesiae ab eo fiat, ad quem spectabit eam conferre. Si vero juris patronatus ecclesiastici erit, ac institutio ad episcopum et non ad alium pertineat, is, quem patronus digniorem inter probatos ab examinatoribus judicabit, episcopo praesentare teneatur, ut ab eo instituatur.[88] Cum vero institutio ab alio, quam ab episcopo, erit facienda, tunc episcopus solus ex dignis eligat digniorem, quem patronus ei praesentet, ad quem institutio spectat. Quod si juris patronatus laicorum fuerit,[89] debeat qui a patrono praesentatus fuerit ab eisdem deputatis ut supra examinari, et non nisi idoneus repertus fuerit admitti. In omnibusque supradictis casibus non cuiquam alteri, quam uni ex praedictis examinatis et ab examinatoribus approbatis, juxta supradictam regulam, de ecclesia provideatur, nec praedictorum examinatorum relationem, quominus executionem habeat, ulla devolutio aut appellatio, etiam ad Sedem Apostolicam sive ejusdem Sedis legatos aut vicelegatos aut nuncios, seu episcopos aut metropolitanos, primates vel patriarchas interposita impediat aut suspendat; alioquin vicarius, quem ecclesiae vacanti antea episcopus arbitrio suo ad tempus deputavit, vel forsan postea deputabit, ab ejus ecclesiae custodia et administratione non amoveatur, donec aut eidem, aut alteri, qui probatus et electus fuerit, ut supra, sit provisum. Alias provisiones omnes seu institutiones, praeter supradictam formam factae, surreptitiae esse censeantur, non obstantibus huic decreto exemptionibus, indultis, privilegiis, praeventionibus, affectionibus, novis provisionibus, indultis concessis quibuscumque universitatibus,[90] etiam ad certam summam, et aliis impedimentis quibuscumque. Si tamen adeo exigui reditus dictae parochiales fuerint, ut totius hujus examinationis operam non ferant, aut nemo sit qui se examini quaerat subjicere, aut ob apertas factiones seu dissidia, quae in aliquibus locis

---

[87] Cf. Sess. XXV, cap. 9 de ref.
[88] Cf. Sess. VII, cap. 13 de ref. et Sess. XIV, cap. 13 de ref.
[89] Cf. cc.8, 21, X, De jur. patr., III, 38 (Alex. III).
[90] Cf. Sess. VII, cap. 9 de ref.

reperiuntur, facile graviores rixae ac tumultus possint excitari: poterit ordinarius, si pro sua conscientia cum deputatorum consilio ita expedire arbitrabitur, hac forma omissa privatum aliud examen, ceteris tamen ut supra servatis, adhibere. Licebit etiam synodo provinciali, si qua in supradictis circa examinationis formam addenda remittendave esse censuerit, providere.

Caput XIX

MANDATA DE PROVIDENDO; EXSPECTATIVAE ET ALIA ID GENUS ANTIQUANTUR

Decernit sancta synodus, mandata de providendo et gratias, quae exspectativae dicuntur, nemini amplius, etiam collegiis, universitatibus, senatoribus et aliis singularibus personis, etiam sub nomine indulti, aut ad certam summam vel alio quovis colore concedi, nec hactenus concessis cuiquam uti licere.[91] Sed nec reservationes mentales, nec aliae quaecumque gratiae ad vacatura,[92] nec indulta ad alienas ecclesias vel monasteria alicui, etiam ex sanctae Romanae ecclesiae cardinalibus, concedantur, et hactenus concessa abrogata esse censeantur.

Caput XX

RATIO TRACTANDI CAUSAS AD FORUM ECCLESIASTICUM PERTINENTES PRAESCRIBITUR

Causae omnes ad forum ecclesiasticum quomodolibet pertinentes, etiamsi beneficiales sint, in prima instantia coram ordinariis locorum dumtaxat cognoscantur, atque omnino saltem infra biennium a die motae litis terminentur; alioquin post id spatium liberum sit partibus vel alteri illarum judices superiores, alias tamen competentes, adire, qui causam in eo statu, quo fuerit, assumant et quam primum terminari curent; nec antea aliis committantur, nec avocentur, neque appellationes ab eisdem interpositae per superiores quoscumque recipiantur, earumve commissio aut inhibitio fiat, nisi a definitiva vel a definitivae vim habente, et cujus gravamen per appellationem a definitiva reparari

[91] Cf. Sess. XXV, cap. 9 de ref. et tot. tit. X, De conc. praeb. non vac., III, 8; in VI°, III, 7; in Clem., III, 3.
[92] Cf. c. 2, X (Lat. III) et in VI° (Bonif. VIII), tit. cit.

nequeat. Ab his excipiantur causae, quae juxta canonicas sanctiones apud Sedem Apostolicam sunt tractandae,[93] vel quas ex urgenti rationabilique causa judicaverit summus Romanus pontifex per speciale rescriptum signaturae sanctitatis suae manu propria subscribendum committere aut avocare. Ad haec causae matrimoniales et criminales non decani, archidiaconi aut aliorum inferiorum judicio, etiam visitando, sed episcopi tantum examini et jurisdictioni relinquantur, etiamsi in praesenti inter episcopum et decanum seu archidiaconum, aut alios inferiores super causarum istarum cognitione lis aliqua in quacumque instantia pendeat, coram quo, si pars vere paupertatem probaverit, non cogatur extra provinciam nec in secunda nec in tertia instantia in eadem causa matrimoniali litigare, nisi pars altera et alimenta et expenses litis velit subministrare. Legati quoque, etiam de latere, nuncii, gubernatores ecclesiastici aut alii, quarumcumque facultatum vigore non solum episcopos in praedictis causis impedire, aut aliquo modo eorum jurisdictionem iis praeripere aut turbare non praesumant, sed nec etiam contra clericos aliasve personas ecclesiasticas, nisi episcopo prius requisito, eoque negligente, procedant. Alias eorum processus ordinationesve nullius momenti sint, atque ad damni satisfactionem partibus illati teneantur. Praeterea, si quis in casibus a jure permissis appellaverit,[94] aut de aliquo gravamine conquestus fuerit, seu alias ob lapsum biennii, de quo supra, ad alium judicem recurrerit, teneatur acta omnia coram episcopo gesta ad judicem appellationis expensis suis transferre, eodem tamen episcopo prius admonito, ut, si quid ei pro causae instructione videbitur, possit judici appellationis significare. Quod si appellatus compareat, cogatur tunc is quoque actorum, quae translata sunt, expensas pro portione sua, si illis uti voluerit, subire, nisi aliter ex loci consuetudine servetur, ut scilicet ad appellantem integrum hoc onus pertineat. Porro ipsam actorum copiam teneatur notarius congrua mercede accepta appellanti quanto citius et ad minus intra mensem exhibere. Qui notarius si in differenda exhibitione fraudem fecerit, ab officii administratione arbitrio ordinarii suspendatur, et ad dupli poenam, quanti ea lis fuerit, inter appellantem et pauperes loci distribuendam compellatur. Judex vero, si et ipse impedimenti hujus conscius particepsve fuerit, aliterve obstiterit, ne appellanti integre acta intra tempus traderentur, ad eamdem dupli poenam, prout supra, teneatur; non obstantibus quoad omnia suprascripta privi-

[93] Cf. c.7, C.VI, q.4 (conc. Sardicen.); Sess. XXV, cap. 10 de ref.
[94] Cf. fere tot. tit. X, De appell., II, 28; in VI°, II, 15; in Clem., II, 12.

legiis, indultis, concordiis, quae suos tantum teneant auctores, et aliis quibuscumque consuetudinibus.

Caput XXI

DECLARATUR, EX CERTIS VERBIS SUPRA POSITIS NON IMMUTARI SOLITAM RATIONEM TRACTANDI NEGOTIA IN GENERALIBUS CONCILIIS

Cupiens sancta synodus, ut ex decretis ab ea editis nulla unquam futuris temporibus dubitandi occasio oriatur, verba illa posita in decreto publicato sessione prima sub beatissimo domino nostro Pio IV,[95] videlicet: *Quae proponentibus legatis ac praesidentibus ad horum temporum levandas calamitates, sedandas de religione controversias, coercendas linguas dolosas, depravatorum morum abusus corrigendos, ecclesiae veram et Christianam pacem conciliandam, apta et idonea ipsi sanctae synodo videbuntur*, explicando declarat, mentis suae non fuisse, ut ex praedictis verbis solita ratio tractandi negotia in generalibus conciliis ulla ex parte immutaretur, neque novi quidquam, praeter id, quod a sacris canonibus vel generalium synodorum forma hactenus statutum est, cuiquam adderetur vel detraheretur.

INDICTIO FUTURAE SESSIONIS

Insuper eadem sacrosancta synodus proximam futuram sessionem feria quinta post conceptionem beatae Mariae Virginis, quae erit dies nona mensis Decembris proxime venturi, habendam esse statuit et decernit, cum potestate etiam abbreviandi. In qua sessione tractabitur de sexto nunc in eam dilato capite, et de reliquis reformationis capitibus jam exhibitis, deque aliis ad eam pertinentibus. Si vero opportunum videbitur, et tempus patietur, poterit etiam de nonnullis dogmatibus tractari, prout suo tempore in congregationibus proponentur.

Abbreviata est dies sessionis.

---

[95] Cf. Sess. XVII in princ.

SESSIO VIGESIMA QUINTA

QUAE EST NONA ET ULTIMA

SUB PIO IV PONT. MAX.

coepta die III, absoluta die IV Decembris, MDLXIII

DECRETUM DE PURGATORIO

Cum catholica ecclesia, Spiritu Sancto edocta ex sacris litteris et antiqua patrum traditione, in sacris conciliis et novissime in hac oecumenica synodo docuerit, purgatorium esse,[1] animasque ibi detentas fidelium suffragiis, potissimum vero acceptabili altaris sacrificio juvari, praecipit sancta synodus episcopis, ut sanam de purgatorio doctrinam a sanctis patribus et sacris conciliis traditam [2] a Christi fidelibus credi, teneri, doceri et ubique praedicari diligenter studeant. Apud rudem vero plebem difficiliores ac subtiliores quaestiones, quaeque ad aedificationem non faciunt,[3] et ex quibus plerumque nulla sit pietatis accessio, a popularibus concionibus secludantur. Incerta item vel quae specie falsi laborant evulgari ac tractari non permittant. Ea vero, quae ad curiositatem quamdam aut superstitionem spectant, vel turpe lucrum sapiunt, tamquam scandala et fidelium offendicula prohibeant. Curent autem episcopi,[4] ut fidelium vivorum suffragia, missarum scilicet sacrificia, orationes, eleemosynae, aliaque pietatis opera, quae a fidelibus pro aliis fidelibus defunctis fieri consueverunt, secundum ecclesiae instituta pie et devote fiant, et quae pro illis ex testatorum fundationibus vel alia ratione debentur, non perfunctorie, sed a sacerdotibus et ecclesiae ministris et aliis, qui hoc praestare tenentur, diligenter et accurate persolvantur.

---

1 Sess. VI, can. 30; Sess. XXII, cap. 2 et can. 3.

2 Testimonia patrum de purgatorio collegit Rouët de Journel, *Enchiridion patristicum* sub rubrica "Novissima hominis," p. 783, n.587. Vide etiam Denzinger, *Enchiridion* sub rubrica "Novissima singulorum hominum," XIV a, p. [54], qui recenset testimonia conciliorum.

3 Cf. I Tim. 1:4; II Tim. 2:23; Tit. 3:9.

4 Cf. *infra*, cap. 4 de ref.

DE INVOCATIONE, VENERATIONE ET RELIQUIIS SANCTORUM, ET SACRIS IMAGINIBUS

Mandat sancta synodus omnibus episcopis et ceteris docendi munus curamque sustinentibus, ut juxta catholicae et apostolicae ecclesiae usum a primaevis Christianae religionis temporibus receptum, sanctorumque patrum consensionem [5] et sacrorum conciliorum [6] decreta, in primis de sanctorum intercessione, invocatione, reliquiarum honore, et legitimo imaginum usu fideles diligenter instruant, docentes eos, sanctos una cum Christo regnantes orationes suas pro hominibus Deo offerre, bonum atque utile esse suppliciter eos invocare, et ob beneficia impetranda a Deo per Filium ejus Jesum Christum Dominum nostrum, qui solus noster redemptor et salvator est, ad eorum orationes, opem auxiliumque confugere; [7] illos vero, qui negant sanctos aeterna felicitate in coelo fruentes invocandos esse, aut qui asserunt, vel illos pro hominibus non orare, vel eorum, ut pro nobis etiam singulis orent, invocationem esse idololatriam, vel pugnare cum verbo Dei adversarique honori unius mediatoris Dei et hominum Jesu Christi,[8] vel stultum esse in coelo regnantibus voce vel mente supplicare, impie sentire. Sanctorum quoque martyrum et aliorum cum Christo viventium sancta corpora, quae viva membra fuerunt Christi et templum Spiritus Sancti,[9] ab ipso ad aeternam vitam suscitanda et glorificanda a fidelibus veneranda esse,[10] per quae multa beneficia a Deo hominibus praestantur, ita ut affirmantes, sanctorum reliquiis venerationem atque honorem non deberi, vel eas aliaque sacra monumenta a fidelibus inutiliter honorari, atque eorum opis impetrandae causae sanctorum memorias frustra frequentari, omnino damnandos esse, prout jam pridem eos damnavit, et nunc etiam damnat ecclesia.

Imagines porro Christi, deiparae Virginis et aliorum sanctorum in templis praesertim habendas et retinendas, eisque debitum honorem et venerationem impertiendam, non quod credatur inesse aliqua in iis divinitas vel virtus, propter quam sint colendae, vel quod ab eis sit aliquid petendum, vel quod fiducia in imaginibus sit figenda, velut

---

[5] Cf. Rouët de Journel sub rubrica "Religio et cultus sanctorum," p. 770, n. 283.

[6] Eorum testimonia habentur apud Denzinger sub rubrica "Primum Decalogi praeceptum," XI e, p. [34].

[7] Cf. Sess. XXII, de sacrific. miss., cap. 3.

[8] Cf. I Tim. 2:5.

[9] Cf. I Cor. 3:16; 6:19; II Cor. 6:16.

[10] Testimonium traditionis Christianae de cultu reliquiarum exhibet Rouët de Journel, p. 770, n. 285. Illud conciliorum, cf. Denzinger, *loc. cit.*

olim fiebat a gentibus, quae in idolis spem suam collocabant: [11] sed quoniam honos, qui eis exhibetur, refertur ad prototypa, quae illae repraesentant, ita ut per imagines, quas osculamur et coram quibus caput aperimus et procumbimus, Christum adoremus, et sanctos, quorum illae similitudinem gerunt, veneremur. Id quod conciliorum, praesertim vero secundae Nicaenae synodi, decretis contra imaginum oppugnatores est sancitum.[12]

Illud vero diligenter doceant episcopi, per historias mysteriorum nostrae redemptionis, picturis vel aliis similitudinibus expressas, erudiri et confirmari populum in articulis fidei commemorandis et assidue recolendis; tum vero ex omnibus sacris imaginibus magnum fructum percipi, non solum quia admonetur populus beneficiorum et munerum, quae a Christo sibi collata sunt, sed etiam quia Dei per sanctos miracula et salutaria exempla oculis fidelium subjiciuntur, ut pro iis Deo gratias agant, ad sanctorumque imitationem vitam moresque suos componant, excitenturque ad adorandum ac diligendum Deum, et ad pietatem colendam. Si quis autem his decretis contraria docuerit aut senserit: anathema sit.

In has autem sanctas et salutares observationes si qui abusus irrepserint, eos prorsus aboleri sancta synodus vehementer cupit, ita ut nullae falsi dogmatis imagines et rudibus periculosi erroris occasionem praebentes statuantur. Quod si aliquando historias et narrationes sacrae scripturae, cum id indoctae plebi expediet, exprimi et figurari contigerit, doceatur populus, non propterea divinitatem figurari, quasi corporeis oculis conspici vel coloribus aut figuris exprimi possit. Omnis porro superstitio in sanctorum invocatione, reliquiarum veneratione et imaginum sacro usu tollatur,[13] omnis turpis quaestus eliminetur, omnis denique lascivia vitetur, ita ut procaci venustate imagines non pingantur nec ornentur, et sanctorum celebratione ac reliquiarum visitatione homines ad comessationes atque ebrietates non abutantur,[14] quasi festi dies in honorem sanctorum per luxum ac lasciviam agantur. Postremo tanta circa haec diligentia et cura ab episcopis adhibeatur, ut nihil inordinatum aut praepostere et tumultuarie accommodatum, nihil profanum nihilque inhonestum appareat, cum domum Dei deceat sanctitudo.[15]

---

[11] Ps. 134:15 ff.
[12] Cf. Denzinger, nn. 302–304, 306; Rouët de Journel, p. 770, n. 286.
[13] Cf. c. ult., X, De reliq. et ven. sanct., III, 45 (Lat. IV).
[14] Cf. c. 2, D. III de cons. (conc. Toletan. IV).
[15] Ps. 92:5.

Haec ut fidelius observentur, statuit sancta synodus, nemini licere ullo in loco vel ecclesia, etiam quomodolibet exempta, ullam insolitam ponere vel ponendam curare imaginem, nisi ab episcopo approbata fuerit; nulla etiam admittenda esse nova miracula,[16] nec novas reliquias recipiendas,[17] nisi eodem recognoscente et approbante episcopo, qui, simul atque de iis aliquid compertum habuerit, adhibitis in consilium theologis et aliis piis viris ea faciat, quae veritati et pietati consentanea judicaverit. Quod si aliquis dubius aut difficilis abusus sit extirpandus, vel omnino aliqua de iis rebus gravior quaestio incidat, episcopus, antequam controversiam dirimat, metropolitani et comprovincialium episcoporum in concilio provinciali sententiam expectet, ita tamen, ut nihil inconsulto sanctissimo Romano pontifice novum aut in ecclesia hactenus inusitatum decernatur.

DE REGULARIBUS ET MONIALIBUS

Eadem sacrosancta synodus, reformationem prosequens, ea, quae sequuntur, statuenda esse censuit.

Caput I

REGULARES OMNES AD REGULAE, QUAM PROFESSI SUNT, PRAESCRIPTUM VITAM INSTITUANT; ID UT FIAT SUPERIORES SEDULO CURENT

Quoniam non ignorat sancta synodus, quantum ex monasteriis pie institutis et recte administratis in ecclesia Dei splendoris atque utilitatis oriatur, necessarium esse censuit, quo facilius ac maturius, ubi collapsa est, vetus et regularis disciplina instauretur, et constantius, ubi conservata est, perseveret, praecipere, prout hoc decreto praecipit, ut omnes regulares, tam viri quam mulieres, ad regulae, quam professi sunt, praescriptum vitam instituant et componant, atque in primis quae ad suae professionis perfectionem proprie pertinent, ut obedientiae, paupertatis et castitatis,[18] ac si quae alia sunt alicujus regulae et ordinis peculiaria vota et praecepta, ad eorum respective essentiam, necnon ad communem vitam, victum et vestitum conservanda perti-

[16] C. I, X, De reliq. et ven sanct., III, 45.
[17] Cf. adn. 13.
[18] Cf. c. I (§ Quum igitur in primis), De verb. sig. in Clem., V, 11.

nentia fideliter observent. Omnisque cura et diligentia a superioribus adhibeatur tam in capitulis generalibus et provincialibus, quam in eorum visitationibus, quae suis temporibus facere non praetermittant, ut ab illis non recedatur; cum compertum sit, ab eis non posse ea, quae ad substantiam regularis vitae pertinent, relaxari.[19] Si enim illa, quae bases sunt et fundamenta totius regularis disciplinae, exacte non fuerint conservata, totum corruat aedificium necesse est.[20]

Caput II

PROPRIETAS REGULARIBUS OMNINO PROHIBETUR

Nemini igitur regularium, tam virorum quam mulierum, liceat bona immobilia vel mobilia, cujuscumque qualitatis fuerint, etiam quovis modo ab eis acquisita, tamquam propria aut etiam nomine conventus possidere vel tenere; [21] sed statim ea superiori tradantur, conventuique incorporentur. Nec deinceps liceat superioribus bona stabilia alicui regulari concedere, etiam ad usum fructuum vel usum, administrationem aut commendam. Administratio autem bonorum monasteriorum seu conventuum ad solos officiales eorumdem ad nutum superiorum amovibiles pertineat. Mobilium vero usum ita superiores permittant, ut eorum suppellex statui paupertatis, quam professi sunt, conveniat, nihilque superflui in ea sit, nihil etiam, quod sit necessarium, eis denegetur. Quod si quis aliter quidquam tenere deprehensus aut convictus fuerit, is biennio activa et passiva voce privatus sit, atque etiam juxta suae regulae et ordinis constitutiones puniatur.

---

[19] Cf. c.6, X, De stat. monach., III, 35 (Innoc. III).
[20] Cf. c.26, C.I, q.1 (Greg. I).
[21] Cf. c.11, C.XII, q.1 (Aug.), c.13, *ibid.* (Jul. Pom.); c.14 conc. Moguntien. (a.847); c.2, X, De stat. monach., III, 35 (Alex. III), c.6, *ibid.* (Innoc. III).

Caput III

OMNIA MONASTERIA, QUAE HIC NON PROHIBENTUR, POSSUNT POSSIDERE BONA IMMOBILIA; NUMERUS PERSONARUM IN ILLIS PRO MODO FACULTATUM AUT ELEEMOSYNARUM CONSTITUATUR; NULLA SINE LICENTIA EPISCOPI ERIGENDA

Concedit sancta synodus omnibus monasteriis et domibus, tam virorum quam mulierum, et mendicantium (exceptis domibus fratrum sancti Francisci Capucinorum et eorum, qui Minorum de observantia vocantur),[22] etiam quibus aut ex constitutionibus suis erat prohibitum, aut ex privilegio apostolica non erat concessum, ut deinceps bona immobilia eis possidere liceat. Quod si aliqua loca ex praedictis, quibus auctoritate apostolica similia bona possidere permissum erat, eis spoliata sint, eadem omnia illis restituenda esse decernit. In praedictis autem monasteriis et domibus tam virorum quam mulierum, bona immobilia possidentibus vel non possidentibus, is tantum numerus constituatur [23] ac in posterum conservetur, qui vel ex reditibus propriis monasteriorum, vcl ex consuetis eleemosynis commode possit sustentari; nec de cetero similia loca erigantur sine episcopi, in cujus dioecesi erigenda sunt, licentia prius obtenta.[24]

Caput IV

REGULARIS SINE SUPERIORIS LICENTIA NEC SE OBSEQUIO ALTERIUS LOCI AUT PERSONAE SUBJICIAT, NEC A CONVENTU RECEDAT. ABSENS STUDIORUM CAUSA IN CONVENTIBUS COMMORETUR

Prohibet sancta synodus, ne quis regularis sine sui superioris licentia praedicationis vel lectionis aut cujusvis pii operis praetextu subjiciat se obsequio alicujus praelati, principis, vel universitatis vel communitatis, aut alterius cujuscumque personae seu loci,[25] neque ei aliquando

[22] Cf. c.3 (§ Porro), VI°, De verb. sig., V, 12; c.1, h.t. in Clem., V, 11.

[23] Cf. c.9, X, De vit. et hon. cler., III, 1 (Greg. IX); c.1, X, De institut., III, 7 (conc. Arelatan. VI); c. un., VI°, De stat. regular., III, 16 (Bonif. VIII). Cf. etiam const. Pii V *Circa pastoralis,* 29 Maii, 1566.

[24] Cf. const. Clementis VIII *Quoniam,* 23 Jul., 1603.

[25] Cf. c.35, C.XVI, q.1 (conc. Tarraconen.); c.7, X, De off. jud. ord., I, 31 (Innoc. III); cc.3, 4, X, ne cler. vel monach., III, 50 (Alex. III); c.1 (§ 5), in Clem., De stat. monach., III, 10.

privilegium aut facultas ab aliis super iis obtenta suffragetur. Quod si contra fecerit tamquam inobediens arbitrio superioris puniatur. Nec liceat regularibus a suis conventibus recedere, etiam praetextu ad superiores suos accedendi, nisi ab eisdem missi aut vocati fuerint. Qui vero sine praedicto mandato in scriptis obtento repertus fuerit, ab ordinariis locorum tamquam desertor sui instituti puniatur. Illi autem, qui studiorum causa ad universitates mittuntur, in conventibus tantum habitent; alioquin ab ordinariis contra eos procedatur.

Caput V

CLAUSURAE MONIALIUM, PRAESERTIM QUAE EXTRA URBES AGUNT, PROVIDETUR

Bonifacii VIII constitutionem, quae incipit: *Periculoso*,[26] renovans, sancta synodus universis episcopis sub obtestatione divini judicii et interminatione maledictionis aeternae praecipit, ut in omnibus monasteriis sibi subjectis ordinaria, in aliis vero Sedis Apostolicae auctoritate, clausuram sanctimonialium, ubi violata fuerit, diligenter restitui, et ubi inviolata est, conservari maxime procurent, inobedientes atque contradictores per censuras ecclesiasticas aliasque poenas quacumque appellatioine postposita compescentes, invocato etiam ad hoc, si opus fuerit, auxilio brachii saecularis.[27] Quod auxilium ut praebeatur, omnes Christianos principes hortatur sancta synodus, et sub excommunicationis poena ipso facto incurrenda omnibus magistratibus saecularibus injungit. Nemini autem sanctimonialium liceat post professionem exire a monasterio, etiam ad breve tempus, quocumque praetextu, nisi ex aliqua legitima causa ab episcopo approbanda,[28] indultis quibuscumque et privilegiis non obstantibus. Ingredi autem intra septa monasterii nemini liceat,[29] cujuscumque generis aut conditionis, sexus vel aetatis fuerit, sine episcopi vel superioris licentia in scriptis obtenta, sub excommunicationis poena ipso facto incurrenda. Dare autem tantum episcopus vel superior licentiam debet in casibus necessariis, neque

---

[26] C. un., VI°, De stat. regular., III, 16, *infra*, p. 574, lit. AD.

[27] Cf. const. Pii V *Circa pastoralis*, 29 Maii, 1566; *Decori* (§ 2), 1 Feb., 1570; Gregorii XIII *Deo sacris*, 30 Dec., 1572, et *Dubiis*, 23 Dec., 1581.

[28] Cf. c. un., VI°, De stat. regular., III, 16; cc.57, 62 conc. Cabilonen. II (a.813).

[29] Cf. c.2 conc. Matisconen. I (a.581); c.11 (c.24, C.XVIII, q.2), conc. Hispalen. II (a.619); c.63 conc. Cabilonen. II; c.7 conc. Arelaten. VI (a.813); c.8, X, De vit. et hon. cler., III, 1 (Lat. III).

alius ullo modo possit, etiam vigore cujuscumque facultatis vel indulti hactenus concessi vel in posterum concedendi. Et quia monasteria sanctimonialium extra moenia urbis vel oppidi constituta malorum hominum praedae et aliis facinoribus sine ulla saepe custodia sunt exposita, curent episcopi et alii superiores, si ita videbitur expedire, ut sanctimoniales ex iis ad nova vel antiqua monasteria intra urbes vel oppida frequentia reducantur, invocato etiam auxilio, si opus fuerit, brachii saecularis. Impedientes vero vel non obedientes per censuras ecclesiasticas parere compellant.

Caput VI

RATIO ELIGENDI SUPERIORES

In electione superiorum quorumcumque, abbatum temporalium et aliorum officialium ac generalium, et abbatissarum atque aliarum praepositarum, quo omnia recte et sine ulla fraude fiant, in primis sancta synodus districte praecipit, omnes supradictos eligi debere per vota secreta, ita ut singulorum eligentium nomina nunquam publicentur. Nec in posterum liceat provinciales, aut abbates, priores aut alios quoscumque titulares ad effectum electionis faciendae constituere, aut voces et suffragia absentium supplere. Si vero contra hujus decreti constitutionem aliquis electus fuerit, electio irrita sit, et is, qui ad hunc effectum se in provincialem, abbatum aut priorem creari permiserit, deinceps ad omnia officia in religione obtinenda inhabilis exsistat, facultatesque super his concessae eo ipso abrogatae censeantur, et, si in posterum aliae concedantur, tamquam subreptitiae habeantur.

Caput VII

QUAE ET QUOMODO ABBATISSAE ET QUOCUMQUE NOMINE PRAEFECTAE ELIGENDAE. DUOBUS MONASTERIIS NULLA PRAEFICIATUR

Abbatissa et priorissa, et quocumque alio nomine praefecta vel praeposita appelletur, eligatur non minor annis quadraginta,[30] et quae octo annis post expressam professionem laudabiliter vixerit. Quod si his

[30] Cf. c. 12, C. XX, q. 1 (Greg. I).

qualitatibus non reperiatur in eodem monasterio, ex alio ejusdem ordinis eligi possit. Si hoc etiam incommodum superiori, qui electioni praeest, videatur, ex iis, quae in eodem monasterio annum trigesimum excesserint,[31] et quinque saltem annis post professionem recte vixerint, episcopo vel alio superiore consentiente, eligatur. Duobus vero monasteriis nulla praeficiatur.[32] Et si qua duo vel plura quocumque modo obtinet, cogatur, uno excepto, intra sex menses cetera resignare. Post id vero tempus, nisi resignaverit, omnia ipso jure vacent. Is vero, qui electioni praeest, episcopus sive alius superior claustra monasterii non ingrediatur, sed ante cancellorum fenestellam vota singularum audiat vel accipiat. In reliquis serventur singulorum ordinum vel monasteriorum constitutiones.

Caput VIII

REGIMEN MONASTERIORUM NON HABENTIUM ORDINARIOS REGULARES VISITATORES QUOMODO INSTITUENDUM

Monasteria omnia, quae generalibus capitulis aut episcopis non subsunt, nec suos habent ordinarios regulares visitatores, sed sub immediata Sedis Apostolicae protectione ac directione regi consueverunt, teneantur infra annum a fine praesentis concilii et deinde quolibet triennio sese in congregationes redigere juxta formam constitutionis Innocentii III in concilio generali, quae incipit: *In singulis*,[33] ibique certas regulares personas deputare, quae de modo et ordine, de praedictis congregationibus erigendis, ac statutis in eis exequendis deliberent et statuant. Quod si in his negligentes fuerint, liceat metropolitano, in cujus provincia praedicta monasteria sunt, tamquam Sedis Apostolicae delegato, eos pro praedictis causis convocare. Quod si infra limites unius provinciae non sit sufficiens talium monasteriorum numerus ad erigendam congregationem, possint duarum vel trium provinciarum monasteria unam facere congregationem. Ipsis autem congregationibus constitutis, illarum generalia capitula et ab illis electi praesides vel visitatores eamdem habeant auctoritatem in suae congregationis monasteria ac regulares in eis commorantes, quam alii praesides ac visitatores in ceteris habent ordinibus, teneanturque suae congregationis monasteria frequenter visitare, et illorum reformationi

---

[31] Cf. c.43, VI°, De elect., I, 6 (Bonif. VIII).
[32] Cf. c.4, C.XXI, q.1 (conc. Agathen.); c.9 conc. Epaonen. (a.517).
[33] C.7, X, De stat. monach., III, 35, *infra*, p. 576, lit. AE.

incumbere, et ea observare, quae in sacris canonibus [34] et in hoc sacro concilio sunt decreta. Quod si etiam metropolitano instante praedicta exequi non curaverint, episcopis, in quorum dioecesibus loca praedicta sita sunt, tamquam Sedis Apostolicae delegatis subdantur.

Caput IX

MONASTERIA MONIALIUM IMMEDIATE SUBJECTA SEDI APOSTOLICAE AB EPISCOPO REGANTUR; ALIA VERO A DEPUTATIS IN CAPITULIS GENERALIBUS, VEL ALIIS REGULARIBUS

Monasteria sanctimonialium sanctae Sedi Apostolicae immediate subjecta, etiam sub nomine capitulorum S. Petri, vel S. Joannis vel alias quomodocumque nuncupentur, ab episcopis tamquam dictae Sedis delegatis gubernentur, non obstantibus quibuscumque.[35] Quae vero a deputatis in capitulis generalibus vel ab aliis regularibus regun- tur, sub eorum cura et custodia relinquantur.

Caput X

MONIALES UNOQUOQUE MENSE CONFITEANTUR ET COMMUNICENT. DE CONFESSARIO EXTRAORDINARIO IIS AB EPISCOPO PROVIDEATUR. APUD ILLAS EXTRA PUBLICAM ECCLESIAM EUCHARISTIA NON CONSERVETUR

Attendant diligenter episcopi et ceteri superiores monasteriorum sanctimonialium, ut in constitutionibus earum admoneantur sancti- moniales, ut saltem semel singulis mensibus confessionem peccatorum faciant [36] et sacrosanctam Eucharistiam suscipiant, ut eo se salutari praesidio muniant ad omnes oppugnationes daemonis fortiter supe- randas. Praeter ordinarium autem confessarium alius extraordinarius ab episcopo et aliis superioribus bis aut ter in anno offeratur, qui omnium confessiones audire debeat. Quod vero sanctissimum Christi corpus intra chorum vel septa monasterii, et non in publica ecclesia

---

[34] Cf. tot. tit. X, De stat. monach., III, 35; De stat. regular. in VI°, III, 16, et De stat. monach. in Clem., III, 10.

[35] Cf. c.19, C.XVIII, q.2 (Greg. I).

[36] Cf. c.1 (§ 2), De stat. monach. in Clem., III, 10.

conservetur, prohibet sancta synodus, non obstante quocumque indulto aut privilegio.

Caput XI

IN MONASTERIIS, QUIBUS IMMINET CURA PERSONARUM SAECULARIUM, PRAETER EAS, QUAE SUNT DE ILLORUM FAMILIA, VISITET EPISCOPUS, ET EIDEM CURAE PRAEFICIENDAS EXAMINET, CERTIS EXCEPTIS

In monasteriis seu domibus virorum seu mulierum, quibus imminet animarum cura personarum saecularium, praeter eas, quae sunt de illorum monasteriorum seu locorum familia, personae tam regulares quam saeculares hujusmodi curam exercentes subsint immediate in iis, quae ad dictam curam et sacramentorum administrationem pertinent, jurisdictioni, visitationi et correctioni episcopi, in cujus dioecesi sunt sita.[37] Nec ibi aliqui etiam ad nutum amovibiles deputentur, nisi de ejusdem consensu, ac praevio examine per eum aut ejus vicarium faciendo;[38] excepto monasterio Cluniacensi cum suis limitibus, et exceptis etiam iis monasteriis seu locis, in quibus abbates, generales (aut capita ordinum sedem ordinariam principalem habent, atque aliis monasteriis seu domibus, in quibus abbates)[39] aut alii regularium superiores jurisdictionem episcopalem et temporalem in parochos et parochianos exercent;[40] salvo tamen eorum episcoporum jure, qui majorem in praedicta loca vel personas jurisdictionem exercent.

Caput XII

CONFORMENTUR REGULARES SAECULARIBUS IN OBSERVATIONE CENSURARUM EPISCOPALIUM ET FESTORUM DIOECESIS

Censurae et interdicta, nedum a Sede Apostolica emanata, sed etiam ab ordinariis promulgata, mandante episcopo a regularibus in eorum

---

[37] Cf. const. Gregorii XV *Inscrutabili*, 5 Feb., 1622.
[38] Cf. c. 11, C. XVIII, q. 2 (Stat. eccl. antiq.).
[39] Verba intra parentheses posita non habentur in opere "Concilium Tridentinum" (tom. IX, p. 1082) a societate goerresiana edito. Omnes tamen editiones, quas vidi, ea continent. Non est dubium, videtur mihi, omissionem esse errorem impressoris, et verba illa in textu esse ponenda.
[40] Cf. const. Benedicti XIV *Firmandis* (§ 12), 6 Nov., 1744.

ecclesiis publicentur atque serventur.[41] Dies etiam festi, quos in dioecesi sua servandos idem episcopus praeceperit, ab exemptis omnibus, etiam regularibus, serventur.[42]

Caput XIII

CONTROVERSIAS DE PRAECEDENTIA E VESTIGIO COMPONAT EPISCOPUS. EXEMPTI NON IN STRICTIORI CLAUSURA VIVENTES AD SUPPLICATIONES PUBLICAS ACCEDERE COMPELLANTUR

Controversias omnes de praecedentia, quae persaepe maximo cum scandalo oriuntur inter ecclesiasticas personas tam saeculares quam regulares cum in processionibus publicis, tum in iis, quae fiunt in tumulandis defunctorum corporibus, et in deferenda umbella et aliis similibus, episcopus amota omni appellatione et non obstantibus quibuscumque componat.[43] Exempti autem omnes, tam clerici saeculares quam regulares quicumque, etiam monachi, ad publicas processiones vocati accedere compellantur; iis tantum exceptis, qui in strictiori clausura perpetuo vivunt.

Caput XIV

REGULARI PUBLICE DELINQUENTI POENA A QUO IRROGANDA

Regularis non subditus episcopo, qui intra claustra monasterii degit, et extra ea ita notorie deliquerit, ut populo scandalo sit, episcopo instante a suo superiore intra tempus ab episcopo praefigendum severe puniatur, ac de punitione episcopum certiorem faciat. Sin minus, a suo superiore officio privetur, et delinquens ab episcopo puniri possit.[44]

---

[41] Cf. c. 1, De sent. excomm. in Clem., V, 10.

[42] Cf. c. 13, D. XII (conc. Toletan. XI) et const. Pii V *Cum primum* (§ 7), 1 Apr., 1566.

[43] Cf. const. Gregorii XIII *Exposcit*, 15 Jul., 1583.

[44] Super huj. decreti executione, cf. const. Clementis VIII *Suscepti muneris*, 23 Feb., 1596. Cf. etiam c. ult., X, De stat. monach., III, 35 (Honor. III).

CAPUT XV

PROFESSIO NON FIAT NISI ANNO PROBATIONIS EXACTO, ET DECIMO SEXTO AETATIS COMPLETO

In quacumque religione tam virorum quam mulierum professio non fiat ante decimum sextum annum expletum, nec qui minore tempore quam per annum post susceptum habitum in probatione steterit, ad professionem admittatur.[45] Professio autem antea facta sit nulla, nullamque inducat obligationem ad alicujus regulae vel religionis vel ordinis observationem, aut ad alios quoscumque effectus.[46]

CAPUT XVI

RENUNCIATIO AUT OBLIGATIO FACTA ANTE DUOS MENSES PROXIMOS PROFESSIONI SIT NULLA. FINITA PROBATIONE NOVITII AUT PROFITEANTUR AUT EJICIANTUR. IN PIO CLERICORUM SOCIETATIS JESU INSTITUTO NIHIL INNOVATUR. CAVETUR, NE QUID EX BONIS NOVITII MONASTERIO TRIBUATUR ANTE PROFESSIONEM

Nulla quoque renunciatio aut obligatio antea facta, etiam cum juramento vel in favorem cujuscumque causae piae, valeat, nisi cum licentia episcopi sive ejus vicarii fiat intra duos menses proximos ante professionem, ac non alias intelligatur effectum suum sortiri, nisi secuta professione; aliter vero facta, etiamsi cum hujus favoris expressa renunciatione, etiam jurata, sit irrita et nullius effectus. Finito tempore novitiatus superiores novitios, quos habiles invenerint, ad profitendum admittant, aut e monasterio eos ejiciant. Per haec tamen sancta synodus non intendit aliquid innovare aut prohibere, quin religio clericorum societatis Jesu juxta pium eorum institutum a sancta Sede Apostolica approbatum Domino et ejus ecclesiae inservire possit.[47] Sed neque ante professionem, excepto victo et vestitu novitii vel novitiae illius temporis, quo in probatione est, quocumque praetextu a parentibus vel propinquis aut curatoribus ejus monasterio aliquid ex

---

[45] Cf. c.1, C.XVII, q.2 (Alex. II); c.16, X, De regular., III, 31 (Innoc. III); c.2 h.t. in VI°, III, 14 (Alex. III).

[46] Cf. c.8, X, h.t. (Alex. III), c.12, *ibid.* (Clem. III); c.1 h.t. in VI° (Innoc. IV).

[47] Cf. const. Gregorii XIII *Ascendente Domino*, 25 Maii, 1584.

bonis ejusdem tribuatur, ne hac occasione discedere nequeat, quod totam vel majorem partem substantiae suae monasterium possideat, nec facile, si discesserit, id recuperare possit. Quin potius praecipit sancta synodus sub anathematis poena dantibus et recipientibus, ne hoc ullo modo fiat, et ut abeuntibus ante professionem omnia restituantur, quae sua erant. Quod ut recte fiat, episcopus etiam per censuras ecclesiasticas, si opus fuerit, compellat.

Caput XVII

PUELLA MAJOR DUODECIM ANNIS SI HABITUM REGULAREM SUSCIPERE VOLUERIT, EXPLORETUR AB ORDINARIO, ITERUMQUE ANTE PROFESSIONEM. TEMPUS PROFESSIONIS FACIENDAE EPISCOPO ANTE MENSEM ANNUNCIANDUM

Libertati professionis virginum Deo dicandarum prospiciens sancta synodus statuit atque decernit, ut, si puella, quae habitum regularem suscipere voluerit, major duodecim annis sit,[48] non ante eum suscipiat, nec postea ipsa vel alia professionem emittat, quam exploraverit episcopus vel, eo absente vel impedito, ejus vicarius, aut aliquis eorum sumptibus ab eis deputatus, virginis voluntatem diligenter, an coacta,[49] an seducta sit, an sciat quid agat, et si voluntas ejus pia ac libera cognita fuerit, habueritque conditiones requisitas juxta monasterii illius et ordinis regulam, necnon monasterium fuerit idoneum, libere ei profiteri liceat. Cujus professionis tempus ne episcopus ignoret, teneatur praefecta monasterio eum ante mensem certiorem facere. Quod si praefecta certiorem episcopum non fecerit, quamdiu episcopo videbitur, ab officio suspensa sit.

---

[48] Cf. c.12, X, De regular., III, 31.
[49] C.10, C.XX, q.1 (cap. incert.); c.1, X, tit. cit., III, 31 (conc. Moguntien. a.813).

Caput XVIII

NE QUIS, PRAETERQUAM IN CASIBUS A JURE EXPRESSIS, COGAT MULIEREM AD INGREDIENDUM MONASTERIUM, AUT INGREDI VOLENTEM PROHIBEAT. POENITENTIUM SEU CONVERTITARUM CONSTITUTIONES SERVENTUR

Anathemati sancta synodus subjicit omnes et singulas personas, cujuscumque qualitatis vel conditionis fuerint, tam clericos quam laicos, saeculares vel regulares, atque etiam qualibet dignitate fungentes, si quomodocumque coegerint aliquam virginem vel viduam, aut aliam quamcumque mulierem invitam, praeterquam in casibus in jure expressis,[50] ad ingrediendum monasterium, vel ad suscipiendum habitum cujuscumque religionis, vel ad emittendam professionem quique consilium, auxilium vel favorem dederint, quique scientes eam non sponte ingredi monasterium, aut habitum suscipere, aut professionem emittere, quoquo modo eidem actui vel praesentiam, vel consensum vel auctoritatem interposuerint. Simili quoque anathemati subjicit eos, qui sanctam virginum vel aliarum mulierum voluntatem veli accipiendi vel voti emittendi quoquo modo sine justa causa impedierint.[51] Eaque omnia et singula, quae ante professionem vel in ipsa professione fieri oportet, serventur non solum in monasteriis subjectis episcopo, sed et in aliis quibuscumque. Ab his tamen excipiuntur mulieres, quae poenitentes aut convertitae appellantur, in quibus constitutiones earum serventur.

Caput XIX

QUOMODO IN CAUSIS DEFICIENTIUM A RELIGIONE PROCEDENDUM

Quicumque regularis praetendat, se per vim et metum ingressum esse religionem, aut etiam dicat, ante aetatem debitam professum fuisse, aut quid simile, velitque habitum dimittere quacumque de causa, aut etiam cum habitu discedere sine licentia superiorum, non audiatur, nisi intra quinquennium tantum a die professionis, et tunc non aliter, nisi causas, quas praetenderit, deduxerit coram superiore

---

[50] Cf. c.18, X, De conv. conjug., III, 32 (Innoc. III), c.19, *ibid.* (Greg. IX).
[51] Cf. c.2, C.XX, q.2 (conc. Triburien. a.895); c.16, C.XXXII, q.2 (Toletan. III).

suo et ordinario.[52] Quod si antea habitum sponte dimiserit, nullatenus ad allegandam quamcumque causam admittatur, sed ad monasterium redire cogatur, et tamquam apostata puniatur; interim vero nullo privilegio suae religionis juvetur. Nemo etiam regularis cujuscumque facultatis vigore transferatur ad laxiorem religionem,[53] nec detur licentia cuiquam regulari occulte ferendi habitum suae religionis.

Caput XX

SUPERIORES ORDINUM EPISCOPIS NON SUBJECTI, INFERIORA MONASTERIA VISITENT AC CORRIGANT, ETIAM COMMENDATA

Abbates, qui sunt ordinum capita, ac ceteri praedictorum ordinum superiores episcopis non subjecti, quibus est in alia inferiora monasteria prioratusve legitima jurisdictio, eadem illa sibi subdita monasteria et prioratus suo quisque loco atque ordine ex officio visitent, etiamsi commendata exsistant. Quae cum ordinum suorum capitibus subsint, declarat sancta synodus, in iis, quae alias de visitatione monasteriorum commendatorum definita sunt,[54] non esse comprehensa, teneanturque quicumque praedictorum ordinum monasteriis praesunt, praedictos visitatores recipere et illorum ordinationes exequi. Ipsa quoque monasteria, quae sunt ordinum capita, juxta sanctae Sedis Apostolicae et cujusque ordinis constitutiones visitentur. Et quamdiu durabunt hujusmodi commendae, priores claustrales, aut in prioratibus conventum habentibus subpriores, qui correctiones et spirituale regimen exercent, a capitulis generalibus vel ipsorum ordinum visitatoribus instituantur. In ceteris omnibus praefatorum ordinum privilegia et facultates, quae ipsorum personas, loca et jura concernunt, firma sint et illaesa.

Caput XXI

MONASTERIA REGULARIBUS CONFERANTUR. ORDINUM CAPITA NEMINI IN POSTERUM COMMENDENTUR

Cum pleraque monasteria, etiam abbatiae, prioratus et praepositurae, ex mala eorum, quibus commissa fuerunt, administratione non levia

---

[52] Cf. c.18, C.XX, q.1 (Leo I); c.12, X, De regular., III, 31 (Clem. III).
[53] Cf. Sess. XIV, cap. 11 de ref.
[54] Cf. Sess. XXI, cap. 8 de ref., ubi declaratur monasteria commendata, in quibus non viget observantia regularis, ab ordinario esse visitanda.

passa fuerint tam in spiritualibus quam in temporalibus detrimenta, cupit sancta synodus ea ad congruam monasticae vitae disciplinam omnino revocare. Verum adeo dura difficilisque est praesentium temporum conditio, ut nec statim omnibus, nec commune ubique, quod optaret, remedium possit adhiberi. Ut tamen nihil praetermittat, unde praedictis salubriter aliquando provideri possit, primum quidem confidit, sanctissimum Romanum pontificem pro sua pietate et prudentia curaturum, quantum haec tempora ferre posse viderit, ut iis, quae nunc commendata reperiuntur, et quae suos conventus habent, regulares personae, ejusdem ordinis expresse professae, et quae gregi praeire et praeesse possint, praeficiantur. Quae vero in posterum vacabunt non nisi regularibus spectatae virtutis et sanctitatis conferantur.[55] Quoad ea vero monasteria, quae capita sunt ac primates ordinum, sive abbatiae sive prioratus filiae illorum capitum nuncupantur, teneantur illi, qui in praesenti ea in commendam obtinent, nisi sit eis de regulari successore provisum, infra sex menses religionem illorum ordinum propriam solemniter profiteri, aut iis cedere; alias commendae praedictae ipso jure vacare censeantur. Ne autem in praedictis omnibus et singulis fraus aliqua adhiberi possit, mandat sancta synodus, ut in provisionibus dictorum monasteriorum qualitas singulorum nominatim exprimatur, aliterque facta provisio surreptitia esse censeatur, nullaque subsequenti possessione, etiam triennali, adjuvctur.

Caput XXII

PRAEDICTA DE REFORMATIONE REGULARIUM NULLA MORA INTERPOSITA OBSERVENTUR

Haec omnia et singula in superioribus decretis contenta observari sancta synodus praecipit in omnibus coenobiis ac monasteriis, collegiis ac domibus quorumcumque monachorum ac regularium, necnon quarumcumque sanctimonialium virginum ac viduarum, etiamsi illae sub gubernio militiarum, etiam Ierosolymitanae, vivant, et quocumque nomine appellentur, sub quacumque regula vel constitutionibus, et sub custodia vel gubernatione, vel quavis subjectione aut connexione vel dependentia cujuscumque ordinis, mendicantium vel non mendicantium, vel aliorum regularium monachorum aut canonicorum quo-

---

[55] Cf. Sess. XIV, cap. 10 de ref.

rumque; non obstantibus eorum omnium et singulorum privilegiis sub quibuscumque formulis verborum conceptis ac mare magnum appellatis, etiam in fundatione obtentis, necnon constitutionibus et regulis, etiam juratis, atque etiam consuetudinibus vel praescriptionibus, etiam immemorabilibus. Si qui vero regulares tam viri quam mulieres sunt, qui sub arctiori regula vel statutis vivunt, excepta facultate habendi bona stabilia in communi, eos ab eorum instituto et observantia sancta synodus amovere non intendit. Et quia sancta synodus desiderat, ut omnia et singula supradicta quam primum executioni demandentur, praecipit omnibus episcopis, in monasteriis sibi subjectis, et in omnibus aliis ipsis in superioribus decretis specialiter commissis, atque omnibus abbatibus et generalibus, et aliis superioribus ordinum supradictorum, ut statim praedicta exequantur. Et si quid executioni mandatum non sit, episcoporum negligentiam concilia provincialia suppleant et coerceant. Regularium vero capitula provincialia et generalia, et in defectum capitulorum generalium, concilia provincialia, per deputationem aliquorum ejusdem ordinis provideant. Hortatur etiam sancta synodus omnes reges, principes, respublicas et magistratus, et in virtute sanctae obedientiae praecipit, ut velint praedictis episcopis, abbatibus ac generalibus, et ceteris praefectis in superius contentae reformationis executione suum auxilium et auctoritatem interponere, quoties fuerint requisiti, ut sine ullo impedimento praemissa recte exequantur ad laudem Dei omnipotentis.

DECRETUM DE REFORMATIONE

Caput I

CARDINALES ET OMNES ECCLESIARUM PRAELATI MODESTAM SUPELLECTILEM ET MENSAM HABEANT. CONSANGUINEOS FAMILIARESVE SUOS EX BONIS ECCLESIAE NON AUGEANT

Optandum est, ut ii, qui episcopale ministerium suscipiunt, quae suae sint partes agnoscant, ac se non ad propria commoda, non ad divitias aut luxum, sed ad labores et sollicitudines pro Dei gloria vocatos esse intelligant. Nec enim dubitandum est, et fideles reliquos ad religionem innocentiamque facilius inflammandos, si praepositos suos viderint non ea, quae mundi sunt, sed animarum salutem ac coelestem patriam cogitantes.[56] Haec cum ad restituendam ecclesiasticam disciplinam praecipua esse sancta synodus animadvertat, admonet episcopos omnes, ut secum ea saepe meditantes, factis etiam ipsis ac vitae actionibus, quod est velut perpetuum quoddam praedicandi genus, se muneri suo conformes ostendant, in primis vero ita mores suos omnes componant, ut reliqui ab eis frugalitatis, modestiae, continentiae, ac, quae nos tantopere commendat Deo, sanctae humilitatis exempla petere possint.[57] Quapropter, exemplo patrum nostrorum in concilio Carthaginensi,[58] non solum jubet, ut episcopi modesta supellectili et mensa ac frugali victu contenti sint, verum etiam in reliquo vitae genere, ac tota ejus domo caveant, ne quid appareat, quod a sancto hoc instituto sit alienum, quodque non simplicitatem, Dei zelum ac vanitatum contemptum prae se ferat. Omnino vero eis interdicit, ne ex reditibus ecclesiae consanguineos familiaresve suos augere studeant,[59] cum et apostolorum canones prohibeant,[60] ne res ecclesiasticas, quae Dei sunt, consanguineis donent, sed, si pauperes sint, iis ut pauperibus distribuant; eas autem non distrahant nec dissipent illorum causa. Immo, quam maxime potest, eos sancta synodus monet, ut omnem humanum hunc erga fratres, nepotes propinquosque carnis affectum, unde multorum malorum in ecclesia seminarium extat, penitus deponant. Quae vero de episcopis dicta sunt, eadem non solum in quibuscumque beneficia ecclesiastica tam saecularia quam regularia obtinentibus pro gradus sui conditione observari, sed et ad sanctae Romanae ecclesiae cardinales pertinere decernit, quorum consilio apud sanctissimum Romanum pontificem cum universalis ecclesiae administratio nitatur, nefas videri potest, non iis etiam virtutum insignibus ac vivendi disciplina eos fulgere, quae merito omnium in se oculos convertant.

Caput II

A QUIBUS NOMINATIM DECRETA CONCILII SOLEMNITER RECIPI ET DOCERI DEBEANT

Cogit temporum calamitas et invalescentium haeresum malitia, ut nihil sit praetermittendum, quod ad populorum aedificationem et

[56] Cf. Sess. XXII, cap. 1 de ref. in princ.
[57] Ps. 101:18; Ecclus. 3:20; 35:21; Matt. 18:3 f.
[58] C.7, D.XLI, *infra*, p. 578, lit. AF.
[59] Cf. c.23, C.XII, q.1 (conc. Antiochen.); c.19, C.XII, q.2 (Nicaen. II).
[60] Can. Apost., 39.

catholicae fidei praesidium videatur posse pertinere. Praecipit igitur sancta synodus patriarchis, primatibus, archiepiscopis, episcopis et omnibus aliis, qui de jure vel consuetudine in concilio provinciali interesse debent,[61] ut in ipsa prima synodo provinciali, post finem praesentis concilii habenda, ea omnia et singula, quae ab hac sancta synodo definita et statuta sunt, palam recipiant, necnon veram obedientiam summo Romano pontifici spondeant et profiteantur,[62] simulque haereses omnes, a sacris canonibus et generalibus conciliis, praesertimque ab hac eadem synodo damnatas, publice detestentur et anathematizent. Idemque in posterum quicumque in patriarchas, primates, archiepiscopos episcoposque promovendi, in prima synodo provinciali, in qua ipsi interfuerint, omnino observent. Quod si quis ex supradictis omnibus, quod absit, renuerit, episcopi comprovinciales statim summum Romanum pontificem admonere sub poena divinae indignationis teneantur, interimque ab ejusdem communione abstineant. Ceteri vero omnes, sive in praesenti sive in futurum beneficia ecclesiastica habituri, et qui in synodo dioecesana convenire debent, idem ut supra in ea synodo, quae primo quoque tempore celebrabitur, faciant et observent; alias secundum formam sacrorum canonum puniantur. Ad haec omnes ii, ad quos universitatum et studiorum generalium cura, visitatio et reformatio pertinet, diligenter curent, ut ab eisdem universitatibus canones et decreta hujus sanctae synodi integre recipiantur, ad eorumque normam magistri, doctores et alii in eisdem universitatibus ea, quae catholicae fidei sunt,[63] doceant et interpretentur, seque ad hoc institutum initio cujuslibet anni solemni juramento obstringant; sed et si aliqua alia in praedictis universitatibus correctione et reformatione digna fuerint, ab eisdem, ad quos spectat, pro religionis et disciplinae ecclesiasticae augmento emendentur et statuantur. Quae vero universitates immediate summi Romani pontificis protectioni et visitationi sunt subjectae, has sua Beatitudo per ejus delegatos eadem, qua supra, ratione, et prout ei utilius visum fuerit, salubriter visitari et reformari curabit.

---

[61] Cf. Sess. XXIV, cap. 2 de ref.
[62] Cf. const. Pii V *Injunctum nobis*, 13 Nov., 1564, *infra*, p. 540.
[63] Cf. Sess. V, cap. 1 de ref.

Caput III

EXCOMMUNICATIONIS GLADIO TEMERE NON UTENDUM. UBI EXECUTIO REALIS AUT PERSONALIS FIERI POTEST, A CENSURIS ABSTINENDUM, IISQUE CIVILI MAGISTRATUI SE IMMISCERE NEFAS ESTO

Quamvis excommunicationis gladius nervus sit ecclesiasticae disciplinae et ad continendos in officio populos valde salutaris, sobrie tamen magnaque circumspectione exercendus est, cum experientia doceat, si temere aut levibus ex rebus incutiatur, magis contemni quam formidari, et perniciem potius parere quam salutem.[64] Quapropter excommunicationes illae, quae monitionibus praemissis ad finem revelationis, ut aiunt, aut pro deperditis seu subtractis rebus ferri solent, a nemine prorsus praeterquam ab episcopo decernantur, et tunc non alias, quam ex re non vulgari, causaque diligenter ac magna maturitate per episcopum examinata, quae ejus animum moveat.[65] Nec ad eas concedendas cujusvis saecularis, etiam magistratus, auctoritate adducatur, sed totum hoc in ejus arbitrio et conscientia sit positum, quando ipse pro re, loco, persona aut tempore eas decernendas esse judicaverit. In causis vero judicialibus mandatur omnibus judicibus ecclesiasticis, cujuscumque dignitatis exsistant, ut quandocumque executio realis vel personalis in qualibet parte judicii propria auctoritate ab ipsis fieri poterit, abstineant se tam in procedendo quam definiendo a censuris ecclesiasticis seu interdicto; sed liceat eis, si expedire videbitur, in causis civilibus, ad forum ecclesiasticum quomodolibet pertinentibus, contra quoscumque, etiam laicos, per mulctas pecuniarias, quae locis piis ibi exsistentibus eo ipso, quod exactae fuerint, assignentur, seu per captionem pignorum, personarumque districtionem per suos proprios aut alienos executores faciendam, sive etiam per privationem beneficiorum aliaque juris remedia procedere et causas definire. Quod si executio realis vel personalis adversus reos hac ratione fieri non poterit, sitque erga judicem contumacia, tunc eos etiam anathematis mucrone arbitrio suo praeter alias poenas ferire poterit.[66] In causis quoque criminalibus, ubi executio realis vel personalis, ut supra, fieri

[64] Cf. c.18, C.II, q.1 (Aug.).
[65] Cf. c.8, C.XI, q.3 (conc. Agathen.), c.41, *ibid.* (Melden.), c.42, *ibid.* (Arvernen.); omnino concordat hic ult. c. cum c.2 conc. Aurelianen. V a.549 habiti. C.48, X, De sent. excomm., V, 39 (Lat. IV).
[66] C.22, C.XVII, q.4 (cap. incert.).

poterit, erit a censuris abstinendum. Sed si dictae executioni facile locus esse non possit, licebit judici hoc spirituali gladio in delinquentes uti, si tamen delicti qualitas, praecedente bina saltem monitione, etiam per edictum, id postulet. Nefas autem sit saeculari cuilibet magistratui prohibere ecclesiastico judici, ne quem excommunicet, aut mandare, ut latam excommunicationem revocet, sub praetextu, quod contenta in praesenti decreto non sint observata, cum non ad saeculares, sed ad ecclesiasticos haec cognitio pertineat. Excommunicatus vero quicumque, si post legitimas monitiones non resipuerit, non solum ad sacramenta et communionem fidelium ad familiaritatem non recipiatur,[67] sed, si obdurato animo censuris annexus in illis per annum insorduerit, etiam contra eum tamquam de haeresi suspectum procedi possit.

Caput IV

UBI NIMIUS MISSARUM CELEBRANDARUM NUMERUS, STATUANT EPISCOPI, ABBATES ET GENERALES ORDINUM, QUOD EXPEDIRE JUDICAVERINT

Contingit saepe in quibusdam ecclesiis vel tam magnum missarum celebrandarum numerum ex variis defunctorum relictis impositum esse, ut illis pro singulis diebus a testatoribus praescriptis nequeat satisfieri, vel eleemosynam hujusmodi pro illis celebrandis adeo tenuem esse, ut non facile inveniatur qui velit huic se muneri subjicere, unde depereunt piae testantium voluntates, et eorum conscientias, ad quos praedicta spectant, onerandi occasio datur. Sancta synodus, cupiens haec ad pios usus relicta, quo plenius et utilius potest, impleri, facultatem dat episcopis, ut in synodo dioecesana, itemque abbatibus et generalibus ordinum, ut in suis capitulis generalibus re diligenter perspecta possint pro sua conscientia in praedictis ecclesiis, quas hac provisione indigere cognoverint, statuere circa haec quidquid magis ad Dei honorem et cultum atque ecclesiarum utilitatem viderint expedire;[68] ita tamen, ut eorum semper defunctorum commemoratio fiat, qui pro suarum animarum salute legata ea ad pios usus reliquerunt.

---

[67] Cf. c.18, C.XI, q.3 (Isid.), c.19, *ibid.* (Stat. eccl. antiq.), c.25, *ibid.* (Greg. I), c.26, *ibid.* (conc. Toletan. I); cc.8, 9, X, De sent. excomm., V, 39 (Alex. III), cc.15, 18, *ibid.* (Clem. III), cc.29, 30, 31, 38, 39, *ibid.* (Innoc. III).

[68] Cf. Sess. XXII, cap. 6 de ref.

Caput V

REBUS BENE CONSTITUTIS ET ANNEXUM ONUS HABENTIBUS NIHIL DETRAHATUR

Ratio postulat, ut illis, quae bene constituta sunt, contrariis ordinationibus non detrahatur. Quando igitur ex beneficiorum quorumcumque erectione seu fundatione aut aliis constitutionibus qualitates aliquae requiruntur, seu certa illis onera sunt injuncta, in beneficiorum collatione, seu in quacumque alia dispositione eis non derogetur. Idem in praebendis theologalibus, magistralibus, doctoralibus aut presbyteralibus, diaconalibus ac subdiaconalibus, quandocumque ita constituta fuerint, observetur, ut eorum qualitatibus vel ordinibus nihil ulla provisione detrahatur, et aliter facta provisio surreptitia censeatur.

Caput VI

QUI SE GERERE DEBEAT EPISCOPUS QUOAD VISITATIONEM CAPITULORUM EXEMPTORUM

Statuit sancta synodus, ut in omnibus ecclesiis cathedralibus et collegiatis decretum sub fel. rec. Paulo III, quod incipit: *Capitula cathedralium,*[69] observetur, non solum quando episcopus visitaverit, sed et quoties ex officio, vel ad petitionem alicujus contra aliquem ex contentis in dicto decreto procedat; ita tamen, ut, cum extra visitationem processerit, infra scripta omnia locum habeant, videlicet, ut capitulum initio cujuslibet anni eligat ex capitulo duos, de quorum consilio et assensu episcopus vel ejus vicarius tam in formando processum quam in ceteris omnibus actibus usque ad finem causae inclusive, coram notario tamen ipsius episcopi et in ejus domo aut consueto tribunali, procedere teneatur. Unum autem tantum sit utriusque votum, possitque alter episcopo accedere. Quod si ambo ab episcopo discordes in aliquo actu seu interlocutoria vel definitiva sententia fuerint, tunc intra sex dierum spatium cum episcopo tertium eligant, et, si in electione tertii etiam discordent, ad viciniorem episcopum electio devolvatur, et juxta eam partem, cum qua tertius conveniet, articulus, in quo erat discordia, terminetur. Alias processus et inde

[69] Cf. Sess. VI, cap. 4 de ref. et Sess. XIV, cap. 4 de ref.

secuta nulla sint, nullosque producant juris effectus. In criminibus tamen ex incontinentia provenientibus, de qua in decreto de concubinariis,[70] et in atrocioribus delictis depositionem aut degradationem requirentibus,[71] ubi de fuga timetur, ne judicium eludatur, et ideo opus sit personali detentione, possit initio solus episcopus ad summariam informationem et necessariam detentionem procedere, servato tamen in reliquis ordine praemisso. In omnibus autem casibus ea ratio habeatur, ut juxta qualitatem delicti ac personarum delinquentes ipsi in loco decenti custodiantur. Episcopis praeterea ubique is honor tribuatur, qui eorum dignitati par est, eisque in choro, et in capitulo, in processionibus et aliis actibus publicis sit prima sedes,[72] et locus, quem ipsi elegerint, et praecipua omnium rerum agendarum auctoritas. Qui si aliquid canonicis ad deliberandum proponant, nec de re ad suum vel suorum commodum spectante agatur, episcopi ipsi capitulum convocent,[73] vota exquirant, et juxta ea concludant. Absente vero episcopo omnino hoc ab iis de capitulo, ad quos hoc de jure vel consuetudine spectat, perficiatur, nec ad id vicarius episcopi admittatur. Ceteris autem in rebus capituli jurisdictio et potestas, si qua eis competit, et bonorum administratio salva et intacta omnino relinquatur. Qui vero non obtinent dignitates, nec sunt de capitulo, ii omnes in causis ecclesiasticis episcopo subjiciantur; non obstantibus quoad supradicta privilegiis, etiam ex fundatione competentibus, necnon consuetudinibus, etiam immemorabilibus, sententiis, juramentis, concordiis, quae tantum suos obligent auctores; salvis tamen in omnibus privilegiis, quae universitatibus studiorum generalium seu earum personis sunt concessa. Haec autem omnia et singula in iis ecclesiis locum non habeant, in quibus episcopi aut eorum vicarii ex constitutionibus, vel privilegiis, aut consuetudinibus sive concordiis, seu quocumque alio jure majorem habent potestatem, auctoritatem ac jurisdictionem, quam praesenti decreto sit comprehensum, quibus sancta synodus derogare non intendit.

---

[70] Cf. Sess. XXIV, cap. 8 de ref. matr. et infra, cap. 14.
[71] C. 24, X, De accus., V, 1 (Innoc. III); c. 6, X, De poenis, V, 37 (idem).
[72] Cf. c. 10, D. XCV (Stat. eccl. antiq.).
[73] Cf. cc. 4, 5, X, De his, quae fiunt, III, 10 (Alex. III).

Caput VII

ACCESSUS ET REGRESSUS AD BENEFICIA TOLLUNTUR. COADJUTOR QUO MODO, CUI ET EX QUA CAUSA CONCEDENDUS

Cum in beneficiis ecclesiasticis ea, quae hereditariae successionis imaginem referunt, sacris constitutionibus sint odiosa et patrum decretis contraria,[74] nemini in posterum accessus aut regressus, etiam de consensu, ad beneficium ecclesiasticum cujuscumque qualitatis concedatur, nec hactenus concessi suspendantur, extendantur aut transferantur. Hocque decretum in quibuscumque beneficiis ecclesiasticis, ac etiam cathedralibus ecclesiis, ac in quibuscumque personis, etiam cardinalatus honore fulgentibus, locum habeat. In coadjutoriis quoque cum futura successione idem posthac observetur, ut nemini in quibuscumque beneficiis ecclesiasticis permittantur. Quod si quando ecclesiae cathedralis aut monasterii urgens necessitas aut evidens utilitas postulet praelato dari coadjutorem,[75] is non alias cum futura successione detur, quam haec causa prius diligenter a sanctissimo Romano pontifice sit cognita, et qualitates omnes in illo concurrere certum sit, quae a jure et decretis hujus sanctae synodi in episcopis et praelatis requiruntur.[76] Alias concessiones super his factae surreptitiae esse censeantur.

Caput VIII

ADMINISTRATORUM HOSPITALIUM MUNUS. EORUM NEGLIGENTIA A QUIBUS ET QUA RATIONE COERCENDA

Admonet sancta synodus quoscumque ecclesiastica beneficia, saecularia seu regularia, obtinentes, ut hospitalitatis officium a sanctis patribus frequenter commendatum,[77] quantum per eorum proventus licebit, prompte benigneque exercere assuescant, memores, eos qui hospitalitatem amant, Christum in hospitibus recipere.[78] Illis vero,

---

[74] Cf. c.5, C.VIII, q.1 (Hilar. in syn. Rom.), c.7, *ibid.* (Lat. II); cc.7, 10, 11, X, De fil. presb., I, 17 (Alex. III), c.13, *ibid.* (Clem. III); cc.6, 15, X, De jur. patr., III, 38 (Alex. III).

[75] Cf. Sess. XXI, cap. 6 de ref. et cc.1, 14, C.VII, q.1.

[76] Cf. Sess. VII, capp. 1, 3 de ref. et Sess. XXII, cap. 2 de ref.

[77] Cf. c.2, D.XLII (Chrysost.); c. un., D.LXXXV (Greg. I); c.2, D.LXXXIX (idem); c.30, C.XII, q.2 (idem).

[78] Matt. 25:35.

qui hospitalia vulgo nuncupata, seu alia pia loca ad peregrinorum, infirmorum, senum pauperumve usum praecipue instituta in commendam, administrationem aut quemcumque titulum, aut etiam ecclesiis suis unita obtinent, vel si ecclesiae parochiales hospitalibus forte unitae aut in hospitalia erectae, earumque patronis in administrationem concessae sint, praecipit omnino, ut impositum illis onus officiumve administrent, atque hospitalitatem, quam debent, ex fructibus ad id deputatis actu exerceant juxta constitutionem concilii Viennensis, alias in hac eadem synodo sub fel. rec. Paulo III innovatam, quae incipit: *Quia contingit.*[79] Quod si hospitalia haec ad certum peregrinorum, aut infirmorum aut aliarum personarum genus suscipiendum fuerint instituta, nec in loco, ubi sunt dicta hospitalia, similes personae aut perpaucae reperiantur, mandat adhuc, ut fructus illorum in alium pium usum, qui eorum institutioni proximior sit ac pro loco et tempore utilior, convertantur, prout ordinario cum duobus de capitulo, qui rerum usu peritiores sint, per ipsum deligendis, magis expedire visum fuerit; nisi aliter forte, etiam in hunc eventum, in eorum fundatione aut institutione fuerit expressum, quo casu quod ordinatum fuit observari curet episcopus, aut, si id non possit, ipse, prout supra, utiliter provideat. Itaque si praedicti omnes et singuli, cujuscumque ordinis et religionis et dignitatis, etiamsi laici fuerint, qui administrationem hospitalium habent, non tamen regularibus subjecti, ubi viget regularis observantia, ab ordinario moniti hospitalitatis munus adhibitis omnibus, ad quae tenentur, necessariis re ipsa obire cessaverint, non solum per ecclesiasticas censuras et alia juris remedia ad id compelli possint, sed etiam hospitalis ipsius administratione curave perpetuo privari possint, aliique eorum loco ab iis, ad quos spectabit, substituantur. Et praedicti nihilominus etiam ad fructuum restitutionem, quos contra ipsorum hospitalium institutionem perceperunt, quae nulla eis remissione aut compositione indulgeatur, in foro conscientiae teneantur; nec administratio seu gubernatio hujusmodi locorum uni et eidem personae ultra triennium deinceps committatur, nisi aliter in fundatione cautum reperiatur; non obstante, quoad omnia supradicta, quacumque unione, exemptione et consuetudine in contrarium, etiam immemorabili, seu privilegiis aut indultis quibuscumque.

[79] Cf. Sess. VII, cap. 15 de ref.; c. 2, De relig. dom. in Clem., III, 11, *infra*, p. 562, lit. M.

Caput IX

QUOMODO PROBANDUM JUS PATRONATUS. CUI DEFERENDUM MUNUS PATRONORUM; ACCESSIONES VETITAE; QUIBUS ID JURIS NON ACQUIRATUR

Sicuti legitima patronatuum jura tollere, piasque fidelium voluntates in eorum institutione violare aequum non est, sic etiam, ut hoc colore beneficia eccclesiastica in servitutem, quod a multis impudenter fit, redigantur, non est permittendum. Ut igitur debita in omnibus ratio observetur, decernit sancta synodus, ut titulus juris patronatus sit ex fundatione vel dotatione,[80] qui ex authentico documento et aliis jure requisitis ostendatur; sive etiam ex multiplicatis praesentationibus per antiquissimum temporis cursum, qui hominum memoriam excedat, aliasve secundum juris dispositionem. In iis vero personis, seu communitatibus vel universitatibus, in quibus id jus plerumque ex usurpatione potius quaesitum praesumi solet, plenior et exactior probatio ad docendum verum titulum requiratur, nec immemorabilis temporis probatio aliter eis suffragetur, quam si praeter reliqua ad eam necessaria praesentationes etiam continuatae, non minori saltem quam quinquaginta annorum spatio, quae omnes effectum sortitae sint, authenticis scripturis probentur. Reliqui patronatus omnes in beneficiis, tam saecularibus quam regularibus, seu parochialibus, vel dignitatibus, aut quibuscumque aliis beneficiis, in cathedrali vel collegiata ecclesia, seu facultates et privilegia concessa tam in vim patronatus, quam alio quocumque jure nominandi, eligendi, praesentandi ad ea, cum vacant, exceptis patronatibus super cathedralibus ecclesiis competentibus, et exceptis aliis, quae ad imperatorem et reges seu regna possidentes, aliosque sublimes ac supremos principes jura imperii in dominiis suis habentes pertinent, et quae in favorem studiorum generalium concessa sunt,[81] in totum prorsus abrogata et irrita cum quasi possessione inde secuta intelligantur, beneficiaque hujusmodi tamquam libera a suis collatoribus conferantur ac provisiones hujusmodi plenum effectum consequantur. Ad haec liceat episcopo praesentatos a patronis, si idonei non fuerint, repellere. Quod si ad inferiores institutio pertineat, ab episcopo tamen, juxta alias statuta ab hac sancta synodo,

---

[80] Cf. Sess. XIV, cap. 12 de ref.; c.25, X, De jur. patr., III, 38 (Alex. III).
[81] Cf. Sess. XXIV, cap. 19 de ref.

examinentur; [82] alioquin institutio ab inferioribus facta irrita sit et inanis. Patroni autem beneficiorum cujuscumque ordinis et dignitatis, etiamsi communitates, universitates, collegia quaecumque clericorum vel laicorum exsistant, in perceptione fructuum,[83] proventuum, obventionum quorumcumque beneficiorum, etiamsi vere de jure patronatus ipsorum ex fundatione et dotatione essent, nullatenus nullave causa vel occasione se ingerant; sed illos libere rectori seu beneficiato, non obstante etiam quacumque consuetudine, distribuendos dimittant. Nec dictum jus patronatus venditionis aut alio quocumque titulo in alios contra canonicas sanctiones transferre praesumant.[84] Si secus fecerint, excommunicationis et interdicti poenis subjiciantur, et dicto jure patronatus ipso jure privati exsistant.

Insuper accessiones, per viam unionis factae de beneficiis liberis ad ecclesias juri patronatus, etiam laicorum, subjectas, tam ad parochiales quam ad alia quaecumque beneficia, etiam simplicia, seu dignitates, vel hospitalia, ita ut praedicta beneficia libera ejusdem naturae cum iis, quibuscum uniuntur, efficiantur, atque sub jure patronatus constituantur, hae si nondum plenarium sortitae sunt effectum, vel deinceps ad cujusvis instantiam fient, quacumque auctoritate, etiam apostolica, concessae fuerint, simul cum unionibus ipsis per surreptionem obtentae intelligantur, non obstante quacumque in iis verborum forma seu derogatione, quae habeatur pro expressa, nec executioni amplius demandentur, sed beneficia ipsa unita, cum vacaverint, libere ut antea conferantur. Quae vero a quadraginta annis citra factae [85] effectum et plenam incorporationem sunt consecutae, hae nihilominus ab ordinariis tamquam a Sede Apostolica delegatis revideantur et examinentur, ac quae per surreptionem vel obreptionem obtentae fuerint, simul cum unionibus irritae declarentur, ac beneficia ipsa separentur, et aliis conferantur. Similiter quoque patronatus quicumque in ecclesiis et quibuscumque aliis beneficiis, etiam dignitatibus, antea liberis acquisiti a quadraginta annis citra, et in futurum acquirendi seu ex augmento dotis, seu ex nova constructione vel alia simili causa, etiam auctoritate Sedis Apostolicae, ab iisdem ordinariis, uti delegatis, ut supra, qui nullius in his facultatibus aut privilegiis impediantur, diligenter cognos-

---

[82] Cf. Sess. VII, cap. 13 de ref. et Sess. XXIV, cap. 18 de ref.
[83] C. un., X, ut eccles. benef. sine demin. confer., III, 12 (Innoc. III).
[84] Cf. cc.6, 16, X, De jur. patr., III, 38 (Alex. III).
[85] Cf. Sess. VII, cap. 6 de ref.

cantur, et quos non repererint ob maxime evidentem ecclesiae, vel beneficii seu dignitatis necessitatem legitime constitutos esse, in totum revocent, atque beneficia hujusmodi sine damno illa possidentium, et restituto patronis eo, quod ad eis idcirco datum est, in pristinum libertatis statum reducant; non obstantibus privilegiis, constitutionibus et consuetudinibus, etiam immemorabilibus.

Caput X

JUDICES A SYNODO DESIGNANDI, QUI DELEGENTUR A SEDE APOSTOLICA; A QUIBUS ET ORDINARIIS CAUSAE BREVITER TERMINANDAE

Quoniam ob malitiosam petentium suggestionem, et quandoque ob locorum longinquitatem, personarum notitia, quibus causae mandantur, usque adeo haberi non potest, hincque interdum judicibus non undequaque idoneis causae in partibus delegantur, statuit sancta synodus, in singulis conciliis provincialibus aut dioecesanis aliquot personas, quae qualitates habeant juxta constitutionem Bonifacii VIII, quae incipit: *Statutum,*[86] et alioquin ad id aptas designari, ut praeter ordinarios locorum iis etiam posthac causae ecclesiasticae ac spirituales et ad forum ecclesiasticum pertinentes in partibus delegandae committantur. Et si aliquem interim ex designatis mori contigerit, substituat ordinarius loci cum consilio capituli alium in ejus locum usque ad futuram provincialem aut dioecesanam synodum, ita ut habeat quaeque dioecesis quatuor saltem aut etiam plures probatas personas ac ut supra qualificatas, quibus hujusmodi causae a quolibet legato vel nuncio, atque etiam a Sede Apostolica committantur. Alioquin post designationem factam, quam statim episcopi ad summum Romanum pontificem transmittant, delegationes quaecumque aliorum judicum, aliis quam his factae, surreptitiae censeantur. Admonet dehinc sancta synodus tam ordinarios quam alios quoscumque judices, ut terminandis causis quanta fieri poterit brevitate studeant,[87] ac litigatorum artibus seu in litis contestatione seu alia parte judicii differenda modis omnibus, aut termini praefixione, aut competenti alia ratione occurrant.

---

[86] C. 11, VI°, De rescript., I, 3, *infra,* p. 578, lit. AG.

[87] Cf. c. 5, X, De dolo et cont., II, 14 (Innoc. III), c. 10, *ibid.* (Greg. IX); c. 2, X, De sent. et re jud., II, 27 (Greg. I); Sess. XXIV, cap. 20 de ref.

Caput XI

VARIAE LOCATIONES BONORUM ECCLESIASTICORUM PROHIBENTUR; QUAEDAM FACTAE IRRITANTUR

Magnam ecclesiis perniciem afferre solet, cum earum bona repraesentata pecunia in successorum praejudicium aliis locantur. Omnes igitur hae locationes, si anticipatis solutionibus fient, nullatenus in praejudicium successorum validae intelligantur,[88] quocumque indulto aut privilegio non obstante; nec hujusmodi locationes in Romana curia vel extra eam confirmentur. Non liceat etiam jurisdictiones ecclesiasticas seu facultates nominandi aut deputandi vicarios in spiritualibus locare,[89] nec conductoribus per se aut alios eas exercere, aliterque concessiones, etiam a Sede Apostolica factae, surreptitiae censeantur. Locationes vero rerum ecclesiasticarum, etiam auctoritate apostolica confirmatas, sancta synodus irritas decernit; [90] quas a triginta annis citra ad longum tempus, seu, ut in nonnullis partibus, ad viginti novem, seu bis viginti novem annos vocant factas, synodus provincialis vel deputandi ab ea in damnum ecclesiae et contra canonicas sanctiones contractas fuisse judicabunt.

Caput XII

DECIMAE INTEGRE PERSOLVENDAE. EAS SUBTRAHENTES EXCOMMUNICANDI. RECTORIBUS ECCLESIARUM TENUIUM PIE SUBVENIENDUM

Non sunt ferendi qui variis artibus decimas ecclesiis obvenientes subtrahere moliuntur, aut qui ab aliis solvendas temere occupant, et in rem suam vertunt, cum decimarum solutio debita sit Deo,[91] et qui eas dare noluerint, aut dantes impediunt, res alienas invadant. Praecipit igitur sancta synodus omnibus, cujuscumque gradus et conditionis sint, ad quos decimarum solutio spectat, ut eas, ad quas de jure tenentur, in posterum cathedrali aut quibuscumque aliis ecclesiis vel

[88] C.6, C.X, q.2.
[89] Cf. c.1, X, ne prael. vices suas, V, 4 (Lat. III), c.2, *ibid.* (conc. Turonen.).
[90] Cf. c. un., De re eccl. non alien. in Extrav. comm., III, 4.
[91] Ex. 22:29; Lev. 27:30 f.; Num. 18:21 f.; Tob. 1:6; Mal. 3:10. C.66, C.XVI, q.1 et cc.6, 7, *ibid.*, q.7; c.14, X, De dec. et obl., III, 30 (Alex. III), c.23, *ibid.* (Coelest. III), c.26, *ibid.* (Innoc. III).

personis, quibus legitime debentur, integre persolvant. Qui vero eas aut subtrahunt aut impediunt, excommunicentur,[92] nec ab hoc crimine nisi plena restitutione secuta absolvantur. Hortatur dehinc omnes et singulos pro Christiana caritate debitoque erga pastores suos munere, ut de bonis sibi a Deo collatis episcopis et parochis, qui tenuioribus praesunt ecclesiis, large subvenire ad Dei laudem atque ad pastorum suorum, qui pro eis invigilant, dignitatem tuendam non graventur.

Caput XIII

QUARTAM FUNERALIUM CATHEDRALES VEL PAROCHIALES ECCLESIAE RECIPIANT

Decernit sancta synodus, ut quibuscumque in locis jam ante annos quadraginta quarta, quae funeralium dicitur, cathedrali aut parochiali ecclesiae solita esset persolvi,[93] ac postea fuerit ex quocumque privilegio aliis monasteriis, hospitalibus aut quibuscumque locis piis concessa, eadem posthac integro jure, et eadem portione, qua antea solebat, cathedrali seu parochiali ecclesiae persolvatur; non obstantibus concessionibus, gratiis, privilegiis, etiam mari magno nuncupatis, aut aliis quibuscumque.

Caput XIV

PRAESCRIBITUR RATIO PROCEDENDI IN CAUSIS CLERICORUM CONCUBINARIORUM

Quam turpe, ac clericorum nomine, qui se divino cultui addixerunt, sit indignum, in impudicitiae sordibus immundoque concubinatu versari, satis res ipsa communi fidelium omnium offensione summoque clericalis militiae dedecore testatur. Ut igitur ad eam, quam decet, continentiam ac vitae integritatem ministri ecclesiae revocentur, populusque hinc eos magis discat revereri, quo illos vita honestiores cognoverit: prohibet sancta synodus quibuscumque clericis, ne concubinas aut alias mulieres, de quibus possit haberi suspicio, in domo vel extra detinere, aut cum iis ullam consuetudinem habere audeant;

[92] Cf. c.5, C.XVI, q.7 (conc. Rothomagen. *ca.* a.650); c.5, X, tit. cit. (Alex. III), c.22, *ibid.* (Coelest. III), cc.25, 32, *ibid.* (Innoc. III); c.1. h.t. in Clem., III, 8.

[93] Cf. c.8, X, De sepult., III, 28 (Luc. III); c.2 h.t. in VI°, III, 12 (Bonif. VIII); c.2 h.t. in Clem., III, 7.

alioquin poenis a sacris canonibus vel statutis ecclesiarum impositis puniantur.[94] Quod si a superioribus moniti ab iis se non abstinuerint, tertia parte fructuum, obventionum ac proventuum beneficiorum suorum quorumcumque et pensionum ipso facto sint privati,[95] quae fabricae ecclesiae aut alteri pio loco arbitrio episcopi applicetur. Sin vero in delicto eodem cum eadem vel alia femina perseverantes secundae monitioni adhuc non paruerint, non tantum fructus omnes ac proventus suorum beneficiorum et pensiones eo ipso amittant, qui praedictis locis applicentur, sed etiam a beneficiorum ipsorum administratione, quoad ordinarius, etiam uti Sedis Apostolicae delegatus, arbitrabitur, suspendantur, et si ita suspensi nihilominus eas non expellant, aut cum iis etiam versentur, tunc beneficiis, portionibus, ac officiis et pensionibus quibuscumque ecclesiasticis perpetuo priventur, atque inhabiles ac indigni quibuscumque honoribus, dignitatibus, beneficiis ac officiis in posterum reddantur, donec post manifestam vitae emendationem ab eorum superioribus cum iis ex causa visum fuerit dispensandum. Sed si, postquam eas semel dimiserint, intermissum consortium repetere aut alias hujusmodi scandalosas mulieres sibi adjungere ausi fuerint, praeter praedictas poenas excommunicationis gladio plectantur.[96] Nec quaevis appellatio aut exemptio praedictam executionem impediat aut suspendat, supradictorumque omnium cognitio non ad archidiaconos, nec decanos aut alios inferiores, sed ad episcopos ipsos pertineat, qui sine strepitu et figura judicii et sola facti veritate inspecta procedere possint. Clerici vero beneficia ecclesiastica aut pensiones non habentes juxta delicti et contumaciae perseverantiam et qualitatem ab ipso episcopo carceris poena, suspensione ab ordine, ac inhabilitate ad beneficia obtinenda, aliisve modis juxta sacros canones puniantur. Episcopi quoque,[97] quod absit, si ab hujusmodi crimine non abstinuerint, et a synodo provinciali admoniti se non emendaverint, ipso facto sint suspensi, et, si perseverent, etiam ad sanctissimum Romanum pontificem ab eadem synodo deferantur, qui pro qualitate culpae, etiam per privationem, si opus erit, in eos animadvertat.

---

[94] Cf. inter alia tot. tit. X, De cohab. cler. et mul., III, 2.
[95] Cf. cc.4, 6 h.t. (Alex. III).
[96] Cf. c.2, X, De cohab. cler. et mul., III, 2 (Eugen. II), c.3, *ibid.* (Alex. III).
[97] Cf. c.1, D.XXXIV (Nicol. I); c.13, D.LXXXI (cap. incert.), c.16, *ibid.* (Alex. II).

Caput XV

FILII CLERICORUM ILLEGITIMI A QUIBUSDAM BENEFICIIS ARCENDI

Ut paternae incontinentiae memoria a locis Deo consecratis, quos maxime puritas sanctitasque decet, longissime arceatur, non liceat filiis clericorum, qui non ex legitimo nati sunt matrimonio, in ecclesiis, ubi eorum patres beneficium aliquod ecclesiasticum habent aut habuerunt, quodcumque, etiam dissimile, beneficium obtinere,[98] nec in dictis ecclesiis quoquo modo ministrare, nec pensiones super fructibus beneficiorum, quae parentes eorum obtinent vel alias obtinuerunt, habere. Quod si in praesenti pater et filius in eadem ecclesia beneficia obtinere reperiantur, cogatur filius suum beneficium resignare, aut cum alio permutare extra ecclesiam intra trium mensium spatium; alias ipso jure eo privatus exsistat, et super iis quaecumque dispensatio surreptitia censeatur. Ad haec reciprocae resignationes, si quae posthac a parentibus clericis in favorem filiorum fient, ut alter alterius beneficium consequatur, in fraudem hujus decreti et canonicarum sanctionum factae omnino censeantur, nec collationes secutae vigore hujusmodi resignationum, seu aliarum quarumcumque, quae in fraudem factae fuerint, ipsis clericorum filiis suffragentur.

Caput XVI

BENEFICIA CURATA NON CONVERTANTUR IN SIMPLICIA. QUOD UBI, ETIAM AB IMMEMORABILI, FACTUM EST, AUT PERPETUO VICARIO CONGRUA FRUCTUUM PORTIO ASSIGNETUR, AUT PRIMA QUOQUE OCCASIONE VICARIA IN INTEGRUM RESTITUATUR

Statuit sancta synodus, ut ecclesiastica beneficia saecularia, quocumque nomine appellentur, quae curam animarum ex primaeva eorum institutione aut aliter quomodocumque retinent, illa deinceps in simplex beneficium, etiam assignata vicario perpetuo congrua portione, non convertantur, non obstantibus quibuscumque gratiis, quae suum plenarium effectum non sunt consecutae. In iis vero, in quibus contra earum institutionem seu fundationem cura animarum in vicarium per-

---

[98] Cf. tot. tit. X, De fil. presb., I, 17.

petuum translata est, etiamsi in hoc statu ab immemorabili tempore reperiantur, si congrua portio fructuum vicario ecclesiae, quocumque nomine is appelletur, non fuerit assignata, ea quam primum et ad minus intra annum a fine praesentis concilii arbitrio ordinarii juxta formam decreti sub fel. rec. Paulo III assignetur.[99] Quod si id commode fieri non possit, aut intra dictum terminum factum non erit, cum primum per cessum vel decessum vicarii seu rectoris aut quomodolibet alterum eorum vacaverit, beneficium curam animarum recipiat, ac vicariae nomen cesset, et in antiquum statum restituatur.

Caput XVII

EPISCOPI DIGNITATEM SUAM MORUM GRAVITATE COMMENDENT, NEC CUM REGUM MINISTRIS, REGULIS AUT BARONIBUS INDIGNA DEMISSIONE SE GERANT

Non potest sancta synodus non graviter dolere, audiens episcopos aliquos sui status oblitos pontificiam dignitatem non leviter dehonestare, qui cum regum ministris, regulis et baronibus in ecclesia et extra indecenti quadam demissione se gerunt, et velut inferiores ministri altaris nimis indigne non solum loco cedunt, sed etiam personaliter illis inserviunt. Quare haec et similia detestans sancta synodus sacros canones omnes, conciliaque generalia atque alias apostolicas sanctiones ad dignitatis episcopalis decorem et gravitatem pertinentes renovando praecipit, ut ab hujusmodi in posterum episcopi se abstineant, mandans eisdem, ut, tam in ecclesia quam foris suum gradum et ordinem prae oculis habentes, ubique se patres et pastores esse meminerint; reliquis vero tam principibus quam ceteris omnibus, ut eos paterno honore ac debita reverentia prosequatur.

Caput XVIII

CANONES AD AMUSSIM SERVENTUR. SI QUANDO IN EIS DISPENSANDUM, ID VALIDE, MATURE ET GRATIS FIAT

Sicuti publice expedit legis vinculum quandoque relaxare, ut plenius evenientibus casibus et necessitatibus pro communi utilitate satisfiat:

---

[99] Cf. Sess. VII, cap. 7 de ref.

sic frequentius legem solvere, exemploque potius quam certo personarum rerumque delectu petentibus indulgere nihil alius est, quam unicuique ad leges transgrediendas aditum aperire. Quapropter sciant universi, sacratissimos canones exacte ab omnibus, et, quoad ejus fieri poterit, indistincte observandos. Quod si urgens justaque ratio et major quandoque utilitas postulaverit cum aliquibus dispensandum esse, id causa cognita ac summa maturitate atque gratis a quibuscumque, ad quos dispensatio pertinebit, erit praestandum, aliterque facta dispensatio surreptitia censeatur.

Caput XIX

MONOMACHIA POENIS GRAVISSIMIS PUNITUR

Detestabilis duellorum usus fabricante diabolo introductus, ut cruenta corporum morte animarum etiam perniciem lucretur, ex Christiano orbe penitus exterminetur. Imperator, reges, duces, principes, marchiones, comites, et quocumque alio nomine domini temporales, qui locum ad monomachiam in terris suis inter Christianos concesserint, eo ipso sint excommunicati, ac jurisdictione et dominio civitatis, castri aut loci, in quo vel apud quem duellum fieri permiserint, quod ab ecclesia obtinent, privati intelligantur, et, si feudalia sint, directis dominis statim acquirantur. Qui vero pugnam commiserint, et qui eorum patrini vocantur, excommunicationis, ac omnium bonorum suorum proscriptionis, ac perpetuae infamiae poenam incurrant, et ut homicidae juxta sacros canones puniri debeant, et, si in ipso conflictu decesserint, perpetuo careant ecclesiastica sepultura.[100] Illi etiam, qui consilium in causa duelli tam in jure quam facto dederint aut alia quacumque ratione ad id quemquam suaserint, necnon spectatores, excommunicationis ac perpetuae maledictionis vinculo teneantur; non obstante quocumque privilegio, seu prava consuetudine, etiam immemorabili.

---

[100] Cf. c.22, C.II, q.5 (Nicol. I); tot. tit. X, De homicid., V, 12, de torneam., V, 13, et de cler. pugn. in duello, V, 14. Cf. etiam const. Gregorii XIII *Ad tollendum*, 5 Dec., 1582, et Clementis VIII *Illius vices*, 17 Aug., 1592.

CAPUT XX

QUAE SUNT JURIS ECCLESIASTICI PRINCIPIBUS SAECULARIBUS COMMENDANTUR

Cupiens sancta synodus ecclesiasticam disciplinam in Christiano populo non solum restitui, sed etiam perpetuo sartam tectam a quibuscumque impedimentis conservari, praeter ea, quae de ecclesiasticis personis constituit, saeculares quoque principes officii sui admonendos esse censuit, confidens eos, ut catholicos, quos Deus sanctae fidei ecclesiaeque protectores esse voluit,[101] jus suum ecclesiae restitui non tantum esse concessuros, sed etiam subditos suos omnes ad debitam erga clerum, parochos et superiores ordines reverentiam revocaturos; [102] nec permissuros, ut officiales aut inferiores magistratus ecclesiae et personarum ecclesiasticarum immunitatem, Dei ordinatione et canonicis sanctionibus constitutam, aliquo cupiditatis studio seu inconsideratione aliqua violent, sed una cum ipsis principibus debitam sacris summorum pontificum et conciliorum constitutionibus observantiam praestent. Decernit itaque et praecipit, sacros canones et concilia generalia omnia,[103] necnon alias apostolicas sanctiones, in favorem ecclesiasticarum personarum, libertatis ecclesiasticae, et contra ejus violatores editas, quae omnia praesenti etiam decreto innovat, exacte ab omnibus observari debere. Propterea que admonet imperatorem, reges, respublicas, principes, et omnes et singulos, cujuscumque status et dignitatis exstiterint, ut, quo largius bonis temporalibus atque in alios potestate sunt ornati, eo sanctius quae ecclesiastici juris tamquam Dei praecepta ejusque patrocinio tecta venerentur, nec ab ullis baronibus, domicellis, rectoribus, aliisve dominis temporalibus seu magistratibus, maximeque ministris ipsorum principum laedi patiantur; sed severe in eos, qui illius libertatem, immunitatem atque jurisdictionem impediunt, animadvertant. Quibus etiam ipsimet exemplo ad pietatem, religionem ecclesiarumque protectionem exsistant, imitantes anteriores optimos religiosissimosque principes, qui res ecclesiae sua in primis auctoritate ac munificentia auxerunt, nedum ab aliorum injuria vindicarunt. Adeoque ea in re quisque officium suum sedulo praestet, quo cultus divinus

---

[101] Cf. c.20, C.XXIII, q.5 (Isid.).
[102] Cf. c.9, D.XCVI (Greg. VII).
[103] Cf. c.29, C.XVII, q.4 (Lat. II); tot. tit. X, De immun. eccl., III, 49; c.4, VI°, De cens., III, 20.

devote exerceri, et praelati ceterique clerici in residentiis et officiis suis quieti et sine impedimentis cum fructu et aedificatione populi permanere valeant.

Caput XXI

IN OMNIBUS SALVA SEDIS APOSTOLICAE AUCTORITAS MANEAT

Postremo sancta synodus, omnia et singula, sub quibuscumque clausulis et verbis, quae de morum reformatione atque ecclesiastica disciplina tam sub fel. rec. Paulo III ac Julio III, quam sub beatissimo Pio IV, pontificibus maximis, in hoc sacro concilio statuta sunt, declarat ita decreta fuisse, ut in his salva semper auctoritas Sedis Apostolicae et sit et esse intelligatur.[104]

DECRETUM DE PROSEQUENDA SESSIONE IN SUBSEQUENTEM DIEM

Cum ea omnia, quae in praesenti sessione tractanda erant, quia hora tarda est, commode expediri non possint, propterea juxta id, quod in generali congregatione a patribus statutum fuit, ea, quae supersunt, in diem crastinam hanc eamdem sessionem continuando differuntur.

CONTINUATIO SESSIONIS
die IV Decembris

DECRETUM DE INDULGENTIIS

Cum potestas conferendi indulgentias a Christo ecclesiae concessa sit,[105] atque hujusmodi potestate divinitus sibi tradita antiquissimis etiam temporibus illa usa fuerit,[106] sacrosancta synodus indulgentiarum usum, Christiano populo maxime salutarem et sacrorum conciliorum auctoritate probatum, in ecclesia retinendum esse docet et praecipit, eosque anathemate damnat, qui aut inutiles esse asserunt, vel eas concedendi in ecclesia potestatem esse negant. In his tamen concedendis moderationem juxta veterem et probatam in ecclesia con-

---

[104] Cf. Sess. VII de ref. in princ.
[105] Cf. Matt. 16:19; 18:18; Joan. 20:23.
[106] Cf. Rouët de Journel sub rubrica "Indulgentiae," p. 782, nn. 550 f.; Denzinger sub ead. rubrica, XII 1, p. [47 f.].

suetudinem adhiberi cupit, ne nimia facilitate ecclesiastica disciplina enervetur. Abusus vero, qui in his irrepserunt,[107] et quorum occasione insigne hoc indulgentiarum nomen ab haereticis blasphematur, emendatos et correctos cupiens, praesenti decreto generaliter statuit, pravos quaestus omnes pro his consequendis, unde plurima in Christiano populo abusuum causa fluxit, omnino abolendos esse. Ceteros vero, qui ex superstitione, ignorantia, irreverentia aut aliunde quomodocumque provenerunt, cum ob multiplices locorum et provinciarum, apud quas hi committuntur, corruptelas commode nequeant specialiter prohiberi, mandat omnibus episcopis,[108] ut diligenter quisque hujusmodi abusus ecclesiae suae colligat, eosque in prima synodo provinciali referat, ut, aliorum quoque episcoporum sententia cognita, statim ad summum Romanum pontificem deferantur, cujus auctoritate et prudentia quod universali ecclesiae expediet statuatur, ut ita sanctarum indulgentiarum munus pie, sancte et incorrupte omnibus fidelibus dispensetur.

DE DELECTU CIBORUM, JEJUNIIS ET DIEBUS FESTIS

Insuper hortatur sancta synodus, et per sanctissimum Domini nostri atque Salvatoris adventum pastores omnes obtestatur, ut tamquam boni milites illa omnia, quae sancta Romana ecclesia, omnium ecclesiarum mater et magistra, statuit, necnon ea, quae tam in hoc concilio quam in aliis oecumenicis statuta sunt, quibuscumque fidelibus sedulo commendent, omnique diligentia utantur, ut illis omnibus, et iis praecipue sint obsequentes, quae ad mortificandam carnem conducunt, ut ciborum delectus et jejunia, vel etiam, quae faciunt ad pietatem augendam, ut dierum festorum devota et religiosa celebratio; admonentes populos crebro, obedire praepositis suis, quos qui audiunt Deum remuneratorem audient, qui vero contemnunt Deum ipsum ultorem sentient.[109]

DE INDICE LIBRORUM ET CATECHISMO, BREVIARIO ET MISSALI

Sacrosancta synodus in secunda sessione,[110] sub sanctissimo domino nostro Pio IV celebrata, delectis quibusdam patribus commisit, ut de

---

[107] Cf. c. 2, De poenit. et remiss. in Clem., V, 9.
[108] Cf. Sess. XXI, cap. 9 de ref.
[109] Matt. 18:17; Luc. 10:16; Heb. 13:17; c. 9, D. XCIII.
[110] Cf. Sess. XVIII in princ.

variis censuris ac libris, vel suspectis vel perniciosis, quid facto opus esset considerarent atque ad ipsam sanctam synodum referrent. Audiens nunc, huic operi ab eis extremam manum impositam esse, nec tamen ob librorum varietatem et multitudinem possit distincte et commode a sancta synodo dijudicari, praecipit, ut quidquid ab illis praestitum est sanctissimo Romano pontifici exhibeatur, ut ejus judicio atque auctoritate terminetur et evulgetur.[111] Idemque de catechismo a patribus,[112] quibus illud mandatum fuerat, et de missali et breviario fieri mandat.

DE LOCO ORATORUM

Declarat sancta synodus, ex loco assignato oratoribus,[113] tam ecclesiasticis quam saecularibus, in sedendo, incedendo aut quibuscumque aliis actibus, nullum cuiquam eorum factum fuisse praejudicium; sed omnia illorum, et imperatoris, regum, rerumpublicarum ac principum suorum jura et praerogativas illaesas et salvas esse, in eodemque statu permanere, prout ante praesens concilium reperiebantur.

DE RECIPIENDIS ET OBSERVANDIS DECRETIS CONCILII

Tanta fuit horum temporum calamitas et haereticorum inveterata malitia, ut nihil tam clarum in fide nostra asserenda unquam fuerit, aut tam certo statutum, quod non humani generis hoste suadente illi errore aliquo contaminaverint. Ea propter sancta synodus id potissimum curavit, ut praecipuos haereticorum nostri temporis errores damnaret et anathematizaret, veramque et catholicam doctrinam traderet et doceret, prout damnavit, anathematizavit et definivit. Cumque tamdiu tot episcopi ex variis Christiani orbis provinciis evocati sine magna gregis sibi commissi jactura et universali periculo ab ecclesiis abesse non possint, nec ulla spes restet, haereticos toties, fide etiam publica, quam desiderarunt,[114] invitatos, et tamdiu expectatos, huc amplius adventuros, ideoque tamdem huic sacro concilio finem imponere necesse sit: superest nunc, ut principes omnes, quod facit, in Domino moneat ad operam suam ita praestandam, ut quae ab ea decreta sunt ab haereticis depravari aut violari non permittant, sed

---

[111] Cf. *infra*, regulas de libris prohibitis, pp. 545 ff.

[112] Cf. Sess. XXIV, cap. 7 de ref.

[113] Cf. Sess. II, § Insuper, sub fin.

[114] Datus fuit salvus conductus Protestantibus sub Julio III primo in Sess. XIII, deinde ampliatus in Sess. XV; repetitus denique et iterum auctus sub Pio IV in Sess. XVIII.

ab his et omnibus devote recipiantur et fideliter observentur. Quod si in his recipiendis aliqua difficultas oriatur, aut aliqua inciderint, quae declarationem, quod non credit, aut definitionem postulant, praeter alia remedia in hoc concilio instituta confidit sancta synodus, beatissimum Romanum pontificem curaturum, ut vel evocatis ex illis praesertim provinciis, unde difficultas orta fuerit, iis, quos eidem negotio tractando viderit expedire, vel etiam concilii generalis celebratione, si necessarium judicaverit, vel commodiore quacumque ratione ei visum fuerit, provinciarum necessitatibus pro Dei gloria et ecclesiae tranquillitate consulatur.

DE RECITANDIS DECRETIS CONCILII SUB PAULO III ET JULIO III IN SESSIONE

Quoniam diversis temporibus tam sub fel. rec. Paulo III quam Julio III multa in hoc sacro concilio quoad dogmata ac morum reformationem statuta et definita sunt,[115] vult sancta synodus, ut illa nunc recitentur et legantur.
Recitata sunt.

DE FINE CONCILII ET CONFIRMATIONE PETENDA A SANCTISSIMO DOMINO NOSTRO

Illustrissimi domini reverendissimique patres, placetne vobis, ut ad laudem Dei omnipotentis huic sacrae oecumenicae synodo finis imponatur, et omnium et singulorum, quae tam sub fel. rec. Paulo III et Julio III, quam sub sanctissimo domino nostro Pio IV, Romanis pontificibus, in ea decreta et definita sunt, confirmatio nomine sanctae hujus synodi per Apostolicae Sedis legatos et praesidentes a beatissimo Romano pontifice petatur?
Responderunt: Placet.

Postmodum illustrissimus et reverendissimus cardinalis Moronus, primus legatus et praesidens, benedicens sanctae synodo dixit: post gratias Deo actas reverendissimi patres ite in pace. *Qui responderunt:* Amen.

Deinde illustrissimus et reverendissimus dominus cardinalis Lotharingus dixit alta voce infrascripta verba, videlicet:

---

[115] In Sess. V–VII, XIII, XIV

ACCLAMATIONES PATRUM POST FINEM CONCILII

Cardinalis: Beatissimo Pio Papae et domino nostro, sanctae universalis ecclesiae pontifici, multi anni et aeterna memoria.

Responsio patrum: Domine Deus, sanctissimum patrem diutissime ecclesiae tuae conserva multos annos.

Card.: Beatissimorum summorum pontificum animabus, Pauli III et Julii III, quorum auctoritate hoc sacrum generale concilium inchoatum est, pax a Domino, et aeterna gloria, atque felicitas in luce sanctorum.

Resp.: Memoria in benedictione sit.

Card.: Caroli V imperatoris, et serenissimorum regum, qui hoc universale concilium promoverunt et protexerunt, memoria in benedictione sit.

Resp.: Amen, Amen.

Card.: Serenissimo imperatori Ferdinando semper augusto, orthodoxo et pacifico, et omnibus regibus, rebuspublicis et principibus nostris multi anni.

Resp.: Pium et Christianum imperatorem, Domine, conserva; Imperator coelestis, terrenos reges rectae fidei conservatores custodi.

Card.: Apostolicae Romanae Sedis legatis et in hac synodo praesidentibus cum multis annis magnae gratiae.

Resp.: Magnae gratiae; Dominus retribuat.

Card.: Reverendissimis cardinalibus et illustribus oratoribus.

Resp.: Magnas gratias, multos annos.

Card.: Sanctissimis episcopis vita et felix ad ecclesias suas reditus.

Resp.: Praeconibus veritatis perpetua memoria; orthodoxo senatui multos annos.

Card.: Sacrosancta oecumenica Tridentina synodus, ejus fidem confiteamur, ejus decreta semper servemus.

Resp.: Semper confiteamur, semper servemus.

Card.: Omnes ita credimus, omnes id ipsum sentimus, omnes consentientes et amplectentes subscribimus. Haec est fides beati Petri et Apostolorum; haec est fides patrum; haec est fides orthodoxorum.

Resp.: Ita credimus, ita sentimus, ita subscribimus.

Card.: His decretis inhaerentes digni reddamur misericordiis et gratia primi et magni supremi sacerdotis Jesu Christi Dei, intercedente simul inviolata Domina nostra sancta deipara et omnibus sanctis.

Resp.: Fiat, fiat. Amen, Amen.
Card.: Anathema cunctis haereticis.
Resp.: Anathema, anathema.

Post haec mandatum fuit a legatis praesidentibus sub poena excommunicationis omnibus patribus, ut, antequam discederent e civitate Tridentina, subscriberent manu propria decretis concilii, aut ea per publicum instrumentum approbarent; qui omnes deinde subscripserunt, et fuerunt numero CCLV, videlicet, legati IV, cardinales II, patriarchae III, archiepiscopi XXV, episcopi CLXVIII, abbates VII, procuratores absentium cum legitimo mandato XXXIX, generales ordinum VII.

LAUS DEO

Concordat cum originali, in cujus fidem subscripsimus:

Ego Angelus Massarellus, Episcopus Thelesinus, sacri concilii Tridentini secretarius.

Ego Marcus Antonius Peregrinus, Comensis, ejusdem concilii notarius.

Ego Cynthius Pamphilius, clericus Camerinensis dioecesis, ejusdem concilii notarius.

ORATIO HABITA DIE PRIMA SESSIONIS NONAE ET ULTIMAE SACRI CONCILII TRIDENTINI SUB PIO PAPA IV, DIE 3 DECEMBRIS, 1563 A R. P. D. HIERONYMO RAGAZONO, VENETO, EPISCOPO NAZIANZENO ET COADJUTORE FAMAUGUSTANO

Audite haec, omnes gentes, auribus percipite qui habitatis terram.[1] Tridentinum concilium, jam diu coeptum, aliquando intermissum, distractum varie atque divulsum, nunc demum singulari Dei omnipotentis beneficio, summa atque incredibili omnium ordinum ac nationum voluntate connectitur atque perficitur. Dies haec quidem felicissima Christiano populo eluxit, in qua templum Domini, disturbatum frequenter ac dissipatum, reficitur et absolvitur, et navis haec una bonorum omnium ex maximis ac diuturnis turbinibus atque fluctibus tuta in portu collocatur. Quam utinam conscendere nobiscum ii vo-

[1] Ps. 48:2.

luissent, quorum in primis gratia haec ipsa navigatio instituta fuit, atque aedificii hujus construendi participes exsisterent, qui hoc nobis negotium exhibuerunt, majoris nunc profecto laetitiae causam haberemus. Sed nostra id certe culpa non accidit.

Nos urbem hanc in Germaniae faucibus, id est in domus illorum fere limine positam, elegimus; nos custodiam nullam nobis, ne suspicionem illis aliquam minus liberi loci daremus, adhibuimus; nos eam fidem publicam illis concessimus, quam sibi ipsi composuerunt; nos hic illos perdiu exspectavimus, neque hortari ac rogare unquam destitimus, ut ad veritatis lucem cognoscendam accederent. Verum illis etiam absentibus satis, ut puto, a nobis consultum est. Etenim cum duo essent, in quibus aegris atque infirmis illorum animis medicina fuit adhibenda, alterum fidei catholicae ac vere evangelicae, illis in rebus, quae in dubium ab ipsis vocantur, quaeque opportunae his temporibus viderentur, explicata et confirmata, disjectis omnibus et dissipatis errorum tenebris, doctrina; alterum disciplinae ecclesiasticae, cujus potissimum depravatione illi se a nobis defecisse affirmant, restitutio; utrumque, quantum in nobis fuit, pro horum temporum ratione cumulate, praestitimus.

Principio enim sancta haec synodus (facta ex laudabili majorum nostrorum consuetudine suae fidei professione), ut quoddam quasi fundamentum futuris actionibus poneret, et quibus testimoniis atque praesidiis in dogmatibus sanciendis nitendum esset ostenderet, veteris ac novi testamenti libros, qui essent sine ulla dubitatione recipiendi, antiquorum conciliorum probatissimorum exemplo pie et prudenter enumeravit, ac, ne de verbis quidem ulla ex variis versionibus oriri posset difficultas, certam ac definitam de graecis et hebraeis translationem approbavit. Hinc omnium haeresum caput atque arcem aggrediens de humanae naturae corruptis initiis ea statuit, quae veritas ipsa, si loqui posset, exprimeret. De justificatione deinceps (res magna et cum ab antiquis tum a nostri temporis haereticis mirum in modum oppugnata) ea definivit, quibus et perniciosissimis eo in genere opinionibus occurreretur, et recte sentiendi ratio miro quodam ordine atque admirabili sapientia (ut in illis Dei spiritum facile agnoscas) demonstraretur. Praestantissimo hoc post hominum memoriam decreto haereses fere universae jugulantur, et, quasi caligo sole, discutiuntur ac dispelluntur, eaque claritas isque splendor veritatis apparet, ut tantum lumen quin videat dissimulare jam nemo possit.

Subsecuta est salutaris septem divinorum ecclesiae sacramentorum tractatio: primum simul de omnibus, post de unoquoque separatim. Hic vero quis non videt, quam distincte, explicate, abundanter, illuminate et (quod caput est) vere tota coelestium horum mysteriorum ratio contineatur? Quis in tam magna multiplicique doctrina quid aut sequendum aut fugiendum sit potest ullo modo desiderare? Quis in illis omnibus errandi locum aut occasionem inveniet? Quis denique de sacramentorum horum vi atque virtute dubitare in posterum poterit, cum gratiam illam, quae illis ipsis quibusdam quasi stillicidiis in fidelium quotidie mentes illabitur, tunc nobis adfuisse tam copiose perspiciatur? Accesserunt ad haec de sacrosancto missae sacrificio, et de communione sub utraque specie et parvulorum decreta, quibus quidem, nihil sanctius, nihil utilius, ut de coelo lapsa, non ab hominibus composita videantur. Adjungetur his hodie certa de indulgentiis, de purgatorio, de sanctorum veneratione, invocatione, imaginibus et reliquiis doctrina, qua non solum haereticorum fraudibus et calumniis obsistetur, sed piorum etiam catholicorum conscientiis plane satisfiet.

Haec de rebus ad salutem nostram pertinentibus, quae dogmata appellantur, fauste ac feliciter fuerunt peracta, neque aliud quidquam praeterea eo in genere a nobis hoc tempore expectabitur. In eorum autem quisbusdam administrandis cum nonnulla essent, quae non rite omnino ac recte servarentur, accuratissime, patres amplissimi, curastis, ut pure illa et caste, atque ex more institutoque majorum tractarentur. Ita omnem superstitionem, omnem quaestum, omnem (ut dicunt) irreverentiam a divina missarum celebratione abstulistis, vagis, ignotis et criminosis sacerdotibus sanctum hoc offerre sacrificium interdixistis, rei hujus sacratissimae usum a privatis domibus et profanis in sacra et religiosa loca revocastis, molliores cantus et symphonias, deambulationes, colloquia, negotiationes a templo Domini submovistis; ita ecclesiastico unicuique gradui leges illae a vobis praescriptae sunt, ut tradito illis divinitus ordine abutendi nullus utique locus relinquatur. Ita nonnulla matrimonii impedimenta, quae ansam quasi quamdam ad violanda ecclesiae praecepta dare videbantur, removistis, facilem veniae consequendae viam minus legitime connubii foedus ineuntibus interclusistis. Quid de furtivis tenebricosisque matrimoniis commemorem? Equidem ita sentio, si alia nulla causa convocandi concilium fuisset (quae multae et maximae fuerunt), propter unam hanc id omnino fuisse faciendum. Nam cum res haec ad omnes spectet, neque ullus in orbe terrarum universo angulus reperiatur, quem labes haec non invaserit, curandum merito fuisset, ut communi huic malo communi etiam consilio provideretur. Innumerabilium, patres sanctissimi, et gravissimorum delictorum ac scelerum occasio providentissima ista vestra ac prope divina sanctione penitus ablata est, et Christianae reipublicae gubernationi sapientissime consultum. Accedet ad haec utilis in primis ac necessaria multorum in purgatorii, sanctorum venerationis, invocationis, imaginum et reliquiarum, atque etiam indulgentiarum ratione abusuum interdictio, qui rerum ipsarum pulcherrimam faciem inquinare atque turpare mirum in modum videbantur.

Altera vero pars, in qua de labenti ac prope cadenti ecclesiastica disciplina fulcienda erat agendum, diligentissime etiam absoluta fuit atque perfecta. Eligentur in posterum ad ecclesiastica munera obeunda qui virtute, non ambitione praestent, quique populi commodis, non suis inserviant, et prosint potius quam praesint. Enunciabitur atque explanabitur frequentius et studiosius verbum Domini, omni ancipiti gladio penetrantius.[2] Aderunt suis gregibus et invigilabunt episcopi ceterique, quibus animarum cura commissa est, neque extra creditam sibi custodiam vagabuntur. Nihil cuiquam proderunt aut ad impure et flagitiose vivendum, aut ad male et perniciose docendum privilegia; nullum sine poena crimen, nulla sine praemio virtus relinquetur. Pauperum et mendicantium sacerdotum multitudini optime provisum est; certae unusquisque ecclesiae statutoque operi, unde ali possit, adscribetur.

Avaritia, quo nullum vitium est tetrius,[3] praesertim in domo Dei, ab ea omnino tolletur; gratis sacramenta omnia, ut par est, conferentur. Ex una ecclesia plures, ex pluribus una, ut populi commodum et ratio postulabit, constituetur. Eleemosynarum quaestores (ut appellant), qui sua, non quae Jesu Christi quaerentes magnum nostrae religioni damnum, magnam infamiam afferebant, ex omni hominum memoria (quod summae felicitatis loco ponendum est) penitus evellentur. Hinc nostra praesens calamitas sumpsit exordium, hinc serpere infinitum malum, manareque in dies latius non desistebat, neque occurri illi adhuc multorum conciliorum cautionibus ac provisionibus potuit. Quamobrem quis non nisi sapientissime factum dixerit, ut membrum hoc, in quo sanando diu ac multum frustra laboratum est, ne reliquo corpori noceret, excideretur?

Porro Deo cultus tribuetur purius et accuratius, atque ita qui ferunt vasa Domini mundabuntur, ut ad sui imitationem alios trahant. In quo

---

[2] Heb. 4:12.

[3] Ecclus. 10:9.

praeclare illud fuit excogitatum, ut qui sacris essent initiandi iis moribus atque litteris in unaquaque ecclesia a prima aetate instituerentur, ut quoddam quasi virtutum omnium seminarium illud exsisteret. Jam vero provincialibus synodis restitutis; visitationibus ad populorum utilitatem, non ad querelam et sumptum renovatis; tradita pastoribus regendi suos atque pascendi commodius facultate; poenitentia publica in usum revocata; hospitalitate tum ecclesiasticis hominibus, tum piis locis indicta; in curatis sacerdotiis conferendis memorabili ac pene coelesti ratione constituta; beneficiorum (ut aiunt) pluralitate sublata; hereditaria sanctuarii Dei possessione prohibita; modo excommunicationibus imposito ac terminato; primis judiciis iis in locis, ubi lites oriuntur, assignatis; singularibus certaminibus interdictis; omnium hominum ac sacrorum in primis luxuriae, cupiditati atque licentiae freno quasi quodam, quod excuti non facile possit, injecto; regibus ac principibus sui muneris diligenter admonitis; aliisque rebus hujusmodi prudentissime sancitis: quis non videt vestras vos, patres optimi, hac etiam in re partes cumulatissime executos?

Actum saepe est in superioribus conciliis de fide nostra explicanda moribusque corrigendis, sed nescio, an unquam diligentius atque distinctius. Hic, praesertim hoc biennio, omnium populorum ac nationum, in quibus catholicae religionis veritas agnoscitur, non solum patres, sed oratores habuimus. Ad quos viros? Si doctrinam spectemus, eruditissimos; si usum, peritissimos; si ingenia, perspicacissimos; si pietatem, religiosissimos; si vitam, innocentissimos. Numerus is quoque fuit, ut, si praesentes Christiani orbis considerentur angustiae, frequentissima haec omnium, quae antea fuerunt, synodus appareat. Hic singula omnium vulnera detecta, mores expositi fuere, nihil dissimulatum est. Adversariorum nostrorum argumenta et rationes ita tractatae, ut eorum tum causa, non nostra, agi videretur. Tertium nonnulla atque etiam quartum discussa; summa saepe contentione certatum; eo scilicet consilio, ut, quemadmodum igne aurum, ita quibusdam quasi luctationibus veritatis vires ac nervi probarentur. Quae enim inter idem sentientes idemque spectantes discordia potuit exsistere?

Quae cum ita sint, licet optandum, ut initio dicebam, summopere fuisset, ut una cum illis haec agerentur, quorum potissimum causa tractata sunt: absentium tamen etiam incolumitati atque saluti ita provisum est, ut alia ratione provideri, si adfuissent, non potuisse videatur. Legant illi quae de fide nostra statuimus, ut Christianum hominem decet, humiliter; et, si lumen eis aliquod fulserit, ne faciem avertant, et, si vocem Domini audierint, corda sua non obdurent, ac si ad communem matris ecclesiae complexum, unde se illi distraxerunt, redire voluerint, clementiam sibi omnem ac misericordiam tribuendam non dubitent.

Sed praecipua illa ratio est, patres amplissimi, dissentientes a nobis animos conciliandi, consentientes in fide atque officio retinendi, si quae hoc in loco verbis sancivimus, re ipsi in nostris ecclesiis praestemus. Leges etsi optimae sunt, muta tamen res est. Quid hebraeo populo Dei ipsius ore latae leges profuerunt? Quid Lycurgi leges Lacedaemoniis, Solonis Atheniensibus, ad libertatem retinendam, quam ob causam erant conscriptae, utilitatis attulere? Sed cur externa atque antiqua nimis commemoro? Quae ad bene beateque vivendum instituta atque praecepta ex unius Christi Domini nostri vita atque doctrina desiderare aut possumus aut debemus? Quid item fuit a majoribus nostris omissum, quod cum ad recte sentiendum, tum ad praeclare agendum pertineret? Medicamentum quidem salutare compositum ac paratum jamdiu habemus; verum si morbum debet expellere, sumendum est ac per venas in omne corpus diffundendum. Poculo hoc salutis nos primum inebriemur, carissimi, et vivae atque loquentes leges simus et norma quasi quaedam ac regula, ad quam aliorum actiones et studia dirigantur, atque ita sibi unusquisque persuadeat, nihil a Christianae reipublicae commodo ac dignitate successurum nisi quantum in se sit studiose praestiterit.

Id curandum nobis cum antea fuit, tum multo erit in posterum accuratius. Etenim, si magistri nostri ac Salvatoris exemplo facere prius debeamus quam docere,[4] postquam docuimus, quin faciamus, quae esse poterit excusatio? Quis ferre nos ac pati poterit, si, cum non furandum esse demonstravimus, ipsi furemur? Si, cum non moechandum, moechemur? Sanctos a sancto concilio, innocentes atque integros ab integritatis praeceptis et innocentiae, firmos in fide atque constantes a fidei nostrae firmata doctrina discedere minime convenit. Ac tales quidem expectant nos populi nostri, qui nostrum jamdiu reditum sustinentes ea se ipsi ratione consolabantur, fore, ut hanc temporis usuram majori praesentes studio sarciremus. Sed fiet id a vobis, ut spero, patres sanctissimi, diligenter, et, quemadmodum hoc in loco fecistis, ita etiam domi satis Deo atque hominibus facietis.

---

[4] Act. 1:1.

Nunc (quod hujus temporis est) Deo primum ipsi maximo atque immortali maximas atque immortales gratias et agamus et habeamus, qui non secundum peccata, quae fecimus nos, neque secundum iniquitates nostras retribuit nobis,[5] sed diem hunc laetissimum, quem videre multi concupiverunt, nobis non solum videndum, sed etiam celebrandum incredibili cum totius Christiani populi assensu atque approbatione sua magna benignitate concessit. Pio deinde IV, summo nostro atque optimo pontifici, gratiae perpetuae ac singulares habendae sunt, qui, cum primum beati Petri sedem ascendit, tanto synodum hanc instaurandi desiderio exarsit, ut in eo suas omnes curas et cogitationes defigeret. Nuncios statim viros prudentissimos ad indicendum illis nationibus atque provinciis concilium misit, pro quorum in primis salute convocabatur. Hi aquilonis partes prope omnes peragrarunt, rogarunt, obsecrarunt, obtestati sunt; tuta omnia atque amica promiserunt, atque id etiam egerunt, ut in Angliam trajicerent. Legatos postmodum pietate ac doctrina praestantissimos, cum interesse ille synodo, ut mirum in modum cupiebat, non posset, huc misit, ex quibus duos (quorum memoria in benedictione est) statuta die, tametsi nulli fere episcopi convenissent, his esse voluit. Hi, atque additus eis paulo post tertius, novem menses atque eo amplius justum ad synodum instituendam episcoporum numerum hoc in loco nihil agentes expectaverunt, cum interea nihil aliud pontifex ipse aut ageret aut meditaretur, quam ut patres quam plurimi, quam optimi, et quam primum huc accederent, et Christiani nominis reges omnes ac principes suos huc oratores mitterent, ut communi omnium voto atque consilio communis haec causa gravissima omnium atque maxima tractaretur. Quid vero postea omni cura, sollicitudine, sumptibus praetermisit, quod ad concilii hujus amplitudinem, libertatem et commodum pertinere aliquo modo videretur? O singularem pastoris ac patris nostri pietatem atque prudentiam! O summam etiam ejusdem felicitatem, cujus auctoritate atque auspiciis jactatum hoc diu et agitatum concilium constitit et conquiescit! Te Paulum III, te Julium III mortuos appello; quamdiu quantoque studio videre quod nos videmus exoptastis? Quot in eam rem sumptus, quot labores insumpsistis? Quamobrem vere tibi atque ex animo, Pie sanctissime ac beatissime, gratulamur, quod tantam tibi laetitiam, tantam tuo nomini laudem (id quod maximum divinae in te benevolentiae argumentum est) Dominus reservavit, quem nos pre-

---

[5] Ps. 102:10.

cibus omnibus ac votis supplices oramus, ut te nobis incolumem pro ecclesiae suae sanctae commodo atque ornamento et quam citissime reddat, et quam diutissime conservet.

Serenissimo etiam imperatori gratias agere, et gratulari jure optimo debemus. Ille potentissimorum Caesarum, qui propagandae Christianae religionis miro quodam desiderio flagrarunt, animum, ut locum, referens, urbem hanc ab omni periculo liberam conservavit, et nos, ut tutam tranquillamque pacem traheremus, sua vigilantia perfecit, magnamque nostris animis securitatem assidua trium suorum legatorum summorum virorum praesentia ac prope pignore attulit. Ille de nostris his rebus pro sua eximia pietate sollicitus mirifice fuit. Ille a se atque a nobis dissentientes homines ex obscurissimis, in quibus versantur, tenebris eruere, atque ad sanctae hujus synodi clarissimam lucem aspiciendam adducere maximopere laboravit. Regum praeterea Christianorum ac principum in concilio hoc amplissimis suis legationibus ornando, et suos vestrae auctoritati fasces submittendo, pia maxime voluntas grata nobis memoria prosequenda est.

Jam vero quis est, illustrissimi legati et cardinales, qui se vobis debere plurimum non fateatur? Vos nostrarum actionum duces optimi ac moderatores extitistis. Vos, ne nostra aut in dicendo aut decernendo libertas violari aliqua ex parte videretur, incredibili patientia ac diligentia curastis. Vos nulli corporis labori, nulli animi contentioni pepercistis, ut ad optatum res exitum, quod alii multi vestri similes frustra tentaverunt, quamprimum perduceretur. In quo praecipuam quamdam ac propriam laetitiam habere tu, Morone illustrissime atque ornatissime, debes, qui, cum vigesimo ab hinc anno primum praeclaro huic aedificio lapidem posueris, extremam nunc manum post alios multos huic operi architectos adhibitos feliciter pro summa tua ac prope divina sapientia imponis. Factum hoc tuum egregium ac singulare omnium sermone perpetuo celebrabitur, neque ulla unquam aetas de tuis his laudibus conticescet.

Quid de vobis dicam, patres sanctissimi? Quam bene de Christiana republica vestris his praestantissimis actionibus meruistis! Quanta vestrum uniuscujusque nominis commendatio, quanta gloria a Christiano populo universo tribuetur! Vos vere patres, vere pastores et agnoscent omnes et praedicabunt, vobis suam unusquisque vitam atque salutem acceptam libentissime referet. O diem illam populis nostris jucundissimam atque laetissimam, in qua primum revisere illis nos atque amplecti a templi Domini aedificatione redeuntes contigerit!

Sed fac, tu Domine Deus noster, ut tam eximiae de nobis opinioni egregiis factis respondeamus, et semen hoc, quod in agro tuo seminavimus, uberem fructum afferat, fluatque ut ros eloquium tuum, atque, quod fore aliquando pollicitus es, fiat temporibus nostris, ut unum sit omnium ovile, et unus pastor, atque is potissimum Pius IV, in tui nominis gloriam sempiternam. Amen.

PETITIO PRO CONCILII CONFIRMATIONE

Nos Alexander, sancti Laurentii in Damaso diaconus cardinalis de Farnesio, S. R. E. vicecancellarius, fidem facimus et attestamur, qualiter hodie, die Mercurii, XXVI Januarii MDLXIV, pontificatus sanctissimi D. nostri D. Pii, divina providentia Papae quarti, anno quinto, in consistorio secreto apud S. Petrum reverendissimi DD. mei cardinales Moronus et Simoneta, nuper reversi a sacro concilio Tridentino, cui uti Sedis Apostolicae legati praeerant, petierunt ab eodem sanctissimo D. nostro ut infra:

Beatissime Pater: in decreto super fine concilii oecumenici Tridentini, pridie nonas Decembris praeteriti publicato, statutum fuit, ut per Sanctitatis vestrae et sanctae sedis apostolicae legatos et praesidentes peteretur nomine dicti concilii a Sanctitate vestra confirmatio omnium et singulorum, quae tam sub fel. rec. Paulo III et Julio III, quam sub Sanctitate vestra in eo decreta et definita sunt. Quapropter nos Ioannes cardinalis Moronus et Ludovicus cardinalis Simoneta, qui tunc legati et praesidentes eramus, volentes exequi quod in dicto decreto stabilitum fuit, humiliter petimus nomine dicti concilii oecumenici Tridentini, ut Sanctitas vestra dignetur confirmare omnia et singula, quae tam sub fel. rec. Paulo III et Julio III, quam sub Sanctitate vestra in eo decreta et definita sunt.

Quibus auditis Sanctitas sua, viso et lecto tenore dicti decreti, et habitis votis reverendissimorum DD. meorum cardinalium, respondit per haec verba:

Petitioni nomine concilii oecumenici Tridentini super ejus confirmatione per dictos legatos nobis factae annuentes, omnia et singula, quae in dicto concilio tam sub fel. rec. Paulo III et Julio III praedecessoribus nostris, quam pontificatus nostri tempore decreta et definita sunt, auctoritate apostolica, etiam de venerabilium fratrum nostrorum cardinalium consilio et assensu, matura cum illis deliberatione praehabita, confirmamus, atque ab omnibus Christi fidelibus recipi et inviolabiliter observari mandamus, in nomine Patris et Filii et Spiritus Sancti. Amen.

Ita est.

A. Cardinalis Farnesius, Vicecancell.

BULLA S. D. N. PII IV PONT. MAX.

SUPER CONFIRMATIONE

SACRI OECUMENICI CONCILII TRIDENTINI

Romae XXVI Januarii, MDLXIV

PIUS EPISCOPUS, SERVUS SERVORUM DEI, AD PERPETUAM REI MEMORIAM

Benedictus Deus et Pater Domini nostri Jesu Christi, Pater misericordiarum et Deus totius consolationis,[1] qui respicere dignatus ecclesiam suam sanctam, tot procellis et tempestatibus agitatam atque vexatam et gravius in dies laborantem, apto tandem ei subvenit optatoque remedio. Ad plurimas et perniciosissimas haereses extirpandas, ad corrigendos mores et restituendam ecclesiasticam disciplinam, ad pacem et concordiam Christiani populi procurandum, indictum jam pridem in civitate Tridentina oecumenicum et generale concilium a piae memoriae Paulo III, praedecessore nostro, et sessionibus aliquot habitis coeptum fuerat; ab ejus autem successore Julio in eamdem urbem revocatum, post alias sessiones celebratas variis impedimentis et difficultatibus objectis ne tum quidem peragi potuerat, itaque diutius intermissum fuerat, non sine maximo moerore piorum omnium, cum quotidie magis ecclesia ejusmodi remedium imploraret. Nos autem post susceptum Sedis Apostolicae regimen tam necessarium ac salutare opus, sicut pastoralis sollicitudo monebat, divinae misericordiae fiducia perficere aggressi, adjuti pio studio carissimi in Christo filii nostri Ferdinandi Romanorum imperatoris electi, et aliorum Christianorum regum, rerumpublicarum et principum, tandem consecuti sumus quod nec diurnis nec nocturnis curis elaborare destitimus, quodque a Patre luminum assidue precati sumus. Cum enim eam in urbem undique ex Christiani nominis nationibus convenisset, nostris convocata litteris et sua etiam ipsorum pietate excitata,

[1] Cf. II Cor. 1:3.

episcoporum et aliorum insignium praelatorum maxima et oecumenico concilio digna frequentia, praeter plurimos alios pios et sacrarum litterarum scientia divinique et humani juris cognitione praestantes viros, praesidentibus ipsi synodo Sedis Apostolicae legatis, nobis adeo concilii liberati faventibus, ut etiam de rebus Sedi Apostolicae proprie reservatis liberum ipsi concilio arbitrium per litteras ad legatos nostros scriptas ultro permiserimus, quae de sacramentis et aliis rebus, quae quidem necessariae visae sint, tractanda, definienda et statuenda restabant, ad confutandas haereses, ad tollendos abusus, et emendandos mores, a sacrosancta synodo summa libertate diligentiaque tractata et accurate ac mature admodum definita, explicata, statuta sunt. Quibus rebus perfectis concilium tanta omnium, qui illi interfuerunt, concordia peractum fuit, ut consensum eum plane a Domino effectum fuisse constiterit, idque in nostris atque omnium oculis valde mirabile fuerit.[2] Pro quo tam singulari Dei munere supplicationes statim in alma hac Urbe indiximus, quae magna cleri et populi pietate celebratae fuerunt, laudesque et gratias divinae majestati merito persolvendas curavimus, cum ejusmodi concilii exitus spem magnam et prope certam attulerit, fore, ut majores in dies fructus ad ecclesiam ex ipsius decretis et constitutionibus perveniant. Cum autem ipsa sancta synodus pro sua erga Sedem Apostolicam reverentia, antiquorum etiam conciliorum vestigiis inhaerens, decretorum suorum omnium, quae nostro et praedecessorum nostrorum tempore facta sunt, confirmatione a nobis petierit, decreto de ea re in publica sessione facto. Nos, ex legatorum litteris prius, deinde post reditum eorum ex iis, quae synodi nomine diligenter retulerunt, postulatione ipsius synodi cognita, habita super hac re cum venerabilibus fratribus nostris sanctae Romanae ecclesiae cardinalibus deliberatione matura, Sanctique Spiritus in primis auxilio invocato, cum ea decreta omnia catholica et populo Christiano utilia ac salutaria esse cognovissemus, ad Dei omnipotentis laudem de eorumdem fratrum nostrorum consilio et assensu in consistorio nostro secreto illa omnia et singula auctoritate apostolica hodie confirmavimus, et ab omnibus Christi fidelibus suscipienda ac servanda esse decrevimus, sicut harum quoque litterarum tenore ad clariorem omnium notitiam confirmamus, et suscipi observarique decernimus. Mandamus autem in virtute sanctae obedientiae, et sub poenis a sacris canonibus constitutis, aliisque gravioribus,

---

[2] Ps. 117:23.

etiam privationis, arbitrio nostro infligendis, universis et singulis venerabilibus fratribus nostris, patriarchis, archiepiscopis, episcopis et aliis quibusvis ecclesiarum praelatis, cujuscumque status, gradus, ordinis et dignitatis sint, et etiamsi cardinalatus honore praefulgeant, ut eadem decreta et statuta in ecclesiis suis, civitatibus et dioecesibus in judicio et extra judicium diligenter observent, et a subditis quisque suis, ad quos quomodolibet pertinet, inviolabiliter faciant observari, contradictores quoslibet et contumaces per sententias, censuras et poenas ecclesiasticas, etiam iis ipsis decretis contentas, appellatione postposita, compescendo, invocato etiam, si opus fuerit, brachii saecularis auxilio. Ipsum vero carissimum filium nostrum imperatorem electum, ceterosque reges, respublicas ac principes Christianos monemus, et per viscera misericordiae Domini nostri Jesu Christi obtestamur, ut, qua pietate concilio per oratores suos adfuerunt, eadem pietate ac pari studio, divini honoris et populorum suorum salutis causa, pro Sedis quoque Apostolicae et sacrae synodi reverentia, ad ejusdem concilii exequenda et observanda decreta praelatis, cum opus fuerit, auxilio et favore suo adsint, neque adversantes sanae ac salutari concilii doctrinae opiniones a populis ditionis suae recipi permittant, sed eas penitus interdicant. Ad vitandam praeterea perversionem et confusionem, quae oriri posset, si unicuique liceret, prout ei liberet, in decreta concilii commentarios et interpretationes suas edere, apostolica auctoritate inhibemus omnibus, tam ecclesiasticis personis, cujuscumque sint ordinis, conditionis et gradus, quam laicis, quocumque honore ac potestate praeditis, praelatis quidem sub interdicti ingressus ecclesiae, aliis vero, quicumque fuerint, sub excommunicationis latae sententiae poenis, ne quis sine auctoritate nostra audeat ullos commentarios, glossas, adnotationes, scholia, ullumve omnino interpretationis genus super ipsius concilii decretis quocumque modo edere, aut quidquam quocumque nomine, etiam sub praetextu majoris decretorum corroborationis aut executionis, aliove quaesito colore statuere. Si cui vero in eis aliquid obscurius dictum et statutum fuisse, eamque ob causam interpretatione aut decisione aliqua egere visum fuerit, ascendat ad locum, quem Dominus elegit,[3] ad Sedem videlicet Apostolicam, omnium fidelium magistram, cujus auctoritatem etiam ipsa sancta synodus tam reverenter agnovit. Nos enim difficultates et controversias, si quae ex eis decretis ortae fuerint, nobis declarandas et decidendas, quemadmodum

---

[3] Deut. 17:8.

ipsa quoque sancta synodus decrevit, reservamus, parati, sicut ea de nobis merito confisa est, omnium provinciarum necessitatibus ea ratione, quae commodior nobis visa fuerit, providere; decernentes nihilominus irritum et inane, si secus super his a quoquam quavis auctoritate scienter vel ignoranter contigerit attentari. Ut haec autem ad omnium notitiam perveniant, neve quis excusatione ignorationis uti possit: volumus et mandamus, ut hae litterae per aliquos curiae nostrae cursores in basilica Vaticana principis apostolorum et in ecclesia Lateranensi tunc, cum in eis populus, ut missarum solemnibus intersit, congregari solet, palam et clara voce recitentur, et postquam recitatae fuerint, ad valvas earum ecclesiarum, itemque cancellariae apostolicae, et in loco solito Campi Florae affigantur, ibique, ut legi et omnibus innotescere possint, aliquantisper relinquantur; cum autem inde amovebuntur, relictis de more ibidem exemplis in alma Urbe ad impressionem tradantur, quo commodius per Christianas provincias et regna devulgari possint. Transumptis quoque earum, quae manu alicujus publici notarii scripta subscriptave, et sigillo ac subscriptione alicujus personae in dignitate ecclesiastica constitutae munita fuerint, fidem sine ulla dubitatione haberi mandamus atque decernimus. Nulli ergo omnino hominum liceat hanc paginam nostrae confirmationis, monitionis, inhibitionis, reservationis, voluntatis, mandatorum et decretorum infringere, vel ei ausu temerario contraire. Si quis autem hoc attentare praesumpserit, indignationem omnipotentis Dei ac beatorum Petri et Pauli Apostolorum ejus se noverit incursurum. Datum Romae apud S. Petrum anno incarnationis dominicae MDLXIV. VII. Kal. Februarii, pontificatus nostri anno V.

Ego Pius catholicae ecclesiae episcopus.

Ego F. Card. Pisanus, Episcop. Ostien. Decan.
Ego Fed. Card. Caesius, Episcop. Portuen.
Ego Io. Card. Moronus, Episcop. Tuculan.
Ego A. Card. Farnesius, Vice cancell. Episcop. Sab.

....

Ego R. Card. S. Angeli, Major Poeniten.

....

Ego Io. Card. S. Vitalis.
Ego Io. Michael Card. Saracenus.

....

Ego Io. B. Cicada Card. S. Clementis.
Ego Scipio Card. Pisarum.
Ego Io. Card. Romanus.
Ego F. M. G. Card. Alexandrinus.
Ego F. Clemens Card. Arae coeli.
Ego Io. Card. Sabellus.
. . . .
Ego B. Card. Salviatus.
Ego Ph. Card. Aburd.
Ego Lud. Card. Simoneta.
. . . .
Ego F. Card. Pacieccus y de Tol.
Ego M. A. Card. Amulius.
Ego Io. Franc. Card. de Gambara.
Ego Carolus Card. Borromaeus.
Ego M. S. Card. Constant.
Ego Alph. Card. Gesualdus.
Ego Hipp. Card. Ferrar.
Ego Franciscus Card. Gonzaga.
. . . .
Ego Gui. Asc. Diac. Card. Camerar.
Ego Vitellotius Card. Vitellius.
. . . .
. . . .

Ant. Florebellus Lavellinus.
H. Cumyn.

BULLA SS. D. N. PII DIVINA PROVIDENTIA PAPAE QUARTI

super declaratione temporis ad observanda decreta sacri oecumenici et generalis concilii Tridentini

PIUS EPISCOPUS, SERVUS SERVORUM DEI, AD PERPETUAM REI MEMORIAM

Sicut ad sacrorum conciliorum decreta ac canones, auctoritas atque confirmatio Apostolicae Sedis et debet et solet accedere, ita, si qua super eis exorta sit dubitatio, ejusdem Sedis judicio et declaratione tollenda est. Ad aures nostras pervenit, multos esse, qui dubitent, ex quo tempore coeperint decreta sacri generalis concilii Tridentini, ad reformationem et jus positivum dumtaxat spectantia, eos, ad quos pertinent, obligare, illa praesertim, quae tempora certa praestituunt ad provinciales, dioecesanasque synodos celebrandas, ad ordines suscipiendos, ad religionem profitendam, ad parochiales ecclesias aliaque beneficia ecclesiastica, quae ejusdem concilii decretis retineri prohibitum sit, resignanda, et ad complures res hujusmodi exequendas, ac alias omnes ad praedictam reformationem, jusque positivum tantum spectantes, quae observari aut evitari debeant. Nos itaque, ut omnis controversia dubitatioque tollatur, motu proprio eam rem, prout rationi, juri et aequitati convenire censuimus, duximus declarandam. Nam etsi ipsius concilii decreta etiam de venerabilium fratrum nostrorum sanctae Romanae ecclesiae cardinalium consilio et assensu in consistorio nostro secreto confirmata a nobis fuerunt sub finem mensis Januarii, et ab eo etiam tempore apud hanc sanctam Sedem observari coeperunt; quia tamen non parum temporis in eis Romae diligenter emendateque imprimendis necessario consumptum fuit, et jure etiam communi sancitum est, ut constitutiones novae vim non nisi post certum tempus obtineant; aequum nobis et justum visum est, praedicta decreta omnia ad dictam reformationem jusque positivum dumtaxat spectantia, a Kal. Maii proxime praeteriti omnes obligare coepisse, neque post eam diem excusationem cujusquam, quod ea ignoraverit, admittendam, atque ita apostolica auctoritate declaramus ac definimus, et ab omnibus judicari debere mandamus atque statuimus; decernentes irritum et inane, si quid secus a quoquam quacumque dignitate, auctoritate et potestate praedito contigerit judicari; non obstantibus constitutionibus et ordinationibus apostolicis, aliisque in contrarium facientibus quibuscumque. Nulli ergo, etc. Si quis autem, etc. Datum Romae apud S. Petrum anno incarnationis dominicae MDLXIV. XV. Kal. Augusti, pontificatus nostri anno V.

Fed. Card. Caesius.
Caes. Glorierius.
H. Cumyn.

REGISTRATA APUD CAESAREM SECRETARIUM

Anno a Nativitate Domini millesimo quingentesimo sexagesimo quarto, indictione septima, die vero vigesima mensis Julii, pontificatus sanctissimi in Christo Patris et Domini nostri. Domini Pii, divina providentia Papae quarti, anno quinto, retroscriptae litterae affixae, lectae et publicatae fuerunt in valvis basilicarum principis apostolorum de Urbe, et sancti Joannis Lateranen., necnon cancellariae apostolicae, et in acie Campi Florae, per nos Jacobum Carra et Julium Parinum, praelibati S. D. N. Papae cursores.

Antonius Clerici,
Magister Cursorum.

MOTUS PROPRIUS S. D. N. PII DIVINA PROVIDENTIA PAPAE QUARTI

per quem deputantur octo cardinales, qui faciant observari constitutiones et ordinationes ab ipso editas, necnon decreta sacri oecumenici et generalis concilii Tridentini

PIUS PAPA IV

Motu proprio, etc. Alias nos nonnullas constitutiones et ordinationes, reformationem majoris poenitentiarii ac sacrae poenitentiariae nostrae, ac vicarii nostri ac ejus officii, necnon camerarii et camerae apostolicae, ac illius causarum auditoris, necnon palatii apostolici causarum auditorum, ac gubernatoris et capitolinae curiarum, et contradictarum aliorumque almae Urbis nostrae ac Romanae curiae tribunalium et officiorum concernentes edidimus, quae tamen, ut intelleximus, ab eorumdem officiorum et tribunalium praefectis ac officialibus minus diligenter observantur. Cum autem enixae nostrae voluntatis sit, ut illa, et pariter decreta sacri concilii Tridentini, in his, quae ad eorum officia spectant, ab eisdem omnino observentur: nos propterea considerantes, parum esse jura condere, nisi sint qui ea executioni demandari faciant, et in praemissis, prout ex debito pastoralis officii nobis, meritis licet imparibus, injuncti obligamur, salubriter et utiliter providere, praefatasque constitutiones et ordinationes ac decreta concilii, quas et quae hic haberi volumus pro expressis, inviolabiliter observari volentes: venerabili fratri nostro Joanni episcopo Tusculan. Morono, Joan. Michaeli Sanctae Anastasiae Saraceno, ac Joan. Baptistae Sancti Clementis Cicadae, necnon Michaeli Sanctae Sabinae Alexandrino, Clementi Sanctae Mariae in Ara coeli, Ludovico Sancti Cyriaci in Thermis Simonetae, ac Carolo Sancti Martini in

Montibus Borromaeo Presbyteris, necnon Vitellotio Sanctae Mariae in porticu Vitellio nuncupatis titulorum, diacono,[1] cardinalibus committimus et mandamus, quatenus ipsi,[2] seu eorum major pars, conjunctim vel divisim, eorum arbitrio, etiam tamquam executores dictarum litterarum, constitutionum et decretorum praedictorum, constitutiones et ordinationes ac decreta praefata, juxta tenores eorum ac litterarum desuper confectarum, per quoscumque poenitentiariae, vicariae et camerae, ac rotae curiarum ac tribunalium praedictorum judices et officiales, sub excommunicationis latae sententiae ac privationis officiorum, et aliis eisdem cardinalibus bene visis, etiam pecuniarum eo ipso incurrendis poenis, firmiter observari faciant et cum effectu, nisi tam in executione dictorum decretorum concilii, quam dictarum litterarum nostrarum, aliqua dubietas aut difficultas emerserit, quo casu ad nos referant, invocato etiam ad hoc, si opus fuerit, auxilio brachii saecularis, ac eos, qui litteris et decretis praedictis, et eorumdem cardinalium mandatis non paruerint, ex tunc, prout ex eadem die, et e contra, illorum officiis privatos, necnon ad illa et alia Romanae curiae officia in posterum obtinenda inhabiles, ac ipsis ab eisdem officiis sic privatis, illa tamquam per privationem vacantia a datario nostro vendi, et a quibusvis personis idoneis pro pretio convenienti emi libere et licite posse auctoritate nostra curent, nuncient, decernant ac declarent, prout nos harum serie nunciamus, decernimus et declaramus; non obstantibus quibusvis constitutionibus et ordinationibus apostolicis, ac poenitentiariae, et curiarum, necnon tribunalium praedictorum statutis etc., etiam juramento etc., roboratis, privilegiis quoque, indultis et litteris apostolicis, illis ac dictis officialibus et tribunalibus sub quibuscumque tenoribus et formis, ac cum quibusvis clausulis et decretis, etiam motu simili, et alias quomodocumque concessis, etc. Quibus omnibus etc. illorum tenores etc. hac vice latissime derogamus, eaque adversus praemissa nullatenus suffragari volumus, ceterisque contrariis quibuscumque.

Placet motu proprio I.

Datum Romae apud Sanctum Marcum, IV. Nonas Augusti, anno V.

---

[1] Sixtus V istius congregationis facultates declaravit in bulla, quae incipit: *Immensa*, 1588, art. 7.

[2] Confirmatur bulla Pii V, *Cum felicis*, 1566.

BULLA SS. D. N. PII DIVINA PROVIDENTIA PAPAE QUARTI

super forma juramenti professionis fidei

PIUS EPISCOPUS, SERVUS SERVORUM DEI, AD PERPETUAM REI MEMORIAM

Injunctum nobis apostolicae servitutis officium requirit,[1] ut ea, quae Dominus omnipotens ad providam ecclesiae suae directionem sanctis patribus in nomine suo congregatis divinitus inspirare dignatus est, ad ejus laudem et gloriam incunctanter exequi properemus. Cum itaque juxta concilii Tridentini dispositionem omnes, quos deinceps cathedralibus et superioribus ecclesiis praefici, vel quibus de illarum dignitatibus, canonicatibus et aliis quibuscumque beneficiis ecclesiasticis curam animarum habentibus provideri continget, publicam orthodoxae fidei professionem facere, seque in Romanae ecclesiae obedientia permansuros spondere et jurare teneantur: nos volentes, etiam per quoscumque, quibus de monasteriis, conventibus, domibus et aliis quibuscumque locis regularium quorumcumque ordinum, etiam militarium, quocumque nomine vel titulo providebitur, idem item servari, et ad hoc, ut unius ejusdem fidei professio uniformiter ab omnibus exhibeatur, unicaque et certa illius forma cunctis innotescat, nostrae sollicitudinis partes in hoc alicui minime desiderari, formam ipsam praesentibus annotatam publicari, et ubique gentium per eos, ad quos ex decretis ipsius concilii et alios praedictos spectat, recipi et observari, ac sub poenis per concilium ipsum in contravenientes latis, juxta hanc et non aliam formam, professionem praedictam solemniter fieri, auctoritate apostolica tenore praesentium districte praecipiendo mandamus, hujusmodi sub tenore:

Ego N. firma fide credo et profiteor omnia et singula, quae continentur in symbolo fidei, quo sancta Romana ecclesia utitur, videlicet: "Credo in unum Deum Patrem omnipotentem, factorem coeli et terrae, visibilium omnium et invisibilium. Et in unum Dominum Jesum Christum, Filium Dei unigenitum, et ex Patre natum ante omnia saecula; Deum de Deo, lumen de lumine, Deum verum de Deo vero. Genitum, non factum, consubstantialem Patri, per quem omnia facta sunt. Qui propter nos homines et propter nostram salutem de-

[1] Qui praeterea ad fidei professionem teneantur, declarat Pius IV in const. *In sacrosancta*, 13 Nov., 1564.

scendit de coelo, et incarnatus est de Spiritu Sancto ex Maria Virgine et homo factus est; crucifixus etiam pro nobis sub Pontio Pilato, passus et sepultus. Et resurrexit tertia die secundum scripturas, et ascendit in coelum, sedet ad dexteram Patris, et iterum venturus est cum gloria judicare vivos et mortuos, cujus regni non erit finis. Et in Spiritum Sanctum, Dominum et vivificantem, qui ex Patre Filioque procedit; qui cum Patre et Filio simul adoratur et conglorificatur; qui locutus est per prophetas. Et unam, sanctam, catholicam et apostolicam ecclesiam. Confiteor unum baptisma in remissionem peccatorum, et expecto resurrectionem mortuorum et vitam venturi saeculi. Amen." Apostolicas et ecclesiasticas traditiones, reliquasque ejusdem ecclesiae observationes et constitutiones firmissime admitto et amplector. Item sacram scripturam juxta eum sensum, quem tenuit et tenet sancta mater ecclesia, cujus est judicare de vero sensu et interpretatione sacrarum scripturarum, admitto; nec eam unquam nisi juxta unanimem consensum patrum accipiam et interpretabor. Profiteor quoque septem esse vera et proprie sacramenta novae legis a Jesu Christo Domino nostro instituta, atque ad salutem humani generis, licet non omnia singulis necessaria, scilicet baptismum, confirmationem, Eucharistiam, poenitentiam, extremam unctionem, ordinem et matrimonium, illaque gratiam conferre, et ex his baptismum, confirmationem et ordinem sine sacrilegio reiterari non posse. Receptos quoque et approbatos ecclesiae catholicae ritus in supradictorum omnium sacramentorum solemni administratione recipio et admitto. Omnia et singula, quae de peccato originali et de justificatione in sacrosancta Tridentina synodo definita et declarata fuerunt, amplector et recipio. Profiteor pariter in missa offerri Deo verum, proprium et propitiatorium sacrificium pro vivis et defunctis, atque in sanctissimo Eucharistiae sacramento esse vere et realiter et substantialiter corpus et sanguinem, una cum anima et divinitate Domini nostri Jesu Christi, fierique conversionem totius substantiae panis in corpus, et totius substantiae vini in sanguinem, quam conversionem catholica ecclesia transubstantiationem appellat. Fateor etiam sub altera tantum specie totum atque integrum Christum verumque sacramentum sumi. Constanter teneo purgatorium esse, animasque ibi detentas fidelium suffragiis juvari; similiter et sanctos una cum Christo regnantes, venerandos atque invocandos esse, eosque orationes Deo pro nobis offerre, atque eorum reliquias esse venerandas. Firmiter assero, imagines Christi ac deiparae semper Virginis, necnon aliorum sanctorum, habendas et retinendas esse, atque eis debitum honorem ac venerationem impertiendam; indulgentiarum etiam potestatem a Christo in ecclesia relictam fuisse illarumque usum Christiano populo maxime salutarem esse affirmo. Sanctam catholicam et apostolicam Romanam ecclesiam, omnium ecclesiarum matrem et magistram agnosco; Romanoque Pontifici, beati Petri Apostolorum principis successori ac Jesu Christi vicario, veram obedientiam spondeo ac juro. Cetera item omnia a sacris canonibus et oecumenicis conciliis ac praecipue a sacrosancta Tridentina synodo tradita, definita et declarata, indubitanter recipio atque profiteor; simulque contraria omnia atque haereses quascumque ab ecclesia damnatas et rejectas et anathematizatas, ego pariter damno, rejicio et anathematizo. Hanc veram catholicam fidem, extra quam nemo salvus esse potest, quam in praesenti sponte profiteor et veraciter teneo, eamdem integram et immaculatam usque ad extremum vitae spiritum constantissime (Deo adjuvante) retinere et confiteri, atque a meis subditis, vel illis, quorum cura ad me in munere meo spectabit, teneri, doceri et praedicari, quantum in me erit, curaturum, ego idem N. spondeo, voveo ac juro. Sic me Deus adjuvet et haec sancta Dei evangelia.

Volumus autem quod praesentes litterae in cancellaria nostra apostolica de more legantur. Et ut omnibus facilius pateant, in ejus quinterno describantur ac etiam imprimantur.

Nulli ergo, etc. Si quis autem, etc. Datum Romae apud S. Petrum anno incarnationis dominicae MDLXIV., Idibus Novemb., pontificatus nostri anno V.

Fed. Cardinalis Caesius.
Caes. Glorierius.

Lectae et publicatae fuerunt suprascriptae litterae Romae in cancellaria apostolica, anno incarnationis dominicae MDLXIV., die vero sabbati, IX. mensis Decembris, pontificatus sanctissimi in Christo Patris et Domini nostri, Domini Pii Papae IV., anno V.

A. Lomellinus, Custos.

BULLA SS. D. N. PII DIVINA PROVIDENTIA PAPAE QUARTI

revocatoria privilegiorum, exemptionum, immunitatum, facultatum, conservatoriarum, indultorum, confessionalium, maris magni, et aliarum quarumcumque similium gratiarum, quibuscumque locis et personis concessarum; in his, in quibus statutis et decretis sacri concilii Tridentini contrariantur

PIUS EPISCOPUS, SERVUS SERVORUM DEI, AD PERPETUAM REI MEMORIAM

In principis Apostolorum Sede,[1] meritis licet imparibus divina dispositione constituti, nihil neque universali ecclesiae, curae et sollicitudini nostrae commissae salubrius, neque injuncto nobis apostolicae servitutis officio decentius praestare possumus, quam quod providentiae nostrae ministerio oecumenicum concilium Tridentinum, sicut nostris potissimum auspiciis, summaque sanctorum patrum concordia per Dei misericordiam feliciter absolutum fuit, ita per universos, qui Christiana pietate censentur, ubique suscipiatur, et remotis quibuslibet obstaculis, ab omnibus aequaliter observetur. Cum itaque in eodem concilio quamplurima salubria et ad universalem morum reformationem valde utilia decreta atque statuta, maturo praesentium ipsorum examine praecedente, sint edita, quibus multa atque diversa privilegia, exemptiones, immunitates, dispensationes, facultates, conservatoriae, indulta, et, ut vocant, confessionalia, et mare magnum, et aliae gratiae, quae variis tam cathedralibus, etiam metropolitanis, quam collegiatis ecclesiis, monasteriis, conventibus, et aliis religiosis, etiam fratrum mendicantium domibus et ordinibus, necnon Sancti Spiritus in Saxia, Sancti Joannis Lateranensis, ac incurabilium de Urbe, Sancti Antonii Viennensis et Sancti Bernardi Jurensis, aliisque hospitalibus, militiis, eorumque capitulis et conventibus, ac universitatibus, etiam studiorum generalium collegiis, tam saecularibus quam ecclesiasticis, confraternitatibus, societatibus, et tam principis apostolorum de Urbe, quam aliis fabricis, sanctae cruciatae, aliisque piis locis et operibus, necnon patriarchis, archiepiscopis, episcopis, praelatis, abbatibus, abbatissis, prioribus, praepositis, et aliis ecclesiasticis, tam saecularibus quam

[1] Gregorius XIII privilegia regularibus concessa a Pio V iterum reduxit ad terminos concilii per const. *In tanta*, 1573.

diversorum ordinum et militiarum regularibus, ac etiam laicis cujuscumque dignitatis, et status ac gradus, et excellentiae, ac etiam ducali, regia et imperiali dignitate fulgentibus utriusque sexus personis, necnon aliquibus notariis, et etiam de latere legatis atque nunciis, tam perpetuo quam ad tempus, per plures Romanos pontifices praedecessores nostros, ac nos et Sedem Apostolicam ejusque legatos hactenus, etiam motu proprio, et ex certa scientia ac de apostolicae potestatis plenitudine, seu etiam imperatorum, regum, ducum, et aliorum principum contemplatione et intuitu, etiam de fratrum consilio, diversimode, variisque temporibus, in genere vel specie, ex quavis etiam honesta causa concessa, et etiam pluries confirmata et innovata fuerunt, in plerisque contrariantur: nos, quibus in primis cordi est, tam sancta et ecclesiae Dei saluberrima decreta suos, ut par est, effectus ubique consequi, et ab omnibus obedienter observari, privilegiorum, exemptionum, immunitatum, facultatum, conservatoriarum, indultorum, confessionalium, maris magni, et aliarum gratiarum praedictarum, ac quarumcumque apostolicarum et aliarum litterarum desuper confectarum, processuumque, decretorum et aliorum inde secutorum tenores, ac si de verbo ad verbum insererentur, praesentibus pro sufficienter expressis et plene insertis habentes, motu proprio et ex certa scientia, ac de apostolicae potestatis plenitudine, quod eadem omnia et singula privilegia, exemptiones, immunitates, facultates, dispensationes, conservatoriae, indulta, confessionalia, mare magnum, et aliae gratiae in his omnibus et singulis, in quibus illa statutis et decretis concilii hujusmodi contrariantur, ipso jure revocata, cassata et annullata, ac ad ipsius concilii terminos atque limites reducta sint et esse censeantur, nec quidquam adversus ipsa decreta et statuta, quominus ubique et apud omnes observentur, in aliquo suffragari posse, sed ea perinde haberi et reputari debere, ac si nunquam emanassent, auctoritate apostolica tenore praesentium declaramus, ac etiam statuimus et ordinamus. Decernentes nihilominus omnia et singula, quae vigore privilegiorum, exemptionum, immunitatum et dispensationum, facultatum, conservatoriarum, indultorum, confessionalium, et aliarum quarumcumque gratiarum hujusmodi, post id tempus, quo concilium obligare coepit, facta et gesta quomodolibet fuerunt et in posterum fient, in his, in quibus dicti concilii decretis adversantur, nulla, invalida et irrita esse et censeri, ac nemini, etiam quantumlibet, ut praefertur, qualificato, tam in foro, quod aiunt, fori, quam conscientiae, suffragari posse et debere. Et ita per quoscumque locorum ordinarios, aliosque judices et commissarios quavis auctoritate fulgentes, etiam sanctae Romanae ecclesiae cardinales, sublata eis et eorum cuilibet quavis aliter judicandi facultate, in utroque foro judicari et definiri debere, ac quidquid secus a quoquam, quavis auctoritate, scienter vel ignoranter, attentari contigerit, irritum et inane decernimus; non obstantibus praemissis, ac constitutionibus et ordinationibus apostolicis, ceterisque contrariis quibuscumque. Nulli ergo, etc. Si quis autem, etc.

Datum Romae apud S. Petrum anno incarnationis dominicae MDLXV., XIII. Kalend. Martii, pontificatus nostri anno VI.

Caes. Glorierius.
P. Episcopus Narnien.
H. Cumyn.

Anno a Nativitate D. MDLXV., indictione VI., die vero XXIV. mensis Februarii, pontificatus sanctissimi in Christo Patris et D. nostri, Domini Pii, divina providentia Papae IV., anno ejus VI., retroscriptae litterae apostolicae affixae et publicatae fuerunt in acie Campi Florae, et valvis cancellariae apostolicae, per nos Nicolaum de Matthaeis, et Camillum Cherubinum S. D. N. Papae cursores.

Philibertus Phapuis,
Magister Cursorum.

DE LIBRIS PROHIBITIS REGULAE DECEM

per patres a Tridentina synodo delectos concinnatae et a Pio Papa IV. comprobatae constitutione, quae incipit, *Dominici gregis* [1]

Regula I

Libri omnes, quos ante annum MDXV. aut summi pontifices aut concilia oecumenica damnarunt, et in hoc indice non sunt, eodem modo damnati esse censeantur, sicut olim damnati fuerunt.

Regula II

Haeresiarcharum libri, tam eorum, qui post praedictum annum haereses invenerunt vel suscitarunt, quam qui haereticorum capita aut

[1] Cf. Sess. XXV decretum de indice librorum.

duces sunt vel fuerunt, quales sunt Lutherus, Zuinglius, Calvinus, Balthasar Pacimontanus, Swenchfeldius, et his similes, cujuscumque nominis, tituli aut argumenti exsistant, omnino prohibentur. Aliorum autem haereticorum libri, qui de religione quidem ex professo tractant, omnino damnantur. Qui vero de religione non tractant, a theologis catholicis jussu episcoporum et inquisitorum examinati et approbati permittuntur. Libri etiam catholici conscripti, tam ab illis, qui postea in haeresim lapsi sunt, quam ab illis, qui post lapsum ad ecclesiae gremium rediere, approbati a facultate theologica alicujus universitatis catholicae vel ab inquisitione generali permitti poterunt.

Regula III

Versiones scriptorum etiam ecclesiasticorum, quae hactenus editae sunt a damnatis auctoribus, modo nihil contra sanam doctrinam contineant, permittuntur. Librorum autem veteris testamenti versiones viris tantum doctis et piis judicio episcopi concedi poterunt, modo hujusmodi versionibus tamquam elucidationibus vulgatae editionis ad intelligendam sacram scripturam, non autem tamquam sano textu utantur. Versiones vero novi testamenti ab auctoribus primae classis hujus indicis factae nemini concedantur, quia utilitatis parum, periculi vero plurimum lectoribus ex earum lectione manare solet. Si quae vero annotationes cum hujusmodi, quae permittuntur, versionibus, vel cum vulgata editione circumferuntur, expunctis locis suspectis a facultate theologica alicujus universitatis catholicae aut inquisitione generali, permitti eisdem poterunt, quibus et versiones. Quibus conditionibus totum volumen bibliorum, quod vulgo biblia Vatabli dicitur, aut partes ejus concedi viris piis et doctis poterunt. Ex bibliis vero Isidori Clarii Brixiani prologus et prolegomena praecidantur; ejus vero textum, nemo textum vulgatae editionis esse existimet.

Regula IV

Cum experimento manifestum sit, si sacra biblia vulgari lingua passim sine discrimine permittantur, plus inde ob hominum temeritatem detrimenti quam utilitas oriri, hac in parte judicio episcopi aut inquisitoris stetur, ut cum consilio parochi vel confessarii bibliorum a catholicis auctoribus versorum lectionem in vulgari lingua eis concedere possint, quos intellexerint ex hujusmodi lectione non damnum, sed fidei atque pietatis augmentum capere posse; quam facultatem in scriptis habeant. Qui autem absque tali facultate ea legere seu habere praesumpserit, nisi prius bibliis ordinario redditis peccatorum absolutionem percipere non possit. Bibliopolae vero, qui praedictam facultatem non habenti biblia idiomate vulgari conscripta vendiderint vel alio quovis modo concesserint, librorum pretium in usus pios ab episcopo convertendum amittant, aliisque poenis pro delicti qualitate ejusdem episcopi arbitrio subjaceant. Regulares vero non nisi facultate a praelatis suis habita ea legere aut emere possint.

Regula V

Libri illi, qui haereticorum auctorum opera interdum prodeunt, in quibus nulla aut pauca de suo apponunt, sed aliorum dicta colligunt, cujusmodi sunt lexica, concordantiae, apophthegmata, similitudines, indices et hujusmodi, si quae habeant admixta, quae expurgatione indigeant, illis episcopi et inquisitoris una cum theologorum catholicorum consilio sublatis aut emendatis, permittantur.

Regula VI

Libri vulgari idiomate de controversiis inter catholicos et haereticos nostri temporis disserentes non passim permittantur; sed idem de iis servetur, quod de bibliis vulgari lingua scriptis statutum est. Qui vero de ratione bene vivendi, contemplandi, confitendi ac similibus argumentis vulgari sermone conscripti sunt, si sanam doctrinam contineant, non est cur prohibeantur, sicut nec sermones populares vulgari lingua habiti. Quod si hactenus in aliquo regno vel provincia aliqui libri sunt prohibiti, quod nonnulla continerent, quae sine delectu ab omnibus legi non expediat, si eorum auctores catholici sunt, postquam emendati fuerunt, permitti ab episcopo et inquisitore poterunt.

Regula VII

Libri, qui res lascivas seu obscoenas ex professo tractant, narrant aut docent, cum non solum fidei sed et morum, qui hujusmodi librorum lectione facile corrumpi solent, ratio habenda sit, omnino prohibentur, et qui eos habuerint severe ab episcopis puniantur. Antiqui vero ab ethnicis conscripti propter sermonis elegantiam et proprietatem permittuntur; nulla tamen ratione pueris praelegendi erunt.

Regula VIII

Libri, quorum principale argumentum bonum est, in quibus tamen obiter aliqua inserta sunt, quae ad haeresim seu impietatem, divinationem seu superstitionem spectant, a catholicis theologis inquisitionis generalis auctoritate expurgati concedi possint. Idem judicium sit de prologis, summariis seu annotationibus, quae a damnatis auctoribus, libris non damnatis, appositae sunt: sed posthac non nisi emendati excudantur.

Regula IX

Libri omnes et scripta geomantiae, hydromantiae, aeromantiae, pyromantiae, oneiromantiae, chiromantiae, necromantiae, sive in quibus continentur sortilegia, veneficia, auguria, auspicia, incantationes, artes magicae, prorsus rejiciuntur.[2] Episcopi vero diligenter provideant, ne astrologiae judiciariae libri, tractatus, indices legantur vel habeantur, qui de futuris contingentibus successibus, fortuitisve casibus, aut iis actionibus, quae ab humana voluntate pendent, certi aliquid eventurum affirmare audent. Permittuntur autem judicia et naturales observationes, quae navigationis, agriculturae sive medicae artis juvandae gratia conscripta sunt.

Regula X

In librorum aliarumve scripturarum impressione servetur quod in concilio Lateranensi sub Leone X. sess. X. statutum est.[3] Quare, si in alma urbe Roma liber aliquis sit imprimendus, per vicarium summi pontificis et sacri palatii magistrum, vel personas a sanctissimo Domino nostro deputandas prius examinetur. In aliis vero locis ad episcopum vel alium habentem scientiam libri vel scripturae imprimendae, ab eodem episcopo deputandum, ac inquisitorem haereticae pravitatis ejus civitatis vel dioecesis, in qua impressio fiet, ejus approbatio et examen pertineat, et per eorum manum propria subscriptione gratis et sine dilatione imponendam sub poenis et censuris in eodem decreto

---

[2] Cf. bullam Sixti V *Coeli et terrae,* 1586, qua procedi potest non modo per ipsos episcopos et ordinarios, sed etiam per inquisitores locorum.

[3] Lateranense V. Hardouin, IX, 1775–77.

contentis approbetur, hac lege et conditione addita, ut exemplum libri imprimendi authenticum et manu auctoris subscriptum apud examinatorem remaneat; eos vero, qui libellos manuscriptos vulgant, nisi ante examinati probatique fuerint, iisdem poenis subjici debere judicarunt patres deputati, quibus impressores; et qui eos habuerint et legerint, nisi auctores prodiderint, pro auctoribus habeantur. Ipsa vero hujusmodi librorum probatio in scriptis detur, et in fronte libri vel scripti vel impressi authentice appareat, probatioque et examen ac cetera gratis fiant. Praeterea in singulis civitatibus ac dioecesibus domus vel loci, ubi ars impressoria exercetur, et bibliothecae librorum venalium saepius visitentur a personis ad id deputandis ab episcopo sive ejus vicario, atque etiam ab inquisitore haereticae pravitatis, ut nihil eorum, quae prohibentur, aut imprimatur aut vendatur aut habeatur. Omnes vero librarii et quicumque librorum venditores habeant in suis bibliothecis indicem librorum venalium, quos habent, cum subscriptione dictarum personarum, nec alios libros habeant aut vendant aut quacumque ratione tradant sine licentia eorumdem deputandorum, sub poena amissionis librorum, et aliis arbitrio episcoporum vel inquisitorum imponendis. Emptores vero, lectores vel impressores eorumdem arbitrio puniantur. Quod si aliqui libros quoscumque in aliquem civitatem introducant, teneantur eisdem personis deputandis renunciare, vel, si locus publicus mercibus ejusmodi constitutus sit, ministri publici ejus loci praedictis personis significent libros esse adductos. Nemo vero audeat librum, quem ipse vel alius in civitatem introduxit, alicui legendum tradere, vel aliqua ratione alienare aut commodare, nisi ostenso prius libro, et habita licentia a personis deputandis, aut nisi notorie constet, librum jam esse omnibus permissum. Idem quoque servetur ab heredibus et executoribus ultimarum voluntatum, ut libros a defunctis relictos sive eorum indicem illis personis deputandis offerant, et ab iis licentiam obtineant, priusquam eis utantur, aut in alias personas quacumque ratione transferant. In his autem omnibus et singulis poena statuatur vel amissionis librorum, vel alia arbitrio eorumdem episcoporum vel inquisitorum, pro qualitate contumaciae vel delicti.

Circa vero libros, quos patres deputati examinarunt aut expurgarunt, aut expurgandos tradiderunt, aut certis conditionibus ut rursus excuderentur concesserunt, quidquid illos statuisse constiterit, tam bibliopolae quam ceteri observent. Liberum tamen sit episcopis aut inquisitoribus generalibus, secundum facultatem, quam habent, eos etiam libros, qui his regulis permitti videntur, prohibere, si hoc in suis regnis aut provinciis vel dioecesibus expedire judicaverint. Ceterum nomina cum librorum, qui a patribus deputatis purgati sunt, tum eorum, quibus illi hanc provinciam dederunt, eorumdem deputatorum secretarius notario sacrae universalis inquisitionis Romanae descripta sanctissimi Domini nostri jussu tradidit.

Ad extremum vero omnibus fidelibus praecipitur, ne quis audeat contra harum regularum praescriptum, aut hujus indicis prohibitionem libros aliquos legere aut habere. Quod si quis libros haereticorum vel cujusvis auctoris scripta, ob haeresim vel ob falsi dogmatis suspicionem damnata atque prohibita, legerit sive habuerit, statim in excommunicationis sententiam incurrat. Qui vero libros alio nomine interdictos legerit aut habuerit, praeter peccati mortalis reatum, quo afficitur, judicio episcoporum severe puniatur.

BULLA SS. D. N. PII
DIVINA PROVIDENTIA PAPAE QUARTI

Approbatio indicis librorum prohibitorum cum regulis firmatis per patres a sancto concilio Tridentini deputatos, et prohibitio hos libros habendi et legendi

PIUS PAPA IV. AD FUTURAM REI MEMORIAM

Dominici gregis custodiae Domino disponente praepositi, vigilis more pastoris non desistimus ipsi gregi ab imminentibus periculis quanta maxima possumus cura et diligentia praecavere, ne propter negligentiam nostram pereant oves, quae pretiosissimo Domini Jesu Christi sanguine sunt redemptae. Etsi autem quae ad fidei veritatem patefaciendam et ad horum temporum haereses confutandas pertinebant in oecumenico et generali concilio Tridentino Sancti Spiritus assistente gratia nuper adeo enucleata ac definita fuerunt, ut facile jam sit unicuique sanam catholicamque a falsa adulterinaque internoscere; tamen, cum librorum ab haereticis editorum lectio non modo simpliciores homines corrumpere soleat, verum saepe etiam doctos eruditosque in varios errores et a veritate fidei catholicae alienas opiniones inducere, huic quoque rei esse duximus providendum.

Cum autem aptissimum ei malo remedium esse sciremus, si componeretur atque ederetur index sive catalogus librorum, qui vel haeretici sint, vel de haeretica pravitate suspecti, vel certe moribus et pietati noceant, id negotium ad sacram Tridentinam synodum rejeceramus; ea vero ex tanta episcoporum et aliorum doctissimorum virorum copia delegit ad eum conficiendum indicem multos cum doctrina tum judicio insignes praelatos ex omnibus fere nationibus. Qui quidem non sine maximo labore plurimisque vigiliis eum indicem tandem Deo juvante perfecerunt, adhibitis etiam in consilium lectissimis quibusdam theologis. Peracto autem concilio, cum ex ipsius synodi decreto is index nobis oblatus fuisset, ut ne ante ederetur quam a nobis approbatus fuisset, nos doctissimis quibusdam probatissimisque praelatis eum accuratissime legendum examinandumque tradidimus, et ipsi etiam legimus.

Cum igitur eum magno studio, acri judicio, diuturna cura confectum, et praeterea commodissime digestum esse cognoverimus: nos saluti animarum consulere, eamque ob causam providere cupientes, ne libri et scripta cujuscumque generis, quae in eo improbantur sive ut haeretica sive ut de haeretica pravitate suspecta, sive ut pietati ac morum honestati inutilia, aut aliqua correctione saltem indigentia, posthac a Christi fidelibus legantur, ipsum indicem una cum regulis ei praepositis auctoritate apostolica tenore praesentium approbamus, imprimique ac divulgari, et ab omnibus universitatibus catholicis, ac quibuscumque aliis ubique suscipi, easque regulas observari mandamus atque decernimus; inhibentes omnibus et singulis, tam ecclesiasticis personis saecularibus et regularibus, cujuscumque gradus, ordinis et dignitatis sint, quam laicis quocumque honore ac dignitate praeditis, ne quis contra earum regularum praescriptum aut ipsius prohibitionem indicis libros ullos legere habereve audeat.

Si quis autem adversus eas regulas prohibitionemque fecerit, is quidem, qui haereticorum libros vel cujusvis auctoris scripta propter haeresim vel falsi dogmatis suspicionem damnata atque prohibita legerit habueritve, ipso jure in excommunicationis poenam incidat, eamque ob causam in eum tamquam de haeresi suspectum inquiri et procedi liceat, praeter alias poenas super hoc ab Apostolica Sede sacrisque canonibus constitutas. Qui autem libros alia de causa prohibitos legerit habueritve, praeter peccati mortalis reatum episcoporum arbitrio severe se noverit puniendum; non obstantibus constitutionibus et ordinationibus apostolicis contrariis quibuscumque, aut si aliquibus communiter vel divisim ab eadem Sede sit indultum, ne excommunicari possint per litteras apostolicas, non facientes plenam et expressam ac de verbo ad verbum de indulto hujusmodi mentionem.

Ut haec autem ad omnium notitiam perveniant, neve quis excusatione ignorationis uti possit, volumus et mandamus, ut hae litterae per aliquos nostrae curiae cursores in basilica Vaticana principis apostolorum, et in ecclesia Lateranensi tunc, cum in eis populus, ut missarum solemnibus intersit, congregari solet, palam et clara voce recitentur, et postquam recitatae fuerint, ad valvas earum ecclesiarum, itemque cancellariae apostolicae, et in loco solito Campi Florae affigantur, ibique, ut legi et omnibus innotescere possint, aliquantisper relinquantur. Cum autem inde amovebuntur, earum exempla in iisdem locis affixa remaneant. Nos enim per recitationem hanc, publicationem et affixionem omnes et singulos, qui his litteris comprehenduntur, post tres menses a die publicationis et affixionis earum numerandos, volumus perinde adstrictos et obligatos esse, ac si ipsismet illae editae lectaeque fuissent. Transumptis quoque earum, quae manu alicujus publici notarii scripta subscriptave, et sigillo ac subscriptione alicujus personae in dignitate ecclesiastica constitutae munita fuerint, fidem sine ulla dubitatione haberi mandamus atque decernimus.

Datum Romae apud S. Petrum, sub annulo piscatoris die 24, Martii MDLXIV., pontificatus nostri anno V.

Antonius Florebellus Lavellinus.

CONSTITUTIONES

A JURE ANTIQUO DESUMPTAE ET PER

CONCILIUM TRIDENTINUM

memoratae vel ab ipso innovatae

CONCILIUM TOLETANUM XI

(Sess. II, decr. de modo vivendi, etc.)

A In loco benedictionis considentes Domini sacerdotes nullus debet aut indiscretis vocibus perstrepere, aut quibuslibet tumultibus perturbare, nullus etiam vanis fabulis vel risibus agi, et (quod est deterius) obstinatis disceptationibus tumultuosas voces effundere. "Si quis enim putat se religiosum esse, non refrenans linguam suam, sed seducens cor suum, hujus vana est religio" (Jac. 1:26). Cultum enim suum justitia perdit, quando silentia judicii obstrepentium turbo confundit, dicente Propheta: "Erit cultus justitiae silentium" (Is. 32:17). Debet ergo quidquid aut considentium consultationibus agitur, aut ab accusantium parte proponitur, sic mitissima verborum relatione proferri, ut nec contentiosis vocibus sensus audientium turbent, nec judicii vigorem de tumultu enervent. Quicumque ergo in conventu concilii haec, quae premissa sunt, violanda crediderit, et contra haec interdicta aut tumultu, aut contumeliis vel risibus concilium perturbaverit, juxta divinae legis edictum, quae praecipit: "Ejice derisorem, et exibit cum eo jurgium" (Prov. 22:10), cum omni dedecore de consessione abstractus a communi cetu secedat, et trium dierum excommunicationis sententiam ferat. (C. 3, C. V, q. 4.)

LEO X IN CONCILIO LATERANENSI

(Sess. IV, decr. de edit. et usu sacr. lib.)

B Nos, ne id, quod ad Dei gloriam et fidei augmentum, ac bonarum artium propagationem salubriter est inventum, in contrarium convertatur, ac Christi fidelium saluti detrimentum pariat, super librorum impressione curam nostram habendam fore duximus, ne de cetero cum bonis seminibus spinae coalescant, vel medicinis venena intermisceantur. Volentes igitur de opportuno super his remedio providere, hoc sacro approbante concilio, ut negotium impressionis librorum hujusmodi eo prosperetur felicius, quo deinceps indago solertior diligentius et cautius adhibeatur: statuimus et ordinamus, quod de cetero perpetuis futuris temporibus, nullus librum aliquem, seu aliam quamcumque scripturam, tam in Urbe nostra, quam aliis quibusvis civitatibus, et dioecesibus, imprimere seu imprimi facere praesumat, nisi prius in Urbe per vicarium nostrum, et sacri palatii magistrum, in aliis vero civitatibus et dioecesibus per episcopum, vel alium habentem peritiam scientiae, libri seu scripturae hujusmodi imprimendae, ab eodem episcopo ad id deputandum, ac inquisitorem haereticae pravitatis civitatis sive dioecesis, in quibus librorum impressio hujusmodi fieret, diligenter examinentur, et per eorum manu propria subscriptionem, sub excommunicationis sententia, gratis et sine dilatione imponendam, approbentur. Qui autem secus praesumpserit, ultra librorum impressorum amissionem, et illorum publicam combustionem, ac centum ducatorum fabricae principis Apostolorum de Urbe, sine spe remissionis, solutionem, ac anni continui exercitii impressionis suspensionem, excommunicationis sententia innodatus exsistat; ac demum ingravescente contumacia, taliter per episcopum suum, vel vicarium nostrum respective per omnia juris remedia castigetur, quod alii ejus exemplo similia minime attentare praesumant. Nulli ergo, etc. Si quis autem, etc. Datum Romae in publica sessione solemniter celebrata anno incarnationis dominicae MDXV. IV. Nonas Maii, pontificatus nostri anno III. (C. 3, de libr. prohib. in VII, V, 4.)

SIXTUS IV
(Sess. V, decr. de pecc. orig.)

C Cum praeexcelsa meritorum insignia, quibus regina coelorum, Virgo Dei genitrix gloriosa, sedibus praelata aethereis, sideribus quasi stella matutina praerutilat, devotae considerationis indagine perscrutamur, et infra pectoris arcana revolvimus, quod ipsa, utpote via misericordiae, mater gratiae et pietatis, amica humani generis consolatrix, pro salute fidelium, qui delictorum onere gravantur, sedula oratrix et pervigil ad regem, quem genuit, intercedit: dignum, quin potius debitum reputamus, universos Christi fideles, ut omnipotenti Deo (cujus providentia ejusdem Virginis humilitatem ab aeterno respiciens, pro concilianda suo auctori humana natura lapsu primi hominis aeternae morti obnoxia, eam sui unigeniti habitaculum Sancti Spiritus praeparatione constituit, ex qua carnem nostrae mortalitatis pro redemptione populi sui assumeret, et immaculata Virgo nihilominus post partum remaneret), de ipsius immaculatae Virginis mira conceptione gratias et laudes referant, et instituta propterea in Dei ecclesia missas et alia divina officia dicant, et illis intersint, indulgentiis et peccatorum remissionibus invitare, ut exinde fiant ejusdem Virginis meritis et intercessione divinae gratiae aptiores. Hac igitur consideratione inducti, ejusdem omnipotentis Dei ac beatorum Petri et Pauli Apostolorum ejus auctoritate confisi, auctoritate apostolica hac in perpetuum valitura constitutione statuimus et ordinamus, quod omnes et singuli Christi fideles utriusque sexus, qui missam et officium conceptionis ejusdem Virginis gloriosae juxta piam, devotam et laudabilem ordinationem dilecti filii magistri Leonardi de Nogarolis clerici Veronensis, notarii nostri, et quae desuper a nobis emanavit, missae et officii hujusmodi institutionem in die festivitatis conceptionis ejusdem Virginis Mariae et per octavas ejus devote celebraverint et dixerint, aut illis horis canonicis interfuerint, quoties id fecerint, eamdem prorsus indulgentiam et peccatorum remissionem consequantur, quam juxta felicis recordationis Urbani IV in concilio Viennensi approbatae, ac Martini V et aliorum Romanorum pontificum praedecessorum nostrorum constitutiones consequuntur illi, qui missam et horas canonicas in festo corporis et sanguinis Domini nostri Jesu Christi a primis vesperis et per illius octavas juxta Romanae ecclesiae constitutionem celebrant, dicunt, aut missae, officio et horis hujusmodi intersunt, praesentibus perpetuis temporibus valituris. Datum Romae apud S. Petrum anno incarnationis dominicae MCCCCLXXVI. III. Kal. Martii, pontificatus nostri anno VI. (C. 1, de relig. et venerat. sanct., III, 12 in Extrav. comm.)

CONSTITUTIO ALTERA
(Sess. V, decr. de pecc. orig.)

D Grave nimis gerimus et molestum, cum sinistra nobis de quibusdam ecclesiasticis personis referunter. Sed in eorum, qui ad evangelizandum verbum Dei sunt deputati, excessibus praedicando commissis eo gravius provocamur, quo illi periculosius remanent incorrecti, cum facile deleri nequeant, qui multorum cordibus sic publice praedicando diffusius et damnabilius imprimuntur errores. Sane cum sancta Romana ecclesia de intemeratae semperque Virginis Mariae conceptione publice festum solemniter celebret, et speciale ac proprium super hoc officium ordinaverit: nonnulli, ut accepimus, diversorum ordinum praedicatores in suis sermonibus ad populum publice per diversas civitates et terras affirmare hactenus non erubuerunt, et quotidie praedicare non cessant, omnes illos, qui tenent aut asserunt, eamdem gloriosam et immaculatam Dei genitricem absque originalis peccati macula fuisse conceptam, mortaliter peccare vel esse haereticos, ejusdem immaculatae conceptionis officium celebrantes, audientesque sermones illorum, qui eam sine hujusmodi macula conceptam esse affirmant, peccare graviter. Sed et praefatis praedicationibus non contenti, confectos super his suis assertionibus libros in publicum ediderunt, ex quorum assertionibus et praedicationibus non levia scandala in mentibus fidelium exorta sunt, et majora merito exoriri formidantur in dies. Nos igitur hujusmodi temerariis ausibus, ac perversis assertionibus ac scandalosis, quae exinde in Dei ecclesia exoriri possunt (quantum nobis ex alto conceditur), obviare volentes, motu proprio, non ad alicujus nobis super hoc oblatae petitionis instantiam, sed de nostra mera deliberatione et certa scientia hujusmodi assertiones praedicatorum eorumdem, et aliorum quorumlibet, qui affirmare praesumerent, eos, qui crederent aut tenerent, eamdem Dei genitricem ab originalis peccati macula in sua conceptione praeservatam fuisse, propterea alicujus haeresis labe pollutos fore, vel mortaliter peccare, aut hujusmodi officium conceptionis celebrantes, seu hujusmodi sermones audientes alicujus peccati reatum incurrere, utpote falsas et erroneas, et a veritate penitus alienas, editosque desuper libros praedictos, id continentes, quoad hoc auctoritate apostolica tenore praesentium reprobamus et damnamus, ac motu, scientia et auctoritate praedictis statuimus et ordinamus, quod praedicatores verbi Dei et quicumque alii, cujuscumque status, gradus, aut ordinis ac conditionis fuerint, qui de cetero ausu temerario praesumpserint in eorum sermonibus ad populum seu alias quomodolibet affirmare, hujusmodi sic per nos improbatas et damnatas assertiones veras esse, aut dictos libros pro veris legere, tenere vel habere, postquam de praesentibus scientiam habuerint, excommunicationis sententiam eo ipso incurrant, a qua ab alio, quam a Romano pontifice (nisi in mortis articulo) nequeant absolutionis beneficium obtinere; item motu, scientia et auctoritate similibus simili poenae ac censurae subjicientes eos, qui ausi fuerint asserere, contrariam opinionem tenentes, videlicet, gloriosam Virginem Mariam cum originali peccato fuisse conceptam, haeresis crimen vel peccatum incurrere mortale, cum nondum sit a Romana ecclesia et Apostolica Sede decisum, non obstantibus constitutionibus et ordinationibus apostolicis contrariis quibuscumque, quibus communiter vel divisim a Sede Apostolica indultum exsistat, quod interdici, suspendi vel excommunicari non possint per litteras apostolicas, non facientes plenam ac expressam, ac de verbo ad verbum de indulto hujusmodi mentionem. Et ne de praemissis aliquando valeant ignorantiam allegare: volumus, quod locorum ordinarii requisiti praesentes litteras in ecclesiis, consistentibus in eorum civitatibus, et suarum dioecesum, et locis insignibus, dum major ibi multitudo populi ad divina convenerit, sermonibus ad populum mandent et faciant publicari. Praeterea, quia difficile foret praesentes litteras ad singula loca, in quibus expediens fuerit, deferre: etiam volumus et dicta auctoritate decernimus, quod earumdem litterarum transumpto manu publici notarii confecto et authentico alicujus praelati ecclesiastici sigillo munito ubique stetur, prout staretur eisdem originalibus litteris, si forent exhibitae vel ostensae. Nulli ergo, etc. Si quis autem, etc. Datum Romae apud S. Petrum anno incarnationis dominicae MCCCCLXXXIII. prid. Non. Sept., pontificatus nostri anno XIII. (C. 2, de reliq. et venerat. sanct. III, 12 in Extrav. comm.)

INNOCENTIUS III IN CONCILIO LATERANENSI
(Sess. V, cap. 2 de ref.)

E Inter cetera, quae spectant ad salutem populi Christiani, pabulum verbi Dei permaxime sibi noscitur esse necessarium, quia, sicut corpus materiali, sic anima spirituali cibo nutritur, eo quod non in solo pane vivit homo, sed in omni verbo, quod procedit de ore Dei. Unde, cum saepe contingat, quod episcopi propter occupationes multiplices, vel invaletudines corporales, aut hostiles incursiones, seu occasiones alias (ne dicamus defectum scientiae, quod in eis est reprobandum omnino, nec de cetero tolerandum) per se ipsos non sufficiunt ministrare populo verbum Dei, maxime per amplas dioeceses et diffusas: generali constitutione sancimus, ut episcopi viros idoneos ad sanctae praedicationis officium salubriter exsequendum assumant, potentes in opere et sermone, qui plebes sibi commissas vice ipsorum, cum per se idem nequiverint, sollicite visitantes, eas verbo aedificent et exmplo, quibus ipsi, cum indiguerint, necessaria ministrent, ne pro necessariorum defectu compellantur desistere ab incepto. Unde praecipimus, tam in cathedralibus quam in aliis conventualibus ecclesiis viros idoneos ordinari, quos episcopi possint coadjutores et cooperatores habere, non solum in praedicationis officio, verum etiam in audiendis confessionibus et poenitentiis injungendis, ac ceteris, quae ad salutem pertinent animarum. Si quis autem hoc adimplere neglexerit, districtae subjaceat ultioni. (C. 15, X, de off. jud. ord., I, 31.)

ALEXANDER III IN CONCILIO LATERANENSI
(Sess. VII, cap. 1 de ref.)

F Cum in cunctis sacris ordinibus et ecclesiasticis ministeriis sint aetatis maturitas, gravitas morum, et litterarum scientia inquirendae, multo fortius in episcopo haec oportet inquiri, qui, ad aliorum curam positus, in se ipso debet ostendere, qualiter alios in domo Dei oporteat conversari. Ea propter, ne quod de quibusdam pro necessitate temporis factum est trahatur a posteris in exemplum, praesenti decreto statuimus, ut nullus in episcopum eligatur, nisi qui jam trigesimum annum aetatis exegerit, et de legitimo matrimonio sit natus; qui etiam vita et scientia commendabilis demonstretur. (C. 7, X, de elect., I, 6.)

ALEXANDER III IN CONCILIO LATERANENSI
(Sess. VII, cap. 3 de ref.)

G Quia nonnulli, modum avaritiae non ponentes, dignitates diversas ecclesiasticas et plures ecclesias parochiales contra sacrorum canonum instituta nituntur accipere, ut, cum unum officium vix implere sufficiant, stipendia sibi vindicent plurimorum, ne id de cetero fiat districtius inhibemus. Cum igitur ecclesia vel ecclesiasticum ministerium committi debuerit, talis ad hoc persona quaeratur, quae residere in loco et curam ejus per se ipsum valeat exercere. Quod si aliter actum fuerit, et qui receperit quod contra sacros canones accepit amittat, et qui dederit largiendi potestate privetur. (C. 3, X, de cler. non resid., III, 4.)

GREGORIUS X
(Sess. VII, cap. 3 de ref.)

H Licet canon, a felicis recordationis Alexandro Papa III praedecessore nostro editus, inter cetera statuerit, ut nullus regimen ecclesiae parochialis suscipiat, nisi vigesimum quintum aetatis annum attigerit, ac scientia et moribus commendandus exsistat, quodque talis ad regimen assumptus hujusmodi, si monitus non fuerit praefixo a canonibus tempore in presbyterum ordinatus, a regiminis ejusdem amoveatur officio, et alii conferatur; quia tamen in observatione canonis memorati se multi exhibent negligentes: nos, periculosam illorum negligentiam volentes juris executione suppleri, praesenti decreto statuimus, ut nullus ad regimen parochialis ecclesiae assumatur, nisi sit idoneus moribus, scientia et aetate; decernentes, collationes de parochialibus ecclesiis iis, qui non attigerint vigesimum quintum annum, de cetero faciendas viribus omnino carere. Is etiam, qui ad hujusmodi regimen assumetur, ut gregis sibi crediti diligentius curam quaerere possit, in parochiali ecclesia, cujus rector is exstiterit, residere personaliter teneatur, et intra annum, a sibi commissi regiminis tempore numerandum, se faciat ad sacerdotium promoveri. Quod si intra idem tempus promotus non fuerit, ecclesia sibi commissa (nulla etiam praemissa monitione) sit praesentis constitutionis auctoritate privatus. Super residentia vero, ut praemittitur, facienda possit ordinarius gratiam dispensationis ad tempus facere, prout causa rationabilis id exposcit. (C. 14, VI°, de elect., I, 6.)

INNOCENTIUS III IN CONCILIO LATERANENSI
(Sess. VII, cap. 3 de ref.)

I Grave nimis est et absurdum, quod quidam ecclesiarum praelati, cum possint viros idoneos ad ecclesiastica beneficia promovere, assumere non verentur indignos, quibus nec morum honestas, nec litterarum scientia suffragatur, carnalitatis sequentes affectum, non judicium rationis; unde quanta ecclesiis damna proveniant, nemo sanae mentis ignorat. Volentes igitur huic morbo mederi, praecipimus, ut praetermissis indignis idoneos assumant, qui Deo et ecclesiis velint et valeant gratum impendere famulatum, fiatque de hoc in provinciali concilio diligens inquisitio annuatim ita, ut qui post primam et secundam correctionem fuerit repertus culpabilis, a beneficiis conferendis per ipsum concilium suspendatur, instituta in eodem concilio persona provida et honesta, quae suspensi suppleat defectum in beneficiis conferendis. Et hoc ipsum circa capitula, quae in his deliquerint, observetur. Metropolitani vero delictum superioris judicio relinquatur ex parte concilii nunciandum. Ut autem haec salubris provisio pleniorem consequatur effectum, hujusmodi suspensionis sententia praeter Romani pontificis auctoritatem aut proprii patriarchae minime relaxetur, ut in hoc quoque quatuor patriarchales sedes specialiter honorentur. (C. 29, X, de praeb., III, 5.)

INNOCENTIUS III IN CONCILIO LATERANENSI
(Sess. VII, cap. 4 de ref.)

J De multa providentia fuit in Lateranensi concilio prohibitum, ut nullus diversas dignitates ecclesiasticas, vel plures ecclesias parochiales reciperet contra sacrorum canonum instituta; alioquin recipiens sic acceptam amitteret, et largiendi potestate conferens privaretur. Quia vero propter praesumptiones et quorumdam cupiditates nullus hactenus aut rarus de praedicto statuto fructus provenit, nos evidentius et expressius occurrere cupientes, praesenti decreto statuimus, ut quicumque receperit aliquod beneficium curam habens animarum annexam, ei prius tale beneficium habebat, eo sit ipso jure privatus; et si forte illud retinere contenderit, etiam alio spolietur. Is quoque, ad quem prioris spectat donatio, illud post receptionem alterius libere conferat, cui merito viderit conferendum, et si ultra sex menses conferre distulerit, non solum ad alios secundum Lateranensis concilii statutum ejus collatio devolvatur, verum etiam tantum de suis cogatur proventibus in utilitatem ecclesiae, cujus est illud beneficium, assignare, quantum a tempore vacationis ipsius constiterit esse perceptum. Hoc idem in personatibus esse decernimus observandum, addentes, ut in eadem ecclesia nullus plures dignitates aut personatus habere praesumat, etiamsi curam non habeant animarum. Circa sublimes tamen et litteratas personas, quae majoribus beneficiis sunt honorandae, cum ratio postulaverit, per Sedem Apostolicam poterit dispensari. (C. 28, X, de praeb., III, 5.)

GREGORIUS X
(Sess. VII, cap. 5 de ref.)

K Ordinarii locorum subditos suos plures dignitates vel ecclesias, quibus animarum cura imminet, obtinentes, seu personatum aut dignitatem cum alio beneficio, cui cura similis est annexa, districte compellant dispensationes, auctoritate quarum hujusmodi ecclesias, personatus seu dignitates canonice tenere se asserunt, intra tempus pro facti qualitate ipsorum ordinariorum moderandum arbitrio exhibere. Quod si forte justo impedimento cessante nullam dispensationem intra idem tempus contigerit exhiberi, ecclesiae beneficia, personatus seu dignitates, quae sine dispensatione aliqua eos ipsos illicite detineri constabit, per eos, ad quos eorum collatio pertinet, libere personis idoneis conferantur. Ceterum si dispensatio exhibita sufficiens evidentur appareat, exhibens nequaquam in beneficiis hujusmodi, quae canonice obtinet, molestetur. Provideat tamen ordinarius, qualiter nec animarum cura in eisdem ecclesiis, personatibus seu dignitatibus negligatur, nec beneficia ipsa debitis obsequiis defraudentur. Si vero de dispensationis exhibitae sufficientia dubitetur, super hoc erit ad Sedem Apostolicam recurrendum, cujus est aestimare, quem modum sui beneficii esse velit. In conferendis insuper personatibus et dignitatibus et aliis beneficiis, curam habentibus animarum annexam, iidem ordinarii diligentiam illam observent, ut personatum, dignitatem vel aliud beneficium, similem curam habens animarum, alicui plura similia obtinenti non ante conferre praesumant, quam eis super obtentis dispensatio evidenter sufficiens ostendatur; qua etiam ostensa ita demum ad collationem procedi volumus, si appareat per eamdem, quod is, cui est collatio facienda, hujusmodi personatum, dignitatem vel beneficium retinere libere valeat cum obtentis, vel si ea, quae sic obtinet, libere ac sponte resignet. Aliter autem de personatibus, dignitatibus et beneficiis talibus facta collatio nullius penitus sit momenti. (C. 3, VI°, de off. ord., I, 16.)

INNOCENTIUS IV IN CONCILIO LUGDUNENSI
(Sess. VII, cap. 14 de ref.)

L Volentes libertatem (quam nonnullis Apostolica Sedes privilegio exemptionis indulsit) sic integram observari, ut et illam alii non infringant, et ipsi ejus limites non excedant, declaratione irrefragabili definimus, quod quantumcumque sic exempti gaudeant libertate, nihilominus tamen ratione delicti sive contractus aut rei, de qua contra ipsos agitur, rite possunt coram locorum ordinariis conveniri, et illi quoad hoc suam in ipsos jurisdictionem (prout jus exigit) exercere.

Numquid ergo carent omnino in his commodo libertatis? non utique, quia nec coram ordinariis ipsis, dummodo sit in loco exempto commissum delictum vel contractus initus, aut res litigiosa, nec ubi domicilium habent, si alibi delinquant vel contrahant, aut res ipsa consistat, conveniri possunt aliquatenus super istis; nec domiciliorum praetextu locorum dioecesani (si ubi deliquerunt, vel contraxerunt, aut res ipsa consistit, illi conveniantur) remittendi eos illuc, vel ipsis, ut illic respondeant, injungendi habeant aliquam potestatem; salvis nihilominus casibus aliis, in quibus eos episcoporum jurisdictioni subesse canonica praecipiunt instituta. Et id ipsum decernimus circa illos, quibus, ut non nisi sub uno judice teneantur de se conquerentibus respondere, apostolico privilegio est concessum. In eos autem, quibus, ne interdici, suspendi vel excommunicari a quoquam valeant, a Sede Apostolica est indultum, sicut sunt religiosi quam plures, in quorum privilegiis continetur, ne quisquam episcopus vel archiepiscopus monasteriorum suorum monachos pro ulla causa ullove loco interdicere, suspendere vel excommunicare praesumat: iidem ordinarii jurisdictionem suam, quantum ad ista, ubicumque illi fuerint, penitus exercere non possint; nisi forsan ipsi monachi ad monasteriorum suorum prioratus ordinariis iisdem subjectos fuerint destinati. Tunc enim etsi libere possint ad eadem monasteria revocari, ac tam illorum quam ipsorum prioratuum monachi reputentur (cum non sit inconveniens aliquem utrobique locum habere monachicum) unum alteri subesse monasterio, vel ab ipso noscitur dependere; ratione tamen eorumdem prioratuum dicti ordinarii sua jurisdictione in ipsis etiam quoad praemissa (quamdiu morantur in iis) licite uti possunt. (C. 1, VI°, de privil., V, 7.)

CLEMENS V IN CONCILIO VIENNENSI
(Sess. VII, cap. 15 de ref., sess. XXIII, cap. 18 de ref.,
et sess. XXV, cap. 8 de ref.)

M Quia contingit interdum, quod xenodochiorum, leprosarium, eleemosynariarum seu hospitalium rectores, locorum ipsorum cura postposita, bona, res et jura ipsorum interdum ab occupatorum et usurpatorum manibus excutere negligunt, quinimo et collabi et deperdi, domos et aedificia ruinis deformari permittunt, et non attento, quod loca ipsa ad hoc fundata et fidelium erogationibus dotata fuerunt, ut pauperes infectique lepra reciperentur inibi, et ex proventibus sustentarentur illorum, id renuunt inhumaniter facere, proventus eosdem in usus suos damnabiliter convertentes, cum tamen ea, quae ad certum usum largitione sunt destinata fidelium, ad illum debeant, non ad alium (salva quidem Sedis Apostolicae auctoritate) converti: nos incuriam et abusum hujusmodi detestantes, hoc sacro concilio approbante sancimus, ut ii, ad quos id de jure vel statuto in ipsorum fundatione locorum apposito, aut ex consuetudine praescripta legitime, vel privilegio Sedis Apostolicae pertinet, loca ipsa studeant in praedictis omnibus salubriter reformare, ac occupata, deperdita et alienata indebite in statum reduci debitum faciant, et ad ipsarum miserabilium personarum receptionem et sustentationem debitam juxta facultates et proventus locorum ipsorum rectores praedictos compellere non omittant. In quo si forte commiserint negligentiam vel defectum, ordinariis locorum injungimus, ut etiamsi pia loca praedicta exemptionis privilegio munita consistant, per se ipsos vel alios impleant omnia praemissa et singula, et rectores eosdem utique non exemptos propria, exemptos vero et alios privilegiatos apostolica ad id auctoritate compellant; contradictores, cujuscumque status aut conditionis exsistant, aut praebentes eisdem circa praemissa consilium, auxilium vel favorem, per censuram ecclesiasticam et aliis juris remediis compescendo; nullum tamen per hoc exemptionibus seu privilegiis ipsis quoad alia praejudicium generando. Ut autem praemissa promptius observentur, nullus ex locis ipsis saecularibus clericis in beneficium conferatur, etiamsi de consuetudine (quam reprobamus penitus) hoc fuerit observatum, nisi in illorum fundatione secus fuerit constitutum, seu per electionem sit de rectore locis hujusmodi providendum. Sed eorum gubernatio viris providis, idoneis et boni testimonii committatur, qui sciant, velint et valeant loca ipsa, bona eorum ac jura utiliter regere, et eorum proventus et reditus in personarum usum miserabilium fideliter dispensare, et quos in usus alios bona praedicta convertere praesumptio verisimilis non exsistat; in quibus sub obtestatione divini judicii illorum, ad quos dictorum locorum commissio pertinet, conscientias oneramus. Illi etiam, quibus dictorum locorum gubernatio seu administratio committetur, ad instar tutorum et curatorum juramentum praestare, ac de locorum ipsorum bonis inventaria conficere, et ordinariis, seu aliis, quibus subsunt loca hujusmodi, vel deputandis ab eis, annis singulis de administratione sua teneantur reddere rationem. Quod si secus a quoquam fuerit attentatum, collationem, provisionem seu ordinationem ipsam carere decernimus omni robore firmitatis. Praemissa vero ad hospitalia militarium ordinum aut religiosorum etiam aliorum extendi minime volumus. Quorum tamen hospitalium rectoribus in sanctae obedientiae virtute mandamus, ut in illis secundum suorum ordinum instituta et antiquas observantias providere pauperibus, hospitalitatem debitam in illis tenere procurent; ad quod per superiores eorum arcta districtione cogantur, statutis aut consuetudinibus quibuslibet non obstantibus in praemissis. Ceterum nostrae intentionis exsistit, quod, si quae hospitalia, altare vel altaria, et coemeterium ab antiquo habentia, et presbyteros celebrantes, et sacramenta ecclesiastica pauperibus ministrantes, seu si parochiales rectores consueverint in illis exercere, praemissa antiqua consuetudo servetur quoad exercenda et ministranda spiritualia supradicta. (C. 2, in Clem. de relig. dom., III, 11.)

INNOCENTIUS III IN CONCILIO LATERANENSI
(Sess. XIII de Euch., can. 9 et sess. XIV de poenit., can. 8)

N Omnis utriusque sexus fidelis, postquam ad annos discretionis pervenerit, omnia sua solus peccata confiteatur fideliter saltem semel in anno proprio sacerdoti, et injunctam sibi poenitentiam studeat pro viribus adimplere, suscipiens reverenter ad minus in Pascha Eucharistiae sacramentum, nisi forte de consilio proprii sacerdotis ob aliquam rationabilem causam ad tempus ab ejus perceptione duxerit abstinendum; alioquin et vivens ab ingressu ecclesiae arceatur, et moriens Christiana careat sepultura. Unde hoc salutare statutum frequenter in ecclesiis publicetur, ne quispiam ignorantiae caecitate velamen excusationis assumat. Si quis autem alieno sacerdoti voluerit justa de causa sua confiteri peccata, licentiam prius postulet et obtineat a proprio sacerdote, cum aliter ille ipsum non possit solvere vel ligare. (C. 12, X, de poenit., V, 38.)

CLEMENS V IN CONCILIO VIENNENSI
(Sess. XIV, cap. 6 de ref.)

O Quoniam qui abjectis vestibus proprio congruentibus ordini alias assumere, et in publico portare rationabili causa cessante praesumit, professorum illius ordinis praerogativa se reddit indignum, praesenti constitutione sancimus, quod quicumque clericus virgata vel partita veste publice utetur (nisi causa rationabilis subsit), si beneficiatus exstiterit, per sex menses a perceptione fructuum beneficiorum, quae obtinet, sit eo ipso suspensus; si vero beneficiatus non fuerit, in sacris tamen ordinibus citra sacerdotium constitutus, per idem tempus reddatur eo ipso inhabilis ad ecclesiasticum beneficium obtinendum.

Idem quoque censemus de clericis aliis, vestem talarem simul et tonsuram publice deferentibus clericalem. Dignitatem vero, personatum seu beneficium aliud obtinens, cui cura immineat animarum, necnon ceteri in sacerdotio constituti, ac religiosi quilibet, quos oportet per decentiam habitus extrinseci morum intrinsecam honestatem ostendere, si (praeterquam ex causa rationabili) publice vestem ferant hujusmodi, aut infulam seu pileum lineum publice portent in capite, sint eo ipso, beneficiati videlicet, a perceptione fructuum beneficiorum, quae obtinent, suspensi per annum. Ceteri vero sacerdotes et religiosi quilibet per idem tempus reddantur inhabiles ad quodcumque beneficium ecclesiasticum obtinendum. Sed et tales et ceteri quicumque clerici utentes epitogio seu tabardo foderato usque ad oram, et ita brevi, quod vestis inferior notabiliter videatur, epitogium ipsum saeculares clerici et religiosi administrationem habentes teneantur intra mensem dare pauperibus; ceteri vero religiosi, administrationem non habentes, intra idem tempus illud teneantur suis superioribus assignare in pios usus aliquos convertendum. Alioquin beneficiati suspensionis, ceteri vero inhabilitatis poenas praedictas per idem tempus se noverint incurrisse.

Huic insuper adjicimus sanctioni, ut clerici, praesertim beneficiati, caligis soccatis, rubeis aut viridibus publice non utantur. (C. 2 in Clem. de vit. et hon. cler., III, 1.)

ALEXANDER III
(Sess. XXI, cap. 4 de ref.)

P Ad audientiam nostram noveris pervenisse, quod villa quae dicitur H., tantum perhibetur ab ecclesia parochiali distare, ut tempore hiemali, cum pluviae inundant, non possint parochiani sine magna difficultate ipsam adire; unde non valent congruo tempore ecclesiasticis interesse officiis. Quia igitur dicta ecclesia ita dicitur reditibus abundare, quod, praeter illius villae proventus, minister illius convenienter valet sustentationem habere, mandamus, quatenus, si res ita se habet, ecclesiam ibi aedifices, et in ea sacerdotem, sublato appellationis obstaculo, ad praesentationem rectoris ecclesiae majoris cum canonico fundatoris assensu instituas, ad sustentationem suam ejusdem villae obventiones ecclesiasticas percepturum; providens tamen, ut competens in ea honor pro facultate loci matrici servetur, quod quidem fieri posse videtur, cum ejusdem villae dominus viginti acras terrae frugiferae velit ad usus sacerdotis conferre. Si vero persona matricis ecclesiae virum idoneum praesentare distulerit, vel opus illud voluerit impedire, tu nihilominus facias idem opus ad perfectionem deduci, et virum bonum, appellationis cessante diffugio, instituere non omittas. (C. 3, X, de eccl. aedif., III, 48.)

CLEMENS V IN CONCILIO VIENNENSI
(Sess. XXII, cap. 4 de ref.)

Q Ut ii, qui divinis in cathedralibus vel collegiatis, saecularibus vel regularibus ecclesiis sunt mancipati officiis, vel mancipabuntur in posterum, ad suscipiendos sacros ordines propensius inducantur, statuimus, ut nullus de cetero in hujusmodi ecclesiis vocem in capitulo habeat (etiamsi hoc sibi ab aliis libere concedatur), nisi saltem in subdiaconatus ordine fuerit constitutus. Illi vero, qui dignitates, personatus, officia vel praebendas, quibus certi ordines sunt annexi, pacifice nunc obtinent in eisdem ecclesiis, vel obtinuerint in futurum, nisi (justo impedimento cessante) ad hujusmodi ordines se promoveri fecerint intra annum, ex tunc, donec ad eos promoti fuerint, nullo modo vocem in capitulo habeant earumdem; ipsisque distributionum, quae dantur iis, qui certis horis intersunt, pars dimidia subtrahatur, non obstantibus quibuslibet consuetudinibus vel statutis. Poenis aliis, quae contra tales promoveri ad ordines recusantes statuuntur in jure, nihilominus in suo robore permansuris. (C. 2, de aet. et qual. et ord. praef. in Clem., I. 6.)

INNOCENTIUS IV
(Sess. XXII, cap. 7 de ref.)

R Romana ecclesia *et infra:* Cum suffraganeorum Remensis ecclesiae suorumque officialium (qui generaliter de causis ad ipsorum forum pertinentibus eorum vices supplendo cognoscunt) unum et idem consistorium sive auditorium sit censendum, ab ipsis officialibus non ad dictos suffraganeos (ne ab eisdem ad se ipsos interponi appellatio videatur), sed de jure ad Remensem est curiam appellandum. Ab archidiaconis vero aliisque inferioribus praelatis suffraganeis subjectis eisdem, et eorum officialibus, ad suffraganeos ipsos debet, et non ad eamdem curiam (omissis dictis suffraganeis) appellari, nisi aliud Remensi ecclesiae de consuetudine competat in hac parte. Cum autem ad praefatam curiam ab eorumdem suffraganeorum vel suorum officialium audientia fuerit appellatum, Remensis archiepiscopus (qui pro tempore fuerit) vel officialis ipsius nullatenus in appellationis causa interpositae ante definitivam sententiam citent partes, nec etiam aliis illam committant, appellationis ejusdem causa probabili seu legitima non expressa.

Si vero vocatis partibus vel nullatenus, aut non intra decem dies post interlocutoriam vel definitivam sententiam appellatum fuisse, seu aliquid aliud simile, sicque non esse per appellationem ad eumdem archiepiscopum vel ejus officialem devolutum negotium proponatur; iidem (nisi prius ipsis constiterit causam ipsam ad eos totaliter fuisse delatam) prohibere, ne in causa illa, vel ne ad executionem procedatur sententiae, non praesumant.

Quod si objiciatur ex injusta causa seu minus legitima ante sententiam appellationem interpositam exstitisse, et ex eo non esse appellationem hujusmodi admittendam; nequeunt praedicti archiepiscopus vel ejus officialis prohibere, ne procedatur in causa, nisi prius appellatione recepta, velut amissa ex causa probabili, cognoscere incipiant de causa hujusmodi, an sit vera. Si autem post sententiam in casibus a jure prohibitis (utpote a sententia super manifesto et notorio crimine, vel de quo quis in jure confessus exstitit, promulgata) vel consimilibus appellatum fuisse dicatur: possunt, ne sententia executioni mandetur (postquam cognoscere coeperint, utrum sit recipienda vel non appellatio ab eo interposita) inhibere. In alium quoque, qui circa rem, de qua inter appellantem et appellatum controversia vertitur, aliquid post eorum inhibitionem attentat, non valent occasione hujusmodi jurisdictionem aliquam vindicare. Cum vero is, qui ad Remensem curiam super aliqua causa vocem appellationis emittit, nihilominus in causis aliis ordinarii sui jurisdictioni subjiciatur, Remensis archiepiscopus vel officialis ipsius nequaquam jurisdictionem ipsam in aliis impediant, ut ab ejusdem ordinarii potestate totaliter eximant taliter appellantem. Debet autem ad eos ab episcopis praefatae provinciae super causis, in quibus temporalem jurisdictionem exercent, nisi forte de consuetudine aut privilegio, sive jure alio speciali sit appellandum ad alium, appellari. Sententias quoque interdicti vel suspensionis seu excommunicationis in appellantem ab eo, a quo appellatum proponitur, promulgatas, nullatenus, nisi vocatis partibus et de appellatione legitime cognita, revocent aut denuncient, esse nullas. Cum autem ad Remensem archiepiscopum ab audientia suffraganei sui super aliqua causa fuerit ante sententiam appellatum, idem archiepiscopus (postquam de appellatione cognita constiterit eam minus rationabilem exstitisse) causam ad eumdem suffraganeum remittere non postponat. (C. 3, VI°, de appel., II, 15.)

EUGENIUS IV

(Sess. XXIII, cap. 1 de ref. et sess. XXIV, cap. 11 de ref.)

S Divina in eminenti Sedis Apostolicae specula disponente clementia constituti ad ea libenter intendimus, per quae officiales praedictae Sedis obsequiis ejus (ad quam velut fidelium omnium matrem pro animarum salute quaerenda et justitia prosequenda de diversis mundi partibus confluit multitudo), tutius et quietius se promptiores valeant exhibere. Hinc est, quod nos ex certis rationabilibus causis moti, etiam nonnullorum praedecessorum nostrorum vestigiis inhaerentes, districtius inhibemus locorum ordinariis, necnon commissariis et delegatis eorum, ceterisque universis et singulis, quacumque potestate et auctoritate praefulgeant, cujuscumque dignitatis, gradus vel praeeminentiae fuerint, ne contra officiales praefatos, quocumque nomine nuncupentur, in nostris et dictae Sedis obsequiis nunc et pro tempore exsistentes, necnon quoscumque alios pro suis, et eorum causis vel negotiis prosequendis ad Sedem praedictam venientes, ac in ea (durante negotiorum et causarum hujusmodi prosecutione) moram trahentes, et recedentes ab eadem, procedere, aut in eos excommunicationis, suspensionis vel interdicti, aut privationis officiorum aut beneficiorum, seu quamvis aliam sententiam promulgare praesumant.

Nos enim omnes et singulos processus et sententias contra tenorem et mentem nostrae inhibitionis hujusmodi latas et habitas, et in posterum habendas ac etiam promulgandas, et quaecumque inde secuta, declaramus nulla, irrita et inania, nulliusque exstitisse vel exsistere roboris vel momenti. Necnon quidquid in contrarium a quoquam, quavis auctoritate, scienter vel ignoranter attentatum forsan est hactenus, vel in posterum contigerit attentari, etiam decernimus irritum et inane, et nihilominus in omnes et singulos ordinarios et officiales, commissarios, delegatos eorum, qui se de dignitatibus ac beneficiis ecclesiasticis quibuscumque officialium aut negotia hujusmodi apud dictam Sedem prosequentium praedictorum, eos illis forsan privando, atque privatos decernendo seu declarando, vel cujuscumque privationis praetextu illa personis aliis conferendo, seu de illis in eos quomodolibet se intromittendo, tam in dantes quam in recipientes excommunicationis, suspensionis et interdicti latas sententias promulgamus, quas volumus eos ipso facto incurrere; a qua quidem excommunicationis sententia absolvi nequeant, nisi a nobis vel per nos deputandis, praeterquam in mortis articulo constituti.

Praemissa autem a die affixionis praesentium ad valvas basilicae principis apostolorum de Urbe ex certa scientia quoscumque ligare volumus et arctare; non obstantibus apostolicis et quibuscumque generalibus aut provincialibus aut synodalibus conciliis, edictis, constitutionibus, ordinationibus et apostolicis privilegiis, per quas effectus praesentium impediri posset quomodolibet vel differri, etiamsi de illis eorumque totis tenoribus habenda esset in praesentibus mentio specialis, et quae praesentibus volumus haberi pro sufficienter expressis, ceterisque contrariis quibuscumque. Nulli ergo, etc. Si quis autem, etc. Datum Romae apud S. Petrum anno incarnationis dominicae MCCCCXXXII. VIII. Idus Martii, pontificatus nostri anno II. (C. 3 de privil. in Extrav. comm., V, 7.)

BONIFACIUS VIII
(Sess. XXIII, cap. 6 de ref.)

T Clerici, qui cum unicis et virginibus contraxerunt, si tonsuram et vestes deferant clericales, privilegium retineant canonis ab Innocentio secundo praedecessore nostro editi in favorem totius ordinis clericalis (c. 29, C. XVII, q. 4). Et cum juxta Parisiense concilium (c. 2, X, de foro comp., II, 2) nullus clericus distringi debeat aut condemnari a judice saeculari, praesenti declaramus edicto, hujusmodi clericos conjugatos pro commissis ab eis excessibus vel delictis trahi non posse criminaliter aut civiliter ad judicium saeculare, nec ab ipsis saecularibus judicibus eos debere personaliter vel etiam pecunialiter (ne per unam viam concedatur eisdem judicibus quod per aliam denegatus) ullatenus condemnari. In ceteris autem, vel nisi, ut praemittitur, tonsuram vel vestes deferant clericales, etiam in praemissis eos gaudere nolumus privilegio clericali. (C. un. VI°, de cler. conjug., III, 2.)

CONCILIUM CHALCEDONENSE
(Sess. XXIII, cap. 16 de ref.)

U Neminem absolute ordinari presbyterum, vel diaconum, vel quemlibet in ecclesiastica ordinatione constitutum, praecipimus, nisi manifeste in ecclesia civitatis sive possessionis, aut in martyrio, aut in monasterio, qui ordinatur, mereatur ordinationis publicatae vocabulum. Eos autem, qui absolute ordinantur, decrevit sancta synodus vacuam habere manus impositionem, et nullum tale factum valere ad injuriam ipsius, qui eum ordinavit. (C. 1, D. LXX.)

INNOCENTIUS III IN CONCILIO LATERANENSI
(Sess. XXIV, cap. 1 de ref. matr.)

V Cum inhibitio copulae conjugalis sit ultimis tribus gradibus revocata, eam in aliis volumus districte servari. Unde praedecessorum nostrorum vestigiis inhaerendo, clandestina conjugia penitus inhibemus; prohibentes etiam, ne quis sacerdos talibus interesse praesumat. Quare specialem quorumdam locorum consuetudinem ad alia generaliter prorogando statuimus, ut, cum matrimonia fuerint contrahenda, in ecclesiis per presbyteros publice proponantur, competenti termino praefinito, ut infra illum qui voluerit et valuerit legitimum impedimentum opponat, et ipsi presbyteri nihilominus investigent, utrum aliquod impedimentum obsistat. Cum autem apparuerit probabilis conjectura contra copulam contrahendam, contractus interdicatur expresse, donec fieri debeat super eo manifestis constiterit documentis. (C. 3, X, de cland. despons., IV, 3.)

GREGORIUS X IN CONCILIO LUGDUNENSI
(Sess. XXIV, cap. 3 de ref.)

W Exigit perversorum audacia, ut non simus sola delictorum prohibitione contenti, sed etiam poenam delinquentibus imponamus. Constitutionem itaque felicis recordationis Innocentii Papae IV praedecessoris nostri, editam super non recipiendis in pecunia procurationibus, ac super receptione munerum visitantibus eorumque familiaribus interdicta, quam multorum fertur temeritas praeterire, volentes inviolabiliter observari, eam decernimus poenae adjectione juvandam; statuentes, ut universi et singuli, qui ob procurationem sibi ratione visitationis debitam exigere pecuniam, vel etiam a volente recipere, vel alias constitutionem ipsam recipiendo munera, sive visitationis officio non impenso procurationem in victualibus, aut aliquid aliud procurationis occasione, violare praesumpserint, duplum ejus, quod receperint, ecclesiae, a qua id receptum fuerit, intra mensem reddere teneantur. Alioquin ex tunc patriarchae, archiepiscopi, episcopi duplum ipsum ultra praedictum tempus restituere differentes, ingressum sibi ecclesiae sentiant interdictum. Inferiores vero ab officio et beneficio noverint se suspensos, quousque de duplo hujusmodi gravatis ecclesiis plenariam satisfactionem impendant, nulla eis in hoc dantium remissione, liberalitate seu gratia valitura. (C. 2, VI°, de cens., III, 20.)

INNOCENTIUS III IN CONCILIO LATERANENSI
(Sess. XXIV, cap. 5 de ref.)

X Qualiter et quando debeat praelatus procedere ad inquirendum et puniendum subditorum excessus, ex auctoritate novi et veteris testamenti colligitur evidenter, ex quibus postea processerunt canonicae sanctiones, sicut olim aperte distinximus, et nunc sacri approbatione concilii confirmamus. Legitur enim in evangelio, quod villicus ille, qui diffamatus erat apud dominum suum, quasi dissipasset bona ipsius, audivit ab illo: *Quid hoc audio de te? redde rationem villicationis tuae; jam enim non poteris villicare* (Luc. 16:2). Et in Genesi Dominus ait: *Descendam, et videbo, utrum clamorem, qui venit ad me, opere compleverint* (Gen. 18:21). Ex quibus auctoritatibus manifeste comprobatur, quod non solum cum subditus, verum etiam cum praelatus excedit, si per clamorem et famam ad aures superioris pervenerit non quidem a malevolis et maledicis, sed a providis et honestis, nec semel tantum, sed saepe, quod clamor innuit et diffamatio manifestat, debet coram ecclesiae senioribus veritatem diligentius perscrutari, ut, si rei poposcerit qualitas, canonica districtio culpam feriat delinquentis, non tamquam sit actor et judex, sed quasi deferente fama vel denunciante clamore officii sui debitum exsequatur. Licet autem hoc sit observandum in subditis, diligentius tamen observandum est in praelatis, qui quasi signum sunt positi ad sagittam (Thren. 3:12). Et quia non possunt omnibus complacere, cum ex officio teneantur non solum arguere, sed etiam increpare, quin etiam interdum suspendere, nonnunquam vero ligare, frequenter odium multorum incurrunt, et insidias patiuntur: ideo sancti patres provide statuerunt, ut accusatio praelatorum non facile admittatur, ne concussis columnis corruat aedificium, nisi diligens adhibeatur cautela, per quam non solum falsae, sed etiam malignae criminationi janua praecludatur. Verum ita voluerunt providere praelatis, ne criminarentur injuste, ut tamen caverent, ne delinquerent insolenter, contra morbum utrumque invenientes congruam medicinam, videlicet ut criminalis accusatio, quae ad diminutionem capitis (id est degradationem) intenditur, nisi legitima praecedat inscriptio, nullatenus admittatur. Sed cum super excessibus suis quisquam fuerit infamatus ita, ut jam clamor ascendat, qui diutius sine scandalo dissimulari non possit vel sine periculo tolerari, absque dubitationis scrupulo ad inquirendum et puniendum ejus excessus, non ex odii fomite, sed caritatis procedatur affectu, quatenus, si fuerit gravis excessus, etsi non degradetur ad ordine, ab administratione tamen amoveatur omnino, quod est secundum evangelicam sententiam a villicatione villicum amoveri, qui non potest villicationis suae dignam reddere rationem. Debet igitur esse praesens is, contra quem facienda est inquisitio, nisi se per contumaciam absentaverit, et exponenda sunt ei illa capitula, de quibus fuerit inquirendum, ut facultatem habeat defendendi se ipsum. Et non solum dicta, sed etiam nomina ipsa testium sunt ei, ut quid et a quo sit dictum appareat, publicanda; necnon exceptiones et replicationes legitimae admittendae, ne per suppressionem nominum infamandi, per exceptionum vero exclusionem deponendi falsum audacia praebeatur. Ad corrigendos itaque subditorum excessus tanto diligentius debet praelatus assurgere, quanto damnabilius eorum offensas desereret incorrectas; contra quos, ut de notoriis excessibus taceatur, etsi tribus modis possit procedi, per accusationem videlicet, denunciationem et inquisitionem eorum, ut tamen in omnibus diligens adhibeatur cautela, ne forte per leve compendium ad grave dispendium veniatur, sicut accusationem legitime praecedere debet inscriptio, sic et denunciationem caritativa admonitio, et inquisitionem clamosa insinuatio praevenire; illo semper adhibito moderamine, ut juxta formam judicii sententiae quoque forma dictetur. Hunc tamen ordinem circa regulares personas non credimus usquequaque servandum, quae, cum causa requirit, facilius et liberius a suis possunt administrationibus amoveri. (C. 24, X, de accus., V, 1.)

INNOCENTIUS III
(Sess. XXIV, cap. 11 de ref.)

Y Cum capella ducis Burgundiae gaudere dicatur hujusmodi privilegio, quod nullus archiepiscopus vel episcopus in personas canonicorum ejusdem capellae suspensionis vel excommunicationis aut interdicti sententias audeat promulgare, quidam capellae supradictae canonici, qui parochiales ecclesias a te tenent, occasione privilegii praelibati in his etiam, quarum jurisdictio ad te pertinet, ita se dicunt exemptos, ut, quantumcumque graviter interdum excedant, tuae correctioni recusent et sententiae subjacere. Quocirca mandamus, quatenus, in quantum exempti sunt, ejusdem ratione capellae apostolicis privilegiis deferas reverenter, sed in quantum ratione parochialium ecclesiarum vel alias jurisdictionem tuam respicere dignoscuntur, officii tui debitum in eosdem libere prosequaris. (C. 16, X, de privil., V, 33.)

ALEXANDER III IN CONCILIO LATERANENSI
(Sess. XXIV, cap. 12 de ref.)

Z Inferiora etiam ministeria, ut puta decanatum, archidiaconatum, et alia, quae curam animarum habent annexam, nullus omnino suscipiat, sed nec parochialis ecclesiae regimen, nisi qui jam vigesimum quintum annum aetatis attigerit et scientia et moribus commendandus exsistat. Cum autem assumptus fuerit, si archidiaconus in diaconum, et decanus et reliqui admoniti non fuerint praefixo a canonibus tempore in presbyteros ordinati, et ab isto removeantur officio et aliis conferatur, qui et velint et possint illud convenienter implere. Nec prosit eis appellationis refugium, si forte in constitutionis istius transgressionem per appellationem voluerint se tueri. Hoc sane non solum de promovendis, sed etiam de his, qui jam promoti sunt, si canones non obsistant, praecipimus observari. (C. 7 [§ Inferiora], X, de elect., I, 6.)

BONIFACIUS VIII
(Sess. XXIV, cap. 12 de ref.)

AC Consuetudinem, quae in quibusdam partibus inolevit, qua canonici et alii beneficiati seu clerici cathedralium et aliarum collegiatarum ecclesiarum distributiones quotidianas, quae alias manualia beneficia seu victualia nuncupantur, et tantum residentibus tribuuntur, qualitercumque in civitatibus seu aliis locis, in quibus ipsae consistunt ecclesiae, sint praesentes, licet divinis officiis non intersint, ex integro percipiunt, ac si continuo in ipsis ecclesiis in eisdem officiis deservirent, penitus improbantes, statuimus, ut distributiones ipsae quotidianae, in quibuscumque rebus consistant, canonicis ac aliis beneficiatis, et clericis ecclesiarum ipsarum, qui eisdem officiis in ipsis ecclesiis adfuerint, tribuantur juxta ecclesiae cujuslibet ordinationem rationabilem jam factam seu etiam faciendam. Qui vero aliter de distributionibus ipsis quidquam receperit (exceptis illis, quos infirmitas seu justa et rationabilis corporalis necessitas, aut evidens ecclesiae utilitatis excusaret), rerum sic receptarum dominium non acquirat, nec faciat eas suas; immo ad omnium restitutionem, quae contra hujusmodi constitutionem nostram receperit, teneatur. De distributionibus etiam pro defunctorum anniversariis largiendis idem decernimus observandum. (C. un. VI°, de cler. non resid., III, 3.)

BONIFACIUS VIII
(Sess. XXV, cap. 5 de regular.)

AD Periculoso et detestabili quarumdam monialium statui (quae honestatis laxatis habenis et monachali modestia sexusque verecundia impudenter abjectis, extra sua monasteria nonnunquam per habitacula saecularium personarum discurrunt, et frequenter intra eadem monasteria personas suspectas admittunt, in illius, cui suam integritatem voluntate spontanea devoverunt, gravem offensam, religionis opprobrium et scandalum plurimorum), providere salubriter cupientes, praesenti constitutione perpetuo irrefragabiliter valitura sancimus, universas et singulas moniales praesentes atque futuras, cujuscumque religionis sint vel ordinis, in quibuslibet mundi partibus exsistentes, sub perpetua in suis monasteriis debere de cetero permanere clausura, ita, quod nulli earum, religionem tacite vel expresse professae, sit vel esse valeat quacumque ratione vel causa (nisi forte tanto et tali morbo evidenter earum aliquam laborare constaret, quod non posset cum aliis absque gravi periculo seu scandalo commorari), monasteria ipsa deinceps egrediendi facultas, nullique aliquatenus inhonestae personae, nec etiam honestae (nisi rationabilis et manifesta causa exsistat, ac de illius, ad quem pertinuerit, speciali licentia), ingressus vel accessus pateat ad easdem, ut sic a publicis et mundanis conspectibus separatae, omnino servire Deo valeant liberius, et lasciviendi opportunitate sublata eidem corda sua et corpora in omni sanctimonia diligentius custodire.

Sane ut hoc salutare statutum commodius valeat observari, districtius inhibemus, ne in monasteriis ordinum non mendicantium aliquae recipiantur de cetero in sorores, nisi quot poterunt de ipsorum monasteriorum bonis sive proventibus absque penuria sustentari; si secus actum fuerit, irritum decernentes.

Verum quando abbatissa vel priorissa cujusvis monasterii pro feudo, quod monasterium ipsum tenet ab aliquo principe seu domino temporali, sibi debebit homagium vel fidelitatis sacramentum praestare (nisi quod per procuratorem illud praestet, possit efficere apud eum), de monasterio cum honesta et decenti societate exire poterit eo casu licenter; homagio facto, quamprimum commode poterit, seu fidelitatis praestito sacramento, ad ipsum monasterium e vestigio reversura sic, quod in fraudem residentiae sive morae claustralis nihil fiat omnino.

Porro ne moniales causam seu occasionem habeant evagandi, principes saeculares ac alios dominos temporales rogamus, requirimus et obsecramus per viscera misericordiae Jesu Christi, eisdem in remissionem peccaminum nihilominus suadentes, quod abbatissas ipsas et priorissas, ac moniales quascumque, monasteriorum suorum curam, administrationem negotiave gerentes, quibuscumque nominibus censeantur, per procuratores in suis tribunalibus seu curiis litigare permittant, ne pro constituendis procuratoribus (qui adornati in aliquibus partibus nuncupantur), seu aliis ejusmodi easdem oporteat evagari. Si qui vero contra presumpserint, exhortationi hujusmodi rationabili atque sanctae obtemperare nolentes, cum sit juri contrarium, quod mulieres (praesertim religiosae) per se ipsas litigare cogantur, et a via deviet honestatis, et periculum animarum inducat, ad hoc per suos ordinarios ecclesiasticos censura ecclesiastica compellantur. Episcopis autem et aliis praelatis superioribus et inferioribus quibuscumque injungimus, quod et ipsi causas seu negotia, quae praefatae moniales habebunt agere, coram ipsis, aut in curiis eorumdem, sive sint homagia, fidelitatis sacramenta, lites vel quidquid aliud, ipsa per procuratores earum fieri faciunt et tractari.

Et quoniam parum esset condere jura, nisi essent qui ea executioni debitae demandarent, patriarchis, primatibus, archiepiscopis et episcopis universis districte in virtute sanctae obedientiae sub obtestatione divini judicii et interminatione maledictionis aeternae praecipiendo mandamus, quatenus eorum quilibet in civitate ac dioecesi propria in monasteriis monialium sibi ordinario jure subjectis sua, in iis vero, quae ad Romanam immediate spectant ecclesiam, Sedis Apostolicae auctoritate; abbates vero et alii tam exempti quam non exempti praelati ecclesiarum, monasteriorum et ordinum quorumcumque, in monasteriis hujusmodi sibi subjectis de clausura convenienti, ubi non est, ipsorum monasteriorum expensis et fidelium eleemosynis, quas ad hoc procurent diligentius faciendas, et de ipsis monialibus includendis, quamprimum commode poterunt providere procurent, si divinae ac nostrae indignationis voluerint acrimoniam evitare; contradictores atque rebelles per censuram ecclesiasticam appellatione postposita compescendo, invocato ad hoc, si opus fuerit, auxilio brachii saecularis. Per hoc autem in monasteriis exemptis ordinarii locorum quoad alia nullam sibi credant jurisdictionem vel potestatem aliquatenus attributam. (C. un. VI°, de stat. regular., III, 16.)

INNOCENTIUS III IN CONCILIO LATERANENSI
(Sess. XXV, cap. 8 de regular.)

AE In singulis regnis sive provinciis fiat de triennio in triennium, salvo jure dioecesanorum pontificum, commune capitulum abbatum atque priorum abbates proprios non habentium, qui non consueverunt tale capitulum celebrare; ad quod universi conveniant praepeditionem canonicam non habentes, apud unum de monasteriis ad hoc aptum, hoc adhibito moderamine, ut nullus eorum plus quam sex evectiones et octo personas adducat. Advocent autem caritative in hujus novitatis primordiis duos Cisterciensis ordinis abbates vicinos ad praestandum sibi consilium et auxilium opportunum cum sint in hujusmodi capitulis celebrandis ex longa consuetudine plenius informati. Qui absque contradictione duos sibi de ipsis associent, quos viderint expedire. Ac ipsi quatuor praesint capitulo universo ita, quod ex hoc nullus eorum auctoritatem praelationis assumat, unde, cum expedierit, provida possint deliberatione mutari. Hujusmodi vero capitulum aliquot certis diebus continue juxta morem Cisterciensis ordinis celebretur, in quo diligens habeatur tractatus de reformatione ordinis et observantia regulari; et quod statutum fuerit illis quatuor approbantibus, ab omnibus inviolabiliter observetur, omni excusatione et contradictione ac appellatione remotis, proviso nihilominus, ubi sequenti termino debeat capitulum celebrari. Et qui convenerint vitam ducant communem, et faciant proportionabiliter simul omnes communes expensas ita, quod, si non omnes potuerint in eisdem, saltem plures simul in diversis domibus commorentur. Ordinentur etiam in eodem capitulo religiosae ac circumspectae personae, quae singulas abbatias ejusdem regni sive provinciae non solum monachorum, sed etiam monialium, secundum formam sibi praefixam vice nostra studeant visitare, corrigentes et reformantes quae correctionis et reformationis officio viderint indigere, ita quod, si rectorem loci cognoverint ab administratione penitus amovendum, denuncient episcopo proprio, ut illum amovere procuret; quod si non fecerit, ipsi visitatores hoc referant ad Apostolicae Sedis examen. Hoc ipsum regulares canonicos secundum ordinem suum volumus et praecipimus observare. Si vero in hac novitate quidquam difficultatis emerserit, quod per praedictas personas nequeat expediri, ad Apostolicae Sedis judicium absque scandalo referatur, ceteris irrefragabiliter observatis, quae concordi fuerint deliberatione provisa.

Porro dioecesani episcopi monasteria sibi subjecta ita studeant reformare, ut, cum ad ea praedicti visitatores accesserint, plus in illis inveniant, quod commendatione, quam quod correctione sit dignum; attentissime praecaventes, ne per eos dicta monasteria indebitis oneribus aggraventur, quia sic volumus superiorum jura servari, ut inferiorum nolimus injurias sustinere. Ad hoc districte praecipimus tam dioecesanis episcopis quam personis, quae praeerunt capitulis celebrandis, ut per censuram ecclesiasticam appellatione remota, compescant advocatos, patronos, vicedominos, rectores et consules, magnates et milites, seu quoslibet alios, ne monasteria praesumant offendere in personis ac rebus. Et si forsitan offenderint, eos ad satisfactionem compellere non omittant, ut liberius et quietius omnipotenti Deo valeant famulari. (C. 7, X, de stat. monach., III, 35.)

CONCILIUM CARTHAGINENSE IV SIVE STATUTA ECCL. ANTIQUA

(Sess. XXV, cap. 1 de ref.)

AF Episcopus vilem supellectilem et mensam ac victum pauperem habeat, et dignitatis suae auctoritatem fide et vitae meritis quaerat. Hospitium quoque non longe ab ecclesia habeat. (C. 7, D. XLI.)

BONIFACIUS VIII

(Sess. XXV, cap. 10 de ref.)

AG Statutum, quod circa judices a Sede Apostolica deputandos nuper edidimus, cum quaedam contenta in eo, quae pro communi utilitate credebantur inducta, sicut experientia docuit, tendere dignoscantur ad noxam, sanctione praesenti, quam irrefragabiliter observari mandamus, suadente utilitate in melius duximus reformandum. Sancimus igitur, ut nullis, nisi dignitate praeditis, aut personatum obtinentibus, seu ecclesiarum cathedralium canonicis, causae auctoritate litterarum Sedis Apostolicae vel legatorum ejus de cetero committantur; nec audiantur alibi, quam in civitatibus vel locis insignibus, ubi possit commode copia peritorum haberi. (C. 11 de rescrip. in VI°, I, 3.)

INDEX

INDEX RERUM ALPHABETICUS